Integrated Science for CSEC® Examinations

Third edition

June Mitchelmore

Formerly Education Officer (Science)
Ministry of Education, Kingston, Jamaica

John Phillips

Formerly Science Teacher
Harrison College, Bridgetown, Barbados

John Steward

Formerly Science Adviser
Ministry of Education, Georgetown, Guyana
and Curriculum Consultant, Dominica

Cambridge Integrated Science for CSEC® Examinations is an independent publication
and has not been authorised, sponsored, or otherwise approved by CXC.

CAMBRIDGE
UNIVERSITY PRESS

CAMBRIDGE
UNIVERSITY PRESS

University Printing House, Cambridge CB2 8BS, United Kingdom

One Liberty Plaza, 20th Floor, New York, NY 10006, USA

477 Williamstown Road, Port Melbourne, VIC 3207, Australia

314–321, 3rd Floor, Plot 3, Splendor Forum, Jasola District Centre, New Delhi – 110025, India

103 Penang Road, #05-06/07, Visioncrest Commercial, Singapore 238467

Cambridge University Press is part of the University of Cambridge.

It furthers the University's mission by disseminating knowledge in the pursuit of education, learning and research at the highest international levels of excellence.

Information on this title: education.cambridge.org

© Cambridge University Press 1986, 2010

First published 1986
Second edition 2002
Third edition 2010

20 19 18 17 16 15 14 13

Printed in Great Britain by CPI Group (UK) Ltd, Croydon CRO 4YY

A catalogue record for this publication is available from the British Library

ISBN 978-0-521-16882-3 Paperback with CD-ROM for Windows and Mac

Preface

Integrated Science for CSEC® is the third edition of the previously named *CXC Integrated Science*. This third edition has been comprehensively updated in line with the revision of the Caribbean Examination Council's CSEC® Integrated Science syllabus, examined for the first time in 2011.

The content and the design of the book will appeal to students who need simple presentation of the material, while also covering all the key information.

The book features:
- clear text, illustrations and photographs
- extensive coverage of the practical skills needed for School-based assessment (SBA), making the book also useful for private students
- coding of practicals throughout the book that identify the skills covered by each practical
- photocopiable worksheets for over 30 SBA practicals, from which teachers can select the ones they wish to use
- activities for discussion and research, interwoven into the text
- 'Did you know?' boxes, providing extra information and added interest
- a summary on each double-page spread that students complete in their Exercise books using key words
- numerous questions within the text.

Additional features of the book are summarized on the back cover.

The book is arranged within chapters as double-page spreads. Each double-page spread contains a list of the specific objectives for that spread, which are based on the syllabus objectives.

The chapters are arranged in four sections.
- Introduction, which revises important topics studied in previous grades and covers the practical skills required for SBA
- A The organism and its environment
- B The home and workplace
- C Energy

At the back of the book, there is a section about School-based assessment, which contains tables summarizing skills used in science investigating and reporting, and worksheets to accompany selected SBA practicals chosen from throughout the syllabus. The Glossary and Index contains comprehensive descriptions of important terms.

The CD-ROM in the back of the book contains:
- animations that illustrate certain key concepts and present problem situations for students to solve
- sample questions in Integrated Science, including examination-style questions and free-response questions for discussion
- answers to all the 'Key ideas' from within the book, which together provide a summary of the whole course
- notes for teachers about setting up and marking SBA practicals.

Additional information for both students and teachers can be found at www.cambridge.org/education.

The authors would like to record their thanks for the feedback received from the adviser, Sue Cameron-Chambers.

June Mitchelmore
John Phillips
John Steward

Contents

1 Matter, energy and living things

1.1 What are living and non-living things?

Look around you. Try to identify which are the living things, or **organisms**, and which are the non-living things. What do the living things have in common? For example, they are all made of living material, need food and can move parts of themselves. They do their activities on their own. They can also reproduce to make new organisms like themselves.

Let us examine the **characteristics** of living things.

Nutrition

Nutrition is the process of making or eating of food. Food is the fuel needed by living things for all their activities.

Plants can make their own food from simple substances – carbon dioxide, water and mineral salts. Plants contain **chlorophyll** that allows them to carry out **photosynthesis**. They trap energy from the sun and build it into food.

Animals cannot make their own food. They have to take in foods that already contain trapped energy. They eat plants, or animals that have eaten plants.

Respiration

Respiration is the release of energy from food inside all living cells. Carbon dioxide and water are also produced.

Respiration is similar to burning: the combination of oxygen with a fuel to release energy. However, in living things, respiration makes use of special substances called **enzymes** and can happen without high temperatures.

Excretion

Excretion is the removal of wastes made by the activities of living cells. A living thing is a bit like a chemical factory, with lots of chemical reactions going on in the cells all the time. Some of these reactions produce wastes that could be harmful.
Note: getting rid of faeces is not part of excretion, as the wastes are only undigested materials.

Irritability

Irritability is being able to *sense* (be aware of) changes in the environment called **stimuli**. Living things have to react (respond) appropriately to stimuli in order to stay alive.

Plants usually respond slowly to stimuli. For example, roots grow towards water, or sunflowers turn towards the light. A few plants, such as the sensitive plant, respond quickly to touch by closing their leaves.

Animals usually have special sense organs to pick up stimuli, and muscles so they can move quickly to search for food, or to escape their enemies.

Objectives

● Identify the seven characteristics of living things.
● Describe briefly what you understand by each characteristic.

Activity

Living and non-living things

1 Look carefully at the photograph. Make a list of all the things you can see.

2 Make a table in your Exercise book, with two columns labelled 'Living things' and 'Non-living things'. Write the names of the things in the correct columns.

3 Look at your completed tables with a friend. Discuss any differences that you notice.

● Here is a way to remember the characteristics of living things.

REMINDeR!

Respiration
Excretion
Movement
Irritability
Nutrition
Development and growth
Reproduction

(a) Fish

(b) Sunflowers facing the sun

Movement

Movement happens inside all living things. Organisms can also move parts of themselves.

Movement in a plant is usually very slow and is brought about by growth. An exception is the sensitive plant: this can quickly close its leaves when they are touched.

Most animals can move from place to place: this is called **locomotion**. Locomotion is important, for example, for animals to find their food.

Development and growth

Living things grow if they make or eat more food than is needed for their activities. Growth is an increase in mass, length or width. **Development** is the process by which the organism gets more cells and becomes more complicated.

Reproduction

Reproduction means making more of the same kind. The new organisms can later live separately.

Organisms need to grow and develop before they can reproduce. They have to become **mature**. Usually two organisms are needed; for example, many plants make flowers with pollen and eggs, and animals make sperm and eggs. These are examples of **sexual reproduction**.

Other organisms can reproduce on their own by a part growing out and becoming a new organism. We call this **asexual reproduction** (pages 132–5).

Questions

1 What do we mean by (a) a living thing and (b) a non-living thing? Give an example of each.

2 What are the seven characteristics of living things? How is a non-living thing, such as a car, different from a living thing for each characteristic?

3 How do fish and sunflowers carry out the characteristics of living things?

Did you know?

- Organisms can live in the coldest places near the poles and the hottest places near underground volcanoes.

- A blue whale grows from a single cell less than 1 mg in mass to a one year old of 26 tonnes.

- The giant redwood, General Sherman, is the largest living thing. Its diameter is 11 m. Cars can drive through a hole in its trunk.

Key ideas

Use these words to fill in the spaces as you write the sentences in your Exercise book.

respond   excrete   respire   nutrition   reproduce   move   develop

Every day living things have to make or eat food. We call this _____ . Plants make their own food but animals need to _____ in order to find theirs. All living things also sense and _____ to changes in their environment. They all _____ to release energy and _____ to get rid of waste products. As they grow and _____ they can _____ to make new living things.

1.2 What are the units of measurement?

A system of measurement

There is a system of measurement that is used by most of the nations of the world. The system is called the Système International d'Unités, or SI (metric) system, and its units are meant to replace all other types of measurement. These measurements include measurements of mass, length (distance), time, force, pressure, energy, temperature and electricity.

The table below gives the different types of measurements, with their units and symbols, which you are likely to find in science texts. These units have been adopted by all scientists and are essential for accuracy in the recording, transfer and interpretation of data.

SI units

Measurement	Quantity	Standard unit	Symbol
length, mass and time	length	metre	m
	area	square metre	m^2
	volume	cubic metre	m^3
	mass	kilogram	kg
	density	kilogram per cubic metre	kg/m^3
	time	second	s
	frequency	hertz (= per second)	Hz
force and pressure	force	newton	N
	weight	newton	N
	moment of force	newton metre	N m
	pressure	pascal (= newton per square metre)	Pa
energy and heat	energy	joule	J
	work	joule (= newton metre)	J
	power	watt	W
	temperature	degree Celsius	°C
	absolute temperature	Kelvin	K
electricity	electric current	ampere	A
	electromotive force	volt	V
	potential difference	volt	V
	resistance	ohm	Ω
	electrical energy	joule	J

Using prefixes

A **prefix** is a small word that can be added in front of the standard unit, to increase or decrease its value for very large or very small numbers.

Numbers are expressed as powers of ten. For example, one hundred is ten to the power two (or ten squared): $100 = 10 \times 10 = 10^2$.

Increase in value

For example, the term 'kilo' is used with metre to derive the term 'kilometre'. Since kilo stands for 1000, a kilometre is one thousand metres ($1000 = 10 \times 10 \times 10$, or 10^3).

The table below gives a few examples of the powers of ten of large numbers and shows how the prefixes are used.

Multiple	Prefix	Symbol	Example
10^9	giga	G	gigawatt
10^6	mega	M	megajoule
10^3	kilo	k	kilometre

Decrease in value

One metre can be divided into smaller units, for example into one thousand parts, each of which is called a millimetre. The prefix 'milli' means that the particular unit to which it is attached is divided by one thousand.

$$\frac{1}{1000} = \frac{1}{10 \times 10 \times 10} = 10^{-3}$$

This table gives a few examples of the powers of ten for smaller numbers and shows how the prefixes are used.

Multiple	Prefix	Symbol	Example
10^{-1}	deci	d	decimetre
10^{-2}	centi	c	centimetre
10^{-3}	milli	m	millimetre
10^{-6}	micro	µ	micrometre
10^{-9}	nano	n	nanosecond

Common derived units

The common multiples (larger and smaller) derived from SI units are shown in the table below.

Quantity	SI unit and symbol	Common derived units
Length	metre m	km, dm, cm, mm, μm, nm
Area	square metre m²	cm², mm²
Volume	cubic metre cm³	litre (dm³), cm³, mm³, ml
Mass	kilogram kg	g, mg, μg
Weight	newton N	kN
Time	second s	minute, hour, day, week, month, year
Energy	joule J	kJ, MJ
Pressure	pascal Pa	kPa, MPa

Note: in science, weight is a force and therefore measured in newtons, and not in kilograms or grams.

Measuring very, very large distances

To measure distances in space, astronomers use:

- the light-year (the distance that light travels in a year) = 9.45×10^{15} km
- the astronomical unit (AU: the average distance of the Earth from the Sun) = 149.6×10^{6} km.

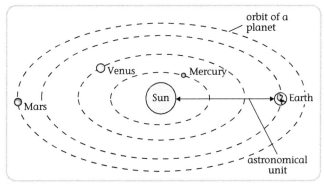

Part of the solar system

Are there other measurements we use?

A visit to the local grocery store or market will soon show that many things are still sold in pounds and pints. Tailors still use inches, cloth may be sold in yards and gallons of paint can be bought from the hardware store. Racehorses still run furlongs, weather reports often give wind speeds in miles per hour and ships travel in knots.

While these units are no longer taught in our schools, they remain part of our everyday experience, and we still need to know how they relate to the SI units we use in science, as shown below.

Unit	How used in everyday life	Metric equivalent
Inch	Length measure	2.54 cm
Foot	Length measure	30.48 cm
Yard	Length measure	0.9144 m
Furlong	Length/distance measure	201.18 m
Mile	Length/distance measure	1.6093 km
Mile per hour	Speed measure	1.61 km/h
Knot	Speed measure	1.85 km/h
Pint (US)	Volume measure	0.473 dm³
Gallon (US)	Volume measure	3.79 dm³
Gallon (Imperial)	Volume measure	4.55 dm³
Ounce	Weight/mass measure	28.38 g
Pound	Weight/mass measure	0.454 kg
Pound/square inch	Pressure measure	7.038 kPa
Ton	Weight/mass measure	1016.05 kg

Questions

1 Choose five quantities (such as length), and give the SI unit and a common derived unit.
2 What is the meaning of each of these prefixes: kilo, milli, centi, micro and mega?
3 What are the scientific units for (a) mass and (b) weight? How are they confused in everyday life?

Key ideas

Use these numbers and words to fill in the spaces as you write the sentences in your Exercise book.

10^{-3} SI light-year 10^{3} prefixes 10^{-2} AU pounds

The _____ system is used by scientists. The _____ units can be made larger or smaller by using

_____ . Some _____ for these measurements are: kilo (_____), centi (_____) and milli

(_____). For very large distances, astronomers use the _____ (astronomical unit) and the

_____ . Non-metric units, such as _____ and stones, are still used to measure weight.

1.3 How are living things built up?

What are the organs in a flowering plant?

The organs of a flowering plant are the:

- flowers
- fruits
- leaves
- stems
- roots

Every living cell in a plant can carry out respiration, but the different parts of the plant have different functions.

flowers
- contain male and female sex organs
- are often brightly coloured to attract insects
- after pollination and fertilization make fruits and seeds

leaves
- carry out photosynthesis and transpiration

stems
- hold up the leaves and flowers
- transport water and minerals up the stem
- transport food down the stem

fruits
- contain the seeds
- store food and can be eaten by animals

roots
- anchor the plant in the soil
- root hairs take in water and mineral salt (they have a large surface area to do this)
- store food and can be eaten by animals

Objectives

- Define cell, tissue, organ, organ system and organism.
- List the functions of some organs and organ systems in a flowering plant and a mammal.

How are organisms built up?

Cells (pages 44–5) are the building blocks of living things, in a similar way that bricks are used in a house. Cells are built into tissues, tissues into organs, organs into systems and systems into the whole organism.

What does it mean?

Cell   The building block of living things.

Tissue   A group of similar cells working together with a certain function, e.g. plant epidermis, a muscle.

Organ   Different tissues working together with certain functions, e.g. a leaf, the heart.

Organ system   Several organs working together to carry out major activities, e.g. transport systems.

Organism   The whole plant or animal.

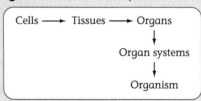

Cells → Tissues → Organs
→ Organ systems
→ Organism

What are the organs and systems in a mammal?

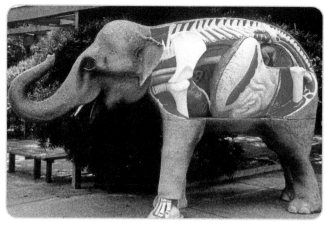

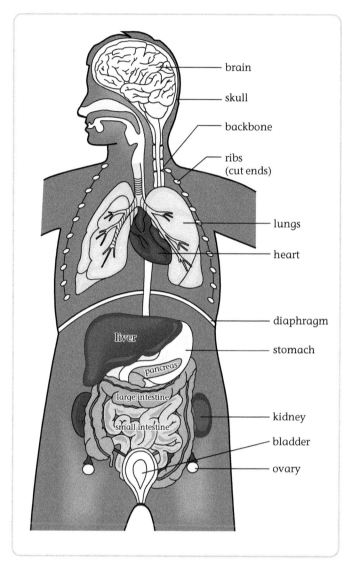

brain
skull
backbone
ribs (cut ends)
lungs
heart
diaphragm
liver
stomach
pancreas
large intestine
small intestine
kidney
bladder
ovary

Systems	Functions and main organs
Digestive system	Digests and absorbs food: alimentary canal, liver, pancreas
Respiratory system	Takes in O_2 and gets rid of CO_2: windpipe, lungs, ribs, diaphragm
Excretory system	Removes waste materials made in the body: kidneys, bladder, liver
Circulatory system	Transports materials around body: heart, blood vessels
Reproductive system	Produces offspring: ovary, uterus; testes, penis
Nervous system	Controls and coordinates body: brain, spinal cord, nerves
Endocrine system	Controls growth rates and some reactions: glands, hormones
Skeletal system	Supports and protects body organs: backbone, skull, limb bones
Muscle system	Allows movement of the body: muscles arranged in pairs

Key ideas

Use these words to fill in the spaces as you write the sentences in your Exercise book.

different　　**digestive**　　**similar**　　**reproductive**　　**organs**　　**respiratory**

A tissue is built up of _____ cells working together. An organ is made up of _____ tissues working together. Several _____ work together to make each organ system. In animals the _____ system is important for breaking down food, the _____ system controls the exchange of gases, and the _____ system produces offspring.

1.4 Who's who among living things?

How do we classify living things?

'To classify' is to put things into groups. These groups are then split into smaller groups. Each group has features in common and is different from other groups. Some important features we use are:

- size: microscopic, or can be seen with the naked eye
- unicellular (one cell) or multicellular (many cells)
- seeds or no seeds
- number of limbs
- kind of body covering
- flowers or no flowers
- backbone or not
- lays eggs or not

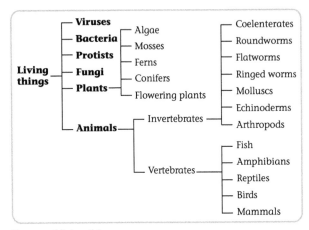

Groups of living things

Number of limbs	Examples of animals
0	Molluscs, echinoderms
4	Amphibians, reptiles, birds, mammals
6	Insects
8	Spiders
2 per segment	Centipedes
4 per segment	Millipedes

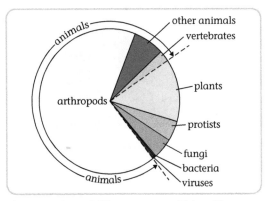

The proportions of different groups of living things

How are plants and animals different?

Look at the photographs and talk about how plants and animals are different. Then read the table below and check if you were right.

A plant	An animal
Uses simple substances to make its own food.	Feeds on complex food substances containing trapped chemical energy.
Has chlorophyll and can carry out photosynthesis.	Does not have chlorophyll and cannot photosynthesize.
Does not digest food.	Has structures to digest food.
Is usually rooted in the ground.	Is not rooted in the ground.
Does not move from place to place.	Moves around to get food and to escape enemies.
Has no nerve or muscle cells.	Has nerves and muscle cells.
Does not have special sense organs.	Has special sense organs.

Viruses About 100 nm, seen only with electron microscope, no cell structure, can only reproduce inside living organisms.

Tobacco mosaic disease virus   Influenza virus

Protists About 10 μm–1 mm, some seen with low power, single-celled, with nucleus. Plant-like with chlorophyll, or animal-like.

Plant-like: diatom   Animal-like: *Entamoeba*

Bacteria About 0.001 mm, seen under high power, single-celled or joined in chains, no nuclei.

Streptococcus (sore throat)   *Bacillus typhosus* (typhoid fever)   *Vibrio* (cholera)

Fungi About 5 μm–20 cm, mostly many-celled with nuclei. No chlorophyll.

Yeast   Pin mould on a banana   Mushroom

Plants

Small to very large, visible to the naked eye (i.e. without a microscope), many-celled with nuclei, chlorophyll, mostly stationary and rooted in the ground.

Non-flowering plants Do not have flowers.

Flowering plants 5 cm–30 m, small to tree-like, roots, stems and leaves, reproduce by seeds inside flowers.

Algae About 5 mm–100 cm, mostly small, no roots, stems or leaves. Threads or divided sheets.

Spirogyra green threads   *Sargassum* brown seaweed

Monocotyledons

Narrow leaves with parallel veins.
Bunch of small roots (fibrous roots).
One seed leaf (cotyledon) in seed.

Dicotyledons

Broad leaves with branching veins.
Main (tap) root with many branches.
Two seed leaves (cotyledons) in seed.

Mosses About 5 mm–15 cm, simple roots, stems and leaves, reproduce by spores.

Moss 'leaves'   Spore case

Grass

Balsam

Ferns About 5 cm–10 cm, small to tree-like, roots, stems and leaves, reproduce by spores.

Fern   Spore cases   Tree fern

Banana

Hibiscus

Conifers About 5 m–30 m, mainly tree-like, roots, stems and leaves, reproduce by seeds inside cones.

Pine tree   Cone

Coconut palm

Mango tree

1.4 Who's who among living things? (continued)

Animals
Small to large, visible to the naked eye, many-celled with nuclei, no chlorophyll, usually move around and feed on other organisms.

INVERTEBRATES Animals without backbones. Mostly small. Either soft-bodied or with a hard outer case (exoskeleton).

Coelenterates About 1 cm–many metres. Bag-like with tentacles around mouth, no legs. Live singly or in groups (coral). Most live in the sea.

Sea anemone   Jellyfish   Coral

Roundworms (nematodes) About 100 mm–30 cm. Body long and thin, round in cross-section, no legs, no rings. Most are parasites; others live in the soil.

Hookworm   Threadworm

Molluscs About 3 cm–30 cm. Soft body, undivided and often inside a shell, no legs. Some with tentacles. Most live in water, a few on land.

Sea snail   Slug   Squid

Flatworms About 10 mm–5 m. Body long and thin, flat in cross-section, no legs, no rings. Have hooks and suckers. Most are parasites of animals.

Tapeworm   Blood fluke

Echinoderms About 10 cm–15 cm. Ball-shaped or star-shaped based on a five-part pattern, no legs, tough outer skin with spines. Live in the sea.

Sea urchin   Starfish

Ringed worms About 5 cm–1 m. Body long and divided up by rings, round in cross-section, no legs. Most are aquatic; others live in the soil.

Pheretima, an earthworm   Leech   Sea worm

Arthropods Mainly small, crawling animals with a hard outer case (exoskeleton). The only invertebrates with jointed legs.

Insects 3 pairs of legs, body divided into head, thorax, abdomen, 2 pairs of wings. Live on land. Examples: butterflies, cockroaches, beetles, termites and lice.

Beetle

Arachnids 4 pairs of legs, head and thorax joined, no wings. Some are parasites. Live on land. Examples: spiders, ticks and mites.

Spider

Crustacea 4–10 pairs of legs, usually with shield over front of body, no wings, breathe with gills. Mostly live in water. Examples: crabs, shrimps, woodlice.

Crab

Myriapods More than 10 pairs of legs, body long and divided into segments, no wings. Live on land. Examples: centipedes and millipedes.

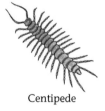

Centipede

VERTEBRATES Animals with backbones. Skeleton inside the body (endoskeleton). Mostly large. Some live in water and have gills. Others live on land or in the air and have lungs. Land forms usually have four limbs.

Fish Covered in scales. Live in water and breathe with gills. Streamlined body and fins for swimming. Eggs laid and develop in water. Examples: Nile perch, flying fish, seahorse, shark.

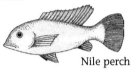

Nile perch

Birds Covered in feathers. Breathe with lungs. Live on land and in the air. Have wings for flying. Eggs laid inside a hard shell in nests. Examples: vulture, egret, chicken, owl. Maintain a constant body temperature.

Vulture

Amphibians No skin outgrowths. Young stage (tadpole) lives in water, breathes with gills. Adult lives on land and in water, has 4 limbs and breathes with lungs. Eggs laid and develop in water or moist places. Examples: toads and frogs.

Tadpole

Adult toad

Reptiles Covered in scales. Breathe with lungs. Most live on land, others in water. Either slide (snakes), swim (turtles) or walk (lizards). Eggs laid inside a leathery shell on land.

Lizard

Crocodile

Mammals Covered in hair. Breathe with lungs. Most live on land, some live in water. Either walk (dog) or swim (whale). Eggs develop inside female, and the young are born. The young are fed on milk. Maintain a constant body temperature.

Dog

Human

How to identify vertebrates
Animals with fins or four limbs are vertebrates. You can identify them even further by their skin covering:

Scales . . . . Fish
Feathers . . . . Birds
Moist, non-scaly skin . . . . Amphibians
Dry, scaly skin . . . . Reptiles
Hair or fur . . . . Mammals

Questions

1 How could you distinguish between each pair of organisms? (a) reptile and amphibian, (b) bird and insect, (c) tapeworm and earthworm, (d) tree fern and pine tree.
2 List three distinguishing features for each of (a) mammals, (b) insects, (c) flowering plants, (d) fish.

Did you know?

● On Earth there are more than one and a half million species and more than 3,000,000,000,000,000,000,000,000,000,000 animals.
● Snakes are reptiles, even though you can't see their limbs.

Key ideas

Use these words to fill in the spaces as you write the sentences in your Exercise book.

backbone   **covering**   **outside**   **flowers**   **unicellular**   **seeds**

Simple organisms may have only one cell: they are _____ . Conifers have _____ but do not have _____ . Many invertebrates have a soft covering, and those that have a skeleton have it on the _____ of their bodies. Vertebrates have a _____ inside their bodies. We can divide vertebrates into groups depending on their skin _____ .

1.5 What is energy?

What are the forms of energy?

Energy is the ability to make things work and to make things change. Energy comes in various forms.

Electrical energy	Light energy
Wherever current is flowing. Easy to change to other forms of energy. electric cell — conventional current flows +ve to –ve	Produced, e.g., by the Sun, light bulbs and candles.
Sound energy	**Movement (kinetic energy)**
Vibrations, produced, e.g., by talking, telephones and musical instruments. 	Everything that moves has kinetic energy. 
Chemical energy	**Heat energy**
This is stored energy, e.g. in food, fuels and electric cells.	Everything has heat energy. The hotter something is, the more heat energy it has.
Potential energy (gravitational)	**Potential energy (elastic)**
Due to the position of an object above the ground, e.g. plane, waterfall. 	Due to stretching or turning, e.g. of rubber bands, springs. 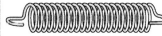

Practical 1

How can energy be stored? (MM)

1 Build a toy tank from a cotton reel, a rubber band and some spent matches. The length of the rubber band should be less than that of the reel.

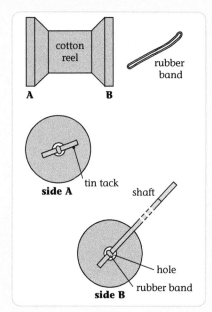

Making a cotton reel tank

2 Insert and pull one end of the band through side **B** and insert the shaft.

3 Hammer a small tack into side **A** to prevent the stick at **A** from spinning.

4 Hold the tank in one hand with side **B** uppermost. Turn the shaft in a circle several times. This twists the rubber band and gives it potential elastic energy.

5 Place the tank on the ground. It will move forward as the rubber band slowly untwists, as the potential energy is changed to kinetic energy of movement.

Activity

How does energy change?

Energy is not 'used up' as work is done. Instead, energy is changed from one form to another to make things change.

1 Look at each picture below. Decide which of these are the main energy changes that are occurring in each case.

- chemical to electrical to light + heat
- potential (gravitational) to kinetic
- chemical to kinetic + heat
- light to electrical
- electrical to sound
- kinetic to electrical

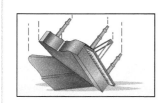 

 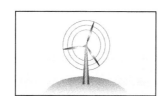

 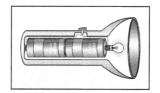

2 Look around you. Find an appliance that is 'working'. List the form of energy that is being changed into other forms.

What is nuclear energy?

The atoms of some elements, such as some forms of uranium, can release energy from their nuclei. They are called **radioactive** substances.

They are made to disintegrate in nuclear power stations. During this process, some mass is changed into an enormous amount of energy (page 341). The original atoms are split into simpler ones and the process is called **nuclear fission**. 1 kg of radioactive uranium can release as much energy as 60 tonnes of coal.

In the Sun and other stars, small atoms are combined to make new atoms. Mass is again changed into energy. This process is called **nuclear fusion**. It also happens in the hydrogen bomb and in some experimental power stations.

Did you know?

- The unit in which we measure energy and work done is the joule (J).
- The work done in throwing a ball is about 20 J, and climbing stairs is 1 kJ.

How is energy 'wasted'?

If an appliance gets hot or is noisy when we use it, then it is probably not changing all the energy into a useful form. But the energy still exists – as heat and sound – it just is not very useful to us.

Key ideas

Use these words to fill in the spaces as you write the sentences in your Exercise book.

heat   **electrical**   **sound**   **light**   **potential**   **kinetic**   **chemical**

As a flashlight works, _____ energy changes into _____ and _____ . The energy something

has because of its position or when it is stretched is called _____ energy. This can change into

_____ energy to cause movement. Energy stored in foods, fuels and electric cells is called _____

energy. When working, appliances can 'waste' energy as _____ and _____ .

1.6 What is matter made of?

Matter is the stuff of which all living and non-living things are made. There is a lot of evidence that matter itself is made up of very, very small pieces, or **particles**.

Practical 2

Finding evidence for particles in matter (ORR, MM, AI)

1 Forming crystals

Particles in a solution come together to build up crystals.
- You start with a very concentrated solution, for example of blue copper sulphate. You add more and more copper sulphate to warm water until no more will dissolve. Then you can suspend a small crystal in the solution and observe the crystal grow during the next 4 to 5 days.

Explanation: the crystal increases in size layer by layer as particles are added to the outside of it.

2 Diluting solutions

As you dilute a solution containing a coloured substance, the solution becomes paler and paler.
- Use a small amount of, for example, copper sulphate or instant coffee, which you dissolve in 10 cm³ of water in a small measuring cylinder. Stir and then pour 9 cm³ of this solution into a test tube. Dilute the remaining 1 cm³ of solution up to the 10 cm³ level in the measuring cylinder. Again, keep 9 cm³ in a second test tube, and dilute the remaining 1 cm³ up to the 10 cm³ level. Repeat this process until the colour disappears.

Explanation: as the solutions become more dilute, the coloured particles are so few we can no longer see them.

3 Particles in gases can move

The smell of a gas spreads out from its starting point as the particles move to fill the space: this is called **diffusion**.
- Everyone should sit facing the front. Then your teacher will squirt some air freshener from a certain point at the back of the room. As each person smells the gas, they raise their right hand. You will observe how the gas travels (diffuses) from its starting point. Record the time it takes for the air freshener to reach the front of the classroom.

Explanation: particles in a gas move quickly as they diffuse out from a place where they are concentrated.

4 Particles in liquids can move

Coloured particles diffuse out to colour a solution.
- Carefully add a small amount of copper sulphate or instant coffee to water in a beaker. Watch as the colour spreads. Record how long it takes to colour the solution.

Explanation: particles move in a solution, but diffusion occurs more slowly in a liquid than in a gas.

Objectives

- Examine evidence for the presence of particles in matter, and see how this helps explain some of our observations.
- Describe solids, liquids and gases and how they change state.

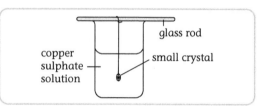

1 Forming crystals

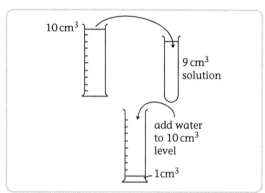

2 Diluting solutions

3 Particles in gases can move

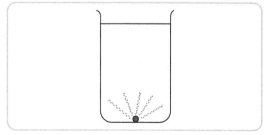

4 Particles in liquids can move

The particle theory of matter

All matter is made up of particles. These are packed closer together or further apart in the three states of matter. This helps us explain the properties of solids, liquids and gases.

Solids

- Particles are held very closely together by strong forces.
- Particles can vibrate, but do not move around.

This explains their properties: solids are not easily squashed, they can conduct heat easily from particle to particle, they have a definite shape and volume, and they expand the least when heated, as the particles are held tightly together.

Liquids

- Particles are close together but have more energy.
- Particles are still attracted to each other but they can move around in the liquid.

This explains their properties: liquids are not easily squashed, they transfer heat mainly by the moving of particles, they have a definite volume but not a definite shape, and they expand more than solids when heated.

Gases

- Particles are far apart and there is only very weak attraction between them.
- Particles move freely until they bump into something.

This explains their properties: gases are easily squashed, they transfer heat by the moving of particles, they do not have a definite shape or volume, they diffuse quickly to fill the space available, and they expand the most when heated.

Heating and cooling

When solids and liquids are heated, their particles take up more space and they expand. They might be heated so much that they can **change state** to liquids and gases.

When gases and liquids are cooled, their particles take up less space and they contract. They might be cooled so much that they change state to liquids and solids.

Changes in state

As a substance changes state it takes in heat to rearrange its particles.

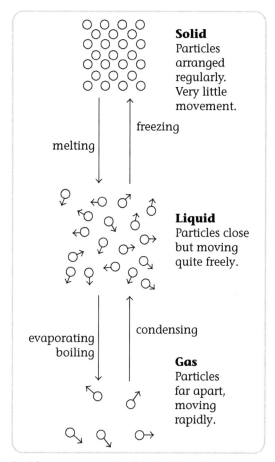

Particle arrangements in solids, liquids and gases

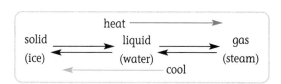

Key ideas

Use these words to fill in the spaces as you write the sentences in your Exercise book.

gas　　**diffuse**　　**liquid**　　**melting**　　**solid**　　**condense**　　**state**

A _____ has a fixed shape and volume, but a _____ can fill any space. A _____ will take the shape of the lower part of its container. Particles in liquids and gases can _____ from their place of origin. When solids are heated sufficiently they can change _____ by _____ to become liquids. When a gas is cooled sufficiently it can _____ to make a liquid.

1.6 What is matter made of? (continued)

You have seen how matter is made up of particles. But what are the particles themselves made of?

Atoms and molecules

If we could cut an element into its smallest particles, we would get to **atoms**. These are the smallest particles that still show the characteristics of the substance. So all the atoms in pure carbon are carbon atoms.

Atoms join together to make **molecules**. So molecules have two or more atoms in them. The atoms can be the same, as in molecules of oxygen, or they can be different, as in molecules of carbon dioxide.

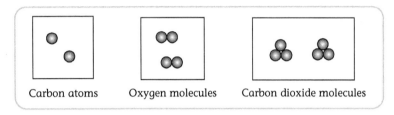

Carbon atoms   Oxygen molecules   Carbon dioxide molecules

Elements, mixtures and compounds

In an **element**, all the particles are the same: carbon and oxygen are elements. When elements combine to form a new substance, this is called a **compound**: carbon dioxide is a compound. Many compounds contain molecules with two or more different kinds of atoms in them.

If elements are mixed up and can be easily separated again, we call this a **mixture**. If the bits of one part of the mixture are big enough, the parts can be separated by sieving or filtering. But if one substance is dissolved in the other and cannot be seen, then the parts cannot be separated by sieving or filtering.

Practical 3

Iron and sulphur (ORR, MM)

Your teacher will give you samples of iron and sulphur. You will also need a magnet, bottle top, tongs and a Bunsen burner.

1 Note the appearance and properties of the elements.

2 Mix small quantities of the elements in a bottle top. Now record the appearance and properties of the mixture.

3 Hold the bottle top in tongs and heat the mixture strongly in a Bunsen flame. Allow it to cool and then note the properties of the compound that has been formed.

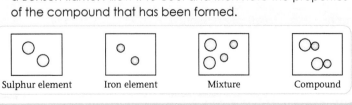

Sulphur element   Iron element   Mixture   Compound

Objectives

- Distinguish between atoms and molecules, and between elements, mixtures and compounds.
- Describe the structure of atoms.

What does it mean?

Element A pure substance that cannot be split into simpler substances. Its particles can be atoms or molecules.

Atom The smallest particle of an element that still has its characteristics.

Molecule This contains two or more atoms. These atoms are the same in an element. The atoms are different in a compound.

Compound A pure substance in which the molecules have different atoms combined in certain proportions. Its properties are different from the elements that made it.

Mixture This contains elements and/or compounds in various amounts that can easily be separated. Its properties are those of the chemicals used to make it.

Uneven mixture The parts that made it can usually be seen and separated, e.g. with a magnet or by sieving or filtering.

Solution The parts of this mixture (solute and solvent) are evenly mixed and cannot be seen or separated by sieving or filtering.

Questions

1 What is (a) an atom, (b) a molecule, (c) an element and (d) a compound?

2 (a) How could you separate a mixture of sand and water?

  (b) Could you use the same method for a mixture of salt and water? Why?

3 How is a mixture of iron and sulphur different from the compound of iron and sulphur?

What does it show?

Match the diagrams to the following:

- an element
- a compound
- a mixture of an element and a compound
- a mixture of elements
- a mixture of compounds

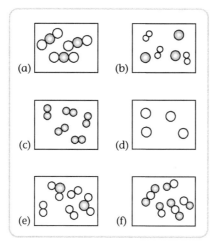

What are atoms made of?

All atoms have a similar structure. Differences between atoms, and therefore between elements, are based on the numbers of particles and the arrangement of electrons.

Particle	Position	Relative mass	Charge
Proton	In nucleus (p)	1	Positive
Neutron	In nucleus (n)	1	Neutral
Electron	In shells around nucleus	about 1/2000	Negative

For example, the simplest atom is hydrogen. It has one proton and one electron. The next simplest atom is helium, with two protons, two neutrons and two electrons. After this, extra electrons go into a second shell, as in the carbon atom.

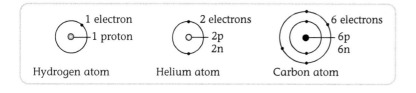

Hydrogen atom   Helium atom   Carbon atom

What does it mean?

Atomic structure Shows what an atom is made of: a central nucleus of protons and neutrons, surrounded by electrons.

Proton A particle in the nucleus. It is given a mass of 1. It has a positive charge.

Neutron A particle in the nucleus with the same mass as a proton but no charge.

Electrons Very tiny particles, with a negative charge, that orbit the nucleus at various distances.

Shells The positions around the nucleus where the electrons are most often.

Charge A characteristic of some particles: they can be positive (+) or negative (–).

Neutral The numbers of protons (+) and electrons (–) in any atom are the same, so an atom is neutral: it has no charge.

Ion A charged particle. It is made, for example, when an atom gains or loses electrons.

Key ideas

Use these words to fill in the spaces as you write the sentences in your Exercise book.

protons   **compound**   **atoms**   **element**   **electrons**   **molecule**   **mixture**

An _____ is a pure substance that cannot be split into simpler substances. The _____ in a _____ can be similar or different. If they are different the substance is called a _____ . If elements and compounds are just mixed together and can be separated, the substance is called a _____ . Inside an atom the positively charged particles are _____ and the negatively charged particles are _____ . There are equal numbers of each of them in an atom.

1.7 How can matter change?

Physical and chemical changes

Physical changes

When you mixed iron and sulphur (page 20), you found that the mixture kept the properties of the elements. Using a magnet could separate them. No new substances were formed.

Here are some other examples of physical changes:

- change of state, e.g. solid to liquid to gas
- grinding a solid to make a powder
- many examples of making solutions, e.g. salt and water.

Chemical changes

When you heated iron and sulphur together, you made a new compound. This had different properties from the elements that made it. Those elements could no longer be easily separated from each other.

How are chemical changes brought about?

Heating

You can heat a substance on its own, for example, blue copper sulphate crystals, and drive off the water. Or you can heat two substances together, such as burning magnesium in air, where it combines with oxygen to give out lots of light and heat and produce magnesium oxide.

Electric current

If electricity is passed through some substances, it can supply energy to break up the compound to release the elements. For example, water can be broken down in this way to release oxygen and hydrogen.

Mixing

If the chemicals we mix can react together, we get a chemical change. For example, mixing iodine solution with starch solution gives a new blue-black substance. And when we add magnesium to a dilute acid we get bubbles of hydrogen gas and another new substance.

How can we show chemical reactions?

To show what happens in a chemical reaction we write a **word equation**. The substances that react we put on the left-hand side, and they are called the **reactants**. The new substances that are made we put on the right-hand side, and they are called the **products**. Here is an example:

magnesium + oxygen	—heat→	magnesium oxide + energy
reactants		*products*

Objectives

- Distinguish between physical and chemical changes.
- Identify some changes caused by heat, electricity and chemical reactions.
- Represent chemical changes using word equations and models of the atoms and molecules involved.

What does it mean?

Physical change A change that can fairly easily be reversed, e.g. change of state, or mixing substances that do not react. No new substances are formed.

Chemical change The chemical reaction between substances that produces new substances with different properties. It cannot usually be easily reversed.

Word equation Shows the substances that react (**reactants**) and the new ones that are produced (**products**) during a chemical reaction.

State symbols These record the state of matter of each substance in a chemical reaction: solid (s), liquid (l), gas (g).

Aqueous solution When a substance is dissolved in water: symbol (aq).

What's in a name?

When iron and sulphur combine they make iron sulph**ide**. Sodium and chlorine make sodium chlor**ide**. Compounds made from two elements have a name ending in **–ide**.

Name the compounds made from:

1 calcium and oxygen
2 aluminium and iodine
3 iron and chlorine.

Then write all the word equations.

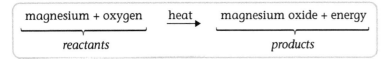

State symbols

We can add information to a word equation by showing the state: solid(s), liquid(l) or gas(g) of each substance.

$$\text{magnesium(s)} + \text{oxygen(g)} \xrightarrow{\text{heat}} \text{magnesium oxide(s)}$$

If a substance is dissolved in water, we say it is an **aqueous solution**(aq). For example, when we dissolve solid sodium hydroxide pellets in water we can show this as:

$$\text{sodium hydroxide(s)} + \text{water(l)} \longrightarrow \text{sodium hydroxide(aq)}$$

How else can we show chemical reactions?

We can use diagrams to represent the atoms and molecules as circles, and show how they react. You need to have the same numbers of atoms of each chemical on each side of the equation.

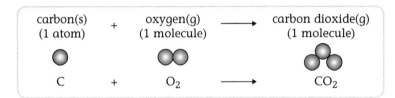

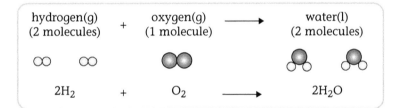

What actually happens in a chemical reaction?

In a chemical reaction, the electrons are very important.

- Atoms in the substances that are reacting can lose or gain electrons. This makes positive or negative **ions**. These ions then attract each other to make a new compound.
- In some chemical reactions, the electrons are shared between the atoms, to form molecules, when a new compound is made.

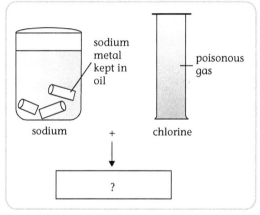

Compounds have very different properties from their elements!

Questions

For the reaction shown above:

1 Write a word equation, with state symbols.

2 Explain how the properties of the elements and the compound differ.

Key ideas

Use these words to fill in the spaces as you write the sentences in your Exercise book.

chemical   **word**   **physical**   **products**   **state**   **atoms**   **reactants**

During a _____ change no new substances are made. But during a _____ change the _____ interact to make new _____ . We can show what happens in a _____ reaction by making a diagram to show the _____ and molecules that are involved, and by writing a _____ equation. We can also add _____ symbols to the _____ equation.

1.8 Why is carbon so important?

What do you think the following things have in common: sugar, cheese, a tree, kerosene, gasoline, a CD, a lizard and a plastic cup? The answer is that they all contain carbon. Carbon is a very important element in every living thing, as well as in foods, fuels and plastics. Carbon is an element that can be found pure in the form of diamonds (which are very hard and transparent) and graphite (which is soft and black).

Activity

Where can we find carbon?

Your teacher will carry out this activity.
- When wood is heated without much air, black charcoal is formed. This is an impure form of carbon.
- If you hold a tin lid in a candle flame or yellow flame of a Bunsen burner, you will find bits of black soot on it. These came from the carbon in the wax or fuel.
- If a little concentrated sulphuric acid is poured onto white sugar, it draws water molecules out of it. What is left behind is a frothy mass of black carbon.
- If a little kerosene is lit in a bottle top and a tin lid is held over the flame, you will again see bits of black carbon. These have come from the kerosene.

What does it mean?

Organic compounds Complex carbon compounds containing a lot of trapped energy. Usually made by living things.

Hydrocarbons Compounds containing carbon and hydrogen only.

In the activity above, the substances containing carbon are called **organic compounds**. Organic compounds are complex carbon compounds, usually made by living things, that contain a lot of trapped energy. This is why some of them can be used as food and fuels.

How can carbon form so many compounds?

Each atom of carbon has four electrons in its outer shell. When it takes part in chemical reactions it fills up this shell to have eight electrons. It does this by sharing electrons with other atoms. It can form very many compounds with other elements. It is often combined just with hydrogen to make **hydrocarbons**.

- An example of a hydrocarbon is shown in the top diagram on the right (a). Each carbon atom combines with four hydrogen atoms to make a molecule called *methane*.

- In the next diagram (b) is an *ethane* molecule. You can count the numbers of carbon and hydrogen atoms. See how each carbon atom bonds to four other atoms.

- Carbon can also form compounds containing oxygen. An example of this is *ethanol* (alcohol) (c).

- There are also many examples in which carbon forms rings, on its own, or with oxygen – as in *glucose* sugar (d). You can count the numbers of carbon, hydrogen and oxygen atoms in a glucose molecule.

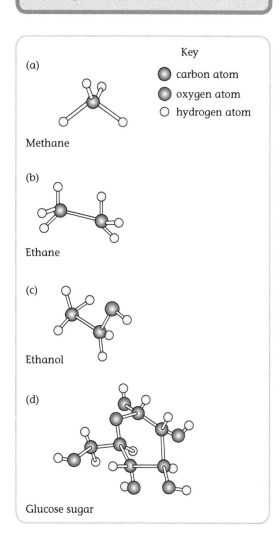

Key
- carbon atom
- oxygen atom
- hydrogen atom

(a) Methane

(b) Ethane

(c) Ethanol

(d) Glucose sugar

What are some of the important groups of carbon compounds?

Fuels

Fuels are compounds that burn in air with the release of energy, usually as light and heat. Wood, charcoal, gasoline and kerosene are examples of fuels, as are the hydrocarbons methane (pages 24 and 237) and ethane.

Many fuels were originally made from living things, from long ago, and we call these **fossil fuels**. The energy from the Sun was trapped in the fuels, and this is released when the fuel is burnt. At the same time, compounds of carbon and hydrogen are made (see page 81).

Foods

Plants make foods during **photosynthesis**. Foods therefore contain trapped energy that can be released during **respiration** (pages 76–80). Foods act as fuels for living things as they release their energy slowly, by the use of enzymes.

Carbohydrates These contain carbon, hydrogen and oxygen, for example glucose sugar (d) on page 24. Count the numbers of atoms, and you will find twice as many hydrogen as oxygen atoms. Other carbohydrates are cane sugar, starch and cellulose (page 55).

Fats These also contain carbon, hydrogen and oxygen. They contain and release more energy than other foods. There are different kinds of fats (page 55).

Proteins These contain carbon, hydrogen and oxygen, but also nitrogen (page 54). Some proteins contain sulphur as well. Fish, meat and many seeds contain proteins.

Polymers

These are very large compounds, with chains of carbon atoms joined together in a repeating pattern. An example is *polyethene* (polythene) containing carbon and hydrogen atoms. A small part of a polythene molecule is shown in the diagram on the right. Some natural polymers are cotton, silk and wool. Humans also make synthetic polymers, such as plastics (pages 260–1).

What does it mean?

Fuel   A compound able to release a lot of energy when burnt or respired.

Food   A kind of fuel used by living things to release energy in respiration.

Polymer   Very large molecules with a carbon backbone and repeated pattern.

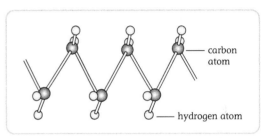

— carbon atom

— hydrogen atom

Part of the polymer polythene

Objects made from a common polymer: plastic

Key ideas

Use these words to fill in the spaces as you write the sentences in your Exercise book.

carbohydrates   **fuels**   **hydrocarbons**   **proteins**   **polymers**   **organic**

Complex compounds containing carbon and trapped energy are called _____ compounds. Some examples are _____ , which contain just carbon and hydrogen and are used as _____ . Fats and _____ contain carbon, hydrogen and oxygen, and in _____ we also find nitrogen. Small _____ can also be combined to make _____ , as in plastics.

2 Practical skills

2.1 How do we study Integrated Science?

Why study science?

Why should you study science if you do not want to work as a scientist? The science covered in this text is called **Integrated Science** because it involves many branches of science. For example, movement in animals involves biology for the muscles and nerves, physics for lever action and forces, and chemistry for the release of energy.

What mental skills are needed to study science?

The 'facts' of science can be read from books and memorized, but these have to be properly understood. There are higher-order skills beyond memorizing facts that will help you examine information critically, reorganize information and produce new ideas. Some of these skills are comprehension, analysis and application.

Science is very practical. In some cases the only way science can be understood is through practical work and demonstrations. When you do something practical, the experience becomes your own and you will learn and understand more quickly. Practical approaches to the study of science involve skills such as drawing, measuring, observing and recording (page 27 and pages 32–41).

While you study science, keep in mind that you have many different abilities or aptitudes, which influence the way you learn. Different people learn in different ways.

How is science useful?

- **For artists** Artistic people are usually good at visualizing and expressing their ideas through drawing, painting and design. They have a high spatial intelligence. They can benefit from the study of science, to understand the properties of the materials they work with, colour mixing, staining, fabrics, lighting, angles, photography, etc.

- **For sports people** Sports people are usually very aware of how the body works. They can benefit from the scientific knowledge of the corrosion of materials, and of the body's functioning, such as circulation and muscles.

- **For musicians** Musicians gain an understanding of the principles of sound production, materials and how the various instruments generate different sounds.

- **For everyone** The study of science helps improve your logical–mathematical problem-solving skills. For example, jury members must use logic and reason to come to a conclusion. The restaurant chef too must realize the logical outcome of the mixing and heating of various ingredients to produce the desired outcome.

Objectives

- Describe why science is so important.
- Describe the main profiles of your CSEC® examination: KC, UK and PS.
- Set up your SBA Practical workbook.

What science does a chef need?

Activity

What science do they need?

Work with a partner. Record some of the science information needed by:

- a pilot
- a musician
- a politician
- a parent
- a photographer
- a seamstress
- your teacher
- you

Questions

1 Discuss how science can help someone to become a better (a) taxi driver, (b) nursery nurse, (c) security guard and (d) dentist.
2 Can science help someone develop the skills when arguing a case? Discuss.
3 Can science help someone to make decisions on current issues? Discuss.

What is covered in Integrated Science?

Knowledge and comprehension (KC)

An ability to:

- remember what you have been taught as you recall, state and identify basic facts and ideas
- show understanding by selecting appropriate facts and ideas, and giving examples for familiar situations.

Use of knowledge (UK)

An ability to:

- adapt information for new situations, classify living and non-living things, and use formulae correctly
- identify parts of a whole and the relationship between them – for example, studying a local habitat
- combine parts to form a whole – for example, studying parts of the systems of a mammal, making predictions and solving problems
- evaluate (give reasons for the value of) ideas and actions, and make recommendations based on them.

Practical skills (PS)

These are outlined in the box, and on pages 30–43. Some practicals will be assessed by your teacher as part of the School Based Assessment (SBA): 20% of your final grade.

How do you keep records?

You need to set up two record books:

(a) an Exercise book to record results from activities, write answers to questions and complete the 'Key ideas'
(b) a practical workbook to record your practicals, some of which will be assessed for SBA; number all the pages in the book and set up a contents page:

Page number	Date	Aim of the practical	* (star) if assessed	Skills assessed
				etc.

What else is important?

You have to deal with numbers: this is covered in your CSEC® Mathematics course. You can also use:

- SI units, and units used in measurement (pages 8–9)
- Units used with measuring instruments (page 34)
- Preparing tables, bar charts, histograms, pie charts and line graphs (pages 39–41)
- Analysing and interpreting information (pages 42–3)

What are the examination papers?

Paper 1	(1¼ hours)	A multiple choice paper of 60 items
Paper 2	(2 hours)	Part A: four compulsory structured questions (one based on practicals)
		Part B: two essay-style questions.

Practical skills

The student:

PD
- thinks of a possible explanation: this is a **hypothesis**
- designs methods to make a **fair test** of the hypothesis
- collects materials and modifies plans in the light of difficulties

MM
- shows correct and careful handling of equipment, and is able to carry out laboratory techniques
- makes accurate readings using measuring equipment

D
- makes large, clear drawings and diagrams of specimens, apparatus or models, and labels them correctly

ORR
- uses the senses to make and record accurate observations
- displays information correctly in tables, bar charts, histograms, pie charts and line graphs
- uses appropriate headings and sequence for writing the report

AI
- identifies relationships and patterns, for example from graphs
- predicts from data
- makes accurate calculations and logical inferences
- evaluates data including errors.

Where to find help

- Science investigations and planning practical work (pages 361–2)
- Planning and designing (PD) (pages 30–1, 362)
- Manipulation and measurement (MM) (pages 32–5)
- Drawing (D) (pages 36–7)
- Observation, recording and reporting (ORR) (pages 38–41, 363)
- Analysis and interpretation (AI) (pages 42–3)

2.2 How do we use information?

Why is information needed?

Living organisms, even single cells, are aware of their surroundings. Being sensitive to stimuli and making the appropriate response are important characteristics of life (see page 6). Complex organisms have highly developed sense organs that are sensitive to stimuli. They have also devised and developed apparatus and instruments that can extend their senses.

How is information stored by living organisms?

All cellular organisms use DNA (page 44) to store information. This ensures basic functions of the cell are carried out, and information is passed to the next generation. Organisms also learn, and those with a nervous system and a brain have a very large capacity for storing information. This is especially true for humans.

How is information stored today?

The written word in newspapers, magazines and books is still our most important means of recording and storing information. Other information systems include photographic film, video tapes, computer chips, hard discs, floppy discs, flash drives, CDs and DVDs.

How is a computer used?

A computer system has five main parts, the computer **hardware**, as shown below.

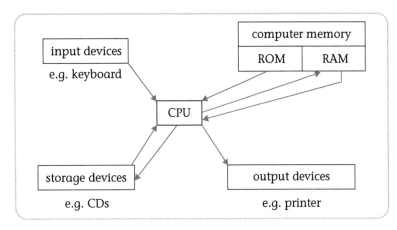

Parts of the computer hardware

The computer also needs **software**. These are the programs for instructing the computer. The main types are:

- operating systems, e.g. Windows and Mac OS, which control the hardware
- applications, e.g. word-processing and spreadsheet programs, and web browsers. They work through the operating system to access the hardware so that their programs can run.

What does it mean?

Input devices   Change information into binary code. Examples: keyboard, touch screen, microphone, scanner, digital camera, mobile phone and webcam.

Binary code   Code used by a computer, that has a series of 0s and 1s to show characters such as letters and numbers.

CPU   Central processing unit (the 'brain') that interprets the programs and performs the computer's activities.

Computer memory   ROM and RAM.

- ROM (read-only memory): the permanent memory that can be used for the start-up, but cannot be changed.
- RAM (random access memory): the memory in which you can save the changes that were made in the CPU.

Output devices   Change binary code into a form that is useful for humans. Examples: VDU (the screen or monitor), printers, loudspeakers.

Storage devices   These allow information to be stored and then accessed.

- Hard disc: built into the computer and can contain over 100 GB of data.
- Floppy discs: hold less than 1 GB of data.
- Flash drives: hold over 10 GB of data.
- CDs: contain over 700 MB of data.
- CD-ROMs: used to distribute software and multimedia programs. They cannot be changed by the user.
- CD-RW: used for recording data.
- DVDs: can be used to store movies for showing on a TV screen.

Computer hardware: can you name each piece of equipment?

How do we use the Internet?

The Internet (Net) is made up of linked computers. You can access the Net and send or receive text, sound and pictures to or from anywhere in the world in an instant.

- ISPs: Internet Service Providers allow access to the Net, and may provide search engines for gaining information.
- Modem: this connects the computer to the Net.
- Broadband: this makes the connection very quickly using a special modem.
- Email software: this connects with the user's ISP account, so that text, pictures and photographs can be sent and received between email addresses.
- Website: a place on the Net with information available on 'web pages'. You can set up your own website.
- World wide web (www): the huge collection of web pages that can be searched.
- Search engines, such as Google or Yahoo: these allow the user to search websites or to input a word or phrase and download articles on particular topics.

Questions

1 Give examples of hardware and software and how they are used.
2 Find out how computers are useful in an industry or business near you.
3 List some problems with using the Net.

The binary code

Computers only deal in 0s and 1s. 0 and 1 are called **bits** (short for 'binary digits'). These are strung together in groups of eight (a **byte**) to represent letters and larger numbers; e.g. the binary code for capital A is 01000001. For coding large amounts of data we need:
- one kilobyte (kB) = 1024 bytes
- one megabyte (MB) = 1024 kB
- one gigabyte (GB) = 1024 MB.

Other uses of computers

Electronic games

These allow different amounts of user participation. They can keep records of responses and scores.

Educational software

Learning programs may be simulations of physical systems, which are too difficult to explore in reality.

Business use

- Word-processors and spreadsheets.
- Data analysis and data processing.
- Reading the unique bar codes at the checkout in a supermarket. This allows records to be kept of items sold, prices controlled and replacements ordered.

Key ideas

Use these words to fill in the spaces as you write the sentences in your Exercise book.

CDs	input	software	Net	output	hardware	CPU

Our sense organs are like _____ devices, and our brain has a function similar to the _____ of a computer. The keyboard is an _____ device, and the printer is an _____ device. _____ are common storage devices. The computer equipment is called _____ , and the programs are the _____ . The _____ allows interaction with other computer users.

2.3 How do we plan and design?

How is SBA arranged?

The Integrated Science syllabus needs a teaching time of at least five 40-minute periods over two academic years. The practical skills of SBA are assessed during this time.

- In Form 4, the skills ORR, D, MM and AI are assessed.
- In Form 5, the skills ORR, D, MM, AI and PD are assessed.

In Form 4, your teacher will usually give you the method and title of the practical. Then you will carry out the practical and record, report and interpret your results. But you should also practise planning and designing, to give you a good basis for the assessment when you are in Form 5. There is a table that you can use on page 362, which outlines the main steps in planning and designing.

What is involved in planning and designing?

Planning and designing covers the first stage in how we try to find the answer to a scientific problem. For example, the problem and question might be 'Is water necessary for germination?' We then make a statement or **hypothesis** about what might happen, such as 'Seeds left without water will not germinate, but seeds left moist will germinate.' We then set up a **fair test** to find out if the hypothesis is supported by the results. For a fair test we must change only one thing or **variable**, in this case water: dry or moist. Our experiment should also be repeated several times and an average taken of the readings. For experiments with living material, such as seeds, you should always include large numbers. This is to guard against some of the seeds not germinating.

How can I do well in planning and designing?

- The hypothesis should be written as a statement and not as a question. It is based on observations.
- You should be able test the hypothesis.
- The method should relate directly to the hypothesis.
- The one variable to be changed must be clearly stated.
- All the other variables, such as volumes, masses and temperatures, must be listed and kept constant, to make the experiment a fair test from which you will be able to draw conclusions.
- The method should include the number of times the experiment is repeated, or include large numbers, such as 20 seeds, so the results will not just be the result of chance.
- You are likely to be asked to plan and design an experiment you have never done.
- You may not have to do the experiment. But your plan should be sensible and clear enough to enable someone else to do it.
- You should list the materials and equipment you need.
- You should also include the results you expect and when observations and measurements should be taken.
- You should list any safety precautions.
- You should also list any possible sources of error.

Objectives

- Describe what is involved in planning and designing (PD).
- Practise setting up fair tests as part of planning and designing.

What does it mean?

Problem   What you want to find out about. The question you want to investigate.

Hypothesis   A statement that says what you think the explanation could be. It might not be correct, but it should be sensible.

Variables   The conditions in an experiment, such as water, temperature, height.

Fair test   An experiment set up so only one variable is changed, so you can find its effect. You keep the other variables the same (*constant*). Then you can see if the hypothesis was supported or not.

Results   What happens: your observations or measurements.

Control   This has all the variables, so you compare your experiment (missing just one variable) to it, and draw a conclusion.

Method   Steps to take in setting up and carrying out an experiment. It should be clear enough for someone else to use.

Assessment   Checking if what you have done has achieved what you wanted; e.g. can you say your hypothesis is correct?

Questions

1 How do you use (a) variables and (b) a fair test in setting up an experiment?
2 Your friend says that small seeds germinate faster than larger seeds. How could you set up a fair test to find out?

Setting up a fair test

1 Susan and Jane were given this problem:
   Is the blue flame of a Bunsen burner hotter than the yellow flame?
   They were told they could heat some water to find out the answer.
2 They both wrote this hypothesis:
   The blue flame will heat water more quickly than a yellow flame does.
3 They then designed their experiments and set up their apparatus
   as shown below. Talk with a friend about the following.
   (a) Some mistakes Susan has made.

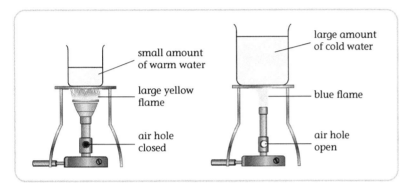

What Susan set up

   (b) How Jane has set up a fair test.

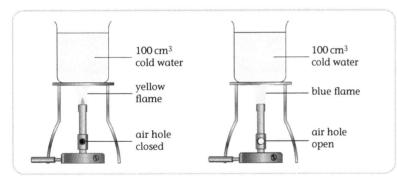

What Jane set up

   (c) Which of the girls will be able to say if her results agree or
   disagree with the hypothesis? How did her test make it possible
   to draw a correct conclusion?

Practical 4

Planning and designing

Use the outline on page 362 to help you
plan and design experiments to explain
these observations.

1 You observe a Coleus plant in a pot
   on a windowsill is bent towards the
   window. How could you find out
   the reason?

2 You are making bread on a very hot
   day and the dough rises very high.
   Why do you think this is and how could
   you test it?

3 Your friend has bought a new ball,
   which he says bounces better than
   yours. How could you find out if it does?

How will I be marked for planning and designing?

Here is a possible marking scheme.
Hypothesis:
- Clear statement of hypothesis   1
- Hypothesis testable/manageable   1

Design:
- Generally workable/suitable   1
- List of apparatus/materials   1
- Description of method   1
- Modifications where necessary   1
- Method can be duplicated   1
- Precautions taken, large numbers
  used, or repeated measurements 1
- Control clearly set up   1
- Limitations listed   1

Key ideas

Use these words to fill in the spaces as you write the sentences in your Exercise book.

problems   variable   method   hypothesis   fair test   variables   results

In science we make observations and want to solve _____ . We begin by stating a possible

solution, which we call a _____ . We then experiment to see if it is true by setting up a _____ .

We should change only one _____ and keep all the other _____ the same. We list the _____

we expect and describe our _____ so someone else could carry out our test.

2.4 How do we manipulate and measure?

What is manipulation?

Manipulation is the safe and correct handling of equipment, materials and living things. At all times follow the general instructions for safety in the laboratory (pages 246–8) and keep your workspace tidy and well organized.

What should I be able to do?

Handle glassware, chemicals, circuits and living things

1 Use two hands when carrying glassware and chemicals.
2 Put equipment down gently away from the edge of the bench.
3 Keep the label of a reagent bottle uppermost when you are pouring liquids. Hold the stopper in your hand.
4 Use separate clean spatulas to transfer solid chemicals.
5 Use only small amounts of chemicals and do not return unused chemicals to the bottle.
6 Dispose of wastes in the appropriate containers.
7 Check circuits with your teacher before using them.
8 Use dry hands to plug in electrical appliances.
9 Handle living things with care – use gloves if necessary.
10 Lift soft organisms carefully so you do not squash them.

Light a Bunsen burner

1 Set up the Bunsen burner with plenty of space around it, in a place that is not windy.
2 Turn the collar so the air hole is *closed*.
3 Light the match or splint.
4 Turn on the gas gently.
5 Hold your light near the top of the tube: you will get a yellow flame.
6 Slowly open the air hole until the flame becomes blue.
7 Adjust the gas supply to use the flame.
8 Do not leave the flame unattended.
9 After use, close the gas tap.
10 For more information, see page 248.

Use a test tube for heating

1 Make sure the test tube is clean before use – let it cool before you wash it, then leave it to drain in a rack.
2 Protect your hair and clothing from the Bunsen flame and wear safety goggles if necessary.
3 If you are heating solids, start with a dry test tube.
4 If you are using liquids, be careful not to spill any. Do not use more than about a third of the volume of the tube.
5 Hold the test tube near the top with a test-tube holder.
6 Hold it at an angle and with its top pointing away from other people and yourself.
7 Move the tube gently from side to side as you heat it in the flame (do not shake it up and down).
8 Heat as instructed, and do not use a finger as a stopper.
9 When you have finished, rest the hot test tube in a rack.

Objectives

- Set up simple laboratory apparatus and use it safely and correctly.
- Prepare specimens for observation.

More things to do

You should also be able to carry out these activities safely and correctly.
- Set up circuits   pages 292–5
- Filter   page 213
- Do simple distillation   page 214
- Test for gases
  O_2 page 49
  CO_2 page 73
  H_2 page 262
- Use a water bath   page 71

Questions

1 Choose one technique from this topic. Write your own instructions on how it should be done.
2 How do you get (a) a yellow flame and (b) a blue flame from a Bunsen burner? When should they each be used?

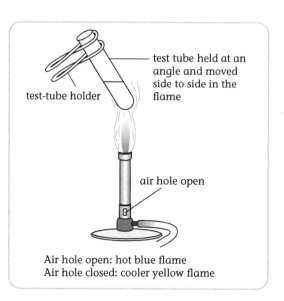

test tube held at an angle and moved side to side in the flame

test-tube holder

air hole open

Air hole open: hot blue flame
Air hole closed: cooler yellow flame

How do I prepare and observe specimens?

Use a hand lens

1 Hold the hand lens close to your eye.
2 Move the lens towards the object until it comes into focus.

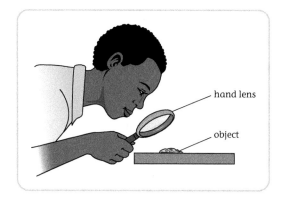

Cut sections and make slides

1 Choose a stem that is stiff but not thickened with wood.
2 Use a sharp safety razor blade.
3 Either cut across the stem (transverse section) or down the stem (longitudinal section).

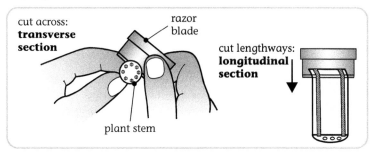

4 Cut very thin sections and put them in water or a stain.
5 Put the thinnest piece in a drop of water on a slide.
6 Use a pointed needle or large pin to carefully lower a coverslip over the material, without catching air bubbles.

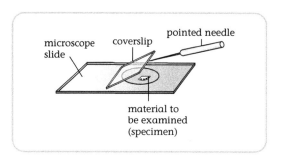

Use a microscope

1 Carry it carefully with two hands. Put it down gently onto a flat surface away from the edge of the bench.
2 Clean the lenses with soft tissue paper.
3 Put the eyepiece lens into the top of the body tube.
4 Screw the objective lens into the nosepiece, and turn it so it is above the hole in the stage.
5 Adjust the mirror and iris diaphragm to give a clear but not too bright view when looking down the eyepiece.
6 Place the slide on the stage and hold it with clips.
7 *Looking from the side*, lower the body tube with the coarse adjustment *down* until the objective lens is close to (but not touching) the slide.
8 *Looking though the eyepiece*, use the fine adjustment to *raise* the body tube until the specimen is in focus.

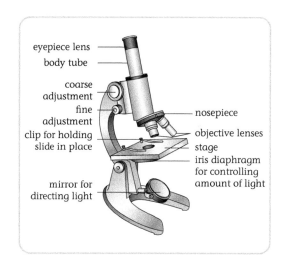

Key ideas

Use these words to fill in the spaces as you write the sentences in your Exercise book.

safe   open   side   raise   eyepiece   lower   close

Before you light a Bunsen burner you should _____ the hole. When the burner is lit you can

_____ the hole to adjust the flame. To focus a specimen with a microscope you should first

_____ the body tube while looking from the _____ . You can then _____ the body tube while

looking down the _____ . Always handle equipment in a _____ way.

2.4 How do we manipulate and measure? (continued)

What is measurement?

Measurement is finding the quantity of something, for example length or mass. We use a measuring instrument marked with a **scale**. The scale has lines and numbers. We need to look at these at the correct angle and read the value. Then we add the correct **units**, such as cm or g.

Which instruments should I be able to use?

Ruler and metre rule

These are marked in centimetres (cm) each with ten smaller markings in millimetres (mm).

1 Place the object to be measured at the zero line and read the scale looking from above at right angles.
2 You can also use these instruments to find the surface area in cm², or the volume of regular objects in cm³.

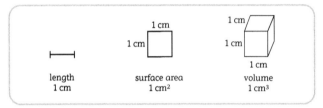

| length | surface area | volume |
| 1 cm | 1 cm² | 1 cm³ |

Measuring cylinder

This is used to find the volume in cm³.

1 Pour in the liquid, and read the level by looking at right angles at the lower curve (meniscus).
2 For an irregular solid: measure the volume of some water. Then put the solid in the water and work out its volume by taking the first reading away from the second.

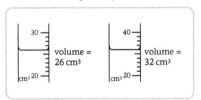

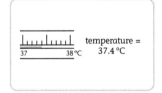

Thermometer

This tells us the average temperature ('hotness' or 'coldness') of something. There are several kinds of thermometer (pages 168–9).

1 Never put a thermometer into substances likely to be above its top reading, and never near a Bunsen flame.
2 Carry it by the top end and put it down gently.
3 For a mercury-in-glass clinical thermometer, give it a quick flick to shake down the mercury before using it.
4 Put the bulb completely in the liquid. Leave it for two minutes before reading it, to allow the thermometer to become the same temperature as the liquid.
5 Never use a thermometer as a stirrer.
6 Read the top of the meniscus in mercury thermometers.

Questions

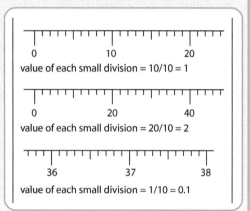

1 Find a measuring instrument for each of the scales shown below.

value of each small division = 10/10 = 1

value of each small division = 20/10 = 2

value of each small division = 1/10 = 0.1

2 Make a table to show the quantities we measure, and the units we use.
3 List six measuring instruments, with an instruction for the use of each one.

How accurately should we measure quantities?

- Ruler or metre rule:
  length to nearest 1 mm (0.1 cm)
- Measuring cylinder:
  volume to nearest 1 cm³
- Thermometer:
  temperature to nearest 0.1, 0.5 or 1.0 °C
- Lever-arm balance:
  mass to nearest 1 g
- Stop clock:
  time to nearest second (s)

Note: it is best to take three readings, and then work out the average.

Lever-arm balance

This measures the mass: the amount of 'stuff' in an object.

1 Make sure the bench is level and the balance is upright.
2 Check that the original reading is zero, or adjust it.
3 Add the object to the pan, and read its mass from the scale while looking straight at it.
4 To find the mass of a liquid, first measure a beaker and then add the liquid and find the mass again. Then take the first reading away from the second.

Note: we sometimes use 'weight' when we mean mass.
- **Mass** is the amount of substance in a thing. It is measured in grams (g) and kilograms (kg), for example.
- **Weight** is the force with which gravity attracts an object. It is measured in newtons (N) (page 336).

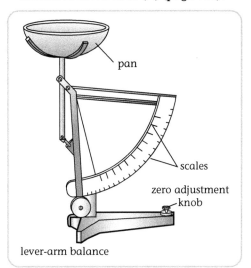

lever-arm balance

Stop clock (spring wound)

This measures time in seconds (s).

1 Ensure the spring is fully wound up.
2 Start the clock at the same moment as the event to be measured (you can use a count-down method: 3, 2, 1, 0).
3 Ensure the clock is stopped exactly as the event stops.
4 Read the scale by looking straight on at the marks.
5 Leave the clock working to run down the spring.

stop clock

More things to use

You should be able to set up and use these measuring instruments safely and correctly.
- Voltmeter and ammeter   page 294
- Burette   page 280
- Newton-meter (spring balance) to measure weight   page 336

Practical 5

Manipulating and measuring

Look at this hypothesis:
'The blue flame of a Bunsen burner will heat water to 60 °C more quickly than a yellow flame does.'

Use the planning sheet on page 362 to help carry out this practical. Practise your manipulation and measurement skills.

How will I be marked for manipulating and measuring?

Here is a possible marking scheme.
- Selects correct equipment   1
- Uses equipment safely and tidily   2
- Sets up equipment correctly   1
- Makes accurate readings   1
- Takes 3 readings and an average 1
- Masters laboratory techniques in a competent and safe way   3
- Handles and prepares living material   1

Key ideas

Use these words to fill in the spaces as you write the sentences in your Exercise book.

length   temperature   volume   scale   mass   surface area   weight   time

Every measuring instrument has a _____ made of lines and numbers. To measure _____ and

_____ we can use a metre rule. To measure _____ we usually use a measuring cylinder.

_____ is measured with a thermometer, and _____ with a clock. The amount of stuff in an

object is its _____ , and the force with which gravity attracts it is called its _____ .

2.5 How do we draw?

How are drawings and diagrams different?

Drawings

- Drawings should be large and look like the 'real thing'.
- They should be in the same proportion as the original.
- You should show the magnification, for example ×2.

$$\text{magnification} = \frac{\text{size of drawing}}{\text{size of original}}$$

Diagrams

- Diagrams of living things are made to show the main features – for example, a diagram of parts of the heart. They do not have to be exactly like the real thing, but they should show important points and how they are related.
- Diagrams of equipment should be an imagined cut surface view. They should be drawn carefully using a ruler.

How can I draw living things?

Here are some guidelines for drawing living things.

Not like this

- ✗ Drawing is small and unclear.
- ✗ Drawing is not in proportion and not accurate.
- ✗ Lines are not continuous.
- ✗ Drawing is shaded and coloured.
- ✗ Label lines are not drawn with a ruler.
- ✗ Label lines have arrowheads.
- ✗ Label lines cross each other.
- ✗ Labels are in capitals and lowercase.
- ✗ Labels are not horizontal.
- ✗ No title or view is given.
- ✗ No magnification is shown.

Like this

- ✓ Drawing is large and clear.
- ✓ Drawing is in proportion and accurate.
- ✓ It is drawn with continuous lines.
- ✓ There is no shading or use of colour.
- ✓ Label lines are drawn with a ruler.
- ✓ There are no arrowheads on label lines.
- ✓ Label lines are neatly arranged and not crossing.
- ✓ Labels are in lowercase only.
- ✓ Labels are horizontal.
- ✓ A suitable title and view are given.
- ✓ Magnification is shown.

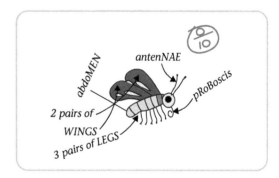

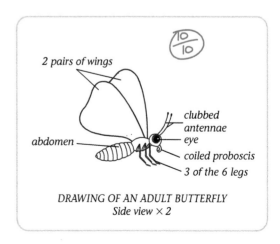

DRAWING OF AN ADULT BUTTERFLY
Side view × 2

How can I make diagrams of apparatus?

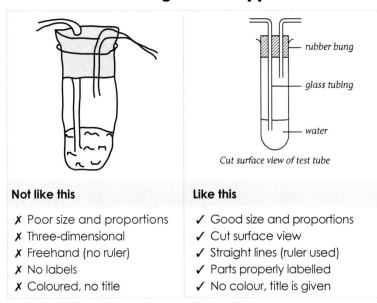

Cut surface view of test tube

Not like this	**Like this**
✗ Poor size and proportions	✓ Good size and proportions
✗ Three-dimensional	✓ Cut surface view
✗ Freehand (no ruler)	✓ Straight lines (ruler used)
✗ No labels	✓ Parts properly labelled
✗ Coloured, no title	✓ No colour, title is given

Remember your drawing skills

1. You have to draw from 'real life', not copy from a textbook or overhead projector.
2. Use a sharp pencil with an eraser.
3. Draw with clean, clear, continuous lines.
4. Do not use shading or coloured crayons.
5. Plan your drawing at least twice the size of the original.
6. Make a pale rough sketch first to get the proportions correct, and rub it out as you fill in the details.
7. Make your drawing two-dimensional.
8. Make your diagram of apparatus big enough to show the details. It should also be labelled and have a title.
9. Show a Bunsen burner by drawing an arrow (page 48).
10. Label lines should be drawn with a ruler to just touch the part being labelled. There should be no arrowheads.
11. Label lines should not cross each other.
12. All labels should be in lowercase letters.
13. Give a title to your drawing, and the magnification.
14. If you are asked to 'annotate' a drawing, it means you should write the functions of the parts you label.

Practical 6

Drawing

Make a large, clear, labelled drawing of the photograph of the fish. Practise the drawing skills on these pages.

Questions

1. Describe exactly how label lines and labels should be added to a drawing.
2. How should you use your ruler for (a) drawings and (b) diagrams of apparatus?

How will I be marked for drawing?

Here is a possible marking scheme.

- Large, with clear lines — 2
- Important details shown — 1
- Two-dimensional and no shading — 1
- Title correctly stated — 1
- Proportions accurate — 1
- View and magnification given — 1
- Label lines accurate, level and ruled — 2
- Labels in lowercase print — 1

Key ideas

Use these words to fill in the spaces as you write the sentences in your Exercise book.

ruler **magnification** **cut surface** **labelled** **freehand** **specimen**

Drawings are made _____ . They should look like the original _____ . They are usually bigger than the specimen and the _____ should be given. Diagrams of apparatus should be made with a _____ . They should show a _____ of the apparatus. Both drawings and diagrams should be _____ using ruled label lines.

2.6 How do we observe, record and report?

What is observation?

Observation is using all your senses to find out about your surroundings, but with due regard to safety. You use your senses of sight, touch and hearing. You use taste and smell only when following the teacher's instructions.

1 Do not breathe in an unknown gas. Just waft a little towards your nose, to see if it has a recognizable smell.
2 Observe organisms or parts of organisms using a hand lens or microscope.
3 Note overall features and fine details.
4 Find similarities or differences between organisms.
5 Wear goggles when appropriate.
6 Identify colour changes in food tests, changes in volume or mass, or stages of growth.
7 Observe on several occasions.
8 Record your observations in a table or in the form of drawings or diagrams.

Observing measuring equipment

For water and most other liquids read the lower curve of the meniscus. In mercury thermometers, read the top curve. When using measuring equipment, position yourself correctly so that your eye is directly in line with the scale.

Observing living things

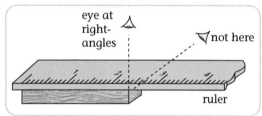

When reading a scale, look straight at the markings

Observations on animals	Observations on flowers
Outgrowths: legs, wings **B**ody cover: colour, hairy **S**hape: long, rounded **E**nd (front): head, organs **R**elative size: compare **V**iew: upper or lower **E**nd (back): openings	**S**hape: open or tube-like, regular or irregular **O**utgrowths: sizes of stamens and style **A**rrangement: single, disc **P**etals: colour, size, number **S**ize: compare to others

Key ideas

Use these words to fill in the spaces as you write the sentences in your Exercise book.

nose   **sight**   **tongue**   **sense organs**   **hearing**   **touch**   **hand lens**

We use our _____ to make observations. We use our _____ and _____ to detect the smell and taste of food. For our senses of _____ and _____ we use our eyes and ears. Our skin is the organ of _____, so we can feel things all over our bodies. We also use instruments such as a measuring cylinder and _____ to help us make more accurate observations.

What is recording?

Recording is presenting observations or numbers (numerical data) in useful ways, to help us to see patterns.

Preparing tables

Use a table to record descriptions or numbers.

1 Set up your table before you begin your practical work.
2 Decide what you are going to observe or the measurements you are going to take.
3 List items to be described down the left-hand side, and add headings to the columns on the top. Then add the descriptions or numbers to the table.
4 Write the heading of each column with the quantity being measured (e.g. temperature) and the units (e.g. °C). You do not need to repeat the units in the table. If decimal points are needed, they must be used correctly.
5 For comparing two organisms, compare similar features in the same row.
6 Enter your results in the table as you go along, and not on scraps of paper.
7 Write a title in capital letters above the table.

Preparing bar charts

Use a bar chart when only one variable is numerical.

1 Use graph paper and a ruler.
2 Make your bar chart large and clear.
3 On the upright (vertical) axis make a scale of numbers evenly spaced.
4 On the horizontal axis enter the items to be described.
5 Use your ruler to carefully draw the bars of the correct height. They can be separate or touching.
6 You can shade or colour the bars. Use pale colours so that the graph lines still show through.
7 Label each axis with what is being measured or described.
8 Give the bar chart a title above or below in capital letters.

Preparing histograms

Histograms are a special kind of bar chart. We use histograms when both of the variables are numerical and one of them can be grouped into sets.

1 Use graph paper and a ruler.
2 Group the information into sets with the same ranges, e.g. sets with 5 cm heights.
3 Enter the ranges on the horizontal axis. Note that the ranges should not overlap.
4 Enter the numbers, e.g. of students, up the vertical axis.
5 Use your ruler to draw the bars. The bars should touch each other. You can shade or colour the bars. Use pale colours so that the graph lines still show through.
6 Label each axis with what is being measured.
7 Give the histogram a title above or below in capitals.

Objectives

- Choose the most appropriate way in which to record observations or data.
- Set up tables, bar charts, histograms, pie charts and line graphs.

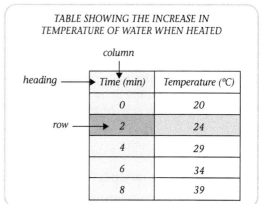

TABLE SHOWING THE INCREASE IN TEMPERATURE OF WATER WHEN HEATED

Time (min)	Temperature (°C)
0	20
2	24
4	29
6	34
8	39

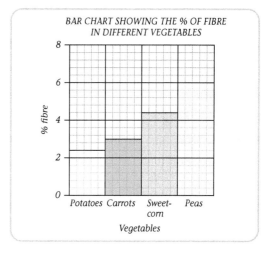

BAR CHART SHOWING THE % OF FIBRE IN DIFFERENT VEGETABLES

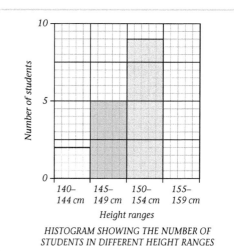

HISTOGRAM SHOWING THE NUMBER OF STUDENTS IN DIFFERENT HEIGHT RANGES

39

2.6 How do we observe, record and report? (continued)

Preparing pie charts

Pie charts are like pizzas cut into various parts, or **sectors**. The sectors show the relative sizes of the parts that make up the whole.

1 Work out the angle for each of the sectors. The angle at the centre of a circle is 360°, so work out:

$$\frac{\text{number or percentage in group}}{\text{total number or percentage}} \times 360°$$

For example: water sector $= \dfrac{50}{100} \times 360° = 180°$

2 Use a pair of compasses to draw a large circle.
3 Use a ruler and protractor to enter the sectors – the angles at the centre are the ones you worked out.
4 Colour and label the sectors.
5 Give the pie chart a title above or below in capital letters.

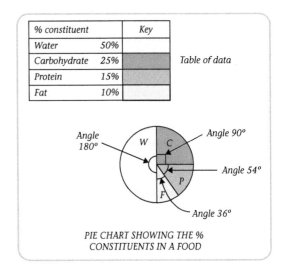

% constituent		Key
Water	50%	
Carbohydrate	25%	
Protein	15%	
Fat	10%	

Table of data

PIE CHART SHOWING THE %
CONSTITUENTS IN A FOOD

Preparing line graphs

A line graph shows the relationship between two numerical variables. The experimenter changes the values of one of these.

1 Make the graph large: use at least half of the length of the graph paper in each direction.
2 The horizontal (*x*-axis) has the measurements you have changed, e.g. time (the **independent** variable).
3 The vertical (*y*-axis) has the record of the results you find in the experiment, e.g. mass (the **dependent** variable).
4 Choose the scales: evenly divide each axis by making small lines with numbers. They do not need to start at zero.
5 Label the axes: the quantities together with their units.
6 Mark the points in pencil: record where the readings meet. Use a cross or a dot inside a circle for each point.
7 Join the points in pencil by drawing a curve that best fits the points (the best-fit curve). Ignore any single points far away from the curve, but say what you have done.
8 Draw short straight lines for graphs showing growth.
9 Give the line graph a title above or below in capitals.

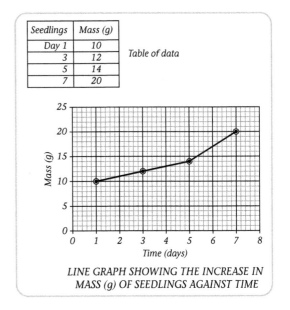

Seedlings	Mass (g)
Day 1	10
3	12
5	14
7	20

Table of data

LINE GRAPH SHOWING THE INCREASE IN
MASS (g) OF SEEDLINGS AGAINST TIME

Key ideas

Use these words to fill in the spaces as you write the sentences in your Exercise book.

table	data	line graph	histogram	pie chart	bar chart

The numbers we record in an experiment are called _____ . We can make a _____ to record results in columns and rows. We can then display this information as a _____ . Sometimes we can make a _____ where the sectors show the sizes of different parts. Where there are two sets of related data with numbers, then we can prepare a _____ or a _____ .

How can I report?

You should report your practical under headings. Use a planning sheet first (page 363), then write your report. It should be in a logical order under the headings shown below. You should use the correct terms, and have few or no grammatical or spelling errors.

Aim

This is what you are trying to find out. Write it in capital letters. It often begins with the words: To find out ...

It might also be a statement (hypothesis) you are testing. List it on the contents page of your Practical workbook.

Materials and apparatus

Here you list all the things you used, including equipment and chemicals. It tells other people what they would need in order to do a similar activity.

Method

Here you describe, in the passive tense, what was done. For example, 'A beaker with $100\,cm^3$ water was heated.' This should help another person repeat your activity. Write complete sentences and do not use numbered notes.

Results

Here you write your description of observations or record your measurements. Decide the best way to show them. Then prepare your table, bar chart, pie chart or line graph, etc.

Discussion

Here you report what your observations and results mean. Analyse and interpret your results (pages 42–3).

Conclusion

Here you sum up and say if you have achieved your aim or if your results agree or disagree with your hypothesis.

Note: there should be proper use of diagrams (drawn with a ruler, in two dimensions and with no shading); see page 37. The diagrams should also be neatly labelled.

Objective

- Display data and write a logical report in sentences under given headings.

Practical 7

Observing, recording and reporting

Plan, design and carry out a practical comparing the heating effects of the blue and yellow flames of a burner. Record your observations and results and write up your report.

How will I be marked for observing, recording and reporting?

Here is a possible marking scheme.

- Accurate observations — 2
- Written account:
  Logical order of report — 2
  Sections named with headings — 1
  Correct terms and grammar — 1
- Accurate display of data — 3
  (marks awarded will vary for a table, bar chart, pie chart or line graph)
  Diagrams where useful — 1

Questions

1 Why is a pie chart so called?
2 Describe when you would use each kind of recording method for data.

Key ideas

Use these words to fill in the spaces as you write the sentences in your Exercise book.

materials   method   diagram   apparatus   results   aim   conclusion

We begin our report by listing the title (name of the practical) and the _____ : what we want to find out. Then we record the _____ and _____ we used, and can include a labelled _____ . We then write what we did in the _____ . As we make our observations we record the _____ in tables, bar charts or line graphs etc. After this we discuss our results and interpret them. We finish with the _____ , which sums up whether we have achieved our aim.

2.7 How do we analyse and interpret?

What are analysis and interpretation?

When you have carried out your practical, and collected and recorded your data, you have to show you understand and can explain it. You should be able to:

- read values
- make predictions
- draw conclusions
- identify patterns and relationships
- carry out calculations
- evaluate what you have found.

Interpret tables

Average mass of caterpillars from day 4 after hatching											
Day	4	5	6	7	8	9	10	11	12	13	14
Av. mass (g)	12	13	13	15	17	20	24	24	24	26	29

Answer these questions. Write your answers as complete sentences.

- Values: what is the average mass on day 9?
- Calculate: on what day is the mass twice what it was on day 5?
- Patterns: what pattern can you see in the data?
- Explain: suggest a reason for the pattern. (The explanation should be based on scientific facts.)
- Interpret: when do you think the caterpillars moulted?
- Predict: what do you think will be the mass on day 15?

Interpret bar charts

Look at the bar chart on page 39. Answer these questions.

- Values: which vegetable has the lowest percentage of fibre?
- Calculate: which vegetable would you have to eat twice as much of to get the same percentage of fibre as in peas?
- Patterns: from the data shown, do underground vegetables have less or more fibre than other kinds?
- Predict: from this data, can you predict the percentage of fibre there would be in a cabbage? Note that the bars on a bar chart are independent, you cannot make predictions about other things from the information you have on a bar chart.
- Evaluate: can we draw conclusions from these few examples? What else should we do?

Interpret histograms

The histogram on the right shows the heights of students for each of six ranges of height. Answer these questions.

- Values: what is the range of heights of all the students? What is the range of each set of students?
- Calculate: what is the mode (most common reading)? How could you work out the average height? How many students were in the class altogether?
- Patterns: what pattern do you notice in the data?
- Predict: would you expect a similar pattern if you measured a different group of students?

What calculations?

You should be able to:

- use the four basic operations $(+, -, \times, \div)$
- calculate decimals and percentages
- change the subject in simple formulae
- put values into simple formulae
- identify significant figures
- find means and modes.

Remember: always include the units.

How to do well

- *Explain* results (i.e. give *reasons* for them), don't just repeat them.
- When explaining your results compare the experimental set-up with the control.
- The conclusion should be linked back to the aim of the experiment, to say if you have achieved it or not.
- Sources of error should be noted, together with the reasons for them.

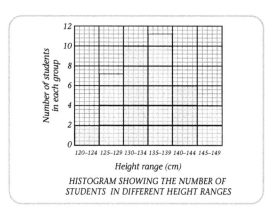

Height range (cm)

HISTOGRAM SHOWING THE NUMBER OF STUDENTS IN DIFFERENT HEIGHT RANGES

Interpret pie charts

You need to change sectors to percentages, using:

$$\frac{\text{angle at the centre of the circle}}{360°} \times 100 = \text{percentage}$$

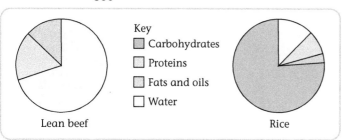

Key
- ■ Carbohydrates
- □ Proteins
- ▨ Fats and oils
- □ Water

Lean beef   Rice

Answer these questions in complete sentences.

- Calculate: find the percentage of each constituent in (a) lean meat and (b) rice.
- Interpret: explain the differences between the foods.

Interpret line graphs

The average mass of a group of rats is given below in a table and shown on the right in a line graph.

Days	0	5	10	15	20	25	30	35
Mass (g)	45	55	65	73	80	85	87	87

Answer these questions.

- Values: what do you notice when comparing the slope of the graph from days 0–20 compared with days 25–35?
- Calculate: how does the rate of growth compare between days 0–10 and days 20–30?
- Interpret: how do you explain the shape of the graph?
- Draw your conclusion: what is your conclusion?

Evaluate and draw a conclusion

- To **evaluate** is to consider the value of something. So you need to say if you can trust the results you have found, or if there are sources of error in them so that they are unreliable.
- To **draw a conclusion** is to sum up whether you have found out what you set out to do in the aim – whether your results agree or disagree with your hypothesis.

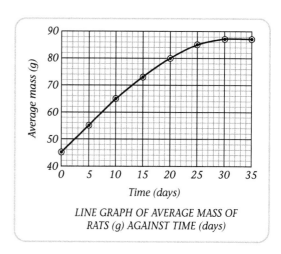

LINE GRAPH OF AVERAGE MASS OF RATS (g) AGAINST TIME (days)

What does it mean?

Relationship How variables are related, e.g. the line drawn on a graph shows if the values increase together.

Pattern Data that are repeated in a similar way so we can make predictions.

Key ideas

Use these words to fill in the spaces as you write the sentences in your Exercise book.

relationship   **prediction**   **slope**   **table**   **bars**   **evaluate**   **bar chart**

We can find the values of particular readings by looking at a _____ or _____ . We should also

be able to interpret the heights of the _____ on a bar chart. The shape and _____ of the line

on a graph can tell us the _____ between the two variables. We can also continue the line on a

graph to make a _____ of readings in the future. We can also _____ our data.

3 The cell

3.1 What are cells like?

Matter and energy make up our Universe of living and non-living things, and allow things to work. Matter is the 'stuff' of which everything is made. It is built into living and non-living things. An important characteristic of living things is that they are made up of very small building blocks called **cells**. These cells allow the organisms to show the characteristics of life (pages 6–7).

Unspecialized cells

The photographs below show typical animal and plant cells. Use the diagrams on page 45 to identify the parts.

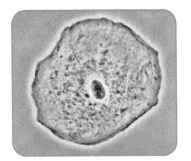

Unspecialized animal cell
(from inside the mouth)

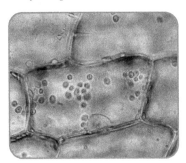

Unspecialized plant cell
(from inside a leaf)

How are plant and animal cells the same?

Plant and animal cells have certain features in common.

Cell membrane

This encloses the cell contents and controls what can come into and out of the cell. It is **partially permeable** and important in diffusion and osmosis (pages 46–7).

Cytoplasm

This is a jelly-like substance, in which most of the chemical reactions of everyday life occur. It is about 70% water. Inside it are small structures called **mitochondria**. The first stage of respiration occurs in the cytoplasm, but the combination with oxygen and release of large amounts of energy occur in the mitochondria.

Nucleus

This is essential for life. It controls the processes of the cell and its division. It contains the **chromosomes**. In humans there are 22 pairs of chromosomes, and another pair that can be XY in males or XX in females (see opposite).

The chromosomes carry genetic information in the DNA in the form of **genes**. It is the genes that carry the instructions for our characteristics. The genes and chromosomes are passed on to the next generation.

Objectives

- Draw, label and compare the parts of unspecialized plant and animal cells.
- Explain the importance of the parts found in the cells.
- Make models of unspecialized plant and animal cells.

How can we look at cells?

Instrument	Magnification	Can see
Naked eye	Life size (×1)	Many multicellular organisms
Hand lens	×10	Cell as a dot
Low-power microscope	×100	Nucleus in a cell
High-power microscope	×400 to ×1000	Some cell structures
Electron microscope	×40,000 to ×500,000	Internal structure of mitochondria

1000 nm (nanometres) = 1 μm	10 mm = 1 cm
1000 μm (micrometres) = 1 mm	100 cm = 1 m

Practical 8

Making model cells (PD, MM)

1 Choose suitable materials to make a model of an animal cell.

2 Now make the necessary changes to the model to make it into a plant cell.

3 Use modelling clay to make a model of some chromosomes inside the nucleus.

Human chromosomes

How are plant and animal cells different?

Plant cells have additional features not found in animals.

Cell wall

This is made of **cellulose** and is tough (it is the fibre we eat). It is outside the cell membrane and helps a plant cell keep its shape. It lets anything in or out of the cell.

Chloroplasts

These are in the cytoplasm and contain green pigment, **chlorophyll**. Chloroplasts are present in plant cells in the light. It is here that photosynthesis occurs. Roots and underground storage organs do not have chloroplasts.

Large vacuoles with cell sap

In the centre of a plant cell is a large hole or **vacuole**. It is filled with cell sap that is a weak solution of sugars and mineral salts. The vacuole helps the cell keep its shape.

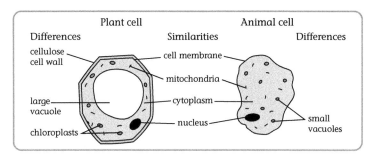

Special cells

The special cells shown below are: a sperm cell, red blood cells, a root hair, a leaf cell and a nerve cell. Can you say which is which?

Plant and animal cells (see also page 365)	
Plant cells	**Animal cells**
Similarities	
Cell membrane	Cell membrane
Cytoplasm	Cytoplasm
Mitochondria	Mitochondria
Nucleus	Nucleus
Chromosomes	Chromosomes
Differences	
Cellulose cell wall	No cell wall
Chloroplasts	No chloroplasts
Chlorophyll	No chlorophyll
Large vacuoles	Small vacuoles
Cell sap	No cell sap

Did you know?

- Humans have 46 chromosomes, fruit flies have 8 and mice have 40.
- Typical plant and animal cells are about 20 μm wide (1000 μm = 1 mm).
- Nerve cells, from your toes to your spinal cord, can be around a metre long.

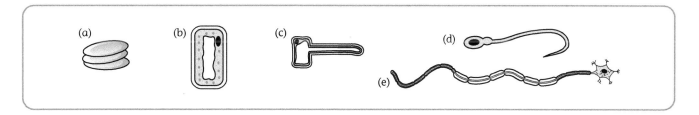

Key ideas

Use these words to fill in the spaces as you write the sentences in your Exercise book.

nucleus   **chloroplasts**   **cell wall**   **cell membrane**   **cytoplasm**   **vacuole**

The three features that plant and animal cells have in common are: _____ , _____ and _____ . The chromosomes, which carry the genes, are found inside the _____ . In addition, a plant cell has a cellulose _____ and a large _____ containing cell sap. Apart from some cells, such as root hairs, plant cells also contain _____ .

3.2 Investigating diffusion and osmosis

- Substances are made of tiny particles, and the particles in gases and liquids are constantly moving (see pages 18–19).
- Particles therefore tend to spread themselves out evenly into any available space. This is called **diffusion**.
- Particles move – **diffuse** – from a place where they are numerous (in *high* concentration) to a place where they are less numerous (in *lower* concentration). We say they are moving along their **concentration gradient**.
- We can illustrate this as follows (see the diagram below): the coloured particles (red) diffuse from high to low concentration (from left to right); the water molecules (black) diffuse from high to low concentration (from right to left).

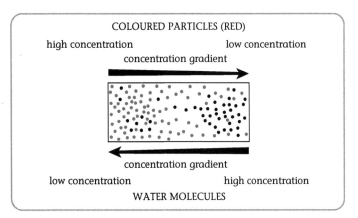

Coloured particles and water molecules move along their concentration gradients

Explaining diffusion

We can put starch and glucose into a porous bag and suspend it in a beaker of water. We can imagine the bag (**membrane**) to have very, very small holes. The molecules of starch are too big to go through the holes. But the glucose molecules can pass through – diffuse – from an area where they are at high concentration (in the bag) to the lower concentration (in the water). They diffuse along their concentration gradient. The membrane is said to be **partially permeable**, because it allows glucose, but not starch, to go through. We can show this in a diagram.

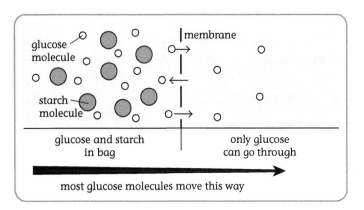

Where do diffusion and osmosis occur?

Diffusion and osmosis are the processes by which substances enter and leave all living cells all the time. The living cell membrane is partially permeable: it controls what exactly can enter and leave the cell. Surfaces through which diffusion and osmosis occur are large and moist.

- Water enters the roots and passes from cell to cell by osmosis.
- Water vapour diffuses into the leaf spaces and is lost by transpiration.
- Carbon dioxide diffuses into cells and oxygen diffuses out during photosynthesis.
- Soluble molecules from digestion are small enough to diffuse through the walls of the villi (page 66).
- Oxygen diffuses into cells and carbon dioxide diffuses out during respiration.

Practical 9

Observing osmosis (MM, ORR, AI)

Your teacher will supply you with an 8 cm length of Visking tubing and a salt solution (30 g of sodium chloride with 100 cm³ water).

1 Collect the tubing. Tie one end very tightly with thread.

2 Add the solution to the bag. Leave some space at the top.

3 Put a length of capillary tube (a narrow glass tube) into the bag, and tie the top of the bag tightly with thread.

4 Use thread to firmly support the bag on a clamp. Hold the tube gently in the claws of the clamp.

5 Lower the bag into a beaker of water and use a felt tip to mark the starting level of the liquid in the tube.

6 Every five minutes, use a ruler to measure, in mm, the height of the liquid in the tube (until it reaches the top).

7 Make a table of your results.

8 Draw a line graph, with time along the horizontal axis and height of the liquid on the vertical axis.

9 Try to explain your observations. (See also page 366.)

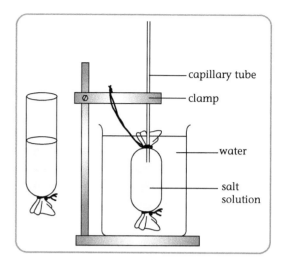

Explaining osmosis

In the experiment above, water moves into the bag by **osmosis**. As water comes in, the solution rises up the tube. This is because the bag is partially permeable and allows water molecules to pass through, but not salt. So water moves from its higher concentration in the beaker to its lower concentration in the salt solution.

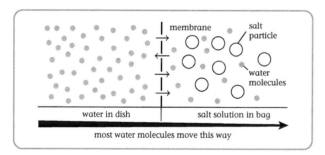

Questions

1 Students made a potato cup and placed sugar inside. They left the potato in a dish of water. The sugar became wet and then dissolved. Explain what happened.

2 Another group boiled a potato cup for 10 minutes before putting sugar into it. When they left it in a dish of water, the sugar remained dry. Why?

3 Mother placed some lettuce leaves in tap water, but Sandra placed hers in salty water. What will the leaves look like after 2 hours? Explain the differences.

4 Explain: (a) why seeds swell when left in water; (b) why water comes out of slices of eggplant sprinkled with salt; (c) why it is important not to make fertilizer solution too strong, especially when adding it to potted plants.

Key ideas

Use these words to fill in the spaces as you write the sentences in your Exercise book.

high   diffuse   lower   osmosis   partially   diffusion   gradient

Particles move (_____) from a place where they are in _____ concentration to a place

of _____ concentration, along a concentration _____ . We call this _____ . When water

moves through a _____ permeable membrane, we call this _____ . _____ is a special case of

_____ . They are both important processes in living things.

4 Food and nutrition

4.1 How do plants make food?

Photosynthesis is the process by which plants use simple substances and combine them using the energy in sunlight. The light energy is changed into chemical energy in the food. The food they make is **glucose**, but this is quickly changed to **starch**. So if we want to know if a plant has been carrying out photosynthesis, we test a leaf for starch. But a leaf is green, so we first need to remove the chlorophyll (Practical 10).

How do we find out about photosynthesis?

Remove the starch from the plant

If we want to find out what is needed for photosynthesis, we have to start with a plant without starch. We call this a **de-starched** plant. We leave a potted plant in the dark for 24 hours. Any starch in the leaves will be changed to sugars and sent around the plant. To make sure, we test a leaf as in Practical 10. We want no starch to be present.

Choose the variables

- The starting substances (**reactants**) for photosynthesis are water and carbon dioxide. It is impossible to remove water from a plant to find out its effect, as it would kill the plant. But the importance of water has been confirmed by scientists. We can, however, leave plants with and without carbon dioxide to see if that is important.
- The conditions for photosynthesis to take place are the presence of chlorophyll and sunlight. We need to design tests with and without each of these variables.
- The substances produced (**products**) are oxygen (which is given off), and glucose (which is changed to starch). We can test for the production of oxygen and starch.

Objectives

- Define photosynthesis.
- Investigate the reactants, the conditions and the products.
- Write a word equation for the process.

Practical 10

How do we test a leaf for starch? (MM, ORR)

1 Hold a leaf in boiling water for a minute. This will soften it.

2 Turn off the Bunsen burner (this is because you are going to use alcohol, which can easily catch alight).

3 Fill a test tube with alcohol, and put the leaf in it. Stand the test tube in the hot water. This will decolourize the leaf (remove the chlorophyll from it).

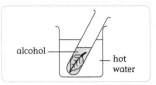

alcohol — hot water

4 Wash the leaf to remove the alcohol.

5 Put the leaf on a white tile and add iodine solution. If the iodine goes blue-black, then the leaf contained starch.

iodine solution

Practical 11

Are chlorophyll and light necessary for photosynthesis? (PD)

You have to design two separate experiments. You can refer to pages 361 and 362 for help in your planning. Use a copy of page 363 to write your notes.

- Make sure you state your problem and your hypothesis.
- Make sure you control for all the other variables besides the one you are testing.
- Say how you test the result, and what you expect it to be.
- List the equipment you will need.
- Outline the method you will use – it should be workable.
- Say how you will assess if the hypothesis was tested.

Show your work to your teacher. (See also page 367.)

Practical 12

Is carbon dioxide necessary for photosynthesis? (MM, ORR, AI)

Answer the questions and carry out the practical.

1 Use a de-starched plant. (Why?)

2 Arrange for some leaves to receive carbon dioxide, and some to receive none. (Why?)

3 Use sodium hydroxide pellets to absorb carbon dioxide. (How are these useful?)

4 You can use one leaf as your experiment, and the other as the control. (Why is this useful?)

5 Set up the apparatus as shown below. (Why is everything arranged as it is?)

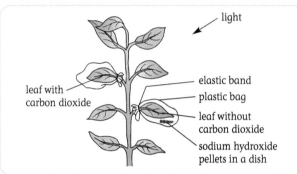

light

leaf with carbon dioxide

elastic band
plastic bag
leaf without carbon dioxide
sodium hydroxide pellets in a dish

6 Put the plant in sunlight for 2 to 3 hours. (Why?)

7 Then test the leaves. (How will you do this?)

8 What are your results? What do they mean?

Practical 13

Is oxygen produced during photosynthesis? (MM, ORR, AI)

Answer the questions and carry out the practical.

1 Use a water plant such as pondweed. (Why?)

2 Fill a test tube with water and put your finger over the open end. (Why?) Carefully lower it over an upturned filter funnel, as below. (Why?)

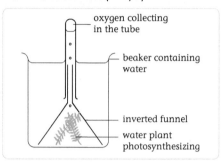

oxygen collecting in the tube

beaker containing water

inverted funnel
water plant photosynthesizing

3 Observe what happens when the apparatus is left in sunlight. (Can you explain your observation?)

4 Test the gas in the test tube for oxygen. (See if it re-lights a glowing splint. What happens? Why?)

5 What could you use as a control? Why?

Summary on photosynthesis

Carbon dioxide and water are simple inorganic compounds that do not contain much energy. They are combined using the energy in sunlight that is trapped by chlorophyll. The result is complex organic compounds – food – containing a large amount of chemical energy. The gas oxygen is also produced.

Photosynthesis can occur in any green parts of the plant. But most of it occurs in the leaves (pages 50–1).

Questions

1 (a) Animals depend on a gas produced by plants. Name it.
(b) In return, animals produce a gas that plants use. Name it.

2 Explain 'de-starched' and 'decolourized' and why each one is important.

Key ideas

Use these words to fill in the spaces as you write the sentences in your Exercise book.

oxygen   chlorophyll   glucose   carbon dioxide   starch   water   sunlight

During photosynthesis the reactants are _____ and _____ . For photosynthesis to occur

_____ and _____ must also be present. The products of photosynthesis are _____ and

_____ . To see if photosynthesis has occurred we test for _____ .

4.1 How do plants make food? (continued)

What is needed for photosynthesis?

Leaves with a flat shape

If you squash a small ball of modelling clay flat, you can see how the surface area increases for the same volume. This is like a leaf, and the thin shape helps gases to **diffuse**.

Reactants: water and carbon dioxide

- Water comes in through the roots and travels up in the xylem vessels of the veins. The veins are spread throughout the leaf, taking water to the leaf cells. Water vapour is continually lost from the leaf, so more is drawn up.
- There is less carbon dioxide inside the leaf than outside. So it tends to diffuse in through the stomata. It dissolves in the water around the cells and enters them. As it is used up in photosynthesis, so more diffuses in.

Conditions: chlorophyll and light

- Chlorophyll is in the chloroplasts, especially of the palisade cells. It traps the light energy for photosynthesis.
- Light shines on the leaf and can easily pass through the epidermis, which is only one cell thick. It is light energy that is converted to chemical energy during photosynthesis. There are more details on page 52.

Products: oxygen and glucose

- Oxygen is made in photosynthesis, so there is more inside the leaf than outside. Oxygen diffuses out of the large air spaces, through the stomata and into the air.
- Glucose is made in photosynthesis. It is soluble and sugars can be transported away in the phloem to other parts of the plant. Some is changed into starch, which is insoluble, and therefore good for storage. Glucose is also used in respiration to release energy (pages 76–80) and is also changed to other compounds (pages 54–5).

Diffusion

Particles in liquids and gases are always moving. They spread out from an area of high concentration to a lower one. This is called **diffusion** (page 46). It is how carbon dioxide, oxygen and water vapour move in and out of cells and leaves. It is most efficient over short distances – which is why cell walls and leaves are thin.

Objectives

- Describe how leaf structure is adapted to allow photosynthesis to occur.
- Write a word equation and a chemical equation for photosynthesis.

smaller veins

main vein (mid-rib)

leaf blade

leaf stalk

Photosynthesis occurs mainly in the leaves

Practical 14

How do gases enter and leave the leaf? (MM, ORR, D)

1 Fold an *Hibiscus* leaf in half, with the pale under-surfaces together.
2 Slide the halves past each other, to strip off a piece of the transparent under-surface (called the **epidermis**).

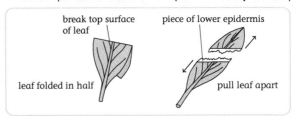

break top surface of leaf

piece of lower epidermis

leaf folded in half

pull leaf apart

3 Put a small piece of epidermis in a drop of water on a slide and cover it with a coverslip.
4 Observe the slide under low power. You will see ordinary epidermis cells, and pairs of **guard cells** each side of small holes, the **stomata**. Draw and label what you see.

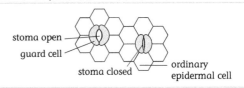

stoma open

guard cell

stoma closed

ordinary epidermal cell

A chemical equation for photosynthesis

We can describe what happens in photosynthesis by using symbols to show the compounds (see pages 20 and 23). The starting substances (reactants) are water (H_2O) and carbon dioxide (CO_2). The products are oxygen (O_2) and glucose ($C_6H_{12}O_6$). Chlorophyll (to trap energy) and light (to provide the energy) are the conditions that make the reaction possible.

Word equation: water + carbon dioxide $\xrightarrow[\text{chlorophyll}]{\text{light}}$ glucose + oxygen

Chemical equation: $6H_2O(l) + 6CO_2(g) \longrightarrow C_6H_{12}O_6(s) + 6O_2(g)$

Leaf structure	Importance in photosynthesis
1 Leaves arranged with little overlap	1 Light can reach most of the leaves for photosynthesis
2 Main vein and branching network of veins	2 Hold the softer tissues of the leaf up to the light
3 Many chloroplasts with chlorophyll in palisade layer	3 Chlorophyll absorbs sunlight for photosynthesis
4 Leaf blade is thin and flat	4 Gives a large surface area to volume for diffusion
5 Spongy layer with many air spaces	5 Allow O_2, CO_2 and H_2O vapour to diffuse easily
6 Many pores – stomata – in lower epidermis	6 Allow O_2, CO_2 and H_2O vapour to diffuse easily
7 Guard cells each side of the pores	7 Control the movement of gases in and out
8 Veins contain xylem vessels	8 Xylem vessels bring water from the roots to the leaf
9 Veins contain phloem sieve tubes	9 Phloem sieve tubes take food away from the leaf

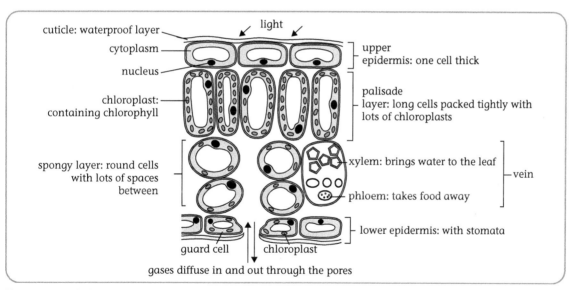

The structure of a leaf (transverse section)

Key ideas

Use these words to fill in the spaces as you write the sentences in your Exercise book.

chloroplasts   carbon dioxide   out of   water   into   oxygen   light

The roots take in _____ and it passes up to the leaves. The _____ needed for photosynthesis

diffuses _____ the leaf. The chlorophyll in the _____ traps _____ . During photosynthesis

glucose is formed, and _____ that diffuses _____ the leaf.

4.2 Photosynthesis and photography

Photochemical reactions

A photochemical reaction is where light causes a chemical change. The change cannot usually be easily reversed. Some examples are:

- photosynthesis
- suntanning
- photography
- reactive spectacle lenses
- fading of clothes and pictures
- yellowing of old newspapers

Photosynthesis

Photosynthesis is the combination of water and carbon dioxide, in the presence of chlorophyll and light, to make glucose and oxygen. The light energy is changed to chemical energy in the bonds of the glucose molecules.

It has been found by experiments that photosynthesis has two phases.

- Light phase – this can happen only in the light; it depends on light energy.

  Light energy is trapped by chlorophyll. The energy is used to break water into hydrogen and oxygen. The oxygen is given off as a gas.

> water + light energy ⟶ hydrogen + oxygen ↑

- Dark phase – this can happen in the light or the dark.

  The hydrogen that is produced in the light is combined with carbon dioxide to make glucose.

> hydrogen + carbon dioxide ⟶ glucose

Reactive spectacle lenses

You may have seen spectacles where the lenses go dark in sunlight, and then go clear again when taken indoors. In this case the chemical change is reversible. The lenses contain a chemical, often silver bromide. When sunlight shines on them, the silver bromide breaks into silver and bromine. The silver metal shows up as a grey tint, and this helps to block further sunlight coming into the eyes. When the spectacles are taken out of the light, the silver and bromine recombine and the lenses become clear again.

Suntanning

Energy from the Sun arrives on Earth in three forms: infrared (heat), visible light and ultraviolet. It is ultraviolet radiation that causes a suntan. Chemicals in the skin absorb ultraviolet radiation to make melanin. This is coloured, and so makes the skin look darker – the person gets a suntan. The melanin can then absorb other ultraviolet radiation, so that this does not damage the skin cells underneath. However, if a light-skinned person stays out in the Sun, the ultraviolet may burn their skin before melanin is produced.

Objectives

- Define a photochemical reaction.
- Describe the reactions in photosynthesis and photography.

Practical 15

How does photographic paper work? (MM, ORR)

1 You will need some photographic paper, about 6 cm square (in its lightproof wrapping).
2 Collect three small objects. Open the paper and quickly put the objects on it.
3 Place the arrangement in bright sunlight or under a powerful lamp. Observe what happens over the next 10 minutes. Does the film get dark? We say it has been exposed.
4 Remove the paper from the light. Take away the objects and immediately examine the areas underneath (the unexposed parts). Do they still look white?

Photographic paper

Photographic paper is sensitive to light. The areas that are exposed to light become dark. When you remove the objects obstructing the light, the whole piece of paper would eventually become dark. This is why it is important that unused paper or film is kept in lightproof packets or boxes.

Questions

1 What is a photochemical reaction?
2 What happens in the two phases of photosynthesis?
3 What is the main chemical change that light causes in reactive spectacle lenses?
4 (a) What is a photographic negative? (b) How is this changed into a photographic positive?

Photography

Black-and-white photography is based on the light-sensitive properties of silver salts (halides), especially silver chloride and silver bromide. There are various stages.

Photographic film

When a photograph is being taken, a camera is used with photographic film rather than paper. The film contains a layer of gelatine with particles of silver halide. The shutter is opened for only a very short time to let light fall onto the film. Where the light from the object falls on the film, the silver halide is changed to make an image.

However, if you could examine exposed film straight after a picture was taken you would see nothing on it, as the image is hidden.

Making a photographic negative

The completed roll of film is processed in a darkroom. (This is lit only by wavelengths of light that do not affect the film.) The image is first **developed** (shown up) by treating the film with special mixtures of different chemicals. This image would slowly disappear, and so it is has to be **fixed** using another set of chemicals. This makes a photographic negative, where the black-and-white areas are the opposite of how they will be in the final photograph.

Making the final photograph

The photographic negative is projected onto photographic paper, which also contains light-sensitive chemicals. The dark areas of the negative become light areas on the finished photograph, and vice versa.

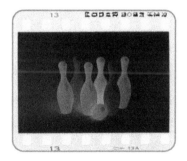

(a) Black and white negative

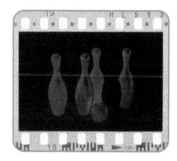

(b) Colour negative

Did you know?

- Photo = 'light'; synthesis = 'building up'. Photosynthesis is the building up of complex molecules using light energy.
- Photo = 'light'; graphy = 'writing'. Photography is the making of pictures using light energy.

What about colour photography?

A special colour film is used. It has three light-sensitive layers. The layers are sensitive to blue, green or red light. The three layers record the different amounts of light of the different colours given off by the object. The film is developed into negatives and then reversed to make the positive. In the process the three colours are changed to yellow, magenta and cyan. The result is a colour transparency, and from this colour prints can be made. For more on colour mixing see page 315.

What about digital photography?

This does not use film. The light that bounces off the object is changed directly into a digital image made of a long series of 1s and 0s. These represent all the tiny coloured dots – or pixels – that together make up the image. The image can be stored on a memory stick or computer, sent by email to someone else, or printed out to make a photograph.

Key ideas

Use these words to fill in the spaces as you write the sentences in your Exercise book.

photosynthesis   **light energy**   **film**   **hydrogen**   **chemical**   **silver**

In a photochemical reaction, _____ produces a _____ change. In _____ , the _____ splits water into _____ and oxygen. The _____ then combines with carbon dioxide to make glucose. In photography, the _____ splits a compound, such as silver bromide, into _____ and bromine on light-sensitive photographic _____ .

4.3 Uses of food nutrients

What happens to glucose made in the leaves?

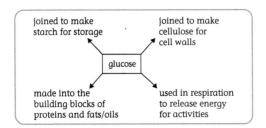

Objectives

● Describe how plants and animals use food.
● List the building blocks and some sources of common food nutrients.

● Glucose molecules can be joined together into long chains to form **starch**. This is what we test for to see whether photosynthesis has occurred. Starch is used for storage.
● Glucose molecules can also be built up into **cellulose**. This forms cell walls and is part of the fibre in our food.
● Glucose is combined with mineral salts to make **amino acids**. These are the building blocks of **proteins**. These are used for growth and for food storage.
● Glucose can also be made into fatty acids and glycerol. These are the building blocks of **fats** and **oils**. They are used for storage.
● Glucose contains trapped energy. This energy can be released by plants and animals during **respiration** (pages 76–80). You can find the amount of energy released from a food (see page 370).
● The food present in seeds, fruits and other plant storage organs becomes the **food for animals**.

Questions

1 Trace the pathway by which an animal gets its energy from sunlight.
2 List three examples each of how plants and animals use food.
3 Make a table to show the building blocks and some sources of proteins, sugars, starch, fibre, and fats and oils.
4 The equation below shows what happens in respiration. How does this compare to what happens in photosynthesis?

Respiration
glucose + oxygen $\longrightarrow$ carbon dioxide + water + energy

How do plants use stored food?	How do animals use stored food?
When stored food is needed it is broken down into its building blocks: glucose, amino acids, fatty acids and glycerol. These can then be used for growth and respiration. Food stores are also useful to the plant:	Animals, including humans, eat plants (especially the storage organs) to obtain food and fibre. The foods are broken down during digestion, and then the building blocks are used for growth and respiration.
1 during poor conditions such as drought, when plants may not be able to make enough food	1 Storage crops such as cassava, yam, eddo, dasheen and sweet potato are a major source of starch.
2 for the growth and development of the plant	2 Grains (cereals) such as rice, maize, oats and wheat (flour) provide animals with starch and some vitamins.
3 for vegetative reproduction (page 133) as buds grow out to make new plants	3 Seeds, beans and peas provide starch and protein.
4 for the developing embryo, from food stores in the seeds and fruits.	4 Fruits such as mango, tomato, pawpaw and citrus provide sugars, fibre and vitamins.

Proteins

Proteins are built up from amino acids. Proteins contain carbon, hydrogen, oxygen and nitrogen, and often sulphur and phosphorus as well. We use proteins for growth and repair and, for example, to make muscles, enzymes, antibodies and haemoglobin.

Foods rich in protein are meat, fish, eggs, milk, peas and beans.

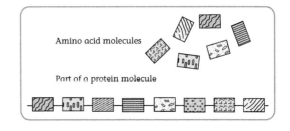

Amino acid molecules

Part of a protein molecule

Fats and oils

Fats and oils contain carbon, hydrogen and oxygen only. They are used for insulation and energy release. They are built up from fatty acids and glycerol.

- Fats from animals are mainly **saturated fats**. These are found in red meat, butter and full-fat cheese. Eating too much of these can raise blood **cholesterol** (page 97).
- Fats from plants (e.g. nuts), and most of those in fish and chicken, are mainly **unsaturated**. The best fats for health are **polyunsaturated**: examples are olive, corn and soya oil.
- Animal fats are usually solid, and plant fats (oils) are usually liquid at room temperature.

It is best to try to reduce our fat intake, especially of saturated fat, by cutting away visible fat and skin from the food.

Carbohydrates

Sugars

These usually taste sweet. Some, for example glucose and fructose, are simple sugars (monosaccharides), which are 'reducing sugars'. Others are disaccharides: for example maltose (a reducing sugar) and sucrose (a non-reducing sugar).

Sucrose is the refined sugar from sugar cane, which is used in sweets, biscuits, cakes etc. Glucose and fructose are found in fresh fruit – which are better for our health.

Starch

Starch is a polysaccharide made of chains of glucose molecules. It provides glucose as a source of energy.

Foods rich in starch are plant storage organs such as yams, cassava, dasheen, Irish and sweet potatoes, some grains such as rice and maize, and also peas and beans, and food made from flour, such as bread and cakes.

Cellulose (fibre)

This is also built up of glucose. It makes the cell walls of plants. It is found in fruits, vegetables, storage organs and wholemeal bread. We cannot digest cellulose. Its function in our body is as **roughage** to give bulk to the material in the alimentary canal and help prevent constipation.

What does it mean?

Saturated fat   The fatty acid parts have as many hydrogen atoms as possible.

Unsaturated fat   The fatty acids could contain more hydrogen atoms.

Polyunsaturated fats   The fatty acids could contain many more hydrogen atoms.

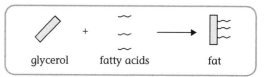

glycerol   fatty acids   fat

What does it mean?

Monosaccharides   Only one sugar unit.

Disaccharides   Contain two sugar units.

Polysaccharides   Contain many sugar units.

Reducing sugar   Gives a red precipitate when heated with Benedict's solution, e.g. glucose, fructose and maltose.

Non-reducing sugar   Does not give a red precipitate with Benedict's solution, e.g. sucrose (see page 57).

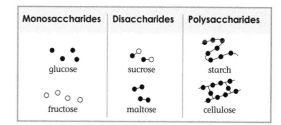

Monosaccharides	Disaccharides	Polysaccharides
glucose	sucrose	starch
fructose	maltose	cellulose

Key ideas

Use these words to fill in the spaces as you write the sentences in your Exercise book.

amino acids   **glucose**   **starch**   **fatty acids**   **proteins**   **cellulose**

The _____ that plants make in their leaves during photosynthesis is very important. It can be built up into other sugars, _____ and _____ . Other substances made are _____ , which form part of fats and oils. With the addition of nitrogen and other elements, _____ are made, which are the building blocks of _____ .

4.4 Food groups and food tests

Food groups

Food groups have been described by the Caribbean Food and Nutrition Institute (CFNI). This is a classification based on the different foods as we buy or grow them.

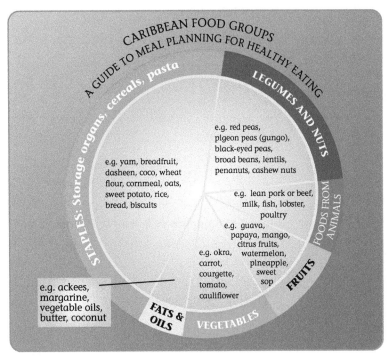

Notes: the 'Fruits' group is limited to sweet fruits, such as pawpaw and mango. The 'Vegetables' group includes e.g. cucumbers and tomatoes, and non-starchy leafy vegetables. Starchy vegetables, e.g. breadfruit, are in the 'Staples' group.

Food nutrients

We can also classify foods based on the main chemicals or nutrients they contain (these are described on pages 58–9). We can make a table to show the main nutrients (and fibre) present in each of the food groups.

Food groups	Food nutrients					
	Pro	Car	Fat	Vits	Mins	Fibre
Staples	+	+++	+	++	+	+
Legumes and nuts	+++	+++	+	+	+	+
Food from animals	+++		++	++	++	
Fats and oils			+++	++		
Fruits		++		+++	++	++
Vegetables		+		+++	+++	+++

Key: Pro = Protein, Car = Carbohydrates, Vits = Vitamins, Mins = Minerals,
+, ++ and +++ = increasing amount of nutrient

Food tests (MM, ORR, AI)

Practical 16

Testing for proteins (Biuret test)

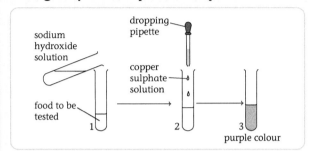

First test milk, then try other food items.

1 Put 2 cm³ of the food in a test tube and add the same amount of dilute sodium hydroxide solution.
2 Add 1% copper sulphate solution from a pipette, drop by drop. Shake the test tube.
3 A purple colour shows the presence of protein.

Practical 17

Testing for fats (emulsion test)

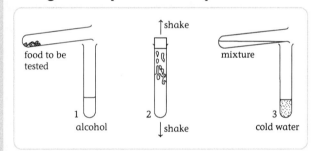

First test margarine, then try other food items.
1 Add 1 cm³ of the food to 2 cm³ of alcohol (for example, ethanol) in a test tube.
2 Put a cork over the top of the test tube and shake the tube thoroughly.
3 Add the mixture to a test tube with of 2 cm³ water. A milky appearance (drops of fat) shows the presence of fat.

Practical 18

Testing for starch (iodine test)

First test cut-up rice grains, then try other food items.

1 The food can be either solid or liquid. Add a few drops of iodine solution.
2 The straw-coloured iodine solution will go blue-black to show the presence of starch.

Practical 19

Testing for reducing sugars (Benedict's test)

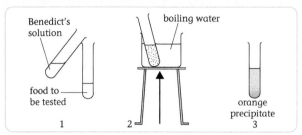

First test glucose, then try other food items.

1 Add 2 cm³ of Benedict's solution to 1 cm³ of the food in a test tube.
2 Put the test tube into a beaker of boiling water for about 5 minutes.
3 An orange-red precipitate shows the presence of a reducing sugar.

Practical 20

Testing for non-reducing sugars

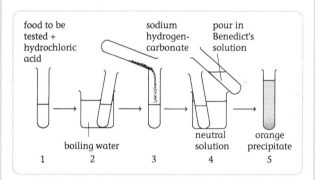

First test sucrose, then try other food items. The substance to be tested must have given a negative result in the test for reducing sugar.

1 Add a few drops of dilute hydrochloric acid to 1 cm³ of the food in a test tube.
2 Put the test tube into a water bath of boiling water for about 3 minutes to break down any sugar into reducing sugars.
3 Cool. Then add a little sodium hydrogencarbonate until the fizzing stops. (This is to neutralize any left-over acid.)
4 Add 2 cm³ of Benedict's solution and put it back into the water bath for about 5 minutes.
5 An orange-red precipitate shows the presence of a reducing sugar. This means the food originally contained a non-reducing sugar.

4.5 What is a balanced diet?

A balanced diet provides an adequate supply of energy and nutrients (in the correct proportions) to suit the needs of the individual. The artwork shows foods rich in various nutrients. We also need water. Our diet also should *not* contain additives that might harm us (pages 62–3).

(pages 62–3)

Objectives
- Identify good food sources for the different nutrients in a balanced diet.
- Discuss how age, gender, pregnancy and occupation affect energy needs.

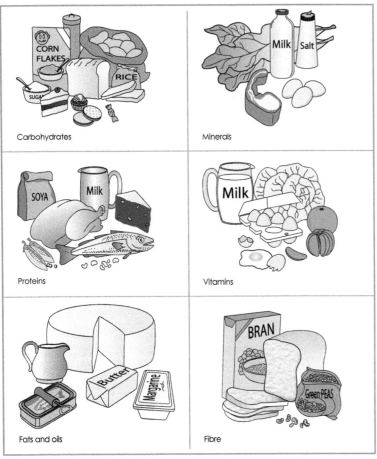

Carbohydrates

Minerals

Proteins

Vitamins

Fats and oils

Fibre

A balanced diet	
55% carbohydrates ⎫ 15% fats and oils ⎬	Energy-giving
20% protein	Body-building
10% water, minerals, vitamins and fibre	To maintain health

Energy requirements in kJ	
Child 2–3 years	5900
Child 5–7 years	7500
Girl 12–15 years	9600
Boy 12–15 years	12,000
Sedentary job:	
woman	9000
man	10,000
Active job:	
woman	12,000
man	13,000
Pregnant or nursing woman	13,000
Very active job	16,000

The vitamins we need

Vitamins	Some sources	Why they are needed	Results of deficiency
A	Carrots, mangoes, spinach, red peppers, liver, margarine, butter, milk	Aid growth and help maintain healthy tissues in throat and lungs. Part of pigment in rod cells of retina	Infections of respiratory system. **Night blindness**, from lack of production of pigment in retina
B complex	Wholemeal, cereals (including brown rice), milk, liver, meat, green vegetables	Help in chemical reactions such as respiration. Also for healthy skin and muscles and prevention of anaemia	Tiredness, loss of energy and mouth sores. **Beri-beri** (muscular weakness and paralysis) where white rice is major part of diet
C	Fresh vegetables and fruit, especially citrus fruits (oranges, limes, grapefruit)	For healthy skin and gums. Helps cuts and sores to heal properly. May help combat colds	Bleeding gums and slow-healing sores. **Scurvy** (pains in joints, bleeding gums) with lack of fresh fruits and vegetables
D	Fish oils, butter, eggs. (Made in the skin in sunny places like the Caribbean)	Helps body absorb calcium from our food for strong bones and teeth. Especially important during growth	Poor bones and teeth. **Rickets** (soft leg bones which curve) found in children with deficiency
E	Wheat germ, eggs, dark green vegetables	Probably helps protect cells from damage	Deficiency unlikely

Nutritional value of common Caribbean food

Constituents of food/100 g edible portion

Name of food	Protein (g)	Fat (g)	Carbohydrate (g)	Calcium	Iron	Vitamin A	Vitamin B complex	Vitamin C	kJ
Bread (brown)	8	1.1	49	+	++	–	++	–	1000
Carrot	1	0.3	10	+	+	+++	+	++	202
Coconut flesh	4	38	12	+	++	–	+	–	1697
Groundnut	26	46	10	++	++	–	++++	–	2344
Irish potato	2	–	19	+	+	+	++	++	353
Kidney bean	24	2	48	+++	+++	–	++	–	1285
Maize grains	10	4.5	70	+	++	+	++	–	1461
Pawpaw	0.6	–	9	+	+	++	+	++++	160
Pumpkin	1.2	0.1	7	+	+	++	+	++	147
Rice (unpolished)	8	2.0	76	+	++	–	++	–	1487
Soya bean	35	18	12	+++	+++	–	+++	–	1470
Spinach	4	–	5	+++	++	+++	++	++++	168
Sugar (brown)	0.2	–	96	+	++	–	+	–	1634
Sweet potato root	1.8	0.7	27	+	+	+++	++	++	508
Sweet potato leaves	2.3	–	4	+++	++	+++	+	++++	118
Tomatoes	1	–	4	+	+	++	+	+++	88
Yam	2	–	25	+	++	–	+	++	454
Beef (lean)	22	8	–	+	++	–	+++	–	672
Butter	0.6	82	0.4	+	–	++	+	–	3108
Chicken	19	7	–	+	++	–	+++	–	584
Eggs	13	11	–	++	++	++	+	–	634
Fish, sea-water	19	1.0	–	+	++	+	+++	–	340
Liver	18	5	–	+	++++	++++	++++	–	491
Milk (cow's)	4	4	4.6	+++	–	+	+	+	294

Key: – = none present or not known; +, ++, +++ and ++++ = increasing amounts of particular constituent

The minerals we need

Minerals	Some sources	Function in the body
Sodium chloride (salt)	Seafood, processed food, especially meat	Part of blood plasma. Needed for digestion and nervous system
Potassium	Banana, avocado, citrus, milk, vegetables	Healthy skin, normal growth and functioning of nervous system
Phosphorus	Milk	Bones and teeth. Needed in chemical reactions of respiration
Calcium	Beans and peas, milk, spinach (callaloo)	Bones and teeth. Deficiency causes soft bones and teeth.
Iron	Liver, spinach, beans and peas	Part of haemoglobin. Deficiency causes **anaemia** (weakness/tiredness)
Iodine	Seafood, table salt	Part of thyroxine. Deficiency causes goitre (swollen neck)

Questions

1 What are the parts of a balanced diet? Give examples of foods containing them.

2 Why are vitamins and minerals important in the body? Choose three of each: name some foods that contain it, and what problems a deficiency can cause.

3 Use the information on energy requirements on page 58 to prepare a bar chart. How do (a) age, (b) gender, (c) pregnancy and (d) occupation affect energy needs?

Key ideas

Use these words to fill in the spaces as you write the sentences in your Exercise book.

proteins   fats and oils   fibre   carbohydrates   vitamins   minerals   water

The parts of a balanced diet should be in the right proportion. We also need to drink _____.

The _____ and _____ are used to release energy. The _____ are needed for growth, and the

_____ , _____ , _____ and _____ are needed for healthy body functioning.

4.5 What is a balanced diet? (continued)

Balanced diets

What is needed in a balanced diet will vary, for example, with the age, gender and occupation of the individual.

Age

Younger children need smaller portions (as energy requirements are less), but more protein, vitamins and minerals for greater growth. Teenagers also need extra protein, minerals and vitamins for active growth, and larger portions for additional activities.

Gender

Men need larger portions than women, as they are usually heavier and have more muscle mass. Men use up energy more quickly and often have more physical jobs.

Pregnancy

Pregnant women need more unsaturated fats, proteins and minerals, e.g. calcium for the growth of the baby. Iron supplies from the food may be adequate, as there are no periods. They need larger portions of carbohydrates in the last 3 months as more energy is needed to carry around the weight of the developing baby.

State of health

If a person is ill they need additional protein for repair of tissues, and vitamins and minerals to restore health. If they have a deficiency disease (pages 58–9) they need additional foods with specific vitamins or minerals, e.g. for scurvy a person needs extra foods rich in vitamin C.

Occupation and physical activity

The amount of physical activity determines the amount of energy foods (carbohydrates and fat) that are needed, as well as other specific needs.

- Office worker: will need fewer energy foods compared with someone of the same age and sex doing more active work.
- Weightlifter: will need more protein to build muscles, and more energy foods to provide additional energy, than an average person.
- Farmer or cane cutter: will need very many more carbohydrates and fats, as this job uses a great deal of energy, than an average person.
- Athlete: will need more carbohydrates for energy and more protein for building muscles, than an average person.

Special diets

Vegetarians: if a person does not eat meat, they have to ensure they get a full range of nutrients. Some vegetarians eat eggs, milk and shellfish. If they do not do this, they need a wide variety of beans, peas, nuts and soya to supply the range of necessary amino acids needed to build proteins. They may also need extra minerals, e.g. iron (especially girls and women having their periods).

Objectives

- Relate balanced diets to age, gender, pregnancy and occupation.
- Describe unbalanced diets, e.g. obesity, deficiencies and PEM.

Did you know?

- Peanuts and meat have the same amount of protein. But soya beans have more than either of them.
- There is more water in an apple than in milk.

Timing of meals

You should not take strenuous exercise soon after a heavy meal. This is because, as food is digested, it is transported away from the small intestine by the blood. If the blood is required for this purpose, then there may be an insufficient blood supply to the legs and this can cause **cramp**. If, for example, you are swimming at this time, it might mean that you could drown. Exercising too soon after a meal can also produce a pain in the abdomen called a **'stitch'**.

Leave 1–2 hours after a meal before vigorous physical activity.

Questions

1 Part of a chocolate bar gave a red precipitate with the Biuret test and turned blue-black with iodine solution. Is it a balanced snack? Why?
2 A vegetarian ate a baked potato with margarine. Which food nutrients are missing? Suggest food items to add to make the meal more balanced.
3 What specific advice would you give a pregnant woman for her diet, and why?

Unbalanced diets

People need all the constituents of a balanced diet, and in the right proportions, to stay healthy. Unbalanced diets can cause **malnutrition**. Some examples of unbalanced diets and malnutrition follow.

Obesity

People who continually eat foods with more energy than they use will become heavier. In time, they may become **obese** (page 145). They need to reduce their food intake, especially of fatty foods, and become more active.

Deficiency diseases

If people do not eat foods rich in vitamins or minerals, they can suffer, for example, from beri-beri, scurvy, rickets or anaemia. They need to add specific foods to their diets.

Undernourished

Many older people may eat too little of most of the food groups. They need to add a wide range of food nutrients.

Slimming

When slimming, people eat less food, especially saturated fat, and may also increase their activity. The body uses the person's fat stores, and the person become thinner. It is important still to eat foods high in vitamins and minerals.

Anorexia

Anorexia is a disorder that describes a person who avoids food in order to lose body mass in a desire to become slim. The person, often a teenage girl, still sees herself as too fat, and so eats less. She may require treatment in hospital, or may die.

PEM

PEM is **protein energy malnutrition** seen in children with unbalanced and insufficient meals. It has two causes. Both show that the child is suffering from starvation.

- A lack of energy foods (carbohydrates and fats) causes the body to use its fat stores. This can result in **marasmus**.
- A lack of proteins causes the body to use the protein of the muscles, and this results in **kwashiorkor**.

Questions

4 The Brown family had a meal of roast chicken and bread. Is this a balanced meal? Give three reasons for your answer.

5 A pregnant woman is feeling very tired and is told her baby is small for its age. How should she adjust her diet?

6 A young child is allergic to cow's milk. What could the mother give her instead?

7 What precautions should a person take if they want to slim?

8 Your grandma has stomach cramps and constipation. Which food constituent should she increase in her diet? List two food items that contain it.

9 Which groups of people might need to add vitamin pills and minerals to their diets, and why?

10 What are the (a) advantages and (b) disadvantages of a vegetarian diet?

11 What are the causes of (a) kwashiorkor, (b) marasmus and (c) anorexia? How can each be treated?

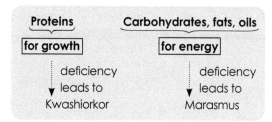

Key ideas

Use these words to fill in the spaces as you write the sentences in your Exercise book.

age　　**kwashiorkor**　　**malnutrition**　　**marasmus**　　**obesity**　　**physical activity**

The proportions and amounts of nutrients in a balanced diet depend, for example, on _____ and _____ . An unbalanced diet can cause _____ . If too much food is eaten, it can cause _____ . PEM (protein energy malnutrition) found especially in children is caused by insufficient proteins (_____) or insufficient carbohydrates and fats (_____).

4.6 Food additives

Activity

What is in our food?

1 The picture above shows labels taken from various foods. Look at them. The substances can be divided into two groups: **natural products** (e.g. nutrients and fibre) and **food additives** (e.g. food colourings and preservatives).

2 Make a full list of the natural products: the substances that occur naturally in our food.
   (a) Energy-providing foods such as green peas, beef, brown sugar, fat.
   (b) Minerals, e.g. salt, iron.
   (c) Vitamins, e.g. A, C.
   (d) Natural flavourings, e.g. salt, pepper, spices.
   (e) Fibre.
   (f) Water. If no water is present the food has been dried or **dehydrated.**

3 Make a full list of the food additives: the synthetic compounds added to the food.
   (a) Food colouring, e.g. yellow colouring.
   (b) Preservatives, e.g. sodium nitrite.
   (c) Flavour enhancers, e.g. monosodium glutamate.
   (d) Gelling agents, e.g. gelatine and agar (to 'set' the food).
   (e) Emulsifiers, e.g. lecithin, which keep fat particles evenly mixed in the food.

Repeat steps 2 and 3 with the labels from other foodstuffs.

Objectives

- Define natural products, food additives and food contaminants.
- Name groups of food additives and what they are used for.
- Discuss the effects of food additives and contaminants on health.

Hints for healthy living

(Adapted from the World Cancer Research Fund, and pages 58–61 and 97–9)

- Avoid sugary drinks.
- Limit high-energy foods (especially processed foods high in added sugar, salt or fat, or low in fibre).
- Eat more of a variety of vegetables, fruits, wholegrain, and legumes.
- Limit red meat, e.g. beef, pork, lamb.
- Avoid processed meats, e.g. bacon.
- Be as lean as possible without being underweight.
- Be physically active for at least 30 minutes each day.
- Limit alcoholic drinks.
- Do not smoke or chew tobacco.

Food additives

These are mainly synthetic compounds added, in small amounts, for particular reasons, such as to make the food look or taste more attractive or to make it last longer. Food additives should be listed on the ingredients label.

Some additives may cause problems.

Colours

These are mostly synthetic dyes added to almost all processed food, to improve the appearance and encourage people to buy it. However, tartrazine (a yellow food colouring used in margarine and orange-coloured rice) has been withdrawn from use because it could cause cancer.

Preservatives

Preservatives are added to most foods that are sold moist, because in the presence of water and oxygen bacteria can grow on the food (page 232). For example, processed meats, e.g. bacon and corned beef, may contain sodium nitrite. This makes the food safe from botulism bacteria, which could kill us. But the nitrite produces chemicals in the body that can be carcinogenic. For this reason processed meats should never be given to babies.

Flavourings and flavour enhancers

These are synthetic compounds, which are added to 'improve' flavour and make food more attractive. Many of them are given E numbers.

- An example of a flavouring is saccharin which was added to increase the sweetness of certain foods and bottled drinks. In large quantities it was found to be carcinogenic in mice, and is no longer used on a large scale. People can, however, still use it in small quantities to sweeten tea and coffee, although there are now safer alternatives. For example, a sugar substitute can be made from the leaves of a plant called *Stevia*.
- An example of a flavour enhancer is monosodium glutamate, which is used in many Chinese dishes. This can cause an allergic reaction in people who are sensitive to it.

What can we do about food additives?

- Avoid processed foods as far as possible.
- Read labels carefully and avoid products with harmful additives, e.g. sodium nitrite and saccharin.
- Keep informed about other harmful additives.
- Eat fresh food whenever possible.
- Eat foods that have been preserved by drying rather than by adding chemicals.

Food contaminants

These are chemicals or microorganisms that have got onto or into our food by accident. We do not usually know that they are there, unless they make us ill!

Microorganisms

These may have got onto the food from flies or from handling (pages 232 and 239).

Pesticides

Pesticides may be applied to crops at too high a dose, or too close to harvest time. Pesticide residues may then be found on or inside our food. Some insecticides are very resistant to being broken down, and they accumulate, especially in fatty meat, fish and poultry and in dairy products.

EDB (ethane dibromide) is a pesticide used in the growing of grain that has been found to cause cancer. EDB residues were found in flour, peanuts and corn-bread mix in the USA and 77 products were withdrawn from the stores.

Animal hormones

Animal hormones, for example diethylstilbestrol (DES), have been fed to beef cattle and chickens to improve growth. DES is related to the female hormone oestrogen, and when it is found in the food we eat it can cause the development of breasts in young children of both sexes. It may cause cancer.

Pollutants

Pollutants such as lead (from gasoline), sulphur dioxide (from burning coal) and caustic fumes (from processing bauxite) can end up on our food.

Fertilizers

Fertilizers added to the land may be washed into rivers used for irrigation and for drinking purposes (page 224).

What can we do about food contaminants?

- Wash all fresh fruit and vegetables before eating or cooking them. This will remove any microorganisms, pesticides, pollutants or fertilizers.
- Remove the outer skin, unless this would remove valuable nutrients, for example in Irish potato.
- Trim off fat from meat to remove pesticides.
- Reduce meat consumption and increase fresh vegetables, fruit, legumes and nuts in the diet.
- Use dried foods, e.g. milk that can be made up with water just when we need it.

4.7 How do we use our teeth?

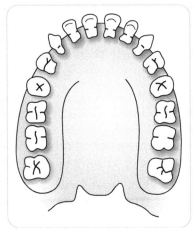

What do our teeth do?

Humans are **omnivores**: we eat a wide variety of plant and animal food, and so we need teeth of every kind.

Incisors

These **bite** pieces from the food. There are four in each jaw. They have a narrow ridge along the top of the tooth and work against each other like scissors. Mainly used for plant food.

Well developed in **herbivores**, e.g. rabbits.

Canines

These **tear** pieces from the food. There are two in each jaw. They have a pointed top to the crown and are longer than other teeth.

Well developed in **carnivores**, e.g. lions.

Premolars and molars (cheek teeth)

These **crush** and **grind** food. There are four premolars and six molars in each jaw. They have flat wide tops with small bumps and hollows on them. When food has been cut or torn off it is pushed to the back of the mouth. The cheek teeth then work against each other to crush and grind the food into small pieces.

Well developed in herbivores, e.g. cows.

Dental formula of humans $= I \frac{2}{2} \quad C \frac{1}{1} \quad PM \frac{2}{2} \quad M \frac{3}{3}$

Mechanical digestion

Our teeth cut, crush and grind our food into small pieces of the *same* kind. We call this **mechanical** digestion.

● We can then swallow the pieces more easily.

● The smaller pieces have a larger surface area and so can be digested more quickly by enzymes in the gut.

Without using our teeth, our food would not be properly chewed, and digestion would therefore be slower.

A vertical section of a tooth

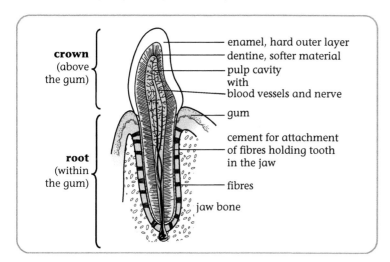

Looking after our teeth

The teeth we have as children are the **milk teeth**. It is important to clean these carefully, as they keep spaces for the **adult teeth**, which grow later. We can strengthen teeth by drinking water or using toothpaste with fluorides.

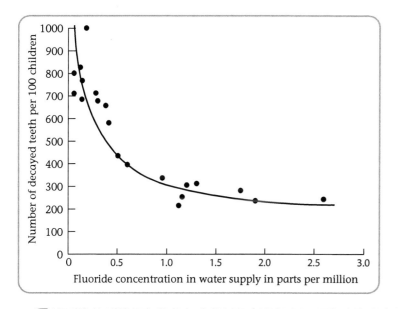

Caring for our teeth

Cleaning

When we eat, food pieces get stuck between our teeth to form **plaque**. We need to clean this away with crisp foods or with a brush. If plaque remains, especially from sticky starch or sugary foods, it is acted on by bacteria. These produce acids that attack the enamel.

Tooth decay

The acids can wear away the enamel, and then the softer dentine. This exposes the nerves in the pulp cavity, and we feel toothache. We need to go to a dentist, who drills away the decayed tooth, and fills the hole with a filling. If there is too much decay, the dentist will remove or extract the tooth.

What we can do

To make strong teeth:
- eat milk and cheese with calcium and phosphorus to build strong teeth
- expose the skin to make vitamin D, needed to use calcium, and eat foods with vitamin C for healthy gums.

Fluoridation

Fluoridation is the adding of fluorides to toothpaste or drinking water.
- Fluorides in toothpaste harden only the outer surface of the teeth. They become more resistant to decay by 15% to 30%.
- Small amounts of fluoride added to drinking water harden the teeth and reduce decay by 54% to 84%. The graph on the left shows how different concentrations of fluoride reduce the number of decayed teeth. But too much fluoride can blacken the enamel.

Key ideas

Use these words to fill in the spaces as you write the sentences in your Exercise book.

rabbits   grind   canines   incisors   enamel   lions   crown   nerves

The part of a tooth above the gum is the _____ . The cutting teeth are the _____ , which are well developed in _____ . Carnivores, such as _____ , have well-developed _____ . The premolars and molars _____ the food. Fluoridation helps to harden the _____ of the teeth. If our teeth decay, we feel toothache when the pulp cavity and _____ are exposed.

4.8 How do we digest our food?

The lining of our gut (**alimentary canal**) is like a sieve with very, very small holes. Our food is made of big pieces, like starch, that cannot pass through the holes. **Digestion** is the process by which insoluble food is made soluble, so it can **diffuse** (page 46) through the holes in the gut wall and into the blood. Undigested bits are **defecated** as faeces.

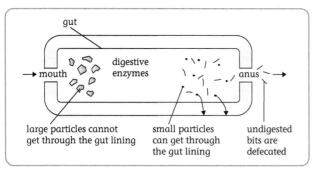

Digestion and defecation

Absorption of digested food

Food is broken down and changed to soluble substances via **mechanical** and **chemical** digestion.

- The small intestine is 5 m long – digestion is completed.
- Soluble end products of digestion are: glucose, amino acids, glycerol and fatty acids.
- The inner wall of the small intestine has small holes.
- The wall has many finger-like projections (**villi**) that increase the surface area for absorption of food.
- The wall of the villus is only one cell thick.
- Soluble food diffuses in: glucose and amino acids go into the blood to the liver, where their concentration is adjusted (page 120); glycerol and fatty acids enter the lacteals (part of the lymph system) and then the blood.

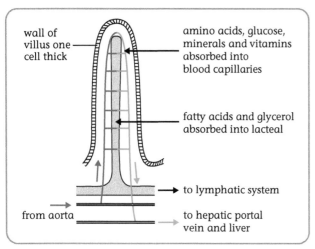

How a villus works

Objectives

- Distinguish between mechanical and chemical digestion.
- Demonstrate the diffusion of soluble substances and describe absorption.
- Draw and label the digestive system and state the functions of each part.

Mechanical digestion   This breaks food into smaller pieces of the same kind. It occurs in the mouth (teeth), the stomach (churning action) and duodenum (bile salts emulsifying fats and oils).

Chemical digestion   This makes use of enzymes to change the food from large insoluble substances to different small soluble ones.

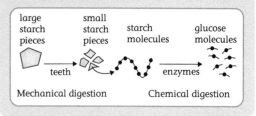

Mechanical digestion   Chemical digestion

What does it mean?

Ingestion   The taking in of food into the mouth.

Digestion   The mechanical and chemical breakdown of large molecules of food to make small, soluble molecules.

Absorption   The uptake of soluble molecules into the blood in the villi.

Assimilation   The use the body makes of the absorbed food. The food is used for growth and respiration, for example.

Egestion   The passing out through the anus of dried remains (faeces) from parts of the food that cannot be digested.

Functions of parts of the alimentary canal

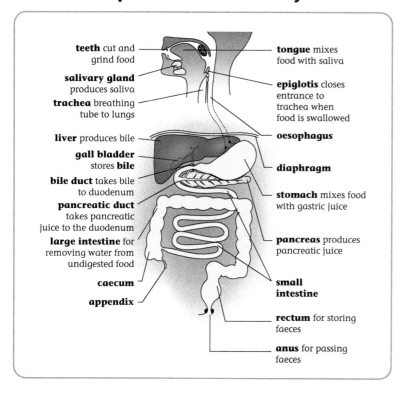

teeth cut and grind food

salivary gland produces saliva

trachea breathing tube to lungs

liver produces bile

gall bladder stores bile

bile duct takes bile to duodenum

pancreatic duct takes pancreatic juice to the duodenum

large intestine for removing water from undigested food

caecum

appendix

tongue mixes food with saliva

epiglotis closes entrance to trachea when food is swallowed

oesophagus

diaphragm

stomach mixes food with gastric juice

pancreas produces pancreatic juice

small intestine

rectum for storing faeces

anus for passing faeces

As the food passes down the alimentary canal, it is well mixed with the digestive juices containing the enzymes.

- In the mouth, the teeth and tongue mix the food with saliva, and this starts the digestion of cooked starch.
- In the stomach, the muscular walls squash and squeeze the food to mix it with stomach (gastric) juice.
- The small intestine, where most of the digestion occurs, is very long and has folded walls. Theses features assist in mixing the food with digestive juices.
- All along the alimentary canal the walls alternately squeeze and relax on the food (**peristalsis**). Fibre in the food gives bulk, and helps this process. So the food is mixed with the juices and pushed along to the next stage.

What does it mean?

Vomiting This means 'being sick'. It happens when contents from the stomach are sent back up because the body has been upset by an infection, alcohol, stress, or the hormone changes of pregnancy.

Faeces The fibre (cellulose, roughage) in our food cannot be digested into soluble substances. It passes through the gut to the large intestine, where water is removed from it. This waste then goes to the rectum and is passed out as faeces.

Diarrhoea Large amounts of runny faeces because water has not been removed in the large intestine. It is due to infection, stress or spicy foods. It can lead to dangerous dehydration, especially in children. Check at a clinic if it does not improve in 2 days.

Constipation The faeces are hard, and passing them may cause pain. Prevent it by a diet high in fibre such as cereals, bran, wholemeal bread, fruit and vegetables.

Did you know?

- On average, food takes 24 hours to pass right through the alimentary canal.
- If laid out straight, your whole gut would be six times as long as you are tall.
- An empty stomach has a volume of half a litre (0.5 dm^3); when full it can stretch to 4 dm^3.

Key ideas

Use these words to fill in the spaces as you write the sentences in your Exercise book.

soluble   chemical   small intestine   diffuse   mechanical   villi   enzymes

The breaking of food into smaller pieces that occurs in the mouth is called _____ digestion.

The change of insoluble molecules to different _____ ones is called _____ digestion, and it is

brought about by _____ . In the _____ the _____ end products of digestion _____ into

the _____ and into the blood.

4.8 How do we digest our food? (continued)

Digestive enzymes are in three main groups:

- carbohydrases to digest carbohydrates
- proteases to digest proteins
- lipases to digest fats and oils.

The action of the various enzymes is shown in the table on page 69.

The action of the various enzymes is shown in the table on page 69.

Objectives

- Describe the role of enzymes in digestion, and the effect of pH.
- Explain the importance of bile salts.

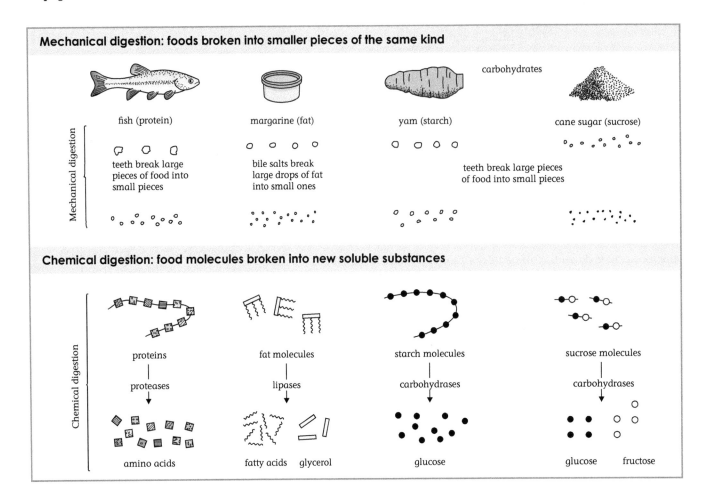

Key ideas

Use these words to fill in the spaces as you write the sentences in your Exercise book.

amino acids   enzymes   proteases   bile   lipases   carbohydrases   pH

Different _____ work on different substrates and at different _____ values. Proteins are digested by _____ to make _____ . Carbohydrates are digested by _____ to make simple sugars such as glucose. Fats and oils are made into small droplets by _____ salts, and digested by _____ to make fatty acids and glycerol.

What do the enzymes do in the alimentary canal?

Part	pH	Digestive juice	Enzyme group	Enzyme example	Substrate	End products
Mouth	Alkaline	Saliva	Carbohydrases	Salivary amylase	Cooked starch	Maltose (a sugar)
Stomach	Acid	Gastric juice	Proteases	Pepsin	Protein	Smaller proteins
Pancreas	Alkaline	Pancreatic juice	Carbohydrases Lipases	Amylase Lipase	All starch Emulsified fat	Sugars Fatty acids and glycerol
			Proteases	Trypsin	Small proteins	Smaller proteins
Small intestine	Alkaline	Intestinal juice	Carbohydrases	Maltase	Maltose	Glucose (a simple sugar)
			Lipases	Lipase	Emulsified fat	Fatty acids and glycerol
			Proteases	Peptidases	Small proteins	Amino acids

Note: bile (from the liver) is *not* an enzyme. It emulsifies fats (breaks it into small droplets).

Digestive juices

The juices usually contain enzymes, and chemicals that make the juice a certain pH. This pH is important for the most efficient working of particular enzymes.

Saliva

This is made in the salivary glands in the **mouth**. Its pH is slightly alkaline. It contains one enzyme, salivary **amylase**, which begins the digestion of cooked starch. This is the only chemical digestion that occurs in the mouth.

Gastric juice

This is made by glands in the wall of the **stomach**. Its pH is acid. This is the only part of the gut with an acid pH, and it is needed only for the action of the protease **pepsin**. This begins the digestion of proteins (the only chemical digestion that occurs in the stomach).

Bile

This is made by the **liver**, and is stored in a sac called the **gall bladder**. It passes along a tube into the beginning of the small intestine. Its pH is alkaline because of sodium hydrogencarbonate, which helps to neutralize the acidity from the stomach. It does *not* contain any enzymes. It does contain **bile salts**, which break up (**emulsify**) fats and oils. This is mechanical digestion, and it allows the enzyme lipase, in the small intestine, to work more efficiently.

Pancreatic juice

This is made in the **pancreas**. Its pH is alkaline. It passes along a tube into the first part of the small intestine. There it makes conditions alkaline for the protease **trypsin**. It also contains an amylase and lipase. So chemical digestion occurs on all the types of food.

Intestinal juice

This is made by glands in the **intestine** wall. Its pH is alkaline. It contains amylases, lipases and proteases, which complete the digestion of all food groups to simple sugars, fatty acids and glycerol, and amino acids.

Practical 22

Importance of mechanical digestion (PD)

Pretend that you have a cracker and want to design a fair test of the hypothesis that 'smaller pieces of food are digested more quickly than larger ones'.
  List all the steps you will follow, and the chemical reagents you will need.

Questions

1 Which of the following are mechanical and which are chemical digestion?
  (a) Biting and chewing of food.
  (b) Action of pepsin on protein.
  (c) Action of bile salts on fats and oils.
  (d) Churning action of the stomach.
  (e) Action on cooked starch in the mouth.
  (f) Action on protein in the mouth.
  (g) Action of lipase on emulsified fats.
2 You are eating a meat patty or beef pie.
  (a) What groups of food are present?
  (b) Which groups of enzymes are used?
  (c) List all substrates and end products.
3 In what conditions of pH do:
  (a) amylases work best?
  (b) lipases work best?
4 Give an example of a protease that:
  (a) works best in acid conditions
  (b) works best in alkaline conditions.

4.9 How do enzymes work?

Enzymes are biological **catalysts**. They make the reactions go more quickly but are not themselves used up in the reaction. They cannot make reactions occur that would not usually happen. But they act as a 'go-between' to bring molecules together, so they interact more quickly.

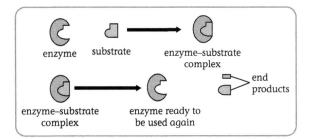

The characteristics of enzymes	
Characteristics	**Notes**
1 Most are proteins.	Enzymes are made from the amino acids in our food.
2 Work best at body temperature (37°C).	This is because most are proteins, and these are destroyed above 40°C.
3 Needed in very small amounts, as re-used.	They catalyse (speed up) the reaction but are not changed by it.
4 They do a particular job (are specific).	Each enzyme is important for one special reaction.
5 They are sensitive to pH.	Different enzymes work best at different pH values.
6 They are sensitive to poisons.	For example, arsenic and cyanide destroy respiratory enzymes and so kill the person.
7 They are helped by vitamins and minerals.	This is one reason why we need these for health, e.g. the B vitamins help the respiratory enzymes.

Objectives

- Define what is meant by an enzyme.
- Give examples of enzyme action.
- Show how enzyme action is affected by temperature and pH.

Enzymes in living things

Enzymes help to build up or break down molecules in a step-by-step way without the need for high temperatures.

- Photosynthesis: the stages are assisted by enzymes.
- Digestion: different enzymes help in the breakdown of foods to produce soluble end products.
- Respiration: a series of respiratory enzymes help the combination of oxygen with glucose to release energy.

Questions

1 Which characteristic of enzymes can explain each of these observations?
   (a) Boiling enzymes stops their activity.
   (b) Pepsin digests protein, but not starch.
   (c) Enzymes are only needed in very small amounts.
2 You have been given three enzymes – pepsin, trypsin and salivary amylase – but you do not know which is which. How could you find out, using a cracker, an egg and some acid and alkali? (Say which reagents you need for testing the end products.)

Key ideas

Use these words to fill in the spaces as you write the sentences in your Exercise book.

salivary amylase   temperature   pepsin   body   acid   alkaline   protein

The enzyme in our mouth is _____ and it works best in slightly _____ conditions. The enzyme in our stomach is _____ and it works best in _____ conditions. Enzyme activity increases with _____ up to about 37°C, which is _____ temperature. Above this _____ , many enzymes are destroyed, as the _____ of which they are made is damaged.

Practical 23

Action of enzymes (PD, ORR, AI)

1 Find out about the enzymes amylase (in germinating seeds), catalase (in liver) and papain (in pawpaw).

2 Design experiments to investigate their actions. (You will need the substrates, equipment and reagents for testing the end products.)

3 Check your plans with your teacher, then carry out the activity with one of the enzymes.

4 Compare your results with those from other groups.

Practical 24

How does pH affect enzymes? (PD)

Set up a fair test to compare how well amylase works at different pH values. Include:

● three different values for the pH

● a set-up where the only difference between the test tubes is the pH (everything else is constant)

● measurements to find out in which conditions the reaction occurs most quickly

● a chemical check of the end products.

(Show your teacher your plan, and see page 368.) What different results would you expect if you used pepsin instead of amylase? Explain.

Enzymes in everyday life

● Pawpaw leaves and cubes of green pawpaw are used to make meat tender. They contain a protease, papain, that starts to digest the meat.

● Biological washing powders contain proteases and lipases to digest protein and fat stains.

● Bio-yogurts contain living bacteria whose enzymes help improve the digestion of our food.

● Fresh fruit drinks, e.g. those from banana, contain enzymes that can also help digestion.

● Fermentation of sugar solutions by enzymes in the yeast can be used to make beer and wine.

● Cheese and yogurt are made by the action of enzymes on milk.

● Baby foods contain trypsin to pre-digest proteins in the food.

● Catalase is used to help make foam rubber.

● Testing strips for diabetics contain enzymes.

Practical 25

How does temperature affect salivary amylase? (MM, ORR, AI)

1 Make a sample of cooked starch as on page 368.

2 Divide your sample equally into four test tubes, labelled **A**, **B**, **C** and **D**.

3 Add two drops of saliva and boil the contents for 3 minutes (**A**).

4 Set up the other three test tubes, like this, before adding saliva: put one into a beaker with ice, or put it into the refrigerator (**B**); put one into a beaker with water at room temperature and record the temperature (**C**); put one into a water bath (**D** – a beaker with water kept at about 37°C, which is body temperature).

5 Add two drops of saliva to tubes **B**, **C** and **D**. Record the time.

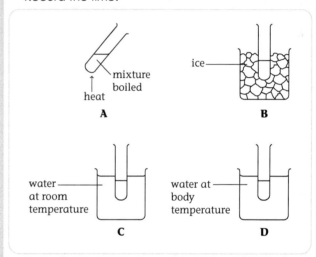

6 At one-minute intervals, use a dropping pipette to take out a little of each solution from each test-tube. Test it with iodine solution on a tile.

	A	B	C	D
1 minute	o	o	o	o
2 minutes	o	o	o	o
3 minutes	o	o	o	o

7 Record what happens in each of test tubes **A**, **B**, **C** and **D**. Explain your findings.

8 In which conditions did the salivary amylase work most quickly to break down the starch?

9 Describe how temperature affects the enzyme.

5 Respiration and air pollution

5.1 How do we breathe?

Breathing is the process of taking in, and pushing out, air.

- Taking in air is called **inhalation**. Pressure in the chest decreases, and the lung volume increases to pull in air.
- Pushing out air is called **exhalation**. Pressure in the chest increases, and the lung volume decreases to push out air.

Air enters the respiratory system through the nose and mouth to the throat. It passes through the voice box into the windpipe (**trachea**) and the two **bronchi**. All these have rings of cartilage that help to keep them open. The bronchi go into the lungs, where they divide into small **bronchioles**. These then lead into many small air sacs (**alveoli**), where gas exchange takes place.

The lungs are enclosed, at the front, back and sides, within the **ribcage**. At the base of the chest cavity is a muscular sheet, the **diaphragm**.

Inhalation

The left-hand diagram below shows what happens when you breathe in. The diaphragm is pulled down and the volume inside the chest cavity increases. The ribs are drawn up and outwards, which also increases the volume. This increase in volume causes a decrease of pressure on the lungs, which therefore expand and draw in air from outside.

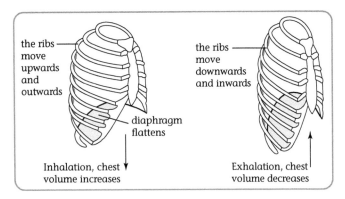

Chest movements during breathing

Exhalation

The right-hand diagram above shows what happens when you breathe out. The diaphragm is pushed up and the volume inside the chest cavity deceases. The ribs are drawn in and downwards, which also decreases the volume. This decrease in volume causes an increase in pressure on the lungs, so that the air inside them is pushed out.

Objectives

- Explain how inhalation and exhalation occur.
- Account for the composition of inhaled and exhaled air.

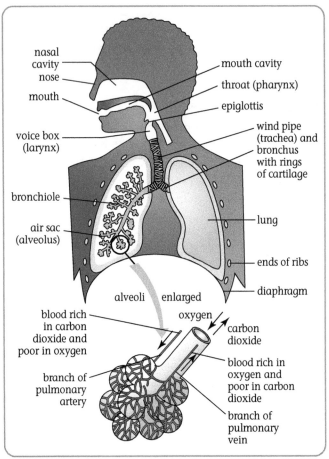

Respiratory system

Inhalation	Exhalation
Ribs pulled up and out	Ribs moved down and in
Diaphragm pulled flat by diaphragm muscles	Diaphragm goes up into the chest cavity
Chest volume increases	Chest volume decreases
Pressure inside chest decreases, so air is drawn in	Pressure inside chest increases, so air is pushed out

Practical 26

Making a model (MM, ORR)

1 Set up a model as shown below of the chest cavity. Identify each part on the diagrams.

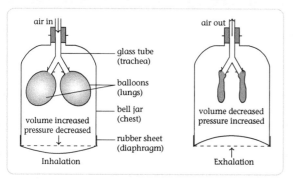

2 Pull down the diaphragm to represent inhalation.
3 Push up the diaphragm to represent exhalation.
4 How is the model (a) like and (b) unlike the real respiratory system?

Differences between inhaled and exhaled air

● **Oxygen:** there is more oxygen in inhaled than exhaled air because some is removed in the lungs and passed to the cells for respiration.
● **Carbon dioxide:** there is more carbon dioxide in exhaled than in inhaled air. This is because, during respiration, carbon dioxide is made and is returned to the lungs to be breathed out.
● **Nitrogen and other gases:** these gases stay the same, as they are not involved in respiration.
● **Heat:** exhaled air is usually warmer than inhaled air because heat energy is released during respiration.
● **Water vapour:** exhaled air usually has more water vapour than inhaled air as water is released in respiration and some is breathed out.

Practical 27

Testing inhaled and exhaled air (MM, ORR)

1 Set up two test tubes as shown below.

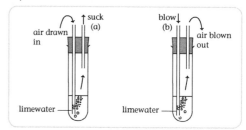

2 *Suck* air in through the *short* tube in (a). Air from the atmosphere (which is like inhaled air) will be drawn in to bubble through the limewater.
3 Now *blow* out through the *long* tube in (b). Your exhaled air will bubble through the limewater.
4 Carbon dioxide makes limewater go milky. Explain what you find out.
5 To test for oxygen: use similar candles in inhaled and exhaled air, and compare how long they burn.
6 Use a thermometer to find the temperature of inhaled and exhaled air. Breathe out onto a glass surface to see the water vapour in exhaled air.

Constituent	Inhaled air	Exhaled air
Oxygen	20%	16%
Carbon dioxide	about 0.03%	4%
Nitrogen and other gases	about 80%	about 80%
Heat	usually less than exhaled air	body temperature
Water vapour	usually less than exhaled air	saturated air

Key ideas

Use these words to fill in the spaces as you write the sentences in your Exercise book.

exhaled   20%   flattened   inhaled   4%   16%   up and out   decreases

During inhalation the ribs are pulled _____ and the diaphragm is _____ . This increases the chest volume and _____ the pressure. _____ air with _____ oxygen is drawn in. During exhalation the volume of the chest cavity _____ , which increases the pressure, and _____ air with _____ oxygen and _____ carbon dioxide is pushed out.

5.2 How are gases exchanged?

Gaseous exchange is the exchange of gases through moist surfaces, called **respiratory surfaces**; in animals and plants it occurs by diffusion (see page 46).

Characteristics of respiratory surfaces

- **Large and thin**: respiratory surfaces are large, so there is a large surface area (pages 84–5) for diffusion. They are very thin (usually one cell thick), so gases only have a short distance to diffuse.
- **Moist**: the surfaces are moist; gases have to dissolve in moisture before they diffuse.
- **Supplied with gases**: in animals, gases are brought to and from the respiratory surface by breathing movements.
- **Supplied with blood**: in animals, respiratory surfaces are well supplied with blood vessels to transport some gases to and from the surface.

Gaseous exchange in mammals

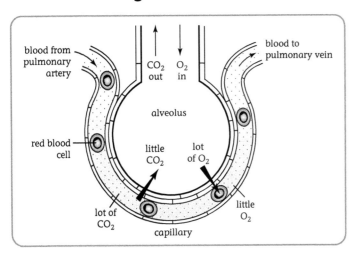

The lung is divided into very many **alveoli** (air sacs). These give a large respiratory surface and the walls are one cell thick. They also have a layer of moisture in which gases can dissolve.

Blood with a lot of carbon dioxide is brought close to the alveolus in a capillary from the pulmonary artery. There is less carbon dioxide in the alveolus and so a **concentration gradient** is set up. Carbon dioxide diffuses from the capillary into the alveolus and is breathed out.

There is more oxygen in the alveolus (from the inhaled air) than is in the capillary. So a concentration gradient is set up and oxygen passes from the alveolus into the capillary of the pulmonary vein.

Deoxygenated blood leaves the heart in the pulmonary artery to go the lungs. When carbon dioxide has left the blood, and oxygen has been picked up, the oxygenated blood returns to the heart in the pulmonary vein.

Objectives

- Discuss the features common to respiratory surfaces.
- Describe gas exchange in mammals, amphibians, fish and flowering plants.

Gaseous exchange in fish

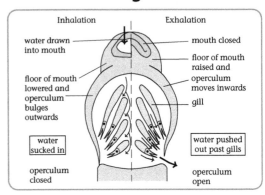

Breathing movements in a fish

Water, containing dissolved oxygen, is drawn into the fish and passes over its **gills** during inhalation. The gills have a large surface area, and are thin and well supplied with blood.

The blood that is brought to the gills has a lot of carbon dioxide, and not much oxygen, in it. Concentration gradients are set up so that oxygen diffuses from the water into the blood, and carbon dioxide diffuses from the blood out into the water. The water passes out of the operculum during exhalation.

Questions

1. Distinguish between breathing and gaseous exchange in an animal. Explain why each is important.
2. How do alveoli in a mammal show the characteristics of respiratory surfaces?
3. (a) How do fish breathe? (b) How do fish obtain oxygen from the water and lose carbon dioxide?
4. How are respiratory surfaces of a flowering plant simpler than those of animals? Why are they simpler?

Comparison of gaseous exchange in living organisms				
Organism	Large respiratory surface	Moist respiratory surface	Supplied with gases	Supplied with blood
Fish	**Gills:** divided into small thin parts with large surface area	Gills surrounded by water	Breathing movements: water comes in through the mouth and out through the operculum	Gases diffuse into and out of the blood supplied to the gills
Amphibian	**Gills:** large surface area **Skin:** all over the body **Lungs:** fairly small	Gills in the water Skin kept moist Lungs kept moist	Water currents Air movements Breathing movements	Gases diffuse into and out of blood vessels in the gills, skin and lungs
Mammal	**Alveoli** in lungs: very many make a very large surface area	Cells in the alveoli secrete fluid	Breathing movements: ribs and diaphragm; air enters and leaves lungs (see pages 72–3)	Gases diffuse into and out of the blood supplied to the lungs
Flowering plant	**Large surface of cells** near the stomata inside the leaves (see page 51)	Cells with covering of water brought in xylem vessels	No breathing movements; gases just diffuse into and out of stomata	No blood system; gases just diffuse into and out of stomata

Gaseous exchange in amphibians

Amphibians, such as toads and frogs, have three respiratory surfaces. The young tadpole has **gills**, which are thin and feathery with a large surface area. Gills are well supplied with blood, and oxygen diffuses in and carbon dioxide diffuses out along their concentration gradients.

Older tadpoles and adults use their **skin and lungs**. The skin is kept moist and well supplied with blood for gaseous exchange. The lungs have thin walls supplied with blood vessels, but they are less important as respiratory surfaces than the skin.

Did you know?

- Lungs contain about 300,000 million capillaries – a total length of 2400 km.
- The area of all the alveoli together is about 100 m^2, which is half of a doubles tennis court.

Gaseous exchange in flowering plants

The respiratory surface is the large, moist surface of cells near the stomata in the leaves (see page 51). Gases high in concentration in the air outside diffuse into the air spaces. Other gases diffuse out along their concentration gradients (see pages 50–1).

Differences between plants and animals

- Plants use less energy than animals and do not need rapid gas exchange to support respiration in the cells. They are rooted in the ground, and are simpler and less active. So there is no need for breathing movements or blood to transport the gases.
- Complex, active animals need rapid gaseous exchange assisted by breathing movements and a good supply of blood. This allows for additional energy release.
- Animals always take in oxygen and give out carbon dioxide. Plants also do this at night; but in the daytime plants take in carbon dioxide and give out oxygen (see pages 110–11).

Key ideas

Use these words to fill in the spaces as you write the sentences in your Exercise book.

moist   breathing   oxygen   concentration   carbon dioxide   large   blood

The respiratory surfaces where gases are exchanged are _____ , thin and _____ . In animals

there are also _____ movements, and the surfaces are well supplied with _____ . The gases

that are exchanged are _____ and _____ . They diffuse along their _____ gradients. Fish are

able to take in _____ from the water and pass out _____ .

5.3 What is respiration?

Respiration is a very important process occurring in each cell, all the time, in all living things. It uses food to release energy and carbon dioxide. The energy released is essential for all life processes (pages 6–7).

- **Aerobic** respiration requires oxygen:

  glucose + oxygen → carbon dioxide + water + energy

- **Anaerobic** respiration does not need oxygen (see pages 78–80), but releases much less energy.

What happens when living things respire?

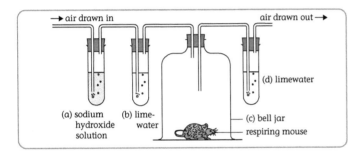

Air is drawn through the apparatus from left to right.

- Test tube (a) contains sodium or potassium hydroxide solution. This absorbs carbon dioxide from the air. Why is this important?
- Test tube (b) contains limewater. It stays clear and shows there is no carbon dioxide entering the bell jar (c). (If this limewater does go milky, the apparatus is wrongly set up.)
- Bell jar (c) contains a live, respiring mouse. The bell jar is sealed with petroleum jelly to stop the outside air from entering.
- Test tube (d) contains limewater. This tests if there is any carbon dioxide in the air coming from the mouse.

Questions

1 Do you expect the limewater in test tube (d) to go milky? If yes, why? What would this show?

2 A student observes mist on the inside of the bell jar. What could this be, and how could it be tested?

3 This experiment is not allowed to run for more than half an hour. Why do you think this is so? What would be the effect on the mouse, and what would be the reason?

4 Could the apparatus be used with other animals? Explain any changes you would make.

5 If the apparatus was used with (a) a flowering plant or (b) a water weed, what changes would you make?

6 Name two substances that are produced during aerobic respiration.

7 How is aerobic respiration (a) similar to and (b) different from combustion of fossil fuels?

Objectives

- Define respiration, and give the substrate, products and equations.
- Carry out experiments to show how respiration occurs.
- List the importance of energy release.

Practical 28

Do respiring seeds release energy? (ORR)

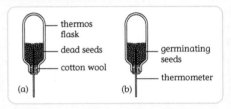

1 Set up thermos flasks as shown above.

2 Seeds in flask (a) were killed by boiling in water for 5 minutes.

3 Seeds in flask (b) were germinating. Both sets of seeds were washed in disinfectant to kill any bacteria on them.

4 Record the initial temperature and after 3 days. What has happened?

5 Why were the two kinds of seeds used?

Practical 29

Do respiring seeds release carbon dioxide? (MM, ORR)

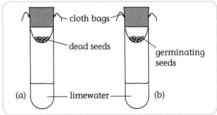

1 Use test tubes, cloth bags, bungs, limewater and dead and germinating seeds (washed in disinfectant).

2 What do you observe after 3 hours? What does this mean?

How do we show respiration in plants?

Green plants carry out respiration all the time, to combine food with oxygen and release energy, carbon dioxide and water. But in the daytime plants also carry out photosynthesis – which uses up the carbon dioxide released during respiration. So if we want to record the changes due to respiration alone, we need to put the apparatus in a dark room, or cover the bell jar with a dark cloth. If we want to show respiration in a water plant, we put it in a flask with water.

The following set-ups would be used instead of the bell jar containing the mouse. All the other containers would be the same as shown on page 76.

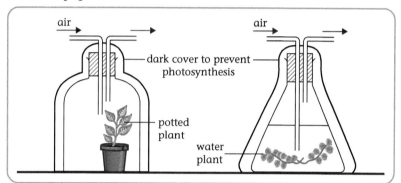

Showing respiration in plants

Testing for the products of respiration

- Carbon dioxide: turns limewater milky.
- Water: turns dry cobalt chloride paper (blue) to pink.
- Energy (heat): record temperature rise with a thermometer.

Why is energy release important?

Energy is needed, all the time, to keep cells alive. If a cell cannot release energy, then it dies, and so might the organism.
Energy is needed:

- by the cell membrane to control what enters and leaves the cells
- in plant roots, to take up mineral salts
- to build new compounds for growth of plants and animals
- to build new chromosomes during cell division and reproduction
- to build new compounds as seeds and animal embryos grow and develop.

Respiratory substrates

The energy released from 1 g of food is as follows.

Carbohydrate: about 17 kJ. The respiratory substrate is glucose. Carbohydrates are digested to make glucose for respiration.

Fat: about 39 kJ. Used to release energy if insufficient carbohydrates are eaten.

Protein: about 18 kJ. Only used if other food is not available. Use of muscles for respiration occurs (see PEM, page 61).

Comparison of aerobic respiration and photosynthesis	
Aerobic respiration	**Photosynthesis**
Occurs in cytoplasm and mitochondria	Occurs in chloroplasts
Does not need chlorophyll	Needs chlorophyll to trap the Sun's energy
Takes place all the time in plants and animals	Takes place only in the daytime, and only in plants
Energy is released	Energy is needed
glucose + oxygen → carbon dioxide + water + energy $C_6H_{12}O_6 + 6O_2 \rightarrow 6CO_2 + 6H_2O$ + energy	carbon dioxide + water + energy → glucose + oxygen $6CO_2 + 6H_2O$ + energy $\rightarrow C_6H_{12}O_6 + 6O_2$

Key ideas

Use these words to fill in the spaces as you write the sentences in your Exercise book.

oxygen   carbon dioxide   glucose   photosynthesis   heat   fat

Respiration uses food, such as _____ , to release _____ and energy, shown as _____ . In aerobic respiration _____ is needed. The energy released by respiration was stored in the food during _____ . _____ releases more energy than _____ .

5.4 Aerobic and anaerobic respiration

Aerobic respiration

This requires oxygen. All the energy trapped in the glucose, during photosynthesis, is released. Aerobic respiration occurs all the time in plants and animals.

glucose + oxygen → carbon dioxide + water + energy

$$C_6H_{12}O_6 + 6O_2 \rightarrow 6CO_2 + 6H_2O + energy$$

Anaerobic respiration

This takes place when there is no oxygen. The glucose is only partly broken down and releases only a little of the energy. There is still energy trapped in the products of anaerobic respiration (**ethanol** and **lactic acid**).

- Anaerobic respiration occurs in germinating seeds and yeast. It also occurs in bacteria in waterlogged soil that has little oxygen. Ethanol, carbon dioxide and a little energy are produced. This is called **fermentation**. It is an important process in the making of bread and wine.

glucose → ethanol + carbon dioxide + energy

$$C_6H_{12}O_6 \rightarrow 2C_2H_5OH + 2CO_2 + energy$$

- It also occurs in animal muscles during exercise. For example, in humans, when insufficient oxygen has been brought to the muscles by the blood, anaerobic respiration occurs. The muscles respire anaerobically to make lactic acid. This is called **lactic acid fermentation**.

glucose → lactic acid + energy

- The build-up of lactic acid causes our muscles to feel weak and to ache. This is called **muscle fatigue**. This is what happens if you sprint for 100 m without taking a breath. The lactic acid is a poison and has to be got rid of when the exercise is over. You have to breathe in extra oxygen to break down the lactic acid. The amount of oxygen that is needed is called the **oxygen debt**. A further amount of energy is released as the lactic acid is respired.

lactic acid + oxygen → carbon dioxide + water + energy

- Lactic acid fermentation also occurs in some bacteria, which act on the sugar in milk. This process is important in the making of sour cream, yoghurt and cheese.

Questions

1 Yeast can respire aerobically and anaerobically. Write the word equations for each process.
2 Work with a friend to design the apparatus to test whether yeast and sugar in anaerobic conditions produce alcohol and carbon dioxide (then see page 369).
3 What are the advantages to the plant for seeds to be able to respire both anaerobically and aerobically?

Objectives

- Compare aerobic and anaerobic respiration energy release and products.
- Describe industrial uses of anaerobic respiration.
- Measure the energy value of foods.
- Relate the amount of energy released to the type of substrate.

Practical 30

Anaerobic respiration in germinating seeds (ORR)

On page 76 you found that germinating seeds released heat energy and carbon dioxide when respiring aerobically. Seeds can also carry out anaerobic respiration.

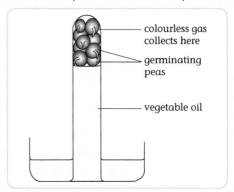

colourless gas collects here

germinating peas

vegetable oil

1 Fill a test tube with vegetable oil and put it upside down in a dish of oil.
2 Push some germinating seeds up into the test tube as shown above. At the top of the test tube there is very little air.
3 Set up another test tube and dish but with seeds that have been boiled. Both sets of seeds are washed in disinfectant.
4 After a few days examine your two test tubes. What do you notice?
5 Put your finger over the mouth of each test tube in turn and remove it carefully from the dish. Pour in a little limewater. What do you notice? Why is this?
6 How do your results support the conclusion that live germinating seeds can carry out anaerobic respiration? Account for any unexpected results.

Uses of anaerobic respiration

Making bread

We make use of the fact that the anaerobic respiration of sugar by yeast produces carbon dioxide. It is the bubbles of carbon dioxide that make the bread light and fluffy.

Yeast is mixed with sugar (sucrose). This is first converted to glucose by enzymes in the yeast. The yeast and sugar are mixed with warm water (which has been boiled to remove oxygen).

The yeast respires anaerobically, grows and produces carbon dioxide and ethanol (this is shown by it bubbling). When mixed with the flour to make dough, this continues to rise in a warm place as more carbon dioxide is made. When shaped into loaves and baked, the heating kills the yeast before very much ethanol has been produced, causes the carbon dioxide to expand to make gas bubbles and evaporates any alcohol. The gas spaces can be seen when we cut the finished loaf of bread.

Making alcoholic drinks

We make use of the fact that the anaerobic respiration of sugar by yeast produces alcohol (ethanol).

The starting material and added flavourings make different drinks. For example, beer is made by fermentation of hops, and red and white wine are made by fermentation of different kinds of grapes (with or without their skins). Beers contain about 5–8% alcohol by volume and wines 10–14%.

If the fermenting liquid contains more than about 14% alcohol, then it kills the yeast. To make rum, whisky and gin, the fermented liquid is distilled in a special chamber (see the photo on the right). This raises the proportion of alcohol in the finished drink to over 40% by volume.

Large amounts of alcoholic drinks can have a bad effect on our health (see pages 100 and 102).

Making sour cream, yoghurt and cheese

We make use of the fact that some bacteria can respire anaerobically. They act on milk sugar (lactose) to make lactic acid, which gives flavour to the foods. Different bacteria help to make different varieties of the foods. Note that anaerobic bacteria are also involved in making biogas (see pages 237 and 322).

Making bread

Using your knowledge of respiration, explain why each of the following steps in the making of bread is important:

- sugar is mixed with warm water
- live yeast is added to the mixture
- when the mixture is bubbling it is added to flour to make a dough
- the dough is left in a warm place
- after rising, the dough is made into loaves and placed in a heated oven.

Questions

4 When might anaerobic respiration occur in our muscles? What is its effect, and how does our body deal with it?

5 Explain examples of the industrial importance of anaerobic respiration.

Distillation chamber: the water and alcohol mixture is heated and alcohol vaporizes at about 80 °C

Key ideas

Use these words to fill in the spaces as you write the sentences in your Exercise book.

oxygen   **carbon dioxide**   **ethanol**   **aerobic**   **lactic acid**   **anaerobic**

_____ respiration occurs in the presence of _____ and releases more energy than _____ respiration. _____ respiration in yeast produces _____ and _____ . _____ respiration in muscles produces only _____ and creates an _____ debt. _____ and _____ can be further respired with _____ to release more energy.

5.4 Aerobic and anaerobic respiration (continued)

Aerobic and anaerobic respiration

Glucose is the usual respiratory substrate for respiration. In the cells of all plants and animals, a series of chemical reactions takes place under the control of enzymes. The first stage takes place in the cytoplasm and releases only a small amount of energy.

The remaining stages:

- for anaerobic respiration also occur in the cytoplasm; the end products, lactic acid and ethanol, still contain trapped energy
- for aerobic respiration occur in **mitochondria**, and release a large amount of energy; the end products, carbon dioxide and water, contain none of the energy trapped in photosynthesis.

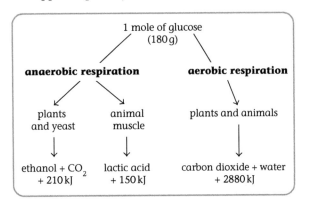

How do we measure energy release?

We can find out how much energy there is in a food by burning a known amount and using the heat energy to heat water (see page 370). To get a more accurate result we use a **calorimeter**.

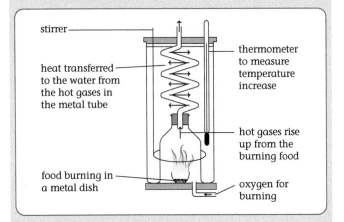

The food is placed in the metal dish and set alight by a small electric current. It is supplied with air. It burns and releases energy, which heats a known amount of water. From the increase in temperature we find the energy in joules (J) or kilojoules (kJ).

The temperature of 1 g (1 cm³) of water is raised by 1 °C by 4.2 joules (J) of energy.

Energy released (J) = temperature increase (°C) × mass of water × 4.2

Then divide the number of joules by the mass of the food to give energy release in J/g.

Questions

1 From where do (a) plants and (b) animals get the glucose they need for respiration?

2 What determines whether an organism will carry out aerobic or anaerobic respiration?

Comparison of aerobic and anaerobic respiration		
Aerobic respiration	**Anaerobic respiration**	
Occurs in the cytoplasm and mitochondria	Occurs in the cytoplasm	
Usually uses glucose as respiratory substrate	Usually uses glucose as respiratory substrate	
Requires oxygen	Does not require oxygen	
Releases all the energy from the glucose	Releases only part of the energy from the glucose	
In all plants and animals when oxygen is supplied Products: carbon dioxide and water	Plants, yeast, bacteria Products: ethanol and carbon dioxide	Animal muscle Product: lactic acid
glucose + oxygen → carbon dioxide + water + energy $C_6H_{12}O_6 + 6O_2 \rightarrow 6CO_2 + 6H_2O$ + energy	glucose → ethanol + carbon dioxide + energy $C_6H_{12}O_6 \rightarrow 2C_2H_5OH + 2CO_2$ + energy	glucose → lactic acid + energy

5.5 Pollution and the respiratory system

Pollution in the air

Pollution is the accumulation in the environment of waste products (**pollutants**), such as dangerous chemicals, or excess energy, such as heat.

We are at constant risk from dangerous chemicals, fine particles, microorganisms and other substances in the air we breathe in. If any part of the respiratory system becomes blocked or diseased, we cannot get sufficient fresh air into our bodies. We may cough, become breathless or develop serious diseases.

Pollutants from burning fossil fuels

The combustion of fossil fuels, such as coal and charcoal (in factories and homes), and gasoline and diesel (by motor vehicles), produces a range of pollutants.

Sulphur dioxide

There is sulphur in fossil fuels. When this burns in air, it forms sulphur dioxide. This can cause additional coughing in people with asthma. It is the main gas involved in making **acid rain** (see page 321).

Carbon dioxide

Fossil fuels contain carbon, which burns in air to make carbon dioxide. It contributes to the **greenhouse effect**, **global warming** (see page 321) and acid rain. It does not have a direct effect on respiration.

Carbon monoxide

This is made when carbon is not fully burnt. Carbon monoxide is colourless and odourless. It can enter the lungs and is taken up by the blood. It combines with haemoglobin in the red cells, more readily than oxygen does, and so prevents the distribution of oxygen to the cells. It can cause death.

Nitrogen oxides

These form at high temperatures as nitrogen and oxygen interact. Nitrogen dioxide can irritate the lungs and lower our resistance to flu infections.

Lead

This was formed by the combustion of gasoline containing lead. It was especially harmful to infants, and could be transferred via the mother to unborn babies. It caused damage to the nervous system. Levels are now lower where unleaded gasoline is used.

Fine particles

These come from the combustion of fossil fuels (from road vehicles), dust (e.g. from the Sahara or volcanoes), sea salt and particles from construction work (e.g. cement, quarrying, rock drilling and metal work). Fine particles can enter deep into the lungs, where they cause inflammation and worsen the symptoms of people with lung and heart diseases. They may also carry chemicals into the lungs that are **carcinogenic** (can cause cancer).

The exhaust from vehicles contains many pollutants

Other pollutants

Asbestos

This has fine particles that are breathed into the lungs. Over time they cause patches of irritation that produce scar tissue. This makes the lungs less flexible and causes breathlessness.

Methane

This is made by the anaerobic respiration of organic matter. This can be by humans, e.g. landfills, fermentation, rice growing, burning biomass. Or it can be natural, e.g. wetlands, termites and oceans. Methane in the air traps 20 times the heat of carbon dioxide. In high concentrations it can replace oxygen and causes breathlessness.

Caustic fumes

These escape into the air, e.g. around bauxite factories. The fumes can irritate the lungs, especially in people who already have lung disease.

Radon

This is an invisible, odourless, tasteless radioactive gas that occurs naturally in soil and rocks. Radon gradually escapes and can cause lung cancer. Areas with high levels should not be used for building houses.

5.5 Pollution and the respiratory system (continued)

You have seen (page 81) how pollutants in the air can cause problems to the respiratory system. But people can also cause damage to themselves by smoking cigarettes and breathing in smoke.

Smoking

Cigarette smoke contains dangerous substances.

- **Tar**: this forms a sticky syrup-like substance in the lungs. It kills cells and can cause bronchitis and lung cancer.
- **Nicotine**: this is a drug that raises the heartbeat and increases the risk of blood clots. It can become addictive. This is why smoking is so difficult to give up.
- **Carbon monoxide**: this can combine with haemoglobin in the red cells, so they cannot transport oxygen.

'Breathed-out' smoke also causes damage to other people: this is called **passive smoking**.

Bronchitis

This is inflammation of the bronchioles in the lungs. It is usually caused by cold and flu viruses but is made worse by cigarette smoke and pollution. There is a cough, with a heavy fluid called **phlegm**, breathlessness and wheezing.

Emphysema

The alveoli become stretched so that gaseous exchange is less efficient. It often occurs after long-standing bronchitis in smokers, and those living in polluted areas.

Lung cancer

Cells in the lungs may become damaged, and some of them can form tumours that lead to cancer in the lungs. This causes grave ill health and may be fatal. Only about 1 in 1000 cases of lung cancer occur in non-smokers.

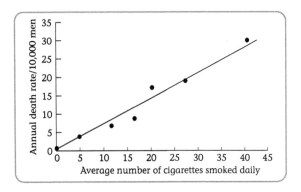

Questions

1. What is the overall relationship between the average number of cigarettes smoked, and risk of lung cancer?
2. On average, how many men who smoke 40 cigarettes a day die from lung cancer in a year?

Lung cancer, pipes and cigarettes

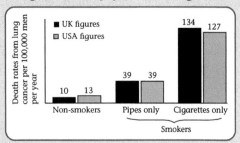

Look at the bar chart. Describe how the annual death rate differs between non-smokers, pipe smokers and cigarette smokers. Also, smoking three to five marijuana joints a week has the same effect as smoking 16 cigarettes a day.

Giving up smoking

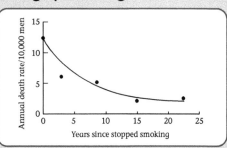

Look at the graph. What is the effect of giving up smoking? Research ways in which people may be helped to quit smoking (e.g. using nicotine patches and dummy cigarettes). Make a poster in support of the message of never starting to smoke.

Did you know?

- Forty per cent of people who smoke more than 20 cigarettes a day die before retirement, compared with fifteen per cent of non-smokers.
- Mothers-to-be who smoke can cause damage to their unborn baby: miscarriage, or premature birth and low birth weight.

Smoking and heart attacks

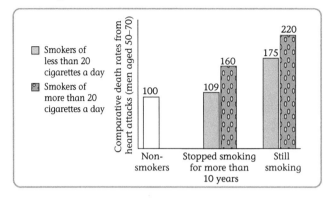

Smoking and pollution

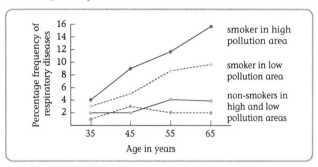

Allergies

Allergies are excessive reactions to substances breathed in or eaten. The substance causing the reaction is called an **allergen**. Examples are pollen, dust, certain drugs and foods.

In an allergic reaction, chemicals called **histamines** are released. It is these that cause the symptoms of the attack.

- **Asthma**: caused by inhaling pollen, dust and fur from pets. The bronchi and bronchioles become partly blocked and the person suffers from breathlessness.
- **Hay fever**: caused by pollen. The person sneezes and has a runny nose.
- **Food allergies**: caused by certain foods, which lead to reactions such as diarrhoea. Peanut allergy can cause difficulty in breathing.
- **Drug allergies**: some people get an allergic reaction to penicillin.

Questions

3 How do the numbers of people dying from heart attacks compare for non-smokers and for smokers of more than 20 cigarettes a day?

4 What is the effect of stopping smoking?

5 How does smoking affect the frequency of respiratory diseases? (Compare smokers with non-smokers.)

6 How does pollution affect the frequency of respiratory diseases? (Compare high- and low-pollution areas.)

7 Which people are (a) at highest risk and (b) lowest risk?

How to treat allergies

- **Inhalers**: used by people having an asthma attack. Breathing is relaxed.
- **Avoid allergens**: do not eat foods that produce an allergic response. Also limit the time in dusty or outside conditions.
- **Antihistamines**: these are pills given to neutralize the effects of the histamines produced in an allergic reaction.
- **'Desensitizing'**: small amounts of an allergen are given, and then increased until the person gets used to it.

Key ideas

Use these words to fill in the spaces as you write the sentences in your Exercise book.

lung cancer   **pollution**   **bronchitis**   **heart attacks**   **asthma**   **passive**

Some effects of long-term smoking are _____ , _____ and _____ . _____ can increase respiratory diseases. Smokers also increase their risks of _____ . Non-smokers, including babies and children, can also be affected by _____ smoking.

6 Transport systems

6.1 Why are transport systems needed?

Diffusion and osmosis (see pages 46–7) are important over short distances. What features make them efficient?

The importance of surface area and volume

Substances diffuse more quickly into the centre of a small cube than a larger one. The smaller cube has a larger **surface area** in relation to its bulk or **volume** – it has a larger surface area to volume ratio (SA:V ratio). The distance to the centre of the smaller cube is also shorter than in the larger cube, and so diffusion occurs more quickly.

Let us compare the SA:V ratio of two shapes that have the same volume, but different amounts of surface.

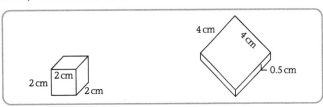

$V = 2 \times 2 \times 2 = 8\,cm^3$
$SA = (2 \times 2) \times 6 = 24\,cm^2$
SA:V ratio = 24:8 = 3:1

$V = 4 \times 4 \times 0.5 = 8\,cm^3$
$SA = (4 \times 4) \times 2 + (4 \times 0.5) \times 4$
$32 + 8 = 40\,cm^2$
SA:V ratio = 40:8 = 5:1

These ideas help us to explain certain observations

- Leaves are flat and not round. A round leaf would have a small surface area to its volume. But a flat leaf has a much bigger surface area through which diffusion occurs.
- The outer surface of a root has long projections from the root hairs. These increase the surface area in relation to the volume.
- The inner surface of the large intestine is folded and bears finger-like projections, the villi, which increase the surface area through which absorption can occur.
- The inner surface of the lungs is folded into numerous air sacs, which increase the surface area through which oxygen can diffuse in, and carbon dioxide diffuse out.

Objectives

- Explain the importance of a surface area to volume (SA:V) ratio.
- Discuss why transport systems are needed in animals and plants.

Surface area The total area of an object in square centimetres (cm^2).

Volume The amount of space an object takes up in cubic centimetres (cm^3).

Activity

Diffusion with agar blocks

1 Your teacher will cut some blocks of agar of different sizes.
2 These are placed in a coloured solution.

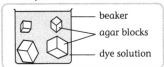

3 After 2 minutes, one cube of each size is removed by forceps, and cut.

4 Why do you think the dye diffused all the way through the smaller cube, but only into the outer part of the larger one?
5 Predict what will happen in 8 minutes, then find out if you were right.

Key ideas

Use these words to fill in the spaces as you write the sentences in your Exercise book.

longer   **transport**   **diffusion**   **large**   **one**   **osmosis**   **short**   **ratio**

Substances enter and leave the cells by _____ and _____ . These processes are only efficient if there is a _____ surface area to volume _____ , and only over very _____ distances. Walls through which _____ occurs are usually only _____ cell thick. In large animals and plants a _____ system is needed to move substances over _____ distances.

The importance of diffusion and osmosis

Organisms that have only one cell can take in and get rid of all they need using diffusion.

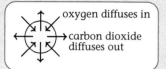 (a) Small organism with high surface area to volume ratio; can exchange gases by diffusion across its surface

Larger organisms need to increase the surface area through which diffusion occurs.

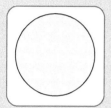

(b) Large organism has low surface to volume ratio

(c) The surface to volume ratio is increased

The surface area to volume ratio is large for:
- the alveoli in the lungs
- the villi in the small intestine
- the long tubules in the kidney
- the chewing of food and emulsifying of fats, which increase the surface for enzymes to work.

Diffusion occurs over short distances, which is why many walls are one-cell thick:
- the walls of the villi in the small intestine
- the walls of the alveoli in the lungs
- the walls of the capillaries.

Diffusion and osmosis are also important in flowering plants, so there are places where the surface area to volume ratio is large.
- Leaves are thin and have many loosely packed cells that give a large surface inside the leaf for diffusion of gases in and out.
- The root hairs give a large surface in contact with the soil. This helps with intake of water by osmosis, and diffusion in of mineral salts.

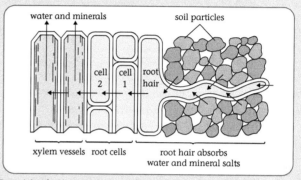

Root hairs have a partially permeable cell membrane. There is a higher concentration of water in the soil than in the root hair. Water therefore enters the root hair by osmosis along its concentration gradient. In the same way water can pass, by osmosis, from the root hair into the next cell, and so on.

Why do large animals need transport systems?

One-celled organisms are very small, have a high surface area to volume ratio and are not very active. They do not need a transport system to transfer substances.

But animals are large and would not be able to satisfy their needs by diffusion alone. They are also more active and therefore need more oxygen to get to their cells, and to get rid of carbon dioxide and other wastes. Substances need to be moved long distances around the body. So there has to be a transport system, the circulatory system, with a pump, the heart, to push the blood around.

Why is a plant transport system less complex?

Plants are often smaller than animals, except for large trees. And they are much less active. They remain rooted in the ground and do not have to go and search for food, or escape from enemies. They have a simple transport system based on xylem vessels that carry water and minerals up to the leaves, and phloem vessels that carry food from the leaves to all the parts of the plant body.

Questions

1. What processes are important for substances entering and leaving cells?
2. (a) What is a surface area to volume ratio? (b) Why is it important?
3. What is the surface area to volume ratio of a cube with sides of 3 cm? Show all your working.
4. Give two examples where diffusion occurs in (a) plants and (b) animals. What are the characteristics of these places?
5. How is a plant well adapted for taking in water? How does it happen?
6. Give two reasons why a transport system is needed in animals.
7. Why is the transport system in plants less complex than in animals?

6.2 How are things moved around in plants?

Water and mineral salts enter through the roots

Root hairs have a large surface area and water enters by **osmosis**. So these cells then contain more water than the ones next to them, and water moves along, by osmosis, into the next cells (page 85).

Mineral salts **diffuse** into the root hairs. If there is no concentration gradient to make this possible, then energy has to be used (in **active transport**) to take them in against their concentration gradient.

Water and mineral salts rise up in the xylem

- This is mainly due to **transpiration**: as water is lost from the leaves, more water is pulled up to take its place.
- Also, as more water enters from below, this pushes the other water up, by **root pressure**.
- Water molecules are also attracted to each other, and to the sides of the vessels, and can rise up by **capillarity**.

Practical 31

How fast do substances rise? (MM, AI)

1 Use a plant such as *Balsam* (Busy Lizzie). Wash the roots and put the plant in red dye solution. Stand it next to an upright ruler marked in centimetres.

2 Read off the height of the dye every 20 minutes.

3 Here are some readings obtained by a class.

Time (minutes)	0	20	40	60	80	100
Height (cm)	0	0.8	1.7	2.7	3.5	4.4

Prepare a line graph of these results, or use your own.

4 Calculate the rate of transport for your results. See the panel on the right.

What are the substances transported in?

Below are diagrams showing the transport vessels in a stem.

Objectives

- Describe xylem and phloem, and the structure of the stem.
- Discuss the processes important in the transport of materials.

What does it mean?

Veins Made of xylem, phloem and cambium.

Xylem Dead vessels on the inner side of a vein. They are thickened with woody tissue. They transport water and mineral salts **up** the stem to the leaves.

Phloem Living vessels on the outer side of the vein. They are called **sieve tubes** as they have areas of holes, the sieves. When food has been made in the leaves, the sieve tubes transport it **up** and **down** the stem to places where it is needed. Excess food is taken to storage organs.

Cambium Cells that can divide; important in the thickening of stems.

Rate = Distance/Time

Rate of transport = $\dfrac{\text{Distance travelled}}{\text{Time taken}}$

Rate = 4.4 cm/100 minutes
= 0.044 cm/min, or 0.04 cm/min

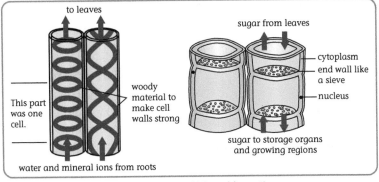

Transverse section of a dicotyledonous stem

Dead xylem tissue

Living phloem tissue

Xylem and phloem

Xylem

This is made of dead cells joined end to end, and with no connecting walls. The tubes are thickened with patterns or rings of lignin. Xylem vessels take water and mineral salts all the way up the plant from the roots to the stem and leaves. The forces that cause this movement are transpiration pull, root pressure and capillarity.

Phloem

This is made mainly of sieve tubes, which are long cells connected to each other by holes (sieves) in the end walls. There are also smaller companion cells. The phloem cells are living cells. Phloem transports food from the leaves both up and down to the cells of the plant including the storage organs and fruits. This is mostly done by diffusion (from areas where there is a lot of food to areas where there is little food). However, as the phloem has living cytoplasm, it is also possible for energy to be used (in active transport) to move food against its concentration gradient.

How is transpiration important?

Water is brought to the leaf in the xylem vessels. Some is used in photosynthesis, to make food for the plant. The rest of the water is lost in transpiration.

The water changes to vapour, and this evaporation takes heat from the plant, and so cools it. The spaces inside the leaves usually have more water vapour than is in the outside air, so it **diffuses** out along its concentration gradient. This is **transpiration**. As water is lost through the stomata more is pulled up from below. This is **transpiration pull** and is the main force pulling up water and minerals.

We can measure the rate of transpiration by:

- finding the decrease in mass of a potted plant, e.g. left in still air and in windy conditions
- passing air over a plant and through calcium chloride, which absorbs the water (the mass of the calcium chloride is measured before and after the experiment)
- observing the movement of an air bubble as water is taken into a leafy shoot (see page 371) to replace that which is being lost by transpiration.

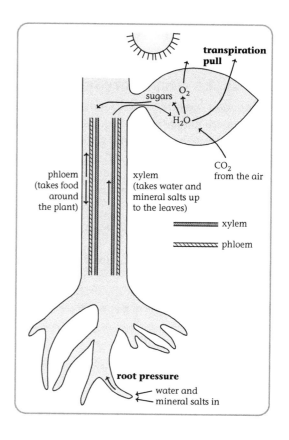

Questions

1 List all the liquids, gases and solutions that enter, leave or travel in a plant. Briefly describe how each one is transported (including the processes involved, such as osmosis and diffusion).

2 How are the xylem and phloem (a) similar and (b) different?

3 How are (a) root pressure and (b) transpiration pull important?

Key ideas

Use these words to fill in the spaces as you write the sentences in your Exercise book.

down   transpiration   diffusion   xylem   up   osmosis   phloem   dead

Water enters the roots by _____ and mineral salts by _____ . Water and salts are pulled

_____ in the _____ vessels as water is lost from the leaves during _____ . When food has

been made in the leaves, it travels _____ and _____ in the _____ . The _____ vessels are

living and the _____ vessels are _____ .

6.3 How are things moved around in humans?

What is the circulatory system?

Large animals are active and cannot rely on diffusion to move substances around in their bodies. They need a transport system. This is the blood, or **circulatory**, system, which takes oxygen and food to the cells and removes carbon dioxide, water and other wastes. It also distributes heat, hormones and antibodies.

The circulatory system consists of:

- the blood (a liquid plasma that contains blood cells)
- the blood vessels (arteries, veins and capillaries that carry the blood around the body)
- the heart (the organ that pumps the blood through the vessels).

Objective

- Describe the structure and function of parts of the blood.

Did you know?

- Red cells are replaced every 120 days.
- An adult contains about $5\,dm^3$ of blood; a child has about half of this.

Structure and functions of parts of the blood		
Part of the blood	**What it is**	**What it does**
Plasma	The liquid part of the blood. It is water that contains salts, proteins and antibodies.	It transports carbon dioxide, food substances and wastes such as urea. It also distributes heat, hormones and antibodies. It contains substances used in blood clotting.
Red blood cells	Red discs that have a hollow on each side. They do not have a nucleus. They contain haemoglobin. They are made in the bone marrow.	They carry oxygen from the lungs to all parts of the body. They also carry some carbon dioxide from the body cells to the lungs.
White blood cells	Two kinds, phagocytes and lymphocytes. They are colourless and each has a nucleus.	They protect the body from infection by germs (bacteria and viruses). See also page 94.
	Phagocytes: the nucleus is made of several lobes joined together. The cytoplasm has granules in it. They are made in the bone marrow	Phagocytes (cell eaters) attack and engulf any germs that enter the body. They are the chief defence against disease-causing microorganisms.
	Lymphocytes: the nucleus is roughly circular. The cytoplasm is clear. They are made in the lymph glands.	Lymphocytes protect the body by producing antibodies, which either kill the microorganisms, or make them clump together so that they can be removed in the lymph glands.
Platelets	Very small pieces of cells from the linings of the blood vessels.	They gather where a blood vessel has been cut, and they plug up the hole as the first part of the blood-clotting process.

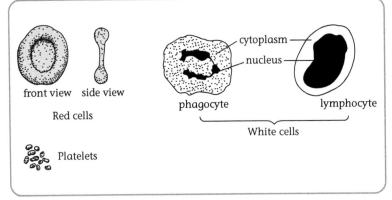

Cells in the blood

front view   side view

Red cells

Platelets

cytoplasm
nucleus
phagocyte
lymphocyte
White cells

How does blood clot?

If you cut yourself, a blood vessel may be damaged and blood comes out. You should clean the cut in running water. Then hold the edges together to help them heal and to keep out germs. The platelets help to plug the hole, and chemicals in the blood make a **clot** of fibres in which platelets and red blood cells are mixed. This stops the blood flow and protects the tissues underneath, which begin to heal.

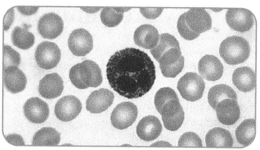

Human blood cells (magnified)

Circulation of oxygen and carbon dioxide

Oxygen

The red cells are hollowed out on each side to increase their surface area, through which oxygen can diffuse in and out. They also do not have nuclei, giving more space for the red pigment, **haemoglobin**.

- In the lungs, oxygen is in high concentration and diffuses into the red cells, to make **oxyhaemoglobin**. The blood becomes **oxygenated**.
- The red cells circulate in the blood until they come near to body cells, which have a low concentration of oxygen. Then the oxygen diffuses out of the red cells and into the body cells. The blood becomes **deoxygenated**.

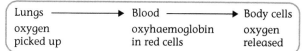

Lungs	Blood	Body cells
oxygen picked up	oxyhaemoglobin in red cells	oxygen released

Carbon dioxide

This can dissolve in the plasma, and some is carried by the red blood cells.

- In the cells, carbon dioxide is in high concentration and diffuses along a concentration gradient into the blood plasma. The blood becomes deoxygenated.
- The carbon dioxide is taken to the lungs, where it diffuses into the air sacs, along a concentration gradient, and is breathed out.

The whole process keeps repeating itself.

What does it mean?

Artery Blood vessel taking blood *away* from the heart. Usually with oxygenated blood (except for the pulmonary artery).

Vein Blood vessel taking blood *towards* the heart. Usually with deoxygenated blood (except for the pulmonary vein).

Oxygenated Blood containing a lot of oxygen picked up in the lungs, and only a little carbon dioxide.

Deoxygenated Blood containing a lot of carbon dioxide picked up in the cells, and only a little oxygen.

Key ideas

6.3 How are things moved around in humans? (continued)

How does our blood circulate?

To push the blood around the body, there is a muscular pump, the **heart**. Its muscles are of a special kind which does not get tired. The heart is divided into two separate halves, with a dividing wall, to keep the blood separate:

- the right side contains deoxygenated blood
- the left side contains oxygenated blood.

Circulation in mammals is called a **double circulation**, as the blood travels twice through the heart on each circuit, e.g. from the kidneys and back to the kidneys. There are two pathways when the blood leaves the heart:

- to the lungs (deoxygenated blood goes to the lungs)
- to the body (oxygenated blood to all body organs).

Structure of the heart

- The right atrium receives deoxygenated blood from the body via the **venae cavae** (veins).
- The deoxygenated blood passes to the right ventricle and is pumped to the lungs in the **pulmonary artery**.
- The blood loses carbon dioxide, gains oxygen and returns to the left atrium in the **pulmonary vein** as oxygenated blood.
- The oxygenated blood passes to the left ventricle from where it is pumped to the body in the **aorta** (an artery).

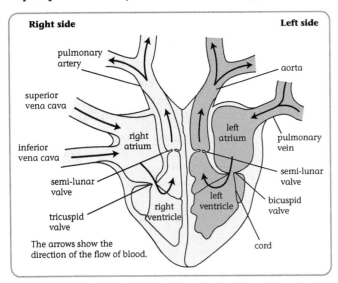

The diagram above shows a longitudinal section of the heart. Notice that:

- the walls of the atria are thinner than those of the ventricles, as they only receive blood and pass it on
- the left ventricle wall is thicker and more muscular (it has to pump blood to the whole body) than that of the right ventricle (it just pumps blood to the lungs)
- there are flaps (valves) and cords between the atria and ventricles to stop blood flowing back the wrong way.

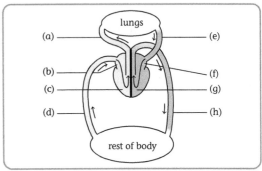

Double circulation: name the parts (a) – (h)

What are our blood vessels like?

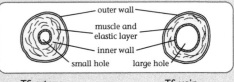

Arteries
- take blood from the heart
- have a thick muscle and elastic layer, as blood is pushed through at high pressure
- have no valves, as blood is pumped strongly.

Veins
- take blood to the heart
- have a thinner muscle and elastic layer, as blood returns to heart at lower pressure
- have valves to stop blood flowing backwards as it returns to the heart.

Capillaries
- link the arteries and veins
- are only one cell thick, as nutrients and wastes have to diffuse to and from cells.

TS capillary

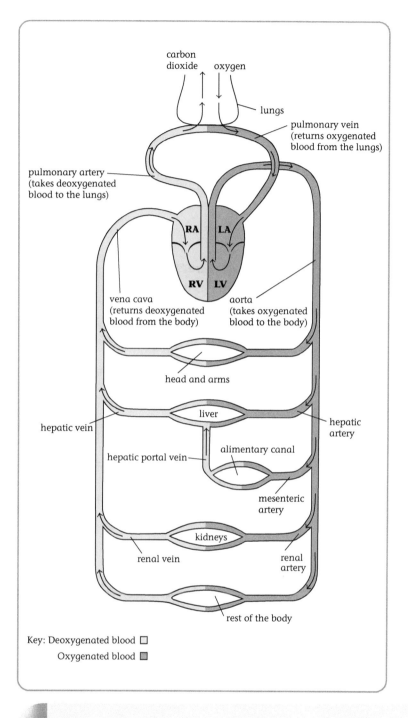

carbon dioxide   oxygen

lungs

pulmonary vein (returns oxygenated blood from the lungs)

pulmonary artery (takes deoxygenated blood to the lungs)

RA   LA

RV   LV

vena cava (returns deoxygenated blood from the body)

aorta (takes oxygenated blood to the body)

head and arms

liver

hepatic vein

hepatic artery

hepatic portal vein

alimentary canal

mesenteric artery

kidneys

renal vein

renal artery

rest of the body

Key: Deoxygenated blood ☐
      Oxygenated blood ■

Did you know?

1 A human contains 100,000 km of blood vessels.
2 Your heart beats all the time, about once every second, all your life.

Practical 33

Measuring your pulse (MM, ORR)

As the heart beats it pumps blood into the arteries. This makes the pulse.
1 Feel for the pulse in your wrist (see the photo below).
2 Count the number of pulse beats in a minute (see also page 98).

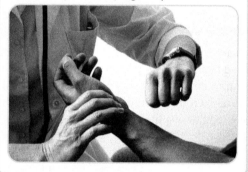

Questions

In the diagram on the left:
1 What is the RA? What kind of blood enters it, and where did it come from?
2 What is the RV? Which blood vessel leaves from it, and where does it go?
3 What is the LA? What kind of blood enters it, and where did it come from?
4 What is the LV? Which blood vessel leaves from it, and where does it go?

Key ideas

Use these words to fill in the spaces as you write the sentences in your Exercise book.

left   oxygenated   veins   deoxygenated   pulmonary   right   arteries

_____ carry blood away from the heart. _____ carry blood to the heart. The _____ atrium of the heart receives _____ blood from the body. This is pumped from the _____ ventricle to the lungs in the _____ artery. _____ blood returns from the lungs to the _____ atrium. It is pumped from the _____ ventricle through the aorta to the body.

6.4 How are blood groups important?

What are blood groups?

There are chemicals, called **antigens**, on the red cells. Different people have different antigens. If they have A antigens, the person has group A blood. This person will also have anti-B antibodies in their plasma. (If they had anti-A antibodies these would react with the A antigens and make the blood clump together, or **agglutinate**.) There are four groupings of antigens and antibodies, called the A, B, AB and O blood groups (as shown below).

Blood groups	A	B	AB	O
Antigens on red cells	A	B	A and B	none
Antibodies in plasma	anti-B	anti-A	none	anti-A and anti-B

Why are blood groups important?

A person who needs a blood transfusion (**recipient**) must be given blood from a **donor** of the same group, or a matching group, e.g. group A can give to groups A and AB. Only some combinations are safe (shown by a ✓ in the table below). Unsafe combinations cause the blood to agglutinate (shown by an ✗ in the table below).

		Donor			
		A	B	AB	O
	A	✓	✗	✗	✓
Recipient	B	✗	✓	✗	✓
	AB	✓	✓	✓	✓
	O	✗	✗	✗	✓

- Everyone can give blood to the same blood group as their own.
- Group A can give to groups A and AB, and group B can give to groups B and AB.
- Group AB can give only to group AB. But people with blood group AB are called **universal recipients**, as they can receive blood from all other groups.
- People with blood group O are called **universal donors**, as they can give blood to all other groups.

Blood donors

Donors give their blood, which is kept in a **blood bank**. The donors will replace the plasma in their blood in a few hours and the red cells in a few days.

- Anyone handling blood should take extreme care not to become infected with any microorganisms.
- The donated blood is treated to kill viruses, such as HIV.
- The blood is stored carefully until it is needed for a blood transfusion.
- The blood must be carefully matched to the recipient. If the wrong blood were given, the clumping of blood cells could block blood vessels, cutting off oxygen to the cells.

Finding a person's blood group

- **Serum** is prepared at the hospital or Blood Transfusion Service. This is plasma with the clotting agents removed. There are two kinds: anti-A and anti-B serums.
- Blood is taken from the person and mixed on a tile with each serum.
  - Group A clots only with anti-A serum.
  - Group B clots only with anti-B serum.
  - Group AB clots with both anti-A and anti-B.
  - Group O clots with neither serum.
- If you donate blood, you will be told your blood group.
  - Group O is most common: 50%.
  - Group A is found in 24% of people.
  - Group B is found in 22% of people.
  - Group AB is the least common: 4%.

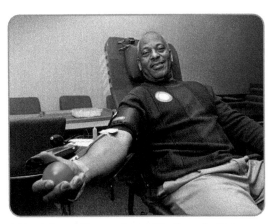

A blood donor. The needle used for the collection of blood is used only once, to ensure no transfer of infections

Why is blood needed?

- To replace blood lost, e.g. because of a car accident, stab wound or severe burn.
- To provide blood during operations, e.g. for heart surgery or for bleeding in pregnancy or at birth.
- To treat people with haemophilia or anaemia. For all these uses the blood should be of a compatible blood group and have been treated to kill any microorganisms.
- As a source of anti-D (see below).

The Rhesus factor

The **Rhesus factor** is an antigen that is found on most people's red blood cells. These people are said to have Rhesus positive (Rh+) blood (93% of the population). People without the Rhesus factor have Rhesus negative (Rh–) blood (7% of the population).

A problem can arise with a Rh– mother and a Rh+ father: the foetus that is being carried may be Rh+ (having inherited the Rhesus gene from the father). This can cause problems if any of the baby's blood gets into the mother. The mother is Rh– and is not used to Rh+ blood, and so she makes **antibodies** to try to kill off this strange substance.

There is unlikely to be a problem with the first pregnancy, but the antibodies will stay in the mother's bloodstream. If she becomes pregnant again with a Rh+ baby, then these antibodies may attack the baby's blood and destroy it. With each pregnancy, there will be more and more antibodies, and these may cause a baby's death. This will be worse in additional pregnancies. If a baby survives, it needs to be given a large blood transfusion at birth to completely change its blood.

These problems can be avoided in the following ways.

- At the beginning of pregnancy the mother should have a blood test to see of she is Rh–. This can be done as part of pre-natal care (see page 154).
- If her partner is Rh+, then the mother should be tested to see if she has made antibodies.
- If so, then after the baby is born, the mother is given a serum containing anti-D. This destroys any Rh+ blood cells in the mother, so she will not make any antibodies during future pregnancies.

Did you know?

- Blood cannot be manufactured, and neither is it sold in most countries.
- The blood given by one person (a unit) can help save the lives of six other people.
- A donor could give blood again after about 2 months.

Questions

1 Which blood group do you think the Blood Bank needs most? Explain why.
2 Why is the Rhesus factor important?
3 Would a Rh+ mother have problems with her babies? Explain why.

Key ideas

Use these letters and words to fill in the spaces as you write the sentences in your Exercise book.

| A | antigens | B | Rh+ | antibodies | O | Rh– |

The chemicals on the red cells are _____ . A person with anti-A _____ and B antigens has the _____ blood group. Such a person should not receive blood from a group _____ person, but can receive group _____ blood. If a woman with _____ blood is carrying a foetus with _____ blood, there may sometimes be problems.

6.5 Control of diseases

What is disease?

'Disease' is anything that upsets the normal functioning of the body: it causes 'dis-ease'. Examples of the various kinds of disease are shown on the right. This topic looks at infections by microorganisms (bacteria and viruses).

How does the blood help to fight infection?

Blood clotting

If the skin and a small blood vessel are cut, blood will come out. On contact with the air, chemical changes take place to thicken and **clot** the blood (see page 88). Platelets and chemicals in the blood form a plug that hardens to make a scab. This keeps out microorganisms until the blood vessel and skin can re-grow underneath.

Role of phagocytes

These are white cells (see page 88) made in the bone marrow. They have a lobed nucleus and granules in the cytoplasm. They can change their shape (like an amoeba) and engulf (surround and digest) any bacteria or viruses that get into the blood.

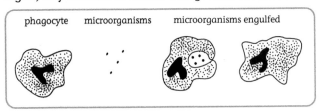

A phagocyte engulfing microorganisms

Role of lymphocytes

These are white cells (see page 88) made in the lymph glands. They have a round nucleus and clear cytoplasm. They cannot change their shape. They produce chemicals to kill the bacteria and viruses.

- Some bacteria and all viruses carry proteins called **antigens**. The proteins are special to a particular species. The lymphocytes produce matching **antibodies**, which can neutralize the antigen and kill the microorganism.
- Some bacteria release chemicals called **toxins**, which cause the disease. The lymphocytes respond by producing matching **anti-toxins**, which neutralize the effect of the toxins. So the person does not become ill.

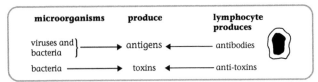

Role of lymphocytes

Note: there are also special drugs called **antibiotics**, e.g. penicillin, given as medicines. These can kill bacteria, e.g. gonorrhoea, but not viruses, e.g. HIV. They work only if given in the correct dosage and for a particular length of time.

Objectives

- Identify different kinds of disease.
- Discuss the role of antigens and antibodies in the natural and artificial control of disease.

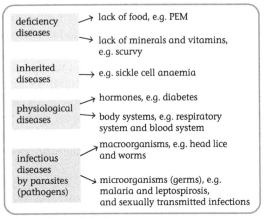

Different kinds of disease

What does it mean?

Antigens Specific chemicals carried on red cells, bacteria and viruses.

Antibodies Chemicals in the plasma or produced by lymphocytes that can neutralize specific antigens.

Toxins Specific chemicals, produced by some bacteria, which cause disease.

Anti-toxins Chemicals produced by lymphocytes to neutralize specific toxins.

Questions

1 List ways in which the blood helps to protect us against infectious diseases.
2 Distinguish between (a) antigens and toxins, (b) antibodies and antibiotics, and (c) natural and artificial immunity.

HIV/AIDS and the immune system

HIV stands for human immunodeficiency virus. This is because the virus actually gets into the nuclei of some kinds of lymphocyte, where they multiply and then infect other white cells. This damages the immune system. The person is no longer protected against the virus, and develops AIDS (page 157). The lymphocytes that are still healthy cannot produce sufficient antibodies and anti-toxins to fight against a range of viruses and bacteria. As the lymphocytes are damaged, the person may die from other infections, such as tuberculosis.

Immunity

Immunity is protection against a specific disease. This can either be **natural** immunity (developed after an infection) or **artificial** immunity (as a result of the person receiving vaccinations).

Natural immunity

Natural immunity describes the situation where the body makes its own antibodies in response to microorganisms. When we are infected by microorganisms it may take the lymphocytes some time to respond and make the specific matching antibodies. We may become ill, but we recover when the lymphocytes have killed off the microorganisms. After this, a few lymphocytes remain with the 'memory' of the infecting microorganisms. If we are infected again with the same kind, then large numbers of antibodies are made much more quickly. We have developed our own natural immunity to that disease.

The degree of immunity we develop depends on the disease. For example, for measles and mumps, once we have had them we develop a life-long immunity. They will not make us ill again. When we get flu we produce antibodies against that particular kind of flu and become immune. But there new kinds of flu produced each year, or outbreaks of special strains, such as swine flu. We may catch a strain of flu against which we are not protected, and so become ill again.

Artificial immunity

Artificial immunity occurs after action is taken by someone else, such as a doctor or nurse.

- In an emergency, a doctor can inject us with ready-made antibodies against specific diseases, such as cholera and a kind of hepatitis. This protection lasts only about 6 months.
- For longer-term protection we can be given **vaccinations**. These contain dead or weakened viruses or bacteria, or the toxins from bacteria, which are put into the blood. They do not cause us harm, and we may hardly notice them. But they make the body produce the matching antibodies or anti-toxins. These remain in the blood, in case we are infected with those microorganisms. 'Top-ups', or boosters, are given at later dates. We become immune to those diseases. The table of vaccinations recommended in a Caribbean country, such as Jamaica, is given below.

Time	Vaccine	Method
3rd–7th month of pregnancy	Tetanus	Injection of tetanus toxin
Birth to 3 months	BCG (tuberculosis)	Injection of weakened bacteria
3 months 5 months 7 months	Three doses of polio vaccine and DPT*	Polio: by mouth (weakened virus) DPT: injection of toxins (T) and weakened bacteria (D and P)
12 months	Measles	Injection of weakened virus
18 months 3 to 6 years	Two polio boosters	As before
9 to 12 years (girls only)	German measles	Injection of weakened virus

* DPT = diphtheria, pertussis (whooping cough) and tetanus

Key ideas

Use these words to fill in the spaces as you write the sentences in your Exercise book.

antibiotics   **lymphocytes**   **antigens**   **artificial**   **antibodies**   **natural**

Disease microorganisms produce toxins and _____ . The _____ in the blood produce

anti-toxins and _____ to neutralize them. Drugs called _____ also kill bacteria. We can

become immune to particular diseases, either by getting the disease and making our own

anti-toxins or _____ (_____ immunity), or by having a vaccination (_____ immunity).

6.6 Problems with our circulatory system

Problems with our veins

Veins carry blood from the body back to the heart. They contain **valves** so that blood travels in one direction only (see (a) in the diagram on the right). However, in people who stand a lot, the veins may become swollen and wider (varicose veins), so the valves do not close properly. Then blood can flow both ways (see (b) in the diagram)

We can overcome the problem by exercise, because the muscles in the legs help to push the blood up in the veins back to the heart. The person should avoid standing still, and should raise the feet when sitting down. If the veins become too swollen, it may be necessary to have an operation to re-route the blood.

Problems with our arteries

Arteries carry blood away from the heart. Most of them carry oxygen and food to the body. Arteries can become:

- narrowed; this happens when fatty deposits, called **plaque**, are laid down in the arteries
- hardened; substances are laid down in the walls so that they are less elastic.

In both these cases it is harder for blood to be pumped through the arteries, and this can cause **high blood pressure** (**hypertension**). It also means that organs may not get sufficient oxygen and food for their needs, and so die. And because the blood vessels are narrower, it is more likely that blood clots will form and block them.

The major problems are with the blood supply to the brain and heart. If there is a blot clot in the brain, the person may have a **stroke**, followed by paralysis and even death. The heart is supplied with blood through the **coronary** arteries. If this supply is reduced, it can cause **angina** or a **heart attack**.

Heart problems

Angina

This is pain in the heart felt across the middle of the chest. It may occur when there is additional strain on the heart, as with exercise or stress. It is not usually severe and goes away when the person rests. But it is a warning sign. It is caused by slight narrowing of the coronary arteries, so insufficient blood gets to the heart muscles during exercise or stress. When angina is felt, special tablets can be taken. These widen the blood vessels to the heart.

A heart attack

This is a crushing pain like a heavy weight across the chest. It can come on at any time. It is usually very severe and does not stop when resting. It can cause death. It is caused by the coronary arteries becoming so narrow that blood cannot reach the heart muscles. This is often because there is a blood clot in the vessels (a **thrombosis**). If the muscles cells do not get food and oxygen they will not be able to contract and so the heart cannot work properly.

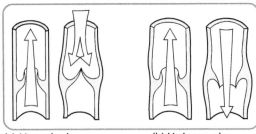

(a) Normal veins   (b) Varicose veins

High blood pressure

Blood pressure is a measure of how hard the heart pumps blood. A reading of 120/80 is 'normal' for a healthy adult. The '120' is the pressure when the ventricles contract to push out blood, and the '80' is when the heart muscles relax.

A person with numbers higher than these has 'high blood pressure' or hypertension. In this case the heart has to pump much more strongly to force blood through the arteries. This is because they have been partly blocked (with **plaque**) or hardened. Hypertension puts a strain on the heart and could make small blood vessels break.

Questions

1 What is meant by (a) hypertension, (b) stroke and (c) heart attack?
2 Describe four possible causes of hypertension, and the action to be taken.
3 Describe two possible results of hypertension.
4 What information can you find on hypertension and heart attacks from clinics, hospitals, doctors and the Internet?

Heart surgery

After a severe heart attack, a person may need to have a **coronary bypass**. In this operation a new piece of blood vessel, taken from the person's leg, is used to renew the blood supply to the heart muscles (see the artwork on the right). The person is advised on lifestyle changes (see below). The patients may also be given drugs that thin the blood and reduce the likelihood of blood clots forming in the vessels.

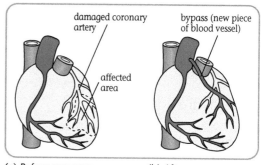

(a) Before coronary bypass operation   (b) After coronary bypass operation

Can we reduce hypertension and heart attacks?

There are certain things we can do to reduce the problems, or to help ourselves if a problem has already developed.

Improve the diet

- **Reduce obesity**: obese people have a higher blood pressure and heart rate, so a greater risk of heart attack. They also have a higher risk of developing diabetes.
- **Reduce some fats**: reduce hydrogenated and trans fats. Also reduce saturated animal fats, as they contain more cholesterol. Eat unsaturated plant and fish oils instead.
- **Reduce cholesterol**: this is found in eggs and animal fats, which should be eaten in moderation. High cholesterol levels have been linked to plaque formation and developing hypertension. The diet should be improved, and drugs such as statins can be used.
- **Reduce salt**: reducing the amount of salty foods can help to reduce hypertension.

Reduce stress

Aggressive behaviour increases the hormone adrenaline, and can cause extra plaque formation in the arteries.

Increase exercise

This helps with overall fitness, reduces weight, tones the muscles, exercises the heart and helps to reduce stress.

Be aware of family tendencies

If there is heart disease in the family, then be especially careful to try to avoid the risk factors discussed.

Some factors that are linked with hypertension and heart attacks

Key ideas

Use these words to fill in the spaces as you write the sentences in your Exercise book.

saturated	stress	stroke	hypertension	heart	salt	varicose

A person with _____ has narrowed or hardened arteries. This may be caused by a diet high in _____ fats and _____ . The person may also suffer from _____ , or have _____ disease in the family. As a result there is a higher risk of a _____ attack or a _____ . People who stand a lot may develop _____ veins, where the valves do not work properly.

6.7 Why do we need exercise?

We may not be able to develop our muscles like this athlete, but we can exercise to be healthy

What are the effects of exercise?

Exercise is any physical movement that is done vigorously enough to make you breathe deeply and become warm and sweaty, e.g. digging the garden or walking briskly. It has various effects.

Lungs

During exercise you breathe more deeply to take in more oxygen. Your lungs become stronger and their capacity increases. So your muscles get more oxygen and work better. You are less likely to get cramp or become easily fatigued.

Heart and circulation

During exercise the heart beats harder and more quickly. Over time it becomes more efficient, so a heart attack is less likely.

Exercise also widens the arteries. So if there is any plaque in the arteries (see page 96), it is less likely to cause a blockage. The strong heartbeat and extra movements of the leg muscles means blood flows more readily back to the heart through the veins. This reduces the likelihood of varicose veins.

Muscles and joints

During exercise the muscles work more and need more oxygen. As they are used regularly they become 'toned up' and ready for further exercise. Exercise also helps to keep joints moving easily and helps guard against arthritis.

Mass

Regular exercise and an energy-controlled diet help to balance energy intake and output and can lead to loss of mass. This is especially important if you are too heavy (see page 145), as this puts an extra strain on the heart.

Overall functioning

Digestion and regularity of bowel movements improve with exercise. Kidney function improves, and extra perspiration gets rid of more wastes. Exercise is enjoyable and you sleep better. The social pleasures of team games are also important.

Which exercise should you choose?

There are several points to bear in mind.

1 Do you want an exercise to do on your own, e.g. swimming, or with a companion, e.g. table tennis, or with a team, e.g. cricket or football?

2 Do you want a 'dynamic' exercise to move your whole body, e.g. swimming or jogging? Or a 'static' exercise to develop muscles, e.g. weight lifting?

3 Are you fit enough to take on strenuous exercise, such as jogging, which may be a strain on your heart and muscles? Or would it be better at first to do something less strenuous such as brisk walking?

4 Do you have enough money to buy or rent any necessary equipment for the exercise?

5 Do you have enough time for your exercise to improve and to feel a sense of achievement?

6 Are the exercises interesting and varied enough for someone of your age, so you will not be bored?

7 Different exercises use up different amounts of energy. They also have different effects on improving the heart, lungs, joints and muscles.

Exercise	Joules used in 20 min	Improvements in		
		heart and lungs	joints	muscles
Walking	240	*	*	*
Housework	360	*	**	**
Gardening	360	*	**	**
Brisk walk	400	**	*	**
Gymnastics	560	**	****	**
Digging	560	**	****	**
Easy jogging	640	***	*	**
Tennis	640	***	***	**
Disco	640	***	****	*
Squash	800	***	***	**
Brisk jogging	840	****	**	**
Cycling	880	****	**	***
Swimming	960	****	****	****

Key: * Negligible, ** Fair, *** Good, **** Excellent

What are the possible problems with exercise?

Heart attack

If you are very unfit the coronary arteries may be narrowed by plaque (see page 96). If you start heavy exercise, e.g. prolonged jogging, there is a sudden strain on the heart, which may not get enough oxygen. This can cause angina or a heart attack.

Cramps and 'stitch'

Do not take strenuous exercise soon after a heavy meal. It can cause **cramp** or 'stitch' (see page 60).

Effect of the Sun

In the Caribbean the effect of the Sun is usually beneficial and leads to a feeling of well-being. But if we exercise too much in the hot Sun and do not drink enough we may lose too much liquid because of sweating to keep cool. This can lead to heat exhaustion or heatstroke (see page 253).

Too much exposure to the Sun can also cause sunburn, with blisters and peeling skin. The ultraviolet rays (see page 345) in sunlight are also associated with the development of skin cancer, especially in fair-skinned albino people. Bright sunlight can also affect our eyes, and we must never look directly at the Sun (see page 127).

Questions

1 In what ways does exercise help people to become healthier?

2 Here are four kinds of sport: (a) long-distance running, (b) gymnastics, (c) cricket, (d) sprinting. Which person do you think would enjoy and do well in each one? A person:
   (i) who enjoys team games
   (ii) who is small and with a lot of stamina
   (iii) with strong muscles and supple joints
   (iv) with strong muscles and large lungs.

3 What are some of the problems you should think about before you begin strenuous exercise?

Key ideas

Use these words to fill in the spaces as you write the sentences in your Exercise book.

lungs   **pulse**   **Sun**   **heart**   **veins**   **cramp**

We breathe more deeply and our _____ rate increases when we exercise. So exercise helps to make our _____ and _____ work more efficiently. Muscular contractions also help the return of blood in the _____ . We should not exercise after a heavy meal, or we may get _____ . We should also take care when exercising in the _____ .

6.8 Use and mis-use of drugs

How are drugs useful?

Drugs are chemicals, other than food, that have effects on our body. They are transported in the blood and may have effects on various organs.

Useful drugs are medicines, e.g. antibiotics, insulin and painkillers. But treat them carefully!

- **Antibiotics**, e.g. penicillin, can treat bacterial diseases, e.g. gonorrhoea and syphilis. They cannot treat viral diseases such as AIDS. The full course of antibiotics must be taken, or strains of bacteria resistant to the drug may develop.
- **Insulin** is used to treat diabetes and saves lives. But too little or too much can be dangerous. Measured amounts are given after the glucose level in the patient's blood has been tested.
- **Painkillers**, e.g. aspirin and paracetamol. Aspirin is useful when used properly, and aspirin with a special coating reduces the risk of heart attack, clots and stroke. But an overdose can cause serious damage, or even death. Paracetamol must also be used with great care, as it can cause liver damage.

How are drugs harmful?

There are other drugs that are harmful in excess.

- **Nicotine** in cigarettes is an addictive drug (see page 102) that raises the heartbeat and blood pressure, and can increase the risk of blood clots. In pregnancy it can cause miscarriage.
- **Caffeine** in coffee, tea and cola drinks is a stimulant (see page 102). More than five cups a day can cause restlessness and trembling. It should be avoided in early pregnancy.
- **Alcohol** is a relaxant (see page 102), but large amounts cause loss of concentration and coordination, slurred speech, blurred vision and vomiting. Heavy long-term drinking can cause damage to the heart and the liver (cirrhosis).

Objectives

- Define drug, useful drug and harmful drug, and give examples of each one.
- Discuss short- and long-term effects of drug mis-use.
- Describe how to avoid drug mis-use.

Dangers of drug mis-use

- There is *no* safe dose for most illegal drugs. Many people have died after their first try.
- The 'down' that comes after a hit or a trip is much worse than you felt before using the drug.
- Many drugs 'hook' you, so you need to keep taking it, or larger amounts, to get the effect.
- Drugs are expensive, so a habit can lead to stealing to get money for the habit.
- It is very dangerous to mix drugs, or take them with alcohol – the combined risks are worse.
- Injected drugs, e.g. heroin, have an extra risk of hepatitis or HIV/AIDS though infected needles.
- Drugs may have been mixed with other substances, which can increase health risks.
- Using or supplying illegal drugs can lead to fines, imprisonment, poor health or even death.

Avoiding harmful drugs

Coming off drugs causes unpleasant 'withdrawal' symptoms. It is better *never* to take drugs.

- It is *not* necessary to do as your friends do. Find other friends, and form a **Say No to Drugs** club (SND). Make slogans and posters for saying NO!
- Tell everyone that drugs *don't* solve problems. Collect information and arrange for speakers.
- Find other ways to spend your time, e.g. with a hobby, or a science, church or adventure club.
- Drugs can ruin your life – they aren't worth it.

Key ideas

Use these words to fill in the spaces as you write the sentences in your Exercise book.

solvents   **depressants**   **heroin**   **stimulants**   **LSD**   **NO!**

Crack and Ecstasy are examples of _____ . Sedatives are called _____ . _____ is an example of a narcotic. _____ is an example of an hallucinogen, which can produce bad trips. _____ are chemicals sniffed as a vapour. It is best to say _____ to illegal drugs.

A few of the drugs shown in this table can be prescribed medicinally, but most have bad effects on health if mis-used.

Types of drugs	Use and short-term effects	Long-term effects
Stimulants ('pep' pills)		
Amphetamine (speed, uppers)	Powder sniffed or injected. Increases physical and mental processes. Weight loss. Dilated (enlarged) pupils, sleeplessness	To maintain the effect users take increasing amounts. High doses can give panic attacks and the body sometimes needs two days to recover. Feel depressed and very hungry. Resistance to disease is lowered, with serious effects on health
Cocaine (coke, snow)	Powder sniffed or injected. Stimulates and heightens sensations. Dilated pupils. Short 'high' leads to addiction	Cocaine, including crack (more dangerous), gives an exhilarating effect which comes quickly and goes quickly. The drug then has to be taken more often to maintain the high and this can lead to dependence, or going on to other drugs, such as heroin. Over time, exhilaration is replaced by sickness, sleeplessness and weight loss. Sniffing cocaine can damage the nose membranes which is very painful
Crack cocaine (rock)	As with cocaine. Made into crystals. Smoked, or heated and vapours inhaled. Hard come-down	
Ecstasy (E, MDMA)	Tablets, liquid or powder. Gives feeling of energy and friendliness, followed by a feeling of misery	Large amounts cause anxiety, confusion and lack of coordination, making driving dangerous. May damage certain brain cells and the liver. Can cause death
Depressants		
Barbiturates, for example Phenobarbitone	Sedative. Extreme tiredness, lack of coordination	Sleeplessness, double vision, possible death from overdose, especially if used with alcohol. Ulcers at injection site
Tranquillizers, for example Benzodiazapines, such as Valium, Librium, Mogadon	Sedatives. Relieve anxiety. Can be prescribed as medicines in small amounts. Very dangerous with alcohol or if injected. Users drowsy and forgetful	Some tranquillizers that are intended for short-term support, become addictive and cause more problems. Can cause temporary memory loss and users trying to quit may suffer panic attacks. Withdrawal has to be very slow over a long period of time
Narcotics		
Opiates, for example opium, morphine, Methadone, Pethidine	Prescribed as short-term medicines for relief of pain. Can become addictive	Small amounts can be prescribed: morphine to relieve pain, for example in cancer patients; Pethidine during childbirth; Methadone helps addicts kick heroin addiction. Opiates can become addictive drugs
Heroin (smack)	Injected, sniffed or smoked. Gives 'high' but bad come-down	Some addicted users may need the drug just to feel normal. Overdose can cause coma and death. Injecting can damage veins and users risk infections of hepatitis or HIV/AIDS
Hallucinogens		
Cannabis (ganja, dope, grass, weed, marijuana)	Smoked as joints. Relaxant, mood swings, dilated pupils, red watery eyes, lethargy	Takes effect quickly. Impairs learning and concentration – therefore dangerous to drive. Long-term smoking of cannabis is more dangerous than tobacco. Users are tired, lacking energy, anxious. Not considered addictive, but users come to rely on it to feel more relaxed socially
Hashish (hash)	Hash is concentrated cannabis usually smoked in a pipe	
LSD ('acid')	On squares of paper dissolved on the tongue. After about an hour have a long 'trip' with distorted vision and depression	'Trip' involves distorted vision and hearing or feeling of being outside the body. Bad trip can be terrifying but can't be stopped. Later you may relive parts of trips as flashbacks. Use complicates mental health problems
Magic mushrooms	From special wild mushrooms. Raw, dried, cooked. Quicker effect and shorter trip than LSD	Problem to distinguish edible mushroom from poisonous ones can cause death. Cause vomiting, diarrhoea, stomach pains. Use complicates mental health problems
Solvents		
Solvents sniffed as vapour, for example glue, paint thinner, aerosols, dry cleaning solvents, lighter fuel, gasoline	Vapours sniffed. Causes vomiting, nose bleeds, fatigue, lack of appetite and coordination. Effect similar to alcohol. Can become unconscious and choke on vomit	Effects short but users repeat the dose. When affected, accidents can occur. Vomiting, black-outs and heart problems can be fatal. Squirting gas down the throat can also cause a reaction which floods the lungs and causes death. Long-term abuse damages brain, liver and kidneys

6.9 How can athletes train their bodies?

The general effects of exercise on the body are given on pages 98–9. But athletes have to train harder to become physically fit to withstand the strain of performing, without injury, and to excel over their opponents.

Objective

● Discuss the effects of and ethics of using drugs and other techniques in the performance enhancement of athletes.

Activity

How do training programmes compare?

1 Compare the training programmes of a sprinter and a long-distance runner (ask your sports teacher).

2 Do both emphasize physical fitness? How are they different? Do the athletes look different?

Training increases the strength, stamina and efficiency of muscle action, blood circulation and improvement in oxygen intake and absorption. Athletes also practise sequences of actions so these become conditioned responses, which are performed smoothly and automatically. All sports also require a supply of energy. During training, the proportion of carbohydrates is often increased (to increase the glycogen stores in the muscles). Foods rich in iron are also needed for the red blood cells.

There are also special needs for particular sports.

● Aerobic sports, e.g. football, tennis and endurance events such as marathons, require increase in stamina and an efficient long-term energy supply.
● Anaerobic sports, with short, intense bursts of activity, e.g. sprinting, require increased muscles and lung capacity.
● Strength sports, e.g. weight lifting and throwing a discus, require special development of muscles, which requires additional protein.

Common drugs (pages 100–1) can have harmful effects on everyone. But they can be especially damaging to the performance of athletes.

Nicotine

This is the active drug in tobacco. It causes changes in mood, which may have effects on athletic performance. The cigarette smoke also contains tar. This stimulates cells in the lung to make excess mucus, which then interferes with gaseous exchange, particularly the uptake of oxygen from inspired air. Athletic achievements that call for a sustained effort and a prolonged demand for oxygen are severely hampered and long-term damage can also be done (see page 82).

Caffeine

The stimulant caffeine, found in tea, coffee and cola, is harmless in small amounts. In large quantities, it is a performance-enhancing drug with harmful side effects and is banned by the International Olympics Committee.

Alcohol

Alcohol (ethanol) is the drug found in alcoholic drinks, such as beers, wine and 'alco-pops'. Alcohol has many effects on the body. When taken in small quantities (e.g. 500 cm³ of beer over 2 hours) it is easily metabolized in the liver and used as a source of energy, like sugars or fats. In larger amounts, alcohol goes directly into the bloodstream. It circulates in the body and affects the thinking and learning areas of the brain. Activities that require alertness and concentration are carried out less effectively. Alcohol also impairs muscle coordination, and this would reduce an athlete's performance.

Parts of the brain that control the functioning of the blood vessels are also affected. Vessels near the skin expand and the person feels warmer. But body temperature actually falls. In cold weather, this leads to a dangerously low body temperature.

Also, the water balance in the body may be upset, leading to dehydration. If the water balance is upset, it could affect the athlete's cooling system, and the effect on brain function could affect judgement. All of these effects could lead to a serious drop in athletic performance.

What happens during training?

Many changes occur. Some tissues are built up, such as muscles, and others broken down, such as fat. An adequate diet is important. Exercise may increase the demand for certain foods, e.g. carbohydrates, proteins, vitamins and iron.

Physical activity causes the body's temperature to rise. If athletes are not prepared for this, they may become heat exhausted. Training to cope with higher body temperatures or high external temperatures is part of most athletes' training.

In 1968 the Olympic Games were held in Mexico City, which is more than 2000 m above sea level. People who normally live at sea level found it difficult to breathe at this altitude. People who always live at high altitude become adapted to these conditions by increasing their lung capacity and number of red blood cells, so taking up oxygen more efficiently. Many athletes for the Mexico Olympics trained at similar high altitudes, to train their bodies for the Olympic conditions.

Drugs and techniques that can be mis-used by athletes

- **Blood boosting** or **blood doping** is an illegal method to increase the numbers of red blood cells in a simpler way. A doctor withdraws some blood from the athlete. The body soon manufactures more red cells. Just before the competition, the red cells, previously withdrawn, are re-injected. The overall effect is there are now extra red blood cells so that the ability of the athlete to use oxygen efficiently is increased. So more oxygen goes to the muscles. The athlete is then able to perform better, particularly if a lot of stamina is required.
  Dangers: increasing the numbers of red blood cells makes the blood thicker, so it clots more easily; this can increase the risks of heart attacks and strokes. Blood contamination during the collection, storage or re-injection can also lead to blood poisoning, affecting the whole body.
- **EPO** is a hormone produced by the kidneys, but now made artificially. It causes an increase in the number of red blood cells and can be used instead of blood boosting. It is injected into the blood, usually in the build-up to a major event.
  Dangers: as for blood boosting, and EPO can also lead to liver failure and pituitary gland problems.
- **Anabolic steroids** are naturally occurring or synthetic substances related to the male sex hormone, testosterone. They boost muscle size and power, especially together with body-building activities.
  Dangers: major mood changes, violent behaviour, kidney and liver problems, tearing of ligaments and reduced sperm production.
- **Stimulants** are drugs such as amphetamines and cocaine. They are similar to adrenaline, which is produced by the body. They reduce tiredness, while increasing competition and aggression. They raise heart rate and may help improve performance. They also lead to weight loss.
  Dangers: with lack of sleep, the body is taken beyond safe limits of exertion, which can be fatal.

Should athletes use drugs?

Most athletes and sports organizations are not in favour of using drugs, as they harm the body in the long term, and the assistance to athletic performance is temporary and may be dangerous. Their use also sets a bad example to younger people. But many athletes claim certain drugs, used with medical supervision, can be useful. What do you think?

Questions

1 What body modifications take place during athletic training?
2 How can drugs affect muscular coordination?
3 Athletes who smoke tend to be sprinters rather than distance runners. Discuss.
4 Do you think blood doping is wrong?

Key ideas

Use these words to fill in the spaces as you write the sentences in your Exercise book.

drugs　　　　**injection**　　　　**diets**　　　　**red**　　　　**steroids**　　　　**EPO**

Training programmes for athletes involve strenuous physical exercise and special _____ .

Some athletes mis-use _____ , such as amphetamines and _____ . Blood doping increases

the numbers of _____ blood cells, either by _____ or by using _____ .

7 Excretion

7.1 Excretion: our lungs and skin

Excretion and egestion

Excretion is the removal of the waste products made during **metabolism** (chemical reactions inside the cells). Excretion is necessary because a build-up of wastes (**excretory products** such as urea, sweat, water and carbon dioxide) would otherwise damage the cells.

Excretion occurs from **excretory organs** (kidneys, lungs and skin). The kidneys are the most important of these; they form part of the **excretory system**.

Egestion is the removal of undigested food remains from the alimentary canal. This waste is not a product of metabolism and has never been part of the cells. The egested material is called **faeces** and the process is called **defecation**.

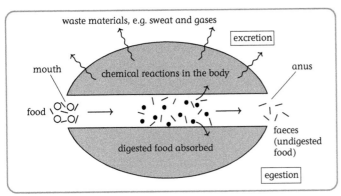

Simplified diagram of a section of an animal to illustrate the difference between excretion and egestion

Excretion in humans

The excretory products come from reactions in the body.

- **Urea**: made in the liver (from the nitrogen part of excess amino acids from proteins eaten in the food) and transported to the kidneys for excretion.
- **Carbon dioxide, water** and **excess energy**: waste products from respiration in the cells.
- **Salts**: from food and not needed by the body.

The excretory organs are the kidneys, lungs and skin.

- **Kidneys** (most important): excrete urine, containing urea, water, salts and energy.
- **Lungs**: excrete carbon dioxide, water and energy.
- **Skin**: excretes sweat (water, urea, salts and energy) and other substances from sweat glands in the armpit.

Note: heat is lost from the body when liquid water evaporates to water vapour. The change of state needs energy, which is taken from the blood in the skin or lungs. The effect is to cool the body.

Excretion in flowering plants is on pages 110–11.

Objectives

- Distinguish between excretion and egestion.
- Identify the excretory organs and excretory products in humans.
- Explain the functioning of the lungs and skin as excretory organs.

Excretion from the lungs

- Carbon dioxide. Blood brought to the lungs in the pulmonary artery from the heart contains a lot of carbon dioxide. In the alveoli (see page 74) there is a concentration gradient so that carbon dioxide passes from the blood into the space of the alveoli and is breathed out.
- Water. Blood coming to the lungs contains a lot of water. Some of this passes as a vapour into the space of the alveoli. On cold, damp days the amount of water vapour will be less, but on warm, dry days it will be more. The water vapour is then breathed out.
- Energy. Blood coming to the lungs is warmer than the air in the alveoli. So some heat can pass from the blood and be breathed out with the air. Heat is also used to evaporate liquid water into water vapour.

Average water balance (24 hours)

Input	(in cm³)
Food and drink	1400
From respiration	350
Output	**(in cm³)**
From the lungs	400
From the skin	500
From the kidneys	700
In the faeces	150

The amount of water lost from the lungs and skin varies depending on outside temperature and moisture in the air. The kidneys then 'balance' this amount (osmoregulation; see pages 108–9).

Excretion from the skin

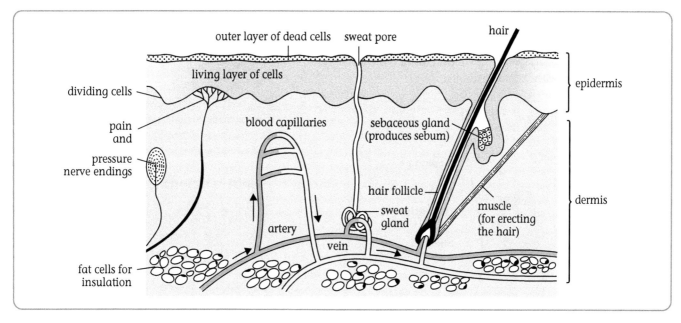

Vertical section through the human skin

How the sweat glands work

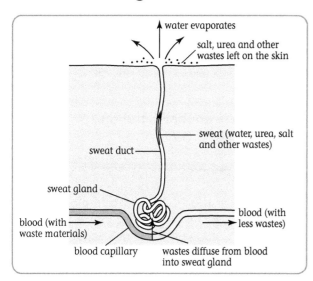

Sweat is mostly water, with urea (about 1.2%) and 1–2% salts. The main function of the sweat glands is to help keep the body temperature constant by evaporation of water (page 121). But the loss of water also helps with the excretion of the urea and salts that are in the sweat.

Blood containing urea, salts and water passes close to the sweat gland. They are in higher concentration in the blood than in the sweat gland and so pass by diffusion along concentration gradients into the sweat gland and up the sweat duct to the surface of the skin. The water evaporates and cools the skin (page 170). The urea and salts are left behind on the surface. Bacteria can break these down to make unpleasant odours, so it is important to wash them away with soap and water, especially when we sweat more on hot days.

Key ideas

Use these words to fill in the spaces as you write the sentences in your Exercise book.

urea	energy	excretion	skin	carbon dioxide	lungs	egestion

The removal of the food remains of digestion is _____. The removal of waste products of metabolism is _____. The excretory products are water, salts, _____, _____ and _____. The main excretory organs are the kidneys, but the _____ and _____ are also involved in _____.

7.2 Our kidneys and osmoregulation

The **kidneys** are the main excretory organs and are found inside the abdomen near the back wall. They form part of the **excretory system**, shown below with its blood supply.

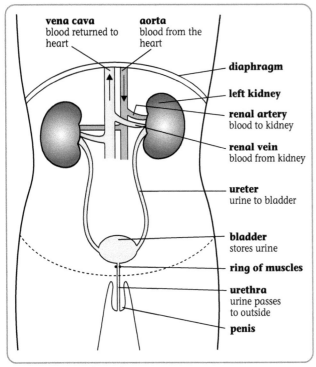

Excretory system of a male

In males, the urethra is the passageway out of the body for both urine and sperm, although both fluids cannot pass down the penis at the same time.

In females, urine is made and stored in the bladder in the same way as in a male. But the urethra (carrying urine) is separate from the vagina (the female passageway from the reproductive system) (see below).

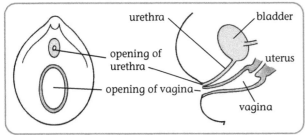

Excretory system of a female

Having two exits is very important in the female because the vagina has other separate functions. During intercourse it has to receive sperm from the male and during the birth of a baby it has to expand a great deal to allow the baby's head and body to come out. The vagina has muscles in its wall to allow it to expand.

Objectives

● Identify the parts of the excretory system, and its blood supply.
● Examine and label a section of a mammalian kidney.

What happens to the urine?

A tube called the **ureter** runs from each of the kidneys to the **bladder**. As urine is made in the kidneys, it flows down the ureters and is stored in the bladder, which increases in size. A ring of muscles keeps the opening of the bladder closed, until the person **urinates** and urine passes out of the body through the **urethra**.

Adults can keep the ring of muscles tight, so that they only urinate when it is convenient. But in a young baby, the bladder is emptied automatically by a reflex action. As a child grows older it gradually learns to control the muscles, although some bedwetting may still occur.

More frequent urination

This may be noticed in:
● early pregnancy because of hormone changes and the uterus pressing on the bladder
● older men if the **prostate gland** (page 149) increases in size and presses on the urethra; urination may become difficult
● people suffering from **diabetes** (page 109); the body passes out extra liquid with the excretion of excess sugar.

Did you know?

● A baby's bladder can contain only a cupful of water before it is emptied.
● Adults vary in the sizes of their bladder and how often they urinate.
● During 24 hours we excrete about 1.4 dm³ of urine.

Practical 34

What is a kidney like inside? (D)

1 Obtain a whole small kidney of a mammal such as a pig or sheep.
2 With a sharp knife, cut it along its length.
3 Look at the cut surface (vertical section) and identify the parts below.
4 Make a labelled diagram of your specimen.

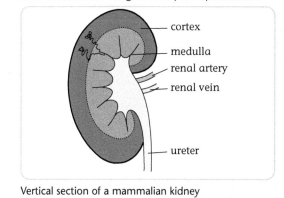

Vertical section of a mammalian kidney

What do the kidneys do?

Blood comes to the kidney in the renal artery. This blood contains urea and salts that the body does not need. Small tubes, called **kidney tubules**, remove the urea and salts together with some water. This liquid is called urine and it leaves the kidney in the ureter to go to the bladder. The blood continues into the renal vein and leaves the kidney. Urine contains more water, salts and urea than the blood, as shown below.

	Blood (%)	Urine (%)
Water	90–93	97.5
Salts	0.35	0.5
Urea	0.03	2.0
Other substances	7.1	none

The roles of the liver and kidneys

The body cannot store amino acids. If we eat more protein than our body needs then it is excreted. The nitrogen part of amino acids is broken off (in a process called **deamination**) in the liver. The liver makes this into **urea**, which is passed on in the blood to be excreted by the kidneys.

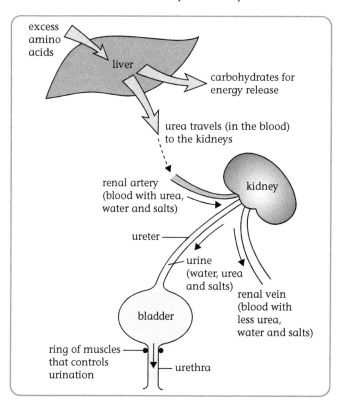

Questions

1 How do the male and female excretory systems differ? Account for the differences.
2 How does blood vary between the renal artery and the renal vein? Account for the differences.
3 Where is urea (a) formed and (b) excreted?

Key ideas

Use these words to fill in the spaces as you write the sentences in your Exercise book.

artery   **vena cava**   **cortex**   **vein**   **bladder**   **aorta**   **medulla**   **ureter**

Blood is brought to the kidney in the renal _____ from the _____ . Blood without urea leaves the kidney in the renal _____ , which joins the _____ . There are kidney tubules in the _____ where blood is filtered. Urine collects in small tubes in the _____ and leaves the kidney in the _____ . The ureter carries the urine to the _____ .

7.2 Our kidneys and osmoregulation (continued)

The blood is taken to very small kidney **tubules**. Each tubule has a cup and a long twisted tube. The kidney tubules filter the blood, and then reabsorb useful materials. The structure and function of the kidney tubule is shown below.

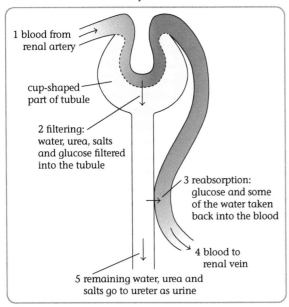

Objectives

- Describe the functions of the kidney tubules (filtration and reabsorption).
- Discuss osmoregulation and its relation to environmental factors.

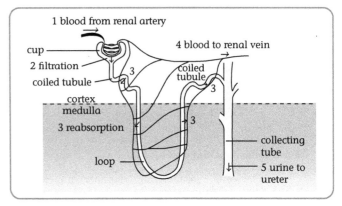

More detail of the coiling of the kidney tubule. The five stages are the same as in the diagram on the left

How the tubule works

1 **Blood to tubule** in branch of renal artery. Has water, urea, salts, glucose and blood proteins.
2 **Filtering** through the cup of small molecules: water, urea, salts and glucose into the tube.
3 **Reabsorption** of useful substances along the tube: all the glucose and some of the water. This is an active process that requires energy.
4 **Blood from tubule** in branch of renal vein. Has less water and salts, no urea, and the same amount of glucose as the renal artery.
5 **Urine formed** from the water, urea and salts left in the tubes. Collects and passes to the ureter.

Water balance, or osmoregulation

The amount of water in the blood is kept constant by the kidneys (**osmoregulation**). This is important for proper cell functioning. It is controlled by a hormone, ADH (page 121), from the pituitary.

- If there is more water in the blood than usual, then less is reabsorbed by the kidneys. The urine is greater in amount, pale and less concentrated.
- If there is less water in the blood than usual, then more is reabsorbed by the kidneys in order to conserve it. The urine is smaller in amount, dark and more concentrated.

Key ideas

Use these words to fill in the spaces as you write the sentences in your Exercise book.

diabetic   **urea**   **water**   **salts**   **filtered**   **reabsorbed**   **glucose**

In the capsule of each kidney tubule the blood is _____ . All the _____ , _____ , and _____ pass down the tubule. The _____ and _____ continue into the urine. But useful substances are _____ . In healthy people all of the _____ and some of the _____ are taken back into the blood. _____ is excreted in the urine of a _____ person.

Osmoregulation and environmental factors

The lungs and skin lose water depending on the temperature of the body, and the temperature, moisture and amount of wind in the outside air. The kidneys 'balance' the amount of water lost, so the amount in the blood remains constant.

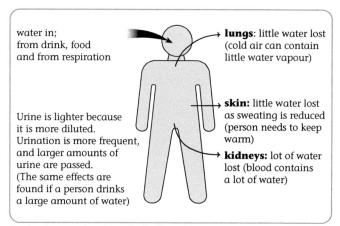

water in; from drink, food and from respiration

lungs: little water lost (cold air can contain little water vapour)

skin: little water lost as sweating is reduced (person needs to keep warm)

kidneys: lot of water lost (blood contains a lot of water)

Urine is lighter because it is more diluted. Urination is more frequent, and larger amounts of urine are passed. (The same effects are found if a person drinks a large amount of water)

Cooler day, or when less physically active

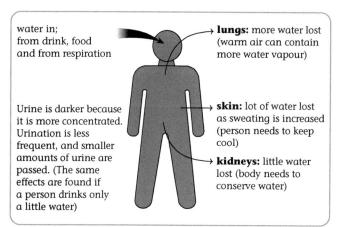

water in; from drink, food and from respiration

lungs: more water lost (warm air can contain more water vapour)

skin: lot of water lost as sweating is increased (person needs to keep cool)

kidneys: little water lost (body needs to conserve water)

Urine is darker because it is more concentrated. Urination is less frequent, and smaller amounts of urine are passed. (The same effects are found if a person drinks only a little water)

Hotter day, or when more physically active

Diabetes

In a healthy person, there is about 0.1% by volume of glucose in the blood. This rises after a meal and then returns to a similar level. A person with **diabetes** has a larger amount of glucose in the blood. This rises after a meal, and stays high. The diabetic person is not producing enough **insulin** in the pancreas to control the blood sugar level.

Kidney problems

If the kidneys are damaged, urea, salts and water could accumulate in the body and cause problems. An **artificial kidney** is used to filter and adjust the blood. This process is called **dialysis**.

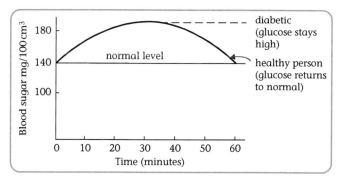

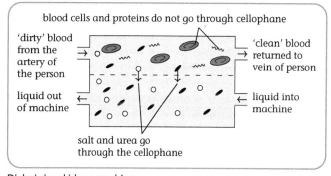

blood cells and proteins do not go through cellophane

'dirty' blood from the artery of the person

'clean' blood returned to vein of person

liquid out of machine

liquid into machine

salt and urea go through the cellophane

Dialysis in a kidney machine

Blood is pumped from an artery to the machine. Small molecules of salt and urea **diffuse** through the membrane along their concentration gradients and are removed. The water content is adjusted, and the clean blood is returned to a vein. This process needs to be repeated.

When blood goes to the kidneys, the glucose passes into the tubes along with the water. In a healthy person this amount of glucose can be reabsorbed, and no glucose goes into the urine. But in a diabetic person the amount of glucose is very high, and it cannot all be reabsorbed. This is why glucose is found in the urine in diabetic people.

Treatment of diabetes is to reduce the amount of glucose in the blood by diet and by giving injections of insulin. These lower the amount of glucose, so it can be reabsorbed in the kidneys.

Questions

1 What is meant by (a) filtration, (b) reabsorption and (c) dialysis? Where does each occur?
2 Under what conditions would a person's urine (a) be darker and (b) contain glucose?
3 Why is osmoregulation important?

7.3 Excretion in flowering plants

Flowering plants carry out chemical reactions, such as photosynthesis, respiration and growth, which produce wastes. They can store some of the wastes, in their leaves and bark, for later removal. They also make only as much protein as they need for growth, and to produce seeds, fruits and storage organs. So they do not produce urea.

However, photosynthesis and respiration produce waste gases and energy that have to be excreted all the time. Water also has to be excreted, to provide the force for water and salts to rise up in the xylem (page 87). The excretion of water involves the loss of another waste, energy, and this helps to keep the plant cool.

The excretory products are: oxygen (from photosynthesis); carbon dioxide, water and energy (from respiration); and wastes, such as tannins from other chemical reactions.

The excretory organs of flowering plants are the leaves and bark.

The excretion of oxygen and carbon dioxide

Animals take in oxygen and give out carbon dioxide all the time. But plants are different: it depends on whether it is night-time or daytime. Respiration occurs all the time, but photosynthesis only occurs when it is light. The gases that are excreted by a plant depend on the balance between photosynthesis and respiration.

At night: carbon dioxide is excreted. There is no light and so no photosynthesis. All of the carbon dioxide from respiration is released. Water and energy are also excreted.

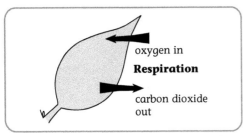

A plant at night: respiration is like that in animals

In the daytime: oxygen is excreted. This was formed during photosynthesis. Any carbon dioxide that the plant releases during respiration is used up in photosynthesis in the light.

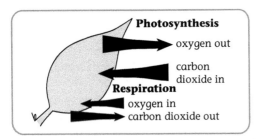

A plant during the day: carbon dioxide is taken in and oxygen is excreted

Objectives

- Identify and explain the excretory products in flowering plants at night and in the daytime.
- Relate transpiration and osmoregulation to environmental factors.
- Describe the use of bark and leaf fall.

Storage of wastes in the bark

Many waste products, other than gases and water, are taken to the outside cells of the stem. They are changed into substances that will not harm the plant. The wastes become part of the tough outer layer of the stem: the **bark**. As trees grow wider, the bark often splits and many pieces of bark drop off; the wastes are lost with the bark.

Excretion from the leaves

The respiratory surface (page 74) in the plant is the large, moist surface of the cells near the stomata (page 51). Gases in the outside air and in the leaf diffuse along their concentration gradients.

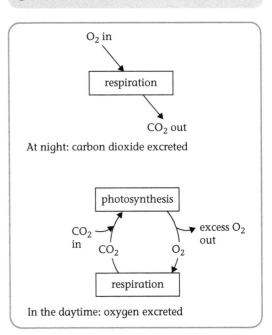

At night: carbon dioxide excreted

In the daytime: oxygen excreted

The excretion of water and energy

Water and energy loss occur by **transpiration**. Water evaporates from the cell surfaces that line the spaces near to the stomata (page 51). As liquid water changes to water vapour, heat energy is needed for the change in state, and this is taken from the cells of the plant. The effect is to lose energy, and so cool the plant.

Inevitable water loss occurs through the stomata that are open for the plant to take in and lose oxygen and carbon dioxide. Most plants have a waterproof cuticle on the outside of the leaves to restrict water loss to the stomata, and many have stomata only on the lower leaf surface.

Where conditions are dry, and water has to be conserved, the plants have other modifications.

- Stomata are hidden in pits or the leaves have hairy surfaces. The pits or hairs trap moist air, and so cut down on the rate of transpiration.
- Desert plants, such as cacti, have leaves reduced to spines (so cutting down on the number of stomata) and photosynthesis occurs in green water-storing stems.

The rate of transpiration from the plant depends on the **humidity** of the air close to the stomata (how much water vapour there is in it). If the saturated air is also blown away, then this also increases the rate of transpiration.

Storage of wastes and leaf fall

Many waste products, as well as gases and water, are taken to the leaves. They are stored in the leaf cells as substances that will not harm the plant. From time to time old leaves drop off (**leaf fall**) and the wastes are also lost.

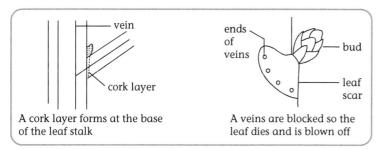

A cork layer forms at the base of the leaf stalk

A veins are blocked so the leaf dies and is blown off

Stages in leaf fall

Osmoregulation compared in humans and flowering plants

Similarities: sweating (in animals) and transpiration (in plants) gets rid of water and energy. Both are affected by environmental conditions: they increase in sunny, dry and windy weather.

Differences: in animals, water is also lost by the kidneys (in urine) and from the lungs; it is under the overall control of the hormone ADH (page 121). Water loss in plants is not under hormonal control; it occurs whenever the stomata are open. However, some plants growing in dry conditions have modifications to cut down on transpiration.

What factors affect transpiration?

- Low humidity, on a sunny, dry, windy day, increases transpiration.
- High humidity, on a cloudy, cool, calm day, decreases transpiration.

Questions

1 List (a) three similarities and (b) two differences in excretory products of humans and flowering plants. (c) Give a reason for one of the differences.

2 How, and why, are the excretory products different in a flowering plant at night and in the daytime?

3 Describe leaf fall and its importance.

Key ideas

Use these words to fill in the spaces as you write the sentences in your Exercise book.

daytime   **energy**   **dry**   **transpiration**   **oxygen**   **night**   **carbon dioxide**   **hot**

In the _____ a plant carries out photosynthesis and excretes _____ . At _____ a plant excretes _____ . During _____ a plant gets rid of water and _____ . The _____ is needed to change liquid water to vapour. The rate of _____ is greater in _____ and _____ conditions.

Plants also lose wastes in the bark and leaf fall.

8 Sense organs and coordination

8.1 What is the nervous system?

The nervous system controls what happens in the body.

- It controls our thinking, planning and learning (voluntary actions).
- It collects information from the sense organs, and allows us to understand it.
- It controls our automatic (involuntary) actions, so we can react quickly to danger by reflex actions.
- It controls the activities of the other systems. For example, it controls the movement of our limbs and regulates our body temperature.

Parts of the nervous system

There are two main parts to the nervous system.

- The **central nervous system**: this includes the brain and the spinal cord.
- The **peripheral nervous system**: this includes the cranial and spinal nerves, the nerve fibres and the sense organs.

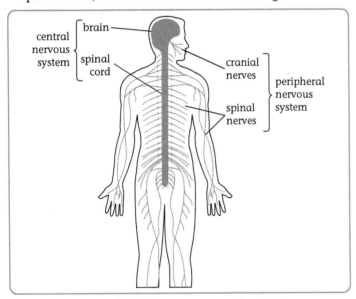

The nervous system links the **receptors** to the **effectors**.

- The receptors are the sensory cells inside all our sense organs. They are sensitive to changes called **stimuli**.
- The effectors are our muscles and glands.

Stimuli, such as light or sound, cause the setting up of tiny pulses of electricity called **nervous impulses**. These pass from the receptor along the nerves to the spinal cord or the brain. Corresponding nervous impulses are sent from the spinal cord or brain to the effector, which responds. Where nerve endings are close together, there is a junction called a **synapse**. The messages are passed across the synapse by release of chemicals. So nerves carry messages using electrical and chemical energy.

Objectives

- Identify the parts and functions of the nervous system.
- Describe the brain and spinal cord and how they are protected.

Protecting the nervous system

The brain   This is protected from physical harm inside the flat bones of the skull.

The sense organs
- The eyes are protected within holes in the bone at the front of the skull.
- Most parts of the ear are protected inside the skull.

The spinal cord   This is protected inside the backbone, which is made up of **vertebrae**. Each vertebra has a central space, and the cord runs though it. The spinal nerves come out at the sides.

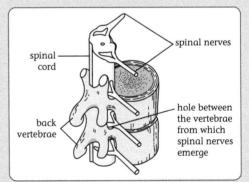

Two back vertebrae, showing how the spinal cord is protected

Questions

1 List two functions of the nervous system. Give examples from actions you carried out today.
2 Choose one part of the nervous system and describe how it is protected from physical harm.

What is the brain like?

The brain lies within the skull. It consists of three parts.

- **Cerebral hemispheres** (cerebrum): this makes up the largest part. It has a twisted and bumpy surface.
- **Cerebellum**: this is smaller and has a ridged surface.
- **Medulla oblongata**: this is like a stalk, and it continues on into the spinal cord.

The cerebrum is mainly concerned with **voluntary** actions that involve thinking. The cerebellum and medulla oblongata are concerned with automatic or **involuntary** actions that do not need thought.

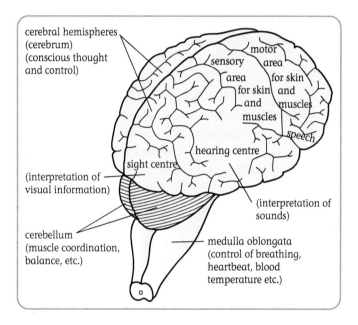

cerebral hemispheres (cerebrum) (conscious thought and control)

motor area for skin and muscles

sensory area for skin and muscles

speech

hearing centre

sight centre

(interpretation of visual information)

cerebellum (muscle coordination, balance, etc.)

medulla oblongata (control of breathing, heartbeat, blood temperature etc.)

(interpretation of sounds)

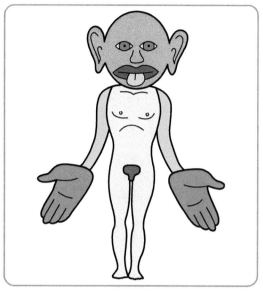

A diagram to show the proportion of brain cells concerned with the various parts of the body. See how important the senses of sight and hearing are, and the lips and hands

Did you know?

- The brain makes up only about 3% of the weight of the body.
- However, the brain uses 20% of the oxygen we breathe in, 20% of the energy from the food we eat and about 15% of the body's blood supply.
- The brain contains about 10,000 million nerve cells.
- Each nerve cell is linked by up to 50,000 connections to other nerve cells.
- The thumb is so important that a larger proportion of the brain is concerned with it than with the chest and abdomen.

What is the spinal cord like?

The spinal cord lies within the cavity of the vertebrae. It is a thick white cord running from the base of the brain to the end of the backbone. Near the top are the cranial nerves (connecting the eye and ear to the brain) and along its length are pairs of spinal nerves. The spinal nerves contain the nerve fibres that branch out to all parts of the body. These nerve fibres are of two kinds: the **sensory** fibres bring in messages, for example from the skin; and the **motor** fibres return the corresponding messages, for example to the muscles (see page 116).

Key ideas

Use these words to fill in the spaces as you write the sentences in your Exercise book.

cerebrum   central   automatic   peripheral   spinal cord   nerves   thinking

The _____ nervous system consists of the brain and _____ . The _____ nervous system

consists of the _____ and sense organs. The largest part of the brain is the _____ , which is

concerned with _____ . The other parts of the brain are concerned with _____ responses.

8.1 What is the nervous system? (continued)

We will now look more closely at the:

- **receptors** (sensory cells inside the sense organs) that set up messages sent in to the spinal cord or brain, and
- **effectors** (muscles and glands) that respond to messages received from the spinal cord or brain.

Which sense organs are being used by the student?

Receptors

The receptors are the sensory cells inside the sense organs. They are sensitive to different **stimuli**. For example, nervous impulses are set up in the eye by the stimulus of light.

The eye (pages 124–5)

The sensory cells in the eye are the **rods** and **cones** in the **retina**. The rods are sensitive to the presence or absence of light, so we see light and dark. The cones are sensitive to different wavelengths of light, so we see in colour.

Nervous impulses are sent along the optic nerve to the sight centre of the brain. This interprets the upside-down image from the retina, so that we see the upright object in front of us.

The ear (pages 130–1)

The **semicircular canals** have cells sensitive to changes in position, so they help us to balance.

The sensory cells in the **cochlea** respond to different frequencies of sound. Nervous impulses pass along the auditory nerve to the hearing centre of the brain, which interprets the impulses as sounds we can understand.

The nervous impulses are sent (along sensory neurones) into the spinal cord. There may be an immediate response, an involuntary action. It is only if the nervous impulses are also sent to the brain that we can see, hear, smell, taste or feel.

Objectives

- Briefly describe the sense organs and the stimuli to which they are sensitive.
- Identify receptors in the sense organs, and effectors (muscles and glands).

The nose

When we draw air in through our noses it goes into the **nasal cavity** (see page 72). There are sensory cells in the lining of the cavity, which are sensitive to different chemical particles in the air. Nervous impulses are sent from the sensory cells to the brain, and so we can interpret the smell.

The tongue

The sensory cells responsible for our sense of taste are found in the **taste buds**, which are buried in pits on the tongue (in diagram (a) below).

Chemicals in food stimulate different sensory cells, and impulses are sent to the brain. Different parts of the tongue are sensitive to different kinds of taste (in diagram (b) below).

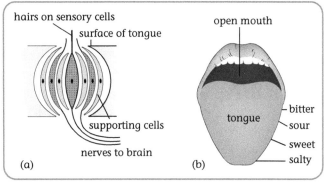

The senses of taste and smell are related. A large part of what we 'taste' actually depends upon the vapours from our food. These rise up into the nasal cavity and stimulate the cells sensitive to smell. We know this is true because when we have a blocked nose due to a cold, it is hard for us to 'taste' our food – it seems less flavoured.

Did you know?

- The skin is the body's largest organ: an adult male has about 1.9 m² and an adult female 1.6 m².
- The smallest human muscle is in the ear: it is a little over 1 mm long.
- The retina in the eye covers about 650 mm². It contains 130 million rods and 7 million cones.

The skin

There are special receptors in the skin. They are the ends of the sensory nerves that are connected to the spinal cord and the brain. These nerve endings are sensitive to touch, pain, pressure, heat and cold. When the receptors are affected by these stimuli, they set up nervous impulses.

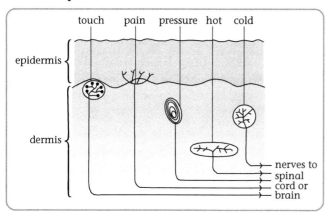

Sensory nerve endings in the skin

In the skin in different parts of the body there are different numbers of receptors. For example, there are more receptors sensitive to touch on our fingertips than on our elbows. When the receptors are stimulated, nervous impulses are sent along nerves to the spinal cord or brain.

Summary of the sense organs

Sense	Sense organ and receptors
Balance	Ear (semicircular canals)
Hearing	Ear (nerve endings in cochlea)
Sight	Eye (rods and cones)
Taste	Tongue (taste buds)
Smell	Nose (lining of nasal cavity)
Touch	Skin (nerve endings)
Pain, hot and cold	Skin (nerve endings)

Effectors

Sensory cells of the receptors send nervous impulses to the spinal cord or brain, and appropriate impulses are sent back to the effectors – muscles and glands – to make them respond.

Muscles

Muscles respond by **contracting** (getting shorter) or **relaxing** (returning to their normal length). In our arms and legs the muscles occur in pairs, attached to the bones by inelastic tendons. As a muscle contracts it pulls the bones to which it is attached closer together. At the same time the other muscle of the pair relaxes.

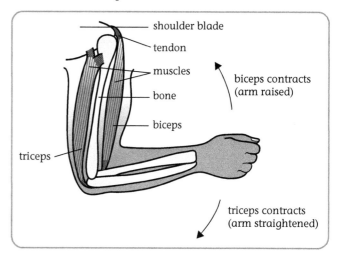

Glands

Glands respond to impulses by secreting **juices**. For example, when we are eating food our salivary glands are stimulated to secrete saliva.

Questions

1 List the stimuli to which the sensory cells in each sense organ are sensitive.
2 Give an example of (a) a sense organ, (b) a stimulus, (c) a receptor and (d) an effector.

Key ideas

Use these words to fill in the spaces as you write the sentences in your Exercise book.

stimuli   nervous impulses   effectors   sense organ   receptors   spinal cord

A _____ , such as the eye, contains _____ . These _____ are sensitive to _____ , such as light. They set up _____ that are sent in to the _____ or brain. Corresponding _____ are sent out to the _____ , such as the muscles, which respond.

8.2 Involuntary and voluntary actions

The brain, spinal cord and nerves are built up of nerve cells, or **neurones**. Each neurone has:

- a **cell body**: this contains the nucleus and cytoplasm
- two kinds of projections: nerve endings and **dendrites**. These are close to other neurones or to muscles, etc.
- a long nerve fibre, the **axon**. This has a fatty covering.

There are three kinds of neurones.

- Sensory neurones have sensory nerve fibres that bring impulses in to the central nervous system from receptors.
- Motor neurones have motor nerve fibres that take impulses from the central nervous system to the effectors.
- Connector neurones connect the other two types.

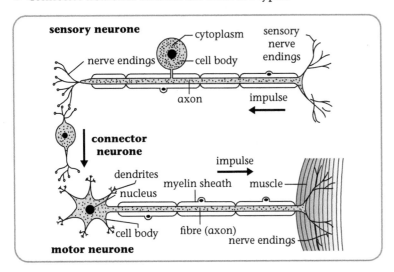

Involuntary action (reflex action)

The reaction occurs automatically to give a response to a stimulus, as shown in the reflex arc below.

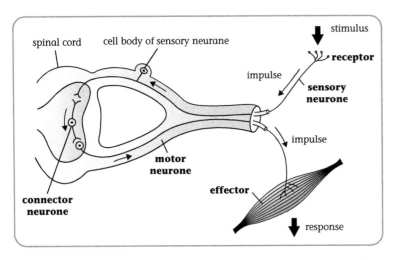

Reflex action: the pathway is from the receptor to the sensory nerve to the spinal cord, to the motor nerve and then to the effector (the muscle)

Involuntary action (knee jerk reflex)

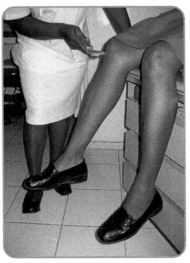

When the doctor hits the knee just below the knee cap, the lower leg automatically springs up – a reflex action

Voluntary action (thinking action)

Voluntary actions are *not* automatic. Impulses from the receptors are sent to the spinal cord and cerebrum (fore-brain, responsible for thought).

In an involuntary action, if your hand touches a hot object, an impulse is sent in along the sensory neurone, and, via the connector neurone, a corresponding impulse is sent out to the muscles of the arm to draw away your hand.

But if you pick up a valuable hot object, something additional happens. When the impulse arrives at the spinal cord, it also travels up to the fore-brain. Here a decision is taken, and an impulse is sent back that goes to the muscles instructing them to put the object down carefully. The voluntary action has involved thought.

	Involuntary actions	Voluntary actions
Action	Reflex, not using thought	Involves thought by the brain
Speed	Very rapid	Response may be slower
Purpose	Protection from danger by reacting quickly	Use of experience to decide on consequences
Control	Spinal cord or hind-brain	Fore-brain (cerebrum)

Damage to the nervous system

- **Blindness** can be caused by damage to the eye, to the neurones carrying the impulses or to part of the brain.
- **Polio** is a paralysis caused by a virus that attacks the motor nerve fibres controlling the muscles. It can be prevented by vaccination with weakened polio virus.
- **Multiple sclerosis** is caused by damage to the myelin sheath that covers the nerve fibres. It can cause gradual loss of control of muscles and paralysis.
- **Parkinson's disease** affects nerve centres in the brain, so that muscles become weak and arms and legs shake.
- **Synapses** between nerves are very important. They are readily affected by drugs and poisons. For example, alcohol affects the synapses in the brain, slowing down our reactions. This is why we should not drink and drive.

Endocrine system

All the actions described above involve electrical impulses sent along nerves. But activities can also be controlled by chemicals called **hormones**, which are released into the blood by the **endocrine system** (see pages 118–19). The two systems are compared in the table below.

	Nervous system	Endocrine system
Produces	Nervous impulses	Hormones
Transport	Along nerves	In the blood
Target	Direct to effector	Not directly to target
Speed	Rapid	Slow
Effect	Immediate, short term	Delayed, long term
Example	Reflex action	Control of growth

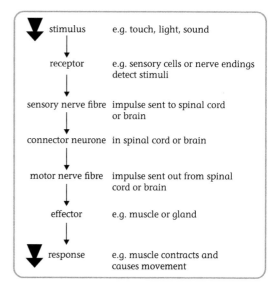

stimulus	e.g. touch, light, sound
receptor	e.g. sensory cells or nerve endings detect stimuli
sensory nerve fibre	impulse sent to spinal cord or brain
connector neurone	in spinal cord or brain
motor nerve fibre	impulse sent out from spinal cord or brain
effector	e.g. muscle or gland
response	e.g. muscle contracts and causes movement

Did you know?

- The brain does not feel pain: it does not have pain receptors. This is why brain operations can be performed on patients who are still awake.
- Axons of neurones connecting the toes and the spinal cord can be more than a metre long: the longest cells in the body.
- Impulses to and from the brain travel as fast as racing cars: 290 km/h.

Questions

1 You accidentally touch a hot pan. Outline, with a diagram, what happens.

2 List three differences between involuntary and voluntary actions.

Key ideas

Use these words to fill in the spaces as you write the sentences in your Exercise book.

voluntary   effector   motor   involuntary   receptor   sensory   spinal cord

A _____ action involves the brain. A reflex action is _____ : it occurs without thought. A stimulus sets up a nervous impulse in a _____ . The impulse passes along the _____ nerve fibre to the _____ . Here it passes through a connector neurone to the _____ nerve fibre, which takes it to the _____ . The _____ , such as a muscle, responds.

8.3 What is the endocrine system?

The **endocrine system** controls some of the activities inside our bodies. It is made up of the endocrine glands, which secrete chemicals called **hormones**. The hormones pass directly into the blood and are carried around the body. Each one affects a particular organ, causing it to slow down or speed up its activity. The endocrine system is responsible for keeping conditions in the body within certain limits, and for growth and development. It is compared to the **nervous system** on page 117.

Secretion   A liquid produced by a gland, e.g. a digestive juice or a hormone.

Hormone   A chemical secreted by an endocrine gland directly into the blood. It slows down or activates a particular organ.

Endocrine gland   A gland without a duct. It secretes hormones into the blood.

Metabolic rate   The rate at which all the chemical processes of an organism occur.

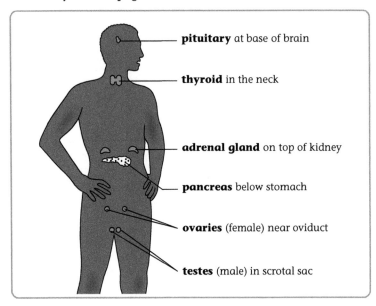

pituitary at base of brain

thyroid in the neck

adrenal gland on top of kidney

pancreas below stomach

ovaries (female) near oviduct

testes (male) in scrotal sac

Pituitary hormones

- Growth hormone: controls amount of growth. With too much it can produce a giant; with too little it can produce a dwarf.
- ADH: controls amount of water in the blood by the amount of water reabsorbed by the kidneys (pages 108–9).
- Control of thyroid: activates thyroid to produce thyroxine.
- Control of sex organs: testes produce sperm and testosterone; ovaries produce eggs, oestrogen and progesterone.

Endocrine glands

Pituitary gland

This is the 'master gland', as it secretes so many hormones. These in turn control the growth and development of the body and the functions of other glands (see page 119).

Gland	Hormones	Functions	Results of deficiency
Pituitary	Growth hormone	Controls rate of growth	Dwarf, or poor overall growth
	ADH	Regulates water content of blood	Excess water loss from kidneys
	Controlling hormones	Activate the thyroid	Thyroid does not secrete its hormone
		Activate testes	Testes does not secrete its hormone
		Activate ovaries	Ovary does not release eggs, nor secrete its hormones
Pancreas	Insulin	Amount of glucose in blood	High glucose in the blood and urine
Thyroid	Thyroxine	Basic metabolic rate	Tiredness, sluggishness, weight gain
Adrenal	Adrenaline	Prepares body for action	Slow response to emergencies
Testis	Testosterone	Sexual development	Delayed sexual development
Ovary	Oestrogen and progesterone	Sexual development and menstrual cycle	Delayed sexual development, irregular menstrual cycle

Pancreas

This produces **insulin**, which controls the amount of glucose in the blood. Insulin makes the cells take up glucose for releasing energy. It also makes the liver absorb and store it as glycogen.

If there is too little insulin, the amount of glucose rises in the blood. Then some glucose is excreted by the kidney in the urine (page 109). The person suffers from **diabetes**.

A diabetic person urinates more often, and will be tired and weak because the cells cannot use glucose. There may be a decrease in mass as fat and protein (muscles) are burnt to provide energy. Diabetic people should eat a diet low in carbohydrates. Daily injections of insulin may also be needed.

Thyroid

This produces **thyroxine**, which controls the metabolic rate.

- With too little thyroxine during childhood, the person will be a dwarf and mentally disabled.
- With too little thyroxine as an adult, body processes slow down so people become fat, tired and worn out.
- With too much thyroxine, metabolism speeds up so people become thin and overactive.

Adrenal glands

These produce **adrenaline**, the 'fright, fight or flight' hormone preparing us for emergencies.

> Effects of adrenaline
> • breathing and heart rates increased
> • extra glucose released into the blood
> • extra blood with oxygen and food pumped to muscles
>
>
>
> therefore the person can be more active

Adrenaline is also produced during stress. This can affect the blood system (page 97).

Testes

At puberty (page 146), the testes are activated by a hormone from the pituitary. As a result the testes produce **testosterone**, which causes the development of secondary sexual characteristics.

Testosterone and the related anabolic steroids have a body-building effect and are sometimes taken (usually illegally) by male and female athletes (page 103). They are taken as tablets, by injection or implanted in muscle tissue. Both men and women become stronger and more muscular, but also face health problems.

Ovaries

At puberty (page 146), the ovaries are activated by hormones from the pituitary. These cause eggs to be developed and released, and the ovaries to produce **oestrogen** and **progesterone**. These hormones then cause the development of secondary sexual characteristics.

The hormones are important in the menstrual cycle (page 146). Oestrogen causes the repair of the uterus wall, and progesterone causes the uterus wall to become thick and full of blood.

Questions

1 Miss Brown has an underactive pituitary. Describe one external effect and one internal effect this might have.

2 John has put on weight and become very tired and sluggish. Suggest a possible cause that the doctor would investigate.

3 Susan's urine shows a positive test for reducing sugars. What might be the cause?

4 You are on the sidewalk and a car swerves towards you. List four things that would happen to you automatically.

Key ideas

Use these words to fill in the spaces as you write the sentences in your Exercise book.

adrenaline   hormones   ducts   insulin   sex   blood   pituitary   thyroid

The endocrine glands do not have _____ ; they secrete their _____ directly into the _____ .

The 'master' gland is the _____ ; it controls other glands, such as the _____ and the _____

organs. _____ , from the adrenal glands, prepares the body for emergencies. _____ , from the

pancreas, controls the amount of glucose in the blood.

8.4 How are life processes controlled?

The various systems of the body are interrelated, so that the living cells are supplied with what they need, and waste products are taken away.

In plants, which are usually less complex than animals, **photosynthesis** and **respiration** are interrelated. The gases produced by one process are used up by the other, and vice versa (page 110).

In animals, the cells are surrounded by tissue fluid. Substances that are needed by the cells are brought in capillaries from an artery and diffuse through the tissue fluid to the cell. The cell carries out **respiration**. It produces waste products that diffuse into the tissue fluid.

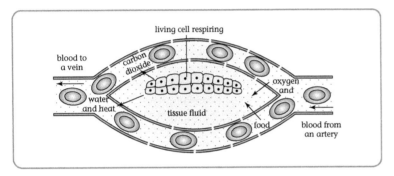

Most of the tissue fluid returns to capillaries and then to a vein. But some of the tissue fluid enters **lymph vessels**, which are part of the **lymphatic system**. This system has:

- swellings, the **lymph glands**, where the white cells (the **lymphocytes**) are made (pages 88 and 94)
- finger-like projections, the **lacteals**, which are inside the villi (page 66). Fatty acids and glycerol enter the lacteals, and are later taken to the liver.

Homeostasis

Living cells can work properly only within fairly narrow limits of pH, temperature, water and glucose. **Homeostasis** keeps conditions in the body constant at a steady level.

Feedback control is the mechanism by which, if one of the conditions starts to increase or decrease beyond set values, that condition is lowered or raised again.

Objectives

- Define homeostasis and feedback control, and give an example of each.
- Use flow charts to show feedback mechanisms for temperature control and osmoregulation.

The role of the liver in homeostasis

When we digest our food, the products of digestion are absorbed into the villi (page 66), and pass to the liver.

- After a meal, there are large amounts of food. The liver reduces the amount passed on in the blood, and stores some.
- After several hours of not eating, the amount of food would be low. The liver releases some of the food it had stored.

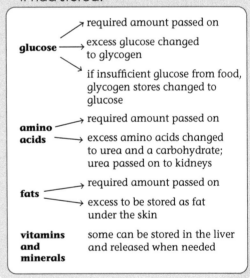

Key ideas

Use these words to fill in the spaces as you write the sentences in your Exercise book.

increases   **feedback control**   **decreases**   **lower**   **homeostasis**   **raise**   **constant**

_____ is the maintenance of constant conditions in the body. It is brought about by _____ .

If a feature _____, then mechanisms occur to _____ it again. If a feature _____ , then

mechanisms occur to _____ it again. So conditions are kept _____.

Feedback control

Feedback control depends on there being:

- a set value or range of some characteristic
- a sensor that is sensitive to an increase or decrease away from the set value
- mechanisms in the body that can restore the set value.

The general process of feedback control is shown in the first diagram below. You should also study the other three diagrams to identify the similarities.

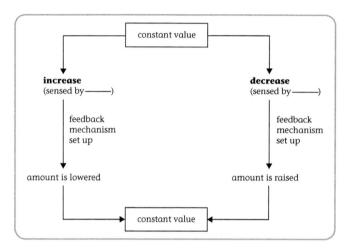

Control of glucose in the blood

Set value: 0.1% by volume
Sensor: hypothalamus affects pancreas
Mechanisms: insulin – glucose to glycogen;
           adrenaline and other hormones – glycogen
           to glucose

Note: **diabetes** (page 109) occurs if a person does not secrete sufficient insulin. Glucose is then excreted by the kidneys. The person may need to have daily injections of insulin in order to control the glucose level of their blood.

Control of water in the blood

Set value: around 65%
Sensor: pituitary gland (page 118)
Mechanisms: water-balance hormone (ADH) acting on the
           kidneys (see pages 108–9)

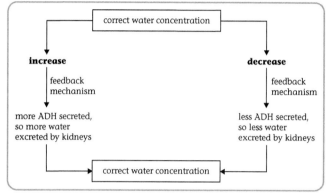

Control of body temperature

Set value: around 37 °C
Sensor: medulla oblongata
Mechanisms: skin changes, changing clothes (see also
           pages 123 and 171)

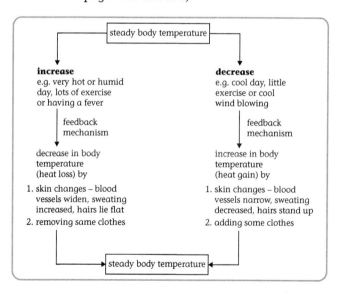

Questions

1 How do your body cells stay alive?

2 Why is the liver important?

3 How are (a) water concentration and (b) temperature of the blood kept constant? Include in your answer the importance of a set value, the sensor and how adjustments are made. Illustrate with diagrams.

8.4 How are life processes controlled? (continued)

You have seen that it is important for body conditions to be kept within a narrow range. In order to do this, the body has sensors and uses feedback control. Now we will look in more detail at how some animals control their body temperature.

Ectothermic animals

Ectothermic animals cannot keep their body temperature constant. They are also described as 'poikilothermic' ('poikilo' means 'changing'). When it is hot outside, their body temperature is higher. When it is cold outside, their body temperature is lower. They vary all the time.

Fish and amphibians

- Fish cannot control their temperature; it goes up and down with the water in which they live.
- Amphibians, such as frogs and toads, often hide under stones when the Sun is hot, to keep cooler. In cold conditions they may hibernate.

Reptiles

Reptiles, such as lizards, do not have feathers or hair to help them control their temperature. But they behave in certain ways to reduce variation. During the morning they 'warm up' in the Sun. At the hottest time they hide in the shade, to keep cool. At night they also hide, to keep warm.

Transpiration and sweating

Transpiration in plants and sweating in animals depend on evaporation. The rates of both are controlled partly by the surroundings and partly by the organism. As water evaporates it takes heat from the plant or animal, and so cools it. In mammals, the feedback control process allows the temperature to be kept constant (see page 121).

Objectives

- Describe and give examples of ectothermic and endothermic animals.
- Describe in detail how the human body temperature is kept constant.

Endothermic animals

Endothermic animals can keep their body temperature constant. They are also called 'homoiothermic' ('homoio' means 'the same'). When it is hot outside, their body temperature does not go up. When it is cold outside, their body temperature does not go down.

Birds

In birds, the small feathers close to the skin trap a layer of warm air. As moisture evaporates from the skin it builds up, and this reduces further evaporation. However, birds may have to migrate to cooler or warmer places at different times of the year.

Mammals

Mammals have hair. There is also a heat-sensitive centre in the brain that controls body temperature (see page 113). Mammals also have fat deposits under their skin to keep them warm.

Humans are an unusual type of mammal. We do not have a thick covering of hair, although our fine hairs do help us with temperature control. We also wear appropriate clothing (see page 171).

Evaporation of sweat cools the body. During exercise, drops of perspiration may collect on the skin. This should be dried off with a towel, because when it evaporates quickly it might cool the body too much.

Key ideas

Use these words to fill in the spaces as you write the sentences in your Exercise book.

decreases   **evaporation**   **endothermic**   **increases**   **dilate**   **ectothermic**

Animals that cannot control their body temperature are called _____ . Animals that can keep a constant temperature are called _____ . In hot conditions, blood vessels in the skin of a mammal _____ so more blood comes to the surface to be cooled. In hot conditions the rate of sweating also _____ so more heat is lost by _____ . In cold conditions sweating _____ .

Cold day: skin retains heat and becomes warmer

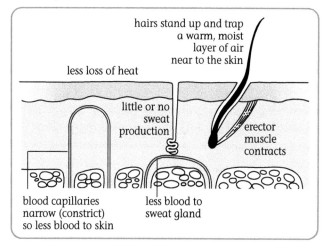

1 Blood vessels in the skin become narrower (**constrict**) so less blood is brought to the skin to be cooled. Therefore, heat radiation does not occur.
2 The amount of sweat production decreases so less heat is lost by evaporation of water.
3 The erector muscles contract so the hairs stand on end ('goose pimples'). So a lot of moist air is trapped near the skin and this reduces sweating.

Advantages of endothermy

- **Ectothermic animals**: fish, amphibians and reptiles are dependent on their surroundings.
- **Endothermic animals**: birds and mammals are independent of their surroundings.

1 Chemical reactions, such as those involving enzymes, work best at 37 °C. If the temperature is lower, the reactions will be slower. If the temperature is too high, the enzymes may be damaged and not work properly (see page 71).
2 In the early morning, an ectothermic animal would take time to 'warm up'. It could not be immediately active to look for prey or to escape from enemies. But an endothermic animal can be active earlier to hunt for prey or to escape enemies, and so has an advantage.
3 An ectothermic animal, dependent on outside conditions, can live only in places with a fairly constant temperature during the day. However, an endothermic animal, independent of outside conditions, is able to live where the temperature varies a lot during the day.
4 A constant body temperature also allows animals such as humans to live in very hot and very cold areas of the world. In these places, we can help regulate our temperature by wearing appropriate clothing (see page 171). We also adjust our surroundings by using fans and air conditioners (see page 175).

Hot day: skin loses heat and becomes cooler

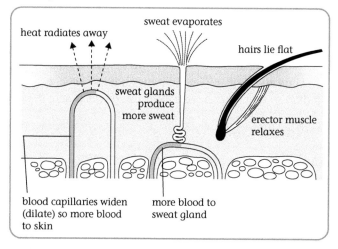

1 Blood vessels in the skin widen (**dilate**) so more blood is brought to the skin to be cooled. Heat is lost by radiation (see page 165).
2 The amount of sweat production increases and the person is cooled as the water evaporates.
3 Hairs close to the skin lie flat, so only a little air (a poor conductor) is trapped, and sweating occurs very easily.

What does it mean?

Radiation Heat radiates away from a warm skin.

Convection Warm air above the skin rises from the body and is replaced by cooler air.

Conduction Air is a poor conductor of heat, so if air is trapped by the hairs, heat loss is slower.

Evaporation Water evaporates and takes heat from the skin, so cooling it.

Question

The graph below shows the body temperature of three animals during the day. Which of **A**, **B** and **C** are a fish, a lizard or a human? Give your reasons.

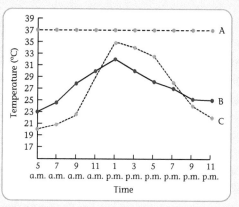

8.5 How do our eyes work?

Light rays come to our eyes from the **objects** around us. Some of these objects make their own light. We see other objects because light bounces off them. The light rays have to be **focused** (brought together) so that we can see a clear **image** (picture of the object).

Objectives

- Compare the eye and a box camera.
- Describe the structure and functions of the parts of the mammalian eye.

Practical 35

Making a pinhole camera (MM, ORR)

1 Use a hammer to make a hole in the base of a clean tin. Stick dark paper over it, and make a small pinhole in the centre of the paper.
2 Use a rubber band to hold a piece of wax paper over the open end of the tin to make a screen.
3 Wrap and secure a roll of newspaper around the tin.
4 Point the end with the hole towards a tree outside.
5 Describe the image that is formed on the screen.

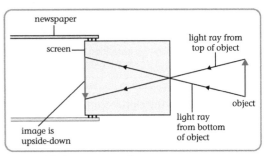

How a pinhole camera works

How is the eye like a simple box camera?

Look at the diagrams below of the eye and a simple box camera. The table underneath compares the structure and functions of the parts.

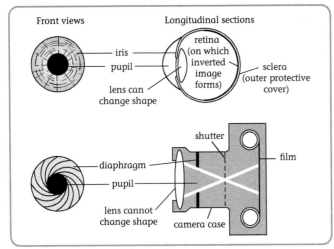

Comparison of the eye and a simple camera

Practical 36

What is a pupil reflex? (ORR, D)

1 Work with a partner. In bright light, sketch the appearance of the iris (coloured part) and the pupil (dark hole) at the front of the eye.
2 Ask your partner to close their eyes for 5 minutes. As soon as they open them, again sketch the iris and pupil. This is an automatic reflex action: the pupil reflex.

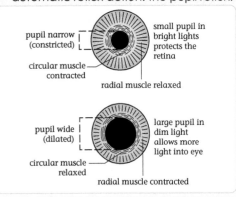

Similarities	Eye	Camera
1 Outer protective case	Sclera	Camera case
2 Control of light	Pupil and iris	Pupil and diaphragm
3 Convex lens	Eye lens	Camera lens
4 Formation of image	Inverted image	Inverted image
5 Light-sensitive layer	Retina	Photographic film

Differences	Eye	Camera
1 Structure	Living	Non-living
2 Humours	Aqueous and vitreous humours	No humours
3 Focusing	Lens changes shape	Lens cannot change
4 Image	Only 'seen' in the brain	Developed on film

Did you know?

- Predators, e.g. owls and cats, have eyes at the front of their heads. This gives them 3D vision.
- Prey, e.g. rats and mice, have eyes on the sides of their heads. Each eye sees in one direction.

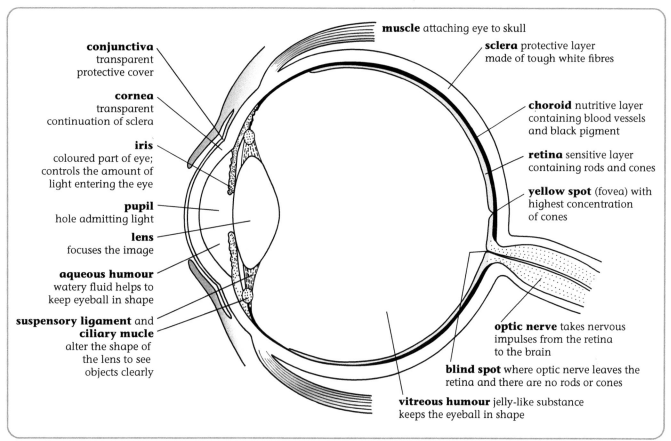

conjunctiva transparent protective cover

cornea transparent continuation of sclera

iris coloured part of eye; controls the amount of light entering the eye

pupil hole admitting light

lens focuses the image

aqueous humour watery fluid helps to keep eyeball in shape

suspensory ligament and **ciliary mucle** alter the shape of the lens to see objects clearly

muscle attaching eye to skull

sclera protective layer made of tough white fibres

choroid nutritive layer containing blood vessels and black pigment

retina sensitive layer containing rods and cones

yellow spot (fovea) with highest concentration of cones

optic nerve takes nervous impulses from the retina to the brain

blind spot where optic nerve leaves the retina and there are no rods or cones

vitreous humour jelly-like substance keeps the eyeball in shape

Section of the mammalian eye

How do we see?

Light enters through the pupil and focuses on the retina. As in photosynthesis and photography, the light causes a chemical reaction: a **photochemical reaction** (page 52). The sensory cells, **rods** and **cones**, set up nervous impulses sent by sensory nerve fibres into the **optic nerve** to the sight centre of the brain. Here the upside-down (**inverted**) image is interpreted as the right way up and we 'see' the object.

The **yellow spot** (fovea) has the most cones: this is where we see the clearest. The **blind spot** has no rods or cones, only nerve fibres, and we cannot see an image if it falls there.

Questions

1 Where exactly are the following and why are they each important? (a) The pupil and iris, (b) the sclera and retina, (c) the rods and cones, (d) the yellow spot and the blind spot.
2 Compare the structure and functioning of the eye and a simple camera.
3 Suggest four ways in which a person may become blind.

Key ideas

Use these words to fill in the spaces as you write the sentences in your Exercise book.

case   **light**   **sclera**   **retina**   **shape**   **film**   **lens**   **position**   **inverted**

A box camera has an outer protective _____ and light-sensitive _____ . In the eye, these functions are carried out by the _____ and the _____ . In the camera the _____ changes in _____ to focus the _____ . In the eye, the _____ changes in _____ to focus the _____ . In both cases an _____ image is formed.

8.6 Lenses and caring for our eyes

Practical 37

Investigating the properties of lenses (MM, ORR)

1 Use several lenses, as shown below. Those with shapes 1, 2 and 3 are convex lenses; 4, 5 and 6 are concave lenses.

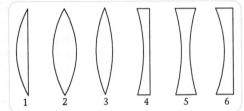

2 How do the two groups of lenses differ in appearance?
3 Look at some objects through each of the lenses in turn. Look at close objects and distant ones. Which set of lenses, convex or concave, can magnify objects?
4 Try to focus the rays of the Sun with each lens onto a piece of dark paper. Do **not** look at the Sun. What do you notice? Which set of lenses can focus the light to a point?
5 Set up the apparatus shown below.

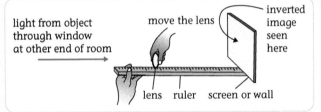

light from object through window at other end of room — move the lens — inverted image seen here — lens ruler screen or wall

6 Use a building or tree seen through a window as the object. Move the convex lens along the metre rule until you get a sharp image focused on a wall or screen. The image will be upside down (**inverted**) and smaller than the object. When the image forms, the distance between the lens and the screen is roughly the **focal length** of that lens.

The convex lens in the eye

The pupil and iris control how much light enters the eye (see page 124). The cornea and lens then focus the light onto the retina. The light rays from the object are shown in the diagram below. An inverted image of the object is made on the retina.

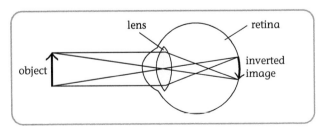

lens   retina   inverted image   object

Focusing in the eye

Objectives

● Investigate the properties of convex and concave lenses.
● Explain accommodation and what happens with loss of accommodation.
● Give advice on caring for the eyes.
● Describe short and long sight, and how they can be corrected.

What does it mean?

Lens   A clear curved piece of glass, plastic or living tissue that can bend light rays.

Convex lens   This is wide in the middle. **Conv**ex **conv**erges (brings together) light rays.

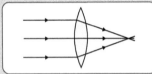

Concave lens   This is narrow ('**cav**ed in') in the middle. It diverges light rays.

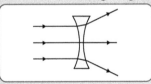

Focus   To bring light rays together. A clear image forms, e.g. on the retina.

Properties of convex and concave lenses

Convex lenses

These can be used to magnify objects, such as text. They form real images that can be seen on a screen. Convex lenses are used as magnifying glasses, in reading glasses, in cameras and to correct long sight.

Concave lenses

These always form images smaller than the object, and the images cannot be shown on a screen. Concave lenses are used as the eyepiece lens in some instruments, and to correct short sight.

Accommodation

Accommodation is the change in the shape of the **lens** that allows us to see near and distant objects clearly. The changes are brought about by the ciliary muscles and the suspensory ligaments of the eye. The changes happen automatically.

Near object

The lens has to be fat to converge the rays. The ciliary muscles contract and the suspensory ligaments relax. This allows the lens to bulge. The fatter lens converges the light rays more, so that they focus on the retina.

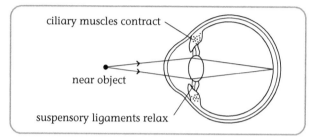

Distant object

The lens has to be thin. The suspensory ligaments contract and the ciliary muscles relax. This pulls the lens thin. The thinner lens is needed because the rays do not have to be converged much in order to focus on the retina.

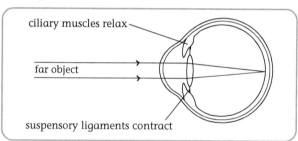

Loss of accommodation

As a person gets older, the lens may harden, and its shape cannot be changed so easily. This is called **loss of accommodation**. It means the person cannot focus on near objects, such as reading a book. They have to hold the book a longer distance away. Special 'reading glasses' can be prescribed to help overcome the problem.

Questions

1 Describe (a) a convex and (b) a concave lens.
2 Name the parts of the eye used in accommodation. What is the function of each?
3 What is the effect of loss of elasticity of the lens?
4 Describe, using diagrams, what is meant by short sight and long sight. Show how each is corrected.

Caring for our eyes

Cleanliness

The surface of the eye is washed with tears. If something gets into the eye, it should be carefully removed with a clean cloth or washed with water. Goggles should be worn when handling dangerous chemicals.

- A **stye** may develop if the base of an eyelash becomes infected. This is a painful red swelling like a boil. It should be kept clean.
- '**Pink**' or '**red**' eye is an infection of the conjunctiva. It can be caught by use of contaminated towels or face cloths. Antibiotic drops are put into the infected eye.

Cataract

This is the gradual clouding up of the lens. If it becomes too severe, the lens can be replaced by a plastic one during an operation.

Light

When light is focused by a lens, the pinpoint of light is very hot. This is why we must never look at the Sun, because ultraviolet rays can burn a circle onto the retina and cause permanent blindness.

Very bright light

- Ordinary sunglasses do not give protection against ultraviolet light, but good-quality sunglasses can block it.
- When reading or writing, sit with a light source behind you, which will be reflected from the paper to your eyes.
- Light sources such as an electric arc, used in welding, produce ultraviolet. Workers using this must wear protective goggles.
- Welders also use protective goggles to prevent sparks or particles of metal from entering the eyes, which can cause burning or irritation.

Very dim light

- In dim light the pupil is wide open, and light comes in from many angles. The eye muscles have a more difficult job to focus the objects and this can cause eyestrain, tiredness and poor vision. The result is that objects can be misjudged for shape, size and position and serious accidents can occur, for example while driving at night.
- Do not look at a television or a computer screen in a dark room. This is because there would be too much contrast between light and dark, which can produce eyestrain. It is better to have on some other low-level lighting as well.
- Correct any short sight or long sight by wearing glasses with the correct lenses (see page 128).
- Have adequate lighting in the home, especially on stairs and in kitchens, where accidents can occur.

8.6 Lenses and caring for our eyes (continued)

Short sight

For a short-sighted person:

- near objects are clearly seen
- distant objects look blurred.

In a short-sighted person, the image of a distant object falls short of the retina (see (a) below). This is because the eyeball is too long, or the lens is too fat and has brought together (**converged**) the rays of light too much.

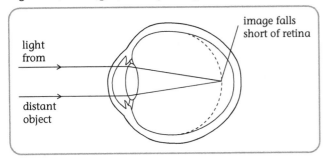

(a) Short sight

What can be done?

The image is falling short of the retina. The light rays need to be spread out more before they enter the eye. This can be done with spectacles containing diverging (**concave**) lenses.

The concave lens spreads out (diverges) the light rays so that they are now focused on the retina. The person sees a clear image.

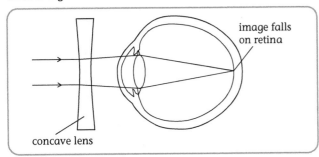

Correction of short sight with a concave lens

Long sight

For a long-sighted person:

- distant objects are clearly seen
- near objects look blurred.

In a long-sighted person, the image of a near object falls behind the retina (see (b) below). This is because the eyeball is too short, or the lens is too thin and has not converged the rays of light enough.

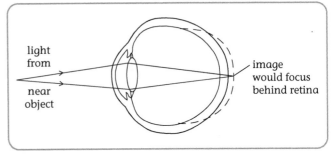

(b) Long sight

What can be done?

The image is falling behind the retina. The light rays need to be converged more before they enter the eye. This can be done with spectacles containing converging (**convex**) lenses.

The convex lens brings together (converges) the light rays so that they are now focused on the retina. The person sees a clear image.

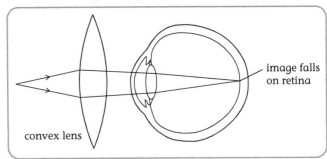

Correction of long sight with a convex lens

Key ideas

Use these words to fill in the spaces as you write the sentences in your Exercise book.

convex   **fat**   **lens**   **concave**   **thin**   **converges**   **diverges**

A _____ lens _____ light. A _____ lens _____ light. Accommodation is a change in the shape of the _____ . To see near objects clearly the _____ is made _____ . To see distant objects clearly the _____ is made _____ . Short sight is corrected using a _____ lens, and long sight is corrected with a _____ lens.

8.7 Sounds and how our ears work

Practical 38

How are sounds produced? (MM, ORR, AI)

1 Take a 30 cm plastic ruler and hold it firmly (or clamp it) at the edge of your desk so that about 20 cm overhangs.
2 With your free hand, pluck the overhanging portion of the ruler and observe what happens. Does the ruler vibrate? Can you see it vibrating?
3 Place your ear directly over it as you pluck the ruler end once more. Do you hear sound?
4 Slide another 2 cm onto the desk to make the overhang shorter and pluck the end again. Does it vibrate faster? Do you hear sound? Is the note the same as before?
5 Continue sliding the ruler onto the desk to make the overhang shorter. Observe what happens to the vibrating part of the ruler and the kind of sound produced. See also page 372.

Plucking the overhanging part of the ruler sets it vibrating. This causes vibrations of air particles to produce a sound.

- When the ruler is overhanging a long way the vibration is easily seen, although it can hardly be heard.
- As the length of the vibrating portion is reduced, the notes are heard more distinctly. As the overhang is made shorter the notes become higher and it is impossible to see the individual vibrations of the tip of the ruler.
- Low notes are said to have a low pitch (low frequency) and high notes have a high pitch (high frequency). One vibration per second is known as 1 hertz, or 1 Hz for short.
- The loudness of sounds can be increased by supplying more energy to the action that produces the sound, e.g. by hitting harder or plucking a string more vigorously.

Can sound waves be seen?

A microphone can convert sound waves into electrical signals. These can be displayed (as traces), on the screen of an oscilloscope. This makes a picture of a sound wave.

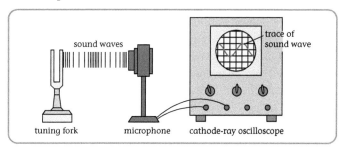

sound waves — trace of sound wave

tuning fork   microphone   cathode-ray oscilloscope

- The height of the trace shows the strength (loudness) of a sound. This is known as the **amplitude**.
- The number of peaks in a given time shows the **frequency** of the vibration.

Objectives

- Investigate loudness and pitch and their effects on humans.
- Describe the functions of the parts of the mammalian ear.

What does it mean?

Sound The result of vibration in a medium – it is set up as objects vibrate.

Loudness How strongly something vibrates determines whether the sound is loud or soft. It is measured in decibels (dB).

Frequency How quickly something vibrates determines whether the sound has high or low pitch. It is measured in hertz (Hz).

Frequency spectrum The range of high and low pitch that can be heard. Humans have a range from 20 to 20,000 Hz.

Practical 39

Investigating vibrations (PD)

Plan controlled experiments to find out how the vibrating lengths of columns of air, rubber bands or wires affect the pitch of the sounds they produce.

Question

Describe how the traces of these sounds compare in loudness and pitch.

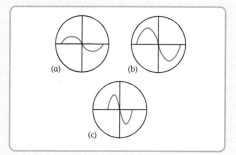

(a)   (b)

(c)

8.7 Sounds and how our ears work (continued)

How do we hear?

The ear has three parts, as shown in the diagram opposite.

Outer ear

This consists of the earflap (**pinna**) and **ear canal**. The pinna helps to catch sound waves (the **vibrations** of the air) and direct them down the ear canal towards the **eardrum**.

Middle ear

The eardrum

This is between the ear canal and the middle ear. As sound waves hit against it, the eardrum vibrates, as the surface of a drum vibrates.

The Eustachian tube

The eardrum vibrates properly only if the air pressure on each side of it is the same. Unequal air pressure (as in an aeroplane or underwater) means we become slightly deaf, as the eardrum cannot vibrate properly.

The Eustachian tube is a tube between the middle ear and the back of the throat. Air passes along here to equalize the pressure, and then we can hear well again.

The ear bones or ossicles

These are three small bones: the hammer, anvil and stirrup. The hammer is attached to the eardrum, so when the eardrum vibrates the hammer also vibrates. These vibrations are passed to the anvil and then to the stirrup. The stirrup is attached to the inner ear.

Inner ear

The inner ear is filled with fluid. It contains the **semicircular canals**, which are concerned with balance, and the **cochlea**, which is concerned with hearing.

The stirrup hits against the **oval window** and makes it vibrate. These vibrations make the fluid move, and these movements are felt in the cochlea. Opposite movements occur in the **round window** to keep the pressure constant.

Along the walls of the cochlea are tiny hairs attached to sensory cells that respond to the vibrations and change them into nerve impulses. Cells near the base of the cochlea respond to high-frequency vibrations (high pitch) and those near the tip respond to low-frequency vibrations (low pitch). They all respond more strongly to loud rather than soft sounds.

The nerve impulses pass along the **auditory nerve** to the hearing centre in the brain. This interprets the message, and so we hear.

Caring for our ears

Cleanliness

You can clean the pinna of the ear with soap and water, but you should *never* push objects into the ear canal. Wax is produced in the ear canal to clean and moisten it. This can sometimes build up and may cause temporary deafness. The wax can be removed by a nurse, who squeezes warm water into the canal.

Deafness

If some part of the ear, the auditory nerve or the brain is damaged, it can lead to deafness. With age we also lose the ability to hear sounds of some frequencies, especially high-pitched ones. Hearing aids may be needed to help correct the problem.

Noise pollution

The sounds and noises (non-musical sounds) around us can harm the ears. There are effects from loudness and pitch.

Loudness

- Loudness (sound intensity) above 120 dB can have serious consequences for humans. Loud noises at night have caused dangerous blood pressure rises in sleepers. A sudden loud noise, such as an explosion, can in extreme cases cause eardrums to rupture and even cause death due to blast pressure.
- People who work in constantly noisy places such as factories may become deaf, and their ears can become insensitive to lesser sounds. Constant loud noises can damage the sensory cells or nerve cells in the inner ear. Research carried out in Trinidad on the effects of loud sounds produced in steel bands on the hearing of pan men supports these findings.
- As far as possible, it is best to avoid loud noises, especially continuous ones, or to wear high-quality earmuffs to reduce the effects.

Pitch

- High-frequency sounds, outside the range of human hearing (ultrasound), may be dangerous. People in the path of ultrasonic waves of high intensity may become confused and depressed and may even lose control over their movements. This effect can last for days.
- Low-frequency sound, below the threshold of hearing (infrasound), is known to have serious effects on the body. Infrasound in the region of 7 Hz can cause serious internal injury, by making the internal organs vibrate.

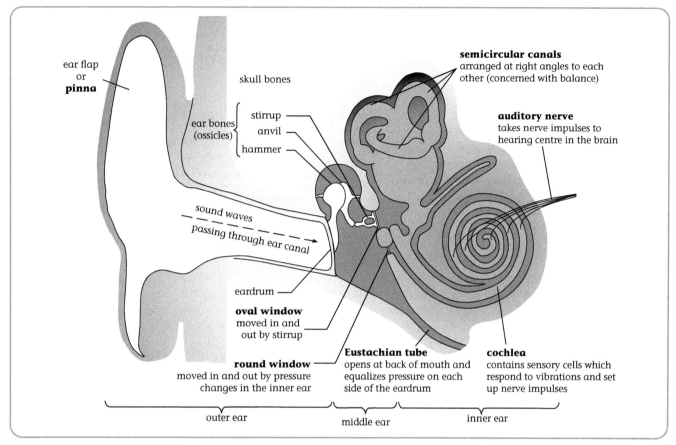

Section of the mammalian ear

How do we keep our balance?

The semicircular canals in the inner ear are responsible for our sense of balance. The canals are arranged at right angles to each other, and together they respond to movement in every direction.

As we move, fluid flows past the sensory cells in the canals, and nerve impulses are set up and sent to the brain. This is combined with information from our eyes and muscles, so we respond and keep our balance.

If you spin around quickly or are in a boat on rough water, the fluid in the canals also moves. This can make you feel dizzy, even after you have stopped moving.

Questions

1 What are the functions of (a) the ear bones, (b) the Eustachian tube, (c) the oval window and (d) the auditory nerve?
2 Describe what happens from the moment a steel drum is hit to the moment we hear it and realize it is a steel drum.
3 Describe four different ways in which a person could become deaf.
4 How may sounds be harmful?

Key ideas

Use these words to fill in the spaces as you write the sentences in your Exercise book.

auditory　　**balance**　　**pitch**　　**sensory cells**　　**hearing**　　**cochlea**　　**loudness**

_____ is measured in decibels. Frequency (in Hz) describes the _____ of a sound. The ear is responsible for our senses of _____ and of _____ . The sound vibrations pass through the ear to the _____ . The _____ in the _____ then set up nerve impulses, which are sent along the _____ nerve to the brain, and we hear.

9 Reproduction and growth

9.1 What are sexual and asexual reproduction?

Living things can **reproduce**. They can make new organisms of a similar kind. They do this in two ways:

- by the joining of gametes from two parents in **sexual reproduction**: this gives variety in the offspring
- by one organism making new ones on its own using **asexual reproduction**: all the offspring are identical.

Objectives

- Describe sexual and asexual reproduction and give examples.
- Compare the advantages and disadvantages of sexual and asexual reproduction.

Asexual reproduction

Cloning

Asexual reproduction produces offspring that have the same genes as the parent. This is called **cloning**, and the organisms are **clones**. Cell division is by **mitosis**, which produces new cells with the same numbers of identical chromosomes.

- Simple organisms, e.g. amoeba, and flowering plants often carry out asexual reproduction.
- Humans make use of this in order to produce new identical plants.
- Some animals have now been cloned, e.g. 'Dolly' the sheep, which was identical to its mother (see page 151).

Budding, e.g. yeast

The parent yeast cell produces a small bump on its surface. The nucleus of the parent cell divides into two by mitosis, with one nucleus inside the bump. The new cells can also bud, so that a chain can be formed.

parent cell   all cells identical

Binary fission, e.g. *Amoeba*

The amoeba grows to a certain size, and the nucleus divides by mitosis. Then the cytoplasm divides to make two identical offspring, which can grow and later divide. *Entamoeba*, which causes diarrhoea, reproduces in the same way.

two identical offspring

parent cell   divides

Multiple fission, e.g. *Plasmodium*

Plasmodium is a single-celled organism that causes malaria. Inside humans a *Plasmodium* organism burrows into a red blood cell and divides asexually. It makes many small cells like itself, each with a similar nucleus. The red cell splits and the new *Plasmodium* organisms can infect other cells.

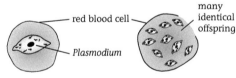

red blood cell   many identical offspring

Plasmodium

Tissue culture, e.g. orchid

A small piece, even a few cells, can be taken from the parent plant. This is grown on an artificial medium of agar, which contains all the nutrients needed for growth. Each small piece grows into a plant identical to the parent.

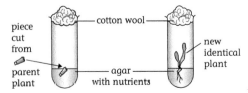

piece cut from parent plant — cotton wool — agar with nutrients — new identical plant

Grafting, e.g. rose

One plant (the stock) is used as the base; it is usually resistant to disease. A branch of a plant, e.g. with special flowers (the scion), is fitted into a cut on the stock. The plant parts grow together.

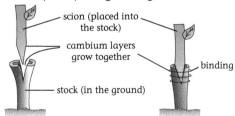

scion (placed into the stock)
cambium layers grow together
binding
stock (in the ground)

Food storage and asexual reproduction

Excess food that the plant makes is stored for future use in roots, stems, leaves, seeds and fruits.

Many of these **storage organs** are important in asexual reproduction. The store of food is used as the buds grow and develop to make new plants identical to the parent. We can also use cuttings and runners to make new plants.

Practical 41

Food tests on storage organs (MM, ORR, AI)

Use pieces of corms, bulbs, rhizomes and root tubers. Carry out food tests (see page 57) to find the nutrients present in them.

Practical 40

Asexual (vegetative) reproduction in flowering plants (D, ORR)
Draw your own examples of these plant parts. Describe how asexual reproduction occurs.

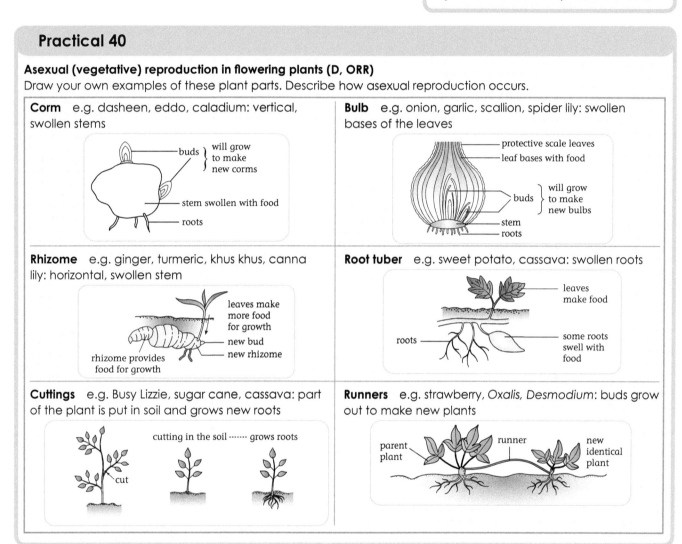

Corm   e.g. dasheen, eddo, caladium: vertical, swollen stems

- buds } will grow to make new corms
- stem swollen with food
- roots

Bulb   e.g. onion, garlic, scallion, spider lily: swollen bases of the leaves

- protective scale leaves
- leaf bases with food
- buds } will grow to make new bulbs
- stem
- roots

Rhizome   e.g. ginger, turmeric, khus khus, canna lily: horizontal, swollen stem

- leaves make more food for growth
- new bud
- new rhizome
- rhizome provides food for growth

Root tuber   e.g. sweet potato, cassava: swollen roots

- leaves make food
- roots
- some roots swell with food

Cuttings   e.g. Busy Lizzie, sugar cane, cassava: part of the plant is put in soil and grows new roots

- cut
- cutting in the soil ······ grows roots

Runners   e.g. strawberry, *Oxalis*, *Desmodium*: buds grow out to make new plants

- parent plant
- runner
- new identical plant

Key ideas

Use these words to fill in the spaces as you write the sentences in your Exercise book.

corms   **binary**   **tissue**   **budding**   **rhizomes**   **bulbs**   **runners**

Yeast reproduces asexually by _____ , and amoeba by _____ fission. _____ culture and

_____ are other examples of asexual reproduction. In _____ the leaves are swollen with

food. Swollen, vertical stems are found in _____ , and horizontal underground stems are called

_____ . Buds use the food and grow to become new plants.

Sexual reproduction	Asexual reproduction
• Two parents are usually needed.	• One parent.
• Making and joining of gametes (e.g. sperm and egg).	• No making or joining of gametes.
• Fertilized egg grows into a new organism.	• Cells divide, or outgrowths are made.
• New organisms (**offspring**) are *not* identical to the parents or to each other.	• The offspring are identical to each other and to their parent.

Sexual reproduction in humans

There are male and female organisms that look different. They make a wide variety of gametes, by meiosis, with half the usual number of chromosomes.

- The male makes the sperm.
- The female makes the eggs.

A sperm and egg join together in **fertilization** to make a fertilized egg (**zygote**) with the normal number of chromosomes. This grows into the offspring. Because the gametes are different from each other, then so are the offspring. Also see pages 150–1.

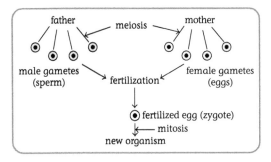

Sexual reproduction in flowering plants

In many plants the male and female gametes are made in the same flower.

- The male gamete is the pollen in the stamen.
- The female gamete is the egg in the ovary.

These gametes are formed by meiosis and have half the usual number of chromosomes. With fertilization they make a fertilized egg (zygote) with the normal number of chromosomes. The zygote grows into the offspring. The gametes are different from each other, and so are the offspring. See also page 138.

Questions

1 How are asexual and sexual reproduction different?

2 A gardener has a new plant and wants to make copies of it. Which method of reproduction should she choose? Why?

3 A company wants a new variety of rice to grow where it is cool. Which method of reproduction should it choose? Why?

What does it mean?

Mitosis Ordinary cell division involved in growth and asexual reproduction. The new cells have the same numbers and kinds of chromosomes as the parent cell.

Meiosis Reduction division. Occurs in the formation of gametes, to halve the number of chromosomes.

Gametes Sex cells, e.g. sperm and egg. Produced as part of sexual reproduction. They are all different from each other.

Fertilization The joining of gametes to restore the full number of chromosomes.

Practical 42

How does bread mould reproduce? (O, D)

1 Take a piece of bread and dampen it. Put it on a plate underneath a jar. Why?

2 Look at the bread every day. Soon you will see white threads of mould.

3 After 2 or 3 more days you will see upright threads with swollen heads (like pins). The mould is reproducing asexually, and inside the heads are **spores**. When the head breaks, the spores are shot out and grow into identical threads.

4 After a few more days you will see small, dark balls on the surface of the mould. These contain the zygotes, made by simple gametes joining together. This is sexual reproduction.

5 Look at spore cases, spores and zygotes with a hand lens and the low power of the microscope. Make labelled drawings.

Asexual reproduction	
Advantages	**Disadvantages**
• Offspring are identical, so copies can be made, e.g. of a disease-resistant or an attractive strain. • It is usually quick, and some methods, e.g. tissue culture, can produce very large numbers. • Producing offspring is less risky, as pollination, fertilization and seed dispersal are not needed. • Food resources of the parent are available for the growth of the new organism. • Rapid growth of the offspring, as no resting stage is needed because there are no seeds. • Essential, e.g. in banana, where seeds are not produced.	• As the offspring are identical, no improvement of quality or plant breeding is possible. • Special facilities may be needed to carry out tissue culture. • Lack of variation means that organisms are unable to adapt to changing conditions. • Any disease or other bad features of the parent will be automatically passed to the offspring. • Overcrowding results from many offspring being close together, or they may all die in dry weather. • Plants that are continually reproduced asexually may be less able to withstand harsh conditions.

Sexual reproduction	
Advantages	**Disadvantages**
• Offspring are varied, so it is likely that new useful strains can be developed. • Large numbers of seeds can be made. • Seeds can remain resting during a drought, and germinate only when water is available. • Seed and fruit dispersal can deposit offspring into new conditions. • New varieties may withstand difficult conditions, or produce bigger seeds or fruits.	• A useful feature in the parent plant cannot be expected to be present in all the offspring. • Each seed will have only a limited food store. • Flower production, pollination and fertilization are more risky than with asexual reproduction. • Some seeds and fruits will land in poor soil, and not grow well. • Weak plants might be produced as well as strong or useful ones.

Asexual reproduction in Busy Lizzie using a cutting

Sexual reproduction in marrow with flowers and fruits

Key ideas

Use these words to fill in the spaces as you write the sentences in your Exercise book.

identical **gametes** **asexual** **variation** **sexual** **male** **one**

In _____ reproduction there is only _____ parent and all the offspring are _____ to each other and to their parent. In _____ reproduction _____ are formed with half the usual number of chromosomes. The _____ gamete fertilizes the female gamete to make a fertilized egg. The gametes are different from each other and this causes _____ in the offspring.

9.2 How do flowering plants reproduce?

Many flowering plants can reproduce asexually (see page 133). If they only reproduced in this way they would all be the same and might be killed by drought or disease. But most plants also reproduce sexually – by making and fertilizing gametes, so that there is variation. Some of these plants may be resistant to drought or to disease.

Practical 43

What are the parts of a flower? (D, ORR)

Use a flowering shoot of Pride of Barbados.

1 Look at a flower bud. The outer covering is made of **sepals**. Draw and describe the function of sepals.

2 Look into an open flower to find the **petals**. Draw and describe the appearance and function of the petals.

3 Inside the petals you will find the **stamens**. These have a head (**anther**) and a stalk (**filament**). See if you can find yellow powder (**pollen**) on an anther. Draw and label the parts of the stamens and give their functions.

4 In the centre of the flower you will find the **carpel**. This has a base (**ovary**), stalk (**style**) and head (**stigma**). Draw and label the parts of the carpel and give their functions.

5 Near the base of the stamens you may find small bumps. These are the **nectaries**, which make nectar.

6 Cut an ovary in half along its length. Inside you will find small white **ovules**. Each of these contains a female gamete. Draw and label the ovary.

7 Find a pod on your plant. Open it up. The seeds inside were made when the ovules were fertilized.

8 Make a labelled display of all the flower parts.

9 Take an undamaged flower and cut it in half. Draw and label all the parts as shown below. (See also page 373.)

What does it mean?

Sepals Protect other parts in the bud.

Petals Often large, colourful and scented. They attract insects.

Stamen Made of the anther and filament. The anther produces pollen containing the male gamete.

Carpel Made up of the ovary, style and stigma. Ovules (containing the female gamete) are made in the ovary.

Pistil Made up of one or many carpels.

Nectary Makes sweet-tasting liquid collected by birds, insects, etc.

Receptacle The top of the flower stalk to which the other parts are connected.

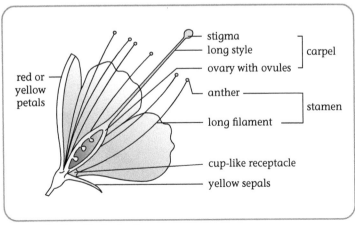

Section of Pride of Barbados flower

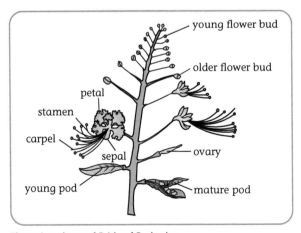

Flowering shoot of Pride of Barbados

What is pollination?

Pollination is the transfer of pollen from the anther to the stigma. Pollination is carried out:

- by animals such as insects (for example, butterflies, moths and flies) or by bats, birds or humans
- by the wind blowing the pollen.

The structure of the flowers helps us to know if they are pollinated by insects or the wind.

Questions

1 Where would you expect to find (a) dry pollen and (b) sticky pollen, and why?
2 Account for the differences in stigmas of wind- and insect-pollinated flowers.
3 A plant has brightly coloured, scented flowers. How might it be pollinated?

Insect pollination

While a bee feeds it picks up pollen from the stamens. This may then be taken to an older flower where the stamens have withered and the stigma picks up the pollen

1 Flowers are usually large and attractive.
2 Petals are large, brightly coloured and with lines on them to guide insects to the nectar.
3 There is scent and nectar to attract insects. The insects use nectar for food.
4 Anthers are usually inside the flower where an insect will touch them.
5 Pollen is larger and sticky, so it becomes attached to an insect's body.
6 Stigmas are shorter and sticky, so pollen on an insect's body will become stuck to them.

Wind pollination

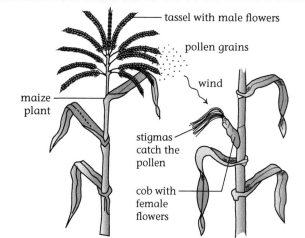

tassel with male flowers

pollen grains

wind

maize plant

stigmas catch the pollen

cob with female flowers

Pollen is shed into the wind to the stigmas

1 Flowers are usually small and green.
2 Petals are small or absent and so do not get in the way of the pollen.
3 There is no scent or nectar because there is no need to attract insects.
4 Anthers hang out of the flower and they can be shaken by the wind.
5 Pollen is very small and dry so it blows in the wind. There is a large amount of it.
6 Stigmas hang out of the flowers; they are feathery and sticky and can catch pollen.

Key ideas

Use these words to fill in the spaces as you write the sentences in your Exercise book.

carpel   **insects**   **stamen**   **ovule**   **wind**   **pollen**   **pollination**

The female gamete is inside the _____ in the ovary of the _____. The male gamete is inside the _____ that forms in the anther of the _____. During _____ the _____ is transferred from the _____ to the stigma. Large, coloured, scented flowers are likely to be pollinated by _____ , while small, green flowers are usually pollinated by the _____.

9.2 How do flowering plants reproduce? (continued)

What are self-pollination and cross-pollination?

- **Self-pollination**: the transfer of pollen from the anther to the stigma of the same flower or another flower of the same plant. Each flower, therefore, has both male and female parts. Self-pollinated plants are usually weaker and have less variation than cross-pollinated plants.

- **Cross-pollination**: the transfer of pollen from the anther of one flower to the stigma of a different flower on another plant of the same species. Anthers and stigmas of the flowers often ripen at different times to avoid self-pollination. Some flowers may contain only stamens or carpels, and so have to be cross-pollinated.

- **Advantages of cross-pollination**: the gametes come from different flowers, so there will be more variation. At least some of the plants will be healthier, stronger and better adapted to new conditions than the parents.

Objectives

- Distinguish between self- and cross-pollination.
- Identify changes that occur after fertilization, to develop seeds and fruits.
- Relate seed and fruit structures to their modes of dispersal.

Questions

1 You want to develop a wide variety of seeds. Should you self-pollinate or cross-pollinate the parent flowers? Why?
2 What features would suggest that a flower was cross-pollinated?

What happens after pollination?

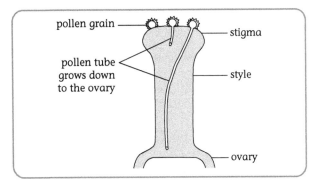

(a) After the pollen grains land on the stigma (**pollination**), small tubes grow out of the pollen grains and grow down the style and into the ovary

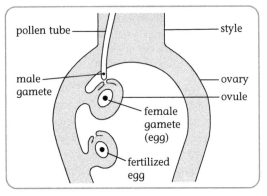

(b) Inside each pollen tube is a male gamete, and inside each ovule is an egg (female gamete). The tube grows into the ovule and the gametes fuse together (**fertilization**)

What happens after fertilization?

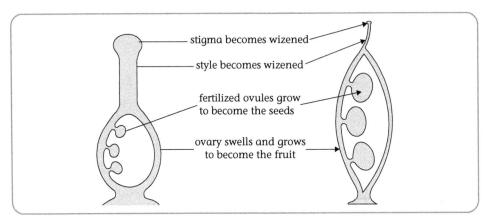

(c) The fertilized ovule becomes the seed. The ovary grows into a fruit

Seeds and fruits

There may be one seed (e.g. mango) or many seeds (e.g. tomato) inside each fruit. The cover of the seed (**testa**) may become hard or fleshy.

The fruit wall may become hard and dry (e.g. pods of Pride of Barbados) or soft and fleshy (e.g. pawpaw).

Seeds and fruits (see also page 373) are adapted to allow for distribution (**dispersal**) of the seeds. This reduces competition for light and water, prevents diseases spreading and allows seeds to get into new environments, where they might grow well.

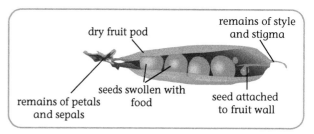

Seeds inside a pod

Different methods of dispersal

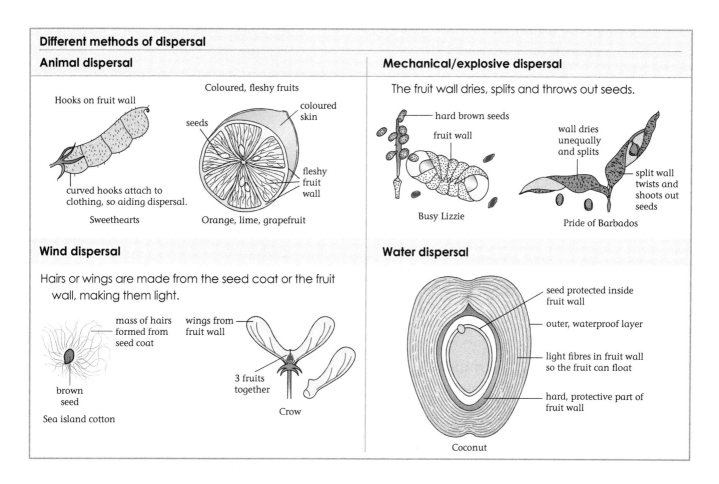

Key ideas

Use these words to fill in the spaces as you write the sentences in your Exercise book.

self-   **wind**   **cross-**   **fleshy**   **fruit**   **sticky**   **water**   **ovules**

In _____ pollination pollen stays inside the same flower. Plants that are _____ pollinated tend to be strong. After pollination, the _____ are fertilized to become seeds and the ovary becomes the _____. Small, light seeds and fruits are dispersed by the _____. The waterproof cover on the coconut helps it to be dispersed by _____. Animals and humans can disperse _____ fruits on their skin or clothing, or can eat _____ fruits to disperse the seeds.

9.3 Seeds and germination

We will now look at the structure of seeds and how they **germinate** and grow.

Practical 44

What is a seed made of? (D)

1 Soak kidney beans (or red peas) in water for an hour.
2 Examine dry and soaked seeds. Compare their sizes and appearance. Draw them. Explain the differences.
3 Find a scar on the seed. The scar shows where the seed was attached inside the fruit.
4 Remove the outer coat (**testa**). Inside it is the **embryo**. It has seed leaves (**cotyledons**) and a small root and shoot (a).
5 Repeat steps 1–4 with a maize grain. Note that the maize has only one cotyledon, but has extra food stores. Cut the maize grain through the centre of the embryo (b).
6 Make labelled drawings of the inside of the bean or pea, and the cut surface of the maize grain.

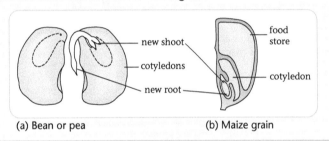

(a) Bean or pea   (b) Maize grain

What do seeds need to germinate?

You may think that seeds need water to germinate. But how could you *prove* this? You need to set up a **fair test**. You would leave some seeds damp, and others dry. All other conditions would be the same, and you would use large numbers to be sure of your results.

● The control has all the conditions (**variables**) you think are important for germination to occur.
● The experiment changes just one of the variables.

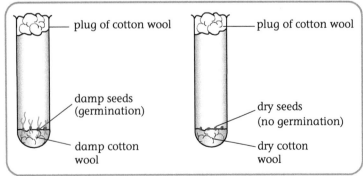

Control: all conditions   Experiment: left dry

If seeds in the experiment do not germinate, then you know water is needed for germination (see page 374).

(see page 374)

Objectives

● Examine and draw seed structure.
● Use fair tests to investigate how seeds germinate.

What does it mean?

Testa   The outer coat of a seed.
Embryo   The baby plant inside the seed.
Cotyledon   The 'seed leaf' of an embryo; it contains food for the developing plant.
Germination   When the seed coat splits and the embryo plant starts to grow out.
Seedling   The young plant; it gets food from the cotyledons and first leaves.

Questions

1 What is a fair test?
2 During germination and early growth of the seedling, how are cotyledons useful in (a) maize and (b) kidney beans?

Practical 45

What happens during germination? (PD)

Plan and design your own experiment to answer a question about germination. Make sure it is a fair test. Here are some ideas:

1 Do large seeds germinate quicker than small ones?
2 What happens if seeds are (a) planted deep in the soil and (b) planted the 'wrong way up'?
3 In which seeds do cotyledons stay below ground?
4 What happens to cotyledons above ground?
5 Do small seeds drop their cotyledons before large seeds do?

Germination of kidney bean

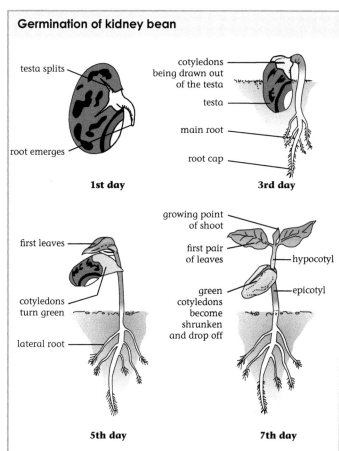

testa splits

root emerges

1st day

cotyledons being drawn out of the testa

testa

main root

root cap

3rd day

first leaves

cotyledons turn green

lateral root

5th day

growing point of shoot

first pair of leaves

hypocotyl

green cotyledons become shrunken and drop off

epicotyl

7th day

Germination of maize

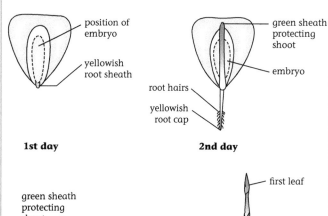

position of embryo

yellowish root sheath

1st day

green sheath protecting shoot

embryo

root hairs

yellowish root cap

2nd day

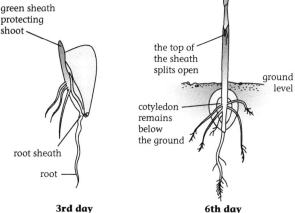

green sheath protecting shoot

first leaf

the top of the sheath splits open

ground level

cotyledon remains below the ground

root sheath

root

3rd day

6th day

In the kidney bean the cotyledons grow up above ground (**epigeal** germination). This also happens in red peas and sunflowers.

In the kidney bean:
- the new root splits through the testa in germination
- the cotyledons come out of the testa (with the new shoot protected between them)
- below ground roots grow to take in water and minerals
- the cotyledons pass on food to the new seedling and when they come above ground they turn green and carry out photosynthesis
- the shoot opens out with the first leaves.

In maize (and in broad bean and peanut) the cotyledon stays under the ground (**hypogeal** germination).

In maize:
- the new root splits through the testa in germination
- the cotyledon stays below ground
- a covering sheath protects the new shoot as it comes up through the ground
- below ground roots grow to take in water and minerals
- the cotyledon passes on food from the food stores to the new seedling
- the cotyledon and food stores are all used up
- the shoot opens out with the first leaves.

Key ideas

Use these words to fill in the spaces as you write the sentences in your Exercise book.

root   above   cotyledons   testa   water   below   oxygen   light

Germination occurs when the _____ comes through the seed coat (_____). The _____

provide food for growth. In maize the cotyledon stays _____ ground, whereas in kidney beans the

cotyledons come _____ ground. To germinate, seeds need _____ , _____ and warmth. Most

seeds do not need _____ for germination, but they do need it for continued healthy growth.

9.4 Growth in plants and animals

Growth is *not* just an increase in size. For example, a seed placed in water will get bigger, but this can be reversed if the seed dries out. Growth is an irreversible increase in size, together with the production of new protoplasm.

The main ways we measure growth are:

- increase in height, e.g. height of a stem, or human height, measured over time
- increase in mass, e.g. mass of seedlings, or of a growing child, measured over time.

Objectives

- Define terms associated with growth.
- Compare the stages in the life cycles of plants and animals.
- Record height and mass readings, and construct and analyse line graphs.
- Make and check predictions.

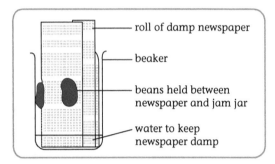

roll of damp newspaper

beaker

beans held between newspaper and jam jar

water to keep newspaper damp

What does it mean?

Growth An irreversible increase in size due to the making of new protoplasm.

Development An increase in complexity and production of tissues and organs.

Maturation Reaching the stage of development (**maturity**) when reproduction is possible. Marked by flower bud formation in plants and puberty in humans.

Reproduction Making new organisms (by asexual or sexual reproduction).

Control of growth and development

- **Flowering plants:** growth is controlled by plant hormones (**auxins**). For example, these cause the growth of stems towards light coming from one direction.
- **Humans:** the overall control is by the growth hormone from the pituitary. At puberty other pituitary hormones cause the release of eggs and sperm. They also stimulate the ovaries and testes to produce their sex hormones, causing the development of secondary sexual characteristics (see pages 146–7).

Growth and development in flowering plants	Growth and development in humans
• Occurs at root and shoot tip and leaf tips. • Leads to a branched shape of root and shoot. • Growth continues throughout life. • More branches can grow if some are cut off. • Growth recorded by measuring height or drying plants to constant mass (dry mass) and comparing them. • Growth controlled by plant hormones (auxins). • Maturation often depends on a flowering hormone produced in response to length of day. • Reproduction is asexual or sexual.	• Occurs as cells divide all over the body. • Leads to a compact shape with trunk and limbs. • Growth ceases at maturity; repair continues. • A new arm or leg cannot grow if one is cut off. • Growth recorded by measuring height, mass or length of parts at certain intervals of time. • Growth controlled by pituitary and thyroid hormones. • Maturation controlled by pituitary hormones and sex hormones from the ovaries and testes. • Reproduction is sexual.
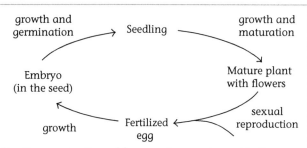	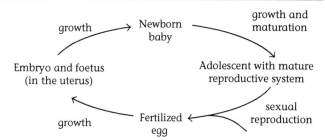
After the production of flowers, the seeds and fruits are formed. The seeds then germinate and grow to make new plants, and the life cycle is repeated	After puberty, sperm and eggs are produced, and sexual reproduction can occur. The baby is born and grows into a new individual, and the life cycle is repeated

Life cycles of flowering plants and humans

Questions

1 What is the importance of maturation for (a) flowering plants and (b) humans?
2 'Not all plants have to be mature in order to reproduce.' Explain what is meant by this statement.
3 How are the life cycles of flowering plants and humans (a) similar and (b) different?

Practical 47

Growth in height (MM, ORR, AI)

You will measure height in humans. Visit other classes (you need a range of students between 11 and 17 years of age).
1 Measure and record the height of each student in cm (without their shoes on) and ask for their age in years and months. Also record if they are a boy or girl.
2 Set up a graph, with the scale for age on the horizontal axis (make marks for every 6 months), and the height (cm) on the vertical axis.
3 Find the average height for each 6-month period.
4 Plot the points; make separate lines for boys and girls.
5 How does the growth of boys and girls differ?
6 Compare your data and graph with those on page 144.

What does it mean?

Embryo First 8 weeks in the uterus.

Foetus Growth in the uterus from 8 weeks to birth.

Childhood The first years of life; in the first year the rate of growth is fastest.

Puberty When egg and sperm production begins; it is the beginning of adolescence.

Adolescence The change from childhood to adulthood, with the development of secondary sexual characteristics.

Menstruation The beginning of 'periods' in girls, usually between 10 and 13 years.

Adulthood By about 16 or 18 years the rapid rate of growth has slowed down, and this marks the beginning of adulthood.

Menopause When a woman stops having periods, usually between 40 and 55 years. Men continue to make sperm.

9.4 Growth in plants and animals (continued)

Growth: increase in height with age

Information is shown below on the average height of males and females from birth to 18 years of age. The graph of the figures is shown on the right. You will notice that:

- the curve is steepest during the first 2 years, and especially in the first year when growth is greatest
- the growth spurt in females is around 10–12 years, and that in males is around 12–13 years
- males keep growing after females have slowed down, and males are finally, on average, taller than females.

Age	Male height (cm)	Female height (cm)
Birth	50.6	50.2
1 year	75.2	74.2
2 years	92.2	86.6
3 years	98.2	95.7
4 years	103.4	103.2
5 years	110.0	109.4
6 years	117.5	115.9
7 years	125.1	122.3
8 years	130.0	128.0
9 years	135.5	132.9
10 years	140.3	138.6
11 years	144.2	144.7
12 years	149.6	151.9
13 years	155.0	157.1
14 years	162.7	159.6
15 years	167.8	161.1
16 years	171.6	162.2
17 years	173.7	162.5
18 years	174.5	162.5

Growth: changes in proportion

Not all parts of the body grow at the same rate. For example, a baby's head is much larger in proportion to its trunk than that in an adult, and most of the increase in height in adolescence is because the legs get longer.

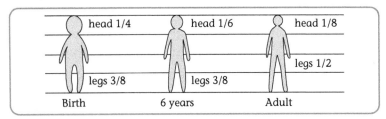

Growth: increase in mass with age

There is a general increase in mass with age. But we have more control over our mass than our height. The amount of food we eat, in relation to the amount of exercise we do, will greatly determine our mass, whereas our height is also determined by the genes we inherit.

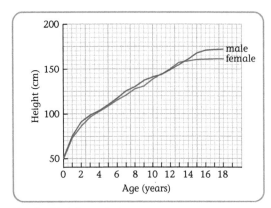

Graph of height against age

Questions

Use either your own graph of increase in height or that shown above.

1 During which year is growth greatest? (Growth rate = increase in height/time)
2 During which years are (a) boys taller than girls and (b) girls taller than boys?
3 When does the growth rate begin to taper off in (a) boys and (b) girls?

Practical 48

Increase in mass (MM, ORR, AI)

You will measure mass in humans. Include students between 11 and 17 years of age.

1 Measure and record the mass of each student to the nearest kg. They should be measured in indoor school uniform and without their shoes on. Also ask for their age in years and months, and record if they are a boy or girl.
2 Set up a graph, with the scale for age on the horizontal axis (make marks for every 6 months), and the mass (kg) on the vertical axis.
3 Find the average mass for each 6-month period.
4 Plot the points; make separate lines for boys and girls.
5 (a) How does the increase in mass of boys and girls differ? (b) How do increases in height and mass compare?

Height and mass

Tables have been prepared for the average mass of adults of different heights. People under 25 years of age should subtract half a kilogram for every year under 25.

Height (cm)	Average mass (kg)		
	Small build	Medium build	Large build
Males			
157	59	62	65
160	60	63	66
163	61	64	68
165	62	65	69
168	63	66	70
170	64	67	72
173	65	68	73
175	66	70	75
178	68	71	77
180	69	73	78
183	70	74	80
Females			
147	48	52	56
150	49	53	58
152	50	54	59
155	51	55	60
157	52	57	61
160	53	58	63
163	55	60	65
165	56	61	66
168	57	62	68
170	59	64	69
173	60	65	71

- Find your height on the left (with 2.5 cm heels). Read the mass (with indoor clothing).
- If your actual mass is more than the amount in the table then you may be too heavy.
- A person more than 20% heavier than recommended for their height is called **obese**. This is becoming an increasing problem in the Caribbean. It can be linked with an increased risk of diabetes, stroke and high blood pressure (pages 96–7). Someone who is more than 40% heavier has twice the risk of dying from a heart attack.

Did you know?

- Robert Wadlow, the tallest person, was 2.72 m tall when he died at age 22.
- By age 75 a person will be about 5 cm shorter than their tallest height.

Abnormal growth: cancer

Cancer is when the growth and division of some body cells gets out of control. A mass of cells called a **tumour** is formed. A benign tumour stays in one place and can be removed. But a malignant tumour can spread and cause secondary cancers. Early treatment is important.

Surgery removes the cancer, or radiotherapy (X-rays) or chemotherapy (drugs) are used to kill it. But these treatments have side effects.

Cancer: any of these could be an early warning sign

- A sore in the mouth or on the body that does not heal in 3 weeks.
- Any unusual bleeding, for example from the vagina, or in the urine or faeces.
- A change in the kind of faeces, which continues for more than 3 weeks.
- Any slow-growing lump or pain, for example in the breast or testes.
- Rapid loss of mass without a reason.
- Persistent cough that suddenly gets worse, especially in smokers.

Key ideas

Use these words to fill in the spaces as you write the sentences in your Exercise book.

males   **menstruation**   **females**   **maturity**   **menopause**   **puberty**

Plants and animals grow and develop. At _____ the production of pollen, eggs and sperm

begins. In humans this is called _____ and _____ begin to have their periods (_____).

The increase in height (growth spurt) and _____ occur earlier in _____ than in _____.

_____ stop making eggs at the _____ , but _____ still continue to make sperm.

9.5 Adolescence and the menstrual cycle

Puberty begins in girls from 8 to 16 years (most often 10 or 11 years) and in boys from 10 to 17 years (most often 12 or 13 years). The pituitary gland (see page 118) produces hormones that activate the ovaries (in girls) and the testes (in boys).

- The testes start to produce the male hormone **testosterone**, which in turn causes the development of the male **secondary sexual characteristics**.
- The ovaries start producing female hormones called **oestrogen** and **progesterone**, which then cause development of the female secondary sexual characteristics.
- Girls also start their monthly bleeding (periods, or **menstruation**). The cycle is roughly 28 days. It begins with the period, after which the uterus lining is built up under the control of oestrogen.

The egg is released on about day 14 (ovulation), under the control of the hormone **LH** from the pituitary. Under the control of progesterone the uterus wall is filled with blood.

If the egg is fertilized, the uterus lining develops as the placenta. If fertilization does not occur, the lining is shed as the next period.

The diagram shows what happens during the menstrual cycle to (a) the ovary, (b) hormones and (c) the uterus lining.

Objectives

- Describe the stages in the menstrual cycle.
- Identify the secondary sexual characteristics of females and males.

Stages in the menstrual cycle

Days 1–5: period – bleeding occurs as the lining of the uterus breaks down.

Days 5-14: uterus lining builds up again with lots of blood vessels.

Day 14: ovulation – egg is released.

Days 14-28: uterus wall is maintained – if fertilization does not occur, the cycle begins again with the next period.

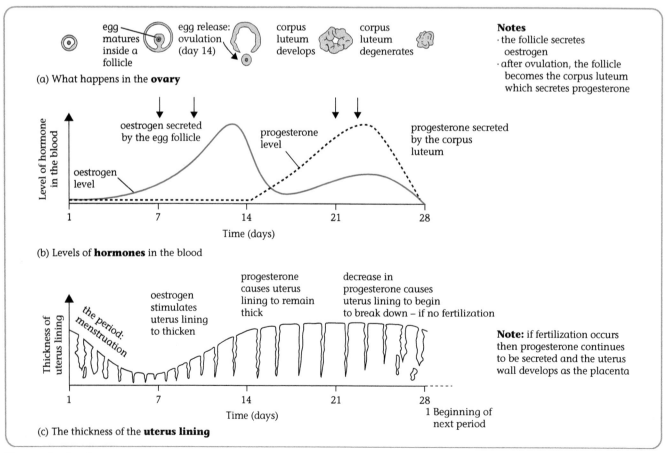

The menstrual cycle

Secondary sexual characteristics

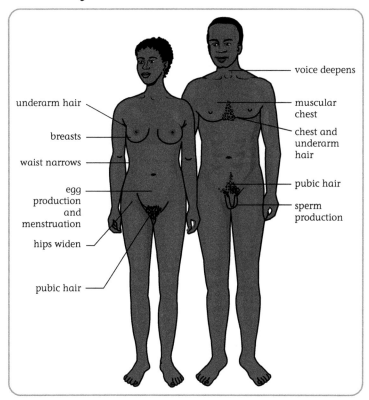

voice deepens

muscular chest

chest and underarm hair

pubic hair

sperm production

underarm hair

breasts

waist narrows

egg production and menstruation

hips widen

pubic hair

Females	Males
Puberty starts at 8 to 16 years	Puberty starts at 10 to 17 years
Cause: female hormones	Cause: male hormones
Breasts enlarge	Testes and penis enlarge
Egg production begins and periods start	Sperm production begins and ejaculation of semen
Hair grows under the arms and around the pubic area	Hair grows on face, chest, under the arms and around the pubic area
Fat is laid down under the skin	Voice 'breaks' and deepens
Female shape develops: waist narrows, hips widen	Male shape develops: chest becomes muscular

Special problems of adolescence

Emotional changes   Adolescents want to be more independent, and this can cause rebelliousness. The hormone changes of adolescence can also lead to mood swings between happiness and sadness. This is normal. But loss of sleep and appetite, and deep depression, may show a more serious problem that requires a doctor's help.

Homosexual feelings   This is the attraction between members of the same sex. But if these develop into deep physical attraction, it is **homosexuality**. During adolescence there will also be the development of **heterosexual** feelings to members of the opposite sex.

Acne   This is the development of lots of spots and pimples, as small holes in the skin become blocked. It is most common in adolescent boys, and in girls during their periods. Thorough cleaning of the skin, and use of special soap and cream, may help to reduce acne.

Teenage pregnancies   A girl can become pregnant before she sees her first period. An egg will be shed from her ovary, and if she has sexual intercourse the egg may be fertilized (page 149). A young teenager is not yet fully developed. For one thing, her bone structure may not be wide enough to allow for the easy birth of her baby. Having a baby also disrupts her schooling and can cause emotional and financial problems for many years. Serious thought must be given to this by both teenage girls *and* boys.

Key ideas

Use these words to fill in the spaces as you write the sentences in your Exercise book.

testosterone   progesterone   pituitary   oestrogen   egg   sperm   secondary

At puberty, hormones from the _____ gland activate the ovary and testes. Then the ovary makes

_____ and _____ , and the testis makes _____ . These hormones cause the development of

_____ sexual characteristics, such as _____ and _____ production.

9.6 How do we reproduce?

Humans, as with many other animals, have two sexes: female and male. The reproductive organs of each sex produce the gametes: eggs and sperm. In humans, and other mammals, the female has a uterus in which the fertilized egg develops.

The human reproductive systems are shown below. The female reproductive system is shown on the left, and the male reproductive system is shown on the right. The upper diagrams show the front views, and the lower ones show the side views.

Copy the unlabelled side-view diagrams into your Exercise book and label them. Make a table listing the female and male organs in the reproductive systems. Then add columns for the position of each organ and its functions.

Objectives

- Name and give the functions of parts of the human reproductive systems.
- Describe how fertilization occurs.

Activity

Looking at models

1 Examine models of female and male reproductive systems.
2 Try to find the organs as shown on the diagrams below.

Human reproductive systems

| Female reproductive system | Male reproductive system |

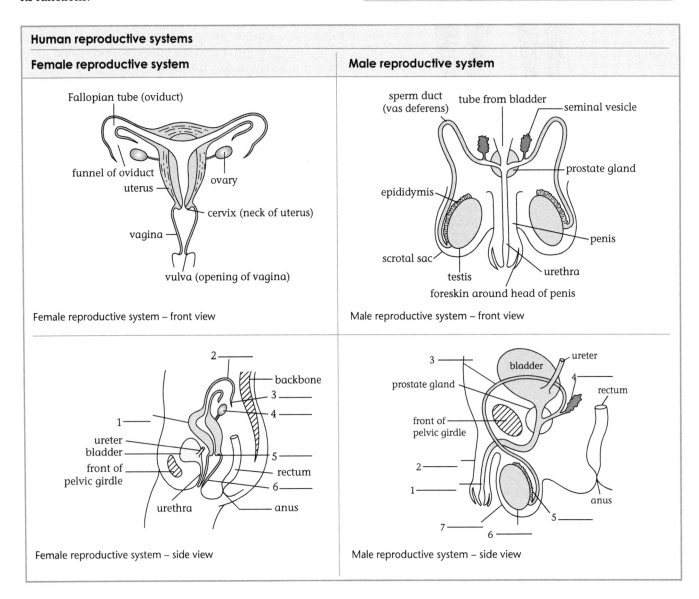

Female reproductive system – front view

Male reproductive system – front view

Female reproductive system – side view

Male reproductive system – side view

Human reproduction

Male reproductive system

The **sperm** (the male gametes) are made in the **testes**, which hang outside the body in the **scrotal sacs**. Sperm are first produced at puberty (see page 147). The release of fluid (**semen**), containing the sperm, may occur at night and take the form of 'wet dreams' during adolescence.

Sperm pass from the testes into a coiled tube, the **epididymis**, and then along the **vas deferens**. They are stored in the **seminal vesicles**, which together with the **prostate gland** make the liquid part of the **semen**.

Female reproductive system

The **eggs** (the female gametes) are produced in the **ovaries**, which are on each side of the uterus. After puberty (see pages 146–7), one egg ripens each month and is shed from the ovary. This happens on about day 14 (halfway between two periods).

The egg travels into the funnel of the **Fallopian tube** (oviduct) and passes towards the **uterus**.

Fertilization

Stimulation of the **penis** causes it to become filled with blood and erect. During sexual intercourse the penis is placed inside the **vagina**. Sexual stimulation eventually leads to **ejaculation** and the release of semen into the female. There may be pleasurable feelings of orgasm.

If intercourse takes place a few days before or after egg release, then **fertilization** can occur. The sperm swim through the uterus and into the oviducts, where fertilization usually occurs when one sperm fertilizes the egg.

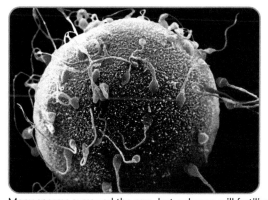

Many sperms surround the egg, but only one will fertilize it

Cancer and the reproductive systems

Cancer is the uncontrolled growth of cells that can cause death (see page 145). Early treatment can save lives.

Breasts Women should feel their breasts regularly for lumps, and have a breast screen every 5 years. Special tests will distinguish if the lumps are benign or malignant, and if treatment is needed.

Uterus Heavy periods can be reduced by the uterus wall being scraped in an operation (D and C). A Pap test can check for cancer of the cervix. This should be done every 5 years. Bad-smelling discharge or bleeding from the uterus between the periods should also be investigated.

Testes Men should make a monthly examination of their testes for any unusual lumps, heaviness or pain. These can be early signs of possible cancer, and quick treatment can save lives. This is especially important for young men.

Prostate gland In older men the prostate often enlarges. This makes urination difficult. Part of the gland can be cut away in an operation. Regular PSA tests can check the health of the prostate and could identify possible cancer at an early date, and lead to treatment.

Key ideas

Use these words to fill in the spaces as you write the sentences in your Exercise book.

urethra	testes	vagina	uterus	oviduct	vas deferens	ovary

Male gametes are formed in the _____ and female gametes in the _____ . In a male the _____ can carry both urine and sperm. In a female there is a _____ connected to the _____ . The sperm travel from the _____ along the _____ to the _____ . If an egg is present during intercourse, fertilization will most likely occur in the _____ .

9.7 How are characteristics passed on?

Characteristics

Our characteristics are what we look like and how we behave. Many of these characteristics are determined by our **genes**, which are carried on our chromosomes. The genes have a code that tells our body which chemicals to make – for example, to develop blue or brown eyes. Look at the photograph of pigeons. It shows the variety of colours, shapes and sizes of these birds. All groups of animals and plants show a similar range of **variation**.

Variation

- Some characteristics, such as height and mass, vary a lot from one person to another. You can have lots of values. These characteristics depend on your genes and also on how you live – for example, how much you eat.
- Other characteristics, such as your blood group or your eye colour, have just a few different options. These are determined just by your genes. We can find out how such characteristics are passed on from parents to children.

Genetic transfer

Human cells have 22 pairs of chromosomes, and another pair that can be XY in males, or XX in females (page 44).

- In ordinary cell division (**mitosis**), each cell divides into two parts, like the amoeba on page 132. Each chromosome splits in half, and each half becomes a whole new chromosome. So the new cells have the same number of chromosomes as the original cell. This is the kind of cell division that occurs during asexual reproduction and growth.
- When gametes are made, there is a special kind of cell division called **meiosis**. The original cell divides twice, but the chromosomes only divide once. The result is that four cells are made, each with only 22 chromosomes and either an X (in eggs), or an X or a Y (in sperm). This is the kind of cell division that occurs during sexual reproduction. When fertilization occurs, the 22 pairs plus XY or XX are reinstated (see on the right). The diagram also shows how boys and girls are formed.
- During meiosis one of each pair of chromosomes goes into a particular gamete. There is therefore a mixing up of chromosomes. Also, the parts of the chromosomes can wind around each other (**cross-over**) and so parts of one chromosome can end up on the other one.
- This means the gametes contain slightly different chromosomes and genes from each other, and also from the parents. This makes a variety of gametes and a variety of offspring (see pages 134–5), different from each other and from their parents. This is why *you* are just like you are – you have a unique mix of genes (unless you are an identical twin), so you have unique characteristics. However, even identical twins have some differences: they have different fingerprints.

Objectives

- Describe how chromosomes transfer genes to determine our characteristics.
- Describe the inheritance of tongue rolling and sickle cell disease.

Range of variation in pigeons

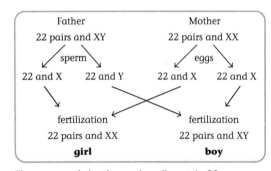

The eggs made by the mother all contain 22 chromosomes plus an X chromosome. The sperm made by the father are of two kinds.

- If a sperm containing an X chromosome fertilizes an egg, it will grow into a girl.
- If a sperm containing a Y chromosome fertilizes an egg, it will grow into a boy.

Did you know?

- There are more than 30,000 genes inside each cell of your body.
- It is the sperm, and therefore the father, that determine the sex of a baby.

How are genes inherited?

Many genes come in pairs. If both forms are present in a person, one may show its effect: it is called **dominant**. The one that does not show its effect is called **recessive**.

Tongue rolling

Tongue rolling is determined by one pair of genes. If the person has at least one T gene (for tongue rolling) they will be able to roll their tongue. The T gene is dominant. But if a person has two t genes (for non-rolling), then they cannot roll their tongue. The t gene is recessive.

Two tongue rollers (both Tt) may have children who cannot roll their tongues (tt). In this way the child shows a 'new' characteristic that is different from the parents.

Sickle cell disease

The gene that causes the disease produces damaged haemoglobin. This makes the red cells twisted when the oxygen concentration in the blood is reduced. This in turn leads to a **crisis** resulting in joint pains and fever.

The person with sickle cell disease has two recessive (SS) genes: they are called **homozygous**. A person with one normal and one sickle gene (AS) has sickle cell trait with minor problems. They are called **heterozygous** and are carriers of the sickle genes, which they can pass on.

Research using genes

Animal cloning

Clones, like 'Dolly' the sheep, are made from adult cells. Cells from humans can be cloned in the laboratory to make tissue with the same genes as the adult. These could make new tissues to transplant back into the adult to cure diseases such as Parkinson's and Alzheimer's. Cloning has also been used to clone animals such as cats and racehorses, exactly like their parent.

Genetic engineering

Genes are moved by the researcher from one organism to another. For example, the human genes that control the making of insulin have been put into bacteria. The bacteria then make human insulin, which can be collected and used.

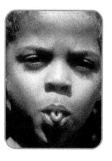

Find out who in your family can or cannot roll their tongues. Can you explain your findings?

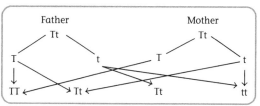

Inheritance of tongue rolling

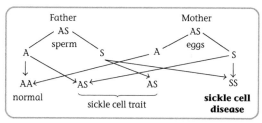

Inheritance of sickle cell disease

Questions

1 Where would (a) mitosis and (b) meiosis occur? How are they different?

2 How many chromosomes are in humans in (a) an egg, (b) a liver cell, (c) a zygote?

3 Do you think that research should be done on trying to clone humans?

4 In what ways might genetic engineering be (a) useful and (b) harmful?

Key ideas

Use these words to fill in the spaces as you write the sentences in your Exercise book.

genes **dominant** **XX** **sickle cell** **recessive** **XY** **chromosomes**

Males have 22 pairs of _____ and _____ . Females have 22 pairs of _____ and _____ . The

_____ that determine our characteristics are carried on the _____ . If the genes of a pair are

different, the one that shows its effect is called the _____ gene and the other is called _____ .

A person needs two recessive genes to have _____ disease.

9.8 What were we like before we were born?

A baby is **conceived** when a sperm fertilizes an egg. This often happens in one of the oviducts. The zygote divides into a ball of cells that becomes **implanted** in the uterus wall. It is supplied with what it needs by the placenta. Growth is about 38 weeks from conception until birth.

In order to calculate the probable date of birth we count 40 weeks from the date of the start of the last period of the mother-to-be. This is because her last period would be about 2 weeks before she became pregnant. For the first 8 weeks of pregnancy the developing baby is called an **embryo**. After this, as it begins to look more like a human, it is called a **foetus**.

Look at the pictures of the developing embryo. In the first few weeks it looks more like a fish than a human being (see (a) and (b) in the diagram below). Only bumps show where the arms and legs will be. But in a very short time the general shape of the limbs can be seen (c), and then the fingers and toes develop (d). A special machine using high-frequency sound waves can be used to show an image (ultrasound scan) of the developing foetus. The mother-to-be should be tested for the Rhesus factor (see page 93) and attend a pre-natal clinic (see page 154).

(see page 93)
(see page 154)

Objective

- Describe the development of the embryo and foetus in humans.

The signs of pregnancy

- The mother-to-be will miss her periods. As soon as she becomes pregnant, her periods stop, She can find out with a pregnancy test, or a visit the clinic.
- Her breasts may feel heavy and tender, because of hormones in her body.
- She may need to urinate more. As the uterus grows it presses on the bladder.
- She may feel sick early in the morning, because of hormones in her body.
- Her waist will become larger (before any increase in her abdomen).

Note: In early adolescence and women approaching menopause, the periods may be irregular. In this case a missed period may not indicate that the woman is pregnant. This is why she should have a pregnancy test.

Questions

1 Explain what is meant by (a) foetus, (b) embryo, (c) amnion and (d) placenta.
2 How is the umbilical cord important?

The developing embryo and foetus: (a) to (d) show different stages

The fertilized egg divides into a ball of cells, which becomes implanted in the uterus wall. This becomes the embryo, which is attached to the placenta by the umbilical cord. The embryo develops extremely rapidly. At 5 weeks it is about the size of a grain of rice, but by 12 weeks it is over 7 cm long.

At 28 days the largest, most developed organ is the heart. The limbs first develop as buds; the nervous system, eyes and ears are present by 6 weeks. The proportions of a developing embryo are very different from those of an adult human being.

Structure	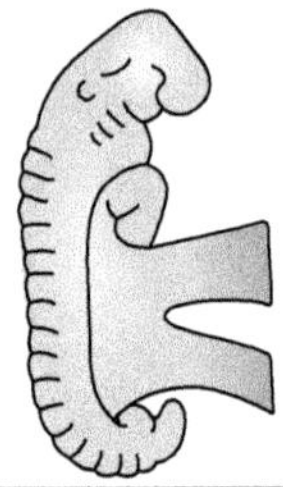	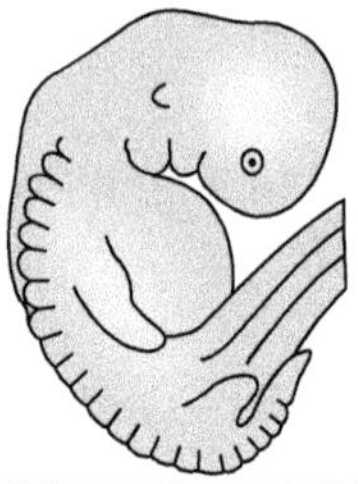	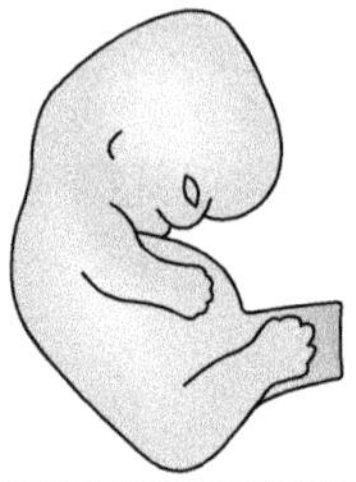	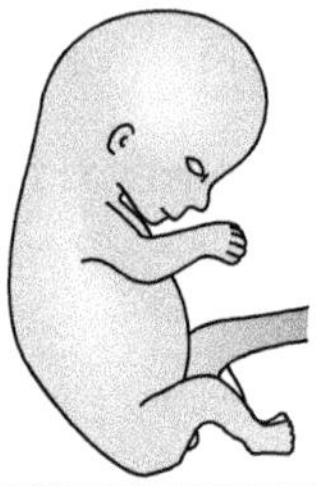
Time since last period	(a) 6 weeks	(b) 7 weeks	(c) 9 weeks	(d) 10 weeks
Actual length	0.5 cm	1.3 cm	3.0 cm	4.0 cm

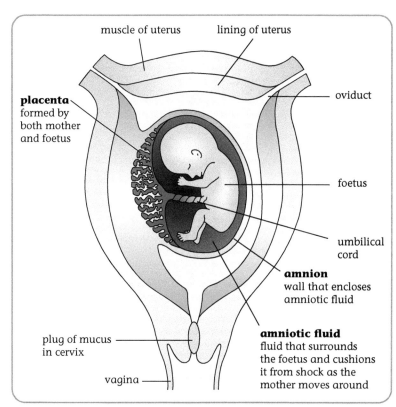

muscle of uterus   lining of uterus

placenta formed by both mother and foetus

oviduct

foetus

umbilical cord

amnion wall that encloses amniotic fluid

plug of mucus in cervix

vagina

amniotic fluid fluid that surrounds the foetus and cushions it from shock as the mother moves around

The developing foetus inside the uterus. Blood capillaries from the foetus are in close contact with the mother's blood. The foetus gets all it needs through the placenta and gets rid of its waste materials.

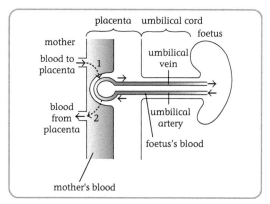

placenta   umbilical cord

foetus

mother

blood to placenta

umbilical vein

blood from placenta

umbilical artery

foetus's blood

mother's blood

1 Materials pass from the mother to the foetus. The umbilical vein takes oxygen, food and some antibodies to the foetus.
2 Materials pass from the foetus to the mother. The umbilical artery brings carbon dioxide and other waste substances from the foetus.

Did you know?

- During pregnancy a woman makes 30% more blood.
- The most babies born to one woman was 69.
- The oldest mother to give birth was over 70 years old.

Development of the embryo and foetus	Effect of development on mother-to-be
1 Conception and implantation in the uterus.	1 The mother misses her period.
2 First 3 months: embryo develops basic structures and is very sensitive to drugs, microorganisms, etc.	2 The mother urinates more, has tender breasts, morning sickness and increase in size of her waist.
3 At about 4 months, the foetus is moving actively in the uterus.	3 The mother feels the movements of the foetus in the uterus ('quickening').
4 In the fourth to eighth months, the foetus continues to grow.	4 The mother's abdomen gets larger and larger.
5 In the eighth month, the uterus is high up near the diaphragm.	5 The mother may suffer from indigestion (heartburn) and feel uncomfortable.
6 In the ninth month, the baby's head usually drops down ready for birth.	6 The mother feels a dropping sensation ('lightening') and also urinates more with pressure on the bladder.

Key ideas

Use these words to fill in the spaces as you write the sentences in your Exercise book.

umbilical   foetus   uterus   oxygen   placenta   embryo   carbon dioxide

In the first 8 weeks the developing baby is called an _____ . After this it is called a _____ . It grows in the _____ connected to the _____ by the _____ cord. It is through the cord that it gets its _____ and food, and gets rid of its _____ and other wastes.

9.9 Pre- and post-natal care

Pre-natal care

Before a woman knows she is pregnant, her baby's brain and heart have started to form. If a woman and her partner are trying for a baby, it is important they both cut down on alcohol and smoking, and have a healthy diet and exercise. The woman should also have supplements of folic acid for 3 months before and after conception, and visit a pre-natal clinic for advice. The additional folic acid can reduce the likelihood of the embryo developing spina bifida. The pre-natal clinic will check blood pressure, haemoglobin levels and monitor development.

Nutrition

It is important that the mother eats the right kinds of food (see pages 58–60). The baby relies on her for the protein, vitamins and minerals such as calcium and iron that are needed to build up its developing skeleton, blood, brain, muscles and so on. She will also need some additional carbohydrates and fats to supply her with energy.

Drugs

Drugs can easily travel from the mother to the foetus. This is especially dangerous during the first 3 months when the nervous system and other organs are developing.

The drug thalidomide, used in the 1960s, caused some babies to be born without fully formed arms and legs. Mothers who smoke (see page 82) are more likely than non-smokers to have a miscarriage, abnormalities of the placenta, and to produce smaller babies. If the mother drinks alcohol, it may also damage her baby. Even the use of aspirin has been linked with certain birth defects. The best advice is NOT to drink alcohol, smoke or use drugs (especially hard drugs; see page 101) during pregnancy.

X-rays

X-rays can cause damage to the developing tissues of the foetus. They have been largely replaced by the use of ultrasound examination, which works like an echo and from which the doctor can see the developing baby.

Diseases

Some diseases travel from the mother to the foetus. For example, if a mother has German measles in the first month of pregnancy there is a 50% chance the baby will be born deaf or with brain damage or heart disease. The mother should be vaccinated (see page 95) when younger.

If the mother suffers from syphilis, herpes or AIDS (see pages 156–7), the baby may catch the disease and become seriously ill or even die. These diseases must be treated.

Rhesus factor

The pregnant mother should be tested to see if the Rhesus factor might cause a problem (see page 93).

Objective

- Discuss the importance of pre- and post-natal care of mothers and babies.

Twins

- Identical twins are formed by division of a single fertilized egg. They have the same genes and will look the same.
- Non-identical twins grow from two separate fertilized eggs. They will be no more alike than any brothers and sisters.
- When a mother is pregnant with two or more babies, they may be smaller and may be born early (be **premature**).

Labour and birth

- The mother will receive advice in pre-natal classes and given exercises to help with the labour.
- **Labour:** this begins as the muscles in the uterus wall start to contract and begin to open the cervix (the exit from the uterus). The amnion bursts and releases the amniotic fluid (breaking of the waters). When the cervix is open, the contractions are more powerful and they push out the baby – usually head first. Then the **placenta** is also pushed out – as the 'afterbirth'.
- **Newborn baby:** the baby cries as it takes its first breath. It is still attached to the umbilical cord, and this is tied and cut so a stump is left on its abdomen. This is kept dry and later drops off – to leave the navel.
- **Immediate care:** the baby is wrapped up and given to the mother to feed.

Did you know?

- A baby's head is three-quarters of the adult size and a quarter of its body mass.
- The baby's head takes 40% of the blood circulation.
- On average, a newborn has a mass of about 3 kg, with boys heavier than girls.

Post-natal care

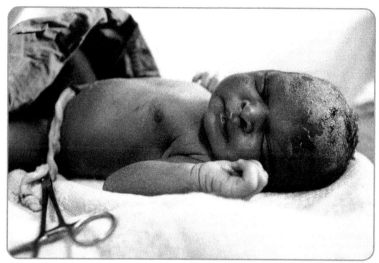

A clamp has been put on the cut end of the umbilical cord of this newborn baby. Notice how its head has been squashed as it came down the vagina.

Breast-feeding

Breast milk is the best food for a young baby. It is also a happy time for the mother and baby. During the first few days a special liquid, **colostrum**, is produced that contains antibodies from the mother. Cow's milk has a different composition and is not suitable for babies.

If a baby has to be bottle-fed on baby formula, extreme care must be taken to boil and cool the water used, and to thoroughly clean the bottle and teat. This is because gastroenteritis (diarrhoea) is easily spread. It can cause death. The baby has watery stools and may become dangerously dehydrated; it should be taken to the clinic.

The mother's milk becomes more concentrated as the baby grows. But after a few weeks, baby cereal, orange juice and vitamins can also be given.

Immunization

Babies need to be immunized (see page 95) against various diseases. This is very important for their health.

Post-natal check-up

This should take place 6 weeks after the birth. At that time both the mother and baby will be checked to see if they are in good health. These visits should be continued.

Before birth a baby:

- is kept at a constant temperature by the amniotic fluid
- receives oxygen and food from the placenta through the umbilical vein
- gets rid of carbon dioxide and other wastes through the umbilical artery.

After birth a baby:

- is wrapped up and must keep its own temperature constant
- has to breathe and feed for itself
- has to breathe, defecate and urinate for itself, to get rid of wastes.

Role of the father

Although many women bring up their children alone, the father is important – both during pregnancy and afterwards. He can help by caring for the mother and helping her to have a good diet. As she becomes larger, she will need more help in the house. Fathers may also be present at the birth of their babies. The father can also help take care of the baby after it is born. The mother should show love and understanding to the father, who may feel jealous of the attention given to the baby.

Questions

1 'Two people make a baby, and two people are needed to look after it!' What do you think?
2 Calculate the cost of a baby (a) before birth and (b) to one year old.

Key ideas

Use these words to fill in the spaces as you write the sentences in your Exercise book.

alcohol	lungs	smoke	drugs	infection	breast

To protect her developing baby a mother should not _____ , drink _____ or use _____ . If she has a sexually transmitted _____ , she should be treated before the baby's birth. When a baby is born it cries as it uses its _____ . It is important for a baby to be fed on _____ milk.

9.10 What are sexually transmitted infections?

Sexually transmitted infections (STIs) can be passed on during any form of sexual intercourse. They may also be passed on during childbirth, and, for HIV, through infected blood or saliva. STIs vary in their seriousness. But if a person has a lifestyle that means they might pick up STIs, then it is possible they could pick up HIV and later suffer from AIDS. It is better to take precautions, such as using a condom, to help prevent infection by STIs.

Seek early treatment

1 If treatment is begun at once, an infection is much easier to treat.
2 If a person continues to have sex while infected, then the disease will be passed on to other people.
3 If certain STIs are not treated, the person may become sterile, or a mother may pass on the disease to her baby.
4 If HIV/AIDS is not treated, the person is very likely to die.

Sexually transmitted infections

Candida (thrush)

Thrush is caused by a fungus but does not harm general health. It is very common in small amounts and is controlled by acid secretions from the woman. But if she uses douches or antibiotics, or is pregnant or on the pill, then the thrush infection may increase. It causes itching around the vulva and a thick white secretion. Wearing cotton pants can help prevent infection. Medication is a pessary containing an anti-fungal drug that is pushed into the vagina. Her partner may be given a cream to apply to his penis to stop any re-infection.

Gonorrhoea

Gonorrhoea is caused by a bacterium. Symptoms occur 1 to 2 weeks from infection. In the man there is some discomfort on passing urine, and perhaps some pus. Samples are taken and tested. As there may not be visible symptoms in the woman, a man will have to ask for his sexual partner to be examined and treated. Treatment is a full course of antibiotics such as penicillin.

Syphilis

Syphilis is caused by a bacterium. Symptoms occur 9 to 90 days from infection. A hard sore or bump develops on the penis (or the anus in homosexuals) and around the vulva in women. At this stage it is very infectious, and this is when it should be treated. The sore may heal, but the infection has not been cured unless antibiotics have been given.

If the infection is ignored, it goes into a second and third stage, getting worse and worse, and can eventually lead to damage of body systems and death.

Treatment is a full course of antibiotic injections, given as early as possible.

Objectives

- Describe sexually transmitted infections (STIs), and how to avoid them.
- Link AIDS with damage done to the immune system.
- Discuss issues related to STIs, and especially to AIDS.

How can I avoid STIs?

Follow the **A**, **B**, **C** of prevention.
- **A**bstain from sexual intercourse.
- **B**e faithful to one partner who is not infected.
- **C**ondoms – use them if you do have sexual intercourse.
- Do not have casual sex.
- Seek prompt medical treatment if you think you are infected.
- Avoid contact with other people's blood (e.g. no sharing of needles for injections).

What you need to know about AIDS

- AIDS develops, sometimes after many years, after infection by the virus HIV.
- HIV weakens the immune system, so the person gets other diseases.
- About one-third of babies born to mothers with HIV are infected during pregnancy, at birth or by breast-feeding.
- Before giving birth, mothers can take anti-retroviral drugs to reduce the likelihood of infecting their babies.
- AIDS cannot yet be cured, but anti-retroviral drugs can improve the health and quality of life of people living with HIV/AIDS (PLWHA).
- HIV can be passed on in infected blood or saliva. Wash and cover any cuts.
- Touching or hugging does not pass on HIV/AIDS. Care, help and affection should be given to people with HIV/AIDS.

Herpes

Herpes is caused by a virus. Symptoms occur 4 to 7 days after infection. In both men and women there is itchiness around the sexual organs, followed by blisters and painful sores, high temperature and feeling unwell.

There is no simple treatment, although half the people do develop resistance. Otherwise anti-viral ointments can be used. This is especially important for mothers, as 40% of babies are infected during birth, and this can cause serious brain damage, blood poisoning or even death.

Acquired immune deficiency syndrome (AIDS)

AIDS is caused by the virus HIV. The virus infects white cells and so weakens the immune system, which usually helps a person fight disease (see page 95). People suffer from skin rashes, diarrhoea, weight loss, fevers and certain cancers. They can also become infected, for example with tuberculosis – which causes about one-third of total HIV/AIDS deaths.

Incubation and symptoms

Incubation is from several months to many years. This is very dangerous, because a person can infect others before knowing they have the disease. The symptoms are swelling of lymph glands all over the body, excessive tiredness and respiratory diseases.

Spread

The virus can be passed on when infected semen enters the bloodstream through breaks in the vagina, anus or mouth of the partner. It can be passed between drug users by infected needles, by blood transfusions from infected people, from infected mothers to their babies and by infected blood or saliva getting into a cut.

Treatment

Combinations (cocktails) of anti-retroviral drugs can be taken to slow the disease. But so far it cannot be cured, as the virus becomes part of the blood cells.

What can be done?

As the disease cannot be cured, it is vitally important not to become infected with HIV (see page 156). If you think you have run a risk of infection – then get tested and start treatment early.

You may also meet people who are living with HIV/AIDS. Please show care and consideration to them.

HIV/AIDS in the Caribbean

Figures from UNAIDS 2008 show that there were an estimated 230,000 people living with AIDS in the Caribbean in 2007, with some 14,000 dying of AIDS.

One high-risk group is female sex workers, with a reported rate of HIV of 9% in Jamaica and 31% in Guyana. Rates in this group have been reduced in the Dominican Republic through greater use of condoms.

Up to 12% of reported HIV infections occur by unprotected sex between men. This is the main mode of transfer in Cuba and Dominica. HIV infection was found in 20% of homosexuals in Trinidad and Tobago, 21% in Guyana and 11% in the Dominican Republic.

Activity

A survey

For your country, find out and report on the number of people with HIV/AIDS, and the treatment, services and help available to them.

Did you know?

In the Caribbean:
- AIDS is the leading cause of death for 15 to 44 year olds
- by the end of 2007, 30,000 people were receiving anti-retroviral treatment.

Worldwide, in 2007:
- there were nearly 7500 new infections a day
- 33 million people living with AIDS
- 2 million people died of AIDS.

Key ideas

Use these words to fill in the spaces as you write the sentences in your Exercise book.

antibiotics	HIV	viruses	TB	bacteria	immune	STIs

Treatment for sexually transmitted infections (_____) should be started as soon as possible.

STIs caused by _____ can be treated with _____ , but those caused by _____ are much more difficult to treat. The virus _____ gradually weakens the _____ system of a person, who may then suffer from _____ and other infections the body cannot fight against.

9.11 The need for population control

The world population is over 7 billion (7 thousand million). Each year it increases by about 80 million: that's 9000 an hour, or 150 a minute! Of the 80 million, about 65 million are in developing countries. The graph below also shows the predictions for 2050 (9 billion) and 2100 (10 billion).

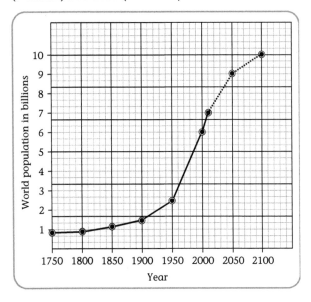

What controls population growth?

Population growth = **birth rate** minus **death rate**. Immigration (people coming into a country) and emigration (people leaving) also affect the growth rates of countries.

Medical progress

Until the 1900s there were high birth rates but also high death rates of children. But death rates have been reduced by reducing malaria, smallpox, etc., so fewer children die, and adults live longer.

Starvation and wars

Famines and wars reduce the populations of some countries.

Birth control

In some Caribbean countries, such as Barbados, there has been more use of birth control, and therefore lower birth rates. But in many countries, birth rates are still high. Parents may want large numbers of children as a sign of fertility, to help with their work, or to care for them in old age.

AIDS (see pages 156–7)

Recently, infection with HIV, and death caused by AIDS and diseases such as tuberculosis, have affected population growth. Over 95% of people with HIV/AIDS live in developing countries. In nine countries in sub-Saharan Africa, it is expected that life expectancy in 2010 will be only 47 years, and it is already less than this in some of them, such as Botswana.

Objectives

- Describe in general terms how human populations have been growing.
- Describe the effects of population growth on quality of life, world food production and mineral resources.

Did you know?

- Industrialized countries have 25% of the world's population, but use 80% of its energy and 70% of its fossil fuels.
- Developing countries have 75% of the world's population, but use only 20% of its energy and 30% of its fossil fuels.

A crowded scene in the Caribbean during a festival. What problems might population growth cause?

Questions

1 Are there areas of your country where there are problems of over- or under-population? What might be done about it?
2 Greater development requires greater energy and water resources. What might be the results, and what might be done?
3 What effects will teenage pregnancies have (a) on the people involved and (b) on the country?

Problems of over-population

It has been estimated that, if the human population kept on rising without control, within 600 years the whole world would be covered by people standing side by side.

Problems of food production

It is difficult to supply food for increasing numbers of people. Yet, in industrialized countries many people are overweight, while in other countries there are famines. If fewer people ate meat, then plant foods could feed more people.

Water supplies

Water is needed for drinking and for development. Where water is scarce, over-population makes it worse and can lead to loss of crops, starvation and perhaps future wars.

How the land is used

With increase in population, more land is needed for houses, factories, roads, etc., and so there is less for growing food.

Limited material resources

More energy is needed, and so fossil fuels are used up more quickly. This also contributes to global warming. More people also make more wastes to be disposed of.

Quality of life

Overcrowding means poor living conditions, increased problems from crime, and unemployment.

Activity

Industrialized and developing countries (AI)

Use the comparisons below, and others on these pages and elsewhere, to prepare your own table of comparison, and discuss the various points with a friend.

- Industrialized countries have over 85% of the industries, use over $350\,dm^3$ of water each day per person, eat more than 25% more protein than the recommended amount, have less than 10% of their people in farming, and many people earning more than US$25,000 per year.

- Developing countries have less than 15% of the industries, use under $50\,dm^3$ of water each day per person, eat less than half of the recommended amount of protein, have about 70% of their people in farming, and many people earning less than US$600 per year.

However, people living in different countries may have different points of view. Discuss the following ideas with some of your friends.

Population growth should be decreased	Population growth should stay as it is
1 More people means we need more food.	1 More people mean more hands to work.
2 High birth rates means lots of young children.	2 More children means a younger population.
3 We will quickly run out of resources.	3 We will find more natural resources.
4 More people means more pollution.	4 We could re-use and recycle more wastes.
5 Cities become overcrowded.	5 Many countries have under-populated areas.
6 More people means more crime/unemployment.	6 More people can create more jobs.

Key ideas

Use these numbers and words to fill in the spaces as you write the sentences in your Exercise book.

developing   **80%**   **nearly 7 billion**   **75%**   **10 billion**   **industrialized**

By the year 2010, the world's population was _____ , and the population is predicted to be about _____ by 2100. _____ of people live in _____ countries, and the rise in population is also greater in _____ countries than in _____ ones. However, the _____ countries use about _____ of the world's energy resources.

9.12 What are some birth control methods?

Couples may wish to limit the number of children they have. They can use a variety of **contraceptive** methods to prevent fertilization from occurring.

The rhythm method

This is the method approved by the Catholic Church. It depends upon the couple not having sex on the 'unsafe days' each side of **ovulation** (release of the egg).

However, it is difficult to work out the 'unsafe' days (see the box). So the method is not very reliable, especially if the woman has a menstrual cycle that varies in length. (The menstrual cycle is explained on page 146.)

There are two ways in which reliability can be improved.

- **Temperature records**: the woman records her temperature each day for 3 months. There is a drop and then a rise in temperature at ovulation, and so she can tell when, in her cycle, ovulation occurs. The 4 days before and the 3 days after this date are her 'unsafe' days.
- **Billings method**: expert advice is needed to help the woman record changes in the mucus that comes from her vagina. This helps to predict when ovulation is expected and intercourse can be avoided around this time.

Spermicides

Spermicides are a chemical method of contraception, as they kill sperm. They are inserted into the vagina shortly before intercourse (the instructions are on the packet). A fresh amount of spermicide is needed for each occasion of intercourse.

Spermicides are not very reliable when used on their own. This is because a single ejaculation contains hundreds of millions of sperm, and only one needs to escape to fertilize the egg. Spermicides should be used together with a condom or diaphragm to give physical protection.

Condom

A condom is a rubber sheath that acts as a barrier to sperm. It is put onto the erect penis before intercourse. When sperm are produced they are caught in the closed end of the condom. So sperm are prevented from getting into the vagina. When removing the condom, the open end must be held carefully so that sperm do not spill into the vagina.

The condom is fairly reliable on its own, but much more so if the woman also inserts spermicide before intercourse. A condom has the disadvantage that putting it on may interrupt the process of lovemaking. There may also be an attitude, especially among men, against its use. But the condom has the great advantage of being easily available and giving some protection against STIs (pages 156–7).

Objectives

- Describe the rhythm method.
- Understand how some artificial contraceptive methods work.

Rhythm method for a 28-day cycle		
Days		
1–9	No egg present	Safe days
10–11	Live sperm may fertilize egg	Unsafe days
12–16	Ripe egg may be released	Unsafe days
17	Egg may still be present	Unsafe days
18–28	No egg present	Safe days

If a woman has a cycle of other than 28 days, she should record the lengths for a year, and calculate:
Shortest cycle, e.g. 25 days – 18 = 7
Longest cycle, e.g. 30 days – 11 = 19
In this case, the unsafe days would be from day 7 to day 19 (counting day 1 as the first day of the period).

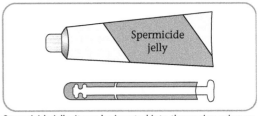

Spermicide jelly. It can be inserted into the vagina using an applicator, and the partner should also wear a condom. Or the jelly can be put onto a diaphragm before insertion.

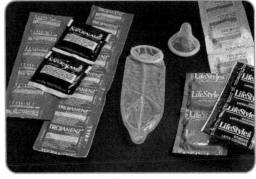

Condom. A rubber sheath that also gives some protection against STIs (see pages 156–7).

Diaphragm

This is a round rubber cap with a stiff outer edge. It acts as a physical barrier to stop sperm getting to the egg, and, used with spermicide, is quite reliable.

A nurse finds the correct size for the woman and shows her how to insert it. The surface is first covered with spermicide cream. It is then squashed and pushed into the vagina and placed over the **cervix** (neck of the uterus). The outside edge springs into place and so keeps the diaphragm securely over the cervix.

It has the advantage that it can be inserted some time before intercourse occurs. It must then be left in place for at least 6 hours after intercourse. Then it should be cleaned carefully, dried and stored. It should be reinserted with more spermicide on the next occasion.

The contraceptive pill

What they contain

The most common contraceptive pills contain types of the female hormones, oestrogen and progesterone. The pills stop the monthly release of eggs but the woman still has her periods. The pill is a very reliable contraceptive.

How they are taken

The contraceptive pills are taken at the same time of day for 21 days (starting on day 5 of the woman's menstrual cycle). As she will not be protected during the first 2 weeks, she should use an additional contraceptive method during this time. If she forgets a pill, she should take it as soon as she remembers, and also the pill for that day. If a pill is forgotten for 12 hours, then she is no longer protected for that month.

After the 21 days she takes the pills containing iron. During this time she will have her period. Then she should start the next packet of pills on the fifth day of her period.

Side effects

The pills may cause nausea (feeling sick), uncomfortable breasts, spotting of blood between periods and high blood pressure in some women.

Precautions

These pills are not suitable for smokers, or for women who are breast-feeding. (Progesterone-only pills can be taken in these cases.) Contraceptive pills may not work well if the woman is vomiting, has severe diarrhoea or is taking medicines such as antibiotics. At these times the couple should use an additional contraceptive method.

A woman may be advised *not to use the pill* if there are circulatory diseases in the family, or if she has sickle-cell anaemia, jaundice or diabetes. There is also a correlation between use of the pill and cervical cancer, especially if the woman also smokes. A nurse or doctor will advise on which pills are most suitable.

If a woman is on the pill, she might take less care when having intercourse. But the pill does NOT prevent the spread of STIs, and for this reason a condom should also be used.

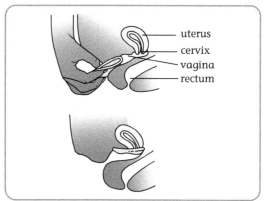

Before the diaphragm is inserted, it should be covered with spermicide cream.

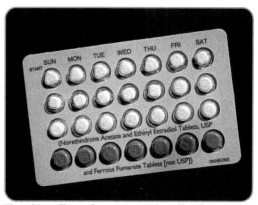

The white pills are the contraceptive pills. They contain hormones to stop the release of eggs. The first pill (at top left) is taken on the fifth day after the period starts. They are taken for 21 days. The dark pills do not contain hormones, but provide iron to replace what is lost during the period.

What does it mean?

Contraceptive   A method preventing fertilization and pregnancy.

Natural method   Does not use chemicals, barriers etc., e.g. the rhythm method.

Chemical methods   These use chemicals, such as spermicides or contraceptive pills.

Barrier methods   Prevent sperm and egg from meeting, e.g. condom and diaphragm.

Surgical methods   Tubes are cut to prevent sperm or eggs being released from the body, e.g. vasectomy and tubal ligation.

9.12 What are some birth control methods? (continued)

Intra-uterine devices

The commonest intra-uterine device (IUD) is a coil or T-shaped structure made of plastic and copper. A doctor or nurse puts it into the uterus, where it is held securely. It has a thread attached to it, which hangs out of the cervix.

Because the IUD can be kept in place, there is no preparation needed before intercourse. It is a reliable contraceptive method. It is believed that it irritates the lining of the uterus and so prevents implantation of the fertilized egg. The woman continues to ovulate and have her periods. If she wants to become pregnant, then a doctor or nurse can remove the coil.

One disadvantage is that there may be heavier periods. There is also the possibility of infections, which might cause infertility.

A similar device, but which contains progesterone, can be used. This is called an intra-uterine system (IUS). It has the advantage that periods are not so heavy. Both IUDs and IUSs can be left in place for 5 years and are 99% effective as contraceptives.

As with the contraceptive pill, an IUD or IUS does NOT give any protection against the spread of STIs. To have some protection against that problem, then a condom should be used.

Sterilization

After careful discussion, if a couple decide they do not want any more children then one of them can have a sterilization operation. Counselling is recommended before people make this decision. They have to be very sure, because the operation usually cannot be reversed.

Vasectomy

This operation, for a man, is usually not reversible. The doctor makes a small cut in the scrotal sac. He then ties the **vas deferens** in two places, and cuts out the piece between. This stops sperm getting into the semen. The male hormones are not affected, so there is no change in masculinity, orgasms etc.

A vasectomy is usually done under local anaesthetic and takes only 15 minutes. The man will feel discomfort for a few days. There will still be sperm in his semen for a few months and he should use another method of contraception during this time. He can then be checked at a clinic to see that he is no longer releasing sperm.

Tubal ligation

This is for the woman. The operation is done under general anaesthetic and takes about 20 minutes. A small cut is made in the abdominal wall and the surgeon seals or cuts off parts of the **oviducts** (Fallopian tubes). As the eggs can no longer reach the uterus, they cannot be fertilized.

Hysterectomy

Under certain circumstances (for example, if a woman develops cancer of the uterus), the uterus, oviducts and ovaries will be removed. This is a hysterectomy.

Objectives

- Understand how some artificial contraceptive methods work.
- Evaluate contraceptive methods.
- Discuss issues relating to life and death.

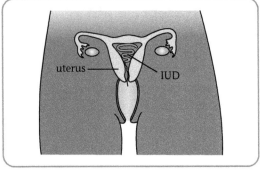

An IUD in the uterus. This cannot be felt by the woman. It is a reliable contraceptive.

Vasectomy. The vas deferens are tied and cut. Sperm no longer reach the semen.

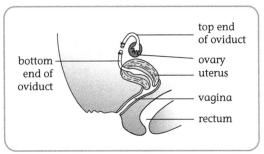

Tubal ligation. The oviducts are tied and cut. Eggs no longer reach the uterus.

Newer methods of contraception

Injectable hormones

Depo-Provera (a progesterone) can be injected under the skin and gives contraceptive protection for 12 weeks. Then it needs to be repeated. It is very reliable but it may take a woman a year to return to regular periods, after stopping.

Contraceptive under the skin

Small plastic tubes containing a progesterone are placed under the skin. These release their hormone slowly and can prevent pregnancy for 3 to 6 years. When removed, the woman's fertility is immediately restored.

A male contraceptive

This is being trialled. Injections to stop sperm production have been tested, but they had unpleasant side effects. If male contraceptives were produced, it might reduce the use of condoms – which might lead to greater spread of STIs.

'Morning-after' pill

This is a pill that can be taken in the 2 days after a woman thinks she might have become pregnant. Implanting of a fertilized egg is prevented.

Some important issues

You can discuss these issues in small groups.

Abortion

Abortion is the artificial ending of a pregnancy. People have different ideas about whether this should be allowed. What do you think?

'Test tube' babies

Genetic engineering could give much more control over the genes a baby receives. Should humans be doing this?

When does a person die?

In the photo on the right a person is attached to a kidney (dialysis) machine (see page 109). Without it, she would die – unless she had a kidney transplant. Also, a person in a coma can be kept alive just by machines. Should the machines be switched off, and who decides?

Average number of pregnancies for 100 couples using the method for 1 year	
No contraceptive method	90
Spermicide alone	25
Rhythm method	20
Condom alone	15
Diaphragm alone	15
Diaphragm with spermicide	4
Condom with spermicide	2
IUD	1–2
IUS	1
Contraceptive pill	less than 1

Questions

1 For each contraceptive method in the table above, say how pregnancy is prevented.

2 What factors would a person consider when deciding which method to use?

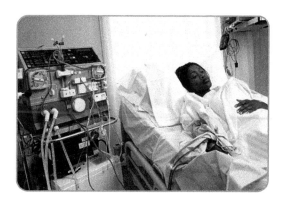

Key ideas

Use these words to fill in the spaces as you write the sentences in your Exercise book.

condom   contraceptive pill   rhythm   vasectomy   spermicide   diaphragm

A natural method of birth control is the _____ method. Barrier methods use a _____ or a _____ , and they are more reliable if a _____ is also used. Two chemical methods use _____ cream or jelly, and the _____ . The _____ contains hormones that prevent ovulation.

A surgical method is having a _____ , which is when the vas deferens are cut.

10 Temperature control and ventilation

10.1 How is heat transferred?

Heat energy can be transferred as the particles vibrate more quickly (in solids) – **conduction** – or move around more quickly (in liquids and gases) – **convection**. Heat energy can also be transferred directly as special waves through empty space without the need for particles – **radiation**.

Conduction

If we leave a metal spoon in a hot cup of tea, we soon notice that the whole spoon becomes hot. Why? The particles of metal in contact with the liquid become hot: they vibrate more quickly. Metal is a good **conductor** of heat (see page 375), and so these vibrations make nearby particles also vibrate so that the whole spoon gradually heats up. This is why we use metal for making cooking pans (see page 266). Metals heat up quickly and pass heat on to the liquid or food in the pan.

But if we made the handles of the pan of metal we would not be able to touch it safely. We need to use materials such as wood, or a covering of plastic or rubber that are poor conductors of heat (see page 257). These are **insulators**.

Gases, such as air, are also poor conductors of heat. Particles in gases are far apart, and so they do not easily pass on the heat. A layer of air, or air trapped in materials, works as insulation against heat transfer. The temperature control, by hairs on the skin and the wearing of clothes, makes use of the same idea of air as a poor conductor of heat.

Convection

If we heat a test tube of water at the bottom, the whole liquid becomes gradually warmer and eventually boils. The flame heats the glass, and heat is transferred from the glass to the water by conduction. As the water at the bottom gets hot, its particles move further apart and it becomes less dense. This warmer water is more buoyant, so it rises in the test tube. At the same time, colder water sinks because it is more dense. This continues until all the water has been heated. This transfer of heat, by movement of particles, is called **convection**. It is the most important method of heat transfer in liquids and gases. The currents set up are **convection currents** (see pages 165 and 375).

Ocean currents

Ocean currents are convection currents in water. At the Equator the Sun warms the surface water. The water in the temperate and polar regions remains relatively cold. The warm water spreads northwards and southwards from the Equator, forming a warm surface current. The cold water becomes covered with warm water and sinks, forming a deep cold current flowing back to the Equator. The process is continually repeated.

Objective

● Describe and give examples of conduction, convection and radiation.

What does it mean?

Conduction The transfer of heat from one particle to another without the substance itself moving. Conduction occurs fastest in solids.

Convection The transfer of heat by the movement of particles of liquids and gases. Convection currents are set up.

Radiation The transfer of heat by electromagnetic waves such as infrared and microwaves. It can occur through empty space.

Practical 49

Heat insulation (PD)

A fisherman wants to build a box to store his fish in ice. He has samples of wood and polystyrene to use. Suggest how he could use small samples of the material to find which one would give the better insulation.
In your plan make sure you:
● set up a fair test
● say how measurements will be taken
● explain what the results will mean
● include a repeat of your experiment.

Questions

1 Which are the main methods of heat transfer when we cook potatoes by (a) boiling in water, (b) grilling and (c) microwaving?
2 Give examples of a good conductor and a poor conductor of heat. Explain how each one could be useful.
3 Explain the importance of convection currents in (a) water and (b) air.

Sea and land breezes

These depend on convection currents in the air.

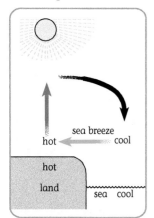 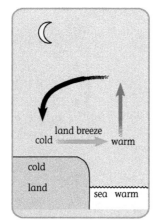

Daytime: sea breezes form   At night: land breezes form

- In the daytime the land is heated up quickly by the Sun. The air above the ground also becomes hot, and rises. The sea remains cool. Air from above the sea flows across the land to take the place of the warm land air that is rising. This makes a cool **sea breeze** in the daytime. (You can remember this by: CD = sea D = sea breeze in daytime.)
- At night, the land cools quickly, but the sea retains its warmth, so the land is cooler than the sea. Warm air rises above the sea, and cooler air flows from the land to fill its place. So a **land breeze** flowing from the land is set up.

Methods of heat transfer

Conduction	Convection	Radiation
In solids	In liquids and gases	In gases and a vacuum
Particles need to be touching	Particles need to be able to move	Particles are not necessary
Metals are good conductors of heat	Solids cannot transfer heat by convection	Transfer of heat from the Sun
Non-metals, liquids and gases are poor conductors	Convection currents in the ocean, and sea and land breezes	Transfer by rays, e.g. infrared rays and microwaves

Radiation

The Sun is about 1.5×10^8 km from Earth. There are no connecting particles, so the heat cannot be transferred by conduction or convection. Instead it comes by **radiation** of infrared waves, which are always given off by hot bodies such as the Sun. Infrared radiation is not visible to the human eye, but it warms up the Earth's atmosphere, land and oceans.

The land heats up more quickly than the sea, and also loses its heat more quickly. This is the basis of the formation of sea and land breezes (see the diagram and discussion on the left).

Heating with microwaves

Microwaves are similar to infrared waves (see page 345). They can be easily absorbed by water, and cause a rise in temperature. For this reason they are used in microwave ovens.

Microwaves easily pass through glassware or plastic containers and are then absorbed by the water in the food, so heating it up. The food cooks on the outside and the inside at the same time. This means food can be cooked more quickly and loses much less of its food value than with other cooking methods.

Microwave ovens are fitted with safety devices so they cannot be operated if the procedures are not followed.

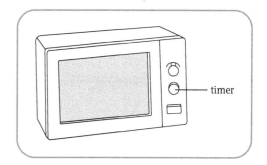
timer

Key ideas

Use these words to fill in the spaces as you write the sentences in your Exercise book.

conduction   **sea**   **metals**   **convection**   **radiation**   **land**   **air**

Heat can be transferred by _____ , _____ and _____ . _____ is a poor conductor of heat; _____ occurs most quickly in _____ . We get energy from the Sun by _____ . _____ is important in setting up ocean currents and for _____ breezes during the day and _____ breezes at night.

10.1 How is heat transferred? (continued)

Many of the appliances used at home work because they either increase or decrease heat transfer.

The importance of radiation

- **Radiant heater**: this is used in cold countries. When it is first switched on, we feel the infrared rays. When it is hot enough, the heater glows and sends out light rays as well.
- **Absorption and reflection**: white or shiny surfaces absorb fewer infrared waves and reflect more than black surfaces, which are good absorbers and poor reflectors of infrared. Black surfaces get hotter than white ones. Explain the pictures below.

We feel hot in dark clothes

Tarmac on the roads can melt in the Sun

Caribbean houses are often white

The importance of convection

We use convection to heat and to cool.

- **Heat from below**
  Use diagrams (a) and (b) below to explain how we use convection currents for heating.

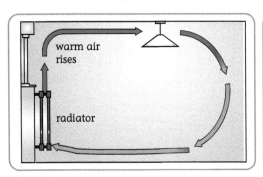

(a) Warming a room

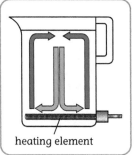

(b) Heating a kettle

- **Cool from above**
  In a refrigerator, the cold air is at the top below the cooler compartment. This cold air is dense, and so it sinks down. As the cold air sinks it pushes warmer air upwards. So a convection current is set up that cools all the food in the refrigerator.

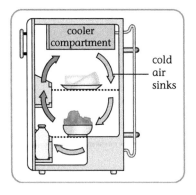

The vacuum flask

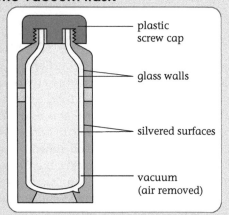

A vacuum, or thermos, flask is used to keep cold things cold, or hot things hot. Heat transfer in and out is reduced.

- Conduction is reduced by having a plastic stopper, and an inner case made of two layers of glass with a vacuum in between (these are all poor conductors).
- Convection is reduced by the inner glass walls being kept away from air currents. The vacuum also reduces convection.
- Radiation is reduced by the glass being silvered. Infrared waves are reflected back into the liquid inside the flask.

Practical 50

Thermos flasks (MM, AI)

1 Set up two similar thermos flasks, one with boiling water and the other with ice.
2 Carefully, and quickly, record the temperatures. Plan how you will record them again after 6, 12 and 24 hours.
3 Make graphs of your results and explain what has happened in each case.

Importance of conduction

● **Good conductors**
We use good conductors of heat, such as metals and alloys, for making cooking and frying pans (see page 266). They heat up quickly and pass on the heat by conduction to the water, oil or food.

● **Poor conductors (insulators)**
We use non-metals, such as plastic or wood, for handles. Polystyrene, which contains many small separated air bubbles, is also a poor conductor of heat.

Temperature control in household appliances

We need to control the temperature of some household appliances, such as electric irons and ovens. To do this we make use of a **bimetallic strip**. This is made of two metals fixed together. They are chosen so that one expands more than the other when heated (see (a) below).

The strip is part of the **thermostat** (see (b) below). The current going to the heating element passes through the bimetallic strip. The strip becomes hot and expands to bend away from the contacts. This breaks the circuit and stops the heating process. When the strip cools down it straightens again, and makes contact in the circuit. The cycle is repeated.

There is also a knob that can be turned to set the temperature that is required in the iron or oven.

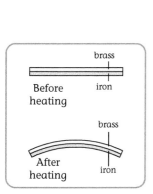

(a) A bimetallic strip

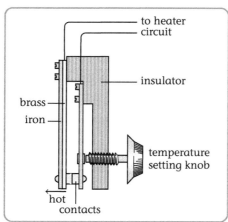

(b) A thermostat as used in, for example, an electric iron

Gas thermostat

The thermostat in a gas oven also uses differences in expansion of metals. It has a brass tube and an **invar** rod. Invar is an alloy of steel and nickel that expands very little when heated.

When the oven is lit, gas flows through the valve head to the burners. As the oven heats, the brass tube expands. This causes the invar rod to rise up, together with the valve head, which then cuts off the flow of gas. When the temperature of the oven falls, the brass contracts. This pushes down the rod and gas flows again.

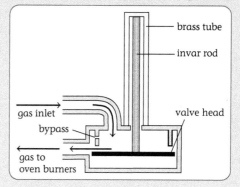

Questions

1 Explain how conduction, convection and radiation are used in named appliances.
2 Why is the heating element of an electric kettle placed close to the base?
3 Why are brass and iron used to make a bimetallic strip?
4 How does a gas thermostat differ from a thermostat used in an electric oven?

Key ideas

Use these words to fill in the spaces as you write the sentences in your Exercise book.

bimetallic   **infrared**   **expand**   **heat**   **control**   **convection**   **metals**

Radiation is the transfer of _____ , for example by _____ waves. To heat water by _____ we

supply the _____ from below. We make cooking pans from _____ because they are good

conductors of _____ . A _____ strip can be used to _____ the temperature of appliances

because the two _____ it is made of _____ different amounts when heated.

10.2 How do thermometers work?

Heat is a form of energy. It is the total kinetic energy of the motion and vibrations of particles in an object. Heat can also be the effect of electromagnetic radiation.

The **temperature** of an object is defined as the average kinetic energy of its particles.

We use thermometers to measure temperature.

- In a cold object, the particles move more slowly.
- In a hot object, the particles move more quickly.

How can we measure temperature?

Most thermometers contain a liquid in a bulb that is connected to a narrow tube, with a scale behind it.

The principles on which thermometers work are:

- as the liquid is heated, its particles move more quickly and take up more space – it expands
- liquid rises up from the bulb into the tube
- the tube is very narrow, and so the expansion of the liquid is easily seen (when cooled, the liquid contracts)
- the temperature can be read from the scale
- the liquid used depends on the temperature range that is needed.

Thermometer scale

In a mercury thermometer, the scale is made using two fixed points: the melting point of ice (0 °C) and the boiling point of water (100 °C). Then the distance between these two points is divided into 100 equal parts to make the Celsius scale.

Mercury and alcohol thermometers

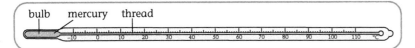

Mercury thermometer as used in the laboratory

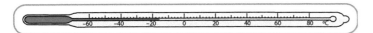

Alcohol thermometer as used in a refrigerator or a deep freeze

Practical 51

Make your own thermometer (MM, AI)

1 Choose a very narrow capillary tube and fit it into a tight-fitting rubber bung.

2 Fill a test tube to overflowing with coloured water and push in the bung. There must be no air left in the tube.

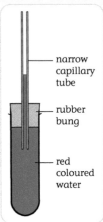

- narrow capillary tube
- rubber bung
- red coloured water

3 Find what happens when you leave the test tube in ice water, and in hot water.

4 What are some inaccuracies in your thermometer? Why is it not possible to use it to record 0 °C or 100 °C?

Mercury thermometer	Alcohol thermometer
Used to measure high temperatures, because mercury does not boil until 365 °C.	Cannot be used to measure high temperatures, because alcohol boils at 78 °C.
Cannot be used to measure very low temperatures, because mercury freezes at –39 °C.	Can be used to measure very low temperatures, because alcohol does not freeze until –117 °C.
Expensive, but can be made to be very accurate.	Cheap, but not so accurate.
Mercury is poisonous.	Small amounts are not poisonous.
Used for example as a laboratory thermometer, as it has a useful range for general laboratory work.	Used for example as a refrigerator thermometer, as it can measure low temperatures in the freezer.

Laboratory and clinical thermometers

Both of these are mercury thermometers.

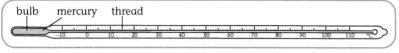

Laboratory thermometer

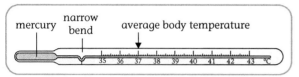

Clinical thermometer

Practical 52

Using thermometers (ORR)

1 Use a laboratory thermometer and then a clinical thermometer to take your temperature. (Wash each bulb in disinfectant before using it, and leave it under the tongue for 2 minutes.)
2 Record the two temperatures.
3 Compare and account for the accuracy of the two thermometers.

Laboratory thermometer	Clinical thermometer
Used for general laboratory measurements.	Used to measure the temperature of the human body.
Range is usually –10°C to 110°C.	Range 35°C to 43°C (normal body temperature is 37°C).
Accurate readings over a wide range.	Very accurate readings over a short range.
Markings are well spread out, so thread can be seen. The glass tube does not magnify the scale.	Thread is very narrow, so the glass is angled like a lens. The glass tube magnifies the scale so it can be read.
There is no bend or constriction to stop the mercury, so the mercury level can change.	There is a bend. When the thermometer is taken out of the mouth the mercury stays in the same position.
The laboratory thermometer does not need to be shaken before use.	The clinical thermometer should be carefully shaken before use, so the mercury goes down below the bend.

Maximum and minimum thermometers

- A **maximum** thermometer uses mercury in the capillary tube, so it will be able to record high temperatures. It also has a bend, as in a clinical thermometer. The mercury expands as the temperature rises. When the temperature falls, the mercury breaks below the bend. The thread above remains to record the highest temperature.
- A **minimum** thermometer uses alcohol, because the lowest temperatures may be well below 0°C. Inside the capillary tube is a small marker. When the temperature is low, the alcohol contracts, pulling the marker down. If the temperature increases again, the alcohol flows around the marker, so the minimum reading is still recorded.
- Some **maximum–minimum** thermometers are combined to make a U-tube containing both mercury and alcohol.

Questions

1 Examine the thermometer below. What liquid is probably inside it, and why is this used?

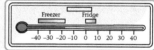

2 Why might it be dangerous to use an alcohol thermometer in the laboratory?
3 Find out what a digital thermometer is. List three ways in which it is different from a mercury thermometer. How do the differences make it useful?

Key ideas

Use these words to fill in the spaces as you write the sentences in your Exercise book.

range   contracts   alcohol   liquids   laboratory   clinical   expands

Thermometers vary in the _____ they use and the _____ of temperatures they can measure.

They work because the liquid inside _____ when it is heated, and _____ when it is cooled.

A thermometer containing _____ can measure very cold temperatures. A _____ thermometer has a larger _____ than a _____ thermometer.

10.3 How is evaporation important?

Boiling and evaporation

Both of these change a liquid to a vapour, and both need energy (latent heat of vaporization) in order to occur.

- Boiling occurs rapidly at a set point called the boiling point.
- Evaporation occurs slowly at lower temperatures.

Where does evaporation occur?

- Evaporation of water occurs from the salt water in salt ponds. Crystals of salt are left behind.
- Evaporation of water occurs from seas, rivers, plants and animals as part of the water cycle (see page 210).
- Evaporation of water occurs from damp pots used to keep milk or wine cool.
- Evaporation of liquid occurs in cooling refrigerators.
- Evaporation of water occurs from the surfaces of living things.

Is the cooling effect of evaporation important?

In order to change liquid water into water vapour, a large amount of energy is needed. This is used to separate the molecules in the liquid to make the vapour. For every 1 kg of water changed into vapour, 2300 kJ of heat energy are needed. This heat for vapour formation (in evaporation and boiling) is called the **latent** (hidden) **heat of vaporization**. The heat energy is taken from the heat source or from surfaces (e.g. skin and leaves) where evaporation occurs.

- **Transpiration** is the name given to evaporation of water in plants. Water travels up the plant in the xylem vessels and wets the surfaces of the cells, especially in the leaves. These wet surfaces are in contact with air spaces that lead out through stomata into the outside air. Water evaporates from the cell surfaces, taking the latent heat of vaporization from the leaf. In this way the plant is cooled. The vapour then diffuses out of the leaf along its concentration gradient.
- **Sweating** is the name given to the evaporation of water from the sweat in animals (see page 105). As the water evaporates, it takes the latent heat of vaporization from the skin. This cools the animal. The water vapour then diffuses away along a concentration gradient.

What affects the rate of evaporation?

In both plants and animals, the movement of the water vapour from the surfaces of leaves and skin depends upon concentration gradients. These affect evaporation.

- If the air is warm, it can take more water vapour and evaporation increases.
- If the air is dry (less humid), it can take more water vapour.
- If there is a wind (or a fan or good ventilation), then moist air will be moved away and more evaporation can occur (see also pages 87 and 376).

Objectives

- Define evaporation and latent heat of vaporization.
- Explain examples of the cooling effects of evaporation.
- Describe the effects of wind, humidity and temperature on evaporation.

Practical 53

Cooling effect due to evaporation (ORR)

1 Put a drop of methylated spirits on the back of your hand. What happens?

2 Wet both hands. Keep one still. Shake the other one, or put it near a fan. Compare the results.

3 (a) Tie a small wet piece of tissue paper around the bulb of a thermometer. Hold it still for a minute, and then record the temperature. (b) Then shake the thermometer and wet paper for a minute. Record the temperature and compare it to the first reading.

Heat control, for example in humans

- Radiation: heat radiates from hot skin.
- Evaporation: as sweat evaporates it takes heat from the skin, so cooling it.
- Convection: hot air rises away from the skin, and cool air replaces it.
- Conduction: if there is a layer of trapped air near the skin this will reduce heat loss because air is a poor conductor of heat.

Did you know?

- A mature tree can take 90 dm^3 of water from the soil each day, and transpire most of it into the air.
- Pigs do not have sweat glands. Instead they wallow in damp mud or water. The water then evaporates and cools them.

Clothing and heat transfer

Our body has various ways of keeping a constant temperature (pages 121 and 123). In addition we wear appropriate clothing that varies, for example, in:

- colour – dark colours absorb heat, light colours reflect it
- the amount of trapped air – air trapped close to the skin will make the evaporation of sweat more difficult
- the nature of the fibres – natural fibres can absorb some water, and so do not interfere with evaporation of sweat.

The tropics

Wearing light colours reflects infrared waves from the Sun. If the clothing is also made of natural fibres and is loose-fitting there will be free circulation of air over the skin, so moisture is carried away and evaporation of sweat can continue and cool the body.

Cold climates

Here clothing is chosen to reduce heat loss. Layers of woollen clothing or garments made of skins and padded with insulating materials are worn. The trapped air reduces heat loss by conduction, and also reduces evaporation.

Natural and synthetic fibres

Natural fibres are cotton, linen, wool and silk. They can absorb some moisture, so evaporation of sweat can cool the body. Synthetic fibres, such as polyester, do not absorb moisture. They become wet, stick to the skin, and slow down the evaporation of sweat.

Questions

1 List, with reasons, three factors that affect the rate of evaporation.
2 Why do (a) transpiration and (b) evaporation of sweat have a cooling effect on plants and animals?
3 Why is light-coloured, loose-fitting clothing best suited for hot conditions?
4 You are travelling to Canada for their winter. Identify, with reasons, five pieces of clothing you will take with you.

Practical 54

Does shape affect heat transfer? (PD)

Design an experiment to test the hypothesis that round shapes lose heat less quickly than long, thin ones. For example:

- Use equal volumes of hot water in differently shaped containers. Make sure it is a fair test.
- Read and record the temperature changes over time and plot the two lines (cooling curves) on a graph.

How could you modify your experiment to find the effect of different clothing?

Nowadays, human body shape is usually not important for survival. However, some body shapes may have advantages over others, depending on the environment.

The shape of Inuit people (left) makes it easy for them to conserve heat in a very cold climate, whereas the shape of Masai people (right) makes it easy for them to lose heat in a very hot climate

Key ideas

Use these words to fill in the spaces as you write the sentences in your Exercise book.

boiling point   vaporization   clothing   transpiration   evaporation   heat   cooling

_____ is the change of a liquid to a gas below the _____ of the liquid. It requires _____ energy, and this is called the latent _____ of _____ . Sweating and _____ are similar because they are both examples of _____ that results in _____ . Our type of _____ and shape can also affect temperature control.

10.4 Temperature, humidity and ventilation

What is humidity?

Humidity is the amount of water vapour in the air.

- The cooler the air, the less moisture it can contain.
- The warmer the air, the more moisture it can contain.

When air contains the maximum amount of water vapour it can hold, it is **saturated**. We compare the amount of water vapour in a sample of air to that in a similar volume of saturated air. We call this the **relative humidity** of the air, and it is a percentage.

$$\text{relative humidity (RH)} = \frac{\begin{array}{c}\text{mass of water vapour in}\\\text{a certain volume of air}\end{array}}{\begin{array}{c}\text{mass of water vapour in the}\\\text{same volume of saturated air}\end{array}} \times 100$$

How is relative humidity measured?

Relative humidity is measured using a **hygrometer**. This is made up of two thermometers. One of these has the bulb covered in wet muslin. The water in the muslin evaporates, making the temperature around the wet bulb cooler than around the dry bulb, so it gives a lower reading compared with the other one. The amount of water that evaporates from the wet bulb increases with the dryness of the air. The two temperature readings are used together with special tables to estimate the relative humidity (RH).

- The greater the temperature difference, the lower the humidity. A temperature difference of 10°C or more may be found on a dry, hot day with less than 10% RH. This is because more water can evaporate from the wet bulb.
- On a slightly humid day (around 65% RH) there may be a 5–10°C difference. This is because the air already contains some water vapour, so there is less evaporation.
- The smaller the temperature difference, the higher the humidity. On a damp, rainy day there may be little or no difference in temperature and an RH of over 95%. The air contains so much moisture that evaporation is very slow.

Why is humidity important?

- If it is hot and humid, for example during the hurricane season, it is very difficult for the body to lose water by evaporation. This means the body has difficulty in cooling itself. We feel hot and sticky with sweat.
- Humid conditions encourage bacteria, viruses and fungi. These may increase respiratory and skin diseases.
- When it is very dry, our mouth and nasal cavities also become dry, and we may also suffer from respiratory diseases.
- People usually find a relative humidity of between 35% and 65% is comfortable. In order to achieve this we can set up air currents using various methods of ventilation, as described on pages 173 and 175.

as described on pages 173 and 175.

Objectives

- Define humidity and describe how it is measured with a hygrometer.
- Define ventilation and account for its importance.
- Outline methods for natural ventilation.

Practical 55

Using a hygrometer (MM, AI)

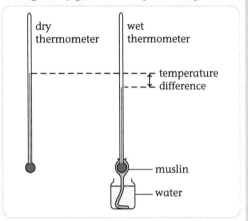

1 Use the hygrometer in two conditions:
  (a) Leave it in the sunshine.
  (b) Put it under a bell jar with an open dish of water, and leave it on the bench.
2 Record the temperature differences in both cases.
3 Which condition had high humidity and which had low humidity? Explain why.
4 Suggest improvements to the activity.

Did you know?

- Seaweed can predict the weather. If the air is dry, the seaweed also dries out and becomes hard. If the air is humid and it may rain, the seaweed will be soft.
- Folklore says that cows lie down when it is humid and about to rain, so they will have a dry place to lie. It is more likely the cows are resting after eating.

What is ventilation?

When humans and other animals are in an enclosed space they make the air 'stale'. This means that:

- the amount of oxygen is reduced, and carbon dioxide is increased, by respiration, cooking and smoking
- the temperature is increased as heat is produced by our body metabolism as we breathe and move, and, for example, by cooking, boiling water, putting on lights
- smoke, smells and particles such as dust and bacteria are added to the air because of our activities
- the humidity increases because of evaporation of sweat from the skin, and also water vapour from cooking, boiling water and drying wet clothes.

Ventilation is the continual replacement of hot, humid, stale air by cool, dryer, fresh air.

Why is ventilation important?

Ventilation helps to keep working conditions pleasant.

- Oxygen is increased and carbon dioxide is decreased. Both these changes let us work better and feel less sleepy.
- Cooler conditions make us feel more comfortable.
- Removal of smoke, other pollutants and bacteria mean that we are less likely to suffer from respiratory diseases.
- Humidity is decreased by the moving currents of air taking away the warm, humid air. This means that evaporation of sweat can occur more easily, and so cool the body.

How can we use natural ventilation?

We build houses to take advantage of natural air movement, so fresh air replaces the stale air.

- We make use of cool sea breezes. Houses can be built so they are positioned to take advantage of the breezes, and have wooden shutters, vents or windows to allow for ventilation using the flow of air (see (a) in the diagram on the right).
- We position shutters, vents and windows so that we set up and make use of convection currents. At a low level the windows, etc. allow for the intake of cool air, and at a higher level for the removal of warmer air (see (b) in the diagram on the right).

Questions

1 Define humidity and ventilation.
2 How would each of these factors affect the quality of air in an office? (a) Number of people, (b) smoking cigarettes, (c) making tea and coffee and (d) a person with flu?
3 Cattle were kept in a poorly ventilated barn for several weeks. (a) What effects might the farmer notice? (b) What should he do to improve the situation?
4 Your parents are going to build a house near the beach. What advice would you give them about using natural ventilation?

Methods of natural ventilation

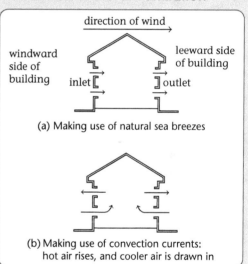

(a) Making use of natural sea breezes

(b) Making use of convection currents: hot air rises, and cooler air is drawn in

Key ideas

Use these words to fill in the spaces as you write the sentences in your Exercise book.

convection   ventilation   humidity   hygrometer   wet   breezes   evaporation

_____ is the amount of water vapour in the air. It is measured using a _____ that has two thermometers. The temperature of the _____ bulb is reduced by _____ , and the amount is determined by the _____ of the air. _____ replaces hot, stale air with cool, fresh air. Natural _____ makes use of sea _____ and the setting up of _____ currents.

10.4 Temperature, humidity and ventilation (continued)

Activity

How can ventilation be assisted?

1 Look at photographs (a) and (b), or visit old-style plantation houses. Look for features that assist natural ventilation, such as style and number of windows, shutters, spacious layout, covered verandas and balconies. Also consider the use made of plants for shading, and high sloping roofs and air vents for convection.

2 Compare these features with those of a modern block of flats (c). Record your findings.

(a) An old-style house

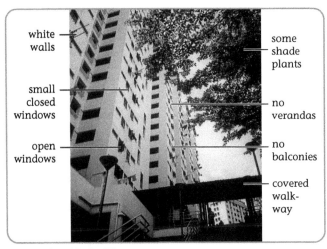

(c) A modern block of flats

Objectives

- Identify features of buildings that will assist or hinder ventilation.
- Explain the use of fans and air conditioners in assisting ventilation.

(b) Another old-style wooden house. Which features assist natural ventilation?

What are the limits of natural ventilation?

Natural ventilation is not very effective:

- if there are no sea breezes or prevailing winds, or if the houses or city blocks are tightly packed together so there is poor circulation of air
- if the outside air is warmer than the air inside the building
- if the air outside is unpleasant, with pollution by fumes from factories or car exhausts.

In the cases above, we may need to use fans to help move the air, and air conditioners and humidifiers to improve the characteristics of the air.

Questions

1 Explain why, in a well-ventilated room, sweating can lower our body temperature better than in a poorly ventilated one.

2 Explain the advantages and disadvantages of using (a) a table fan, (b) an extractor fan and (c) an air conditioner.

Artificial ventilation: fans and air conditioners

Extractor fans

The extractor fan is set high up in the room, e.g. in a kitchen. It has vanes that are turned by the wind or electricity. As the fan turns it takes out (extracts) air and so speeds up the flow of air in through the windows and other openings.

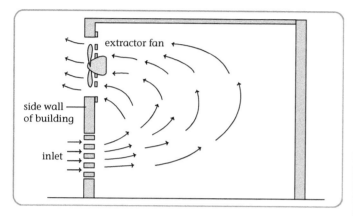

Air conditioners

Extractor fans circulate the air that comes in from outside, and table and ceiling fans circulate the air that is already in the room. But an **air conditioner** *improves* the quality of the air coming into the room.

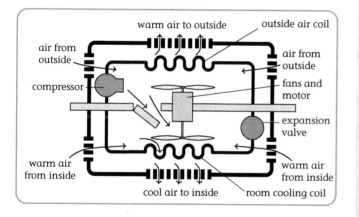

Table and ceiling fans

These have vanes that are turned by electric motors. As they turn they help ventilation by moving the air. Our skin receives moving air, and this takes away any saturated air. This assists with evaporation and therefore cooling of the body, even though no fresh air enters the room.

How do we use air conditioners?

An air conditioner is made up of the following.

- **Cooling coils** containing a liquid refrigerant similar to that in a refrigerator. The refrigerant is controlled by the compressor and expansion valve to keep the coils cool. Warm air from outside comes in and passes over these and is cooled.
- **Fans and motor.** These circulate the air, so the cooled air goes into the room, and warm air leaves to the outside. (This is why it feels warm outside when we stand close to an air conditioner.)
- **Filters.** These keep back dust and other pollutants. They are cleaned when necessary.
- **A thermostat and control knob.** These are used to set the required temperature.

Disadvantages: air conditioners are expensive to put in and to run, and they can break down. They are sometimes set to cool the air too much, making conditions unpleasant and using more electricity.

Advantages: they can cool the air, filter out dust, bacteria and other pollutants, adjust the humidity, and make currents of air around the room. They improve our working conditions.

Key ideas

Use these words to fill in the spaces as you write the sentences in your Exercise book.

natural   **hot**   **convection**   **fans**   **artificial**   **air conditioners**   **evaporation**

Old houses were often built to make use of _____ ventilation. Breezes and _____ currents are important for _____ ventilation. When the outside air is still, or very _____ , we may need _____ ventilation. For _____ ventilation we can use _____ and _____ . In a well-ventilated room, the movement of air over the body is greater and _____ is increased.

11 The terrestrial environment

11.1 How is soil formed?

Soil is formed very slowly, over many thousands of years, from underlying rock and living and dead organisms.

Look at a vertical cut (a **profile**) through soil and rock (as shown on the right). The uppermost layer of soil, **topsoil**, contains a lot of decayed remains (**humus**) and is where most animals, and plants such as crops grow: it may be less than 50 cm deep. Below this is the **subsoil**, which contains more mineral salts and supports the roots of trees. Further down still are the rocks (**bedrock**) from which the soil particles have been derived.

Rocks are broken down – **weathered** – into smaller rock pieces. These are then **eroded**, moved by water, ice, wind and gravity. Plants also carry out biological action. These processes eventually form the soil – made of mineral rock particles, the organic part of the soil (humus) and trapped air and water.

Physical weathering

Physical weathering breaks down the rocks without changing their chemical composition. Water, as rain, rivers, and lakes, wears away at rock surfaces and breaks away small pieces of rock. These rock fragments grind against each other and the rock surface. Water may also be trapped in cracks in the rocks; it expands as it freezes and breaks the rocks up still further.

The wind can blow rock fragments and break them up when they hit against rock surfaces. Sea breezes contain particles of sand and salt, which also wear away rocks. On rocky shores the waves make rocks and stones hit against each other so they break into smaller pieces and become smooth. During a hot day rocks expand, and at night they contract and cool and cracks form in them, especially in desert areas.

Chemical weathering

Rocks can be broken down into new substances by chemical reactions. If water contains acids, from dissolved gases, it may dissolve minerals in the rocks, for example calcium carbonate. The oxygen in the air, on its own or together with water, can oxidize chemical substances in the rock and so help to break the rock apart.

Thus rocks are slowly broken down, and the rock particles can be carried by water and the wind to be deposited and form the mineral part of the soil.

Biological action

Algae and lichens can grow into a rock surface by producing acids which dissolve away the rock. These organisms die and decay and form a thin layer in which other plants can grow. Burrowing animals such as earthworms and termites can eat their way into soft rocks and form channels into which air and water can run. Together with soil bacteria they help to decay the animal and plant materials to produce humus, the organic part of the soil.

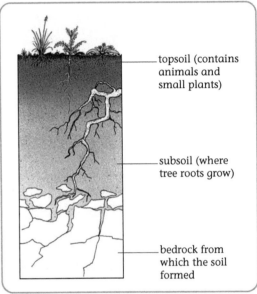

A section showing a soil and rock profile

topsoil (contains animals and small plants)

subsoil (where tree roots grow)

bedrock from which the soil formed

Activity

Looking around you

Over a period of a week look around the school grounds and on your route to school.

1 Find a tarmac or stone path that has plants growing on it. How can the plants live in these places? What effect are the plants having on the path?

2 Look at crevices in a stone or block wall. What do you find there? What effect are the plants having?

3 Look at a stone wall, rocks, or near a tap where water has been running. What is the effect of the water?

4 Find a place where there is an exposed surface down through the soil and rocks. Identify the topsoil, subsoil and underlying rocks.

Practical 56

What is soil made of? (MM, ORR, AI)

Use a spadeful of garden soil, taken from under a tree where there is a layer of decaying leaves.

1 Spread a handful of the soil onto newspaper. Use a hand lens to examine and identify the decayed material, humus and different sizes of particles.

2 Pick out some soil particles and spread a *very* thin layer on a glass slide. Examine using the low power of a microscope and describe their size and shape.

3 Put 50 cm³ of the soil into a 100 cm³ measuring cylinder and add 50 cm³ of water. Stir the contents together. Allow the soil to settle until the next day.

4 The different parts (**components**) of the soil will settle out into different layers depending upon the size and mass of their particles. This is called the **sedimentation method** for examining soils. Look at this picture and identify the components of the soil. Measure the height of each one with a ruler (a rough measure of its amount), and prepare a bar chart.

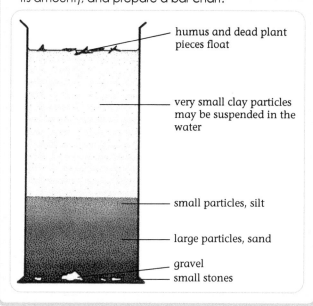

- humus and dead plant pieces float
- very small clay particles may be suspended in the water
- small particles, silt
- large particles, sand
- gravel
- small stones

Functions of different soil components

Humus

This is the decayed remains of plants and animals. Humus contains mineral salts, released by bacteria, which are needed for plant growth. Humus absorbs water, so the soil is better able to keep its water and dissolved minerals.

Clay particles

These are the smallest soil particles. They are so small and light they may stay suspended when soils are mixed with water. Clay particles hold onto water and tend to make the soil sticky (heavy) and waterlogged, without much air.

Sand particles

These are the largest particles, so they do not pack together tightly. The spaces allow water to drain through very quickly. A sandy soil may be dry, and easily blown away.

Air

Plant roots and other living things in the soil need oxygen. Good soil has spaces between the particles, which contain air. Air is also needed by bacteria, which decay materials to form humus.

Water

Soil particles are surrounded by a film of water, which is taken up by the plant roots. In sandy soils water drains through too quickly and in clay soils water tends to fill up the air spaces.

Questions

1 Describe how physical, chemical and biological factors help in the formation of the soil.

2 In the sedimentation method why do the soil particles form different layers?

3 What can you learn about soil formation by looking at different places round about you?

Key ideas

Use these words to fill in the spaces as you write the sentences in your Exercise book.

biological **acids** **physical** **humus** **algae** **chemical** **sand**

_____ weathering breaks rocks into smaller pieces, whereas _____ weathering changes the composition of the rock. _____ and lichen can grow on bare rock and produce _____ to change the rock (_____ action). Rock particles in the soil are of different sizes: _____ has larger particles than clay. Dead and decayed organisms form the _____ in the soil.

11.2 How do soils differ?

Soils differ in the amounts of the different kinds of soil particles they contain, and in the amounts of humus, air and water. You first need to identify sandy, clay and loam soils to use in your experiments.

Objectives

- Compare the characteristics of different soil types.
- Describe ways to improve soils.

Practical 57

Different kinds of soils (ORR)

1 Collect samples of soils from a variety of places. Label them **A**, **B**, **C**, etc. Copy the table below.

Soil	Where it is found	Humus	Clay	Sand	Soil type
A					
B					
C					

2 Use the sedimentation method (page 177) to find the amounts of the components in each sample of soil.

3 Complete the table and use it to identify:
- a sandy soil: lot of sand, little clay, little humus
- a clay soil: lot of clay, little sand, little humus
- a loam soil: sand, clay and humus (about half sand, one-third clay and one-sixth humus).

Practical 58

Describe different soil types (ORR)

Use your results above to collect samples of each of sandy, clay and loam soils.

1 What do the three types of soil look like? (For example, colour, whether particles are visible.)

2 What do they each feel like when they are (a) dry, (b) wet? (For example, fibrous, warm, cold, sticky, gritty.)

3 Use some of the wet soils and see if you can roll each sort out into a long 'worm'.

4 Enter your results in a table like this one.

	Sandy	Clay	Loam
Appearance			
Feel (when dry)			
Feel (when wet)			
Can it be rolled?			

5 Describe how you could distinguish between sandy, clay and loam soils on the basis of the observations you made above.

Practical 59

Measuring the humus in the soil (MM, ORR, AI)

Different groups should do this practical with different types of soil, then compare their results.

1 Measure 20 g of a loam soil into a crucible.

2 Put the soil in an oven at 40 °C for 30 minutes, or out in the Sun for 2 hours (to drive off the water).

3 Let the soil cool down, and then find the mass of dry soil and crucible (the **original mass**).

4 Heat the crucible strongly with a Bunsen flame for about 20 minutes. (This will make the humus burn and it will be driven off, see below.)

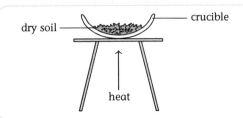

5 Let the remaining soil cool down and then find the mass of the soil and crucible.

6 Continue heating, cooling and finding the mass until the mass is constant (the **final mass**).

7 The percentage by mass of humus is then:

$$\frac{\text{original mass} - \text{final mass}}{\text{original mass}} \times 100$$

8 Work out the percentage of humus in your soil. Then put the class results into a table.

Questions

1 In Practical 59, why are (a) step 2 and (b) step 6 so important?

2 Which type of soil has the most humus?

3 Where was soil with the most humus found?

4 (a) What is humus made from? (b) Why is it important for plant growth?

Practical 60

Measuring water drainage and water retention (MM, ORR, AI)

Water drainage: the amount of water that comes out (drains out) from the soil.

Water retention: the amount of water that is kept back (retained) by the soil.

1 Collect three filter funnels and put cotton wool in the neck of each one.

2 Measure out 30 cm³ of sandy, loam and clay soils.

3 Put the samples into three funnels and rest them in the necks of measuring cylinders. Label each one.

4 Into each sample of soil gently pour 100 cm³ of water (below, and see page 377).

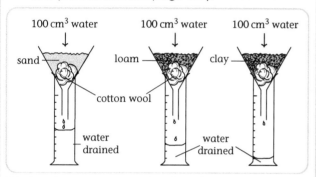

5 The water that drains through is caught in the measuring cylinders. Copy the table below and enter these 'water drained' figures in the *first* column.

	Water drained (cm³)	Water retained (cm³)
Sandy		
Loam		
Clay		

6 You added 100 cm³ of water to each soil. You know the amounts that drained through, so work out the amount of water retained by each soil and enter these figures in the *second* column of the table.

Questions

5 (a) Which soil has greatest water drainage?
(b) What effect will this have on the soil, and on the plants living in this type of soil?

6 (a) Which soil has greatest water retention?
(b) What effect will this have on the soil, and on the plants living in this type of soil?

7 (a) Which soil has 'in-between' values for water drainage and water retention?
(b) What effect will this have on the soil, and on plants living in this type of soil?

Practical 61

Measuring the air in the soil (MM, ORR, AI)

1 Put 50 cm³ of a sample of soil into a 100 cm³ measuring cylinder.

2 Add 50 cm³ of water. Stir the soil and water. Observe the bubbles of air escaping from the air spaces between the soil particles (see below).

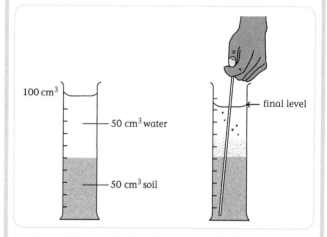

3 The original volume of soil plus water in the measuring cylinder was 100 cm³. Find the final volume of soil plus water.

How much air has escaped?
(Original volume – Final volume)

4 The percentage by volume of air is then:

$$\frac{\text{volume of air that has escaped}}{\text{original volume (50 cm}^3\text{) of soil}} \times 100$$

5 At the beginning of the practical there was air between the soil particles. What is there now in these 'air spaces'? Would this soil be suitable for plants to live in? Explain your answer.

6 Repeat this practical with the same amount of different types of soil.

Questions

8 Which soil contains (a) the most and (b) the least air?

9 Plants need both water *and* air from the soil. Which of these things is likely to be in short supply in (a) a sandy soil and (b) a clay soil? Explain your answer.

10 (a) In what ways is loam a better soil than either sandy or clay soil? (b) How do you think this will affect how well plants can grow in loam soil?

11.2 How do soils differ? (continued)

Comparisons of soil types

Based on the practicals you did on pages 178–9, you can now imagine what the particles are like in the different types of soil. The characteristics are listed below each one.

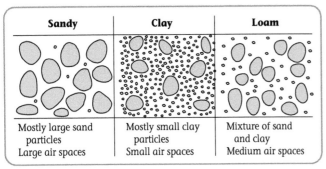

Comparisons of particles in sandy, clay and loam soils

Soils are made from the underlying rocks, and the characteristics of the rocks are important for the kind of soil that develops. For example, sandstone rock will weather to make a sandy soil. The bauxite-bearing limestone rocks in Jamaica and Guyana weather to form red soils containing aluminium and iron salts. The igneous rocks of the volcanic islands of the Eastern Caribbean contain many minerals, which are later found in the soils and give their characteristics to the soils. Soils also differ in their pH, which you can now find out.

Practical 62

Testing soils for pH (ORR)

pH is a measure of acidity or alkalinity. A pH value of less than 7 is acidic, pH 7 is neutral and a pH of more than 7 is alkaline (see page 278).

1 Put a little of the soil in a test tube and mix it with barium sulphate powder and distilled water. (Why do we use distilled water?)

2 Put a bung in the top of the test tube and shake the contents vigorously. Allow them to settle. (Barium sulphate clumps (**flocculates**) the clay particles together so they become larger and sink. This leaves a clear solution to test for pH.)

3 Add a few drops of universal indicator solution or dip in a piece of universal indicator paper. Then compare the colour of the solution or paper with the colour chart provided with the indicator.

4 Is the soil acidic, alkaline or neutral?

5 Test other soil samples, and record your results.

Characteristics of loam soils

The particles in loam soils are a mixture of sand and clay particles, so the air spaces are of medium size. Because of this the water drains properly (without waterlogging) but enough is retained for plant growth. Loam soils have good amounts of both air and water.

Loam soils are the best soils for plant growth, i.e. they are the most fertile. Plants and animals have lived in the soil, and then died and decayed. Loam soils contain humus from the decay of plants and animals.

Loam soils can be improved by adding compost. This decays to make more humus, which improves the texture of the soil and releases its mineral salts slowly into the soil as they are used up by the plants. Chemical fertilizers, such as NPK (containing varying percentages of nitrogen, phosphorus and potassium), do not improve soil texture, but provide extra salts more quickly.

Why are soils important?

● Many animals (including humans) depend, directly or indirectly, on plants that grow in soil.

● Loam soils are used for agriculture: for growing crops, and for grassland to support the rearing of cattle, sheep, goats and other animals.

● Silt is brought down rivers to the sea, and forms the main part of mangrove swamps that form in estuaries around Caribbean shorelines and protect the land behind them from rough weather.

● Sand is important on our beaches, and to support plants such as coconut palms. Sand is also used in making tiles, abrasives, concrete and glass.

● Clay is used to make bricks, and with limestone to make cement for buildings.

● Gravel is used in making macadam, which is mixed with tar to make **tarmac** for road surfaces.

Questions

1 How is the sedimentation method used to distinguish among the three main types of soil?

2 List three characteristics of sandy and clay soil that you can make by observing them.

3 Why are loam soils used in agriculture?

Characteristics of clay soils

- Mostly small clay particles
- Small air spaces
- Water drains poorly (a lot is retained)
- Mineral salts stay attached to clay particles
- Soil stays wet (becomes waterlogged)
- Have little air
- Tend to be acidic

How can we improve clay soils?

Add lime

Lime is calcium oxide or hydroxide (hydrated lime). It is very useful to add lime to clay soils because the lime makes clay particles clump together or **flocculate** to form larger particles. Lime is also alkaline and so helps to reduce the acidity of clay soil. It also adds calcium to the soil, which is needed for plant growth.

Add sand

Sand particles are bigger than clay particles and if they are mixed into clay soil they make the air spaces larger. This means water will drain through better, the soil will not be so wet, and there will be more air for the plants.

Add compost

We can prepare compost (see page 237), which decays to humus in the soil. Humus improves the texture of clay soils because it makes the particles stick together into larger soil crumbs. Humus also absorbs water so the soil becomes less waterlogged. It also contains minerals, which are slowly released for plant growth.

Add chemical fertilizer

If chemical fertilizers are added to clay soils, mineral salts in the fertilizers will stay between the soil particles and may be too concentrated. If this happened, they could draw water out of the plants. It is best to wait until the soil has been improved with lime, sand and humus before adding chemical fertilizers. They do not improve the texture of the soil, but release their chemicals faster than humus does.

Characteristics of sandy soils

- Mostly large sand particles
- Large air spaces
- Water drains easily (little is retained)
- Few mineral salts (they drain away)
- Soil becomes dry
- A lot of air
- Tend to be neutral (can be saline (salty))

How can we improve sandy soils?

Reduce salinity

Sandy soils near to the sea tend to contain a lot of salt. This comes from salt spray and seawater that has drained into them. Only certain plants, such as coconuts, are adapted to live in these conditions. If sea sand is to be used in the garden it should first be washed several times to remove any salt.

Add clay

Clay particles are smaller than sand particles, and if they are mixed into sandy soil they fit into the air spaces, so making the spaces smaller. This means that water will not drain out so quickly, and so the soil will not become so dry and there will be more water for plant growth.

Add compost

Compost decays into humus. Humus improves the texture of sandy soils because it holds onto water, which would otherwise have drained out of the soil. This makes it a better medium for plant growth. It also contains minerals, which are slowly released into the soil for plant growth.

Add chemical fertilizers

If chemical fertilizers are added to sandy soils they will just be washed out by the water that drains through. This might cause a pollution problem (see page 224). It is better to wait until the sandy soil has been improved with clay and humus before adding fertilizers. The smaller air spaces and additional humus of the improved soil will allow the mineral salts to be more useful.

Key ideas

Use these words to fill in the spaces as you write the sentences in your Exercise book.

waterlogging   **sand**   **clay**   **humus**   **water**   **air**

The small _____ particles pack closely together; this can lead to _____ and lack of _____ .

Larger _____ particles have large _____ spaces between them; _____ drains through easily.

Adding lime and _____ can improve _____ soils. Adding compost can improve both kinds of soil, as it decays to make _____ , which slowly releases mineral salts.

11.3 What are good farming methods?

The farming methods we use for a particular soil depend on its physical and chemical properties.

Physical properties

These depend on the nature of the material, such as size of particles, and amounts of water and air in a soil. Copy and complete this table.

Physical property	Sand	Clay	Loam
Size of particles			
Size of air spaces			
Amount of water retained			
Amount of air			

Chemical properties

These depend on the chemical nature of a material. They either assist or harm plant growth.

- **pH** of the soil (see page 180). On the whole, plants prefer neutral or slightly acidic soils.

pH range	Plants that grow best
4.5–6.0	Potatoes
5.5–7.0	Tomato, carrot
6.0–7.0	Lettuce, onion
6.0–7.5	Cabbage, grass

We may need to adjust the soil pH. Add lime if the soil is too acidic. Add ammonium sulphate if the soil is too alkaline.

- **Salinity** is the amount of salt in the soil. Sandy soil near the sea tends to be saline. Only a few plants, e.g. coconuts, are adapted grow there.
- **Mineral salts** are in the form of ions (see page 21), e.g. nitrates, phosphates and potassium, mainly from decayed material, humus and fertilizers.

Effects of properties on fertility

You are going to set up a practical to compare the following soils and watering methods.

Type of soil	Water it with
A Sandy soil (washed to remove salt)	Rainwater
B Clay soil	
C Loam soil	
D Loam soil	Sea water
E Loam soil	0.1 M acid
F Loam soil	0.1 M alkali

Practical 63

Comparing plant growth (MM, ORR, AI)

1 Set up six similar large plastic containers such as those used for ice cream. In each one, make holes in the bottom and put in a layer of stones to allow for drainage.

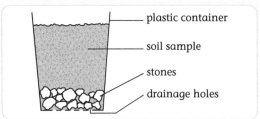

plastic container

soil sample

stones

drainage holes

2 Label the containers **A–F** and fill them with the same amount of different soils, as shown in column 1 of the table at the foot of the page.
3 Put five similar seedlings into the soil in each container, and water them with the same volume of the correct liquid (column 2 of the table) every other day.
4 Measure the heights of the seedlings, and take averages, each week for three weeks, and describe the general appearance of the plants.

Questions

1 (a) How do you predict which plants will grow best in containers **A** to **F**? (b) What did you find out? Account for your findings.
2 Look at the suggestions for good farming practice shown opposite. Describe how each suggestion will result in improved crop yields with the least reduction in soil nutrients.
3 If you are able to talk with farmers in your area, discuss these points with them. Find out which of the actions they carry out, and which ones they think would cost too much time or money or not be very effective.

Good farming practice

Do rotate crops

On a certain plot of land it is best to grow different crops each year and to include a year of fallow (page 184).

Why? Different crops take up different nutrients from the soil. Leguminous plants (beans and peas) should be included in the rotation. Disease organisms left in the soil could attack the same crop the next year, but not a different crop.

Do plough back

Plant remains should usually be ploughed back into the soil. The exceptions are plants that are troublesome weeds, such as nutgrass, or that are infected in some way. These should be removed and burnt.

Why? Nutrients from the old plants are returned to the soil. This is especially important in the case of beans and peas, which have nodules on their roots that contain nitrates (page 187).

Do make compost

Compost is partly decayed plant and animal remains. Farmyard manure can be added to compost heaps (page 237).

Why? Compost returns nutrients to the soil. It further decays to humus, which improves the texture of the soil because it binds small soil particles together as soil crumbs.

Do

Do remove weeds

Before you plant your crop, the ground should be cleared of weeds. While the crop is growing the weeds will also have to be removed by hand or with the careful use of chemical sprays (herbicides).

Why? Weeds compete with the crop you are growing, both in taking up space and in using nutrients from the soil that the crop needs.

Do mulch

Mulch is dried grass. It must be dried in the sun first to kill it, so that it will not start growing again. Mulch is put on the ground as a layer around plants.

Why? Mulch stops water from evaporating from the soil and so less watering is needed for the plants. Mulch also stops weeds from growing, and it can decay slowly into humus.

Do irrigate

Irrigation means watering plant roots as directly as possible. Underground pipes are the best method but these are expensive to install. Irrigation canals can also be useful. Do not water at midday when water will evaporate and not be useful to the plants. Water should go to the plant roots that need it (trickle irrigation).

Why? Irrigation makes the best use of the water available. It also encourages roots to grow down.

Don't

Do not burn off plants

Do not burn off plants unless they are infected or are troublesome weeds. Plants should be returned to the soil so that the nutrients are not lost. Burning sugar cane makes harvesting easier, but it destroys some of the sugar.

Why? Burning the ground breaks down the humus and affects the soil structure. The ash from burning can return some minerals to the soil, but burning usually does more harm than good.

Do not use raw manure

Raw manure is animal faeces. It may contain disease organisms such as pathogenic bacteria and eggs of parasitic worms. Raw manure should be added to compost heaps to be decayed and made harmless.

Why? Disease organisms may infect the humans who work in the fields or may infect the crop plants. Using urine and faeces directly on the fields can be dangerous.

Do not remove ground cover

If a field is not being used for a crop (e.g. in the fallow year of crop rotation) it should still have grass or other plants growing on it (e.g. for feeding cattle).

Why? Ground cover helps to reduce the soil erosion (page 184). This is especially important on sloping ground, where uncovered soil can easily be washed away by the rain.

11.3 What are good farming methods? (continued)

You have looked at physical and chemical properties of soils and how they affect fertility, and considered various farming practices (see pages 182–3). But how do we prevent **soil erosion** in order to keep (**conserve**) the soil in good condition for plant growth?

What is soil erosion?

Soil erosion is when the topsoil is blown away in dry weather, or washed away in wet weather.

Activity

Looking for soil erosion

1 Find examples of soil erosion (a) on flat land and (b) on a slope. Suggest what has caused the erosion.

2 How do (a) plant roots (small plants and trees) and (b) plant leaves help to stop soil erosion?

3 From your experience, is soil erosion worst when the rains are heaviest? Which is more important: the length of time of the rain, or the strength with which it falls? How can you test your suggestion?

How can we conserve the soil?

1 Keep the soil covered
Set up two shallow polystyrene packing trays: one with tightly packed garden soil and the other with turf (soil and its grass cover).

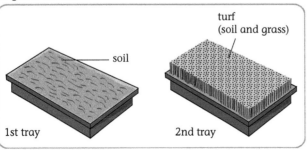

Practical 64

The importance of ground cover (MM, ORR)

1 Lay the trays you prepared flat in a sink.

2 Turn on the tap at a steady rate, and for 2 minutes run water onto the first tray, then the second tray, as each lies flat in the sink. Collect and record the amount of water that runs off each one.

3 Repeat step 2, but with each tray tilted at an angle of about 20°.

Questions

1 (a) How much water ran off and was collected in each of the four cases? Show the results in a table. (b) How much soil was washed off?

2 How did (a) plant cover and (b) slope of the trays affect the amount of soil washed off?

3 In which of the following would you expect most soil erosion, and why? (a) Sloping ground with plant cover. (b) Flat ground with plant cover. (c) Sloping ground with no plant cover.

2 Practise crop rotation
This means growing different crops each year on the same plot of land. The crops take different minerals from the soil, or add nitrates.

Year	Crop	Reasons
1	Root crop (e.g. yams or cassava)	Different crops take different minerals from soil; crops not affected by same diseases
2	Cereal crop (e.g. maize or rice)	
3	Legumes (e.g. beans or peas)	Nodules add nitrates to the soil
4	No crop: fallow (e.g. grass for cattle)	Soil rests; ground cover stops soil erosion

3 Strip planting
Different crops are planted in strips, e.g. around a hill. They take different minerals from the soil. The crops are chosen so they form fruits at different times of year. So when one crop is harvested, the other crop will keep the soil covered to prevent erosion. Permanent trees are also sometimes planted to prevent soil erosion and to give protection from the Sun.

4 Contouring

Contouring means to plough the soil and then plant crops along the contours of the land, which is *around* a hill and *not* up and down the hill.

The photograph (top right) shows crops planted along the contours. Discuss in class how this would be a better arrangement than planting them up and down.

5 Terracing

Terracing is building up flat surfaces of soil around a hillside. It is necessary on sloping ground where erosion and access are problems. A wall is built up from large rocks and boulders, and the space between the wall and the slope is filled in with soil. This is repeated up the hillside; the flat areas are then planted with crops. This prevents run-off of water and soil and also allows the farmer to walk among the crops more easily (see the diagram and bottom photograph on the right).

6 Greenhouse farming

Greenhouse farming uses soil in trays or pots, e.g. for lettuces or sweet peppers. Plants can also be grown in water (**hydroponics** – see page 208), e.g. tomatoes. In both cases there is a high capital cost to build the greenhouses, costs for fertilizers to provide mineral salts, and, because the plants are under cover, an added risk of spread of infection by pests; there may also be a cost for electricity to keep the greenhouses cool. For hydroponics there is an extra cost for electricity to circulate the water containing mineral salts and oxygen that are needed by the plant roots. But some advantages are: conditions for plant growth can be carefully controlled, plants easily harvested, and soils are not depleted.

Contour planting

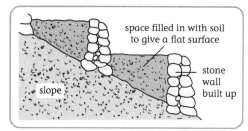

space filled in with soil to give a flat surface

stone wall built up

slope

Making terraces (cross section)

Terracing on a hill

Questions

4 (a) What conditions lead to soil erosion? (b) Choose three methods for reducing it. Compare and contrast the methods, identifying the advantages of each one.

5 When a crop is harvested, it takes with it mineral salts from the soil. Identify three different ways in which mineral salts could be returned to the soil. Which method is (a) most expensive and (b) least expensive?

Questions

6 What are the reasons for including each of the plants grown in a typical four-year cycle of crop rotation?

7 What would be the effects of (a) deforestation without replanting seedlings and (b) soil washed from uncovered land accumulating in a nearby river?

Key ideas

Use these words to fill in the spaces as you write the sentences in your Exercise book.

chemical   **salts**   **pH**   **contouring**   **erosion**   **physical**   **terracing**

Most of the _____ properties of soils depend on the sizes of particles. Some _____ properties of

soil are their _____ , salinity and mineral _____ . _____ is the loss of topsoil as a result of

wind and rain. Some ways of reducing _____ are to keep the soil surface covered, and to practise

crop rotation, _____ and _____ .

11.4 Food chains and food webs

Practical 65

Collecting leaf litter animals (ORR)

1 Dig up a spadeful of soil and decayed leaves (leaf litter) from under a tree.
2 Spread your sample on a newspaper, taking care to catch anything that moves. Use a large spoon or forceps, as some animals bite or sting.
3 Put the animals into separate glass bottles. Try to identify them using the diagram below.
4 When you have finished, return the organisms to where you found them.
5 From the information below, and what you may have observed, try to identify animals that are:
   ● primary consumers (herbivores), which eat plants
   ● secondary consumers (carnivores), which eat animals
   ● omnivores, which eat plants and animals
   ● scavengers, which eat dead material
   ● decomposers, which bring about decay (see page 237).

Note: the producers (which make food) are the plant roots and dead leaves and stems of plants.

Objective

● Discuss food chains and food webs found in a terrestrial environment.

Practical 66

Collecting soil animals (MM, ORR)

1 Make small holes, 2mm diameter, in the bottom of a tin or ice cream container.
2 Fill two-thirds of the container with garden soil.
3 Arrange the apparatus below.
4 Identify any animals that drop out.

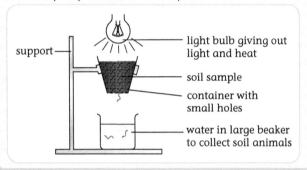

support —

light bulb giving out light and heat

soil sample

container with small holes

water in large beaker to collect soil animals

Soil animals

 **Woodlice** Under leaf litter and stones; eat decaying material	 **Cockroaches** Under leaf litter and stones; eat decaying material	 **Snails** On leaf litter or under stones; feed on living or dead plants	 **Slugs** On leaf litter or under stones; feed on living or dead plants
 **Termites** Burrow in soil and leaf litter; eat dead and decaying wood	**Ants** Burrow in soil and leaf litter; feed on small plants and animals	 **Millipedes** In leaf litter; eat decaying plants	**Centipedes** In leaf litter and stones; eat small animals; can bite humans
 **Earthworms** Active burrowers in soil; eat decaying plants and animals	**Nematodes** Live in water in soil; invade plant roots or eat animals or decaying plants	**Beetle larvae** Burrow in soil; feed on plants and decaying material	 **Insect pupae** Live in soil spaces; resting stage that does not eat

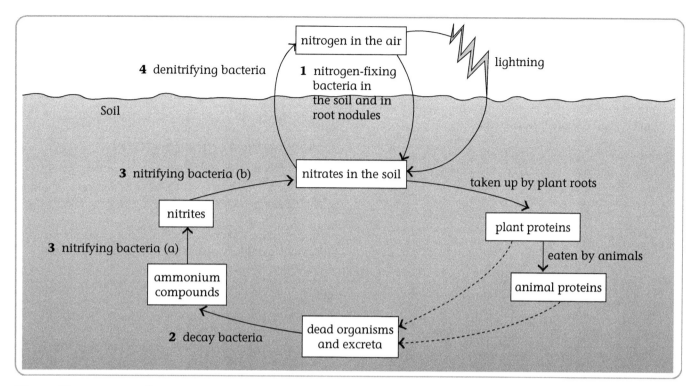

The nitrogen cycle

Most of the organisms in the soil are soil bacteria. They play a role in decaying dead material to produce nitrates that can be recycled for plant growth. This process is called the **nitrogen cycle**. Plants cannot take in nitrogen from the air and they depend upon the bacteria.

There are four main groups of bacteria involved in the nitrogen cycle (labelled 1 to 4 above).

1 Nitrogen-fixing bacteria

Nitrogen-fixing bacteria live freely in the soil or in the bumps (**nodules**) on roots of legumes such as beans and peas. They change nitrogen in the air spaces in the soil into nitrates. This is the reason legumes are planted as part of the process of crop rotation. Small amounts of nitrates are also produced by lightning.

2 Decay bacteria

Decay bacteria act on dead organisms and their wastes (excreta and faeces), to make them into ammonium compounds.

3 Nitrifying bacteria

Nitrifying bacteria are of two types, which (a) convert ammonium compounds to nitrites, and (b) convert nitrites to nitrates (which can be taken up by plant roots).

4 Denitrifying bacteria

Denitrifying bacteria undo the good work of the other bacteria. They are common in waterlogged soils because they can work without oxygen. They convert nitrates back into nitrogen in the air, and so reduce the stock of nitrates in the soil. This is one reason why waterlogged clay soils are deficient in mineral salts.

Important soil animals

Earthworms

Earthworms burrow into the soil, taking decaying leaves into their burrows, which also allow air into the soil. They mix up the soil layers. They take soil into their bodies, digest any juicy bits of decaying material, break up the soil and then pass it out as their faeces (worm casts).

Earthworms are not very common in the hard, dry soils in many parts of the Caribbean. They are also rare in waterlogged soils.

Termites

Termites eat dead and decaying wood, and so damage buildings. They soften the wood with their digestive juices and then chew it. Protists (single-celled organisms) in their guts digest the cellulose in the wood. Some termites make nests underground and so mix up the soil.

Ants

Ants make burrows in the soil. They feed on small animal and plant remains in the soil and they soften and break the soil into fine particles.

Questions

1 Draw three food chains of organisms that eat other organisms in the soil environment.
2 In what ways do (a) plant roots and (b) two named soil animals affect the soil?
3 In what ways are the amount of nitrates in the soil (a) decreased and (b) increased?
4 How can knowledge about the nitrogen cycle help farmers to keep their soil fertile?

11.4 Food chains and food webs (continued)

The groups into which we classify organisms are called **feeding levels**. They are interrelated.

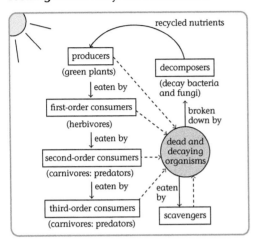

We can classify the organisms from the soil and leaf litter into these feeding levels.

Organism	Food	Feeding level
Plants	Make their own	Producers
Woodlice	Decaying material	Consumer (scavenger)
Cockroaches	Decaying material	Consumer (scavenger)
Snails	Living or dead plants	First-order consumer
Slugs	Living or dead plants	First-order consumer
Termites	Wood	First-order consumer
Ants	Plants and animals	Consumer (omnivore)
Millipedes	Dead or decaying plants	First-order consumer
Centipedes	Animals	Second-order consumer
Earthworms	Decaying material	Consumer (scavenger)
Nematodes	Living plants or animals	Consumer (parasite)
Beetle larvae	Plants, decaying materials	Consumer (omnivore)
Fungi Decay bacteria	Break down dead organisms and wastes	Decomposers

Practical 67

Collecting land organisms (ORR)

1 You will need these things.

- Scissors or shears to cut pieces from plants.
- Knife or penknife to scrape mosses and snails from rocks and stones.
- Long stick to knock organisms out of bushes.
- Thick gardening gloves for handling organisms with spines, or those that bite.
- Notebook and pencil to record where organisms are collected and what they are feeding on.
- Plastic bags and bread ties, tins and plastic jars for transporting organisms.
- Paper tape and pen to write labels for containers.
- Newspaper or plastic bowls for examining the soil and sorting animals.
- Forceps to handle small animals or ones that bite.
- Hand lens to examine small organisms.
- Animal traps and nets for catching organisms.

Food trap: leave 24 hours   Pitfall trap: leave 24 hours

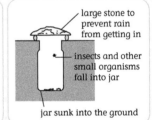

Butterfly net: to catch flying insects   Sweep net: to sweep through long grass

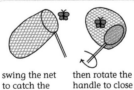
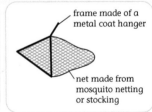

2 In small groups, use the materials to collect organisms in particular places in the school grounds (see page 378). Try to identify them using the diagrams on pages 14 and 186.

3 Record what an animal was eating when you found it, e.g. a butterfly feeding on nectar. You can also collect a piece of the vegetation on which an animal was found to take to the classroom as its food.

Identifying food chains and food webs

The table shows some of the organisms you might observe, together with what eats them.

Organisms that are eaten	Organisms that eat them
Grass	Cows and grasshoppers
Cabbage	Humans and slugs
Plant leaves	Slugs and caterpillars
Decaying plants	Earthworms
Flower (nectar)	Butterflies and hummingbirds
Cows	Humans
Grasshoppers	Praying mantises and toads
Slugs, caterpillars, earthworms and butterflies	Small birds
Praying mantises	Lizards
Toads, small birds and hummingbirds	Large birds

- **Food chains** show which organisms feed on which other ones. An example would be:

Grass ⟶ Grasshopper ⟶ Praying mantis ⟶ Lizard
(producer) (1st-order consumer) (2nd-order consumer) (3rd-order consumer)

- **Food webs** show interrelated food chains. An example of an incomplete food web is shown on the right above.

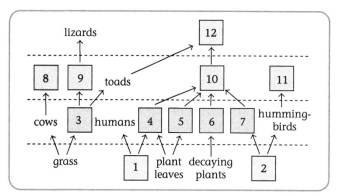

- Look at the incomplete food web above; then find, and write out, the other nine food chains from the table on the left (each starts with a producer).
- Use your information to fill in the spaces 1–12.

Questions

1. What do you understand by each of the following terms? Give an example of each:
   (a) producer, (b) first-order consumer,
   (c) predator, (d) decomposer, (e) herbivore,
   (f) carnivore, (g) omnivore, (h) scavenger,
   (i) parasite, (j) population, (k) community,
   (l) habitat, (m) ecosystem.
2. Why do food webs always start with producers?
3. In the food web, name (a) an omnivore,
   (b) five herbivores and (c) three second-order consumers.

What does it mean?

Population   A group of organisms of the same species living in a particular place, e.g. grasshoppers in a field.

Community   A number of populations living together, e.g. all the populations living on the school grounds.

Habitat   The place where organisms live: aquatic (in water; see pages 218–19) or terrestrial (land and soil).

Environment   The conditions that are found in a habitat, e.g. climatic conditions such as temperature and rain, soil conditions, and other living organisms.

Ecosystem   All the organisms in a particular habitat as they are affected by the environment. The food chains and webs tend to keep the numbers of animals and plants constant. For example, if the numbers of grasshoppers increased, some of them might die as they could not find enough grass to eat. Other ones would be eaten by praying mantises and toads, and so the numbers would return to the usual level.

Key ideas

Use these words to fill in the spaces as you write the sentences in your Exercise book.

ecosystem   **webs**   **producers**   **bacteria**   **chains**   **population**

Food _____ show which organisms eat other ones; food _____ are interrelated food _____ .

Food _____ begin with _____ . Fungi and _____ bring about decay, and different kinds of

_____ are important in making nitrates needed by _____ . A single species is a _____ . The

community interacting with its environment is an _____ .

11.5 How are materials recycled in nature?

Practical 68

Observing an aquarium (ORR, AI)

1 If you have a class aquarium you can observe it. Or your teacher will set up an aquarium. First put in sand and stones; then fill two-thirds of it with rainwater, a little at a time. If you use beach sand, first wash it to remove the salt.

2 Add some plants (producers) such as pondweed, and some animals (consumers) such as tadpoles, some mosquito larvae and pupae, water snails, and an aquatic beetle larva.

3 Close the top of the aquarium with a sheet of glass (see below). Leave it for a week.

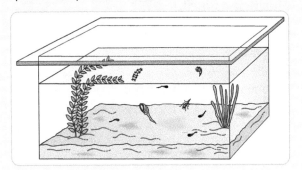

Objective

● Describe the oxygen, carbon, nitrogen and water cycles.

Practical 69

Carbon dioxide levels (ORR)

1 You will be given some hydrogencarbonate indicator solution. This changes colour as follows.

Colour	Amount of carbon dioxide (CO_2) dissolved
Reddish	Same as in the air
Purple	Less than in the air
Yellow	More than in the air

2 Set up two boiling tubes, one containing some plant leaves and the other containing a small animal.

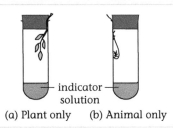

(a) Plant only   (b) Animal only

3 Leave them about 2 hours. Observe and explain what has happened to the indicator solutions.

Questions

1 Observe the inner glass surfaces. Look for small drops of water. What processes produce them?
2 Do the animals stay alive? Explain your answer.
3 Describe three food chains in the aquarium. Make a diagram showing the food web (see page 189).
4 Do the plants produce any bubbles of gas? What are they? How have they been produced?
5 How do animals and plants get oxygen?

Questions

6 Explain how (a) photosynthesis and (b) respiration affect the amount of carbon dioxide in the air.
7 How would covering both boiling tubes with a black cloth have affected the results? (See also page 379.)

Key ideas

Use these words to fill in the spaces as you write the sentences in your Exercise book.

nitrogen   evaporation   oxygen   carbon   nitrates   respiration

The _____ and _____ cycles are interrelated: the _____ produced by plants is used by plants and animals during _____ , and the burning of fuels to produce _____ dioxide . The _____ and condensation of water ensure it is recycled in nature. Various kinds of bacteria are important in the _____ cycle in order to continually replace the _____ taken up by plants.

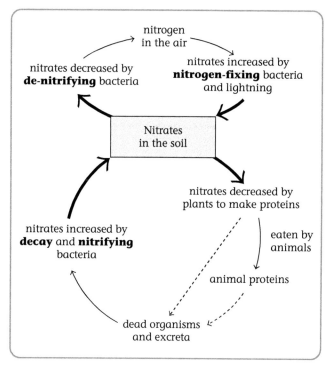

The nitrogen cycle

Nitrogen, water, oxygen and carbon are continually recycled in nature. Humans also affect the cycles, as shown in the diagrams.

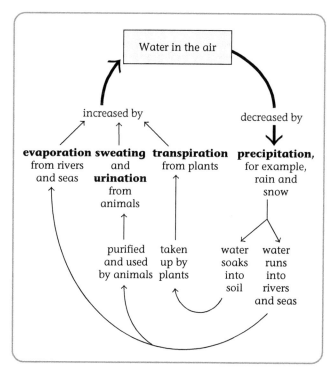

The water cycle

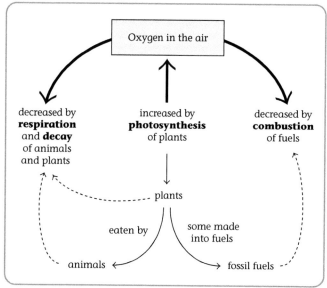

The oxygen cycle

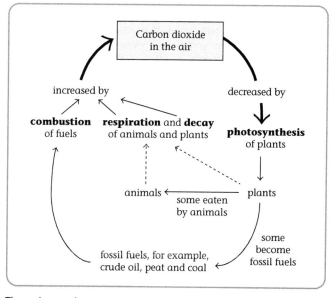

The carbon cycle

Questions

8 For each of the cycles above, list the processes that (a) increase and (b) decrease each substance. Which of these processes are influenced by human activities?

9 How are the oxygen and carbon cycles interrelated?

10 Why are the nitrogen, water, oxygen and carbon cycles important?

11.6 How is pollution spread?

Pollution can be spread by local and global winds. Winds blow from high to lower pressure.

Practical 70

What is pressure? (MM, ORR, AI)

1 Build a small wooden three-legged table. Use a 4 cm square piece of thin plywood and wooden pencil-sized legs that fit snugly into holes bored in the top. Make other sets of legs with ends from blunt to sharp points.

2 Use the bluntest set of legs and stand the table lightly on a flat piece of modelling clay about 5 mm thick. Place a mass of 100 g on the table (see the diagram on the right).

3 After about 30 seconds remove the table and inspect the modelling clay for marks. Record your results.

4 Put the table in a new position and increase the mass to 200 g. Repeat the process using heavier loads.

5 Now keep the mass constant at 100 g but vary the legs, from blunt to very sharp. Discuss your results in class.

Calculating pressure

The force exerted by a mass of 100 g is about 1 N. You should find that:

- with greater force, the holes become deeper
- as the area over which the force is applied becomes smaller, the holes become deeper.

So **pressure** is force/area. The unit is the pascal:

$$\text{pressure (in N) on the area of } 1\,m^2 = N/m^2$$

Does the atmosphere exert pressure?

If a little water is boiled in a can and the can is then corked and cooled, the can collapses. This is because air was pushed out by the steam, which condensed when the can was cooled, leaving a partial vacuum.

This shows that air exerts pressure. You are so used to the air pressure on your body that you hardly notice it, except in your ears.

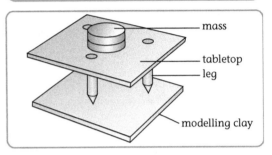

How is atmospheric pressure measured?

Mercury barometer This has a long capillary tube, placed in mercury, with a vacuum at the top. The average pressure of the atmosphere supports a height of 760 mm of mercury. The height can be measured accurately to show changes in atmospheric pressure.

Aneroid barometer

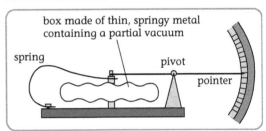

- As atmospheric pressure increases, the box is squashed and the pointer rises.
- As atmospheric pressure decreases, the box expands and the pointer gives a lower reading on the scale.

Global air masses

Around the Earth there are very large air masses of high and low pressure. They form bands around the Earth, parallel with the lines of latitude. At the Equator and at 60°N and 60°S there are low-pressure bands. Then at 30°N and 30°S there are high-pressure bands. The air masses are set up by hot air rising, and cold air sinking, and they give rise to global winds, such as the trade winds.

Air masses are named based on their source, as shown on the diagram on the right: m = maritime (over oceans and seas); c = continental; A = arctic; P = polar; T = tropical; and E = equatorial

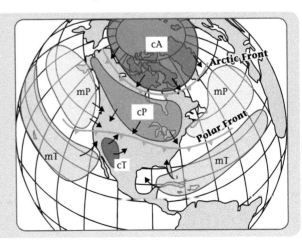

Global winds

Winds blow from areas of high pressure to areas of lower pressure. Winds are named for the direction from which they are blowing. There is a pattern to the world's winds.

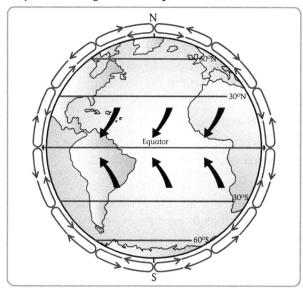

Spreading of pollutants

Short distances

Local winds can spread:
- industrial wastes, such as dust from cement factories or bauxite mining
- landfill fumes, from the waste depots.

Long-range

Global winds can spread:
- volcanic dust from erupting volcanoes
- dust from the Sahara Desert, which is carried to the Caribbean mainly in July by the northeast trade winds. As the air is dry, it causes a reduction in rainfall; the dust reduces air quality for humans, and has contributed to the decline in health of Caribbean coral reefs.
- radioactive fallout from testing of weapons, or accidents at nuclear power stations, such as that which happened at Chernobyl in 1986.

How global winds are formed: The Equator receives the Sun's direct rays all year. The air here is heated and rises, leaving low-pressure areas behind it. Moving to about 30°N and 30°S the warm air spreads out, slowly cools and sinks. Most of this cooling, sinking air moves back to the Equator. These movements give rise to north-east trade winds (north of the Equator) and south-east trade winds (to the south). These are warm, steady winds that blow almost continuously. The general direction of the winds is affected by the spinning of the Earth.

Similar circulation patterns are generated further to the north and south. Cooler air also comes down from the cold, polar regions, so there is a system of winds and a balance of temperature around the world.

Questions

1 How can the idea of pressure explain why sharp knives or needles are more effective than blunt ones?
2 How does an aneroid barometer work?
3 How are the trade winds formed?
4 Name two pollutants spread by winds. How might they be dangerous?

A volcano belching out volcanic dust

Key ideas

Use these words to fill in the spaces as you write the sentences in your Exercise book.

trade	lower	pressure	Saharan	force	760 mm	N/m²

_____ is _____ divided by area and the unit is the pascal (_____) . Average atmospheric

_____ at sea level supports a column of _____ mercury. Winds blow from high _____

to _____ pressure areas. On a global scale, the _____ winds are important in transporting

pollutants, e.g. _____ dust, over long distances.

11.7 What causes changes in the weather?

Weather describes the day-to-day changes in the temperature, humidity and movement of air in a particular place. What the weather is like influences what we wear, what we do and how we feel. A study of the weather includes examination of land and sea breezes along the coast (see page 165), the cooler, wet conditions on windward sides of islands compared to the warmer, drier conditions on the leeward sides, and the extreme power of hurricanes that cause death and destruction.

Air pressure

Underlying many of the changes in the weather are the differences in air pressure (see pages 192–3) of different masses of air. For meteorological purposes (describing the weather) we use the **bar** (10^5 N/m^2) and the **millibar** (mb), which is a pressure of 100 N/m^2.

Standard atmospheric pressure at sea level is about 1013 mb. The lowest low pressure (as in the eye of a hurricane) can be below 960 mb.

On a weather map, places that have the same atmospheric pressure are joined together by lines called **isobars**. Isobars are drawn at 2 or 4 mb intervals.

Winds

Winds blow from areas of high pressure (more dense) towards areas of lower pressure (less dense). The winds are deflected a little to the right (east) in the northern hemisphere by the spinning effect of the Earth (below).

The closer together the isobar lines the stronger the wind. The **Beaufort scale** (see page 196) describes wind speeds all the way from light breezes to storms and hurricanes.

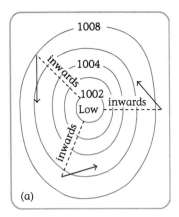
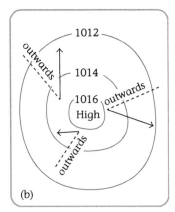

Isobars and winds

The diagrams above show:

(a) low-pressure system with a steep pressure gradient; strong winds tend to blow inwards but are deflected to the right

(b) high-pressure system with a gentle pressure gradient; light winds tend to blow out but are deflected to the right.

Objectives

- Distinguish among the four types of local fronts.
- Consider how the fronts affect the weather.

Clouds

Most clouds are floating collections of very small water droplets (see page 210).

Cirrus

Narrow ribbons of thin, white ice-crystal clouds high in the sky.

Cumulus

Fluffy clouds low in the sky. If they look like separate balls of cotton wool they indicate fine weather. If clumped together from a grey base they may bring rain.

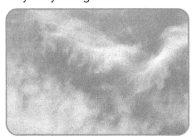

Cirrus above and cumulus below

Stratus

Sheets of clouds at a medium height in the sky.

If the water droplets join together, the cloud changes from white to grey. These are rain clouds and are common, especially in the afternoon, during the rainy season. When the droplets become too heavy they fall as **rain**.

'**Nimbo-**' or '**-nimbus**' can be used to indicate rain-bearing clouds; thus **nimbostratus** are grey sheets of cloud and **cumulonimbus** (below) grey balls of cloud.

Rain-bearing cumulonimbus clouds

Fronts

Over the Caribbean we usually have warm moist air, which has been heated by the Sun and has picked up water vapour from the sea. But colder, drier air may come in, e.g. from North America. When two kinds of air masses meet it is called a **front**. There are four kinds of fronts, and all of them bring rain. Symbols for the fronts are shown on the right. The symbols are added to weather maps to show the direction of movement.

Cold front

The most common type of front in the Caribbean, where cold air comes into a region of warm air and begins to displace it, is called a cold front.

A cold front is preceded by a rapid fall in pressure, deep dense clouds (often cumulonimbus) and rain. As the front passes there are heavy thunderstorms and intense rain for 5–15 hours, with a drop in temperature.

In the Caribbean, the Windward Islands are exposed to the prevailing winds and get more rain than the more protected Leeward Islands.

Warm front

This forms when warm air comes into a region of cold air and displaces it. It is not common in the Caribbean. It is preceded by a slow fall in air pressure, by cirrus clouds which change to become thicker and darker, and by drizzle. As the front passes there are showers for 10–25 hours, the wind may change direction and the temperature rises.

Occluded front

Cold fronts travel more quickly than warm fronts and a cold front may overtake a warm front and lift it off the ground. The warm front is said to be occluded (cut off). Occluded fronts are not common in the Caribbean.

Stationary front

If a cold front passing, for example, from North America over the Caribbean Sea warms up so that the temperature difference between the cold and warm air disappears, then it is called a stationary front.

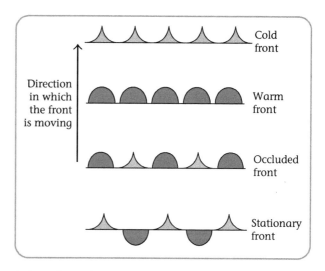

Direction in which the front is moving

Cold front

Warm front

Occluded front

Stationary front

Weather forecasting

We can get a good idea of what the weather will be like in the next few hours by looking at the sky.

- If it is blue with no clouds or only a few cotton wool clouds (cumulus), it is likely to stay fine.
- If the sky is covered with balls (cumulus) or sheets (stratus) of clouds which are grey (nimbus), then we are in for heavy rain or thunderstorms.

We can also look at a barometer.

- When the barometer is *falling* (decreasing pressure, or low pressure air is arriving), it is likely to rain. A falling barometer is associated with the different fronts, which all bring rain.
- When the barometer is *rising* (increasing pressure, or high pressure air is arriving), it is likely to be fine weather.

Questions

1 What kind of weather would you predict if it was hot and sticky (33 °C), with a strong wind from the north-east and a sky covered with cumulonimbus cloud?

2 Explain how the barometer can help us to predict the weather.

Key ideas

Use these words to fill in the spaces as you write the sentences in your Exercise book.

rain   **cumulus**   **isobars**   **fine**   **nimbus**   **pressure**

Differences in air _____ are associated with changes in the weather. A rising barometer predicts

_____ weather; a falling barometer predicts _____ . On a weather map, places with the same

pressure are joined by lines (_____) . _____ clouds predict fine weather, whereas _____

clouds predict _____ . All the fronts are associated with _____ .

11.8 What are hurricanes?

The wind speed of a hurricane is over 120km/h, or force 12 on the Beaufort scale.

Beaufort scale	Wind	Speed (km/h)	Effect
0	Calm	0	Still; smoke rises vertically
1	Light air	1–6	Smoke moves but not wind vanes
2	Light breeze	7–11	Wind felt on face; leaves rustle; wind vanes move
3	Gentle breeze	12–19	Small branches move; raises dust and loose paper
4	Moderate breeze	20–29	Small branches move; raises dust and loose paper
5	Fresh breeze	30–39	Small trees begin to sway
6	Strong breeze	40–50	Large branches move; whistling in overhead wires
7	Near gale	51–62	Whole trees in motion; difficult to walk against wind
8	Fresh gale	63–75	Twigs broken from trees; cars pushed off the roads
9	Strong gale	76–87	Slight damage, such as roof tiles blown off
10	Storm	88–102	Trees uprooted; considerable structural damage
11	Violent storm	103–119	Widespread structural damage
12	Hurricane	>120	Considerable and widespread damage to structures

Objectives

- Describe the characteristics of a cyclonic storm, such as a hurricane.
- Describe storm surges and how they are formed.

Did you know?

- Hurricanes usually form when sea temperatures equal or exceed 28°C.
- The names of hurricanes, alternately male and female e.g. Cindy, Dennis, Emily, are re-used every 6 years.
- For the Caribbean, hurricane information is available from the National Hurricane Center, Miami, Florida.

A cyclone is a region of low atmospheric pressure surrounded by rotating winds. Hurricanes are an extreme form of cyclonic storm. In eastern Asia they are called typhoons.

A cyclonic storm begins when moist air, heated by the Sun, rises from the surface of a tropical sea (below, (a)). As the moist air rises, it cools and condenses into rain. This releases energy to power the hurricane (below, (b)).

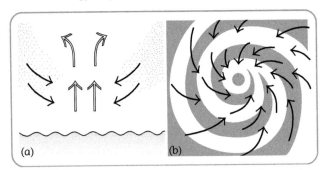

(a)　(b)

Hurricane formation. (a) Warm, moist air over a tropical ocean rises; surrounding air flows in, becomes warm and moist, and rises. (b) Later, top view; as seen from above, winds whirl around; winds are strongest near the eye but calm in the very centre of the eye

Hurricanes in the Caribbean

On average, five hurricanes affect the Caribbean each year during the hurricane season, from July to November. The damage done by a hurricane is caused by high winds, which can blow down buildings and destroy crops, and by flooding caused by the torrential rains and **storm surges** produced in coastal areas.

Hurricane safety measures

Always have available a battery-operated radio (and spare batteries) on which you can listen to weather forecasts. A **hurricane watch** indicates your area may be in danger, and a **hurricane warning** means there is likely to be direct damage. Usually the safest place is at home, if it is well built and above flood level. Keep a record of emergency numbers and plan ahead by shopping for necessities.

If you hear a hurricane warning, bring things inside, such as furniture, plants and garbage bins. Stick wide paper tape over the windows in an X pattern or board them over with wood.

When a hurricane occurs there will be widespread damage, especially from flooding. Do NOT travel to coastal areas, as there may be storm surges. Electricity, gas and water may be cut off and you may not be able to travel freely on the roads. You will therefore have to prepare for a possible emergency. For example, keep a supply of tinned food that does not need cooking or refrigerating. Make sure you have flashlights, spare dry cells, lamps, kerosene, candles and matches. You also need a supply of water for drinking or possible fire fighting.

After a hurricane stay away from disaster areas and, if you drive, take care to avoid fallen electricity cables, trees and other debris.

Follow any instructions from Disaster Preparedness groups. Keep alert for a few days in case of further problems. Boil drinking water until advised otherwise.

Hurricane tracks in the Caribbean

Hurricanes form over water to the east of the Caribbean and sweep across in a north-westerly direction. They are described as categories **1** (120–153 km/h), **2** (154–177 km/h), **3** (178–209 km/h), **4** (210–249 km/h) and **5** (250 km/h and above).

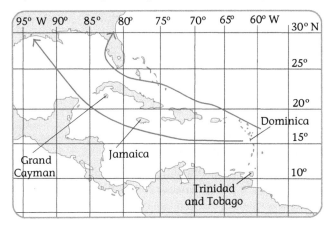

Common hurricane tracks in the Caribbean

Storm surges

The low-pressure eye of a hurricane pulls up a column of water up to 8 m high. As the swirling storm moves towards land, it pushes large waves of a storm surge ahead of it. The surge produces floods, which may cause more damage than the hurricane's winds.

Hurricane Emily (2005); the eye is in the middle

Activity

Tracking hurricanes

1 Use the map of the Caribbean on page 380 to track major hurricanes from the past and recent hurricanes using weather reports.

2 Find the names, dates and damage done by five recent hurricanes in the Caribbean.

Effects of hurricanes

- Short term: people are killed and injured. Houses and many public buildings are damaged and crops destroyed. Roads are impassable, and electricity and waterworks put out of action. Coastal areas are usually the worst hit by winds, floods and storm surges, causing most damage.

- Long term: extra expense because of destruction of crops and need to rebuild and repair services.

Questions

1 Where, and why, do hurricanes form?

2 What is a storm surge?

Key ideas

Use these words to fill in the spaces as you write the sentences in your Exercise book.

5	eye	120 km/h	surge	flooding	hurricane	low

A _____ is a region of rotating winds with very _____ pressure in the central _____ . The

winds travel at _____ and above, and a category _____ hurricane causes catastrophic damage.

The _____ pressure _____ of the _____ pulls up a column of water and pushes a storm

_____ ahead of it, which can cause widespread _____ when it reaches land.

11.9 What are earthquakes?

Earthquakes are movements of the Earth's surface. If we cut an imaginary section through the Earth we would see the parts shown below.

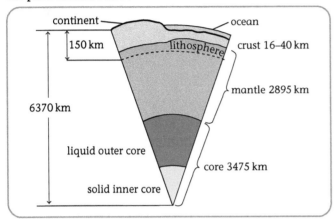

The **crust** lies on top of the **lithosphere**, which is the outer region of the **mantle**. The crust and lithosphere are not a continuous layer over the Earth but are broken up into about 15 large pieces called **plates**. The Earth's core is at about 6000 °C, and at very high pressure. This causes **magma**, or molten (melted) rock, to be pushed up through the mantle towards the crust. This sets up convection currents on which the plates are moved. The movements of the plates cause earthquakes.

Most islands of the Caribbean are on the Caribbean plate, with Cuba on the North American plate and Guyana on the South American plate. Where plates meet we say there is a **plate boundary**.

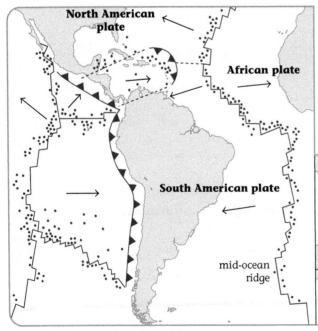

Plate movements that affect the Caribbean

What is the relationship between earthquakes and volcanoes?

An earthquake is a shaking of the ground caused by movements of the plates beneath. When plates collide head on, the released magma can give rise to **volcanoes** (see pages 201–3).

The Caribbean plate is moving to the east (right), and the North American plate is sliding past it to the west (left). Jamaica is sliding eastwards with respect to Cuba, at an estimated rate of about 2 cm per year. This sliding movement gives rise to earthquakes, which usually have their point of origin (**focus**) along a plate boundary. Little or no volcanic action is associated with this kind of boundary.

In the Eastern Caribbean, the Caribbean plate is moving to the east (right) and the South American plate is moving head on into it. The result of this collision is that the South American plate dips down beneath the Caribbean plate. The place where this occurs is called a **subduction zone** (see opposite). The rocks become heated up and melt into **magma**. The magma then works its way to the surface of the land to erupt as a **volcano**.

Question

How are the (a) origin and (b) severity of earthquakes determined and recorded?

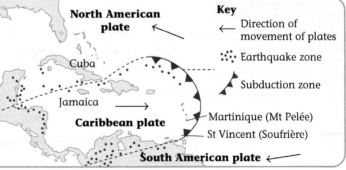

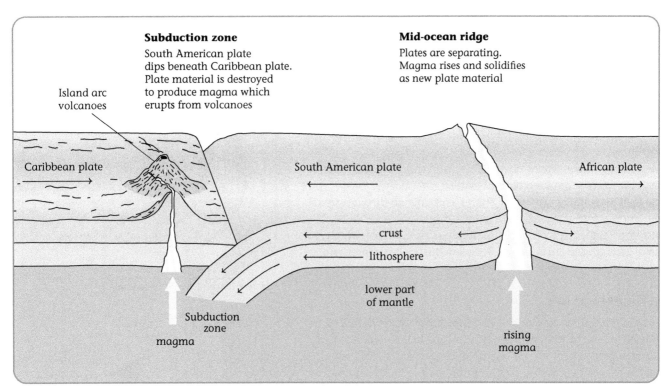

Subduction zone
South American plate dips beneath Caribbean plate. Plate material is destroyed to produce magma which erupts from volcanoes

Mid-ocean ridge
Plates are separating. Magma rises and solidifies as new plate material

Island arc volcanoes

Caribbean plate

South American plate

African plate

crust

lithosphere

Subduction zone magma

lower part of mantle

rising magma

Volcanoes (see pages 201–03) are associated with plate movements and earthquakes. Strato-volcanoes form at the subduction zone, and fissure or shield volcanoes form at the mid-ocean ridge

What effects do earthquakes have?

Most of the problems of an earthquake are caused by the actual movement of the land. But an earthquake under water can also cause high waves called **tsunamis** (see page 200).

Short-term effects of earthquakes

- The effects depend on the severity (**magnitude**) of the earthquake, as expressed by a number from 0–8.9 on the Richter scale (see page 200).
- The Earth cracks open and so destroys the foundations of buildings. Buildings crack and collapse and debris is thrown around, causing injury or loss of life.
- Fires can start very easily because of damaged electricity cables and appliances, or burning of escaped gases.
- Tsunamis cause flooding, which can lead to loss of life and destruction of crops.
- Earthquakes often set off landslides, especially on steep mountains. If these do not have tree cover, then there can be devastating mudslides.

Long-term effects of earthquakes

- Earthquakes cause rivers to change course, which can spoil farmlands and ruin crops.
- People may move away from earthquake areas.
- Buildings have to be designed either to withstand earthquakes or to be very light and easily rebuilt.

Earthquake safety measures

We know the places where earthquakes are *likely* to occur, but do not know exactly *when* they will occur. We have to be prepared.

If you are inside, stay there

- Stand in a strong doorway or get under a strong desk, table or bed.
- Watch out for falling plaster, bricks, lights and other objects. Protect your head and face.
- Do not light a match or turn on a light switch, in case of damage to utilities. Use a flashlight.
- Check your house for serious damage – leave if you are in danger.

If you are outside, stay there

- Stay in the open to avoid flying debris.
- Keep away from buildings that may have been weakened by the earthquake.
- Do NOT go to the beach to watch for tsunamis, as you may get swept away.

In general

- Plan ahead to have supplies of tinned food, clean water, and first-aid emergency materials.
- Stay calm. Check for injuries and give first aid.
- Use a battery-operated radio for earthquake reports.
- Make sure your cell phone is usable.
- Be prepared for additional earthquakes.

11.9 What are earthquakes? (continued)

The seismograph

An earthquake sends out **seismic** waves, which can be recorded on **seismographs**. The times of arrival of various wave forms, and their strength, allow the position and intensity of an earthquake to be determined.

- The **P**, or **primary**, waves travel fastest, and can go through solids and liquids; they are longitudinal waves.
- The **S**, or **secondary**, waves are slower, can only go through solids and are transverse waves.
- The earthquakes also produce longitudinal, or **L**, waves, which move through the Earth's crust. They are the slowest waves and cause the most damage.

The Richter scale

Developed by Charles Richter in 1935, the **Richter scale** describes the **magnitude** of ground movement of an earthquake, as recorded on a seismograph, near the **epicentre** of an earthquake (directly above the focus). Each number on the scale from 0 to 8.9 represents a 10-times increase in strength and size.

Tsunamis

Tsunamis are caused by rapid raising or lowering of the sea floor during an earthquake. The shaking of the Earth shakes the water and sets up 30 cm high waves that travel very fast (at up to 1000 km/h). As the waves reach shallow water near the shore, they slow down and rapidly rise to heights of up to 30 m, causing massive destruction to coastlines, people and buildings.

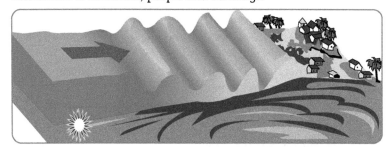

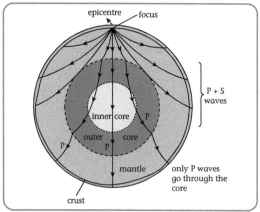

How the different seismic waves travel

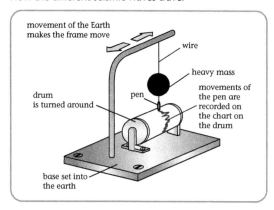

A seismograph. The trace records the different kinds of seismic waves

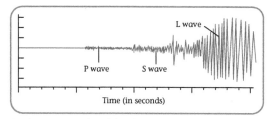

A seismogram. The wider the zigzag bands, the stronger the earthquake is

Key ideas

Use these words and letters to fill in the spaces as you write the sentences in your Exercise book.

plates   **earthquakes**   **Richter**   **S**   **L**   **P**   **tsunamis**

The Earth's crust consists of moving _____ . Where _____ slide past each other, _____ and _____ can occur. _____ set up seismic waves, and the intensity can be used to describe the magnitude on the _____ scale. The waves that travel through the Earth are _____ (fastest waves) and _____ waves. Waves travelling on the surface are _____ waves.

11.10 What are volcanoes?

Volcanoes are often found where plates are moving apart (**mid-ocean ridges**), or one is moving under another (**subduction zone**). At these places hot material from inside the Earth, **magma**, comes to the surface.

The magma contains different amounts of dissolved gases and when it comes to the surface as **lava**, the gases escape to cause an **eruption**. The build-up of lava forms a volcano.

- If the lava is thin and runny, gases escape easily and the eruption is mild.
- If the lava is thick and stiff, the trapped gases explode, breaking the lava into fragments. Large, rock-like pieces are called 'bombs'. If the fragments are very small, it is a fine dust or ash.

Different kinds of volcanoes

The different kinds of volcano depend upon where they are formed, how the magma comes to the surface, and the kind of lava that is present.

Fissure volcanoes

These build up over long cracks in the crust. The magma comes up along the length of the crack. The lava is usually thin and runny and spreads out to form flat plateaux. These volcanoes are found at mid-ocean ridges (see page 199).

Central volcanoes

The magma comes up through a single channel to build a cone around a central crater.

- **Shield volcanoes** form a flat cone (below). The lava is usually thin and runny and spreads out.

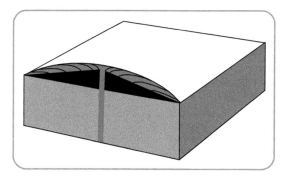

These volcanoes are found at mid-ocean ridges (see page 199). They are therefore under water and may go unnoticed. As the lava is thin, the eruption is fairly mild.

- **Strato volcanoes** form a pointed cone (see page 202). The lava is usually thick and stiff and piles up around the central crater to form steep slopes. These volcanoes occur along a subduction zone (see pages 198–9).

Objectives

- Explain the causes of the different types of volcanic eruptions.
- Describe the short- and long-term consequences of volcanoes.

What effects do volcanoes have?

It is hard to predict exactly when a volcano will erupt. As well as the molten lava, there may also be hot volcanic gases, ash and mud. Related disturbances of the land may lead to tsunamis and floods. Effects can be felt for thousands of kilometres, and dust carried around the world.

Short-term effects

- Molten lava is ejected from the volcano and will kill living things in its path.
- Super-heated gases, which come out under pressure, can cause damage to everything within many kilometres.
- Volcanic ash can blow into cars, machinery, sewers, etc. and block them up. The ash also gets into the lungs and bronchial tubes of people and other animals and can cause death.
- Mud, formed from ash mixed with water, flows into rivers and clogs them up. This can then cause floods, with loss of life, homes and crops.
- The associated winds can uproot mature trees and blow them away.
- Huge tsunamis (see page 200) may form, which can cause great damage to coastal regions.

Long-term effects

- Volcanic eruptions can produce new land masses, as in the case of Kick-'em-Jenny, an underwater volcano off the coast of Grenada. If the lava cools down, and the water level is lowered, it can become an island.
- Some of the ejected materials remain rock-like and sterile and are unsuitable for farming.
- Other materials decompose. The minerals, such as sulphur and phosphorus, which came from the lava, then become available for plant growth. The soils that are formed may be very fertile.
- Where the ash falls there may also be long-term benefits in soil fertility from potassium.
- Where rivers flood onto the land they may cause short-term damage but will also, in the long term, increase the soil fertility.

11.10 What are volcanoes? (continued)

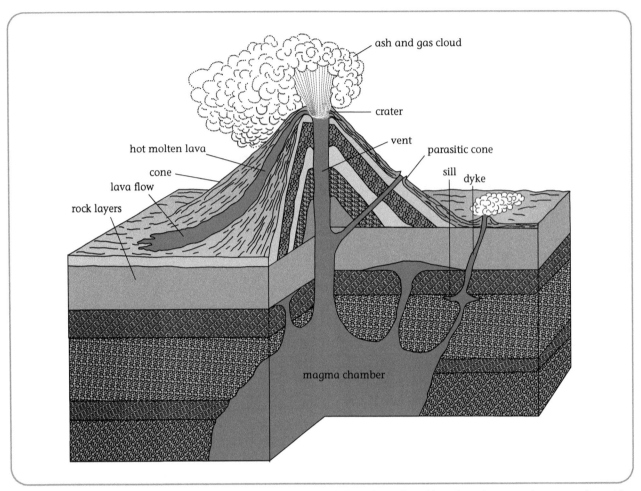

A strato volcano with a pointed cone. Magma rises up the vent and explodes as fine ash and lava. Some lava may also emerge from side vents to form parasitic cones. Other magma is forced into surrounding rock layers as sills (horizontal sheets) and dykes (vertical sheets), which can also reach the surface

Devastating eruption of the Soufrière Hills volcano in Montserrat in 1997, which destroyed the island's capital city, Plymouth. There are three other Caribbean volcanoes called Soufrière, from the French for 'sulphur'

Questions

1 Describe the differences in origin and structure of shield and strato volcanoes. Include diagrams.

2 In what different ways could floods arise as a result of earthquakes and volcanoes?

3 Which of the following islands would you expect to have earthquakes and/or volcanoes? Explain why. (a) Jamaica, (b) St Vincent, (c) Trinidad.

4 Would a large earthquake *always* cause more damage than a small earthquake? What other factors might be involved?

5 In your country, which organizations help to deal with disasters such as hurricanes, earthquakes and volcanoes?

Volcanoes in the Caribbean

As you saw on pages 198–9, volcanoes are associated with movements of the plates of the Earth's crust.

In the Eastern Caribbean, the island arc of the Lesser Antilles has formed in the position where the Caribbean plate collides with the South American plate. The volcanoes have formed in the subduction zone. The islands and their volcanoes are shown below.

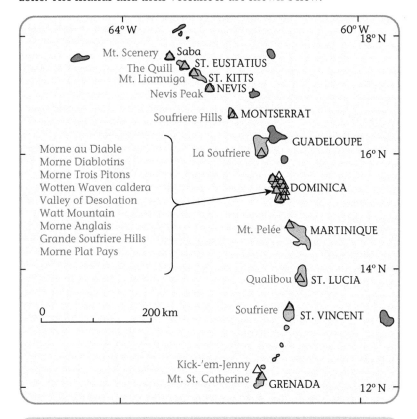

Activity

Earthquakes and volcanoes in the Caribbean

1 Work in small groups. Decide on a country to investigate. Use reference books and the Internet to find information on the origin and activity of earthquakes and volcanoes.

2 Put together a class display of your findings.

Kick-'em-Jenny

This is an active underwater volcano, 8 km north of Grenada, as shown below.

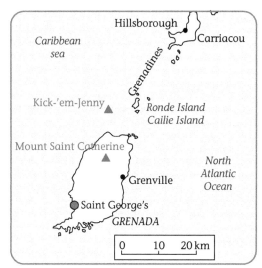

The position of Kick-'em-Jenny

Although the volcano would have erupted many times before then, the first record of Kick-'em-Jenny erupting was in 1939. It sent a cloud of steam and debris 275 m into the air, and generated tsunamis 2 m high when they reached the coasts of northern Grenada and the southern Grenadines.

The volcano has erupted at least 12 more times since then. During the 1974 eruption, the sea above the volcano boiled and spouted steam; many fish were also killed. The shape of the volcano, and its active areas, has been mapped on a image taken by sonar (see page 229).

The volcano rises 1300 m above the sea floor, and, in 2003, the summit had reached 180 m below the sea surface. It is believed this height has been constant since the 1960s.

Key ideas

Use these words to fill in the spaces as you write the sentences in your Exercise book.

subduction   fissure   collide   long   strato   short   magma   apart

_____ volcanoes form in the _____ zone, where plates _____ . _____ volcanoes form at mid-ocean ridges, where plates move _____ . In a volcano, _____ comes from inside the Earth and forms lava to build up the cone. Lava, gases and ash can cause devastating _____-term effects, but the _____-term effects may include increased fertility of the soil.

11.11 How are tides important?

The Earth is in the solar system (see page 357) and has a natural satellite, the Moon. The movements of the Earth and the Moon, in relation to the Sun, produce day and night, the phases of the Moon, and tides.

Day and night

The Earth spins (**rotates**) on its axis. So at different times during 24 hours the Sun shines on different parts.

In the diagrams on the right, the Caribbean is marked with an **X** on the Earth. In the top picture **X** is on the side of the Earth that is receiving light from the Sun, and it will be day in the Caribbean.

In the second picture the Earth has rotated further round. **X** is now in shadow and it is night in the Caribbean.

Phases of the Moon

The Moon travels round the Earth in an anticlockwise direction. It makes one complete orbit in about 28 days (a **lunar month**). The Moon does not produce light of its own. We only see the Moon because it reflects light from the Sun. At different times of the month different parts of the Moon are lit up by the Sun. Then, on Earth, we see the Sun's light reflected from those parts of the Moon. So the Moon appears to be different shapes during the month. We call these the **phases of the Moon** (see bottom picture).

- In position **A** the Sun is shining on the side of the Moon that is facing away from the Earth. So we cannot see the Moon from the Earth: this is the **new Moon**.
- In position **B** the Sun is shining on the right side of the Moon as seen from Earth. When we look at the Moon we see the right side lit up ☽ : this is the **first quarter**.
- In position **C** the Sun is shining on the side of the Moon that is facing towards Earth. When we look at the Moon it is a large, brightly lit circle: this is the **full Moon**.
- In position **D** the Sun is shining on the left side of the Moon. When we look at the Moon we see the left side lit up ☾ : this is the **last quarter**.

Objectives

- Describe how tides are formed.
- Describe the effects of tidal patterns on plant and animal life.

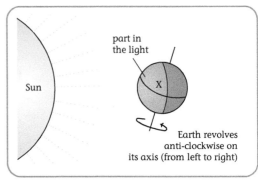

Day in the Caribbean

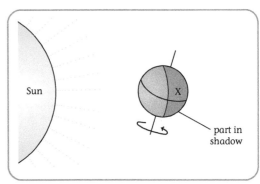

Night in the Caribbean

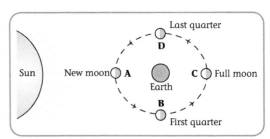

The phases of the Moon

Activity

Observing the Moon

1 On a page in your notebook make a drawing of the shape of the Moon every evening for 30 days. Write the date by the side of each drawing.

2 If the evening is very cloudy, or if you do not see the Moon, then leave a blank, and make the next drawing for the next evening.

3 When you have completed your drawings compare them to those shown on the right and try to identify the different phases of the Moon.

Questions

1 Your younger brother says he sees the 'moonlight'. Explain to him what he is seeing.

2 Does the Moon really change its shape each month? Explain.

Tides

Tides refer to the distance that the sea comes up the shore. At high tide the sea comes far up the shore, whereas at low tide it is farther out. Tides affect shore organisms (see pages 206–7).

Tides are due to the pull or attraction (**force of gravity**) of the Moon and the Sun towards water on Earth. Because the Moon is much closer to the Earth than the Sun, the Moon's effect is more than twice as important as the Sun's.

As the Earth spins on its axis, the Moon is overhead at a certain time in the day. It pulls on the water in the oceans and causes high tide. There is also high tide on the opposite side of the Earth at the same time.

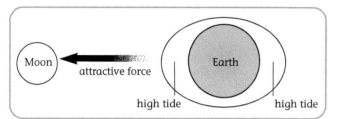

Formation of tides

Approximately 12 hours later, the Moon is overhead on the opposite side of the Earth, and again causes high tide. There are two high tides and two low tides every 24 hours, 50 minutes.

When the pull of the Moon and the Sun are more or less in the same direction, there will be the greatest difference in tides. The attractive force of the Sun is added to the attractive force of the Moon. This happens every month during the periods of new Moon and full Moon. These are called the **spring tides**, when the high tide is highest and the low tide is lowest.

When the Sun and Moon are roughly at right angles, their attractive forces oppose each other and there will be the smallest difference in tides. The attractive force of the Sun is subtracted from the attractive force of the Moon. This happens every month during the periods of the first and last quarters. These are called **neap tides**. High tide is lowest, and low tide is highest.

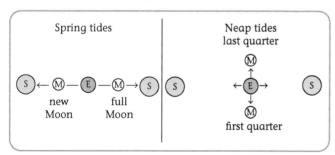

Attractive forces added   Attractive forces subtracted

Waves

The surface of the Earth is approximately 70% water and most of it is in large ocean basins. This water is in continual motion to form **crests** (the tops of the ocean waves) and **troughs** (the hollows in between).

On windy days the waves are highest. The heights of the waves and how fast they travel are related to the speed of the wind and the distance of sea over which it has been blowing. Thus bigger waves are formed in the Caribbean Sea than in sheltered waters, and more on Atlantic coasts than ones within the Caribbean Sea. Also, bigger waves will form during a hurricane (see page 197) than during calm weather.

As the waves reach closer to the shore, where the water is shallow, they become higher and hollow in front. The waves collapse or **break** onto the shore with a lot of force (see page 342).

Effects of Moon phases and tides

On plants

Calendars have been produced for farmers and gardeners to link the phases of the Moon with different activities, but these ideas are not scientific. The new Moon is said to be a time when growth is greatest in the top of the plant and is a good time for taking cuttings. Once the crescent of the new Moon is visible seeds can be sown. In the first quarter grain and seed crops can be sown. The full Moon is a time when root systems store food; it is a time to harvest above-ground crops and to plant root crops. The last quarter is the resting period, which is best for pruning and spraying.

On animals

Many shore animals are affected by the tides, which in turn vary with the phases of the Moon. Female grunion fish produce eggs just after the high point of a spring tide. The eggs are buried in the sand for two weeks until they are washed out by the next spring tide in time for hatching. Some corals also have a monthly reproductive cycle. There are also daily cycles; for example, limpets actively feed every 12.5 hours at high tide, when water covers their part of the shore. They avoid daytime low tide, when they might dry out.

Questions

3 What are the effects of (a) the rotation of the Earth and (b) the Moon orbiting the Earth?

4 What are (a) tides and (b) waves?

11.11 How are tides important? (continued)

The coastal regions at the edge of continents and islands are washed continually by the sea. What effects might the sea have?

- The sea is **saline**: it contains about 3.5 g of dissolved salt in each 100 cm³ of water.
- The sea is in constant motion and **waves** break upon the shore with a lot of force.
- The sea comes in and out (ebbs and flows) with the **tides**. Organisms must survive total immersion, as well as exposure to the Sun.

Rivers

At the mouth of a river, the **estuary**, the full effects of the sea can be felt. The seawater that comes into the estuary at high tide has a high salinity. But when the tide goes out, fresh water from higher up the river flows down, and the salinity drops. Organisms such as crabs and oysters living in the estuary have to be able to live in water with a wide range of salinity.

The movement of the water produces **currents**. Organisms must avoid being washed away. They live in sheltered pools on the riverbank, are attached to rocks, are able to burrow into the soil, or are strong swimmers.

Mangrove swamps

Swamps form in the tropics where mud has been brought down to the coastal region. There are currents, and changes in salinity.

The mud level is always shifting and changing, and the plants that grow there best are mangroves, which have **prop roots** (see (a) below). Animals, such as mudskippers and oysters, live attached to the roots. Also, the mud has a low oxygen concentration compared with normal soil, and some mangroves are adapted by having 'breathing roots' (see (b) below) that take oxygen from the air.

(a) Prop roots

(b) Breathing roots

Seashore

The seashore can be sandy or rocky. On sandy shores, animals such as crabs and clams burrow in the sand as the tide comes in, and come to the surface as the water retreats. So they are protected from the force and current of the waves.

Different organisms are found at different places up the shore depending upon how much they are covered or uncovered by the high and low tides. On rocky shores we can see the effects of high and low tides best (see opposite).

Splash zone

Near the top of the shore is a place where even high tides do not reach. The only water is spray from the waves. This is called the **splash zone**. The organisms that live here are lichens and periwinkles, which can close up their shells to protect themselves from the drying effects of the Sun.

Inter-tidal zone

Between the area where the high tides reach and where the low tides come up, is a zone called the **inter-tidal zone**. Organisms at the *top* of this zone are only covered by the sea at high tide. For most of the day they are left uncovered and are affected by the heating and drying effects of the Sun. In this zone there are many sea snails that can close their shells, and limpets that can pull down tightly onto the rock so that they do not dry out.

Towards the *bottom* of the inter-tidal zone the organisms are covered for a longer period of the day. Here there are seaweeds (sea moss), which are less resistant to drying out than shelled animals. Crabs and sea urchins will also be found here.

Sub-littoral zone

This is below the inter-tidal zone. It is always covered by the sea. Here are different kinds of seaweeds, and soft-skinned animals, such as sea anemones and sponges.

Rock pools

These are hollow areas in the rocks filled with seawater. The conditions are not exactly like the sub-littoral zone, because the water in the pools may not be replenished by the sea very often. It will therefore tend to get hot and very salty as some water evaporates.

If you live near a rocky shore, visit it to observe organisms from the different **zones** and see how they are adapted to life in their habitats. Plan to arrive at high tide, then you can follow the water as it goes down towards low tide.

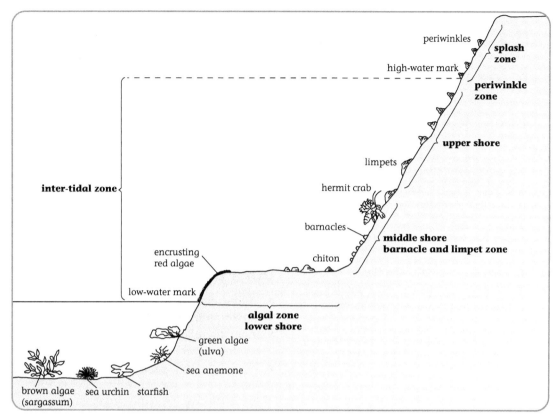

The zones on a rocky shore

High tide and low tide

Approximately every 24 hours and 50 minutes there are two high tides and two low tides. So both tides are a little later each day. The cause of the tides is described on page 205.

For just over 6 hours, water comes in (**flows**) further up the shore until it reaches 'high tide'. Then for just over 6 hours the water goes out (**ebbs**) further down the shore until it reaches 'low tide'. The cycle is then repeated.

The difference between high and low tides varies greatly around the world, and is relatively little in the Caribbean. For this reason it is often difficult to see the zones shown above. This is because splash from the waves may produce as much difference in water heights as the tides.

The cause of the tides is described on page 205.

Questions

1. Describe how a named organism from (a) an estuary and (b) a mangrove swamp is adapted to its conditions.
2. What are the conditions in these areas of a rocky shore? (a) The splash zone, (b) rock pools, (c) the inter-tidal zone. How is a named organism from each zone adapted to the conditions found there?
3. What organisms that live on the shore do humans eat? How does the behaviour of the organisms help us to catch them?
4. If it is high tide at 6:00 am and 6:25 pm on Monday, approximately when will the high tides be on Tuesday?

Key ideas

Use these words to fill in the spaces as you write the sentences in your Exercise book.

mangroves	rock	breathing	splash	prop	adaptations	tides

In the mud found in estuaries, _____ can grow; they have _____ such as _____ roots and _____ roots. On a rocky shore the distribution of organisms is determined by the _____ . Only a few animals are found high on the shore in the _____ zone. Other organisms show _____ to living in _____ pools or the upper shore.

12 Water and the aquatic environment

12.1 Why is water important?

Uses of water

Water is essential for life

- We lose nearly 2 litres of water a day from our lungs, urine, sweat and faeces. We need to replace this in our food and drink (see page 109). This is especially true if the weather is very warm or we undertake any active sport.
- We could only live for a few days without water, but we could live on water and no food for several weeks.
- If humans, and especially babies, lose a lot of water due to diarrhoea they become **dehydrated** and may die. They should be given rehydration fluid – sweetened, slightly salty, boiled water – to replace their body fluids.
- Some animals, such as desert rats and termites, are especially adapted to conserve water, and get all the water they need from their food.
- Desert plants, such as cacti, can survive drought. They have very deep roots, leaves that are often reduced to spines, and a thick green stem that stores water.

Water takes part in body reactions

- Water takes part in the breakdown of food molecules during digestion. The digestive juices, such as saliva, are also mainly water.
- Water is also a very important **solvent** (liquid in which other substances dissolve). For example, dissolved food goes into solution before it can be absorbed. The surface of the alveoli must also be kept moist for gases to dissolve, in order to pass between the blood and the outside air.
- In plants, water is a reactant in photosynthesis and is used in the breakdown of food stores during germination.
- The protoplasm inside living things is about 70% water. The percentage needs to be kept close to normal levels in order for life to continue (osmoregulation; see pages 108–9).

Water is needed for transport

- We use waterways for the transport of goods within countries, for example Guyana.
- The sea is very important for Caribbean trade from one country to another.
- Within animals, blood is mainly water. Animals conserve their water resources by reabsorbing water in the kidneys (see pages 107–8).
- Within plants, water is needed in the xylem and phloem for transport of salts and soluble foods, and in leaf cells for transfer of gases and transpiration (see pages 86–7).

Water is a habitat for organisms

Aquatic habitats (seawater and fresh water) are important for many organisms (see pages 215–19) that could not survive on dry land.

Objectives

- Explain the uses of water.
- Discuss water wastage and suggest methods for water conservation.
- Discuss how the water cycle provides fresh supplies of water.

Other uses of water

- In the home for drinking, cooking, cleaning and disposing of wastes.
- In fire-fighting (see pages 254–5), for helping to put out fires.
- Water from rivers, dams and reservoirs can be used in the generation of electricity (**hydroelectricity**). Find out about schemes in Dominica and St Vincent. The water, or water that has been heated to make steam, is used to drive turbines (see pages 298–9).
- Growing crops in water (**hydroponics**) rather than in soil (see page 381). The water contains mineral salts and has air bubbled through it to supply oxygen to the roots.

Did you know?

- Water spends about:
  a day inside plants
  10 years in a lake
  100 years in the ocean
  before being evaporated into the air.
- The water we use now has been around on Earth for nearly 4 billion years.

How can we make good use of water?

Build dams and reservoirs

These hold water from a river. As water is needed it can be purified (see page 211) for drinking, or used to generate electricity.

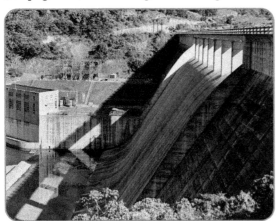

The dam built to hold the water at a hydroelectricity plant

Store water

Use storage tanks or other water containers to store rainwater that falls onto roofs. This water can be led by pipes into the containers, so the surfaces can be kept covered – to avoid the breeding of mosquitoes. Water storage is especially important in Barbados and Antigua, which are very short of surface water. Stored water can be used for the garden and for cleaning cars, etc.

Conserve water

Be careful with water:
- take a short shower rather than have a bath
- soap yourself before opening the shower tap
- use a cup of water when cleaning your teeth, rather than keeping the tap running
- use washing-up water for another use, e.g. cleaning the car or watering plants.

Water plants effectively

Give water to plants in the early morning or late evening. At hotter times of day, a lot of water will evaporate quickly and be lost, rather than go into the soil.

Add dried grass or other plants (**mulch**) around the base of plants to cut down on evaporation of water.

Put water close to the roots, rather than watering the leaves. Provide a larger amount of water less often (for deep roots), rather than a little water each day (which encourages the roots to stay near the top of the soil).

Maintain tree cover and plant more trees

Trees give shade and make cool and humid conditions for smaller plants and animals underneath. The roots hold onto the soil and the leaves transpire water as part of the water cycle. In Haiti, the lack of trees meant that in times of very heavy downpour there was no tree cover to stop the force of the rain. As a result, many people died because of mudslides.

Why should we conserve water?

- In many countries, water becomes scarce as populations increase. Water is needed in households, farming and industry. These needs increase with population growth and affluence.
- Water purification requires energy, and energy is also needed for pumping water from a waterworks to homes and industries. Energy costs money to provide and has to be paid for. The conservation of water and conservation of energy are closely linked.

Practical 71

Do we waste water at home? (MM, ORR, AI)

Do these activities at home.

1 Compare the volumes of water you use to (a) have a bath, (b) take a shower, (c) wash with a basin of water. Calculate the differences over a week, and over a month.

2 Adjust a water tap until it is dripping very slowly, one drop every few seconds. Collect the water drops in a measuring cylinder over 5 minutes. Work out how much water would be collected in (a) 1 day, (b) 1 week, and (c) 1 month. Comment on your findings.

3 (a) What volume of water is used every time the toilet is flushed? (b) How often, on average, is the toilet flushed in a day? (c) If you put a brick in the cistern to reduce the volume by a quarter, how much water is saved in a week, and in a month?

Activity

Water wastage and conservation

1 Work in small groups. Make a list of the different uses of water in your home. Try to work out which requires most water and which the least. Try to estimate roughly how much water is used each day, and how much is wasted.

2 Now brainstorm ways in which you could cut down on wastage and help to conserve water. Collect your ideas.

3 Have a class discussion to prepare a final list of conservation measures.

12.1 Why is water important? (continued)

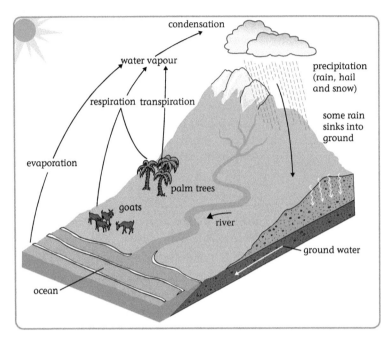

How water is recycled in nature

Water, like many other substances (see page 191), circulates or **recycles** in nature. The **water cycle** shows how we obtain a continuous supply of fresh water.

Water enters the air by evaporation:

- from water surfaces such as oceans, rivers and lakes
- from respiration of plants and animals
- from sweating of animals and transpiration of plants.

The water vapour rises in the air, is cooled and condenses. The droplets form into clouds, and when these are large enough, they drop as rain. Water also falls to Earth as hail and snow. Water seeps into the ground and is taken up by plant roots, or drunk by animals. It also flows into rivers or the sea via groundwater. So the water is recycled.

- 97% of water is salty and is found in the seas.
- Only 3% is fresh – most of this is at the poles as ice.
- 0.036% of water is in lakes and rivers.
- 0.001% of water is in clouds.

Practical 72

Evaporation of water (ORR, AI)

Materials: four similar containers, two with lids, four rubber bands, a measuring cylinder.

1 Measure the same amount of water into each of the containers, until they are three-quarters full.

2 Put the rubber bands around each container to show the initial water level.

3 Leave a covered and an open container in full Sun on a window ledge, and a covered and an open one inside a cupboard.

4 Each day, at the same time, carefully measure the amount of water in each container. Record the amounts and return the water to their original containers.

5 After 4 days prepare a bar chart of your results. Account for your findings.

Questions

1 Describe two examples each that show why water is important for life processes in (a) animals and (b) plants.

2 What are three ways in which you could save water at home, and still be healthy?

3 In the middle of the day some potted Busy Lizzies, in the Sun, were droopy and wilted. Describe *exactly* what you would do to restore them to their upright condition with the *minimum* of water.

4 What will be the effect on the water cycle if we (a) cut down large forests and (b) build large dams and reservoirs?

Key ideas

Use these words to fill in the spaces as you write the sentences in your Exercise book.

solvent   **condenses**   **evaporates**   **chemical**   **transpiration**   **protoplasm**

Water is essential for life. This is because _____ is about 70% water, and water is an important _____ and takes part in _____ reactions. In the water cycle, water _____ from water surfaces, such as the sea. Water vapour is also formed from respiration and _____ . Water _____ to make clouds, and may fall as rain. There is a continual supply of fresh water.

12.2 How is water purified?

Where does our water come from?

Caribbean countries vary in the nature and extent of their water sources. For example, Barbados and Antigua have to rely on underground water supplies, whereas Dominica and Guyana have many rivers. The annual rainfall is of key importance. If there is a lot of rain, it should be possible to store some rainwater in storage tanks or reservoirs so it can be used as a water supply during times of drought.

Water that has been stored or is found in a river, stream or underground well is likely to contain many things besides water. These are called **impurities**, such as garbage, soil, bacteria, fertilizer and detergent. Before we make use of a water source, we need to know what it contains.

Activity

Water sources

1 Make a list of the water sources in your country.
2 Which is the most important source of water in your country? Why?
3 Make a list of the types of impurity you might expect to find in each source. Discuss this with the class.

Water purification

We all need a good, reliable source of clean water. Our water is usually purified at a waterworks. Although this process is more complicated than the way it is explained here, there are five main stages as shown below.

1 A screen sieves out large pieces of garbage.
2 The water is then filtered through coarse sand that removes large solid particles.
3 The filtered water passes through a sedimentation tank. Chemicals such as alum are added to make smaller particles stick together and drop to the bottom.
4 The water is then passed through a fine sand filter to remove the smallest solid particles.
5 Chlorine gas is added. This kills any bacteria.

Objectives

● Outline the stages of water purification at a waterworks.
● Prepare clean water in the laboratory, for example by filtration and distillation.

Practical 73

Impurities in water (MM, ORR)

Work in groups to compare samples of muddy water, rainwater, seawater, storage tank water and tap water.

1 Prepare a table and record the appearance and smell of each sample. Do *not* taste any of the samples. Why not?

2 Record the pH (see page 278) of each.

3 Filter each one and compare the amounts of solid particles left behind, by observation and estimation.

4 Carefully heat a sample of each one, in an evaporating dish, to drive off the water. Compare the amounts of solid remains by observation and estimation.

5 Use the tests for temporary and permanent hardness (see page 288).

6 Your teacher might also perform tests for some specific chemicals.

7 Record and discuss all your results.

8 List the water samples in order from dirtiest to cleanest.

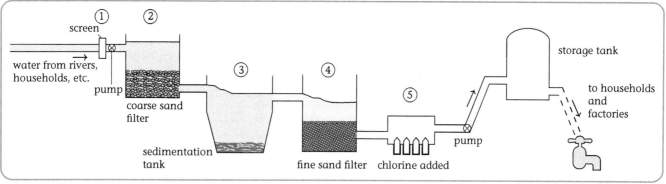

Stages in water purification

12.2 How is water purified? (continued)

Making use of seawater

In many homes in the Caribbean, there is not a reliable source of clean water. But we are surrounded by the sea. Can we process seawater to make fresh water?

When water is heated it evaporates. It is only the pure water that becomes a vapour; any salts that were dissolved in it are left behind. The pure water vapour can then be condensed. This is the principle of **distillation**, and it can be used on a large scale to prepare pure distilled water. The taste of distilled water is different from that obtained from a regular water supply, and some salts should be added back into it for long-term healthy use.

Distillation and other methods can be used to get fresh water from seawater. This process is called **desalination**. There are desalination plants in Antigua, Trinidad and Tobago, Barbados, The Bahamas, The Cayman Islands, US and Virgin Islands, and Turks and Caicos. The Caribbean Desalination Association was formed in 2007, for the exchange of knowledge regarding desalination and water re-use in the region.

A desalination plant in Aruba

How is water desalinated?

Solar distillation This uses the Sun's energy to heat the seawater. The pure water vapour that is formed is then condensed against a cold surface to make pure distilled water. You can try using this process yourself (see the diagram on the right). Suspend a small container above some seawater in a pot. Put ice cubes into the upturned lid and heat the water in the pot. Water will evaporate from the seawater, condense on the cool lid, and drip into the small container, as pure distilled water.

Flash distillation When the pressure in a chamber is reduced, the water in it can evaporate at a lower temperature. Special chambers are kept at low pressure and seawater is passed through them in pipes. The seawater is also heated, so that it evaporates. The condensed pure water is collected.

Salt removal or reverse osmosis Treated seawater is forced at high pressure through special membranes that hold back the salts, and let through only the fresh water.

Freezing This is a new method. The seawater is frozen to give ice crystals. These are then washed to remove salts and allowed to melt back to make fresh water.

What does it mean?

Dirty water Water with soil, organic material, bacteria and other impurities.

River water This may appear clear, but it should be filtered to remove organic material, and boiled to help kill bacteria.

Clean water Water without organic material or bacteria, e.g. tap water supplied from the waterworks.

Fresh water Water with only a small amount of dissolved chemicals, e.g. as found in lakes, rivers and the ice caps.

Seawater Water with about 35 g per litre of dissolved chemicals, such as sodium chloride.

Pure water Water without dissolved chemicals, e.g. as made by distillation.

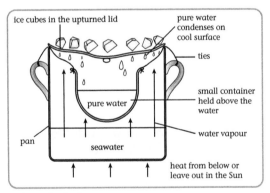

Making distilled water

Questions

1 Why is a supply of clean water important for human life?

2 Try to visit a place where water is purified for use by humans. Describe each of the processes.

3 Water supplied to our homes is likely to be clean but not 'pure'. What is meant by this statement?

How is impure water made safe for use?

You may have lived through a period after a hurricane has struck your country, and the water supply has been cut off or contaminated. Or you may have gone camping and run out of clean water. What can you do?

Here are the steps we can take in an emergency

1 Let a sample of water stand so that most of the suspended material sinks to the bottom. Pour off and keep the top liquid.
2 Filter this liquid through as fine a cloth as you can find. Or you can cut the bottom from a plastic bottle and cover the end with fine cloth. Then fill the bottle with soil and sand and filter your water through it (see the practical on the right).
3 Then boil the filtered liquid for 5 minutes in an open pot, and let it cool in a closed pot. This will kill most microorganisms and could be used in an emergency.
4 If available, add purification or sterilization tablets to the boiled water. As an alternative, add a drop of chlorinated bleach to each litre of your boiled water. In each case, let the water stand for 30 minutes before using it. These chemicals will kill any remaining microorganisms.
5 For babies and young children, it is safer to prepare pure distilled water (see the diagrams on pages 212 and 214). This will be free of chemicals and microorganisms.

Note: It is NOT recommended that these procedures be used except in an emergency, and then only for a short time.

Practical 74

Filtering in the laboratory (ORR, AI)

Use the filtering apparatus below to filter a sample of
(a) muddy water and
(b) salt water (made by adding salt to tap water).
When you have finished, answer the questions in the box on the right.

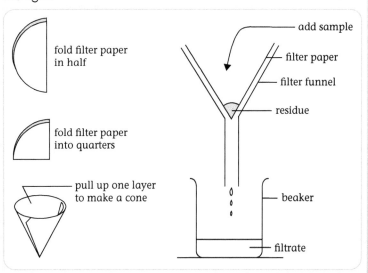

Practical 75

Removing impurities (MM, ORR, AI)

Use the same sample of muddy water you used on page 211. Record the appearance of the water before and after each step.

1 Prepare a tube from a plastic bottle and tie muslin cloth around one open end.

2 Add sand and then soil to the tube. Filter the muddy water, as shown below.

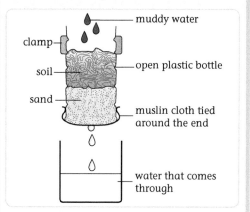

3 Filter the water that comes through from step 2, using proper filter paper.

4 Boil some of the water from step 2.

5 Add bleach to some water from step 2.

6 Take another sample of water from step 2 and distil it.

7 Test each water by putting a few drops onto nutrient agar, and compare which produces fewest microorganisms.

Conclusion: (a) What effect does each of steps 2–6 have on removing impurities? (b) Which is the *only* sample you could be sure was pure for drinking?

Questions

4 **Muddy water** (a) What is in the residue? (b) What is in the filtrate?
5 **Salt water** (a) What is in the residue? (b) What is in the filtrate?
6 **Summary** (a) Does filtering remove solid particles? (b) Does filtering remove dissolved substances?
7 What are the characteristics of a good filter paper?

12.2 How is water purified? (continued)

Practical 76

Distillation in the laboratory (ORR, AI)

Set up the apparatus below to distil a sample of:
(a) salt water (made by adding salt to tap water) and
(b) coloured water (add food colouring to tap water).

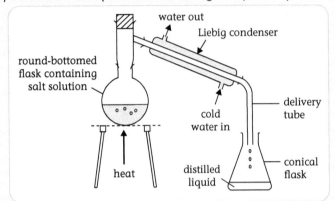

- The liquid is heated gently, so it boils steadily and gives off pure water vapour.
- The vapour enters into the condenser, which is kept cool by water circulating around it.
- The pure water is condensed and collected in the conical flask as distilled water.

Practical 77

Using alum for cleaning water (ORR)

Alum is a sulphate of potassium and aluminium. Your teacher will prepare a 4% solution for you to use with dirty water.

1 Add the alum drop by drop from a pipette. Record your observations. The impurities will be clumped together.

2 Keep adding drops of alum until there is no precipitate.

3 Let the mixture stand for 8 hours, then pour off the clean liquid from the top.

Questions

1 **Salt water** (a) What is left behind in the flask? (b) What is the distilled liquid?
2 **Coloured water** (a) What is left in the flask? (b) What is the distilled liquid?
3 **Summary** Can distillation be used to separate dissolved substances from a solvent? Explain.

Cleaning and purification

- Filtering through coarse sand can remove some larger-sized impurities.
- Filtering through fine sand can remove smaller-sized impurities.
- Filtering through filter paper removes very small solid particles but cannot remove any dissolved ones.
- Boiling can kill most bacteria. Chlorine or purification tablets also kill bacteria.
- Distillation produces pure distilled water with no soluble or insoluble impurities and no bacteria.

Questions

4 Students tested samples of water by putting small amounts onto nutrient agar. In what order do you expect the samples would show most bacteria: seawater, river water, distilled water and filtered water?
5 How is distilled water different from bottled spring water?
6 Why do you think distilled water is used to top up the acid in a car's battery?

Key ideas

Use these words to fill in the spaces as you write the sentences in your Exercise book.

pure   **distillation**   **clean**   **filtering**   **fresh**   **desalination**   **chlorine**

We need to drink _____ water (which is not salty) and _____ water (which does not contain

bacteria). At the waterworks, particles are removed by _____ , and bacteria are killed with

_____ . The process of removing salts from seawater is called _____ . One way of doing this is

by _____ , which produces _____ distilled water.

12.3 Water properties and aquatic life

Chemical properties of fresh water and seawater

Chemical properties are the chemical reactions and the chemical test for a substance. Pure distilled water is a compound of hydrogen and oxygen. The chemical test is that it turns dry (anhydrous) white copper sulphate blue.

- **Seawater** contains large amounts of salts, mainly common salt (sodium chloride) and dissolved gases.
- **Fresh water** contains some salts and dissolved gases.

Physical properties of fresh water and seawater

Physical properties describe how substances behave, such as boiling and melting points, and density.

Why can I swim more easily in the sea than a pool?

In comparing the densities in the activity above, you may have used similar blocks and compared how well they floated in fresh water and seawater. Because seawater contains so many dissolved **solutes**, its density is higher than that of fresh water. When you swim in the sea you get the advantage of this increased **buoyancy** or **upthrust**, compared with being in a swimming pool.

- Fish are also better supported in seawater than in fresh water, can swim more easily, and have less need for a swim bladder to keep them buoyant.
- In fresh water, the fish have to keep swimming to stay up in the water. They also use their swim bladder to control their position: when air is expelled, the fish sinks in the water; when air is let into the bladder, the fish becomes more buoyant and rises in the water.

Water balance in fish

Osmosis is the movement of water from a region of higher concentration to a region of lower concentration.

Freshwater fish

In their natural habitat, the body fluids are more concentrated than the fresh water. Water enters by osmosis, and the fish excretes a lot of dilute urine.

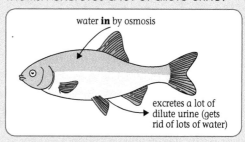

Seawater fish

In their natural habitat, the body fluids are less concentrated than the seawater. So water tends to be lost by osmosis, and the fish conserves as much water as possible.

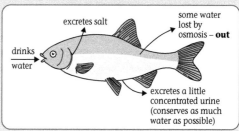

12.3 Water properties and aquatic life (continued)

How can a fish move in water?

Floating and support

If you try to push a balloon below water, you will feel the water pushing back. We call this the **upthrust** of the water. An object also has **weight**. If the upthrust and the weight balance each other, then the object floats. If the weight is greater, then the object sinks.

The same is true for animals. In the case of a fish (see (a)), it adjusts its overall weight by using its swim bladder, and so determines how deep it will be in the water.

Balance

If you are in a boat, you try to keep the weight of people and cargo evenly spread. If a boat is unbalanced it might sink. In the case of a fish, the dorsal and ventral fins keep it balanced (see Practical 81).

Muscles for movement

Fish produce their own force of motion by contracting and relaxing the muscles in their tails (see (b) on the right).

Streamlining

If you try walking in water, you will notice a lot of resistance. This is called **water resistance**, or **drag**. It is much greater than the resistance to moving through air, as water is so much denser. Many fish have a **streamlined** shape, which helps to cut down on the effect of water resistance. This shape has a curved front or one with a gentle point and then becomes wider. It narrows towards the back. You can investigate different shapes.

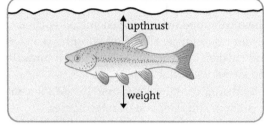

(a) How a fish floats in water: weight is less than, or equal to, upthrust

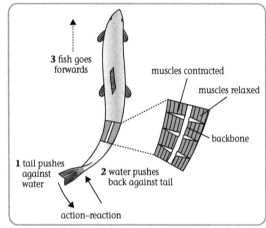

(b) How a fish swims in water: the tail pushes on the water, and the water pushes back

---

Practical 80

Investigating streamlining (MM, ORR, AI)

1 You will need four similar-sized pieces of wood, with different shaped fronts and small hooks.
2 Set up the water tank and pulley as shown below. Use a string over the pulley and attach a 50 g mass.
3 In turn, attach each shape to the other end of the string, and time how long it takes the shape to move the length of the tank.
4 Use each shape five times and take an average. Record all your findings.
5 Which of the shapes travelled the slowest?
6 Which of the shapes travelled the fastest?
7 Explain your results.

Are all fish streamlined?

Streamlining helps fish to move more easily through the water, for the same effort from their muscles. But some fish, such as those adapted for living on a coral reef, have very strange shapes. They are not well streamlined, and so cannot swim away to escape predators. They tend to be camouflaged in some way, and so escape being noticed by predators.

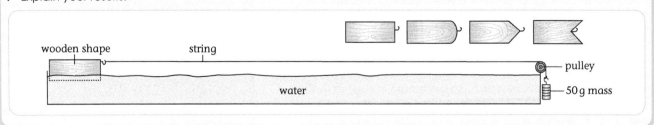

Practical 81

How are fish adapted for life in water? (ORR)

1 Notice how the body is **streamlined**. See how the pointed head goes through the water first and the scales all point backwards. The body is also covered in slippery mucus. The streamlining is similar to that of a boat, bird or plane, and reduces the resistance to the water.

2 See how the fish uses its tail and **fins** in swimming.
 ● **Tail and tail fin** The tail is very muscular. Muscles on either side of the backbone contract and relax alternately. As it pushes against the water (action), the water pushes back (reaction) and drives the fish forward in the water. The world record for swimming 100 m in humans is under 10 km/hour, whereas a sailfish can swim at 108 km/hour.
 ● **Dorsal and ventral fins** keep the fish upright and on a straight course (they stabilize it).
 ● **Pectoral and pelvic fins**, together with the **swim bladder**, control the depth at which the fish swims.

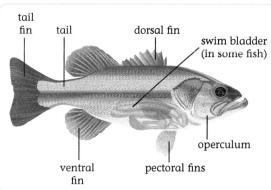

3 See how the fish breathes. Air, containing oxygen, is dissolved in the water. The water goes over the gills, and oxygen moves along a concentration gradient into the blood (see the diagrams on the right).
 ● **Inspiration** The operculum is flat to the body, and the mouth is open. The floor of the mouth cavity is lowered. Water enters the mouth cavity.
 ● **Expiration** The operculum is raised away from the gills, and the mouth is shut. The floor of the mouth cavity is raised so that water is forced out over the gills.

Practical 82

Is there air in water? (ORR, MM)

1 Put a beaker of tap water on a tripod over a very gentle flame. Warm the water slowly, but do not let it boil.
2 As the temperature increases, any air dissolved in the water will come out of solution as small bubbles.
3 Record your observations.

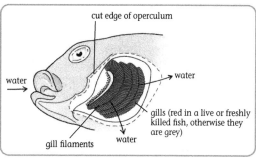

Operculum removed to show the gills

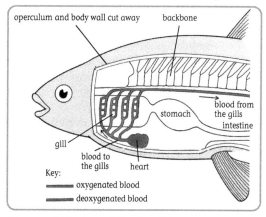

Diagram of blood circulation in a fish

Questions

1 An object sank in fresh water, but floated in seawater. Explain why.
2 How will (a) the buoyancy and (b) water control be affected in a seawater fish transferred to fresh water?
3 How does a fish move through water?
4 Why is the surface area to volume ratio of the gill filaments important?

12.3 Water properties and aquatic life (continued)

How can aquatic organisms live in water?

To be healthy, all aquatic organisms need water that is not polluted (see pages 224–5). They also need other things.

Plants

- They need light for photosynthesis. So plants are often small and light to float, e.g. plankton, or have structures, e.g. bladders in seaweeds, to help keep them up in the water. Light can penetrate to over 100 m in clear water, but corals (which depend on algae in their tissues for photosynthesis) are rarely found deeper than 30 m.
- They need carbon dioxide and water for photosynthesis, and mineral salts for healthy growth. The leaf surfaces are often large and thin, to take in carbon dioxide, water and salts along concentration gradients. Because aquatic plants take in water and salts through their leaves, they often have poorly developed roots. Plants living in fresh water or seawater need to be in water balance with their surroundings (see page 382).
- Excess oxygen, in the daytime, is excreted into the water along its concentration gradient.
- They need oxygen at night for respiration, to release energy. They take this into their leaves from the water.
- They need decomposers to decay the dead remains of plants and animals, to release the mineral salts that are needed for making proteins and ensuring healthy growth.

Animals

- They need food; animals are ultimately dependent on plants for food (see page 219).
- They need oxygen all the time, for respiration. For example, fish have gills to take oxygen from the water and release carbon dioxide (see page 217) along concentration gradients. The reduction of oxygen concentration in the water (see page 224) could cause fish to suffocate.
- They need support from the water and they have to control their water balance (see pages 215–16).

An aquatic plant: in what ways is it adapted for an aquatic habitat?

Questions

1 Describe the meaning of the following terms and give a named example for each one from an aquatic habitat: (a) producer, (b) first-order consumer, (c) herbivore, (d) second-order consumer, (e) carnivore, (f) omnivore.
2 'We depend on plankton for the food that we get from the sea.' Explain why.
3 A large number of small fish were removed from a marine area. What effects will this have on (a) larger fish, (b) animal plankton, (c) plant plankton?
4 How are aquatic plants (a) similar to and (b) different from land plants?
5 Give three examples where concentration gradients are important for aquatic organisms.

Key ideas

Use these words to fill in the spaces as you write the sentences in your Exercise book.

fresh water**gain****seawater****producers****lot of****lose****consumers****little**

_____ contains more solutes and is denser than _____ . A seawater fish in seawater tends to

_____ water by osmosis; it excretes a _____ concentrated urine. A freshwater fish in fresh water

tends to _____ water; it excretes a _____ dilute urine. All food chains begin with _____ , and

have several levels of _____ .

Aquatic food chains

Food chains show which organisms eat other organisms. The complex feeding relationships in a community make up a **food web** (see pages 188–9). We can identify the following.

Producers

These are the green plants at the start of all food chains. They trap the Sun's energy and make food by photosynthesis (see pages 48–9).

Consumers

These are the animals.

- Animals that eat plants are called **first-order** consumers or **herbivores**.
- Animals that eat other animals are called **carnivores** or **predators**. **Second-order** consumers eat first-order consumers, and **third-order** consumers eat them.
- Animals that eat plants and other animals are called **omnivores**, e.g. humans.
- **Parasites** eat other *living* things (see page 234).
- **Scavengers**, e.g. vultures, eat dead and decaying organisms.
- **Decomposers**, e.g. bacteria, cause decay.

Food chains in fresh water

In fresh water the producers are green pondweeds such as *Elodea* (Canadian pondweed) and microscopic green algae (plankton). First-order consumers are animals, such as mosquito larvae, that feed on the plankton, and water snails and tadpoles that eat the pondweed. Second-order consumers, such as young fish (called 'fry') and small fish such as guppies, eat the first-order consumers. In turn, the second-order consumers are eaten by third-order consumers: these may be large fish, such as tilapia, or birds such as the kingfisher.

Food chains in seawater

The basis of the food chains in the sea is **plankton**. Plankton is made up of very small organisms of different kinds.

- Plant plankton are the producers. They are microscopic algae that carry out photosynthesis.
- Animal plankton are the first-order consumers that eat the producers. They are mostly small larvae and crustaceans.

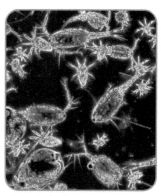

Plant plankton   Animal plankton

In seawater, the food chain begins with the plant plankton, which are eaten by the animal plankton: the first-order consumers. Small fish, such as sardines and the young 'fry' of larger fish, eat the animal plankton and are the second-order consumers. Larger fish such as grouper, snapper, king fish and flying fish are the third-order consumers, and they eat the second-order consumers. They in turn may be caught and eaten by humans, who are fourth-order consumers.

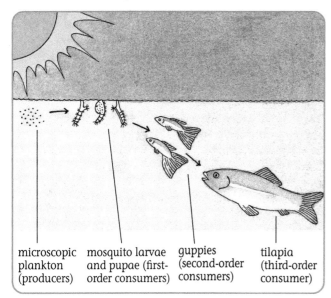

| microscopic plankton (producers) | mosquito larvae and pupae (first-order consumers) | guppies (second-order consumers) | tilapia (third-order consumer) |

A food chain in fresh water

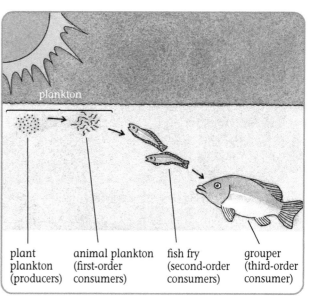

| plant plankton (producers) | animal plankton (first-order consumers) | fish fry (second-order consumers) | grouper (third-order consumer) |

A food chain in seawater

12.4 Why do objects float?

Whether an object floats or not depends on both the object and the medium into which it is put.

Objective

- State the conditions for flotation in terms of upthrust and density.

Object	Length (l)	Breadth (b)	Height (h)	Volume (l × b × h)	Mass (m)	Density (m/v)	Does it float?
Wooden block							
Polystyrene block							
Aluminium block							

Practical 83

Does density affect buoyancy? (ORR, MM, AI)

1 Collect a number of regularly shaped blocks of different materials, both metals and non-metals, e.g. aluminium, wood, candle wax and polystyrene.

2 Measure their length, breadth and height in cm. Weigh each to obtain the mass in grams.

3 Copy the table above and enter your results. Calculate density from the formula:

$$\text{density} = \frac{\text{mass}}{\text{volume}}$$

4 Do the blocks float in water? What are their densities?

Substance	Density g/cm³	Substance	Density g/cm³
Ice	0.92	Zinc	7.1
Tap water	1.0	Steel (iron)	7.8
Glass (varies)	2.6	Copper	8.9
Sand	2.6	Lead	11.3
Aluminium	2.7	Gold	19.3

Did you know?

- Many people laughed when it was first suggested that boats should be built of iron; they expected them to sink.

Practical 84

Finding volume using a measuring cylinder or Eureka can (MM, ORR, AI)

These methods are used for irregular solids, with dimensions that cannot be measured easily. Method (a), displacement in a measuring cylinder, is used for small objects; method (b), using a Eureka can, is for large objects.

1 Find the mass of the object, e.g. a stone, using a balance.

2 Partly fill the measuring cylinder with water and take the reading.

3 Lower the stone into the measuring cylinder until it is completely immersed.

4 Then take the new reading. The volume of the stone is the difference between the two readings.

Finding the volume of irregular objects

Finding the densities of liquids

Use a volume of 50 cm³. Find the mass by measurement. Then calculate the density of each one using density = mass/volume. Find the density of seawater, fresh (tap) water and cooking oil.

The density of seawater is greater than 1 g/cm³. In the Dead Sea, in Israel, the mass of salts is about 370 g in every kg of water and it is almost impossible for a swimmer to sink.

Does temperature affect density?

Convection currents in water (see page 164) depend on the relative differences in density between hot/warm water and cold water. Water is unusual: it decreases in density when heated and increases in density when cooled, with a maximum at 4 °C.

The Plimsoll line

Because fresh water and seawater have different densities, and temperature also affects density, ships will have different degrees of buoyancy depending on whether they are in fresh water or seawater, and whether it is summer or winter. The **Plimsoll line** on the hull of ships (see photograph on the right) shows how far down a ship is in the water, so it is possible to judge the load that can be carried safely. This was first proposed in the British Merchant Shipping Act in 1896 by Samuel Plimsoll MP.

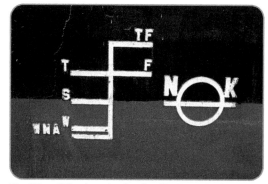

The Plimsoll line is a circular disc 30.47 cm in diameter, with a line drawn through its centre. The upper edge of the line is the maximum summer safe loading line. The lines to the left show the maximum loading lines for different seasons and circumstances

Practical 85

Investigating flotation (ORR, MM)

1 Take the block of wood, the density of which you already know. Float it in a full Eureka can and collect the water displaced. What is the volume of that water? So what is the mass of the displaced water?

2 Repeat the experiment using strong salt water in the Eureka can, e.g. 20% by mass (20 g dissolved in 100 cm³ water). What is the volume of salt water displaced? What is the mass of that water? Are the results the same as for fresh water?

Archimedes' principle

Experiments like the one above show that the mass of liquid displaced is the same for all liquids, e.g. fresh and salt water. This leads to the **law of flotation**: a floating body displaces its own weight of the fluid in which it floats. This means that a boat or a ship, like a piece of wood, when placed in water will sink until the weight of water displaced is just equal to the ship's own weight. So, overall, the ship, including the cargo and all the air spaces in it, must weigh less than the same volume of water. Because of all the air spaces in a ship, the total weight is less than that of an equivalent volume of water – and so the ship floats. If the ship were to get a hole in the side, which released some of the air so it was replaced with water, the denser ship would not be supported – it would sink. You can demonstrate what happens by using a small closed tin as a ship. Try floating the tin when it is full of air, and then when it contains water.

Archimedes' principle

All bodies wholly or partially immersed in a fluid (liquid or gas) are acted upon by an upward force that is equal to the weight of the fluid displaced by the body. This is **Archimedes' principle**. This upward force is called an upthrust. The less dense the material, the greater the upthrust on it. This principle has been applied to the manufacture of water-safety devices.

Questions

1 How does density affect whether an object sinks or floats?

2 How can iron ships float?

3 How can a ship, in the course of one journey, float to a different depth in the water without loading or off-loading?

4 List all the conditions necessary for an object to float.

Key ideas

Use these words to fill in the spaces as you write the sentences in your Exercise book.

volume	density	salinity	float	Plimsoll	upthrust

The _____ of an object is equal to its mass divided by its _____ . An object will _____ in a liquid (or gas) medium if it has a _____ that is less than that of the medium. The supporting force of the medium is the buoyancy (_____). Ships are supported to different degrees depending on the season and _____ of the water, as shown by the _____ line.

12.5 Objects moving through water and air

The shape of an object and the resistance of the medium affect how an object will move through water and air.

The importance of resistance

Resistance or drag

Resistance is the opposing force to movement. The effects of resistance from the medium are much greater in water than in air, as water is nearly 800 times denser than air.

Movement of the medium

The actual movement of the medium affects how quickly an object can move through it. For example, fish travelling **with** an ocean current, rather than **against** it, will travel more quickly. Runners and cyclists will achieve better speeds if the wind speed and direction are in their favour.

   If sprinters run with the wind behind them, this may lead to an improved time. In this case, the time is recorded as 'wind assisted' and is usually disallowed as an official time if the force of the wind is beyond a certain value.

   Sailboats use the wind currents to move them. They cannot sail directly against the wind, as it would blow them backwards. However, they may sail close to the wind, zigzagging from left to right in order to get into the direction of the wind. Kite-flyers also make use of wind currents to lift their kites. There is also usually a tail to keep the kite stable. Games such as table tennis and badminton are very sensitive to wind, so are normally played indoors. Golfers also have to take account of the speed and direction of the wind as they make their shots.

The importance of shape

Streamlining

You saw on page 216 that a streamlined shape (see (a), on the right) moves more quickly through water than one with a flat or incurved front (see (b)). Fish and other animals moving through water are usually streamlined. Humans who compete in swimming events wear close-fitting swimsuits of materials designed to cut down water resistance.

Making use of air resistance

Objects moving though air sometimes take advantage of the principle that air resistance slows down movement. Some examples are parachutes and paragliding, and the shapes of seeds and fruits, with wings or hairs, that keep them floating long enough to be dispersed.

   In cricket, a bowler may make use of air resistance by polishing a cricket ball on one side. The polished side offers less resistance to movement through the air (so it tends to go faster). The rough side has more resistance, so it slows down, and the ball 'swings' (swerves) towards the rough side when the ball is bowled.

Objective

● Discuss the factors affecting the free movement of objects in water and air.

Practical 86

How do different objects fall? (ORR)

1 Drop a flat sheet of paper. Does it fall straight down?

2 Drop a ball or stone from the same height. Does it fall the same way?

3 Fold the paper into different shapes and try it again. Does it behave in the same way? If you screw the paper up into a ball, it will fall in the same way as any other ball.

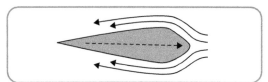

(a) Streamlined shape: less resistance

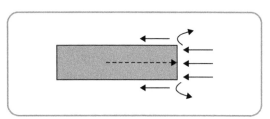

(b) Flat shape: more resistance

A paraglider makes use of air resistance by having a large parachute

Practical 87

What is the best angle for throwing something into the air? (MM, ORR, AI)

The best angle will be that which causes the pellets to travel the furthest.

1 Make a catapult using either a sawn-off syringe, or other type of improvised toy gun, which can fire pellets at different angles. Ensure that the force will be the same every time by using an elastic band stretched to the same amount (see diagram on the right).

2 Start with the catapult horizontal and fire the pellet. Use a metre rule to measure the distance at which it falls.

3 Increase the angle in steps of 10° and repeat. Record your results in a table.

4 Determine, to the nearest 5°, the angle of fire at which a pellet is thrown the furthest.

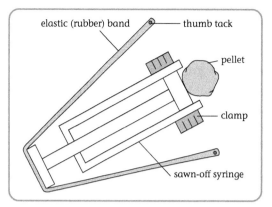

What is the best angle for throwing?

You will find that the best angle is 45°. This is the angle that throwers aim for, in order to attain the maximum distance for the object (projectile) they are throwing.

Apart from throwing the hammer (44°), human throwers are not able to throw their furthest close to the 45° angle, but at lower angles, because more muscle power can then be employed. For the shot-put the best putting angle is 40°, for the javelin the best angle is 30°, and for the discus it is 30°. For the long jump, which is in effect a throwing event involving the whole body, the best angle is again low, at 28°. Check the sequence below for throwing the javelin. Use a protractor to measure the angle of the javelin with the horizontal in the final step.

Putting the shot. Measure the putting angle

Questions

1 List all the conditions affecting movement of objects in water and air.

2 What factors affect the best throwing angles for a projectile?

Key ideas

Use these words to fill in the spaces as you write the sentences in your Exercise book.

angle　　**resistance**　　**shape**　　**air**　　**drag**　　**maximum**

How easily objects move through fluids, such as water or _____ , depends on their _____ and the _____ of the fluid. Water or air _____ (_____) opposes movement of an object. Streamlining reduces the _____ of the fluid. The throwing _____ for a human thrower is influenced by the angle at which the _____ muscle power can be applied.

12.6 How can we control water pollution?

What is pollution?

Pollution is the accumulation in the environment of waste products, or excess energy such as heat. These **pollutants** can cause ill health, disease and death. Here are some pollutants and their effects.

- acid rain (see page 321) – increases the acidity, e.g. of water in lakes, which can kill aquatic plants and animals
- industrial wastes – chemicals and heat can directly kill aquatic organisms, and heat reduces oxygen dissolved in the water
- litter – old containers and food scraps can become breeding grounds for pests that transfer diseases
- fertilizers – nitrates and phosphates enter river water (**eutrophication**) and cause excessive growth of algae
- sewage – disease organisms, smells, affect on movement in the water, and eutrophication
- oil spills – prevent oxygen getting to aquatic organisms, and damage the gills of fish and the feathers of birds
- silt – washed down hills by erosion after deforestation; can cause damage to corals, reefs and mangroves
- pesticides such as herbicides and insecticides – can directly poison aquatic organisms.

Case study: concentration of pesticides

Algae absorb pesticides from the water. The algae are eaten in large numbers by animal plankton, which then contain more pesticide. This is repeated up the food chain. The top consumers, fish or birds, may be killed because of the large amount of pesticides.

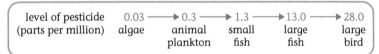

level of pesticide (parts per million)	0.03 algae	→	0.3 animal plankton	→	1.3 small fish	→	13.0 large fish	→	28.0 large bird

Case study: effects of eutrophication

The run-off of fertilizers and sewage into the water provide extra nutrients (eutrophication) for uncontrolled growth of algae (**algal bloom**). This has other effects, as shown below.

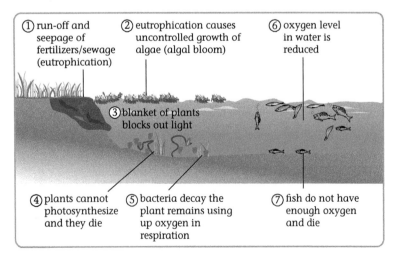

① run-off and seepage of fertilizers/sewage (eutrophication)
② eutrophication causes uncontrolled growth of algae (algal bloom)
⑥ oxygen level in water is reduced
③ blanket of plants blocks out light
④ plants cannot photosynthesize and they die
⑤ bacteria decay the plant remains using up oxygen in respiration
⑦ fish do not have enough oxygen and die

Objectives

- Discuss the effects of water pollution on aquatic life.
- Describe what could be done to reduce pollution.

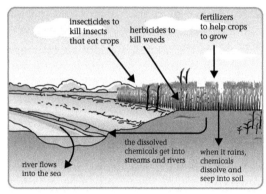

insecticides to kill insects that eat crops
herbicides to kill weeds
fertilizers to help crops to grow
the dissolved chemicals get into streams and rivers
when it rains, chemicals dissolve and seep into soil
river flows into the sea

Sources of pollution

Practical 88

Effect of oxygen removal (MM, ORR)

You need mosquito larvae. Leave a jam jar with rotting plant stems in water outside. Female mosquitoes will lay eggs. There should be larvae by the end of a week.

1 Boil some tap water for 5 minutes, cover and let it cool. You will have removed the dissolved oxygen.
2 Set up three measuring cylinders with equal amounts of water and 10 larvae:
   (a) boiled and cooled tap water
   (b) ordinary tap water left uncovered
   (c) ordinary tap water with oil on top.
3 For each sample, over a 5-minute period, count the number of times the larvae visit the surface to obtain air.
4 Count the number of dead larvae in each container each day.
5 How do you account for your findings?
6 Why is oil sprayed onto stagnant water as a control measure for mosquitoes?

At the end of the activity, kill the larvae so they do not become adult mosquitoes.

Case study: industrial waste

Heavy metals, such as lead and mercury, are very poisonous. In the 1960s a chemical factory in Minamata Bay, Japan, let out waste containing mercury. By 1969, many people were ill and 68 had died.

In Jamaica and Guyana there are problems with 'red mud', which is a waste from the bauxite industries. The chemicals need to be treated so they do not cause damage.

What can be done?

You can work in small groups to discuss an issue relating to water pollution. Research any causes and effects of local pollution, and suggest what could be done about it.

(a) What efforts are made by industries to take care of the water they use and then release into the waterways?

(b) What is being done about the conservation of water by the water supply authority? This might include maintenance of reservoirs, water piping systems, etc.

(c) Is there a local government department responsible for water analysis? What happens in this department?

(d) Are there any regulations about the dumping of industrial and human waste in the sea?

(e) If there is an oil refinery close by, visit it to find out what precautions are taken to prevent pollution.

(f) Are there areas of water in your country that have been so polluted that they cannot be used any longer? Is it possible for this water to be made clean again?

When you discuss your issues, you will probably find there are no simple answers. It is not just a question of scientific principles and how they are used. There are also costs, political control, relations with other countries and so on.

local people catch and eat fish in the bay

waste from the factory containing mercury

Waste water being discharged into the sea. What are the possible dangers of this?

Questions

1 What is meant by (a) eutrophication and (b) algal bloom? What causes each of them, and what are the eventual results on the fish population?

2 Sewage was dumped in an irrigation canal. Suggest (a) two problems this might cause and (b) two health hazards to people who live nearby.

Did you know?

● Oil slicks off the coast of Barbados have prevented flying fish from breeding.

● Heat pollution by global warming is causing part of the polar ice caps to melt, raising water levels.

● Lit sticks of dynamite used to be thrown into the sea to explode and kill fish. But this damaged the seabed and coral reefs, and destroyed other marine life.

Key ideas

Use these words to fill in the spaces as you write the sentences in your Exercise book.

bacteria　　**eutrophication**　　**acid rain**　　**algal**　　**pollutants**　　**fish**

Excess chemicals and heat can be _____ , e.g. _____ . Adding additional nutrients to the water

(as the run-off of fertilizers or sewage) is called _____ , and it can cause excess growth of algae

(an _____ bloom). This can lead to the death of other plants, the increase in numbers of

_____ , reduction of oxygen levels in the water, and the death of _____ .

12.7 What fishing methods are used?

Why do we catch fish?

For relaxation

Young children enjoy catching fish. Individuals and groups can enjoy using a rod and line, with bait, to catch fish as a hobby or sport. Sometimes the fish are returned to the water.

For food

The main purpose is to catch fish to eat. This can be on a small scale, for home use, or as a business.

As a business

- **The fishing industry** This makes its money from catching large numbers of smaller fish, or smaller numbers of very large fish. The purpose is to sell these for profit. For example, a very large fish, such as a yellowfin tuna, in perfect condition, can be sold overseas for several thousands of dollars.
- **Game fishing** Here the business provides an opportunity for tourists and local people to catch large fish, mostly for the sport of catching the fish. It is also the basis of competitions.

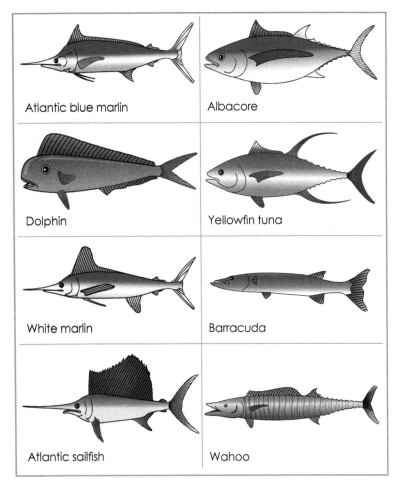

Some game fish caught in the Caribbean

Problems for the fishing industry

Transport Fish have to be transported to land, and then kept fresh until they are sold. They need to be packed in ice, or salted to help them stay fresh.

Consumer choice People have traditions about which fish they like, and which they dislike.

Overfishing If too many fish are taken, this can gradually cause the population to decrease in size. To help prevent this, several countries have quotas (allowed numbers) of fish that can be caught.

Fish farming

Some people set up special enclosures for growing fish. On these **fish farms** young fish, such as *Tilapia*, are reared. They feed on mosquito larvae, small fish and organic wastes, and every month or so the mature fish can be removed and sold.

Advantages: fish farms reduce the pressure on fish populations in the wild, and can produce cheaper fish.

Disadvantages: rearing fish in close conditions can lead to them becoming weak or getting disease. Some fish may escape, and cause problems in the wild.

Questions

1 What procedures are needed to reduce the likelihood of overfishing?
2 Describe and compare three different fishing methods.
3 Imagine you are a local fisherman. List the costs you will have in catching and selling your fish.

How do we catch fish?

By hand This is for sport and requires expertise.

Spear-fishing This is used for catching barracuda. It is a highly skilled method but cannot be used for catching large numbers of fish. Harpoons can be used for larger fish.

Fish pots or traps These have bait and one-way trap doors, so lobsters, crabs or fish that enter cannot get out again. The traps have to be emptied regularly, because if the animals died the smell would deter others from entering.

Fishing rods and lines These have bait (food or other items attractive to the fish) attached to hooks (a). Used for hobby fishing and game fishing. In longlining, which is used by commercial fishers, there is a central fishing line that has extra lines of baited hooks. It is left to trail in the water and is later hauled in with the catch.

Netting If the holes are too big, fish will escape, but if the holes are too small, young fry will be caught. If large numbers of fish, especially fry, are removed there will be fewer fish in the next generation. This is called **overfishing**.

- Scoop nets: these can be small and used in streams, or very large and used by commercial fishers in seawater.
- Trawling: the cone-shaped net (b) is pulled along in the sea by a boat (trawler) to catch large numbers of fish.
- Purse seining: the net (c) is towed in a large circle and then closed up (like a purse) to trap many surface fish. A similar net and procedure can be used close to land.
- Drift net: this is a curtain of netting (d) that hangs in the water. The fish swim into it and get caught.
- Dredging: the boat drags a heavy frame, with an attached mesh bag (e) along the sea floor. Shellfish go into the bag, but the dredger damages the sea floor.

Things to do

1 Collect information from local fishermen and -women, the fisheries department and the Internet, on fishing methods used locally and the fish that are caught.
2 Survey students on their favourite fish dish.

Fishing methods

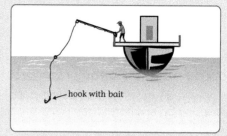

(a) Rod and line

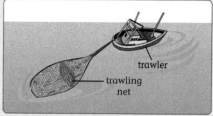

(b) Trawling net

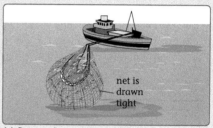

(c) Purse sein

(d) Drift net

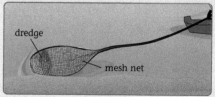

(e) Dredger

Key ideas

Use these words to fill in the spaces as you write the sentences in your Exercise book.

trawling   rod   purse   tuna   overfishing   farm   marlin

Fish can be reared on a fish _____ . A _____ and line is mainly used for sport fishing.

Some game fishes caught in the Caribbean are _____ and _____ . Some methods used for

commercial fishing for large numbers of fish are _____ and _____ seining. It is important to

limit the numbers of fish caught, especially young fry, in order to avoid _____ .

12.8 Can we be safe at sea?

How do magnets behave?

Set up a freely moving magnet in a paper cradle. Carry out and report on each step (see diagrams below).

1 Bring an S-pole close to the S-pole (a). What happens?
2 Bring an N-pole close to the N-pole. What happens?
3 Bring an N-pole close to the S-pole (b). What happens?
4 Lay a compass on the bench and make a sketch of the compass points (c).
5 Suspend the magnet above the sketch (d). What happens?

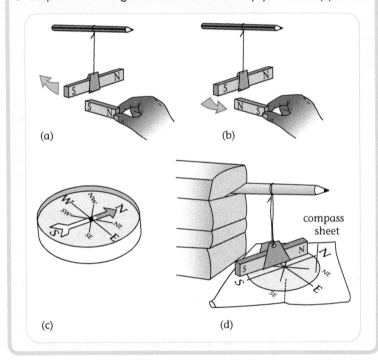

(a)   (b)

compass sheet

(c)   (d)

Objectives

- Describe the various navigational devices used at sea.
- Identify water safety devices.

The more recent **gyroscope** is a navigational instrument that overcomes the difficulties of the magnetic compass. It is a like a spinning compass with its axis set to true north, and it is able to hold this position irrespective of the movement of the ship and is unaffected by magnetism. It is therefore a much more reliable navigational instrument.

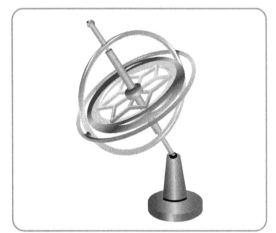

A gyroscope

Navigational devices

Compass

Lodestone (a naturally occurring magnetic material) was probably used first as a navigational aid by the Chinese in the early 12th century. The limitation of a compass is that it points to **magnetic north** rather than **true north**. The needle pointer therefore makes an angle with true north that varies with the position of the observer on Earth.

Global positioning systems

Since 1985 global positioning systems (GPS) became available for general use. All that is required is a GPS receiver and the ability to locate coordinates on a map. To locate a position, the GPS receiver makes contact with three or four of 27 orbiting satellites; each gives estimates of the position. When these estimates are compared, the one common to each of the different estimates is the exact location.

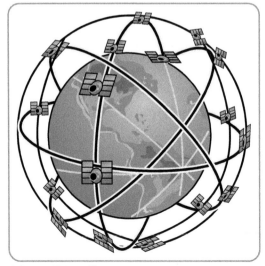

Orbiting GPS satellites

What is sonar?

Sonar refers to devices that produce specific sound-wave frequencies, and the echo is reflected from an object and converted to an electrical signal. Given the speed of sound in water and the echo time, it is possible to calculate distance. As a safety device, sonar is used to detect water depth, bottom contours and the proximity of other objects in poor visibility. Sonar can also be used to detect schools of fish (to assist sport fishing and the fishing industry), and to map underwater features, such as volcanoes (see page 203). The principle is illustrated below.

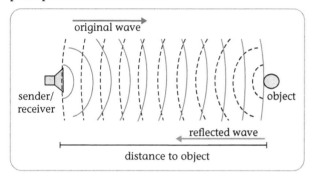

Water safety devices

If the density of an object is less than water, it will float (see page 220–1). This principle has been applied to making water safety devices, as many involve rings, tubes or clothing inflated with air. Some life rafts are made from expanded polystyrene or polyurethane foam with trapped air bubbles. All of these actions reduce the overall density of the safety devices; these can then be used to assist people to float.

General requirements

For safety, lifeboats and rafts are required on ships and large boats and many contain rations and first-aid kits. Flares and signals are also available to indicate their position.

Personal flotation devices

Individual personal flotation devices (PFDs) are also needed. There are different types and sizes, including life jackets, vests, belts and rings. Many are designed to keep an unconscious person face up. A PFD should be worn on recreational vessels at all times.

How is radar used?

Radar uses radio waves in the same way that sonar uses sound waves. So, a transmitter sends out a short pulse or stream of radio waves and a rotating antenna picks up the reflected signal, which is then visually displayed. As radio waves do not penetrate water, radar is always used above the surface. The target may be an object on the surface of the water, on land, or in the air, including cloud masses indicating disturbed weather. Radar is increasingly being used to confirm one's position relative to buoys, landmarks and other vessels in heavy traffic, and through fog and pitch darkness.

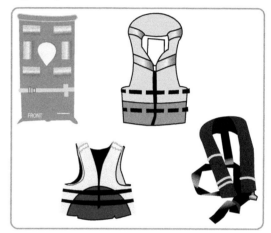

Personal flotation devices

Questions

1 How is sonar different from radar?
2 How would GPS be useful for boats and ships fishing in the Caribbean?
3 Choose three water safety devices. Why and how are they each used?

Key ideas

Use these words to fill in the spaces as you write the sentences in your Exercise book.

| true | magnetic | orbiting | gyroscope | PFDs | position |

A compass points to _____ north rather than _____ north. A _____ always points to _____ north and is unaffected by the movement of the ship. To locate a _____ accurately, the GPS receiver makes contact with three or four of 27 _____ satellites. Water safety devices include flares, signals, lifeboats, life rafts and individual _____ .

12.9 How can we survive under water?

Humans are air breathers, well adapted for life on land. When we wish to enter the strange and fascinating underwater world we may find it fraught with dangers that we must overcome if we are to come out again unharmed.

What are some of the dangers?

How do we get oxygen to breathe?

Have you ever seen **scuba** divers? They use self-contained underwater breathing apparatus (the first letters of each word form the word 'scuba'). This provides oxygen. The divers are supplied with air with the correct percentage of oxygen and delivered at the appropriate pressure.

Is pressure a problem?

The diagram on the right shows water escaping from three similar holes at different heights in a container. The water from the bottom hole travels furthest, whereas water from the top hole travels the least distance. This shows how pressure, which forces the water through the holes, is greatest when the distance from the water surface to the hole is greatest. So, if we go under water we will need a supply of oxygen at the correct pressure.

Does diving affect hearing?

Look at the diagram of the parts of the ear. Note the membrane, the eardrum, and the passage leading from the inner ear to the throat. This is the **Eustachian tube**. At sea level, before the diver descends, the pressure inside and outside the middle ear is balanced. When the diver descends, the increased pressure due to seawater pushes on the eardrum and stretches it – this causes pain, and the eardrum is in danger of rupture. If the diver 'clears' his or her ears, the pressure is relieved and the danger is over. By holding the nose closed and blowing, divers can force air from the throat through the Eustachian tube into the middle ear. This air is then at the same pressure as the surrounding water, so the pressure is relieved.

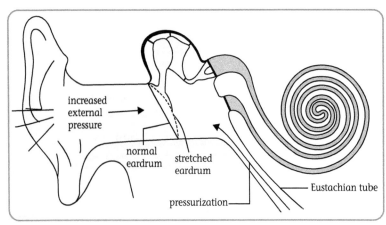

Relieving pressure in the middle ear

The aqualung – the regulator has a mouthpiece attached for breathing and a reduction valve that enables air to be delivered to the diver at safe pressures

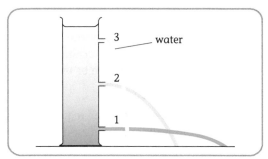

Water pressure increases with depth

Gases and pressure

When you open a soft fizzy drink you can observe how bubbles form in the liquid. Why is this?

The drink in the bottle is produced under pressure. High pressure increases the solubility of gases in liquids. When the stopper is removed, the pressure is reduced and the gas (carbon dioxide in this case) comes out of solution because it is less soluble at the lower pressure.

Similarly, as a diver travels deeper and water pressure increases, more and more gases dissolve in the diver's blood. This may come out as air bubbles when they ascend, causing a type of sickness called 'the bends' (see page 231).

Can air under pressure be harmful?

Nitrogen

High pressure increases the solubility of gases in liquids and this can lead to problems for divers: at deeper depths, more nitrogen dissolves in the blood. Nitrogen can have anaesthetic effects on the brain. This becomes most noticeable at depths of 30 m or more. The effects, known as **nitrogen narcosis**, are lack of coordination, confused thinking and reduced self-preservation instincts. At a depth of 60 m, the effect of nitrogen narcosis becomes very serious indeed.

Oxygen

If pure oxygen were used for a diver's air supply instead of ordinary air, dangerous effects would develop at depths as low as 8 m. Symptoms include coughing, vomiting, convulsions and unconsciousness. If the air or gas mixture contains 20% oxygen, **oxygen poisoning** can occur at depths of 60 m and beyond. At this increased pressure, oxygen has a harmful effect on the central nervous system. So the percentage of oxygen supplied has to be carefully regulated.

What causes 'burst lung'?

This is a serious condition, which can end in death. As the name suggests, the lungs can rupture, causing loss of blood, collapse of the lungs and death. Burst lung can be caused by too rapid an ascent from depth, without taking the precaution of breathing out heavily to release lung pressure. A slow ascent, breathing naturally, helps to avoid this usually fatal occurrence.

Take care

Scuba diving can be a very enjoyable and safe sport, but mistakes can be crippling and fatal. Adequate training with a reputable club or professional body is vital before any scuba diving is attempted.

How can divers avoid the bends?

The bends

'The bends' refers to the cripplingly painful sensations that many of the early scuba divers experienced. Today we know they are caused by air bubbles (air **embolisms**) cutting off circulation of blood in various parts of the body. The pains indicate oxygen-starved and dying tissues. Precautions necessary to avoid the bends include: adequate preparation before dives, learning to dive within safe limits of time and depth, and following regulation decompression procedures.

Decompression

Getting rid of dissolved air is called decompression. Decompression involves slow ascents to predetermined depths and remaining there for a certain time to allow bubbles of dissolved air to be released harmlessly in the lungs. If divers have to return to the surface too quickly they must enter a **recompression chamber** at once, otherwise their health remains at risk. Inside a recompression chamber is a closed compartment, where the air pressure can be controlled to a safe level for the diver. When a diver is being treated in a recompression chamber, compressed air corresponding to the dive conditions is used. This makes any air embolisms redissolve. The pressure in the chamber is then released slowly and safely over a period of time. The diver stays in the chamber until the process is completed.

Questions

1 Why is deep diving much more dangerous than shallow diving?
2 What is the function of the aqualung?
3 Why would it be dangerous to dive with a blocked Eustachian tube?
4 What precautions should a diver take to avoid the bends?

Key ideas

Use these words to fill in the spaces as you write the sentences in your Exercise book.

narcosis　　**decompression**　　**soluble**　　**nitrogen**　　**pressure**　　**oxygen**

The deeper the dive, the greater the _____ and the more _____ the air becomes in the diver's lungs. It is important to provide _____ at the correct percentage. Dissolved _____ in the bloodstream can cause nitrogen _____ . Deep dives have to be carefully planned to allow for adequate air, a slow ascent and time for _____ .

13 Pests and parasites, and sanitation

13.1 How can we stop food from spoiling?

Microorganisms, such as bacteria and moulds, spoil food by decaying it and make it dangerous to eat. Their waste products can make the food smell and taste unpleasant. Some bacteria produce poisonous substances (**toxins**), which pass onto the food and can cause **food poisoning**. Meat, milk and shellfish are often affected. The contents of damaged, bulging or 'blown' cans may cause food poisoning, because the bulge shows bacteria have multiplied inside the can and produced carbon dioxide gas to push out the ends. Such food must not be eaten.

What helps microorganisms grow?

- **Suitable temperature:** 25°C to 38°C is ideal.
- **Oxygen:** needed by most decay organisms; however, some can respire anaerobically (see page 78), but the ethanol or lactic acid produced stops further decay.
- **Water:** needed for germination of spores and growth.
- **Absence of dangerous chemicals:** allows growth.

We can remove one or more of these conditions and so control or kill the microorganisms and **preserve** our food.

How can we preserve our food?

Unsuitable temperature

Freezing does not kill microorganisms; it just slows down their growth rate. The lower the temperature, the slower the growth. The microorganisms resume their normal rate of growth at room temperature and cause decay.

High temperature: most microorganisms die if kept above 50°C for several minutes, but some spores can survive.

Remove oxygen

When food is put into cans the air is removed before the lid is put on. Foods are often preserved in some other way, such as the addition of sugar, before being canned.

Remove water

Drying: Heating food dries it out. Crops such as tobacco leaves, and also fish, can be dried in the Sun (solar drying; see page 328). Dried foods keep for a long time. They also take up less space and are easier to transport and store. When they have water added to them, decay begins.

Add concentrated salt or sugar solution: the water inside the microorganisms will be drawn out by osmosis, and they will die.

Add selected chemicals

Chemicals are added that kill the microorganisms, but should not harm humans. Examples are ethanoic acid (vinegar) used in pickling, and chlorine used to purify water.

Objectives

- Describe the conditions that promote the growth of microorganisms.
- Discuss principles of food preservation.

Practical 90

Slowing down decay (PD)

Use bread mould as your microorganism.
1 Plan and design a fair test to find how it grows under the following conditions. Include a control, with all the conditions you think are needed for growth:
(a) dry, (b) cold, (c) with salt, (d) with sugar, (e) with vinegar.
2 Make predictions about how well the mould will grow in each of the conditions.
Also refer to page 383.

Questions

1 List three foods that could be preserved by each of the methods on the left.
2 Discuss two methods of preservation that you could use yourself and explain the scientific principles underlying them.
3 Explain the following:
   (a) the ends of a can bulging out
   (b) leftover food in a fridge going bad
   (c) dried milk staying good, but liquid milk going bad
   (d) boiling food for a few seconds before preserving it by freezing
   (e) pineapples often being preserved in sugar solution
   (f) frozen food going bad before dried food does.

Did you know?

- Seeds can be dried for many years, and then germinate when given water.
- Bodies have been frozen in deep ice for many years before being thawed out.
- Egyptian mummies were preserved.

Food preservation methods

Heating
- Many microorganisms killed, and too hot for others to grow well.

  If food is cooked and heated in some way, the heat can kill off some of the microorganisms. The food can then be canned or packaged. Liquids can also be boiled to kill the microorganisms. As the food or liquid cools back to room temperature, the remaining microorganisms increase their activity.

Cooling
- Too cold for microorganisms to grow well: slows growth.

  Food can be packed around with ice or put into a refrigerator. Food in the main part of the fridge keeps fresh for a few days, in the freezing compartment for a few weeks and in the deep freeze for a few months. When frozen food has been defrosted, it will begin to decay more quickly.

Drying
- No moisture for growth.

  The proportion of salt and sugar increases, which helps preservation. Drying removes water and is the most effective preservation method. Food can be left to dry in the Sun. The food becomes *dehydrated*. Microorganisms are killed, and spores that land on the food cannot grow. When water is added again, the food starts to decay.

Pickling
- Vinegar (weak acid) kills microorganisms.

  Food can be pickled by soaking it in vinegar. Vinegar is weak ethanoic (acetic) acid. It is harmless to humans, but it kills the microorganisms. The food is kept in the vinegar inside a closed bottle so other microorganisms are unlikely to get inside.

Salting
- Salt draws water out of microorganisms so they are killed.

  Salt is rubbed into the food, or the food is put into a concentrated solution of salt (brine). This same principle is used when sugar is added, for example to preserve fruit.

Preservatives
- Selected chemicals kill microorganisms.

  Chemicals, such as sodium benzoate, are added to food. They are listed on the labels. Some preservatives may also be damaging to humans (see page 63). Preservatives may be added to food that has been treated in other ways, for example dried.

Key ideas

Use these words to fill in the spaces as you write the sentences in your Exercise book.

chemicals **temperature** **preserve** **water** **oxygen** **heat**

Microorganisms, such as bacteria and moulds, need _____ , _____ , a suitable _____ , and absence of dangerous _____ in order to grow. If we change any of these conditions, we can _____ items of food. So we can dry food to remove _____ , and put food in cans and remove _____ . We also _____ the food, and add _____ to it to kill the microorganisms.

13.2 How can we control pests?

Pests and parasites harm people and their crops and farm animals. They reduce productivity and cause economic losses. Some pests transfer parasites to humans. But they are different in these main ways.

Pests	Parasites
Pests live *near* other organisms	Parasites live *on* or *in a* particular host organism
Pests do not depend directly on the other organism for food	Parasites get food directly from the host; they depend on the host
Pests are a nuisance because they spoil or steal our food and can transmit parasites	Parasites harm their host and can cause death
Pests move freely from place to place	Parasites stay with their host unless moving to reproduce

Objectives

- Discuss the conditions that encourage the breeding of household pests.
- Describe different control measures.

Some other pests

- **Ants:** these are a special nuisance if sugar or sweet food is left uncovered.
- **Termites:** these can destroy wooden buildings by eating the wood.
- **Weeds:** these grow among crop plants and take nutrients and water from the soil. They also restrict the light available for the crop.
- **Pests of plants:** caterpillars do a lot of harm as they eat the leaves. However, we need some caterpillars to become butterflies for pollination.

Comparison of common pests

Pests	Where they breed	What trouble they cause	How to control them
Cockroaches	Cockroaches breed in dark places, in drawers and cupboards and in cracks in the floor. The young nymphs are very small and can get into very small cracks. They prefer dirty places with food remains.	Cockroaches eat almost anything and so they carry bacteria around on their bodies. The bacteria can cause food to go bad. They also leave their droppings in the food and make it unpleasant to eat.	We can stop cockroaches from feeding by keeping all food in airtight containers or plastic bags. Drawers and cupboards should be cleaned out regularly. Pesticides can be sprayed to kill them (first cover any food).
Flies	Flies lay eggs on food left open to the air. They are especially attracted to decaying food. Leftover food that is not covered will soon be teeming with maggots (the larvae of the fly).	Flies feed on faeces and on human food. They carry bacteria on their bodies and in their saliva and faeces. They put these on the food, and so make it unsafe to eat. The bacteria can cause decay and disease. The maggots also eat our food.	Wrap up the food or cover it with another dish. Food kept in a food safe, made of fine netting, will also be protected. Catch flies on sticky flypaper, or spray pesticides to kill them, taking care to first cover any food.
Rats	Rats breed in dark cupboards and under floorboards. They also live on ships that are carrying food. They prefer crowded, dirty conditions. They urinate and defecate on our food.	Rats feed in refuse dumps and sewage systems, and so may carry bacteria to our food. Rats can pass on bacteria that cause leptospirosis. They also carry rat fleas, which can bite humans and may pass on plague bacteria. They can also damage wooden buildings.	Food should be stored in airtight containers. Houses and grain stores can be rat-proofed with barriers to stop the entry of rats. Poisoned food (bait) can be put down to kill them, and traps and cats can be used to catch them.
Mosquitoes	Mosquitoes breed in stagnant water in ponds and swamps. They also breed in old tins and pots that contain decaying plant material. Eggs hatch into aquatic larvae, which grow into pupae.	Female mosquitoes suck blood from humans, which causes irritating bites. They also spread diseases. *Anopheles* mosquitoes spread malaria parasites (see page 242). *Culex* mosquitoes spread minute worms causing elephantiasis. *Aedes* mosquitoes spread viruses causing dengue and yellow fever.	We can stop them from feeding by using repellent cream and by keeping ourselves well covered in the evenings. We can stop them from breeding by draining swamps and removing containers that could become filled with water and then serve as a breeding place. We can kill larvae and pupae with kerosene, and adults with insecticides.

What measures can we use to control pests?

Measure	Examples	Advantages	Disadvantages
Sanitary	• Clean the surfaces and cupboards • Cover food, clean the surroundings	• No food, so pests do not feed and breed	• Takes time and money to keep things clean
Chemical	• Spray pesticides to kill pests • Use insecticides to kill insects and herbicides to kill herbaceous weeds • Mix poison with baited food	• Quick and easy to use • Many varieties, so easy to choose best one • Very effective	• Expensive • May kill harmless species • May remain in the environment (see page 224)
Physical	• Use mechanical devices such as fly swatters or traps • Use electronic bug killers	• Less expensive • Does not harm the environment	• May kill harmless species • Traps need emptying • Not very effective
Biological	• Use another animal to specifically eat the pests, such as cats to eat rats and mice • Introduce an infection to kill the pest • Produce infertile males, and release them to breed with females – to reduce numbers	• Can target the choice of predator, infection or control of breeding, to a specific pest • No chemicals released	• A predator might also eat other animals • An infection might spread to other organisms • Upsets balance of nature

Handling pesticides

Pesticides can be pellets for killing rats and slugs, aerosol sprays for killing flies, cockroaches and mosquitoes, or liquid solutions.

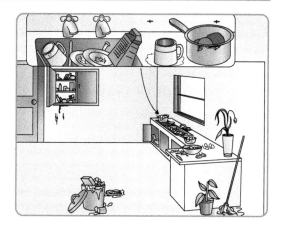

Do

✓ Choose the correct pesticide for the purpose.
✓ Wear gloves and other protective clothing when making up solutions and spraying crops.
✓ Read and follow all instructions carefully.
✓ Cover all foodstuffs before using pesticides.
✓ Spray when the air is still, so pesticide is not blown into other areas. Complete the job, to reduce likelihood of some organisms becoming resistant to the pesticide.
✓ Wash spraying equipment thoroughly after use.
✓ Lock away pesticides when not in use.
✓ Wash your hands carefully after handling pesticides.

Don't

✗ Don't drink, eat or smoke when spraying.
✗ Don't breathe in the fumes of the spray.
✗ Don't spray towards humans.
✗ Don't use up spray left over from the last time.
✗ Don't spray flowers in bloom – you may kill pollinating insects.
✗ Don't spray crops close to harvesting time.

Questions

1 (a) List four pests you might find in the kitchen above. (b) Describe different control measures to use.

2 Summarize the conditions that encourage the breeding of pests.

3 Give (a) two advantages and (b) two disadvantages of using pesticides.

Key ideas

Use these words to fill in the spaces as you write the sentences in your Exercise book.

biological   economic   pesticides   crops   herbicides   chemical   insecticides

Pests cause _____ losses. They harm people, farm animals and _____ . They can be controlled by sanitary, physical, _____ and _____ measures. _____ are chemicals used to kill plant and animal pests; _____ kill insects and _____ kill herbaceous weeds. Great care should be taken in the use of all _____ , as some of them are harmful to humans.

13.3 How can we deal with waste?

We produce domestic, industrial and biological waste. It is important we have state disposal of garbage and adequate toilet and sewage disposal. We can also re-use or recycle some waste, with benefits to the environment.

We produce so much waste. How can we recycle it, or dispose of it safely?

Different kinds of waste

Activity

Domestic waste

This is the **garbage** in our home, school, office, etc.

1 List things in the wastebasket, garbage bin, kitchen and garden waste. *Do not touch them.*
2 Check if you have included:
   • food peelings and waste food (organic waste)
   • detergents, pesticides and dirty water
   • materials: plastics, glass, tin cans, cloth, paper.
3 For each piece of waste, suggest:
   (a) one way in which it might safely be recycled
   (b) a harmful effect associated with it.

Activity

Industrial waste

This is waste from factories and industries.

1 Visit a factory and list the wastes produced.
2 Check if you have included:
   • gases – dirty smoke; sulphur dioxide from fuels
   • liquids – chemical wastes, e.g. from the rum industry, and red mud from bauxite
   • solids – ash, scrap metal and bagasse
   • heat – into the air or as hot water into rivers.
3 For each waste, suggest:
   (a) how it might be recycled or reduced and
   (b) a harmful effect associated with it (see also pages 81, 224–5 and 321).

Objectives

● Discuss different types of waste: domestic, industrial and biological.
● Discuss the need for community hygiene, and beneficial uses for waste.

Activity

Biological waste

This is our liquid waste (urine) and solid waste (faeces). They are organic wastes, and together they are called **sewage**.

1 Do a survey in your school and work out the number of people per toilet or latrine.
2 List what each person could do to keep the toilets/latrines clean and in good order.
3 What problems can arise from improper disposal of (a) urine and (b) faeces? (See pages 240–3.)

Latrines and toilets

● **Pit latrine:** this has a hole over a long drop of at least 3 metres; sewage is decayed in the hole by bacteria and fungi; flies are kept away by screens.
● **Flush toilet:** the toilets are built with tanks that can be flushed, which washes away the sewage into underground pipes, a soak-away or septic tank.

Disposal of sewage

● **Dumping at sea:** sewage is carried in pipes to the sea, but this can harm coral reef and sea life; it can also be washed back to shore and cause disease.
● **Sewage works:** here the sewage is broken down by different bacteria; the solid part, sludge, can be dumped at sea or used as fertilizer; the liquid can be put into rivers. It would need boiling or chlorine added to it, if it were to be used for drinking.
● **Septic tank:** this is a deep household pit in which decay occurs and the liquid drains into the soil.

Questions

1 A lot of domestic waste could be burnt. Give one advantage and one disadvantage of doing this.
2 Describe the main differences between (a) a pit latrine and flush toilet, (b) a septic tank and sewage works, and (c) biodegradable and non-biodegradable waste.
3 Outline four methods by which the amount of waste that needs to be disposed of, for example by burying, could be reduced.

What is done with the waste?

● Storage

For short-term storage use a garbage bin with a secure lid. This stops flies getting in to lay their eggs, and prevents dogs and goats from emptying the garbage bin and spilling out the waste materials.

● Dumping

Dumping in the open means that rats, mice, flies and cockroaches can feed. It is also unsightly, produces smells and may block watercourses. The waste might also be spread by animals, wind and water, to affect other areas and spread diseases.

● Burying

This reduces pests feeding on the waste, and the decayed material enters the soil for plant growth. However, some harmful wastes may also enter the soil, and could get into water supplies.

● Burning

Burning in the open makes toxic fumes causing air pollution and destroys living material that could be recycled as humus in the soil. Waste could instead be burnt in special incinerators, which trap harmful gases.

● Recycling

It would be useful to recycle some of the waste, so there was less to dispose of. We can sort the waste. Food peelings and waste food are **biodegradable**. They can be decayed and broken down by the action of bacteria. Other waste, such as things made of glass, metal or plastics, cannot be decayed. It is **non-biodegradable**.

Recycling non-biodegradable materials

- **Glass bottles** can be re-used at home, or recycled so the glass is re-used by factories.
- **Metal tins** and old metal appliances might be sold for scrap. Metal is melted down and re-used.
- **Plastic** bottles can be recycled and re-used.
- **Newspapers and cardboard** decay slowly but they can also be recycled. The paper is reduced to wood pulp, and this can be re-used.

Recycling biodegradable materials

Direct use as a fuel

Most organic waste can be dried and burnt as a fuel. Cow dung is used like this in India. However, handling the dung can be a health hazard, and harmful gases are produced when it is burnt.

Compost

Decay with oxygen by aerobic bacteria in a compost heap produces **compost**. The compost heap should be open at the bottom. It can have chicken-wire sides supported by poles. The material should be turned over from time to time. These actions allow air circulation.

A compost heap is made up of alternate layers of soil and decaying household materials. Grass cuttings and weeds can be added. The soil provides bacteria that decay the waste. Lime and fertilizer can also be added. As the decay process continues the compost heap becomes very hot. This kills weed seeds and harmful organisms.

The compost heap should be covered with a lid to prevent large animals entering. It should also be kept moist. When the material has decayed it can be used instead of chemical fertilizers.

Compost is good for the soil, because, like humus (see page 177), it improves the texture of the soil and slowly releases mineral salts to be used by the plants.

Biogas

Decay without oxygen, by anaerobic bacteria, in a biogas digester (see page 322) produces **biogas**, which is mainly methane (see page 24). Biodegradable organic waste is added to the digester, which is kept airtight to encourage the anaerobic bacteria. As the biogas is made it is led away in pipes and can be used directly for cooking. Household rubbish contains about a third of the energy of the same amount of coal. Methane is very clean: when it is burnt it produces only carbon dioxide and water. It can also be used to generate electricity. The remaining solid waste, **sludge**, can be used as a fertilizer (the decay process means it is safe to use) and it contains minerals useful for plants. There are many biogas fermenters in the Caribbean.

Key ideas

Use these words to fill in the spaces as you write the sentences in your Exercise book.

biodegradable   compost   non-biodegradable   biogas   industrial   sewage

Different kinds of waste are domestic, _____ and biological (or _____). Some waste cannot be decayed by bacteria: it is _____ . Other waste, such as food remains, can be decayed: it is _____ . Aerobic bacteria can decay _____ material to make _____ . Anaerobic bacteria can decay _____ material to make _____ (methane).

13.4 Why is personal hygiene important?

Every day our skin becomes dirty. We pick up dust and dirt, and our sweat dries on our skin. The top layer of skin dies and the dead cells accumulate. Microorganisms live on our skin (see photograph on the right) and decay the substances there to produce unpleasant odours, and they can also infect us with disease.

What do we use to keep ourselves clean?

Soap and water

When we wash ourselves the soap takes away the surface layer of dirt, grease and sweat. It cleans away the waxy sebum that might otherwise encourage pimples. Some soaps include antiseptics to help kill germs.

Deodorants

These are usually powders, sprays or roll-ons. They contain a substance that absorbs odours and may have a perfume. Some kill odour-producing bacteria.

Antiperspirants

These are designed to block the sweat glands to stop us sweating. This may stop the smell of decaying sweat but is not a good idea, especially in hot weather when we need to sweat to keep cool.

Vaginal douches

These are specially prepared cleaning solutions that a woman can use to wash out her vagina. However, the solutions may kill the natural bacteria that can be useful and may wash any germs higher up into her reproductive system, where they can cause infection.

Antiseptics

These can be fluids, creams or substances added to soaps. An antiseptic is used to kill bacteria and thus prevent infection, e.g. antiseptic mouthwashes. Antiseptic creams are used on wounds to keep them clean.

Manufacturers make claims for their cleaning materials. How could you test scientifically any of the claims made in their advertisements?

If the skin is cut, bacteria can infect us

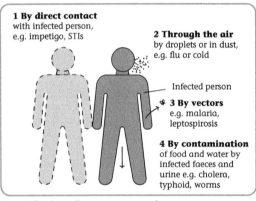

1 By direct contact with infected person, e.g. impetigo, STIs

2 Through the air by droplets or in dust, e.g. flu or cold

Infected person

3 By vectors e.g. malaria, leptospirosis

4 By contamination of food and water by infected faeces and urine e.g. cholera, typhoid, worms

How infectious diseases are spread

Advice for personal hygiene

● Use a tissue when you sneeze.
● Do not spit.
● Wash your hands after using the toilet and before handling food.
● Keep your genital area clean.
● Keep your hair and nails clean.
● Clean and take good care of your teeth.
● Take regular baths or showers.
● Wear clean clothing.
● Wash fresh food before you eat it.
● Boil drinking water if necessary.
● Wear shoes to walk on damp soil.

Activity

Personal hygiene

1 Look at each point of advice for personal hygiene on the previous page. In your group discuss the reasons for each one, and the possible results for the health of the person, or other people, if the advice is ignored.
2 Brainstorm other advice you would suggest relating to personal hygiene and the possible effects on health.
3 List some disease-causing pathogens, such as various microorganisms and parasites such as worms. Suggest how personal hygiene is important in encouraging or discouraging their spread.
4 Prepare a class report.

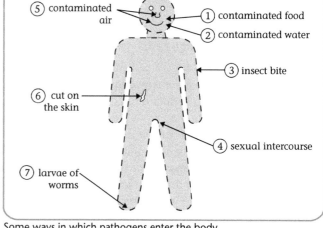

Some ways in which pathogens enter the body

Why do we need to clean our teeth?

When we eat, some of the food particles stay between our teeth. This is especially a problem with foods containing starch and sugar. This builds up a layer called **plaque**. The bacteria in our mouths break down the food particles to produce acids (see page 282). These attack the enamel of the teeth and may cause tooth decay (see page 65).

After you have eaten something sweet, bacteria in your mouth produce acids. These acids attack your teeth for up to an hour. You should therefore limit the sweet things you eat, and clean your teeth after meals.

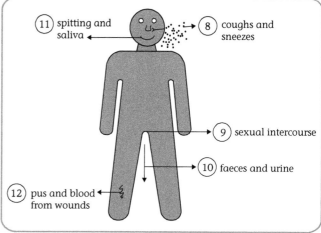

Some ways in which pathogens leave the body

Activity

How do we clean our teeth?

1 Work in small groups. List all the different ways in which you clean your teeth, such as using a toothbrush and toothpaste, chew stick, dental floss and mouthwash.
2 For each method, describe the best procedure for its use, and give the reasons why it is useful.
3 How might crunchy food and cheese be useful in helping to reduce dental decay?

Questions

1 What is the position shown by each of the numbers 1–12, in the diagrams above? For example, 1 and 2 are the mouth.
2 Suggest an example for each of the pathogens 1–12. How could the spread of each one be reduced by attention to good personal hygiene?

Key ideas

Use these words to fill in the spaces as you write the sentences in your Exercise book.

pathogens   **lifestyle**   **sweat**   **teeth**   **personal**   **wash**

_____ hygiene is under the control of each individual. Our skin always has dirt, _____ and

_____ , such as bacteria, on it. We need to _____ our skin regularly, and to clean our _____

to remove plaque and bacteria. _____ hygiene can help reduce the transfer of many _____ ;

our _____ is also important in controlling the transfer of _____ .

13.5 Why is community hygiene important?

What are the dangers of poor hygiene?

There can be a spread of disease-causing pathogens as a result of both poor personal hygiene and inadequate community hygiene. These overlap, because individuals make up the community. For example, the community may provide a proper sanitation system, but if people urinate or defecate on the ground, in rivers or in open drains, then the wastes may accumulate. One result is that harmful microorganisms or worm eggs in the faeces from infected people may get into our food and drinking water.

Many of the parasites that infect humans also live in other organisms, in which part of the life cycle is carried out. This second host may also be a **vector**, as it transmits the disease-causing organisms back to us. The prevention of the spread of these organisms also depends on a combination of personal and community hygiene.

Worms transmitted through contact with faeces

We reduce our chances of infection by practising good community and personal hygiene. Discuss and give reasons for each of the points of advice given for community hygiene in the box. If we do catch worms they can be killed by special medicines. Worms that live inside their host are **endoparasites**.

Bilharzia

This disease is caused by a flatworm, *Schistosoma*. The flatworm is also called a **blood fluke**, as it lives in the blood vessels in the walls of the intestines. It causes diarrhoea, loss of blood, ill health and weakness. The fluke has a special water snail, *Planorbis*, in which it spends part of its life cycle. Humans can be infected by the worm larvae if they walk in water that was previously contaminated with infected faeces, as shown below.

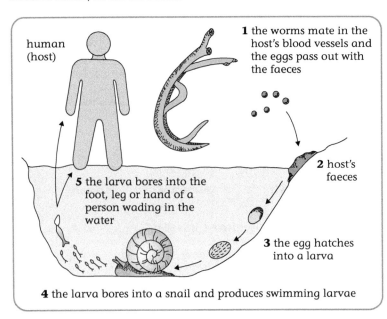

human (host)

1 the worms mate in the host's blood vessels and the eggs pass out with the faeces

2 host's faeces

3 the egg hatches into a larva

4 the larva bores into a snail and produces swimming larvae

5 the larva bores into the foot, leg or hand of a person wading in the water

Objectives

- Describe how parasites are spread by poor hygiene, and by vectors.
- Discuss other ways in which humans are affected by parasites.

What does it mean?

Pathogens Parasites that feed on other living things and cause disease. They can be large, like worms, or be a microorganism, such as bacteria or the malarial parasite. They can live inside the body, e.g. a worm, or outside the body, e.g. a head louse or flea.

Host The organism on which the parasite feeds. It can be an animal, e.g. a human, or a plant, e.g. corn.

Vector An organism that transmits a parasite; e.g. the *Anopheles* mosquito is the vector for the malarial parasite.

Community sanitation services
(see also pages 236–7)

- House and business garbage collection and disposal.
- Emptying of communal litter bins.
- Adequate toilet and sewage disposal, and sewage treatment plants.
- Provision of clean and uncontaminated household and business water supplies.

Community hygiene

- Keep garbage covered until it is collected or disposed of.
- Use proper toilet facilities and flush away faeces and urine.
- Do not bathe in water that others may have used for urinating or defecating.
- Recycle waste materials in community schemes where possible.
- Do not use human or animal urine or faeces directly as manure.

Tapeworm

This is another flatworm. It can be over 10 m long and has many small segments containing eggs. Its head has hooks and suckers to hold onto the intestine wall. Ripe segments pass out with the faeces. If these are eaten by pigs or cattle, cysts form inside their muscles. If meat from these animals is eaten by a human, without being well cooked, the cysts hatch to become tapeworms in the gut.

Hookworm

This is a small roundworm about 1 cm long. Eggs are dropped from infected people in the faeces (up to 6 million per day in a severe infection). The eggs hatch in damp soil and the larvae burrow into the feet or legs of the human. They travel in the blood system via the heart to the lungs and up to the trachea. Here they are swallowed and get into the gut, where they reproduce. They cause lung inflammation, anaemia, diarrhoea and weakness.

Ascaris

This is a pink or white roundworm, which is 20–30 cm long. Perhaps as many as a quarter of humans are infected, via contaminated faeces. The larvae spend time in the lungs and mature in the intestines. A person may have several worms at a time and suffer from abdominal pain, fever, diarrhoea and weight loss.

Pinworm

This is small roundworm, like a piece of thread 1 cm long. It lives in the rectum and causes itching around the anus. Pinworms are common in children. Infection is spread when a person scratches, picks up eggs and later eats them. Or they can be transferred to another person.

External parasites

These live on the outside of the body (**ectoparasites**). Prevention is by good hygiene such as washing regularly.

Head louse

This lives in the hair. It has a flat shape so it can lie close to the skin and has claws for holding on (see (a)). It firmly attaches its eggs, called nits, to the hairs. The adult bites into the skin and sucks blood. Lice cause itching, and can spread typhus and relapsing fever. They spread through sharing combs, brushes and hats. They are killed with special shampoos or creams, and the nits can then be combed out.

Flea

This lives on the skin. It is flattened and has claws to hold onto hairs (see (b)). Its legs are long and strong, and it can jump to other hosts. It bites and sucks blood. The bites are painful and can also spread infections from rats, causing plague, typhus and leptospirosis (see page 242).

Questions

1 What features of a tapeworm help it in its way of life?

2 Some Caribbean countries have *Planorbis* snails, but not the blood fluke causing bilharzia. Why is it very important that the fluke is not introduced there?

3 Explain what problems *might* be associated with each of the following.
   (a) Walking barefoot on damp ground.
   (b) Eating vegetables without washing them first.
   (c) Eating fruit off the ground.
   (d) Paddling in a freshwater stream.

4 With reference to named examples, how can good community and personal hygiene reduce the risk of infection?

Did you know?

- Each adult fluke can produce up to 500,000 eggs.
- Ten billion bacteria live on our skin.
- Bubonic plague, caused by bacteria spread by rat fleas, killed about half the people in Western Europe in the 14th century.

(a) Head louse   (b) Flea

13.5 Why is community hygiene important? (continued)

Food poisoning

This is most often caused by bacteria that produce **toxins**, such as staphylococci and salmonellae. Staphylococci come from infected boils or cuts on the hands of people handling food. Salmonellae are often present in animals, especially chickens, that are used for food. Both kinds of bacteria reproduce in poorly cooked food and food that is left warm.

When food is left uncovered it attracts flies. These flies may previously have fed on faeces, where they may have picked up bacteria that are then transferred to our food.

The main symptom of food poisoning is diarrhoea, often with abdominal pain, vomiting and fever. It is important to drink a lot of fluid. Recovery is usually without antibiotics. If the symptoms continue for 3 days, see a doctor. For a child, take action after 1 day. Information on how to preserve food and keep it safe is given on pages 232–3.

Microorganisms spread by mosquitoes

Malaria

This is caused by a protist called *Plasmodium*, which is injected into the blood in saliva of an infected female *Anopheles* mosquito. The parasite lives in the blood: it enters a red blood cell and multiplies (see page 132). The blood cell breaks open to release new parasites to infect more cells. The release of the parasites causes an attack of fever in the patient. This pattern is repeated every few days.

Special drugs can be given, although some of these are now ineffective. We have the *Anopheles* mosquito in the Caribbean, but few of them are presently infected with malarial parasites.

Yellow fever and dengue

These are caused by viruses and are spread by *Aedes* mosquitoes. Yellow fever is controlled by vaccination. Dengue has symptoms like malaria, but the person often has a rash. There is extreme weakness. Rest and fluids are needed.

Leptospirosis spread by rats and other animals

This is caused by a bacterium. The infection passes via the urine and faeces of infected animals: rats and farm animals such as goats, sheep, horses, cows, dogs and pigs.

The disease causes fever, headache, pains, chills and vomiting. The person has little energy and the eyes become inflamed. Later, the eyes become yellow and blood is passed out in the urine. It can cause death.

Eighty per cent of the people infected in the Caribbean are farmers, garbage collectors or people who work in abattoirs. Infection is a result of poor hygiene, handling infected farm animals and walking barefoot on damp soil. It can be treated by antibiotics.

What harm can parasites do?

- Attack humans, causing ill health or death and reducing the amount of work done.
- Attack animals reared for food, causing poor growth and reducing the food production.
- Attack crop plants, causing poor growth and reducing fruit or seed production.

How can we control parasites?

- **Stop eggs from being transferred:** the eggs of many worms pass out in the faeces and can get onto food or into water. Proper sanitation and hygiene can stop these parasites from spreading.
- **Kill a stage in the life cycle:** for example, use drugs to kill the malarial parasite in human blood.
- **Kill the vector:** for example, killing the water snail controls bilharzia, and killing mosquitoes controls the malarial parasite.

Protection against malarial parasites

1. Avoid being bitten by mosquitoes. Use insect-repellent cream, cover up after dusk and have the house screened.
2. Use drugs to prevent or cure an attack.
3. Report any recurrent fever that begins 1 to 2 weeks after travelling in malarial areas, in case it is malaria.
4. Put kerosene onto stagnant water to kill mosquito larvae and pupae.
5. Use insecticide to kill adult mosquitoes.

Prevention of leptospirosis

1. Do not swim or bathe in stagnant water.
2. Boil water from ponds or rivers before using it for washing fruit and vegetables.
3. Keep your home free of rats by using traps and poisoned bait.
4. Do not allow garbage to accumulate; burn, bury or deliver it to garbage trucks.
5. Wear gloves if handling farm animals.

Water-borne microorganisms

Microorganisms enter water from infected urine or faeces. Bacterial infections can be treated with antibiotics.

Dysentery

This is commonly caused by a protist (*Entamoeba*; see page 132), which lives in the faeces of infected people. It is spread by contaminated water, and careless handling of food. It causes diarrhoea, dehydration and blood in the faeces. Fluids (boiled water with a spoon of sugar and a pinch of salt) should be given to prevent serious dehydration.

Typhoid

This is caused by a bacterium, a kind of *Salmonella*. The infection causes high fever, delirium and intestinal upsets. The bacterium is spread from contaminated water, milk, shellfish and sewage, and by flies, as well as by careless food handling by infected people. Vaccination against typhoid can be given, which lasts for 3 years.

Cholera

This is caused by a bacterium. There is severe diarrhoea, dehydration and collapse. If body fluids are not replaced, dehydration can cause death. Medical help is needed. It spreads via polluted water, raw fruits and vegetables. A vaccination can be given, which lasts for 6 months.

Which parasites affect plants?

Love vine

This is an ectoparasite, with weak yellow stems, which attaches itself to many plants. It puts suckers inside the host, to take away some of its food (see the top photo on the right).

Rusts and smuts

These are endoparasites: parasitic fungi living and feeding inside maize, rice and other cereals. They cause economic losses. **Rusts** can infect maize (see the bottom photo on the right) and are seen as red or brown spots and stripes on the leaves. This reduces photosynthesis, the leaves die and fruits are badly formed. Many spores are produced, which shoot out to infect more plants.

Questions

1 A café worker had an open sore on her hand and complained of diarrhoea. Why should the manager send her home sick?

2 How does killing the vector or second host reduce numbers of parasites?

3 'An important problem for a parasite is to find another host.' Illustrate this statement with two named examples.

4 Describe what precautions you could take to reduce the risk of infection by a named worm or microorganism.

Love vine

Rust infection on maize

Key ideas

Use these words to fill in the spaces as you write the sentences in your Exercise book.

community   **parasitic**   **pathogens**   **food**   **pests**   **malarial**

The state is important in _____ hygiene and the safe disposal of wastes, but individual actions are also involved. _____ can be spread in polluted _____ and water. Unsanitary conditions also lead to the increase in _____ , some of which can transfer _____ . Some examples of _____ are microorganisms (e.g. the _____ parasite), and _____ worms.

14 Safety hazards

14.1 Safety at home

An unsafe kitchen

Objectives

- Identify hazards in the home, and the accidents they may cause.
- Suggest ways to avoid accidents.

What does it mean?

Hazard   Something that could be dangerous or cause an accident.

Accident   A sudden event, usually caused by someone making a mistake, that causes damage, injury or death.

Activity

Guidelines for safety

Many accidents can be prevented.

Work in a group. Discuss and give a reason for each of the following rules. Share your ideas with your classmates.

1 Label all household chemicals clearly.
2 Keep chemicals in their proper bottles.
3 Put pills, medicines and household chemicals where children cannot reach them.
4 Keep pills in 'child-proof' bottles that they cannot open.
5 Keep household chemicals where adults can reach them easily.
6 Keep poisonous chemicals, such as insecticides and rat killer, out of reach of children, or locked up.
7 Replace fraying insulation on electrical appliances.
8 Do not use too hot an iron on clothes.
9 Use the right number of plugs in one electrical fitting (do not 'overload'; see page 301).
10 Light gas burners and cookers safely.
11 On a stove, do not have pot handles projecting over the edge.
12 Handle hot utensils only with protective gloves.
13 Repair any unevenness in floor surfaces.
14 Pick up any toys, papers or food from the floor.
15 If liquids are spilt on the floor, dry them up.
16 Keep floors clean but do not polish them so much that they are slippery.
17 Have adequate lighting in all rooms.

Activity

Hazards at home

1 List as many hazards as you can see in the picture of the kitchen, above left. Beside each one, write down what you would do to stop it causing an accident.
2 Which of the accidents above might also occur (a) in other parts of the house or (b) in the laboratory (see pages 246–8)?
3 Which substances commonly used in the home and garden are dangerous? (Look at labels on the containers and write down ingredients.) Wash your hands afterwards.

Questions

1 Choose a room in the house, such as the kitchen. List the possible hazards and how to avoid them.
2 How are (a) young children and (b) older people at special risk of accidents?
3 In small groups, design a poster to warn people against household hazards. Think of different ways to make your point.

Did you know?

- Bones of young children and the elderly are especially likely to become broken.

Accidents	How to avoid them
Bites and stings: many animals bite or sting, for example ants, centipedes, mosquitoes, wasps, pets, rats and farm animals.	Handle animals carefully, wear gloves if necessary. Do not annoy pets or insects. Use repellent cream against mosquitoes.
Broken bones: falling over, or pulling something heavy onto yourself, could break a bone.	Look where you are walking. Uneven or poorly lit floors, or utensils or liquids left on the floor, may cause falls.
Burns and scalds: burns are caused by touching hot objects; scalds are caused by steam.	Take great care when touching hot liquids, utensils or the stove. Do not bump against pot handles on the stove.
Cuts: these break the surface of the skin and so open it to germs.	Handle all knives carefully. Cut on a flat surface. Point the blade away from you when you cut.
Electric shock: caused by an electric current passing through the body. Can cause burns, unconsciousness or death.	Do not put fingers in electrical sockets or handle electrical appliances while hands are wet. Do not touch electrical wires (see also page 291).
Eye injuries: solid objects or chemicals may fall into the eye; tears are a natural body response.	Avoid very dirty or dusty places. Point boiling liquids away from you. Handle all chemicals carefully.
Explosions: may result from leakage of gas, or delay in lighting burners or cookers.	Check if the gas is leaking from cylinders. Check that the pilot light is on. Have your match ready to light the burner or cooker. Store chemicals away from sources of heat.
Fire: caused by overheating of an iron, electrical faults, burning liquids or gases setting other things alight.	Check iron thermostats, and check for any overloading (see page 301). Take great care with matches and lamps. Mend any frayed electrical wires.
Poisoning: children may eat pills, thinking they are sweets; they may also drink household chemicals. Adults may take overdoses of drugs.	Store pills, household chemicals, etc. safely and in clearly labelled containers. Throw away unwanted drugs. Take special care with sleeping pills.
Sprains: caused by pulling on joints unnaturally or by twisting an arm or leg when falling.	Look where you are walking. If you are falling, try not to let your weight fall onto your wrist or ankle.

Note: see pages 252–3 for first aid for these and other problems.

Key ideas

Use these words to fill in the spaces as you write the sentences in your Exercise book.

lighting　　**label**　　**liquids**　　**overload**　　**store**　　**leakage**　　**frayed**

Some ways in which we can avoid accidents are: _____ all bottles clearly; _____ dangerous chemicals away from children; do not leave objects or _____ on the floor; have adequate

_____ ; mend any _____ electrical wires, and do not _____ electrical sockets. Also check for

any _____ of gas, and do not delay when _____ gas stoves.

14.2 Safety at school

Safety in the laboratory

We have looked at ways to avoid accidents in the home. There are also dangers with using chemicals and equipment in the science laboratory, home economics room and workshop. We also need to be safe in these places.

Activity

Laboratory rules

Work in a group. Give a reason for each of these rules. Choose your own set of rules and design a poster of them.
1. Only enter the laboratory with the teacher's permission.
2. Do not run, play, eat or drink in the laboratory.
3. Put your bags and books out of the way.
4. Keep your work area tidy, and the walkways clear.
5. Do not do any unauthorized experiments.
6. Do not play around with chemicals or equipment.
7. Never push objects into an electrical socket, or touch a socket with wet hands, as these action can cause death.
8. Take care hair does not get close to a Bunsen flame, and do not leave a Bunsen flame unattended.
9. Make sure all equipment is safely positioned on the bench, and be careful not to knock anything over.
10. Wear protective clothing when doing experiments: a laboratory coat or apron, and goggles for the eyes.
11. If a chemical spills, clean it up with water and then dry the area.
12. If equipment or glass is broken, or if there is any other accident, report it immediately to the teacher.

Look at the pictures of the unsafe and safe laboratory on the right, and the unsafe and safe workshop on page 247.
1. Make lists of all the unsafe behaviours.
2. Look at the corresponding pictures to identify how the problems have been improved to make the places safe.
3. Make lists for yourselves of some unsafe behaviour in Home Economics or Crafts. For each possible problem, record the correct and safe behaviour.

Safety with electricity

- Look around you in the laboratory, workshop or home economics room. You will notice that water and electrical outlets should be a certain distance apart. This is because water conducts electricity, and if you handle electrical equipment with wet hands you may get an electric shock.
- There must not be too many electrical appliances plugged into a socket. If there were, there could be overloading of the circuit and a danger of fire occurring.
- Plastic insulation around metal wires must not be damaged to expose bare wires. This is because contact between the wires, or with a person, could also cause an electric shock or electrical fire.

Objectives

- Discuss safety rules important in the school laboratory and workshop.
- Identify various safety symbols.
- Evaluate protective clothing.

Questions

1. In Home Economics, why do you wear an apron, and wash your hands before and after handling food?
2. In the science laboratory, why do you sometimes wear a white coat and goggles?
3. In the workshop, why do you always wear overalls and goggles?

(a) An unsafe science class

(b) A safe science class

Safety with chemicals

We need to know the dangers associated with chemicals we use in the laboratory. The bottles should carry square labels with pictures on them to show the hazards. Refer to the artwork below to find the meanings of the words.

- Most acids and alkalis used in the laboratory are **corrosive**. They need to be poured or heated very carefully. They are all **harmful**, and many of them would be **toxic**.
- Concentrated acids are even more dangerous, and their fumes can be an **irritant** to the eyes and throat.
- Concentrated sulphuric acid is a very strong **oxidizing** agent. It reacts very vigorously with water, making a great deal of heat. You must always add the acid *very slowly* to water. *Never* add water to the acid.
- Some solids and gases, and especially some organic liquids, such as alcohols, can catch fire easily under normal conditions. They are **highly flammable**.
- Many gases, for example cooking gas, are stored under pressure in cylinders. These are **explosive** if heated or lit. It is very important to be careful when lighting a gas stove.
- You are unlikely to see **radioactive** chemicals in the laboratory, but you might see the sign in a hospital.
- Gases, such as chlorine and bromine, are also **irritants** and **toxic**.
- Everyday chemicals may also carry labels, such as bleach (corrosive and irritant), pesticides (harmful, irritant and toxic) and kerosene (highly flammable and toxic).

To be safe: check labels and get advice from a teacher.

(c) An unsafe workshop

(d) A safe workshop

Explosive: these substances may explode if exposed to a flame or heat, or if the storage container is shaken; e.g. cylinder of cooking gas.

Oxidizing: these substances produce a lot of heat in chemical reactions; they therefore are a fire risk; e.g. concentrated sulphuric acid.

Highly flammable: solids, liquids or gases that may easily catch fire under normal conditions; e.g. many organic liquids.

Toxic: these substances are poisonous and can cause death if swallowed, breathed in or absorbed through skin; e.g. many acids, pesticides.

Harmful or **irritant:** these are less dangerous than toxic substances, but still harmful to skin and eyes; e.g. many chemicals.

Corrosive: these chemicals destroy equipment and living flesh, such as eyes and skin; e.g. many acids and alkalis.

Radioactive: these substances give off radiation that can be harmful to living things; must be stored in special ways; e.g. in an X-ray department.

Danger: take care when using the chemicals, and when doing dangerous experiments follow all the safety rules.

14.2 Safety at school (continued)

Practical 91

Using a Bunsen burner safely (MM, ORR)

Look at page 32, where there are instructions for lighting a Bunsen burner. You are going to compare the appearance and properties of the yellow and blue flames.

1 Light the Bunsen burner so you get a yellow flame. The fuel is burning with very little air: there is incomplete combustion with the release of carbon, carbon monoxide and carbon dioxide. This is called a **luminous flame**, as it gives out light as small particles of carbon glow when they are hot (see (a)). What might be the dangers of having a faulty heater or a car that operated with an inadequate air supply?
2 Use the yellow flame to heat $25\,cm^3$ of tap water in a beaker. Record the time taken for the water to boil. Look underneath the gauze. Are there any carbon particles?
3 Open the air-hole to make a blue flame. The fuel now has plenty of air for complete combustion to carbon dioxide; it does not release carbon or carbon monoxide. It is called a **non-luminous** flame, as it does not give out light (see (b)).
4 Use the blue flame to heat another $25\,cm^3$ of tap water (using a clean gauze). Record the time it takes for the water to boil. Are there any carbon particles under the gauze?
5 On page 319 you will also compare the amount of heat released in different parts of a blue flame.

The characteristics of the flames are shown in the table below.

Luminous (yellow) flame	Non-luminous (blue) flame
Unsteady flame	Steady flame
Quiet flame	Noisy flame
Lower temperature	Higher temperature
Gives off carbon, which glows	No carbon; it is all burnt to carbon dioxide
Produces carbon monoxide	No carbon monoxide
Little air: incomplete combustion	Lot of air: complete combustion

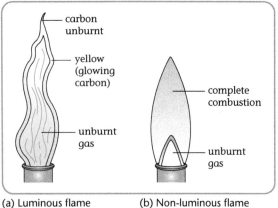

(a) Luminous flame   (b) Non-luminous flame

Activity

Safety on a field trip

Work in small groups.
1 Identify a field trip such as a visit to a beach or wood to study the **ecology**, or to a factory or industrial building to study safety precautions or waste management.
2 Prepare a list of safety precautions to consider before the trip. For example:
 (a) Should parents/guardians sign a letter giving approval for each student?
 (b) Who is legally responsible if there is an accident and a student is injured?
 (c) Is any special clothing required?
 (d) Will each student need to bring their own food and water?
 (e) Will you need to take any collecting equipment? If yes, then make a list.
 (f) Should teachers carry a first aid kit? If yes, then what should be in it, and why?
3 Add any other safety considerations. Then discuss your lists in class with your teacher.

Key ideas

Use these words to fill in the spaces as you write the sentences in your Exercise book.

blue   **monoxide**   **rules**   **yellow**   **dioxide**   **chemicals**   **warning**

We need to follow certain _____ to be safe in the laboratory and workshop. Different

_____ labels are found on hazardous _____ . A flame burning with too little air will be

_____ , and will produce dangerous carbon _____ . A flame where there is plenty of air and

complete combustion occurs will be _____ , with the release of carbon _____ .

14.3 Safety in the workplace

There are hazards present in most working environments.

- Food contamination, for example from flies, chemicals, dirty hands and decay microorganisms (see pages 232–43).
- Wherever we are, we may be bitten by insects or other animals.
- Wherever fuels are used, such as cooking gas or gasoline, there is a danger from fires (see pages 254–5).
- Any electrical appliance can be a potential hazard All wiring should be kept in good order, only a few plugs used in a socket, and hands kept dry (see page 246).
- Uneven floors, combined with poor lighting, can easily cause people to trip and fall and equipment to break.
- Lights that are too bright can harm our eyes.

We can also look at the hazard signs and special precautions that are needed in specific places.

Gas station

- Spilt gasoline could be a source of fire and people should not use flames or smoke cigarettes.
- If cooking gas is sold, there should be a sign warning of possible explosions.

Building site

- This is noisy (so ear protection is needed) and there is a danger of things falling (hard hats should be worn).
- If welding, then full protection and a visor are needed.

Chemicals factory

- Leaking bottles or cylinders of gas, such as chlorine, can affect our breathing, as well as kill aquatic organisms.
- Corrosive chemicals, such as acids and alkalis, can damage hands (so gloves are needed). Careful disposal is also needed so appliances and people are not harmed.
- If toxic chemicals, such as insecticides, are made then there should be the correct warning sign.

Objectives

- Discuss safety in the workplace.
- Identify the meanings of hazard signs.
- Evaluate items of protective clothing recommended for various jobs.

Hazard signs

There are different kinds of hazard signs, and these have a colour coding. Some will be found on the road, on buildings, in the workplace or on bottles. They are there to help us keep safe.

- **Red**: stop, or not allowed. Red indicates danger, and is often used on road signs, in gasoline stations and in the workplace.

No smoking   No pedestrians allowed   No flames

- **Orange**: warning signs to show hazards, such as the possibility of explosions, fires, skin damage etc. (See below and page 247.) Found on bottles of chemicals, and vehicles that transport chemicals.

Toxic hazard   Corrosive substance   Risk of fire

- **Blue**: mandatory signs (action that must be carried out), such as the wearing of certain safety clothing, etc. Displayed in the workplace to help protect workers.

Eye protection must be worn   Breathing protection must be worn   Protective headwear must be worn

- **Green**: safe signs showing no risk, or the action to be taken for safety, such as first aid kit or emergency exits.

First aid   Emergency shower   Eyewash

14.3 Safety in the workplace (continued)

Activity

Hazard signs

1 Survey some workplaces, such as a gasoline station, the outside of a building site and a hospital. Look for and draw the hazard signs you see (including their colours). Write a description for each sign, describe why it is necessary in that place, and what might be the consequences of not following the instruction or advice.

2 Plan and design your own label. It should not contain any words – the picture should give the message. Make a display of the labels that are made in class.

Activity

Spot the workplace

1 The signs and instructions shown below were found in a variety of workplaces. For each item, suggest one or two places where it might be found. In each case explain why the workforce should follow the advice.

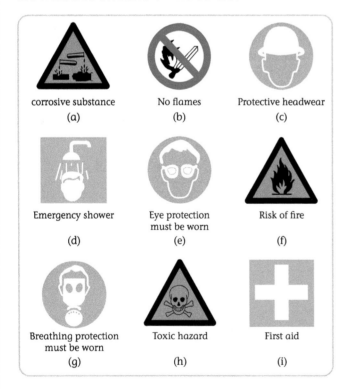

corrosive substance (a)	No flames (b)	Protective headwear (c)
Emergency shower (d)	Eye protection must be worn (e)	Risk of fire (f)
Breathing protection must be worn (g)	Toxic hazard (h)	First aid (i)

2 Where would these items be worn (give as many answers for each one as you can)? Special (a) headgear, (b) clothing, (c) footwear, (d) gloves, (e) goggles, (f) facemasks, (g) leg or knee pads, (h) breathing apparatus.

Practical 92

Evaluating protective wear (PD, MM, ORR, AI)

Work in small groups. Imagine you are a team of researchers who have to evaluate the use of an item of protective clothing, and write a report.

1 Identify what you will test, e.g. a piece of old gardening glove, a plastic surgical glove, a piece of heavy cloth as used for lab coats. Add other materials, but do NOT damage working materials.

2 Design your tests, e.g. the effects of (a) dilute acids and alkalis (use separate dishes and be very careful), (b) rubbing on a rough surface, such as a stone, (c) pulling the material to stretch it. Add in other tests of your own.

3 Summarize your findings, describing how well the material behaves, and the possible effects this would have if it were used as protective clothing. Share your findings in class.

Questions

How is each piece of a firefighter's clothing important?

Protective clothing

Protective clothing is needed in chemical laboratories, workshops and various workplaces such as engineering works and factories. The clothing is worn on the part of the body that needs protection from certain hazards.

- Coats, overalls or aprons are needed in laboratories, workshops, kitchens and some factories. They are strong, fire-resistant and protect against chemicals.
- In laboratories or factories with corrosive chemicals, such as acids and pesticides, rubber aprons and gloves are needed to protect the skin from possible contact with the substances.
- Work gloves made of leather are needed by wood and metal workers to protect their hands from cuts.
- Doctors and surgeons use plastic surgical gloves for reducing the likelihood of cuts and spread of diseases.
- Anyone cutting or welding metal with a hot torch needs leather protection against flying metal and special eye protection (a visor) against the sparks and bright light.
- Head protection (a hard hat) is needed on a building site to prevent getting cuts or a broken skull from falling objects or if the worker falls from a height. It is also needed for a motorcyclist.
- Foot protection (heavy boots with metal over the front part) is also needed on a building site to help prevent damage to toes from falling materials.
- Earplugs or muffs are needed in factories with noisy machinery to prevent damage to ears or even deafness.
- Goggles are needed where there is a risk of splashing chemicals, or bits of flying metal or glass.
- Breathing protection is needed where there are toxic gases or harmful fibres, such as asbestos, in the air. Special filters may be needed for particular chemicals to stop them getting into the lungs, and perhaps causing cancer.
- Firefighters need hard hats, full protective clothing including boots and gloves, breathing protection and perhaps a source of oxygen as well as their firefighting apparatus.
- People playing sports also usually need special protective clothing. You can work with a partner to make your own list (also identify where on the body the item is worn and the reason why each piece is used).

A welder wearing full protection and a visor

A construction worker wearing a hard hat and work gloves

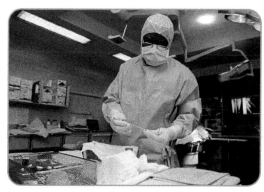

A surgeon needs a sterile gown and gloves

Key ideas

Use these words to fill in the spaces as you write the sentences in your Exercise book.

red **clothing** **colours** **building sites** **hazard** **orange**

_____ signs are of different _____ , which give different information – for example

_____ means 'not allowed' and _____ is used on dangerous chemicals. Different workplaces

need different _____ signs, as the dangers vary. People, for example in factories and on _____ ,

may need special protective _____ .

14.4 How can we give first aid?

> *Warning*: Students wishing to give first aid should first have some basic training and a special course in first aid.

Bites and stings

- Mosquito and other insect bites: relieve the pain with calamine lotion or surgical spirit. Do not scratch. Treat infected bites with gentian violet and cover if necessary. If reactions to poisonous bites are severe (e.g. some spider bites), take the patient to a doctor.
- Stings: treat wasp stings with vinegar. Treat bee stings with sodium hydrogencarbonate solution. Scrape off jellyfish stings with sand and wash with salt water.

Note: also rub onion onto any bite or sting to soothe it.

Broken bones

Move the person as little as possible. Treat any severe bleeding (see cuts). A splint (a rigid object) can be bandaged to the side of the limb to stop it from bending. A sling can be made from a large piece of cloth. Keep the patient warm. Do not give them anything to eat or drink. Get a doctor's help.

Burns and scalds

- Small: cool by putting in cold water or use a cold compress. Do NOT put on petroleum jelly. If a blister forms, leave it uncovered and do not break it. They can be covered with a clean dry cloth or dressing.
- Large: if a person's clothing is on fire, first smother the flames with a blanket (a fire blanket if in the laboratory). Cool and clean the area with cold water. Remove clothing unless it is stuck to the wound. Lightly bandage. Raise the burnt part and give the person small sips of cold water. Treat for shock. Get a doctor's help.

Do NOT burst blisters. Do NOT put on anything fluffy like cotton wool. Do NOT put on ointment or petroleum jelly.

Choking

If something (such as food or a toy) blocks the air passages the person will have trouble breathing. Try to get the person to cough out the object. Hit the person sharply between the shoulder blades. Give artificial respiration if necessary. Get a doctor's help.

Cuts

Wear plastic gloves.

- Small: bleeding stops as a clot forms. Wash the area and remove dirt, etc. Clean with an antiseptic, dry and cover with a clean dressing. If the wound is deep, or if it becomes inflamed, see a doctor, who may give antibiotics and tetanus injections.
- Large: bleeding may be severe if an artery has been cut. Raise the injured part of the body and pick out any pieces of glass, etc. Press on a major artery between the heart and the wound to stop blood flow. Press hard on the wound with a clean pad and bandage tightly to stop blood flow and to prevent entry of germs. Add more bandages if blood seeps through. Get a doctor's help.

Objective

- Outline and evaluate first aid methods for treating accidents.

Aims of first aid

1. To prevent injuries from getting worse.
2. To summon help from a doctor or ambulance.
3. To make the patient comfortable.
4. To provide reassurance.

Mouth-to-mouth resuscitation

This is also called **artificial respiration** and it must be started within 3 minutes if a person stops breathing due to a heart attack (see page 96), drowning, electric shock (see page 291), poisoning or suffocation. Quickly get a doctor's help. Use a facemask to guard against HIV/AIDS.

Here are the steps to take.

(a) Lay the patient face upwards. Tip the head well back and pull the lower jaw forwards and upwards. This will force the tongue forwards and open the air passages.

(b) Sweep around deep inside the patient's mouth with your finger to make sure that nothing is blocking the windpipe.

(c) Pinch the patient's nose. Take a deep breath, then open your mouth and seal your lips against the person's mouth. Breathe out firmly but gently into the person's mouth and lungs.

(d) Lift your mouth off, then turn your head so as to look at the person's chest. If you have been successful you will see that it has risen and is now falling as air comes out of the lungs. Repeat steps (c) and (d) until the person breathes unaided.

Electric shock

Electric current has flowed through the person (see page 291), so before touching the person switch off the current, or separate them from the source of electricity. They may be 'live' and you could also get an electric shock if you touch them. Use a wooden broom (or other non-conducting object) to disconnect them from the source of electricity. Give artificial respiration if necessary and lay the person on his or her side in a comfortable position. Get a doctor's help.

Eye injuries

- Chemicals: wash the eye in running water. Cover it with a pad and see a doctor.
- Small objects: use the corner of a clean cloth or paper tissue to remove the object. Pull the eyelids down and then up to help dislodge the object.

Fainting

The patient feels dizzy and becomes unconscious. This is caused by insufficient blood flow to the head. Sit the patient down with their head between their knees, or lie them down and lift their feet. Blood gets back to the head. People in a faint should regain consciousness in a few minutes.

Heatstroke

This follows exposure to high temperatures. The body's heat-regulating mechanisms (see page 121) are upset, so the body temperature rises from the normal 37 °C to 40 °C or higher. The person looks flushed, with hot, dry skin and rapid pulse, and may become unconscious.

Remove the person's clothing and sponge them with cold water or wrap them in a cold wet sheet. Fan them. Lay them on their side in a comfortable position. Get a doctor's help.

Heat exhaustion

This is less serious than heatstroke. The person has damp skin and may feel sick and dizzy with a headache and muscle cramps. Lay the patient down, with their feet raised. Loosen their clothing and give them salt water to drink (one teaspoon of salt in 1 dm³ of cooled, boiled water).

Poisoning

Common household chemicals taken accidentally by children or others can be harmful, e.g. alcohol, aspirin, bleach, lavatory cleaner, washing-up liquid, weedkiller, insecticide, rat pellets, paint thinner and kerosene.

Follow any instructions on the container from which the poison came. Otherwise do not try to make the person vomit. Wash around the mouth but do not give water to drink. Give artificial respiration if necessary. Lay them on their side in a comfortable position. Get a doctor's help.

Shock

This can follow a severe burn, blood loss or electric shock. The person is pale, faint and sweating with a cold skin. Lay them on their back, with their head low and legs raised. Loosen tight clothing and wrap them in a coat or blanket. Do not give them anything to eat or drink. Get a doctor's help.

Sprains

The joint is pulled unnaturally. These are common in the ankle or wrist due to falls in the home or on the playing field. The joint will swell and be painful and bruised. Sponge it with cold water. Bind the joint in its proper position with light bandaging.

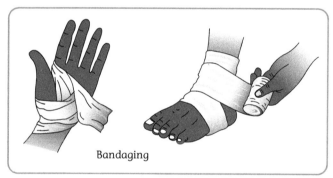
Bandaging

For a sprained wrist or ankle hold the joint in its natural position. Wrap a bandage around it above and below the joint several times. Rest it for as long as necessary.

Key ideas

Use these words to fill in the spaces as you write the sentences in your Exercise book.

bandage **petroleum jelly** **clean** **resuscitation** **cool** **antiseptic** **clots**

If a person stops breathing, mouth-to-mouth _____ is needed urgently. For cuts and burns it is important to keep the wounds _____ and _____ . Do not remove _____ or blisters. Do not put on cotton wool or _____ , but open wounds can be cleaned with _____ before being covered with a _____ . A _____ is also used to bind sprained joints.

14.5 How can we control fires?

The 'fire triangle'

For a fire to start, and to continue, it needs:

- **fuel**: something that can burn, e.g. wood, oil or gas
- **heat**: to warm the fuel to the ignition temperature (the temperature at which it can burn), and
- **oxygen or air**: to allow for the burning process to occur.

Putting out a fire

If fires start, we need to stop them spreading. We remove one or more of the conditions needed for burning, for example:

- **remove the fuel**: switch off a gas tap, or clear away grass or bush so a fire cannot spread
- **cool the fire**: cover a wood or cloth fire with cold water so the temperature is too low for the fire to continue
- **keep out air**: cover a burning oil pan with a heavy wet cloth to keep away the air from the fire.

What do we use to extinguish a fire?

Fire blanket

This is a thick heavy blanket. In an emergency, use an ordinary blanket or thick wet towel.

Sand

This is stored in a fire bucket. The sand can be thrown onto the fire, excluding air and putting the fire out.

Fire extinguishers

These contain chemicals under pressure, which are released through a nozzle when the operating lever is pressed. There are different kinds:

- **Water extinguisher**: the water is stored under pressure and comes out quickly when the lever is operated. The water cools the fire. Do NOT use water on an oil or electical fire.
- **Carbon dioxide extinguisher**: contains carbon dioxide under pressure, or carbon dioxide is made in a chemical reaction. The gas is heavy and forms a layer over the flames, excluding oxygen. Carbon dioxide does not itself allow burning to occur.
- **Foam extinguisher**: contains a foam under pressure, or chemicals to make one. When the lever is operated, the foam comes out, covers the fire and excludes oxygen.
- **Dry powder extinguisher**: usually contains an unreactive powder such as sodium hydrogencarbonate. The powder is pushed out under pressure and covers the fire. It is used on fires with burning metals.

Fire Service

If the fire is getting out of hand, is smoky, or spreading, switch off all fuel, close the doors, quickly leave the building and call the Fire Service. Firefighters are equipped to deal with fires (see page 250).

(see page 250)

Objectives

- Explain the various methods used in extinguishing different kinds of fire.
- Design and make a simple carbon dioxide fire extinguisher.

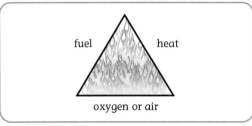

The 'fire triangle'. If a fire goes out it might be rekindled (lit again) by adding more fuel or oxygen.

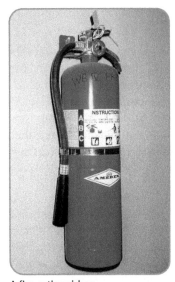

A fire extinguisher

Questions

1 Many organic liquids have low ignition temperatures. Why is it important to keep them away from flames?

2 Explain, with reasons, how you would put out: (a) a fire of spilt gasoline, (b) burning cloth and (c) a bush fire.

3 What are the characteristics of a fire blanket and sand that make them useful?

Different kinds of fire	Which extinguishers to use
Class A Burning solids, e.g. wood, paper, cloth, rubber, plastics.	Water or foam extinguisher. *Reason*: water cools the fire and puts it out. The foam stops air getting to the flames, so the fire goes out.
Class B Burning liquids, e.g. cooking fat, oil, gasoline, kerosene, methylated spirits.	Fire blanket, carbon dioxide, foam or powder extinguisher. *Reason*: all stop air getting to the flames, so the fire goes out. *Never* use water, which could spread the flames.
Class C Electrical fires, e.g. overloading of sockets or the correct fuse is not installed; electrical wiring and appliances can catch fire.	Switch off the electrical supply first. Then use a fire blanket, sand or carbon dioxide extinguisher. *Reason*: all stop air getting to the flames, so the fire goes out. *Never* use water, because it is a conductor of electricity and can cause further fires and electric shocks.
Class D Metal fires, e.g. burning sodium or magnesium.	Dry powder extinguisher. *Reason*: powder excludes air. Makes the chemicals harmless. *Never* use water, which could react with the chemicals.

Questions

4 A burning wood fire and aerobic respiration are examples of combustion. Give two ways in which they are similar, and two ways in which they are different.

5 Look at page 248 on the Bunsen flames. How can you apply the fire triangle to explain the yellow and blue flames, and how quickly they each heat water?

6 Make a list of as many different types of fires as you can. Identify the fuel in each case.

7 Fires can be started in different ways: for example, you can light a piece of paper with a burning match; a gas cooker may have a pilot light. Write down, for each fuel you can think of, how a fire using this fuel can be started.

8 List the special equipment, including clothing, that is needed by members of the Fire Service. For each one explain why it is important.

9 List four ways in which fires can be dangerous to people, animals, crops, buildings and the environment.

Practical 93

Making a fire extinguisher (PD, MM)

1 Design a simple carbon dioxide fire extinguisher, e.g. as shown below.

2 Collect your chemicals and containers and make and test your extinguisher in a safe way.

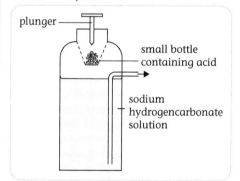

plunger — small bottle containing acid — sodium hydrogencarbonate solution

Key ideas

Use these words to fill in the spaces as you write the sentences in your Exercise book.

cool	electrical	fuel	oil	oxygen or air	remove	heat

For a fire to burn there must be _____ , _____ , and _____ to reach the burning (ignition) temperature. To put out a fire we need to _____ one or more of these conditions: we cut off the _____ , cover the fire to _____ _____ , or _____ the fire by pouring on water. We do not use water for _____ fires or burning _____ , as this would spread the fire.

15 Metals and non-metals

15.1 The properties of metals and non-metals

Physical properties

In your earlier work in science you will have investigated some of the chemical properties of elements, both metals and non-metals. Now you can do some simple practical work on selected **physical properties**. Then you can use data books (or the Internet) to find out about other properties and about some other elements.

Objectives

● Relate the uses of metals, non-metals, plastics and wood to their properties.
● Review properties such as density, heat and electrical conductivity, melting point and tensile strength.

Practical 94

How can we measure the density of some metals and non-metals? (PD, MM, ORR)

1 Use metals, such as an iron nail and a small aluminium block, and a non-metal, such as a graphite rod, to measure density.
2 Use a balance, measuring cylinder and water to find the density (see page 220) of each element.
3 Also add small quantities of the following to a beaker of water: granulated zinc and powdered sulphur. Which do you think is the metal? Why? Record your results in a table.

Practical 95

How can we investigate whether metals and non-metals conduct electricity? (MM, ORR, PD)

1 Set up a simple circuit like that shown in the diagram.

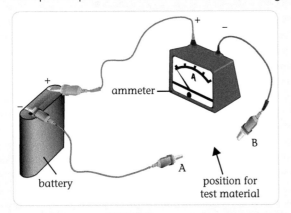

2 Check whether the following elements conduct electricity: copper (wire), iron (nail), sulphur, carbon (graphite) and lead.
3 Which elements conduct electricity?
4 How would you try to investigate whether an element conducts heat well, a little or not at all? Working in groups, design a simple experiment to investigate whether elements conduct heat.

Practical 96

The tensile strength of metals and non-metals (PD, MM, ORR)

1 Use an iron nail, a strip of aluminium foil, a length of copper wire and a graphite rod.
2 Use a hammer on a small sample of each. Which are strong, and which are weak?
3 Use the apparatus below to find the tensile strength of each element.
4 Record all your results in a table.

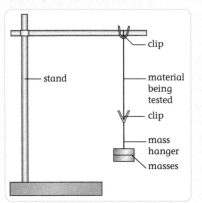

Activity

Metals and non-metals: elements

1 Make a table of the uses of six common metals and six common non-metals.
2 Use a data book or any other source to add the main physical properties (melting point, boiling point, density, tensile strength and electrical and heat conductivity) to your table.
3 List the main differences between the physical properties of metals and non-metals, and identify any unusual examples.

Metals and non-metals

Metals

- Shiny when polished or freshly cut.
- Conduct heat and electricity well.
- Hard and strong, and made into wires.
- High density, except e.g. sodium, potassium.
- High melting points: they are solids at room temperature, except for mercury (a liquid).
- Some, e.g. iron, nickel and cobalt, are magnetic.

Non-metals

- Dull solids, colourless or coloured gases.
- Poor conductors of heat: they are insulators.
- Poor conductors of electricity, except graphite.
- Soft and weak.
- Low density, and many are gases.
- Low melting points: they are solids or gases at room temperature.
- No non-metals are magnetic.

Practical 97

Plastics and woods (ORR, MM, AI)

Plastics and woods are non-metallic compounds.

1 Examine a variety of kinds of plastics (see right) and woods: include appearance (colour, texture) and apparent softness or hardness.
2 Find the densities of the samples.
3 Find (a) the electrical conductivity and (b) the heat conductivity of the samples.
4 Find the tensile strength of the samples.
5 Your teacher will demonstrate to you how to find the melting point of some of these samples. What happens when woods are heated?
6 Record all your results in a table. Compare how the physical properties of these substances are *different* from the properties of metals.

Questions

1 Choose three properties of metals. Give a named example of how a metal with each of the properties is used.
2 Choose three properties of non-metals. Give a named example of how a non-metal with each of the properties is used.

Activity

Properties and uses

1 (a) Make a list of common items used in the home that are made of either plastic or wood. (b) What are the important properties that make them useful?
2 (a) List some items used in the laboratory that are made of metal, plastic or glass. (b) What are the properties that make them useful?

Key ideas

Use these words to fill in the spaces as you write the sentences in your Exercise book.

density	heat	electricity	tensile strength	graphite	high

Sodium and potassium are examples of metals with a low _____ ; most other metals have a high _____ . The _____ of a substance is measured by using a force to stretch it. Metals are good conductors of _____ and _____ . Non-metals are poor conductors of _____ , except for _____ . Most metals have _____ melting and boiling points.

15.2 Materials used in sports equipment

Materials in sports equipment

If you look at some sports equipment, you will observe that it is made from familiar materials with properties that are known or can be investigated. By knowing these properties you can arrive at a fairly good idea of what your sports equipment can withstand. You will then have a better understanding of how to take care of it and get more use from it.

Objective

● Relate the uses of metals and non-metals in sporting equipment to their properties.

What materials are used in cricket?

Activity

What's in your sports equipment?

1 Examine some sports equipment. Copy and complete the table below, adding more columns to the list if necessary.
2 How do the properties of the different materials affect the characteristics of different items of equipment? What would be the effect of leaving them outside? How do they compare for strength and elasticity? What standard of comparison would you use?

Materials which form a major part	Sports equipment	
	Football	Cricket bat
Wood		✗
Rubber		✗
Plastic		
Cotton		
Steel/iron		
Aluminium		
Leather	✗	
Other		

Practical 98

How do materials respond to stretching? (MM, ORR, AI)

1 Hang strings or wires of different materials, one at a time, as shown in the diagram on the right. Make and place a wire pointer somewhere on the material.
2 Load the string with masses appropriately to produce a measurable extension.
3 Plot the results on a graph of load (weight of the masses added) against extension. Compare the shapes of the graphs for different materials (also see page 384).
● As masses are added, the material stretches.
● The value of the load (force) at which the material fails to return to its original length is called the **elastic limit.**
● We can compare the elastic limit of different materials.

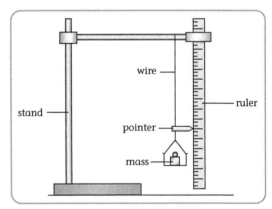
Finding the extension of a wire

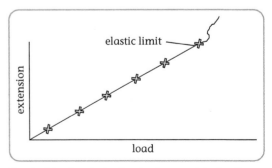
Graph of load against extension for a metal wire. How does it compare to the materials you have tested?

Which material is stronger?

To compare exactly the strength of two materials the mass per unit length is important. For example, if steel wire is compared with nylon, then a metre of nylon string should be compared with a metre of wire of the same mass. Of course, because steel is denser than nylon, the steel wire will be much thinner.

Strength is also important in sports equipment. Strength also has to be considered along with size; for example, ropes used in climbing must be thick enough to give a proper handgrip. Weight, durability and cost are also important.

What care is needed for sports equipment?

- Natural materials, such as cotton and leather, can be attacked and destroyed by microorganisms, such as mildew, unless they are properly treated. They need to be stored in a dry place.
- Cotton must not be kept moist, and leather must not be allowed to become waterlogged.
- The wood of a cricket bat must be oiled; otherwise it is liable to crack.
- Ultraviolet light from the Sun can have a harmful effect on plastics. Clear plastic will eventually become cloudy and then brittle.
- Rubber tends to crack when it has dried in the Sun. Seawater will severely affect leather and speed up corrosion in metals – iron in particular (see page 271). Sea salt, remaining from dried seawater, will also attack rubber.
- The strings on tennis rackets will gradually slacken and have to be tightened.
- The majority of these bad effects will take place gradually and may be unnoticed.
- Because many games involve balls, the bounce of a ball is very important. An older, relatively soft cricket ball bounces differently from a new, hard ball. You could design a test to find out if this is true.

How does bounce affect play?

In games such as tennis and squash, the higher the ball bounces the longer the player has to hit the ball, because it is airborne for longer. On a tennis grass court the grass absorbs some of the energy from the ball and the bounce is lower than on a concrete surface. Players have to make special allowance for this. In squash, the bounce is reduced by using a soft ball, which absorbs a higher proportion of the energy when the ball hits the hard playing surface. In cricket, a very hard pitch will cause a high bounce, which can make life difficult for the person batting. The most difficult playing surfaces have uneven bounce, so the movement of the ball after bouncing is difficult to anticipate.

How can you increase friction?

All ball game players choose suitable footwear to increase frictional contact between the ground and themselves. In this way, they can make quick changes in speed and direction without sliding or falling over. In field sports and athletics, boots and shoes are spiked on the soles to prevent slipping. On hard wooden or concrete floors, rubber-soled shoes are used because they are best able to grip the floor and offer resistance.

Questions

1 (a) Where can you find information on the proper use and care of sports equipment?
    (b) Outline the care of the equipment for a chosen sport.
2 Why might the same type of equipment, e.g. tennis rackets, from different manufacturers need different treatment and maintenance?
3 What makes a playing surface (a) fast or (b) slow? What type of cricket pitch favours (a) fast bowlers and (b) slow bowlers?

Key ideas

Use these words to fill in the spaces as you write the sentences in your Exercise book.

elasticity   **equipment**   **low**   **high**   **damage**   **elastic**

The materials that make up sports _____ may differ in strength, _____ and durability.

Equipment will incur severe _____ if the materials of which it is made are stretched beyond

their _____ limit. On playing surfaces, a hard surface tends to give a _____ bounce, while

a soft ball gives a _____ bounce.

15.3 Using plastics in the home

Plastics

Plastics are very common in our lives. Most plastics are **polymers**. These are very large molecules formed by a process called **polymerization**. Many small molecules are joined together to form one very large molecule.

A good example is polythene, formed when many molecules of ethene are joined together.

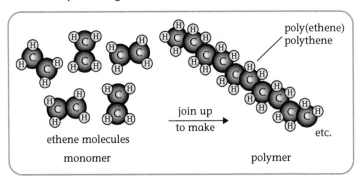

ethene molecules

monomer

join up to make →

poly(ethene) polythene

etc.

polymer

Objectives

- Discuss the advantages and disadvantages of using plastics.
- Consider the negative effects on the environment of using plastics.

Did you know?

- The first plastic, Bakelite, was made in 1907 by Leo Baekeland, in the USA.
- Many plastics can now be sorted and recycled, and many plastic bags used in supermarkets are biodegradable.

Some common plastics

- **Polythene** Low-density polythene is used to make items such as detergent bottles and plastic bags. High-density polythene is used in bowls and dustbins.
- **Polyvinylchloride (PVC)** This is used for making wrapping film and pipes for houses.
- **Polystyrene** This is used to make food containers and disposable cups. Expanded polystyrene is very light and used as an insulator.
- **Polyacrylonitrile** This can be spun into long fibres and used as a fabric.
- **Nylon** This contains nitrogen and oxygen, as well as carbon and hydrogen. It is used as a fibre in clothes and ropes.
- **Terylene** This contains oxygen as well as carbon and hydrogen. It is used for making clothes and sails for boats.

Activity

Using plastics or metals?

1 Examine the photograph on the right. Choose four items made of plastic. Why do you think plastic is used for these items, and not metal? List the special properties of plastics that are being used.
2 Choose four items made of metal in the photograph. Why do you think metal is used for these items, and not plastic? List the special properties of metals that are being used.
3 Make a list of other items used in your home, which are made of plastic.
4 Prepare a list of the advantages of using plastics for certain items. Discuss and then list (a) any limitations for using plastics, and (b) any disadvantages.

Household items made of metals and plastics

Questions

1 What is a polymer?
2 Name three natural polymers (see page 25).
3 How did you identify (a) the plastic items and (b) the metal items from the photograph?
4 List the items you use in the laboratory that are made of plastic.

Why are plastics so useful?

Plastic items are common. Plastics:

- are often cheaper and lighter than similar metal items, e.g. plastic bowls
- do not rust and are long-lasting
- do not conduct electricity, and so can be used as insulation for handles and around wires
- do not break when dropped, as compared with glass or china
- are resistant to many chemicals, but not all
- can make transparent bottles or plastic bags
- can make thin transparent film, e.g. cling film
- can be dyed attractive colours
- can be developed with specific properties, e.g. for adhesives, tyres, aeroplane windows, luggage, hoses and non-stick covering on pans.

Activity

What are some disadvantages of using plastics?

1 Identify a small area in your school or close to your home; check it each day for a week or so. You should note how much plastic waste can be seen each day. Record your observations in a table.

2 When your parents have shopped at a supermarket or large shop, check the amount of plastic used in packaging. What happens to this packaging? How much is (a) re-used in the home, or (b) recycled in special garbage bins?

Problems with using plastics: they are damaged by heat, and they also cause pollution problems as litter or waste.

- Most plastics do not break down into simpler compounds if left in the soil or at a garbage dump (they are **non-biodegradable**).
- However, some plastics do break down over time (they are **biodegradable**).

Practical 99

Testing plastics (ORR, MM)

1 Collect samples of as many plastics as you can.

2 Test the obvious properties of each plastic, such as colour or transparency, approximate density, hardness, resistance to heat (DANGER: only in a fume cupboard and use very small quantities).

3 Test the electrical conductivity of each sample using a simple circuit like the one on page 256.

4 Investigate the reaction of common solvents such as water, ethanol, propanone, aqueous ammonia and dilute acid with small pieces of plastic.

5 Record all your observations in a table.

6 Find a sample of plastic bag that is described as biodegradable. Cut a piece from this, and a similar sized piece from a non-biodegradable bag. Cover both pieces with soil in a container, and keep the soil moist. Examine and comment on the appearance of both pieces after 1 month.

7 Compare the properties of plastics with those of metals and alloys.

8 List the advantages and disadvantages of using plastics.

Questions

5 List (a) the advantages and (b) the disadvantages of using synthetic fibres in clothing.

6 What are the advantages of clothes made of cotton?

7 Many of the raw materials used for making plastics come from petroleum. Why would it therefore be useful to recycle plastic items?

8 Do you know of schemes for collecting and re-using metal cans or plastic objects in your country? Find out what you can about these schemes.

Key ideas

Use these words to fill in the spaces as you write the sentences in your Exercise book.

polymer   **plastic**   **waste**   **litter**   **small**   **nylon**   **biodegradable**

A _____ is made when many _____ molecules are joined together. Terylene is a _____ used in making sails for boats. _____ can be used as a fibre in clothing. A _____ plastic breaks down over time into smaller compounds. But most plastics are non-biodegradable, and two of the biggest problems about using them are _____ and _____ .

15.4 How reactive are some of the metals?

Metals and acids

In your previous work in science, you will have seen that some metals react vigorously with dilute acids, whereas others do not. This is important in everyday life, because we handle both metals and substances containing dilute acids.

You will now investigate how some metals react with dilute hydrochloric and sulphuric acid.

Your teacher may show the reaction of these metals with dilute nitric acid. But dilute nitric acid tends to react more like an oxidizing agent, and oxides of nitrogen are produced. Concentrated nitric and sulphuric acids are also oxidizing agents: hydrogen is not released during reactions with metals. Concentrated hydrochloric acid reacts in a similar way to dilute hydrochloric acid.

Objectives

- Describe the reactions of selected metals with acid, alkali, water, steam and oxygen.
- Write word equations for the reactions.
- Identify the relative activity of the metals and their positions in the Reactivity series.

Practical 100

What happens when metals react with dilute acids? (ORR, MM)

1 Pour dilute sulphuric acid into a test tube to a depth of about 4 cm.

2 Add a small quantity of zinc to the acid. Observe any changes that occur (also see page 387).

3 Repeat steps 1 and 2, but test the gas given off. Put a burning splint in the mouth of the test tube. This is a test for hydrogen gas. Record your observations.

   We can write a simple word equation for this reaction:

   zinc(s) + sulphuric acid(aq) → zinc sulphate(aq) + hydrogen(g)

4 Repeat steps 1 to 3, but use aluminium, copper, iron and tin. If there is no reaction with the acid when the metal is cold, warm the test tube GENTLY. Your teacher may show you the reactions of dilute acid with magnesium and silver.

5 Repeat steps 1 to 3, using each of the metals, but using dilute hydrochloric acid instead of sulphuric acid.

6 Record all your observations in a table. Write simple word equations for any reactions you observe.

Questions

1 How many of the metals produced hydrogen with the dilute acids?

2 Were the reactions similar for dilute hydrochloric and dilute sulphuric acids?

3 Make a list of metals in order of how vigorously they react with dilute acids (the most active metal at the top).

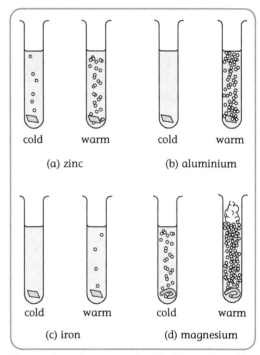

cold   warm   cold   warm

(a) zinc   (b) aluminium

cold   warm   cold   warm

(c) iron   (d) magnesium

The reactions of some metals with dilute acids: cold and warm

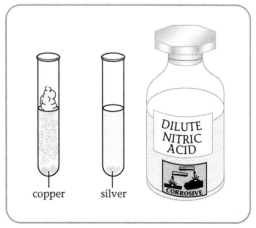

copper   silver

The reactions of copper and silver with dilute nitric acid. Which of these metals is more active?

Practical 101

What happens when metals react with water? (ORR, MM, AI)

You have written a list of some metals, with the most reactive first and the least reactive last. Can you predict how metals will react with water? You can then test your predictions practically.

1 Pour distilled water into a test tube to a depth of 4–5 cm. Add a small amount of zinc.

2 Observe whether a reaction takes place. Identify any gas given off.

3 If there is no reaction, warm the test tube and note whether a reaction takes place.

4 Write a word equation for any reaction observed. Either oxides or hydroxides of the metals will be formed.

5 Repeat the experiment, using separate small amounts of the metals calcium, aluminium, copper, iron and tin. Your teacher may demonstrate the reactions with silver and with sodium.

6 Record your results in the form of a table.

7 How did your observations support your predictions?

Reaction of sodium with water. This vigorous reaction releases hydrogen and makes sodium hydroxide (which can be tested with litmus paper). What would be the colour change with universal indicator?

Metals and water

In Practical 101 you investigated what happens when metals react with water. You will find that only sodium and calcium react quickly, and most metals do not react at all with cold or warm water. You probably predicted this. It is actually useful that many metals do NOT react with water, as it is such a common chemical and it is very important in industry, as a cooling agent, as a source of steam and as a cleaner.

Although many metals do not react with water, a number of metals will react with steam. Your teacher may demonstrate the reaction of either iron or zinc with steam. In the reaction of steam with a metal, an oxide is formed. For example:

iron(s) + water(g) → iron oxide(s) + hydrogen(g)

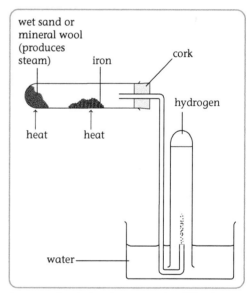

Apparatus for the iron/steam reaction. Why do you think that copper, and not iron, is used for making water pipes in houses?

Key ideas

Use these words to fill in the spaces as you write the sentences in your Exercise book.

acids   **water**   **reactive**   **metals**   **oxides**   **hydrogen**   **hydroxides**

When some metals react with dilute acids, _____ is released. Some _____ react with water to

form _____, and either _____ or _____ . Zinc is more _____ than iron. Most metals do

not react with cold _____ , but will react with _____ . Dilute nitric acid reacts with _____

to form _____ of nitrogen.

15.4 How reactive are some of the metals? (continued)

Metals reacting with oxygen and dilute alkalis

You will now prepare oxygen and investigate how some metals react with it. You will also investigate the reactions between metals and dilute alkalis. But you will NOT use sodium and potassium, which are extremely reactive.

Practical 102

What happens when zinc reacts with oxygen? (ORR, MM)

1 Prepare a number of boiling tubes full of oxygen (see diagram). Seal the tubes with bungs until they are needed.

2 Put a small quantity of zinc in a deflagrating spoon. Heat it strongly in a Bunsen flame. As soon as it gets very hot, put the spoon into one of the boiling tubes full of oxygen.

3 Allow the solid formed to cool down. Then transfer it to a small beaker, and add a small quantity of distilled water. Mix the solid and liquid thoroughly.

4 Add a few drops of universal indicator (UI) solution (see page 278) to the solid/liquid mixture.

5 Record all your observations.

6 Repeat steps 2 to 5 with aluminium, copper, iron and tin. Your teacher will show you the reaction with magnesium.

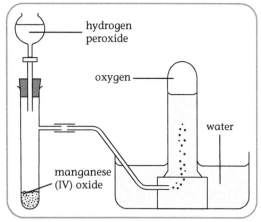

Preparation of oxygen

Zinc reacts with oxygen to form zinc oxide:

zinc(s) + oxygen(g) → zinc oxide(s)

When zinc is added to water and then tested with UI solution, the indicator changes colour to show there is an alkali present. Zinc oxide is only slightly soluble, but a little zinc hydroxide is formed. The oxides of some other metals do not dissolve at all in water; you should record these as insoluble. These oxides are bases, but they do not form hydroxides on reaction with water. Bases react with dilute acids to form a salt and water only (see pages 280–1).

Zinc powder was heated in a deflagrating spoon, which was then put into a gas jar full of oxygen. The white glow shows the formation of zinc oxide

---

Practical 103

What happens when metals react with dilute alkalis? (ORR, MM)

1 Repeat the experiments in which you investigated the reactions of metals with dilute acids. Use dilute sodium hydroxide solution instead of an acid, with zinc, aluminium, copper, iron and tin. If there is no reaction at room temperature, warm the test tube carefully. Identify any gases produced.

2 Record your observations in a table.

3 Repeat the experiments using dilute aqueous ammonia.

4 Record your observations in a table.

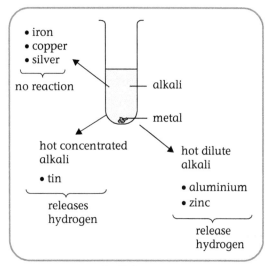

How metals react with alkalis

Activity

Is there a pattern in the reactions of metals?

1 Review the reactions of metals with (a) oxygen, (b) water, (c) steam, (d) dilute acids and (e) dilute alkalis.
2 In each case, make a list of the metals in order of how vigorously they react.
3 Is it possible to put the metals in order of their reactivity with these substances? This list is called a **reactivity series** of metals.

The most reactive metals form compounds very easily, whereas the least reactive form them much less easily. The least reactive metals are elements such as silver, which only reacts with concentrated acid, and gold, which is the least reactive of all.

What happens when metals compete?

A *more* reactive metal can replace a *less* reactive metal from one of its compounds. Iron is above copper in the reactivity series. If an iron nail is placed in a copper sulphate solution, it replaces the copper (see page 385).

iron(s) + copper sulphate(aq) → iron sulphate(aq) + copper(s)

Questions

1 What is the word equation for the preparation of oxygen?
2 Why do you think sodium is stored under oil?
3 What is the reactivity series of metals?
4 Would you expect tin to replace aluminium, or aluminium to replace tin?

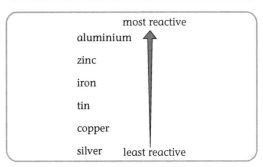

Reactivity series of metals

Reactivity series of metals			
Metal	**With oxygen**	**With water**	**With dilute acid**
Sodium	Reacts rapidly, kept under oil	Vigorous with cold water	Violent
Calcium	Reacts quickly	Rapid with cold water	Vigorous
Magnesium	Becomes coated with a protective layer of the metal oxide	Reacts with steam	Rapid
Aluminium		Red hot, reacts with steam	Less rapid
Zinc		Red hot, reacts with steam	Less rapid
Iron	Rusts slowly with moist air	Red hot, reacts with steam	Less rapid
Tin	Molten metal reacts to form oxide	No reaction	Very slow
Copper	Reacts slowly to form the oxide	No reaction	No hydrogen
Silver	No reaction	No reaction	No hydrogen

(Hydrogen gas released — brace spanning Sodium through Tin in the With dilute acid column)

Key ideas

Use these words to fill in the spaces as you write the sentences in your Exercise book.

copper　　　**oxygen**　　　**reactivity**　　　**hydrogen**　　　**hydroxide**　　　**UI**

Oxygen is formed when _____ peroxide reacts with manganese (IV) oxide. Metals react with _____ to form oxides. When a metal oxide reacts with water to form a metal _____ , the solution turns _____ solution blue. Zinc is above iron in the _____ series, and iron is above _____ . Silver and gold are the least reactive.

15.5 Using metals and alloys in the home

Metals, alloys or plastics?

You have studied the different properties of metals, and non-metals such as plastics (see pages 256–7). Their different properties are made use of when objects are made to use in the home. Mixtures of metals, called **alloys**, have also been designed for special purposes.

You will notice that many of the objects in *both* lists are made of metals or alloys. In many cases, these objects will also contain plastics or wood (see pages 256–7), as insulators. Why are the insulators necessary?

Metals are very common elements. For example, copper is a very good conductor of heat and electricity. It is used to make kitchen utensils such as saucepans, and electrical wiring. It is very important for *both* these uses that copper is low in the reactivity series (see page 265). Why?

Alloys are mixtures of two or more elements, at least one of which is a metal. They have been designed to have special properties different from those of pure metals.

Some common alloys are:

● brass – made of copper and zinc
● bronze – made of copper and tin
● steel – can be made of iron and carbon, although many steels also contain other metals, such as nickel or chromium, which can prevent them from rusting (see page 271: stainless steel).

What are some uses of metals and alloys?

- A lot of cutlery is made from stainless steel. This is more expensive than steel, but less liable to corrode.
- Light bulbs contain a special metal filament.
- Electric kettles have a metal heating element.
- Metals can be made into: tubular frames, used for chairs; sheets, used for making cans; wires, for making copper electrical wiring.
- Metals used outside need to be strong, and may need to be painted or otherwise protected from the corrosive effects of the environment.
- Cars contain a lot of metals and alloys in their engines and bodywork.
- Generally, alloys are harder than the pure metals and have lower melting points. For example, solder is made from tin and lead, and melts at a low temperature using a soldering iron, to be used to join wires in electrical circuits.
- Brass is useful because it is harder than copper, but still resistant to corrosion.
- Duralumin, an alloy of aluminium, still has a low density but is much stronger and more resistant to corrosion than aluminium alone.
- Steel bands use 'steel pans' made from old oil drums, which are made of alloys.

Activity

Different types of metals and alloys

1 Look at all the objects used for cooking and cleaning in your home. Make a list of those that are made of or contain metals.

2 Do the same thing for garden or farm tools. Try to find out which metals or alloys are used.

3 Pick some of the objects you have listed and suggest the properties needed. For example, a saucepan will need a metal or alloy that is a good conductor of heat and is unreactive to boiling water and to dilute acids and alkalis.

What do we use for cooking and canning?

Cooking

Most common cooking utensils are made from copper, iron or aluminium. Many frying pans also now have a non-stick, heat-resistant plastic coating applied to them.

- Copper utensils are the most resistant to attack by water, acids or alkalis but are very expensive.
- In the Caribbean, we often use pots made of cast iron, but these are somewhat reactive.
- Aluminium is light and cheap, and forms a layer of oxide that is very unreactive. But the oxide is a base and reacts with hot acids, such as fruit juice or ethanoic acid, to dissolve the aluminium. Strong salt solutions also react with the oxide to make soluble aluminium salts. There are health concerns about too much aluminium in the diet.

Canning

The cans in which food is kept have to be resistant to acids, as are found in fruit juices. This means that the cans cannot be kept for too long. Common canning materials are aluminium or steel, but these are coated with tin. The tin is less reactive and protects the other metals.

Questions

1 Would plastics be useful for making cooking utensils? Explain your answer.

2 (a) What is an alloy? (b) Describe a particular alloy, and why it is preferred, for a special purpose, than either of the metals it is made from.

3 What are the properties needed for a metal or alloy used in (a) electrical wiring, (b) cooking or canning food, (c) tools for the garden and farm, and (d) making car radiators?

4 What are the advantages and disadvantages of using aluminium for cooking or canning utensils? How do the reasons relate to the properties of the metal?

Key ideas

Use these words to fill in the spaces as you write the sentences in your Exercise book.

metal   alloys   corrosion   conductors   tin   copper   oxide

Aluminium is a _____ that can resist _____ because of the protective layer of _____ that forms on its surface. _____ are mixtures of metals, and sometimes other elements, made for special purposes, e.g. brass, which is made of _____ and zinc. Most metals are good _____ of heat and electricity. _____ is used as a coating inside cans of steel or aluminium.

15.6 How do we clean metal appliances?

Why do household appliances need cleaning?

Metals are used in pans and other household appliances.

- If used for cooking, they get remains of food, or burnt food, on them, which may become dried and stuck on.
- They get dust, dirt and microorganisms on their surfaces from their surroundings. As well as damaging the appearance, these items can be a health hazard.
- They may also react with a range of gases in the air to form a thin layer on the surface, such as the protective oxide, e.g. on aluminium.
- Other chemicals may be formed: sulphides (e.g. on silver and copper), or black copper oxide or green copper carbonate (verdigris) on copper surfaces.
- Iron and steel surfaces left exposed to air and water form a red oxide, **rust**, and this continues to wear away at the metal.

Activity

Cleaning household metals and alloys

1 Look at the list of household objects made of metals or alloys (see page 266).

2 Which of these objects should be cleaned immediately after they are used? Suggest a reason for this.

3 Which have to be cleaned after they have been exposed to the atmosphere for a long time? Why?

4 Which metals are unreactive to the atmosphere?

How can we clean used household appliances?

- Using warm water and washing-up liquid (see page 287). This is sufficient for tin and zinc items. Plates, cutlery and pans of iron and steel used for food can usually also be cleaned this way, which removes oil, grease and food.
- Rubbing with a cloth or sponge usually removes the food remains, otherwise a plastic scourer can be used.
- If food is stuck or burnt onto the surface, the item is left to soak in warm water with detergent. If there is no special finish on the surface, steel wool or an abrasive pad can be used. However, these remove some of the metal surface as well as the food. Do NOT use with non-stick surfaces, or copper or silver items.
- The tarnish on copper items can be removed with a metal polish. You can also use a mixture of equal parts vinegar (which attacks alkalis), flour (which helps spread the cleaner) and salt (which forms soluble compounds with parts of the tarnish).
- Iron and steel objects should be cleaned regularly, to prevent them forming rust. They can be wiped with a vegetable oil to help protect them from corrosion. They should be carefully dried.

Objective

- Discuss methods of cleaning household appliances, including aluminium, copper, iron, tin and zinc.

Activity

Cleaning methods

1 Check the list of appliances that need to be cleaned after use or after being exposed to the atmosphere.

2 How many ways do you know of cleaning metal objects? Make a list of these methods.

3 Which of these methods involve removing part of the metal surface?

Cleaning materials. Detergent (washing-up liquid) in warm water is being used. There are also surface cleaners that will not scratch metal surfaces as much as steel wool would

Questions

1 Vegetable oil is commonly used in cooking. Is this likely to preserve the surface of cooking utensils?

2 What is the advantage of cleaning pots and plates either soon after use, or after soaking in soapy water?

3 Which is (a) the least and (b) the most damaging method to use for cleaning? Name an occasion on which you would use each method.

Using scouring

Plastic scouring pads can be used, with detergent, to clean any surface, except soft metals (copper and silver). Steel wool, a metal scouring pad or a scouring powder can remove burnt-on food, but also removes part of the metal surface. You can check this by looking with a hand lens. If these methods are used with:

- iron and steel, the surfaces are exposed to rusting
- aluminium, the oxide layer is removed, but re-forms
- soft copper or silver, the surface will be scratched.

Using metal cleaners

There is a chemical reaction with the tarnish.

- Tarnished copper can be cleaned with metal polish or other cleaning mixture (see page 268).
- Stainless steel needs a special metal cleaner.
- Silver needs a different special cleaner, and the item is cleaned with a special cleaning cloth, or dipped into a cleaning liquid.

In all cases, the tarnish is removed and leaves the metal clean. All items are then washed in soapy water, to remove traces of the cleaner, and are dried and polished.

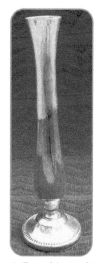

A silver object, which has had part of its tarnish cleaned away using a silver cleaner

Questions

4 You have forgotten about some food cooking in a saucepan, and some of the food is burnt onto the surface. How will you clean it?

5 What special precautions do you need to take when using and cleaning a frying pan with a special non-stick surface?

6 Would you clean all metal appliances with the same metal cleaner? Explain your answer.

7 Why is it better to use scouring powder on aluminium, instead of using an acid or salt?

8 Make a table of metal appliances and the methods best used for cleaning each of them. Include any possible problems to the appliance or our health.

Key ideas

Use these words to fill in the spaces as you write the sentences in your Exercise book.

tarnished	polish	scouring	bleach	steel	corrosion

Metal surfaces that are _____ may be cleaned and protected by using a metal _____ . To clean a metal surface with stuck-on food may require an abrasive pad or _____ powder.

Rusting is an example of the _____ of metals. _____ can be added to a cleaning agent to make it more effective. _____ wool removes part of the surface when it is used for cleaning.

15.7 What causes rusting?

Are air and water important for rusting?

If a machete or cutlass is left out in the rain, you will see it forms some brown spots of rust. Rust forms on the surface of iron (and some steel) objects. Rust contains an oxide of iron, and is an example of corrosion. Unlike aluminium oxide, rust does NOT protect the surface of the metal. The rust spreads and the metal deteriorates. Because of this, we need to check the surface of iron and steel objects regularly. We can investigate the ways in which rust is formed, and this should help us to think about how to prevent rusting.

Objectives

- Investigate the conditions that cause rusting.
- Identify factors that affect the rate of rusting.

Practical 104

How does iron rust? (ORR, MM, AI)

Investigate the ways in which iron rusts by examining what happens to iron nails when they are tested under different conditions.

1 Take four similar iron nails which can fit into a test tube or boiling tube. Clean each nail carefully using emery paper. Make sure the surface is clean.

2 Put one nail in each of the four tubes.

3 Set up the tubes as follows:
   A put in some dry calcium oxide, and close the mouth with cotton wool (calcium oxide absorbs moisture)
   B add water that has been boiled and then allowed to cool in a sealed container; cover the nail entirely, then add a thin layer of oil on top of the water
   C leave the tube open to the air
   D add tap water so that the nail is covered, and leave it open to the air.

4 Describe the different conditions in tubes **A**, **B**, **C** and **D**.

5 Examine the nails each day for about a week. Record your observations in a table.

6 How can you try to explain these observations, based on your answers to step 4?

Questions

1 Would you expect the exhaust pipe of a car to corrode quickly? Why?

2 What would you do to try to protect a garden tool from rusting?

3 Stainless steel does not rust. So why don't we use it to make more items?

Rust on a car. Any damaged surfaces, where the iron is exposed to air and moisture, will rust

What causes rusting?

In the practical, you will have found that the nails in tubes **C** and **D** rusted; those in **A** and **B** did not.

- In **A**, the air has been dried, so it does not contain moisture. These nails have dry air only.
- In **B**, there is water only (the layer of oil prevents air from entering the water, which has already had its air removed by boiling).
- Therefore, air *alone* or water *alone cannot* cause rusting.
- In **C**, there is some water vapour in the atmosphere, so the nail in this tube will rust slowly.
- In **D**, the nail is exposed to plenty of both air and water, and rusts most quickly.

The word equation for the formation of rust is:

iron(s) + oxygen(g) + water(l) → brown iron oxide (rust)

This can also be written as:

iron(s) + oxygen(g) + water(l) → hydrated iron oxide(s)

- Rusting is an example of corrosion of metals.
- Iron objects rust, and need protection from air and water to prevent it.
- Metal objects corrode most quickly close to the coast, or close to an industrial plant that emits gases or other corrosive substances.

We can now further examine these ideas.

Objects close to the sea will be affected by fine sea spray, which contains salts, such as sodium chloride. It may also contain fine particles of sand, which may break the surface and expose it. You may also notice corrosion problems if you live near a bauxite/alumina industrial plant, a cement factory or an oil refinery.

Practical 105

What conditions affect the rate of rusting? (ORR, MM, AI)

In this experiment, you will investigate the effects of different solutions on the surface of iron.

1 Take six iron nails and clean them as in the previous practical.

2 Put each nail into a separate test tube or boiling tube.

3 Cover the nail in tube **A** with distilled water.

4 For tubes **B–F** use the following solutions to cover the nail:

  B dilute sodium chloride

  C dilute sodium hydroxide

  D very dilute acid (sulphuric or ethanoic)

  E dilute sodium carbonate

  F dilute aqueous ammonia

5 Examine the nails each day for at least a week. Record the rate at which rust is formed, and the total final amount in each case (score them from 1 (least) to 6 (most)).

  Tube A is a control. Explain why this is so.

6 Explain your results based on the factors that increase the rate and amount of rusting (also see page 386).

You should find that *all* of the nails corrode. Record the colours of the new substances formed. The test solutions include one acid, two alkalis and two salts. You should find that there is *more* corrosion when these substances are present, than with distilled water. The presence of salts, acids and alkalis speed up the rate of corrosion.

Corrosion and the sea

The sea contains salts, such as sodium and magnesium chloride, that increase the rate of corrosion. Any metal parts of ships and boats are exposed to the sea, and sea spray, all the time. They need to be protected to prevent corrosion. One way of doing this is to use special paint for exposed surfaces, which has to be renewed regularly.

An ocean liner being painted to prevent rusting

Stainless steel

This is an alloy of iron, carbon, chromium and nickel. It is widely used in industry and for some items in the home.

Stainless steel in the kitchen

Key ideas

Use these words to fill in the spaces as you write the sentences in your Exercise book.

stainless   seawater   acids   alkalis   corrosion   paint   air

Rusting needs _____ and water; it is an example of _____ . _____ (which contains salts),

_____ and _____ all cause rusting to occur more quickly than in moist air or distilled water.

The hull of a ship can be protected with a special _____ . Appliances and instruments made of

_____ steel do not rust, but are more expensive than those made of iron or ordinary steel.

15.8 How can we try to prevent rusting?

What can we do about air and water?

You know that *both* air and water are needed for iron to rust. Rusting always starts at the surface of metal objects, so it may be possible to prevent this process by stopping air and water from reaching the surface. You can cover it with paint (see page 273) or try other methods.

Practical 106

Can covering prevent rusting? (ORR, MM, AI)

1 Place four test tubes in a rack and put a little tap water into each one.

2 Clean four iron nails carefully, as in previous practicals. Put one nail in tube **A** (the control).

3 Treat the other three nails as follows, before putting each one into a separate test tube:
  B dip the nail in an oil-based paint and let it dry
  C dip the nail in thick oil or cover it with grease
  D cover the surface of the nail with nickel (you can do this by **electroplating** it with a solution containing a nickel salt – your teacher will help you).

4 Examine each nail every day for at least a week. Record your observations in a table.

5 Compare the appearance of the nail in tube **A** with those of the nails in tubes **B**, **C** and **D**.

6 Try to explain all your observations.

7 What would you expect to happen if the tubes were all kept at a higher temperature, e.g. in a water bath at 60°C? What control would you need?

Results of using surface coverings

You should find that rusting has occurred in test tube **A**, but that preventing air and water from reaching the surface of the iron in tubes **B**, **C** and **D** has reduced or prevented rusting.

However, we have used only four small iron objects at room temperature for a short period of time. We expect iron cooking pots to be used at high temperatures and to last for a long time. The coverings on the surface of the nails might not be so effective at 60°C, and you may have found that some rusting occurred. For industrial items, the covering must survive high temperatures and needs to be checked regularly.

We also need to test the coverings over longer periods of time, and in solutions that might increase the rate of corrosion (as on page 271).

Practical 107

How effective are surface coverings? (ORR, MM, AI)

You will test the effectiveness of the surface coverings on your nails when they are:
- left out in the weather for a long time, *or*
- left in solutions (acid, alkali or solutions of salts).

1 Prepare *two* sets of four nails, covered as in Practical 106.

2 Put one set of nails outside in the school grounds, so they can be checked regularly. Examine and record the appearance of the nails every third day for up to a month.

3 Record your observations in a table.

4 In your group, choose one of the following solutions: dilute sodium chloride, aqueous ammonia, dilute sodium hydroxide or dilute sulphuric acid. Put the remaining nails in test tubes containing the solution chosen.

5 Examine the nails every day for 2 weeks. Record your observations.

6 Check and discuss the results of other groups using different solutions.

7 Try to explain the principles behind the different protection methods.

Questions

1 What are four methods to prevent rusting?

2 If you had to send a car by sea from one country to another, how would you try to protect the bodywork of the car? Why would this be necessary?

3 In cold countries, salt is spread on the roads when there is snow or ice. (a) Why is this done? (b) What might be the effect on the cars? (c) What might be done to reduce these effects?

How do we prevent rusting?

Most methods depend on covering the surface of the iron or steel items so that air and water cannot reach them.

Painting

We can protect an iron bridge by painting it. But it will need to be painted regularly, because the wind and rain will wear the paint away, and rusting may occur.

Greasing

In machinery, engines, or a bicycle, iron and steel parts can be protected by covering them with oil or grease. Different lubricants are used for different purposes.

Galvanizing iron

You may have heard of 'galvanized sheets' or 'zinc sheets' used for roofs and fences. Steel sheet is carefully cleaned to remove any rust, using two or more lots of acid and washing with water. The cleaned sheets are passed into molten zinc, and a protective alloy layer of iron and zinc forms on the surface of the steel.

There are two other methods used to prevent rusting.

Sacrificial protection

Ships can be protected from rusting by the use of sacrificial protection (see right and page 385). This method makes use of knowledge of the reactivity series, by using metal blocks that are more reactive than iron. The blocks are attached, e.g. to the ship's hull or propeller, and they corrode *before* the hull, which is made of steel. The blocks have to be replaced when they are worn away.

A similar method can protect underground steel pipelines or the steel casing around power cables. In this case, the sacrificial material may be magnesium blocks, attached to steel by wires. The magnesium, being much more reactive than iron and steel, will corrode first.

Making stainless steel

The nature of the steel is changed by adding chromium and nickel. This makes a new alloy, stainless steel, which does not rust.

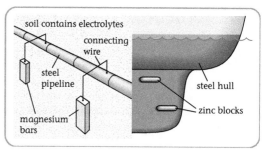

Examples of sacrificial protection

Using sacrificial protection on the iron part of a ship

Questions

4 How would you protect a machete or cutlass from rusting?

5 What do you think would happen if the surface of a galvanized iron sheet was bent or broken?

6 How is the reactivity series related to the use of sacrificial protection?

Key ideas

Use these words to fill in the spaces as you write the sentences in your Exercise book.

| painting | electroplating | galvanizing | surface | grease | iron |

We can protect the _____ of a metal in several ways, e.g. by _____ it. Oil and _____ are used to protect the surfaces of moving parts, e.g. in engines. _____ is the covering of steel sheets with an alloy of _____ and zinc. _____ is the depositing of a nickel layer on top of the _____ or steel using electrolysis in a solution of a nickel salt.

16 Acids, bases and mixtures

16.1 How do we use household chemicals?

Water – a very common household chemical

Water is a very common substance. It is crucial to our existence (see pages 208–9). It has a wide range of uses depending on its unique properties.

Activity

Water in the home

1 Make a list of the common uses of water.
2 We use water in these different ways depending on its properties. In your group, demonstrate one of the properties.

The most important use of water is as a solvent. For example, milk contains fat, milk sugar and proteins as well as water. A common medicine such as milk of magnesia does not contain milk but is a suspension (see page 284) of magnesium hydroxide in water. Hot sauces, common in the Caribbean, also contain a lot of water.

Water can also be found chemically combined in solid substances such as blue (hydrated) copper (II) sulphate.

Look at the table below. You will see that some common food items also contain a high percentage of water.

Percentage composition					
Food	Water	Carbohydrate	Fat	Protein	Other
Cabbage	94	4	–	1	1
Milk	87.5	5	4	3.5	–
Eggs	78	–	10	12	–
Fresh fish	77	–	3	18	2
Meat	63	–	18	18	1
Dried fish	18	–	10	63	9
Maize (corn)	10	78	1	8	3
Soya beans	9	34	18	34	5

Questions

1 Which property of water is the most important for most of its household uses?
2 How important is the boiling point of water for its use in cooking?
3 List some methods of cooking without water. Which foods are used in these cooking methods?

Objectives

● Identify the importance of water as a solvent and as a household chemical.
● Discuss the safe and economic use of some common household chemicals.

THICK BLEACH CONTAINS SODIUM HYDROXIDE
Irritating to eyes and skin.
Warning Do not use with other products.
May release dangerous gases (chlorine).
Store upright in a cool safe place away from babies, children and animals.
Avoid contact with skin and eyes.
In case of contact with eyes, rinse immediately with plenty of water and seek medical advice.
After contact with skin wash immediately with plenty of clean water.
IF SWALLOWED SEEK MEDICAL ADVICE IMMEDIATELY AND SHOW THIS CONTAINER LABEL.

Explain the precautions that should be taken when using a container of bleach

Activity

What is in common chemicals?

1 Collect the containers, or copy the labels, for 10 common household chemicals (do NOT remove labels from chemicals that are in use). Include chemicals used in the garden and at school.
2 Record what each chemical contains. Can you tell whether there are acids or alkalis present?
3 Check whether there are any hazard warning labels (see page 247) on the containers, e.g. pesticides and herbicides. What precautions should you take in handling these chemicals? Why should you wash your hands after handling the containers?
4 Find out whether there is a government policy on the labelling of substances sold to the public.

Questions

4 If a label says a substance contains caustic soda, what precautions should you take in handling it?
5 Many people now use vitamin supplements. How important is it that these have proper labels?

Using household materials properly

- You know that *all* chemicals have to be handled with care; e.g. even water may contain impurities or disease organisms.
- Common chemicals, such as disinfectants, should be handled carefully, and you should not taste or swallow them. Even items that look like food should be checked very carefully; e.g. some mushrooms are poisonous.
- If you are taking medicine, then you should take the dose prescribed. It may be dangerous to take much more – and useless to take much less.
- Materials such as plastics (see page 261) can be dangerous; e.g. some give off poisonous fumes when heated. Plastic bags can also be dangerous, because younger children might be tempted to put a bag over their head and would be suffocated.
- Young children like to explore their environment and will often try to touch or taste things that are potentially dangerous.

There are four basic questions to ask about any household material in common use.
1 What chemicals does the material contain, and what are their properties?
2 Where and how is the material stored?
3 What is the material used for?
4 What precautions should I take when handling the material?

Activity

Using household chemicals safely

1 Make a list of 5–10 common household chemicals.
2 For each chemical, suggest ways in which it might be dangerous if not used properly.
3 Suggest any necessary precautions for storing these substances.

Did you know?

- Drinking too much water can be dangerous. Athletes who sweat a lot lose water and salts. If they then drink a lot of plain water, they can suffer from sodium deficiency and their tissues swell.
- Drinking too little water can also be dangerous. When we sweat a lot in hot weather, or have diarrhoea, we can become dehydrated.
- The water we drink to replace the fluids we have lost should contain a balance of salts.

Questions

6 Do you read the labels on food items? If not, how do you know what you are eating?
7 Would you taste a food item without knowing what it was? Justify your answer.
8 There is often a 'use by' date on processed foods. Why should you take care to use food on or before its 'use by' date?
9 Do you think every chemical sold to the public should have a label listing the substances in it?

Key ideas

Use these words to fill in the spaces as you write the sentences in your Exercise book.

disinfectant   **water**   **poisonous**   **solvent**   **hazard**

One of the most common substances found in many household chemicals is _____ . One of its most important properties is that it can act as a _____ . Pesticides and herbicides contain substances that are _____ . You need to use a _____ to prevent the spread of bacteria in kitchens and bathrooms. It is very important to read any _____ warnings on chemicals.

16.1 How do we use household chemicals? (continued)

Handling household chemicals safely

There are many chemicals and materials used in households, and you need to be aware of how these should be used in a safe and economical way.

Activity

Fuels

1 Make a list of any fuels used in your home, garden or vehicles.
2 Describe the use(s) of each fuel.
3 Are there any special precautions taken for storing them? How are they used safely?

Activity

Insecticides

It is important to keep the numbers of insects in our homes to a minimum. Insecticides can be useful, but we should be careful.

1 List the insecticides used in the home or garden.
2 What is the 'active ingredient' in each of these?
3 Record any warning on the labels about possible dangers, particularly for children and pets.

Activity

Fertilizers and herbicides

Fertilizers encourage growth, whereas herbicides are used to keep down plant pests, such as weeds.

1 Make two lists, one each for the fertilizers and herbicides used in your home or garden.
2 Examine the labels on at least one fertilizer and one herbicide. List the active ingredients.
3 Are there any hazard labels on the herbicides? How should these be stored and used?

Questions

1 Choose one of the groups of chemicals discussed above. Suggest three ways in which you could reduce how much you used, by using it more economically, or using an alternative.
2 If you found an old metal container with some liquid in it, but no label, how would you deal with it? Give reasons for any precautions you take.

Activity

Food additives and preservatives

Chemicals are added to our food for many reasons. For example, hot sauces contain hot peppers but also contain preservatives, such as vinegar (very dilute ethanoic acid).

1 Examine the labels on several processed foods.
2 List the groups of food additives (see pages 62–3). List the additives present in your food items.
3 Make a list of the preservatives in each item.
4 Choose one of the more common preservatives. What are the properties of this substance that make it a good preservative?
5 Find out about methods of food preservation that were used by your grandparents and parents.

Questions

3 Name three common additives. Why is each one used? What would be the effect of NOT using it? Are there any precautions we should take?
4 Does improving the appearance of fruit or vegetables make them a better buy?
5 What are the names of some common preservatives used in processed foods? What can you find out about the use of sulphur dioxide in preserving dried fruit such as apricots?
6 How would you try to preserve fruit such as pineapple or banana?
7 How can you avoid eating too many additives, including preservatives?

Some more safety issues

You know that you have to handle chemicals and equipment in the laboratory safely (see pages 246–8). The laboratory rules of the school may include directions about the wearing of goggles when heating substances or handling acids and alkalis, or wearing protective clothing such as laboratory coats.

Although you probably do not have such rules at home, you should always think about the ways in which you handle household chemicals so that these are safe and cannot cause harm to you, other people or the environment. This means you have to know the various substances in the chemicals, and their properties, so that you know what precautions to take when handling them.

Activity

Household chemicals: what is in them?

1 Choose five common household chemicals, including disinfectant, antiseptic and deodorizer.

2 What precautions, if any, should you take when using each of these chemicals?

3 List the chemicals in a table, together with their trade names. In separate columns, list for each chemical (a) the active ingredients that are responsible for the important properties of the chemical and (b) the actual chemical names of the ingredients.

4 Find out what you can about the properties of the ingredients and record this.

Questions

8 What are the chemical names of (a) common salt, (b) baking soda, (c) washing soda, (d) Epsom salts, (e) quicklime, (f) vinegar?

9 Some solvents and glues are addictive when sniffed. Should their sale be banned or should there be warning labels about their dangers?

Activity

Food supplements

You can have a balanced diet (see pages 58–9) if you choose the right balance of a wide variety of foods. However, many people also choose to have food supplements, e.g. vitamins and minerals. You should know about the properties of the chemicals you put into your body as part of your diet.

1 Make a list of five different food supplements available at your local pharmacy. Find out the purpose of taking one or two of these supplements.

2 Make a list of the vitamins on sale.

3 Use any information resource you can to find out the purpose of taking some (e.g. three or four) of these vitamins. Record your findings.

4 Do you think you could obtain the right amount of these vitamins by choosing the right foods instead of a vitamin supplement?

5 Make a detailed case for *one* vitamin.

6 You can then repeat steps 2–5 for minerals. Exchange your findings with other students.

Questions

10 A famous scientist of the 20th century proposed that very large doses of vitamin C would provide immunity to the common cold. How would you test this hypothesis?

11 Do you take any food supplements on a regular basis? Is there a good reason for this?

12 Why is it recommended that women who are trying to become pregnant should take additional folic acid, and that they should continue doing this until they are three months pregnant?

13 What food supplements are sometimes used by athletes in training, and why?

Key ideas

Use these words to fill in the spaces as you write the sentences in your Exercise book.

fuel   **herbicide**   **insecticide**   **preservative**   **safety**   **supplement**

Kerosene is an example of a _____ ; because it burns with a flame, people handling it have to observe _____ rules. Many governments use 'fogging' with an _____ to reduce the incidence of mosquitoes. Weeds can be removed using an appropriate _____ . Salt can be used as a _____ .
Folic acid is an example of a food _____ .

16.2 Why are acids and bases important?

Acids, bases and alkalis

Acids and bases

- An acid produces hydrogen ions in solution. Common laboratory acids are hydrochloric, sulphuric and nitric acids. As you saw on page 262, acids react with several metals to produce hydrogen.
- A base is a substance that reacts with an acid to form a salt and water only. The word equation is:

  acid + base → salt + water

  Bases are the oxides and hydroxides of metals, such as calcium oxide, zinc oxide and sodium hydroxide.

Bases and alkalis

- Some bases are insoluble, e.g. the oxides of heavy metals, such as copper and iron oxides.
- Some bases are soluble, e.g. oxides such as sodium, potassium and calcium oxides. Soluble bases are called **alkalis**.
- Some common alkalis are sodium hydroxide, potassium hydroxide and aqueous ammonia (ammonia gas dissolved in water). The alkaline solutions contain an excess of hydroxide ions.

The pH scale

It is important to know whether the liquids you are using are acidic or alkaline. For example, concentrated sodium hydroxide solution is corrosive and can harm your skin very quickly, as can concentrated sulphuric acid.

We measure the acidity or alkalinity of a solution using the pH scale. The scale consists of numbers from 0 to 14.

- On the scale, 7 is the neutral point. A solution of pH 7 is neither acidic nor alkaline. This is the pH of pure water.
- Solutions of pH *less* than 7 are acidic. Acid solutions have an excess of hydrogen ions. Acidity *increases* as the pH goes down from 7 towards 0, so a solution of pH 2 is more acidic than one of pH 5.
- Solutions with pH *greater* than 7 are alkaline. Alkaline solutions have an excess of hydroxide ions. Alkalinity *increases* as the pH goes up from 7 towards 14, so a solution of pH 12 is more alkaline than one with pH 9.
- You can estimate the pH of a solution using universal indicator (UI), which contains a mixture of dyes giving different colours through the pH range. You add a few drops of UI to the solution being tested, and compare the colour of the indicator against a colour chart, as shown below.

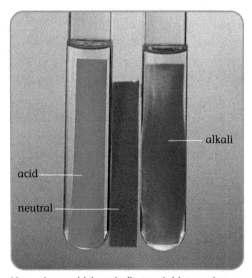

alkali

acid

neutral

Litmus is an acid–base indicator. Acids turn damp blue litmus paper red, and bases turn damp red litmus paper blue

Colour	red			orange		yellow		green	blue		navy blue			purple	
pH	0	1	2	3	4	5	6	7	8	9	10	11	12	13	14

increasingly acidic ← neutral → increasingly alkaline

Practical 108

Using litmus paper (MM, ORR)

1 Put about 5 cm³ of dilute sulphuric acid in a test tube. Test this with small pieces of red and blue litmus paper. Record your observations.

2 Repeat step 1 with different solutions, including dilute hydrochloric acid, aqueous ammonia and sodium hydroxide solution. Record your observations in a table.

Practical 109

Acid–base indicators (MM, ORR)

Repeat Practical 108, using the same solutions. But this time, use other acid–base indicators such as methyl orange, universal indicator and phenolphthalein.

1 What are the colours of these indicators and how do they each change in the different acidity or alkalinity of the solutions tested? Record your observations in a table.

2 Repeat the tests, using other colourless solutions. Record your observations.

Questions

1 Define (a) an acid, (b) a base and (c) an alkali, and give a common example of each one.

2 Which of the following solutions are acidic, and which are alkaline: pH (a) 9, (b) 4, (c) 1, (d) 13?

Did you know?

● The hydrochloric acid in your stomach (pH 1.5) could burn your skin.

● In the home, the most alkaline substance we use is oven cleaner with a pH of 14.

What do some common chemicals contain?

Everything you use at home or in school contains chemical substances. Your body is an example of many chemical substances. The most common chemical is water, pH 7 (when pure). You use many different substances, and we can investigate the properties of some of these.

Practical 110

Are common chemicals acidic or alkaline? (ORR)

1 Collect as many samples as possible of common household chemicals to test with indicators. Avoid chemicals that are coloured. Why?

2 Try to dissolve any solids. Why? Use distilled water. Why?

3 Test a small sample of each chemical or solution with a few drops of universal indicator solution.

4 Record your observations in a table. List the pH values and whether each chemical is acidic or alkaline.

5 Read the label on the chemical. Try to identify the ingredient that makes it acidic or alkaline.

6 Check each of the chemicals to find out whether they contain one or more salts (see page 281).

Questions

3 What are three properties of (a) acids and (b) bases?

4 Acids and alkalis can be corrosive. If you got some aqueous ammonia (a) on your skin or (b) in your eye, what should you do?

5 Why is it important to know whether a substance is acidic or alkaline?

6 Do you store any acidic or alkaline substances at home? If so, what precautions should you take?

Key ideas

Use these words to fill in the spaces as you write the sentences in your Exercise book.

alkalis	hydroxide	base	indicator	acid	hydrogen

An _____ is a pigment that changes colour in acids and _____ . An example of an _____ is hydrochloric _____ , and sodium hydroxide is an example of _____ . Acids have an excess of _____ ions, and _____ have an excess of _____ ions. When an _____ reacts with a _____ , a salt and water only are formed.

16.2 Why are acids and bases important? (continued)

Practical 111

What happens when acids and alkalis react? (MM, ORR)

1 Take about 25 cm³ (using a measuring cylinder) of dilute sulphuric acid and put it in a 100 cm³ beaker. Add a few drops of indicator and record the colour.

2 Add dilute sodium hydroxide solution slowly from another measuring cylinder. Mix the solutions carefully. Stop adding the alkali as soon as there is a *permanent colour change*. Measure the volume of alkali added.

3 Now try a more accurate method. Carefully measure out 5 cm³ of the acid into a test tube.

4 Add the alkali a drop at a time using a dropping pipette.

5 Count the number of drops of alkali used up to the point at which there is a permanent colour change. Record your results. Repeat the experiment to check your result (also see page 387).

Neutralization

When acids and alkalis react, they neutralize each other to give a solution with pH 7. We use an indicator to make sure they have reacted completely, so that there is no acid and no alkali remaining. They react to form a salt and water.

acid(aq) + alkali(aq) → salt(aq) + water(aq)

The salt is formed from the metal (from the base) and the acid group from the acid. The water is formed from the hydrogen and hydroxide ions.

If sodium hydroxide solution reacts with dilute sulphuric acid, the word equation is:

sodium hydroxide(aq) + sulphuric acid(aq)
  → sodium sulphate(aq) + water(aq)

Sodium sulphate is a salt.

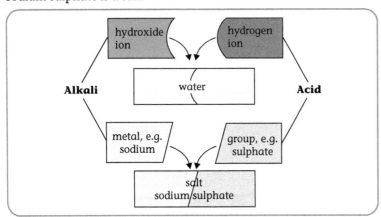

Showing what happens in neutralization

Using a pipette and burette

- You start with an accurately known amount of alkaline solution, measured using a pipette. You usually use 25 cm³.

- This is then reacted with dilute acid, which is contained in a burette. The acid can be added in small quantities, one drop at a time, so that the colour change of the indicator gives a very precise record of the amount of acid needed to neutralize the alkali.

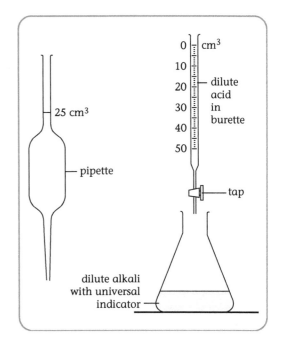

Practical 112

What is formed in neutralization? (MM, ORR, AI)

1 Repeat Practical 111, starting with 50 cm³ of acid, and add just enough alkali to neutralize the acid. Use indicator paper to check. Why is this better than using liquid indicator?

2 Put the neutral solution in an evaporating basin and heat it over a water bath.

3 What do you think is the liquid that is driven off? What do you observe in the basin?

Practical 113

Making salts from acids and alkalis (MM, ORR)

You have made the salt sodium sulphate by reacting sodium hydroxide solution with dilute sulphuric acid. Salts of other metals can be made using the same method.

1 Use dilute solutions of alkalis and acids.

2 Take $50\,cm^3$ of dilute sodium hydroxide and add just enough dilute hydrochloric acid solution to neutralize it.

3 Put the neutral solution in an evaporating basin and heat it over a beaker containing boiling water (see top right).

4 What forms in the basin as the liquid is driven off? You can try to check by putting a glass rod in the liquid, taking it out with a little liquid on it and allowing it to cool.

5 Write a word equation for the reaction.

6 Repeat the experiment, using (a) sodium hydroxide solution and dilute nitric acid, (b) potassium hydroxide solution and dilute sulphuric acid, (c) potassium hydroxide solution and dilute hydrochloric acid.

● Acids and alkalis react (neutralize each other) to form soluble salts. The salts can be obtained from solution by evaporating the water. This is called **crystallization**.

Practical 114

Making salts from acids and bases (MM, ORR)

● Oxides of light, reactive metals, such as sodium and potassium, are soluble in water, forming hydroxides (alkalis). But oxides of heavy, unreactive metals, such as copper and iron, are insoluble in water (they are bases but not alkalis).

● We form salts of these metals by reacting the insoluble bases directly with a dilute acid.

1 Put a small quantity of copper(II) oxide in a boiling tube.

2 Add about $10–15\,cm^3$ of dilute sulphuric acid, and warm gently until there is no further change.

3 Record your observations in a table. How can you explain your observations?

4 Write a word equation for the reaction.

5 How could you obtain a sample of crystals of the salt formed in this reaction?

6 Repeat the experiment, using copper(II) oxide and (a) dilute hydrochloric acid and (b) dilute nitric acid.

7 What is the colour of the salts of copper?

8 Repeat the experiment, starting with iron(II) oxide, and, separately, the three dilute acids.

9 What is the colour of salts of iron?

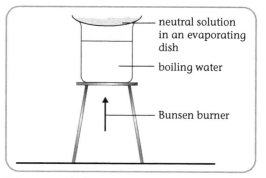

Using a water bath

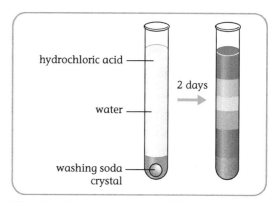

This is the rainbow experiment, in which you can see neutralization taking place. Put a washing soda crystal (an alkali) into a test tube of water. Add dilute hydrochloric acid and a few drops of universal indicator. Observe and describe what you see after two days. How can you explain what has happened? What processes are involved?

Some common salts

Common salt: sodium chloride

Washing soda: sodium carbonate

Baking soda: sodium hydrogencarbonate

Epsom salts: magnesium sulphate

Seasoning salt: monosodium glutamate

Questions

1 What are the names of the salts formed from dilute (a) hydrochloric acid, (b) sulphuric acid and (c) nitric acid?

2 Write word equations for reactions of (a) dilute sodium hydroxide solution and dilute nitric acid, and (b) copper(II) oxide and dilute sulphuric acid.

16.2 Why are acids and bases important? (continued)

Practical 115

Finding the pH of toothpaste (MM, ORR)

1 Use small samples from a range of toothpastes.
2 Place the samples in separate test tubes. Add a little distilled water to each one, and shake gently.
3 Add a few drops of universal indicator solution.
4 Record your observations: colour, pH and if acidic or alkaline. If the toothpaste has a list of ingredients, try to identify the substance making it acidic or alkaline.
5 What is the nature of the inside of your mouth and the surface of your teeth? What effect will each toothpaste sample have on the bacteria in your mouth?

Practical 116

How can we try to remove some food stains? (MM, ORR)

It is often difficult to remove food stains from clothes, particularly if the stains are allowed to dry. Many of these stains contain acids or alkalis – for example, tea and coffee contain tannic acid, and citrus fruits contain citric acid.

1 Find some samples of old cloth.
2 Stain separate small pieces with different substances such as tea, coffee or fruit juice. Let the stains dry.
3 Try to remove these stains, starting with cold water. If that does not work, try warm water. If that does not work either, try warm water with some detergent in it. Keep all the separate pieces of cloth.
4 Record your observations in a table.
5 Now try to remove the difficult stains using a mild alkali, such as a solution of sodium hydrogencarbonate, or a mild acid, such as vinegar (ethanoic acid). (See also page 389.)
6 Record and explain your observations.

Some useful neutralization reactions

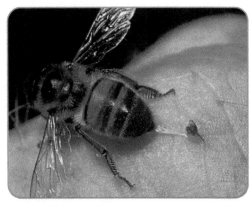

An alkali, such as calamine lotion, neutralizes the acid in a bee sting

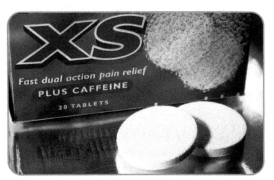

Indigestion tablets neutralize excess stomach acid

Questions

1 How does using toothpaste illustrate the principle of neutralization?
2 How can you use the idea of neutralization when removing stains?

Key ideas

Use these words to fill in the spaces as you write the sentences in your Exercise book.

acid   **toothpaste**   **base**   **neutralization**   **pipette**   **burette**   **alkali**

When an _____ and _____ in solution have reacted completely and the pH is 7, this is called

_____ . You can use a dropping _____ for roughly measuring the volume of liquid added,

or a _____ for more accurate experiments. You can make use of the principle of _____ : the

stains caused by acidic fruits can be removed by using a mild _____ , and bacteria in the

mouth will be affected by the _____ that you use.

16.3 What are different kinds of mixtures?

Solutions

Solutions are examples of mixtures. When a solid is dissolved in a liquid, the solid is called the **solute**. The liquid is called the **solvent**. The commonest solvent is water (see page 208).

- If you dissolve blue copper sulphate in water, a blue solution is formed: the copper sulphate is the solute and water is the solvent.
- It is possible to have solid solutions. For example, many alloys (see pages 267–7) contain solid solutions with one metal dissolved in another.
- The solute can also be a gas, e.g. air dissolved in water, or carbon dioxide in fizzy drinks.
- Solutions are usually transparent, but they can be coloured. They appear the same all the way through: we call them **homogeneous** mixtures. You will also be studying **heterogeneous** mixtures, such as colloids and emulsions (see pages 284–5).

Objective

- Distinguish among solutions, suspensions and colloids, and prepare samples of each one.

Other solvents

Many other liquids can be used as solvents. For example, there are many **organic** solvents (in which the chemical compound contains carbon). Organic compounds usually dissolve in organic solvents; e.g. propanone is used for dissolving fats and resins.

Dry cleaning

One of the most widespread industrial uses of organic solvents is for 'dry cleaning'. This was first used in the 19th century, when some organic solvents such as gasoline and kerosene were the solvents. The most commonly used solvent for much of the 20th century was tetrachloroethene (previously called tetrachloroethylene), but this has been found to be carcinogenic, and its use is likely to be restricted. Other solvents used include glycol ethers and liquid silicone.

When clothes are to be cleaned, you have to check the label. You can damage clothes said to be 'dry clean only' if these are put into a domestic washing machine with water and detergent. You can look at the labels inside some of your clothes. Choose one with the 'dry clean only' sign. What fibres do you think is it made from?

Practical 117

Does everything dissolve easily in water? (MM, ORR)

1 Use a variety of different chemical substances.

2 Put a small quantity of one substance in a test tube.

3 Add a few cm³ of distilled water, and shake the tube. If the substance does not appear to dissolve, add a little more water and shake again.

4 If the substance still does not dissolve, warm the tube gently, but do not allow the water to boil.

5 Record in a table whether the substance is soluble or insoluble in cold and/or warm water.

6 Repeat steps 2–5 with the other substances.

7 For one of the substances you have recorded as insoluble, shake the tube gently and filter. What do you observe on the filter paper?

8 Repeat step 7 with one of the substances recorded as soluble. How do your results differ from above?

Practical 118

Solvents other than water to remove stains (MM, ORR)

1 Use the same stains as you tested in Practical 116 (on page 282). Also include dried egg, grease, biro ink, nail varnish, rust and others.

2 Test small samples of the stains on cloth with, for example, ethanoic acid, borax, propanone, methylated spirits and paint thinner.

3 The stain will be removed if it is soluble in the solvent you use. Test each stain with each liquid when cold. Do NOT heat the test tubes directly – the liquids are flammable. Instead, place the test tubes in a beaker of hot water.

4 Record your results for each stain and solvent in the same way as before. Try to assess which is the best solvent for each of the stains. Do you notice any pattern in your results? (See also page 389.)

Questions

1 What are (a) a solute, (b) a solvent and (c) a solution? Give an example of each.

2 Can (a) an insoluble and (b) a soluble substance be separated from a liquid by filtering?

3 'Solutions are examples of mixtures.' Is this statement correct?

16.3 What are different kinds of mixtures? (continued)

Suspensions

Unlike solutions, suspensions are heterogeneous. In solutions, the particles are very small molecules or ions, and cannot be seen. In suspensions the particles are larger (over 1000 nm), and can usually be seen by the naked eye. The particles stay suspended in the liquid, or settle to the bottom on standing. Examples of suspensions include blood, muddy water and some medicines.

Activity

Solutions and suspensions at home

1 List some of the common liquids used at home.
2 Try to divide the list into (a) solutions and (b) suspensions. Look at the table below to help you.
3 Record your observations in a table (also see page 388).

Practical 119

Making a suspension (MM, ORR)

It is possible to see through a solution. However, when we react some chemicals together or have very fine particles of a substance in a liquid, we have a **suspension**. It is not possible to see clearly through a suspension.

1 Add dilute hydrochloric acid to sodium thiosulphate solution and allow the mixture to stand.
2 Can you see through the substance in the test tube? You should find that there are yellow particles (of sulphur) suspended in the liquid. This is a suspension.
3 Now try to filter the suspension of sulphur. You will find that most of the solid particles remain on the filter paper.
4 How is this different from a solution?

What does it mean?

Mixture   A substance in which two or more substances are mixed, but are not joined together.

Homogeneous mixture   The substance appears the same throughout and is often transparent, e.g. solutions.

Suspension   A heterogeneous mixture in which the parts can be seen with the naked eye, e.g. muddy water.

Colloid   A heterogeneous mixture, in which the parts can be seen with a microscope, e.g. paint, smoke.

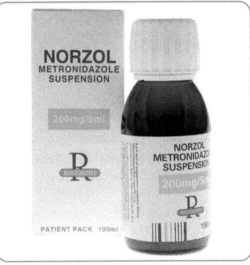

Many medicines are suspensions, and should be shaken before use

Solutions	Colloids	Suspensions
Homogeneous mixture. Solute dissolved in a solvent.	Heterogeneous mixture.	Heterogeneous mixture. Separate parts can be seen.
Solute particles very small.	Colloid particles of in-between size.	Suspended particles are large.
Particles not visible under a microscope.	Particles visible under a microscope.	Particles visible to the naked eye.
Solute and solvent do not separate or settle out.	Particles do not separate or settle out.	Particles suspended, but can settle out when left.
Solute cannot be separated from solvent by filtering.	Particles cannot be separated by filtering.	Particles can be separated from the liquid by filtering.
Examples: salts or carbon dioxide dissolved in water, alloys of metals.	Jelly, shaving cream, egg white. Also emulsions: milk, paint.	Mud, powdered chalk or sulphur in water, some medicines.

Colloids

Colloids are also mixtures; they have properties in between solutions and suspensions. The size of the particles in a colloid is larger than the particles in a solution, but smaller than those in a suspension. The particles in a colloid are usually between 2 and 1000 nm in size, so they can be seen under the microscope. The particles may be solid, liquid or gas, and they can be mixed with a solid, liquid or gas. Light is scattered when it passes through colloids, so that they often appear cloudy or coloured, e.g. smoke. The particles do not separate out on standing. Examples of colloids include:

- solids in liquids: starch solution and the white of egg
- gas in a solid: polystyrene foam
- liquid in a gas: aerosols
- gas in a liquid: shaving cream.

Emulsions

These are particular examples of colloids, in which two liquids that do not usually mix are shaken together and small particles of one liquid in the other are formed. Some examples are milk (fat and water), salad dressing (oil and vinegar), emulsion paint, and kerosene and water.

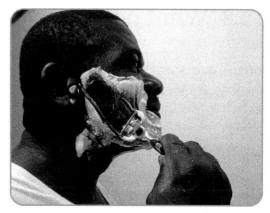

Shaving cream is a colloid of a gas in a liquid

Separating components of mixtures

- **Suspensions:** Components separated using sieves or filters, with holes that let through one component, but not the other.
- **Solutions:** Cannot be separated by filters. We use evaporation or distillation, or chromatography for dyes in solution.
- **Colloids:** Difficult to separate, except for emulsions if the two liquids are of different densities.

Practical 120

Making an emulsion (ORR, MM)

1 Add a little kerosene to water in a test tube. You should find that the two liquids do not mix.

2 Put a rubber bung in the mouth of the test tube to close it and then shake it vigorously. Record what you see.

3 Now allow the test tube to stand for some time. Do the contents remain the same?

4 Shake the test tube again, and then add some soap solution. Allow the test tube to stand. What has happened now?

5 Record all your observations.

- The soap solution acts as an emulsifier, which enables the liquids to mix together (**emulsify**). Examples of emulsions like this include butter and mayonnaise.

Questions

1 How would you classify each of these mixtures in water: (a) soil, (b) salt, (c) oil?

2 Give two examples each of solutions, suspensions and colloids.

3 Why is a suspension so called?

4 What are the liquids in an emulsion paint?

Key ideas

Use these words to fill in the spaces as you write the sentences in your Exercise book.

solute   suspension   colloid   solvent   emulsion   dry cleaning

When sugar is dissolved in water, sugar is the _____ and water is the _____ . Stains can be

removed by using the correct _____ . A _____ is not transparent, because its particles are too

large. An organic _____ is used for _____ clothes. Kerosene and water form an _____ when

mixed. Milk is a good example of a _____ , which is also an _____ .

16.4 What do we use for cleaning?

What are soaps?

Many soaps are made by the reaction of an alkali, such as sodium hydroxide, with an organic acid. They are the salts formed by sodium and complex organic acids.

Making soaps today

The basic principles behind soap making have not changed much. However, we expect soaps not only to wash well, but also to have a smooth texture and an appropriate scent. Compare a bath soap with a bar of washing (laundry) soap, to notice the differences.

In the manufacture of soap, sodium hydroxide is boiled with a mixture of oils and fats – coconut oil is often used. The soap is formed by the reaction of the alkali with the acids in the oils and fats. The process is saponification.

> stearic acid (fatty acid) + sodium hydroxide
> → sodium stearate (soap) + water

The soap is separated from the solution by adding salt (sodium chloride), and the soap then floats on top of the other liquids (which are called lye).

The soap and lye are separated and the soap is washed several times. It is then boiled and water is added. More salt is added to make sure the separation is complete. Then the soap is bleached and perfume is added. The texture of the soap is checked and it is dried in moulds.

Objectives

- Distinguish between soapy detergents (soap) and soapless detergents.
- Explain the cleaning action of detergents.
- Discuss the effectiveness of various types of abrasive materials.

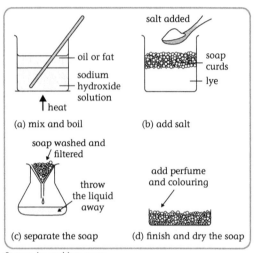

Stages in making soap

Practical 121

Making soap (MM)

1 Place 30 cm³ of vegetable oil in a 250 cm³ beaker.

2 Add 50 cm³ of sodium hydroxide solution (made by dissolving 126 g of pellets in each 50 cm³ of water).

3 Mix them together and boil for about 20–30 minutes.

4 Add one tablespoon of solid sodium chloride to the solution and allow it to cool.

5 Record what you see when the cooled solution is allowed to stand for some time. Describe the appearance of the two layers.

6 Filter off the liquid to separate it from the soapy layer.

7 Wash the soap with water a number of times, to make sure that there is no sodium hydroxide left.

8 You can add colouring and perfume. Then you can dry it in moulds, such as matchboxes.

9 Take a small piece of the soap you have made and shake it with water in a test tube. Compare how well it lathers with a piece of bath soap of similar size. Your soap can be used for cleaning clothes, but not for washing your skin.

Hard water (see page 288) contains chemicals that combine with soap to form a greyish-white scum, which you can see left behind in this bowl.

Questions

1 Why do we call soap a salt?
2 Why is sodium chloride added to the boiling mixture of the alkali and oil/fat?
3 Why are perfumes added to bath soap?

Soapy and soapless detergents

- Soapy detergents (**soaps**), e.g. toilet soap, are formed from natural oils and are unlikely to cause skin allergies, but they do not clean everything and they form a scum with hard water.
- Soapless detergents (synthetic detergents), e.g. washing powder, also contain sulphonate or sulphate groups. They do not form a scum with hard water, but may not be biodegradable.

What do detergents do?

- They reduce the surface tension between water and insoluble compounds such as oil or grease.
- They foam easily, so they spread over surfaces.
- They stabilize insoluble particles removed from your skin or clothes.

How do detergents clean?

All detergent molecules have two parts:
- a water-loving 'head' that is soluble in water
- a water-hating 'tail' that is soluble in fats and oils, but not in water.

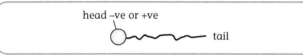

head –ve or +ve

tail

In soapy detergents the head is sodium, whereas in soapless detergents the head is sodium and a sulphonate or sulphate group.

The tail ends of detergent molecules become attracted to the oil or grease. The charged head ends become surrounded by water molecules, and the grease is lifted from the surface.

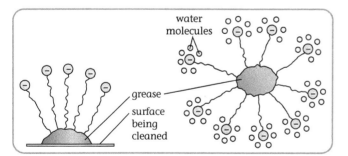

water molecules

grease

surface being cleaned

Cleaning properties

The cleaning property of a detergent may be improved by adding:

- a surfactant, for removing dissolved grease
- a water softener, for using with hard water
- enzymes, for acting on biological stains, e.g. blood or egg
- a fabric softener, for improving the quality of the cleaned product.

Scouring powders

Scouring powders contain:

- small particles of one or more very hard substances, e.g. pumice or silver sand (abrasives)
- a bleaching agent containing chlorine, which bleaches surfaces and kills microorganisms
- detergents, either soapy or soapless.

They may also contain borax, which is alkaline, and can remove acidic stains, such as fruit stains.

Detergents, on their own, work best on recent dirt and grease. If the grime is ingrained, such as layers of scum on skins or baths, a scouring powder is needed. The action of rubbing the powder on the surface removes anything stuck to the surface, and also part of the surface. If bleach is present in the powder, there is also a chemical action that removes other substances. You need to take great care about using such powders, except on metal or ceramic surfaces.

Questions

4 What are the main differences between soaps and soapless detergents?

5 What is the main disadvantage of (a) soapy and (b) most soapless detergents?

6 How would you test (a) two brands of washing-up liquid, and (b) two types of scouring powder, to find which was better?

Key ideas

Use these words to fill in the spaces as you write the sentences in your Exercise book.

soap   **water-hating**   **scouring**   **washing**   **salts**   **soapless**

Detergents are soapy (_____) or _____ , e.g. _____ powder. They are both sodium _____

of organic acids, but _____ detergents also contain other groups. The tails of detergent molecules

are _____ and attracted to grease, whereas the head ends are attracted to water. _____

powders contain small particles of very hard substances, for cleaning surfaces.

16.5 What are hard and soft water?

How can we test the hardness of water?

Water is a solvent and dissolves many things. But we often need to use detergents to make things clean – water alone is not enough. In many parts of the Caribbean, water is obtained from sources where the rock is coral or limestone. Water samples from these areas form a scum with soapy detergents, before they form a lather: this is called **hard water**. Other water samples from other places lather easily: this is called **soft water**.

Temporary hardness

Carbon dioxide in the atmosphere can dissolve in water to form carbonic acid. If rain containing carbonic acid falls in an area with limestone (calcium carbonate), some of this reacts with the acid to form **calcium hydrogencarbonate**. This chemical is soluble and is the cause of temporary hardness of water. Purification at a water treatment plant (see page 211) does not remove calcium hydrogencarbonate.

calcium carbonate(s) + carbonic acid(aq)
→ calcium hydrogencarbonate(aq)

Tap water obtained from limestone areas is hard. When soap is added it reacts with the hydrogencarbonate to make a scum. Only when the hydrogencarbonate has been removed from solution, can the soap form a lather.

When temporarily hard water is boiled, insoluble calcium carbonate is formed. So there is then nothing in solution for the soap to react with, and a lather is formed more easily. So boiling removes temporary hardness, but the calcium carbonate is then deposited. You may have seen this in an electric kettle, as shown in the photograph.

'Scale' or 'fur' inside a kettle

Permanent hardness

Permanent hardness is caused by the presence of either calcium or magnesium sulphate, which was picked up by water travelling over rocks or through soil. These are dissolved in the water and are unaffected by boiling, so permanent hardness cannot be removed by boiling.

Is hard water a problem?

Hard water makes washing more difficult, as more detergent has to be used to obtain a lather, and there is also scum to be washed away. If we have to use temporarily hard water, we may have problems. As the layer of calcium carbonate fur builds up, more energy has to be supplied to heat the same amount of water. In the home, this problem can be reduced by using vinegar (dilute ethanoic acid) to dissolve the carbonate.

How do we remove hardness?

Boiling

This only works to remove temporary hardness, and not permanent hardness. The soluble calcium hydrogencarbonate is changed to insoluble calcium carbonate.

calcium hydrogencarbonate(aq) → calcium
   carbonate(s) + carbon dioxide(g) + water(aq)

Washing soda

This is sodium carbonate. When it is added to hard water, it reacts with some of the calcium ions to form calcium carbonate, which is insoluble. This is precipitated out, and the hard water becomes soft, because the substance causing the hardness has been removed. Washing soda removes both temporary and permanent hardness.

calcium hydrogencarbonate(aq)
   + sodium carbonate(s) → calcium carbonate(s)
   + sodium hydrogencarbonate(aq)
calcium sulphate(aq) + sodium carbonate(aq)
   → calcium carbonate(s) + sodium sulphate(aq)

Distillation

This involves the boiling of water to produce a vapour, which is then condensed back to a liquid. A condenser is used (see page 214). The vapour is pure water, with no dissolved chemicals, so the condensed water is pure distilled water, which can be used for special purposes. Distillation can be used to remove both kinds of hardness.

Practical 123

How can we soften hard water? (MM, ORR)

1 Put about $5 cm^3$ of soft water into a test tube. Add a few drops of soap solution, and shake for about 20 seconds. Leave this to stand as a control.

2 Use several samples of hard water, at least one of which is temporarily hard water and another is permanent hard water. Take about $25 cm^3$ of each and boil them in separate $50 cm^3$ beakers.

3 Allow the boiled samples to cool and use about $5 cm^3$ of each to repeat step 1.

4 Compare the control with the hard water samples. What effect does boiling have on each one?

Practical 124

Can chemicals soften water? (MM, ORR)

1 Take samples of both kinds of hard water, and put $5 cm^3$ of each in separate test tubes.

2 Add a small quantity of washing soda to each sample. Close the test tubes and shake vigorously.

3 Compare the lathering properties of hard water that has been treated with washing soda with untreated hard water.

4 Record your observations.

Questions

4 Why is distilled water used in science laboratories and car batteries?

5 How would you make a sample of temporarily hard water soft without using chemicals?

6 There is some evidence to suggest that hard water is better for your health than soft water. Do some research to find out.

Key ideas

Use these words to fill in the spaces as you write the sentences in your Exercise book.

| temporary | washing soda | distillation | permanent | sulphate | boiling |

_____ hardness of water, caused by calcium hydrogencarbonate, can be removed by _____ .

_____ hardness, caused by calcium or magnesium _____ , cannot be removed by _____ .

_____ hardness causes extra cost due to the production of scum with soap, and fur, due

to _____ . All kinds of water can be softened by _____ or adding _____ .

17 Electricity and lighting

17.1 Which substances conduct electricity?

Electricity is a flow of **electrons**. If materials, such as metals, have electrons that are free to move between the atoms, then they can be **conductors** of electricity.

Practical 125

Testing for conductors (MM, ORR)

1 Use the tester as you did on page 256.

2 (a) This is how to use the tester for solid materials. Connect the clips **A** and **B** to opposite ends of the material.
(b) This is how to use the tester for liquids. Carbon rods are held in the clips and placed in the liquid (close together, but NOT touching; wash them in distilled water between tests).

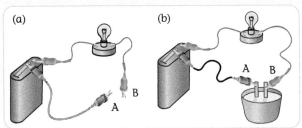

3 Try an iron nail, string, copper coin, a ruler, aluminium foil, eraser, pen, paper, wood, graphite ('lead' in a pencil), glass, dilute acid, dilute alkali, oil, distilled water, salt solution.

4 Make a table like the one below and record your results.

Item	Material	Does bulb light?		Good conductor	Poor conductor
		Yes	No		
Nail	Iron	✓		✓	
String	Fibre				
Coin					
etc.					

5 The diagram below (c) shows another way to test liquids. Movement of the needle on the ammeter shows a flow of electricity.

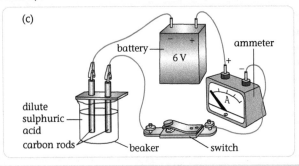

Objectives

● Identify and discuss the uses of good, poor and semi-conductors of electricity.
● List examples of some solid and liquid conductors.

What does it mean?

Free electrons Electrons in metals and graphite that are able to move and so conduct electricity.

Circuit A complete pathway along which electricity can flow; the switch is closed.

Open circuit A circuit with the switch open, or one that contains an insulator.

Insulator A non-conductor that does not allow electricity to flow through it.

Conductor Allows electricity to flow. Can be solid (e.g. metal wire) or liquid that contains ions (e.g. seawater).

Electrolyte A liquid, such as an acid, that can conduct electricity because it has negative and positive ions that can move.

Questions

1 When part of a circuit, which of these would allow electricity to flow: (a) metal wire, (b) glass, (c) salt solution, (d) paper? Give the reason in each case.
2 Give two examples each of (a) conductors and (b) insulators. Explain how their properties are important for how each is used.
3 How would you set up a test to compare the conductivity of salt crystals and salt solution? What result do you expect?

Did you know?

● Copper and aluminium are good conductors of electricity. Gold is better, but it is too expensive for general use.

Conductors and non-conductors

Solid conductors, such as metals, have free electrons. So does the non-metal, carbon, when it is in the form of graphite. When these materials are included as part of a circuit, the electrons can move and the material conducts electricity. We use copper and aluminium as electrical wires, and carbon rods in electrolytes.

Liquid conductors, such as acids, alkalis and salt solution, contain charged ions. The ions are free to move and carry an electric current. The liquids are called electrolytes. We use sulphuric acid in car batteries. Mercury is a metal that is liquid at room temperature, and it is also a conductor.

Non-conductors (insulators), such as rubber, plastic and wood, have electrons that are all tightly held to the atoms. So the electrons cannot move and the material cannot conduct electricity. Plastic and rubber are used for covering wires to protect us from the electricity. (This is why wires with damaged insulation are so dangerous.)

Semi-conductors, such as silicon, behave like insulators when they are cold and like conductors when they are warm. They are used in solar cells and computer chips.

What about water? Distilled water is pure and contains only small numbers of hydrogen and hydroxide ions. At a high voltage, such as connection with high-tension wires or lightning, tap water (which usually contains tiny amounts of dissolved salts) becomes such a good conductor of electricity that it is very dangerous. Seawater, with additional salts, is a better conductor than fresh water.

Current and static electricity

Current electricity

This is the flow of charged particles: electrons (in metals) or ions (in electrolytes).

Static electricity

This is the electric charge on certain materials. Many substances can be electrified by rubbing them. This is static electricity. (Static means stationary.) A motor vehicle, with many moving parts, can build up high electrical charges. Sparks might be made that could ignite flammable vapours such as gasoline. As a precaution, gasoline trucks have an earth chain at the back to carry any sparks of electricity to the ground.

Electric shock

What is it? There is electrical contact between parts of the body and a power source, so electricity flows through the body.

What happens? The electricity stops muscles working properly and so can cause difficulty with breathing and the heart may stop, which could be fatal.

What is the first aid? Remove the person from the power source using an insulator (such as a wooden broom); otherwise you will get a shock. Give mouth-to-mouth resuscitation and heart massage.

When does it happen? Electric shock can happen: (a) if wet hands are used on switches and on electrical appliances; (b) if a kite gets caught in high-tension wires when flying in wet conditions; (c) when standing under a tree in a thunderstorm, especially if there is good electrical contact with the ground due to bare feet or leather-sole shoes (which absorb water), because trees are tall and attract and conduct high-voltage electricity; (d) when using electrical devices anywhere near water (this is why there are no regular sockets in a bathroom).

How can it be avoided? Never handle electrical equipment with wet hands. Always keep water and electricity apart. If a thunderstorm threatens, stay indoors or wear rubber-soled shoes. You are safe in a car (as it has rubber tyres that prevent electric current flow to earth). Also follow the advice on pages 300–3 for using electricity safely.

Key ideas

Use these words to fill in the spaces as you write the sentences in your Exercise book.

metal   insulator   conductor   rubber   electrolyte   shock   water

A material that allows electricity to flow through it is a _____ , for example _____ wire.

A material that cannot be used to complete a circuit is an _____ , for example _____ . A liquid _____ , containing ions, is called an _____ . The combination of electricity and _____ can cause an electric _____ .

17.2 How do electrical circuits work?

Practical 126

How does a flashlight work? (ORR, AI)

1 Take apart a flashlight (see diagram on the right). Observe the light bulb, on/off switch and dry cells. Find out how it works.
2 Remove one dry cell. Does the bulb still light? Why?
3 Look at the dry cell. One end has a bump, the **positive** terminal (**+**), and the other end is the **negative** terminal (**–**).
4 Replace the two cells in different ways, and find out which way(s) work. Try to explain your observations.
5 Put the cells in a way that works, but place a small piece of card between them. Does the bulb still light? Why?

A simple circuit: a flashlight

For electricity to flow in a circuit:
● the pathway must be complete; the switch must be closed, there should be no insulators in the circuit and all parts must be in contact to make a complete pathway
● there must be a source of electrical energy (dry cells); if there is more than one dry cell, these should be facing in the same direction, with a (+) in touch with a (–) terminal
● there should be a part or **component** in the circuit, such as a bulb, that is going to convert electrical energy into another form.

Components of a circuit

We can compare an electrical circuit to a water circuit.

Electrical circuit		Water circuit	
Object	**Job**	**Object**	**Job**
Dry cell	Pushes current around the circuit	Pump	Pushes water around the circuit
Current	Flows around circuit	Water	Flows around circuit
Bulb	Converts energy from current and holds back the current	Paddle wheel	Converts energy from the water and slows down the water
Switch	Breaks the circuit and flow of current	Tap	Stops the flow of water

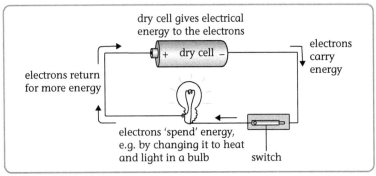

The components of a circuit and how electrons are pushed around

Objectives

● Set up series and parallel circuits and draw diagrams using circuit symbols.
● Describe and measure current and voltage using ammeters and voltmeters.
● Distinguish between dc and ac.

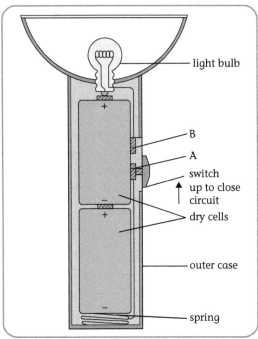

When the switch is pushed up, A connects with B, to complete the circuit and the bulb lights

What does it mean?

Component Part of a circuit, such as a dry cell, switch or bulb.

Circuit symbols Symbols used to show the components of a circuit.

Conventional current By agreement current is said to flow from **+ve** to **–ve**.

dc Direct current that flows in one direction only. Dry cells and batteries (groups of cells) produce dc.

ac Alternating current that keeps changing direction, e.g. mains electricity.

Series and parallel circuits

Series circuit

The bulbs are connected in a line. The current flows through one and then the next (see (a) in the practical on the right). The bulbs share the electrical energy from the cell.

Parallel circuit

The bulbs are parallel to each other and the current divides to go to each one (see (b) in the practical on the right). Each bulb has its own circuit to the dry cell.

Current and voltage

Current

This is the rate of flow of electrons in a circuit. The current (I) is measured in amperes (A) – **amps** for short. A current of one amp means about 6 million, million, million electrons are flowing round the circuit every second. The current is measured using an **ammeter** (see page 294). The electrons keep flowing round and round the circuit; what varies is the amount of electrical energy they carry.

Voltage

This is how energetic the electrons are (how much electrical force they have): how hard the current is being pushed around the circuit. Dry cells vary in the amount of energy they give to the electrons. A dry cell marked 1.5 V (1.5 **volts**) gives electrical energy of 1.5 V to the electrons each time they pass through the dry cell. This electrical energy can be changed into another form, as in a bulb, where the wire becomes hot and then gives out light.

Circuit symbols

When we draw circuit diagrams we use these symbols.

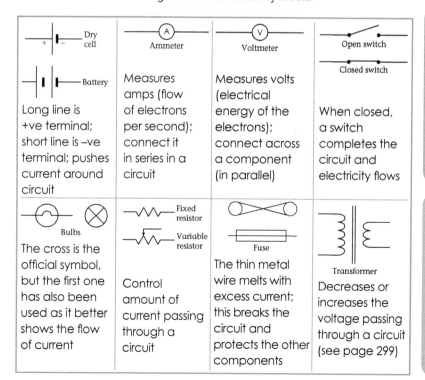

Dry cell Long line is +ve terminal; short line is –ve terminal; pushes current around circuit	(A) Ammeter Measures amps (flow of electrons per second); connect it in series in a circuit	(V) Voltmeter Measures volts (electrical energy of the electrons); connect across a component (in parallel)	Open switch Closed switch When closed, a switch completes the circuit and electricity flows
Bulbs The cross is the official symbol, but the first one has also been used as it better shows the flow of current	Fixed resistor Variable resistor Control amount of current passing through a circuit	Fuse The thin metal wire melts with excess current; this breaks the circuit and protects the other components	Transformer Decreases or increases the voltage passing through a circuit (see page 299)

Practical 127

Series and parallel circuits (MM, ORR)

1 Set up a circuit with one dry cell and two bulbs in series, as shown in (a).

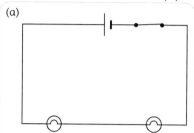

(a)

(i) How bright are the bulbs? Why?
(ii) What happens if one of the bulbs is loosened or is broken? Why?

2 Set up a circuit with one dry cell and two bulbs in parallel, as shown in (b).

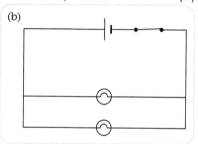

(b)

(i) How bright are the bulbs? Why?
(ii) What happens if one of the bulbs is loosened or is broken? Why?

Did you know?

- The voltage of a cell is not determined by its size, but by the chemical reactions inside it.
- In a circuit, a component is needed where energy can be 'spent' (changed into another form). If not, there is a 'short circuit' and the dry cell can be damaged.

Questions

1 Draw circuit diagrams with symbols, for the circuits (a), (b) and (c) from page 290.
2 Draw circuit diagrams for the flashlight (a) when the switch is open, and (b) when it is closed.
3 Which circuit, series or parallel, would you use for lights in a house?

293

17.2 How do electrical circuits work? (continued)

Using an ammeter and a voltmeter

Ammeter An ammeter measures the current in amperes, amps (A). It is placed in **series** with the other components. Connect the red (+ve) terminal of the ammeter with the +ve terminal of the dry cells, and also the –ve to –ve.

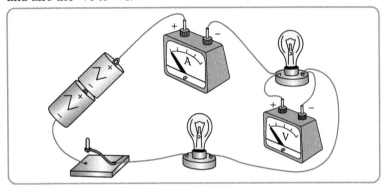

An ammeter and a voltmeter in position in a series circuit with two dry cells and two bulbs

Voltmeter A voltmeter measures voltage in volts (V). The voltage across the dry cell(s) represents the energy transferred to the current, and the voltage across a bulb represents the energy transferred to the bulb. A voltmeter is placed in **parallel** with the dry cell or bulb. Connect the red (+ve) terminal of the voltmeter with the +ve terminal of the dry cells, and also the –ve to –ve.

Questions

1 (a) Draw a series circuit with three bulbs connected to a 4.5 V battery (three 1.5 V cells in series). (b) If I used a voltmeter, what would be the reading across one bulb?

2 (a) Draw a parallel circuit with three bulbs connected to a 4.5 V battery (three 1.5 V cells in series). (b) If I used a voltmeter, what would be the reading across one bulb?

3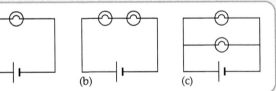

(a)   (b)   (c)

Comment on the brightness of the bulbs in (a) and (b) compared with those in (c). Give reasons for your answers.

4 Draw a circuit diagram to show how a lamp and a fan could be connected to an electric circuit to allow either one to be used at any time.

5 (a) Using a 9 V battery, a student set up a series circuit with three identical bulbs. What would be the voltage across each bulb?
(b) Then she set up a parallel circuit using the same bulbs. She was surprised to find that all the bulbs 'blew' (became broken). Explain what happened.

Practical 128

Measuring current and voltage (MM, ORR, AI)

1 Set up a series circuit, as below, with two dry cells and two bulbs.

2 In turn, place the ammeter in the two positions shown. Record the readings.

3 In turn, place the voltmeter in the three positions shown. Record the readings.

4 What can you say about (a) the current and (b) the voltage in a series circuit?

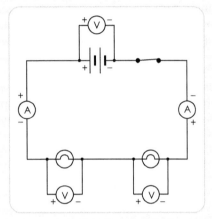

5 Set up a parallel circuit, as below, with two dry cells and two bulbs.

6 In turn, place the ammeter in the four positions shown. Record the readings.

7 In turn, place the voltmeter in the three positions shown. Record the readings.

8 What can you say about (a) the current and (b) the voltage in a parallel circuit?

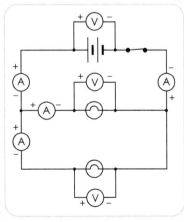

See also page 391.

Series circuits	Parallel circuits
• There is only one pathway for the current. • Current flows through one bulb, and then the next. • Can be turned on and off by a single switch; 'one off, all off'. • If one bulb is broken, the circuit doesn't work. • They have the same current flowing in all parts of the circuit. • With two or more bulbs, they have to share the voltage, and are dim. The sum of voltages across all bulbs is equal to the voltage of the cell.	• There is more than one pathway for the current. • Current flows to each bulb directly along its own pathway. • Switches can be put to either turn off all the circuit, or just part of it. • If one bulb is broken, the other bulbs still light. • The current is divided when it comes to a junction. Current flowing into a junction equals that flowing out. • With two or more bulbs, the voltage across each one is the same as that across the dry cell, so the bulbs are brighter, but the dry cell goes 'flat' more quickly.

<table>
<tr><td>

V_cell

I I

V_1 V_2

Current I is same throughout circuit

Voltage $V_\text{cell} = V_1 + V_2$

</td><td>

V_cell

I

V_1

I_1

I_2

V_2

Current $I = I_1 + I_2$

Voltage $V_\text{cell} = V_1 = V_2$

</td></tr>
</table>

See also page 391.

Work and power

Work

The amount of work that is done in a circuit equals the amount of energy that is transferred to a component, such as a bulb. Work is measured in **joules (J)**. The higher the voltage of the cell, battery or mains electricity, the greater the amount of energy produced.

Power

Power is the rate at which work is done or energy is transferred (joules per second) and it is measured in **watts (W)**. The power equals the current flowing in the circuit, times the voltage:

power (watts) = current (I) × voltage (V)

$$W = I\,V$$

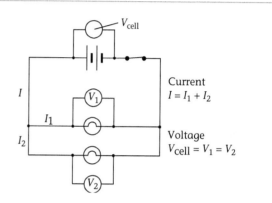

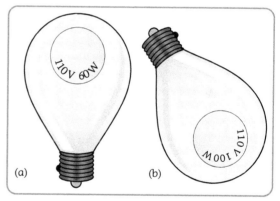

(a)   (b)

Mains light bulbs: which bulb will be brighter? Which converts more energy each second?

Key ideas

Use these words to fill in the spaces as you write the sentences in your Exercise book.

series   amps   circuit   volts   ammeter   parallel   voltmeter

The pathway for flow of electricity is called a _____ . If bulbs are arranged one after another,

it is a _____ _____ . If there are alternative pathways, this is a _____ _____ . The current

is measured with an _____ (placed in _____), and recorded in _____ . The voltage is

measured by a _____ (placed in _____), and recorded in _____ .

17.3 How is resistance important?

Voltage and current

There are two different ways in which these are related.

Voltage × current = power (*VI* = *W*)

- If we know the voltage and the current, we can multiply them to find the power in watts, e.g. of a bulb, $W = VI$.

- If we know the power and voltage, we can calculate the current the lamp will use, with the formula $I = W/V$.

A 40 W bulb used with 110 V mains electricity uses about 0.37 A of current (40 W/110 V). But a 100 W bulb used with 110 V uses about 0.91 A of current (100 W/110 V). This is why a more powerful bulb is brighter and costs more to run (see also page 295).

Voltage/current = resistance (*V/I* = *R*)

- If the temperature of a component stays constant, then the voltage across it divided by the current flowing through it gives the value of its **resistance** (see page 392), that is, $R = V/I$. Resistance is measured in ohms (Ω) and is the opposition to passage of electricity.

- If we know the current and resistance, we can work out the voltage, using $V = IR$. This is called **Ohm's law**.

- If we know the voltage and the resistance, we can work out the current, using $I = V/R$.

Calculations

Example A light bulb operates at 120 V and a current of 0.5 A. What is the resistance of the filament?

$R = V/I$ $V = 120\,V, I = 0.5\,A$ $R = 120\,V/0.5\,A = 240\,\Omega$

Example (a) What is the power in watts of the bulb in the previous example? (b) What is the resistance of a bulb with twice this power output?

(a) power = voltage × current (watts = volts × amps)
$W = VI = 120 \times 0.5 = 60\,W$

(b) A lamp with twice the power output is $60 \times 2 = 120\,W$. To find the resistance we must first find the current.

$I = W/V$ current = power/voltage = 120 W/120 V = 1 A

$R = V/I$ resistance = voltage/current = 120 V/1 A = 120 Ω

Example (a) A resistor is marked as 12 Ω. If a current of 0.25 A flows through it, what would be the voltage across it? (b) What current would flow through the same resistor if it was used with a 6 V battery?

$V = IR$ voltage = current × resistance = 0.25 A × 12 Ω = 3 V

$I = V/R$ current = voltage/resistance = 6 V/12 Ω = 0.5 A

Objectives

- Use power (watts) = current × voltage ($W = IV$) to calculate any unknowns.
- Explain the relationship between current, voltage and resistance.
- Use Ohm's law ($V = IR$) to calculate any unknowns.

Power triangle

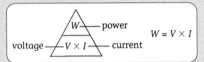

Put your finger over the quantity you want to find. The answer is what is left, so:

I (current) = W (power)/V (volts) $I = W/V$
V (volts) = W (power)/I (current) $V = W/I$

Resistance triangle

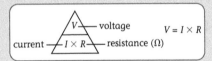

Put your finger over the quantity you want to find. The answer is what is left, so:

R (resistance) = V (voltage)/I (current)
$R = V/I$

I (current) = V (voltage)/R (resistance)
$I = V/R$

Questions

1. If the resistance of a wire is 3 Ω and the current flowing through it is 4 A, what is the voltage?

2. A lamp has a voltage of 20 V and a current flow of 5 A. What is (a) its power and (b) its resistance?

3. Calculate the resistance, *R*, in a series circuit having a battery voltage, *V*, of 9 V and a current, *I*, of 0.5 A.

4. The voltage in a lightning strike was 5 kilovolts. If the resistance of a wet person is $5 \times 10^4\,\Omega$, what current will flow through the person?

Resistance

Resistance is the opposition to the passage of electric current. The higher the resistance of a component, the less current that passes through it at a given voltage.

- Insulators, for example plastic and rubber, have resistances that are measured in millions of ohms.
- Conductors have resistances that allow flow of current.

How is resistance useful?

Resistance causes a heating up of the wire.

- The tungsten filament in an incandescent bulb is very narrow and has a high resistance; this makes it heat up to such a high temperature that it gives out light (see page 310).
- The elements in an electric kettle, hair dryer and iron are made of coils of thin nichrome wire. When current passes through them, their resistance makes them hot, and this heat is used to heat water (in a kettle) or air (in a hair dryer), or the metal in the base of an iron.
- A toaster also has metal elements that become hot. The heat is then used to cook the toast.
- Inside a fuse (see page 302) is a special narrow fuse wire. Its resistance causes it to heat up, melt, and break the circuit if too much current flows that could harm the appliances in the circuit. The thickness of the wire that is chosen determines the current at which it breaks.

How are variable resistors useful?

A variable resistor can be used to vary the current.

- If more current flows, a component in the circuit can be brighter, louder or hotter.
- With less current flowing, a component becomes dimmer, quieter or cooler.

1 Lights can be dimmed or brightened. A dimmer switch can be used in the home, and theatre lights are dimmed and brightened using variable resistors.
2 Sounds can be decreased or increased. Variable resistors are used as volume controls in TVs and radios.
3 Special resistors are used in TV and radio circuits to keep currents and voltages at the correct levels.

How does resistance vary?

- Resistance of a long wire is greater than that of a short wire.
- Resistance of a thin wire is greater than that of a thick wire.
- Some metals have higher resistance than others; e.g. nichrome wire has a higher resistance than copper wire of the same length and thickness.
- When resistors are in series, the total resistance in the circuit is the sum of the resistances.
- When two resistors are in parallel, they give a total resistance that is less than either of the two resistors, as the current has alternative pathways.

Practical 129

How resistance varies (PD)

Choose one of the first three statements above about how resistance varies. Plan a practical to test it. Check your plans with your teacher, then carry them out.

Questions

5 What is the current in a $120\,\Omega$ resistor connected to a 10 V battery?

6 Using similar batteries, two wires of the same metal had a voltage of 3 V across them. Wire X had current through it of 3 A, and wire Y a current through it of 1 A. (a) What is the resistance of each wire? (b) In what ways might wire X be different from wire Y? Give your reasons.

Key ideas

Use these words to fill in the spaces as you write the sentences in your Exercise book.

increase   **decrease**   **current (*I*)**   **voltage (*V*)**   **resistance (Ω)**   **temperature**

Power (watts) = _____ × _____ . Voltage = _____ × _____ . A variable resistance can be

used to _____ or _____ the _____ . If the _____ stays constant, then an _____ in voltage

will lead to an increase in _____ , in the same proportion (Ohm's law). The resistance of a

filament bulb will _____ with an _____ in temperature.

17.4 How is electricity produced?

How do cells produce electricity?

Chemical reactions take place in the cell to produce electricity: chemical energy changes to electrical energy. So it is also called an **electrochemical cell**. Dry cells are used in portable appliances such as flashlights and radios.

A simple type of cell is the zinc–carbon cell. It has a carbon rod inside a zinc case, which contains two separate dry chemicals that interact to make electricity.

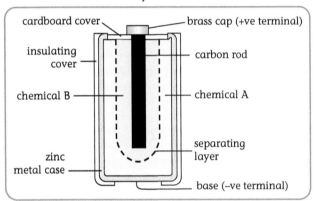

- cardboard cover
- brass cap (+ve terminal)
- insulating cover
- carbon rod
- chemical B
- chemical A
- zinc metal case
- separating layer
- base (–ve terminal)

How does it work?

The cell is made part of a circuit, with wires attached to the top (**+ve**) terminal and the bottom (**–ve**) terminal. Then electrons build up at the –ve terminal, and positive ions build up at the +ve terminal, and there is a flow of energized electrons around the circuit (see page 292).

Current flow is in one direction. So electricity from an electrochemical cell is **direct current** or **dc** electricity.

What kinds of cells are there?

- One common type is the 1.5 V flashlight dry cell (as above).
- Alkaline cells produce a higher current.
- Lead-acid cells are used together to make car batteries. These can be recharged when they are 'flat'.

How does a dynamo produce electricity?

A magnet is turned (spun) within a coil of insulated wire: kinetic energy is changed to electrical energy.

How does it work?

A bicycle dynamo has a spindle that rests on the wheel. As the wheel turns, the spindle turns a magnet inside the dynamo (see right). The turning magnet produces current flow in the coil. This then makes the lights work.

As it turns, the poles of the magnet are reversed; this gives rise to **alternating current** or **ac** electricity.

What kinds of dynamos are there?

- A dynamo is used on a bicycle to make the lights work.
- The same principle is used in huge generators which are used to make the ac electricity we use in the home.

Objectives

- Distinguish between dc and ac.
- Identify energy transfers in a dry cell and a dynamo.
- Describe how electricity is generated.
- Outline the uses of transformers.

Did you know?

- A 'dry' cell is so called because it contains dry chemicals.
- If you connect a working bicycle dynamo to a loudspeaker, the speaker cone vibrates in and out, showing the pulsating alternating current produced.

Dynamo in position on a bicycle

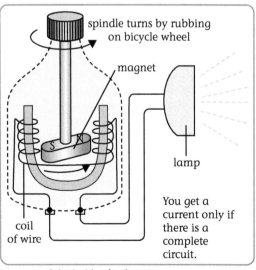

- spindle turns by rubbing on bicycle wheel
- magnet
- lamp
- S N
- coil of wire
- You get a current only if there is a complete circuit.

Diagram of the inside of a dynamo

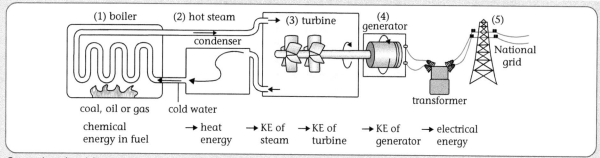

Generating electricity at a power station

1 Fossil fuels such as coal, oil or natural gas are burnt in the boiler to release heat energy.
2 This is used to heat up water, which changes to high-pressure steam.
3 The steam is sent to turn huge turbines (that are like lots of very big fans). This produces kinetic energy (KE).
4 These turbines are attached to a very powerful magnet inside a very large generator, which spins around.
5 The spinning magnets make electricity in the metal wires, which can be passed to the National grid.

What is a transformer?

A transformer consists of two separate coils of wire, called the primary coil and the secondary coil. The wires are wound close together around a soft iron core. When ac electricity flows around one coil, it produces a rapidly changing magnetic field. Because the other coil is near, an ac current flow begins in the other coil.

If there are a different number of turns of wire in one coil compared with the other, voltages can be increased (stepped up, (a) below) or decreased (stepped down, (b) below).

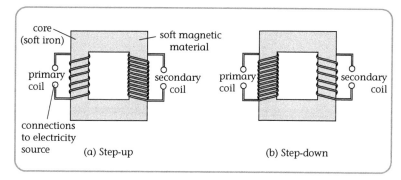

How step-up and step-down transformers are made

How are transformers used?

1 **At the power station** A **step-up** transformer is used to increase voltage. This also reduces the current (total power (watts) = voltage × current)).
● If power were transmitted at high current and low voltage, a lot of energy would be wasted as heat.
● But if the voltage is high and current is low, much thinner wires are satisfactory, and more economical.

2 **For home supply** The high voltages from the transmission lines must be brought down to much lower domestic levels. This is done by a series of **step-down** transformers. These may be located at an electricity sub-station, or fastened to 'electric' telegraph poles.

3 **Within the home** Transformers are used to adjust the voltage we supply to individual appliances, e.g. 110 to 240 V.

Key ideas

Use these words to fill in the spaces as you write the sentences in your Exercise book.

chemical   **generator**   **transformer**   **electricity**   **dynamo**   **kinetic**

A dry cell produces energy from stored _____ energy; this produces a direct current. A magnet that is made to turn within a coil of wire can generate _____ , as in a _____ or _____ ; this produces alternating current. The _____ energy of movement is converted to _____ . A step-up or step-down _____ can be used to change the voltage of an alternating current.

17.5 How do we use electricity safely?

You looked at safety with electricity in the laboratory (see page 246), and electric shock (see page 291). Now we will look at the safety devices we use with electricity.

Fuses

Fuses are pieces of special narrow fuse wire placed in a circuit, in series, with the appliances. Each fuse has a value for the current up to which it can operate safely. But if the current exceeds this, the wire gets hot, melts and breaks (it 'blows'). This stops the current flowing, and protects against possible fire in the wires and damage to the appliances.

Individual fuses are also used inside the plugs (see page 302) that connect appliances to the mains electricity.

It is important to choose the correct fuse: there are different thicknesses for 5, 10, 15 and 30 A. Use the next fuse higher than the amperage of the appliance.

- If the fuse had a lower amperage than the appliance, it would blow below the current needed for operation.
- If the fuse had a much higher amperage, it would not blow and therefore not protect the circuit or appliance.

Example A television has a power rating of 220 W and is working with mains electricity of 110 V. What fuse would it need?

First, work out the current flowing in the TV, using $I = W/V$.

So, $I = 220\,W/110\,V = 2\,A$. Choose a 5 A fuse.

Example An electric kettle has a power rating of 1500 W and is working with mains electricity of 110 V. What fuse would it need?

First, work out the current flowing in the kettle, using $I = W/V$.

So, $I = 1500\,W/110\,V = 13.6\,A$. Choose a 15 A fuse (not 13 A).

Circuit breakers or trip switches

These do not use fuse wire. The current passes through wires round an electromagnet (see page 309), which becomes more powerful as the current increases. Above the safe current value, the electromagnet is strong enough to force apart some contacts, which breaks the circuit. They can break an overloaded circuit in less than 0.01 s (much quicker than a fuse), and can be reset by moving a switch or pressing a button (no melted wire has to be replaced).

Surge protector

For electronic equipment, e.g. a computer, you can plug it into a bank of sockets with a surge protector. If there is an overload, e.g. when the power station supply peaks, or lightning strikes, this causes a surge of electricity, and the surge protector switches off and protects the appliance.

Earth leakage breaker

This can be used with electrical equipment, such as a lawn mower or hedge clipper. It protects against an accident of cutting the cable, which could cause an electric shock. The breaker quickly breaks the circuit.

Objectives

- Explain how a fuse works and how to determine which fuse to use.
- Wire a plug correctly using the colour code and correct choice of flex.
- Consider overloading and safe operation of electrical appliances.

Practical 130

How does a fuse work? (MM, ORR)

1 Set up the series circuit below. Begin with one 1.5 V cell, an ammeter (0–5 A), a 2.4 V flashlight bulb and a strand of steel wool (wire) held by crocodile clips. (The wire represents the fuse.)

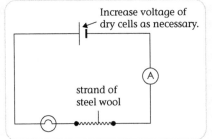

Increase voltage of dry cells as necessary.

strand of steel wool

2 Record the current with the 1.5 V voltage. If nothing happens to the wire, increase the voltage supply by adding an extra 1.5 V dry cell.

3 Repeat step 2 until the wire overheats, burns and breaks the circuit.

Questions

1 A school laboratory bulb is marked 12 V and 24 W. What current will be flowing if it is being operated at 12 V?

2 Why should a fuse wire rated 20 A not be used in a circuit designed for 5 A?

3 Which rating of fuse is suitable for use with a 600 W iron in a 110 V mains circuit?

4 A kitchen has an iron (operating on 9 A of current), an oven (12 A) and a fridge (7 A). A fuse with what value (rating) should be used to protect the circuit? Why?

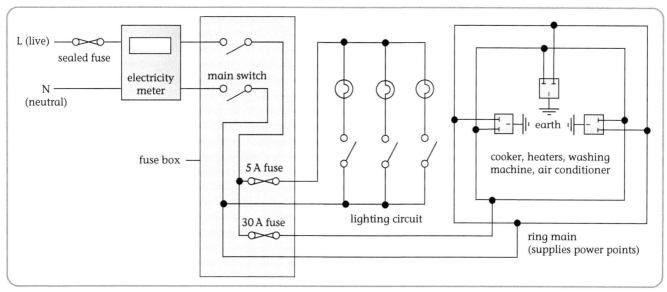

Wiring in a house

House wiring

The lighting circuit is protected by a 5 A fuse and each light can be used separately. If an appliance needing more than 5 A were connected to this circuit, then the fuse would 'blow'. Before replacing a fuse you must make sure that the fault that made the fuse burn out has been traced and fixed. Never use a piece of copper wire or aluminium foil as a fuse, because these are good conductors of electricity and have high melting points. So they would not burn out and protect the wiring and equipment before damage was done.

The main ring circuit in a house has much thicker and stronger wires to meet the demands for current of an electric cooker, washing machine or electric iron. The ring circuit also has a 30 A fuse because of the greater power use of the appliances.

How can house wiring be overloaded?

1 The wrong thickness of wire (flex or cable) might be used. The thin cable used for a lamp can safely carry a current of 2 A. This is appropriate for a 60 W bulb working with 120 V. $I = W/V = 60\,W/120\,V = 0.5\,A$. But an electric iron of 720 W working with the same voltage would have a required current of $I = W/V = 720\,W/120\,V = 6\,A$. The thin cable used for the lamp could not be safely used for the iron because its current limit would be exceeded: it would be overloaded and could cause a fire. Even thicker cables would be needed for a cooker.

2 Too many appliances might be plugged into a socket. For example, a mains socket supplies 13 A. An electric kettle (10 A), hair dryer (3 A), and TV (2 A) should *not* all be plugged in and used at the same time. This overloading can cause a fire.

Results of overloading

- Power outages: these can also be caused, for example at peak times, when households draw off more power than can be supplied.
- Electrical fires: the overheating of wires can set other things alight. Electrical fires are smothered or put out with carbon dioxide (see pages 254–5).
- Malfunctioning outlets: if a socket has been overloaded, it can burn out and be unusable.
- Damage to electrical appliances: if a circuit is overloaded the equipment may be harmed.

Other safety concerns

1 Never mix water and electricity. The water (especially seawater) makes a person a better conductor, so electricity could flow through them (see page 291).

2 If working with electricity, wear rubber-soled shoes, gloves and other protective clothing to insulate you.

3 Check the insulation on wires. Bare wires can come in contact with others to form a short circuit. Or some wires may be broken so the rest become overloaded. In either case, a fire could result.

4 If you are going to investigate an appliance, first switch it off and take the plug out of the wall. *Never* put metal objects into working appliances.

5 Use child-safety caps to stop small children pushing objects into sockets, which can be fatal.

6 Do not confuse a transformer and an adaptor.

- A transformer can convert the voltage supply to an appliance, e.g. a 240 V machine could work at 120 V.
- An adaptor is only a device to make a plug suitable to fit into a socket, e.g. in another country. It does not adjust the voltage.

17.5 How do we use electricity safely? (continued)

A voltage of 50V can kill. In Jamaica, Barbados and Trinidad, the operating supply is 110 or 120V, and in many other places it is 220 or 240V. We need to be careful.

Choose and wire plugs correctly

Cable

The flexible flex or cable used to connect an appliance to the mains supply, via a plug, usually has three wires.

● Live (brown insulation): the source of electricity from the mains to the appliance.
● Neutral (blue insulation): the return path for electricity when it has lost its energy; it completes the circuit.
● Earth (green and yellow): it is connected to the metal casing of an appliance. It is a safety device for you. It provides an alternative route for electricity if the casing became live. If that happened, a large current would flow temporarily and the fuse would blow.

The three wires are held within the outer insulated cable.

What is your cable like?

● If the cable with your appliance has three wires, it must be fitted to a three-pin plug and used with a power circuit that has an earth wire.
● If the cable with your appliance has two wires (live and neutral) it can be used with a two-pin plug.

Does the appliance have a metal case?

● If there is a metal case, e.g. a metal electric kettle, the appliance must be fitted with a three-pin plug and have the appropriate fuse (fuses for appliances come as 1, 3, 5, 10 and 13A). Work out the amperage of the appliance (see page 300) and use the next higher-rated fuse.
● If there is no metal case, e.g. a plastic electric jug, you can use a two-pin plug. If you are not sure, check if the appliance is supplied with a cable with only two wires. The appliances may also carry the sign of one square inside another. This means they are double insulated, and do not need an earth connection. As they are plastic the casing cannot become live and cannot give an electric shock.

How does the fuse work in a plug?

A fuse is a piece of fuse wire inside a glass case, with the wire in contact with the two metal ends. When the wires in a plug have been correctly connected (see the practical on the right), the fuse is placed in contact with both the live wire connection and the live pin. A three-pin plug often has a fuse, placed so that it completes the circuit. Then the appliance is plugged in, switched on and will work.

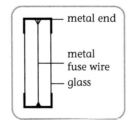

metal end
metal fuse wire
glass

Practical 131

Wiring a plug (MM)

1 Use wire strippers to remove 4 cm of the *outer* insulation from a piece of cable.
2 Cut and trim the wires and coloured insulation as shown below.

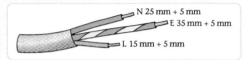

N 25 mm + 5 mm
E 35 mm + 5 mm
L 15 mm + 5 mm

3 Unscrew the cover of the plug.
4 Remove the fuse and the cable grip.
5 Unscrew the live (L) screw and push the bared end of brown wire into the hole and tighten the screw clockwise.

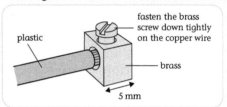

plastic
fasten the brass screw down tightly on the copper wire
brass
5 mm

6 Repeat for the N and E pins.
7 Pull *gently* on the cable. Place the cable grip over the cable and screw it down. Replace the fuse.

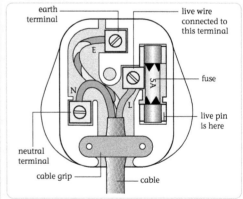

earth terminal
live wire connected to this terminal
fuse
live pin is here
neutral terminal
cable grip
cable

8 Replace the cover and screw it down.
9 You can also wire a two-pin plug using a piece of cable with live and neutral wires.

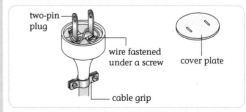

two-pin plug
wire fastened under a screw
cover plate
cable grip

What are the hazards of household electrical appliances?

First make a list of household appliances to show how they use electricity to perform their functions.

Name of appliance	Heavy power users > 250 W	Heavy voltage users > 200 V	Functions performed by the appliance			
			Light	Heat	Turning power	Audio/visual
Washing machine	✓			✓	✓	
Table lamp			✓			
Television						✓
etc.						

High power users

High power users such as electric stoves and water heaters need to have **thick wires** inside the flex connecting them to the electricity supply. They should also be **earthed** and have a **fuse** with a high rating (30 A). They are on a special ring main.

High voltage users

Some household appliances used in the Caribbean have been manufactured to operate with 240 V, rather than the more common 110–120 V. For proper operation, the voltage from the mains has to be increased using a transformer (see page 299). High voltages can cause electric shock.

Light bulbs

These are moderate to low users of electricity. But bulb wattages of 100 W and over produce a lot of heat. So you should choose lampshades carefully, so they do not melt and catch fire. Follow any advice that is given.

Electric hotplates

The rings of an electric cooker can reach over 1000 °C. Paper, oil or cooking fat will burst into flames if in contact with such a hot surface. When switched off it still remains hot.

Motors

Electricity provides the turning power for electric motors. When an appliance is switched on, the motor should spin. If the motor gets stuck, the wiring may become overloaded and burn out. This would damage the appliance.

If the motor in a food mixer, vacuum cleaner or washing machine becomes stuck, switch off immediately and try to find the problem.

Sound systems

High levels of sound can cause deafness (see page 130). Many people buy 50 W hifi sound systems when 10 W ones would be satisfactory. Protect your ears from damage.

Electric lighting

For the effect of high light intensity, see page 127. Special-effects lighting, with the use of ultraviolet light, has also become popular, This can damage the cells in the retina. This is especially so when the general lighting is low and the pupils are wide open. Flashing lights, which correspond to electrical rhythms in the brain, can cause mental disturbances.

Fluorescent tubes and bulbs (see page 311) contain a mixture of different substances which enable white light to be produced. But some of these substances are extremely poisonous. Great care should be taken if you handle broken fluorescent tubes.

Television sets

These contain transformers that produce very high voltages (e.g. 5 kV). Tampering with the inside of a TV is extremely dangerous. Sitting too close to a TV for too long can also cause eye strain and may expose the viewer to radiation that could damage delicate cells of the retina.

Key ideas

Use these words to fill in the spaces as you write the sentences in your Exercise book.

current   **voltage**   **power**   **fuse**   **transformer**   **earth**

A _____ is included as part of a circuit to protect other appliances; it will heat up and melt if excess _____ flows. The _____ wire in a plug helps to prevent an electric shock. The most dangerous household appliances are those with a high _____ or _____ rating. If a country has 110–120 V electricity, you will need a _____ to use 240 V appliances correctly and safely.

17.6 How much does electricity cost?

In this topic you will see how electricity is supplied to your home, find out how much appliances use, how the use is recorded and charged for, and ways in which you can reduce your electricity bill by conserving energy.

Supply of electricity to your home

Electricity is generated at the power station, and the voltage increased by a step-up transformer for distribution through high-voltage cables (see page 299). Cables are usually carried on tall pylons, but they should be underground in regions where hurricanes often occur.

   You will also see pole transformers on telegraph poles (see the top photograph on the right). These reduce the voltage of the electricity for its supply to our homes.

How is electricity charged for?

Energy consumption is measured in kilowatt-hours (kW h). The watt (W) is a unit of power: the rate at which work is done (joules/second, J/s). The watt is also current × voltage ($W = I \times V$) (see page 295). 1 kW is 1000 W.

- 1 kW h is the amount of energy converted by a 1 kW appliance operating for 1 hour.
- It could also be the amount of energy converted by a 500 W appliance operating for 2 hours.

$$
\begin{array}{ccc}
\text{power} & \times & \text{time} & = & \text{energy consumption} \\
\text{in kilowatts (kW)} & & \text{in hours (h)} & & \text{in kilowatt-hours (kW h)}
\end{array}
$$

1 kW h is called an energy unit, or just a **unit**.

How much electricity have you used?

When electricity enters your home it first passes through a meter (see the thick cables entering the meter box in the photograph on the right). The meter records the energy consumption: the number of kW h (energy units) that are used. This is the information used by the electricity company to work out your bill. The meter can have a row of numbers (digital meter) or have dials with pointers (analogue meter).

Digital meter

The diagram below shows the reading on a digital meter at the beginning and end of July (ignore the last column, which shows parts of a unit).

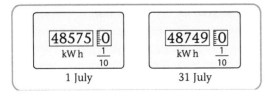

Energy units (kW h) used = second reading − first reading
= 48749   −48575
= 174 kW h

Objectives

- Define W and kW h (energy unit).
- Read digital and analogue meters.
- Calculate energy consumption in kW h of different appliances.
- Calculate electricity bills.
- Discuss energy conservation.

Pole transformer on a utility pole

A digital electricity meter

Questions

1 An oven has a power rating of 3750 W. How many kW h will it use in an hour?

2 The reading on a digital meter on 1 May was 46782 and on 31 May was 46921. (a) How many units of energy were used in May? (b) If each kW h costs the equivalent of US$2, what is the total cost of electricity for May?

Analogue meter

Analogue meters have four or five dials. The last one may show parts of a unit. Dials are numbered alternately in an anticlockwise and clockwise direction. Each dial has a pointer. If the pointer is not exactly on a number, then record the *lower* number.

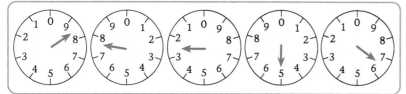

The reading for the Brown family on 1 October is 87256 kWh

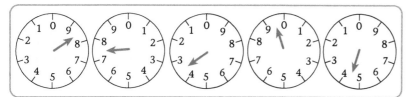

The reading for 31 October is 87394 kWh

So the difference is second reading – first reading
= 87394 – 87256 = 138 kWh (138 units)

Now read these dials, and work out the units used by the Lees.

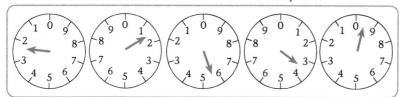

Reading for the Lee family on 1 November

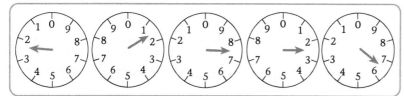

Reading for 30 November

An analogue electricity meter

Work out your own electricity bill

1 Find out, for your country, what other charges there are (see the box on the right, and look at an old bill).
2 Record your meter readings at the beginning and end of a month and work out the number of kWh (units) you used.
3 Multiply the total kWh by the cost of one unit (look at an old bill). If the cost changes depending on the number of units you use, take this into account.
4 Add any other charges to the cost from step 3, e.g.

Reading at the end of the month	= 03782 kWh
Reading at beginning of the month	= 03629 kWh
Units used	= 153 kWh
Charge per unit is $3.00, so cost	= US$ 459
Other charges	= US$ 25
Combined cost	= US$ 484

If GCT is 15%, multiply by 15, and
divide by 100 (484 × 15/100) GCT = US$ 72.60
Total bill = US$ 566.60

Activity

1 Draw a row of five dials. Think of a number with five digits and draw in the pointers to show the number. Ask your teacher to check your answer.

2 If possible, record kWh usage for some appliances by switching them on and off.

3 Take an initial reading of a meter, and read it again every day at the same time for a week. Calculate usage each day and present your results as a bar chart.

4 Look back through old electricity bills. Record the kWh used each month in a bar chart. Try to account for any differences.

What are the other charges?

Look at your own electricity bill or check with the electricity company. Find out which of these charges you have to pay.

● Fixed charge, customer charge or standing charge: this is a fixed charge, which everyone pays.

● Meter rental: a set amount.

● Fuel adjustment charge and exchange rate adjustment charges: additional charges for each kWh used.

● Miscellaneous charges: these may be interest charges on previous unpaid bills or reconnection charges, etc.

Activity

Which appliances cost most to run?

Work in small groups. Use the information in the table below, and other resources you have. Remember:

- the unit of power is the watt (W), the rate at which energy is transferred, and 1000 W = 1 kW

- an energy unit is a kWh (kW × time in hours).

1 Identify (a) four high-wattage users and (b) four low-wattage users. Which ones involve heating?

2 Identify (a) two appliances that we use all the time and (b) four appliances that we use a little.

3 Make a table like that below for the appliances you have in your home.

4 Use a calculator to find the kWh for 1 day. (Multiply W × h and divide by a 1000 to give kWh. Note that 10 minutes is 10/60 hours.)

5 Then calculate kWh used in 30 days.

The cost of running appliances

Remember:
- if the time is given in minutes, you first have to change it to hours (by dividing by 60)
- when you have calculated watts × hours (Wh), you divide your answer by 1000 to get kWh.

Examples

Large air conditioner: 1 day: 1300 W × 10h = 13,000 Wh/1000 = 13 kWh
So, for 30 days = 13 kWh × 30 = 390 kWh

Hair dryer: 10 min = 10/60 h = 0.17 h
1 day: 1250 W × 0.17 h = 213 Wh/1000 = 0.2 kWh, so for 30 days = 0.2 kWh × 30 = 6 kWh

Toaster: 20 min = 20/60 h = 0.33 h
1 day: 1140 W × 0.33 h = 376 Wh/1000 = 0.4 kWh, so for 30 days: 0.4 kWh × 30 = 12 kWh

You will notice that the cost of running appliances depends on two things:
- their wattage (the rate at which they convert energy to do a job)
- the length of time they are used.

Appliance	Typical wattage (W)	Av. use/day	Est. kWh/day	Est. kWh/30 days
Air conditioner	1300 } 750	10h		
Computer	300	2h		
Fan	85	5h		
Freezer				
Small	300	all day,		
Medium	400	every		
Large	500	day		
Hair dryer	1250	10 min		
Clothes iron	750 } 250	20 min		
Light bulb	100 } 60	4h		
Microwave	750	10min		
Sound system	35	1h		
Refrigerator				
Standard	700	all day,		
Large	900	every		
Frost-free	1300	day		
Electric stove				
Small ring	1250 }			
Large ring	2500 }	1h		
Oven	3800 }			
Television	200	4h		
Toaster	1140	20min		
Washing machine	800	1h		
Water heater	4500	3h		
Vacuum cleaner	600	15min		

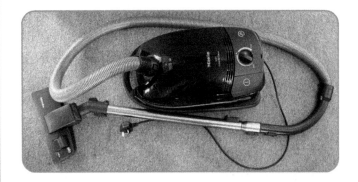

This vacuum cleaner has a wattage of 900 W and the jug 2000 W. If they are used an average of 15 minutes a day, how many kWh do they each use in 30 days?

How can we reduce our electricity costs?

Producing electricity produces pollutants, for example from the burning of fossil fuels. These fuels are also in limited supply. We can help the environment, and reduce our electricity bills, by some simple means.

1 Choice of appliances

- **Power rating** Do not choose an appliance that is more powerful than you need. For example, for sound systems 10 W may be sufficient, and for bulbs a mixture of 60 W and 100 W bulbs is cheaper to run than all being 100 W.
- **Efficiency** Where possible choose fluorescent tubes or bulbs, which convert more of the energy into light, than filament lamps, which waste a lot as heat (see pages 310–11).

2 Operation of appliances

- **Use less** For example, switch off lights that are not being used, wash only full loads of clothes, when washing dishes only just cover them with hot water, use an oven to cook several meals at once, use one pan to cook several vegetables together, take short showers instead of baths, and heat up only as much water as you need for hot drinks.
- **Operate properly** For example, do not open a fridge too much or for too long. You should turn off and take out the plugs of appliances that will be left unused for some time. Check there aren't any dripping taps (especially hot water) or any wasted energy from a faulty seal on a refrigerator. You can also close curtains in the heat of the day to keep a room cooler, and use natural ventilation or a fan rather than an air conditioner.
- **Assess new products** For example, 'frost-free' refrigerators sound good but they use up a lot more energy than one you have to defrost yourself. Some new washing powders work in cold water – with a lot of saving when doing the laundry.

3 Choice of energy supply

- **Use solar power** Install a solar water heater (see page 326) to cut down the cost of heating water by electricity.
- **Switch to bottled gas** for cooking instead of using electricity.
- **Work out costs** If you have a radio that can use either batteries or the mains, work out which is cheaper.

Activity

Energy conservation

Work in a small group.

1 Use the table on page 306, and the information on the left, to suggest five appliance choices that could save money, e.g. buying an iron with a lower wattage.

2 Identify energy savings that could be made (a) in the kitchen and (b) throughout the house on lighting and electricity use.

3 Prepare a brochure giving advice to householders on how to save electricity and reduce their electricity bills.

Questions

1 (a) What is the unit used for measuring power? (b) What is the unit used for measuring energy consumption?

2 (a) What is the power of a machine that draws a current of 5 A at 120 V? (b) What is its energy consumption if it operates continuously for 10 hours?

3 (a) Change 6000 W, 1750 W and 24,500 W to kW. (b) If a refrigerator operates at 900 W for 24 hours, what is its energy consumption in kWh? (c) Does the refrigerator use more or less electrical energy than an air conditioner of 1500 W operating for 20 hours?

4 (a) Compare the energy consumption of a 60 W and a 100 W bulb, both used for 4 hours a day for 30 days. (b) If the cost of 1 kWh is US$2, what is the difference in cost for running the bulbs for 30 days?

Key ideas

Use these words to fill in the spaces as you write the sentences in your Exercise book.

watts   **electricity**   **heating**   **fixed**   **kWh**   **non-heating**   **conserve**

The rate at which energy is converted in an appliance is measured in _____ . The cost of using _____ appliances (iron, stoves, hair dryer) is greater than that of _____ appliances (radio, fluorescent tubes, fans). We are charged for the number of _____ units (_____) that we use, together with a standing or _____ charge. We can _____ energy to save money.

17.7 Magnetic effects of electricity

The first magnets were magnetic rocks found in nature, called lodestone, which consist of magnetite (a kind of iron ore). When magnets are suspended, they align themselves north–south (see page 228). They also attract other objects made of metals or metal alloys containing the ferrous metals: iron (steel), nickel and cobalt.

We can also show that magnets have a magnetic field around them, where their effect can be detected.

(see page 228)

Practical 132

Can magnetic lines of force be shown with a bar magnet? (ORR)

1 Place a stiff piece of white card over a magnet.

2 Sprinkle iron filings lightly but evenly over the card.

3 Tap gently with the edge of a ruler and observe the pattern formed by the filings.

4 Repeat the above steps with two arrangements of bar magnets (as shown on the right).

5 You can make permanent patterns by first sprinkling a card with grated candle wax, before adding the filings. Then pass a Bunsen burner or electric hot plate rapidly over the wax to melt it and fix the pattern.

6 Describe the patterns. How do they relate to the results for attraction and repulsion you found on page 228?

Temporary and permanent magnets

- An iron nail made of 'soft', fairly pure iron, when attracted to a magnet, can in turn attract another ferrous material. It becomes a **temporary** magnet, as it loses that magnetism when it is detached from the magnet.
- However, a steel sewing needle and masonry nail can also retain some magnetism after they are detached from a magnet; they become **permanent** magnets.

The magnetic effect of an electric current

Your teacher may demonstrate the set-up on the right. This shows an electric current being passed through a coil of insulated wire. The magnetic field that is produced can be shown by the movement of small plotting compasses.

If an electric current is passed through a coil of insulated wire, and this is wrapped around an iron bar (core), an **electromagnet** can be produced. This can be shown by the way it attracts iron filings or tacks.

This is a kind of temporary magnet, which lasts only as long as there is a flow of electrical current. Electromagnets are used to pick up and drop iron-containing items, e.g. at scrapyards or rubbish depots. They are found in bells, relays, transformers, circuit breakers and electric motors.

Objectives

- Describe different types of magnets.
- Explain the magnetic effects of electrical current and how it is used.

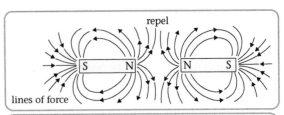

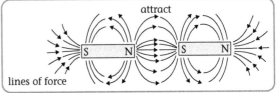

Magnetic lines of force around magnets

What does it mean?

Magnet A material with two poles that can attract ferrous metals or alloys.

Permanent magnet A material that keeps its own magnetism for a long time.

Temporary magnet A magnet that holds its magnetism for only a short time.

Electromagnet A magnet formed due to the magnetic effect of an electric current.

Did you know?

- Soft iron and alloys, e.g. permalloy (iron and nickel), make temporary magnets, used in telephones and electric motors.

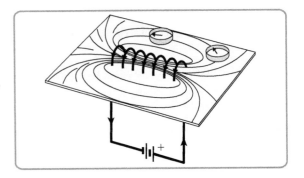

Using electricity to make a magnet

Electricity flowing in a wire has a magnetic effect which can be used to make temporary electromagnets. You can demonstrate this in the practical on the right. You can also make an electric bell.

An electric bell

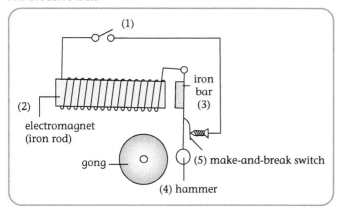

When the switch (1) is pushed down it completes the circuit. Current flows in the wire around the iron rod (2). This becomes an electromagnet that attracts the iron bar (3). So the hammer hits the gong (4) and the bell 'rings'. When the switch is open, the contact at (5) is broken. So no current flows, the iron bar loses its magnetism and the ringing stops.

A relay switch

This is used in the ignition in a car. A small current in one circuit switches on the electric motor in the second circuit.

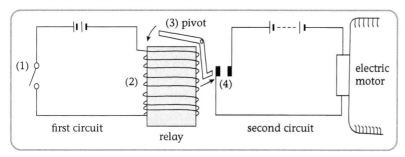

When the switch (1) is closed, an electromagnet (2) is made that pulls down the pivoted iron arm (3). This presses the contacts (4) together, to complete the other circuit.

Practical 133

Making an electromagnet (ORR, PD)

1 Wind insulated copper wire around a nail. Bare the ends, and attach them briefly to terminals of a 1.5 V dry cell.

2 Does the nail now attract iron filings, tacks or pins?

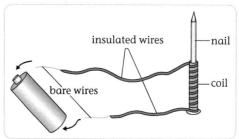

Plan and report on the effect of:
(a) removing the current, (b) increasing the current, (c) increasing the length and number of turns of the wire, and (d) using a steel knitting needle.

Questions

1 List three characteristics of permanent magnets.

2 How can you demonstrate the magnetic field around an electric current?

3 Why does the coil of wire wrapped around an iron bar to make an electromagnet have to be insulated?

4 Why can't steel be used to make an electromagnet?

5 List four uses of electromagnets. How does one of them work?

Key ideas

Use these words to fill in the spaces as you write the sentences in your Exercise book.

magnetic   **lost**   **retains**   **electromagnet**   **current**   **magnetism**

A magnet has a _____ field around it. Wherever there is electric _____ flow, a _____ effect is also produced. A permanent magnet _____ its magnetism for a long time. An _____ is made when electric _____ passes through a coil of wire wrapped around it, but its _____ is _____ when the current stops.

17.8 What are natural and artificial lighting?

Non-luminous and luminous objects

We can see objects only if light comes from them, or if light is reflected from them to our eyes.

- **Non-luminous objects** do not make their own light. We only see them if light shines onto them and is reflected to our eyes. Examples: the Moon, a car, most other objects.
- **Luminous objects** produce or give out light. Examples: the Sun, a lit bulb, a firefly, a burning fire or match.

Natural and artificial lighting

- **Natural** sources of light occur without humans making them. Examples: the Sun, other stars, fireflies, lightning.
- **Artificial** sources of light are made by humans, usually using electricity or a fossil fuel, such as oil or kerosene, as the source of energy to be changed into light. Examples: oil or kerosene lamp, filament lamp, fluorescent tube or bulb.

Filament lamp

Principle involved: the tungsten wire in the bulb becomes very hot as electricity passes through it; it becomes so hot that it glows or gives out light. Your teacher may show you the effect of different currents passing through nichrome wire, which also glows. This giving out of light from very hot objects is called **incandescence**, so the filament lamp is also called an **incandescent** lamp.

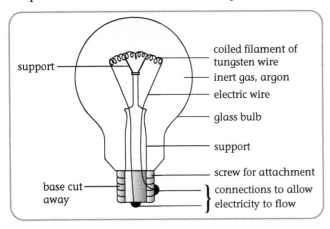

The lamp is made part of an electrical circuit when a switch is closed (it is turned on). Electricity flows in at one connection at the base of the lamp. You can trace the flow of current through the tungsten wire to the other connection, and the lamp lights.

Tungsten is used in a filament lamp because it has a very high melting point (3400 °C). The bulb of the lamp has an inert gas, argon, which does not react with the tungsten. When an electric current passes through the filament, it rises to a temperature of over 2000 °C. It then gives out infrared waves (heat) and visible light. The efficiency of the lamp is the percentage of electricity that is converted to light.

Objectives

- Distinguish between natural and artificial lighting.
- Explain and compare how light is produced in a filament lamp and a fluorescent tube or bulb.

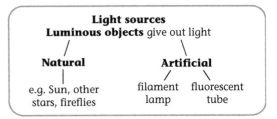

Characteristics of a filament lamp

- As the filament is heated to a very high temperature, it glows to give out light.
- The lamp is only 5% efficient. A lot of energy (95%) is wasted as heat.
- Because so much energy is wasted, filament lamps cost a lot to run.
- However, filament lamps are easy to make and so are cheap to buy.
- Filament lamps produce a spot of strong light and so are useful for lighting a stage or a sports ground at night.
- The light produced is similar to natural light, as produced by the Sun.

Energy transfer in a filament lamp

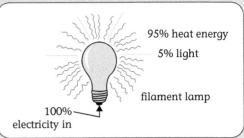

A lamp cannot produce light without producing heat. A filament lamp is said to be 5% efficient, because this is the % of the input energy converted to light.

Fluorescent tube

Principle involved: the tube has a lining of special powder called **phosphor**; the ultraviolet light (UV) produced in the tube is absorbed by the phosphor, which produces visible light (**fluoresces**). Smaller fluorescent bulbs are also available, working on the same principle.

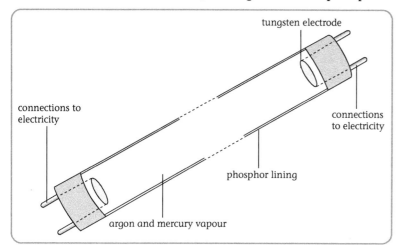

The fluorescent tube is a long glass tube with a lining of phosphor. At each end is an electrode of tungsten connected to the electricity supply. Inside the tube is argon and mercury vapour. When the tube is switched on, electricity flows through the gases and some bluish light and ultraviolet light (UV) are produced. The UV light is absorbed by the phosphor, which fluoresces to give out visible light with a bluish colour (it is deficient in red light). As high temperatures are not involved, more of the input energy is converted to light and less is wasted as heat.

Questions

1 (a) List four luminous objects. (b) Non-luminous objects do not make light, so how do we see them?
2 Explain how light is produced in a filament lamp and a fluorescent tube or bulb.
3 Prepare a table to compare the properties of a filament light with a fluorescent tube or bulb.

Energy transfer in a fluorescent bulb

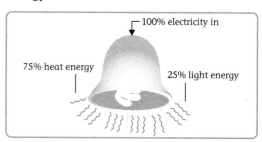

Characteristics of a fluorescent bulb

- Ultraviolet light (UV) produced in the bulb is absorbed by a phosphor lining, and visible light is sent out.
- The fluorescent bulb is 25% efficient. So less energy (75%) is wasted as heat.
- Because less energy is wasted, fluorescent bulbs cost less to run.
- However, fluorescent bulbs are more expensive to make, buy and install.
- Fluorescent bulbs produce light along their length and so give a soft, less dazzling, effect without distinct shadows.
- The light produced has less red light when compared with natural light.

Did you know?

- In order to attract a mate, a female firefly times the number of light flashes per minute to match those of the male.
- The leaves of Morning Glory have a light-sensitive pigment that sends a hormone to the buds to open.

Key ideas

Use these numbers and words to fill in the spaces as you write the sentences in your Exercise book.

fluorescent   25%   incandescent   natural   filament   5%   cheaper

The Sun is a _____ source of light. One artificial source is the _____ lamp, which is also called an _____ lamp, as the hot filament glows to give off light. The _____ lamp also gives off a lot of heat and is only _____ efficient. A _____ tube is more expensive to buy and install, but _____ to run as it is more efficient (_____) at converting electricity to light.

17.9 How do we use light to see?

The workplace, school, office and home are built to include clear-glass windows, at a suitable height, to let in as much natural light as possible. Windows are placed on walls that have clear views, and large trees are planted at some distance from the windows, so as not to block the light. People also sit at tables and desks so that light comes in from behind or from the side of them and falls on the work they are doing. The light is then reflected from the surface of the paper and other objects into our eyes and we see (see pages 124–5).

Natural light is free. But when natural light is inadequate, artificial sources (see pages 310–11) have to be used. Natural light contains all the colours of the spectrum (see the electromagnetic spectrum on pages 314 and 360). We call this combination of colours 'white' light. The filament lamp produces light that is most similar to natural daylight. The fluorescent tube or bulb produces blue-green light that is deficient in red. You can examine the barcharts on page 313 to see the differences.

How do we use filament lamps?

Because the light spreads out from a small area, the filament lamp produces dark, sharp shadows with definite outlines. This makes it easier for us to identify shapes. The filament lamps give a spot of strong light, for example for car headlights or a table lamp, or to illuminate a sports ground at night. With or without coloured filters these lights are also used for lighting a stage.

Because the light is most similar to sunlight, we see the 'natural' colour of any object. This is useful, for example, for a store selling clothing, fabrics and paint.

How do we use fluorescent tubes and bulbs?

Because fluorescent bulbs produce light along their length, shadows are lighter in colour and have soft, indefinite edges. Because they are also economical to run, fluorescent tubes (strip-lights) are useful for lighting large areas such as factories, offices, laboratories and shops, and fluorescent bulbs are now replacing filament lamps. In the home, we often use fluorescent tubes in the kitchen.

We see the colour of an object because of the light it reflects to our eyes: for example, a blue object reflects blue light and a red object reflects red light. But fluorescent light is high in blue and low in red light, so if we shine it on red cloth or lipstick, there is little red light to be reflected. The object therefore looks bluer than it really is. This is the reason that shops selling clothing, fabrics or paint may use filament lamps instead of fluorescent tubes. Alternatively, if buyers are unsure of the colour of an object, they should take it outside to be observed under natural lighting.

Remember:
- light contains wavelengths we see as different colours
- an object appears to be a certain colour because it reflects light of that colour to our eyes
- a filter lets through light only of its own colour.

Objectives

- Give reasons for different uses of filament lamps and fluorescent tubes or bulbs.
- Discuss problems bright lighting and poor lighting may have on our eyes.

Practical 134

Using filters (ORR, AI)

You will need to do this at night or work with a large box and a black cloth.

1 Set up three flashlights, with red, green or blue filters stuck on the front.
2 Check each beam of light produced (a filter lets through only its own light).
3 Collect three objects that are red, green or blue in natural light.
4 In turn shine each of your flashlight beams onto each of the objects and record your results in a table like this.

Appearance of object in			
Daylight	Red light	Green light	Blue light
Red Green Blue			

5 Explain the results you find.
6 Fluorescent lighting is low in red light. Set up a flashlight to observe red and blue objects with this light.
7 Sodium lamps for street lighting give yellow light. Set up a flashlight to observe red and blue objects with this light.
8 Explain your findings in 6 and 7.

Questions

1 A lady visited a store with fluorescent lighting and bought a top she thought would match a skirt she had. However, at home she found the colours were not the same. Why was this?
2 Why are filament lamps used for stage lighting and sports fields at night?
3 What damage is done by lighting that is (a) too intense and (b) too dim?

Different sources of light

The light we receive from a filament lamp is most similar to that from sunlight, whereas light from a fluorescent tube or bulb has more blue light in it. The light used in street lights is often yellow. See the diagram below.

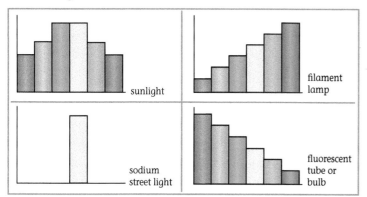

How do our eyes respond to lighting?

Our eyes respond automatically to differences in light intensity (see the diagram and on the right, pages 124 and 127), using the pupil reflex. Some important points are highlighted below.

Various light sources

- Filament lamp: This produces an intense narrow beam of light. Because bright light should not directly enter our eyes, the light should be behind us and fall onto the work we are doing, and then be reflected to our eyes. The filament lamp should also have a shade around it to spread out the light to reduce glare and dark shadows.
- Fluorescent tube: As we have seen, the light is high in blue and low in red. It is therefore not suitable to use when doing any work concerned with colours, as the results will be different from that obtained in natural lighting. So it would be unsuitable, for example, for artists.
- Economy fluorescent bulbs: Lower wattage bulbs can be used, to give the same light output, with savings in electricity costs. But they take some time to come to their full brightness. It is important that the correct replacement bulb is used; otherwise the lighting may be too dim, and cause problems with safety.

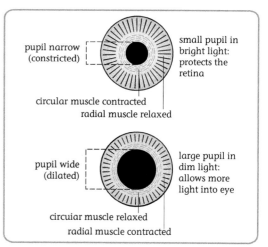

The pupil reflex in bright and dim light

Practical 135

Looking at filament lamps (ORR, D)

1 Look at a filament lamp, such as that shown on page 310. Identify all the parts on your lamp, and make a labelled drawing.

2 Lamps differ in the rate at which they change electricity into light (this is called **wattage**, abbreviated as W). Find lamps marked 40, 60 and 100 W.

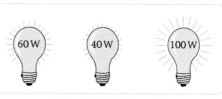

3 Higher wattage lamps cost more to run. Taking cost and the need for adequate lighting into account, suggest where in the home you would use each kind.

4 Take out a small screw-type bulb from a flashlight. Draw and label it to compare it to the lamps above.

Key ideas

Use these words to fill in the spaces as you write the sentences in your Exercise book.

dark   fluorescent   red   spotlights   filament   retina   dim   bright

_____ lamps produce light most similar to natural light and are used for making _____ .

_____ tubes produce light deficient in _____ light. If a red object is seen under fluorescent

lighting it will appear _____ , as there is little _____ light to be reflected from the object. UV and

very _____ lights can damage the _____ . _____ light can cause eye strain.

17.10 White light and its colours

Separating white light

Visible 'white' light is really a very small part of the electromagnetic spectrum (EMS) of the Sun's radiation, as shown on the right. Our brains interpret the band of radiation with wavelengths between 380 and 780 nm as white light. But if a prism is held in the Sun, at a certain angle, the sunlight will be split into different colours. Each colour is a certain band of wavelengths. The wavelengths that correspond to each colour are bent (refracted) to slightly different degrees and so can be separated and shown on a screen as the **visible spectrum**. A similar splitting of white light occurs in water drops, to give rise to a rainbow. Blue is at one end (shorter wavelength) and red is at the other (longer wavelength).

Mixing colours to make white light

Mixing coloured lights of red, green and blue can make white light. To do this we project and overlap the lights onto a white screen. Red, green and blue are known as the **primary** colours of light because they cannot be made by mixing any other colours of light together. If you mix all the primary colours of light together evenly, you get white light (see below).

The colours that are made by mixing light of the two primary colours on each side are known as **secondary** colours. These are magenta (a reddish-blue colour), cyan (a blue-green colour) and yellow (see below).

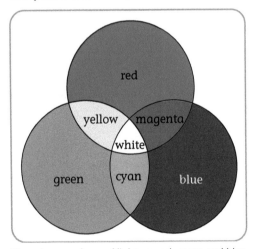

The primary colours of light are red, green and blue

The colour wheel

Colours may be arranged in a colour wheel (see on the right), with the secondary colours opposite the primary colours. The secondary colours lie between the primary colours that can be mixed to make them, e.g. yellow light is formed by mixing red and green light.

Colours opposite to each other on the colour wheel are said to be **complementary** (when mixed together they give white light), e.g. yellow is complementary to blue.

Objectives

- Describe how to separate white light into its component colours.
- Differentiate between primary and secondary colours of light.

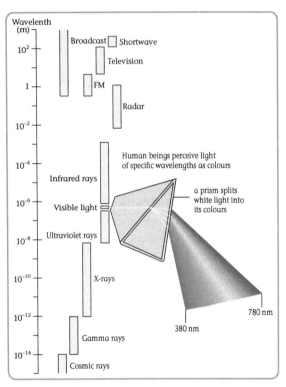

The electromagnetic spectrum

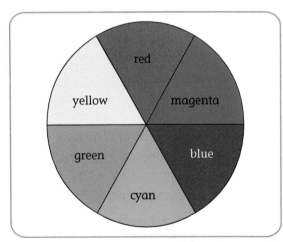

The colour wheel. Primary colours of light: red, green and blue. Secondary colours of light: magenta, cyan and yellow

Practical 136

Mixing coloured lights (MM, ORR, AI)

1 Set up three similar flashlights with green, blue and red filters, or similar colours of cellophane paper, held at the front. Check that you have beams of coloured light.

2 Carry out the next steps at night, or in a darkened room or large box. Shine the flashlights, one by one, onto a sheet of white paper. These are like the spotlights on a stage.

3 Now overlap the beams of red and green. What colour do you see? Carry out the other combinations and record the colours. Check with the artwork on the right. How do your results relate to the primary and secondary colours of light?

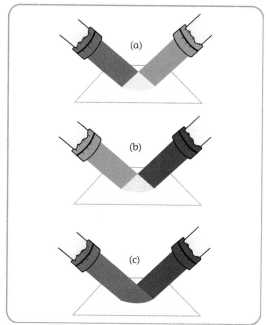

Overlap different primary light colours

Applications of mixing coloured lights

The eye

In the retina of the eye (see page 125) there are three kinds of cones, sensitive to red, green or blue light. When we look at a red object, red light is reflected to our eyes and it stimulates the red-sensitive cones to set up a message to the brain. If we look at a yellow object, then both the red- and green-sensitive cones are stimulated and the brain interprets this as yellow, and so on for all the colours.

Stage lights

Filters are used to make beams of red, green and blue coloured lights that are shone onto the stage. Where these overlap, the secondary colours of light are seen.

Colour TV

If you look closely at a TV screen, you will see coloured spots of red, green and blue light, arranged in sets of three. The combinations give the range of colours.

Colour photography

Look at a colour negative. As with a black and white photograph (see page 53), the dark and light areas are reversed. The colours are also complementary colours of those on the final printed positive photograph. So, for example, areas that are blue on the negative will print as yellow in the final photograph.

Did you know?

- People who are red–green colour blind do not see these colours – they both look grey. It is an inherited characteristic.
- The range of colours we see is determined by the different numbers of red, green or blue cones in the retina that are stimulated.

Questions

1 Refer to the colour wheel opposite. What are all the combinations of coloured lights that will give white?

2 How does the eye see (a) a magenta, (b) a blue and (c) a cyan object?

Key ideas

Use these words to fill in the spaces as you write the sentences in your Exercise book.

prism   **red**   **visible**   **radiation**   **colours**   **spectrum**   **yellow**

Visible light is a small part of the Sun's _____ , known as the electromagnetic _____ . The

colours of light in the _____ spectrum relate to differences in the wavelength. Lights of different

_____ refract differently through a _____ . The primary _____ of light are _____ , green

and blue. Green and _____ lights overlap to give _____ (a secondary colour).

17.11 Mixing and separating pigments

Can pigments produce different colours?

Paints are made from fine particles called **pigments**. These pigments absorb, i.e. subtract from white light, some colours and reflect others. For example, a red object absorbs all colours except red, which it reflects.

The colour mixing for coloured lights is by adding. Colour mixing with pigments is by subtracting. For example, in a mix of blue and yellow paints:

- blue pigment absorbs yellow and red light but reflects some green and violet, as well as blue
- yellow pigment absorbs violet and blue light but reflects some green and red
- so the only colour not fully absorbed by the yellow–blue pigment mixture is green – so the mixture looks green.

What are the primary pigments?

Just as there are primary colours (lights), there are primary pigments. The secondary colours for lights are the primary colours for pigments. These are **magenta**, **yellow** and **cyan**. The primary pigments cannot be made by mixing other pigment colours. (Try to mix yellow from other pigments!) While a mixture of the three primary colours of light will produce white, a mixture of the three primary pigments will produce black (see right).

Objectives

- Discuss the effects of mixing various combinations of primary pigments.
- Separate different coloured inks by chromatography.

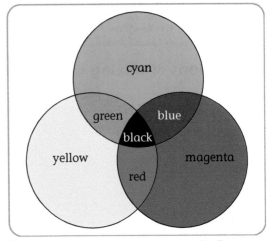

The primary pigments: magenta, cyan and yellow

Practical 137

Mixing primary pigments (ORR, PD)

1 Starting with the three primary pigments, yellow, cyan and magenta, see how many new colours you can produce by combining small quantities in varying proportions. Hint: use flattened toothpicks to take samples of the pigments.

2 Derive a systematic way of relating the colour produced to the proportions of primary pigments in the mixture.

3 Why can you not make white by mixing pigments?

Applications of mixing coloured pigments

Paints

The pigments are mixed together in various proportions to make an extremely wide range of coloured paints.

Pictures

The different shades of colours in pictures in magazines are built up of dots of primary pigments.

Printing

In the printing process to produce a book, the paper is sent four times through the printing machine. First it is printed using cyan, then magenta, and finally yellow. After the colours, the pages are printed with black.

Activity

Looking at pictures

1 Examine a coloured picture postcard or coloured picture from a magazine. List the different colours you can see: include colours such as light brown, beige, light yellow, and all the different shades of blue and green.

2 Now examine the picture with a hand lens. Explain what you see.

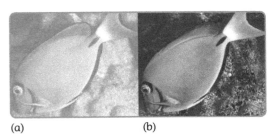

(a)   (b)

This picture has been printed in one colour in (a), and in two colours in (b). What colour(s) do you think were used to print (a) and to print (b)? What would be the effect of adding the third colour?

Practical 138

Does coloured ink contain different pigments? (ORR, MM, AI)

You will use a separation process called **chromatography**.

1 With a knife, cut a split in the underside of a cork that fits a boiling tube.

2 With clean dry hands and a sharp pair of scissors cut a rectangular strip of filter paper about 2 cm wide and 12 cm long. Draw two light pencil lines near one end of the paper 1 cm and 2 cm along. Make a light cross in the middle of the line 2 cm from the end (see diagram on the right).

3 Use a black felt-tip marker to put a tiny spot on the cross. Carefully build up a dense spot by allowing it to dry between applications so there is very little spread.

4 Insert the other end of the paper into the split cork (wedge it in if necessary). Try the cork and paper in the boiling tube to check the length. Adjust the length and width of the paper so that it touches neither side nor the bottom of the tube. Make a mark on the outside of the tube corresponding to the position of the ink spot.

5 Remove the cork and paper and place the solvent (e.g. alcohol–water mixture), from your teacher, into the boiling tube. It should be about 1 cm below the ink spot. Replace the cork and paper and keep the tube upright in a stand.

6 The solvent will rise steadily up the paper. When it nearly touches the cork, remove the paper and make a light pencil mark to show the final position of the solvent. Dry the paper using a fan.

7 How many colours do you see? Do you see different shades of the same colour? Why do you think the colours separated? (See also page 393.)

8 Compare the constituent colours with the original colour.

9 Do you think the results would be the same if other solvent mixtures were used? (You could repeat the process using a different solvent mixture, e.g. a water–acetic acid mixture, to find out.)

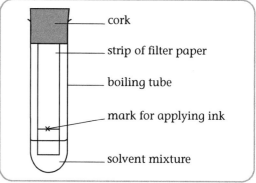

Apparatus for chromatography

Chromatography

Different coloured inks are chemically different substances, which are adsorbed differently to the filter paper. As the solvent rises up, it will push along each chemical substance at a different rate, thus spreading them along the paper.

A mixture containing colourless substances can be separated in the same way, but it will have to be 'developed' with chemical sprays to change the colourless substances into coloured ones.

Some uses of chromatography are:

● forensic work to identify blood samples
● dyeing to separate different pigments
● finding various amino acids in proteins.

Questions

1 Distinguish between (a) primary and secondary colours (light) and (b) primary and secondary colour pigments.

2 What is chromatography? How can it be used to distinguish between pigments?

Key ideas

Use these words to fill in the spaces as you write the sentences in your Exercise book.

solvent   red   pigments   blue   magenta   yellow

The primary pigment colours are cyan, _____ and _____ . The secondary pigment colours

(made by mixing the primary colours) are _____ , green and _____ . Chromatography is

used to separate the _____ in a mixture. In paper chromatography, the individual _____ are

pushed along at different rates by the _____ , so they can be separated and observed.

18 Fossil fuels and alternative sources of energy

18.1 How can we get energy from fuels?

The energy from the Sun, trapped in photosynthesis, is released when fuels (see page 25) are burnt in air. Fuels that were originally made from living things, long ago, we call **fossil fuels**.

Solid fuels

The most common solid fuel is **coal**, which is found in many parts of the world, such as the USA, China and Australia. The substance often called 'coal' in the Caribbean is **charcoal**, which is obtained from wood. If wood is heated in a limited supply of oxygen for a long time, charcoal is the solid produced. The photograph on the right shows charcoal being made. Another solid fuel is **peat**, found in Jamaica.

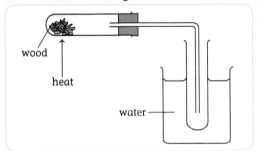
Cutting down trees to get wood for charcoal can have a big effect on the environment, if they are not replaced. The soil will be subject to erosion (see page 184). See what you can find out about the state of the environment in Haiti. Unless more trees are planted to replace those cut down, the environment becomes degraded.

Burning wood to make charcoal ('coal') to use as fuel

Liquid and gaseous fuels

Petroleum (crude oil) is a fossil fuel formed by the action of heat and pressure on the remains of small plants and animals in the earth. The process has taken up to 400 million years. Natural gas accumulates above the crude oil. There are important oil fields (which also contain natural gas) off the coast of Trinidad.

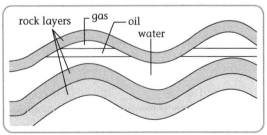

An anti-clinal trap: this is how oil forms under the ground

Practical 140

Do we need oxygen to burn things? (ORR, MM)

Oxygen makes up about 20% of the air by volume. You can prepare it as shown below.

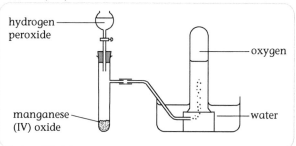

1 Collect four or five boiling tubes of oxygen. Seal each one with a cork or bung.

2 Investigate how materials such as splints and small candles burn in oxygen.

3 Your teacher will demonstrate what happens when magnesium is burnt in oxygen.

4 Record your observations in a table. Do you think that oxygen is necessary for burning? Explain.

Practical 141

What happens when we burn a fuel? (ORR, MM)

Do the following very carefully.

1 Put a *small* quantity of kerosene on a clean tin lid. Light the kerosene, and warm a test tube containing water in the resulting flame.

2 Repeat the same step with a *little* crude oil or diesel. Do the burning fuels release heat energy, and can this warm the water in the test tube?

3 What is the fuel in a Bunsen burner? How do you know it also releases energy when it burns?

Questions

1 Are there any fuel resources in your country? What are they? How much fuel does your country have to import each year?

2 Heat energy is produced in a car engine when fuel is burnt. What else is produced?

3 A candle flame may look similar to one type of flame produced by a Bunsen burner. Why?

4 Trace the flow of energy from the Sun to the production of electricity from the burning of coal.

Practical 142

How hot are the parts of Bunsen flames? (MM, ORR, D)

1 Light a Bunsen burner and adjust the air control so that there is little or no air being burnt in the gas. What is the shape and colour of the flame? How can you explain the nature of the flame based on the combustion of fuels?

2 Adjust the air control so that the input is at a maximum. What is the shape and colour of the flame? How do you explain the nature of the flame?

3 Draw diagrams of the two flames you have seen.

4 With the air supply at maximum, use tongs to hold a piece of wire gauze carefully in the tip of the flame. What do you observe?

5 Move the gauze carefully down until it is just touching the intense blue part of the flame. Then move the gauze slowly down towards the top of the burner.

6 What does this tell you about the heat energy in the different parts of the flame?

When fuels are fully burnt, a lot of heat energy is given out, e.g. for heating water. A useful application is in the generation of electricity (see page 299).

Key ideas

Use these words to fill in the spaces as you write the sentences in your Exercise book.

charcoal   **heat**   **fuels**   **fossil**   **coal**   **petroleum**

Gasoline and kerosene are examples of _____ . _____ has been formed from small plants and animals by the action of heat and pressure (over a long period of time): it is a _____ fuel.

_____ is formed when wood is burnt in a restricted supply of air (oxygen). When _____ are burnt, _____ energy is given out. _____ is an example of a solid _____ fuel.

18.2 Problems of using fossil fuels

What will happen when the fossil fuels run out?

We do not know how long the supplies of coal and crude oil will last. We need to use these fuels as efficiently as possible. We also have to develop alternative sources of energy, such as solar, wind and waves (see pages 322–5).

How does burning fuels affect the atmosphere?

Most of the products of burning fuels go into the atmosphere as gases. One of the most important of these is carbon dioxide. As fuels may contain elements such as sulphur, oxides of this element may be formed too. Nitrogen oxides are also formed when fuels are burnt in air. These gases are harmful to our health (see page 81), particularly if they are present in high concentrations as in some cities such as Los Angeles and Mexico City.

What is the impact of various forms of transport?

The internal combustion engine is used in cars, buses and trucks. The fuel, either gasoline or diesel, is burnt in a cylinder and the heat energy produced is converted to mechanical energy, which drives the vehicle.

Activity

Different methods of transport

1 Working in small groups, record how many students use each kind of transport to get to and from school.
2 Combine the information for the class.
3 Make a list of *all* the types of transport used in your country. Record this in a table, with the type of engine (if any), and the fuel used in each case.
4 Find out how important cars, buses and trucks are in your country: for example, you may be able to find the total numbers registered. If there is a public transport system, find out how much it is used.
5 Try to find out and record the total amount of money spent each year for importing fuel into your country. What is this fuel used for?
6 Try to find out how many people travel to your country by air and by sea each month.

Most forms of transport (except walking and cycling) need an engine, and this requires fuel. Cars usually carry relatively few passengers (one to five perhaps), whereas buses can carry large numbers. A public transport system using buses can be efficient, because large numbers of people can be carried in one vehicle. This helps to reduce the amount of polluting gases entering the atmosphere.

Objectives

- Discuss some of the problems associated with the use of fossil fuels.
- Describe fossil fuels as non-renewable resources, and the environmental effects of acid rain and global warming.

Questions

1 What are the polluting gases formed when fossil fuels are burnt? Outline the effect of these gases.
2 How would you try to measure the impact of exhaust gases from vehicles on your local environment?
3 What are the benefits of an efficient public transport system?

What does it mean?

Non-renewable A fuel that has taken so long to form that we cannot expect the source to be renewed, e.g. crude oil.

Renewable A fuel or energy source that can be renewed and continue to be available, e.g. wood and solar energy.

Alternative source A fuel or energy source other than fossil fuels. It is a renewable source.

Activity

Energy resources

1 Prepare a table of various fuels, with the source of each one; e.g. gasoline comes from crude oil (petroleum).
2 Identify any renewable fuels.
3 How many fuels are non-renewable?
4 What might happen if we go on using non-renewable energy sources?

What is acid rain?

Normal rain has a pH of about 5 due to the presence of carbonic acid (dissolved carbon dioxide). Acid rain occurs when there are oxides of sulphur and nitrogen in the atmosphere; these react with air and water to form acids, such as sulphuric and nitric acids.

The pH of the rain can be as low as 2. Much of the acid rain is caused by burning sulphur-containing coal in power stations. The use of very tall stacks at the power stations has meant that the gases and particles are distributed more widely than before. The parts of the world so far affected by acid rain include Europe (particularly Scandinavia), the USA and Canada.

In lakes where the pH has been lowered by acid rain, fish may be badly affected. For example, at a pH lower than 5, most fish eggs will not hatch. Forests can be badly affected too, with trees not growing properly.

What is global warming?

It has been estimated that the average temperature of the surface of the Earth increased by about 0.75 °C during the 20th century. It seems likely that this change was mainly caused by an increase in 'greenhouse gases'. These affect the way in which radiation enters or leaves the Earth's atmosphere (see the lower diagram on the right).

The most important greenhouse gases are carbon dioxide, methane, water vapour and ozone. The gases are formed by the burning of fossil fuels and the decay process at landfill sites. The increase in average temperature during the 21st century may be as high as 6 °C. In order to try to slow down the increase in temperature, many governments agreed to the Kyoto Protocol, in which targets were set to reduce greenhouse gases. This protocol expires in 2012, so a new agreement is needed. The main effects of global warming include:

- melting of glaciers and sea ice
- a rise in sea level
- an expansion of deserts
- increased intensity of events such as hurricanes.

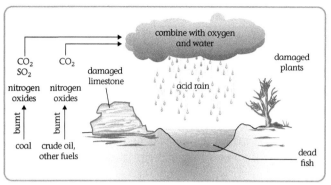

How acid rain is formed

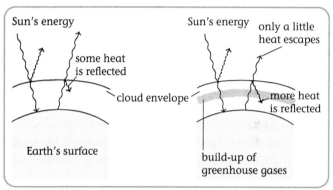

The greenhouse effect: more heat is reflected to Earth, causing global warming

Questions

4 What gases contribute to (a) acid rain and (b) the greenhouse effect? Why is global cooperation needed to help solve these problems?

5 Give three reasons why it is important to limit the use of crude oil as an energy source.

6 What might be the effect of global warming on (a) very low-lying states in the Pacific and (b) islands in the Caribbean?

Key ideas

Use these words to fill in the spaces as you write the sentences in your Exercise book.

acid   **global**   **greenhouse**   **fossil**   **sulphur**   **non-renewable**

We need to use our _____ fuels and energy resources carefully. Crude oil is a _____ _____ fuel. When it is burnt it produces carbon dioxide (a _____ gas) that contributes to _____ warming, and oxides of nitrogen and _____ , which are the main causes of _____ rain. The Kyoto Protocol is about the reduction of _____ gases.

18.3 What are some alternatives to fossil fuels?

Why do we need alternatives?

- The development of the internal combustion engine has meant that we need vast quantities of petroleum.
- Similarly, our demand for energy in factories and homes has meant the use of a great deal of coal (and liquid fuel) for generating electricity (see page 299).
- These non-renewable energy sources cannot last forever. Some of the sources (e.g. crude oil in the North Sea) may not last long into the present century.
- Petroleum has many other uses, as well as being important as a source of fuels (see diagram on the right).
- In addition, there are the pollution problems with acid rain and the greenhouse gases (see page 321).

There is now broad agreement that we need to reduce our greenhouse gas emissions, by 2050, to a level 50% lower than in 2005. If this is so, and we are to continue to travel and make many different things in factories, we will still need large amounts of energy. Now, we should be looking for alternative, renewable sources of energy, so that we can continue using them without depleting the Earth. The sources briefly described below are already being used in many countries – some in the Caribbean.

Solar energy

Uses of solar energy are discussed on pages 326–9.

Biofuels

These can be solid, liquid or gas. They are obtained from recently living biological matter. A good example is agro-fuels, which are obtained from specific crops.

- **Ethanol** is made from the fermentation of sugar cane. This is produced on a large scale in Brazil. The ethanol is then mixed with gasoline and used in cars. Ethanol can also be produced from cellulose, e.g. from grasses.
- **Vegetable oils**, e.g. from plants high in oil, can be used directly in engines, and oils produced from algae.
- **Wood** and **bagasse** (from sugar production) are also biofuels.

Biogas

There is a lot of dead and waste material (**biomass**), including waste from humans and animals. This can be used to produce biogas, by fermentation in the absence of oxygen by anaerobic bacteria. Biogas is a mixture of methane and carbon dioxide and it is used as a fuel. Or it can be burnt and the energy released can be used for generating electricity. The remaining waste can be removed and used as a fertilizer.

Objective

- Identify alternative sources of energy, including solar, biofuels, biogas, biodiesel, wind, waves, geothermal, hydroelectricity and nuclear.

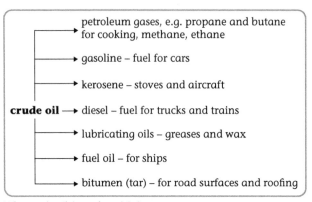

Why crude oil (petroleum) is important

- petroleum gases, e.g. propane and butane for cooking, methane, ethane
- gasoline – fuel for cars
- kerosene – stoves and aircraft
- **crude oil** → diesel – fuel for trucks and trains
- lubricating oils – greases and wax
- fuel oil – for ships
- bitumen (tar) – for road surfaces and roofing

Questions

1 If a food crop is grown and then used for producing a fuel, what might be the consequences for future food supplies?

2 How are biofuels, biogas and biodiesel (a) similar and (b) different? List one advantage and one disadvantage of using each of them.

3 How is solar energy involved in producing (a) the wind and (b) waves?

4 As many Caribbean islands have an Atlantic coast, how could wave energy be useful for them?

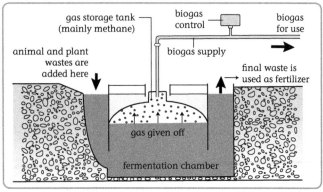

Section through a biogas fermenter

Biodiesel

Diesel fuel is produced from petroleum (by fractional distillation). It is used as a fuel in lorries and trains. When it is used properly, the greenhouse gas emissions are lower than those of a vehicle using gasoline.

Biodiesel is better still. This is produced by a process called transesterification, starting from a vegetable or animal fat. Biodiesel can be used in standard diesel engines. In Europe, starting materials include sunflower oil and rapeseed oil.

Wind energy

Windmills were used in the past, on a large scale throughout the Caribbean, to provide most of the energy needed to produce sugar from cane. The energy supplied by the wind was converted to kinetic energy to grind and press the cane. Small-scale wind turbines can now be used to provide energy for domestic purposes.

Winds (see page 165) are a renewable energy resource, driven by energy from the Sun. There are many parts of the world where there is, on average, a fairly high wind speed. Where this is so, it is possible to develop a wind farm, in which turbines are used to generate electricity (see the diagram on the right). This may be used on site or fed into the National grid. The kinetic energy of the wind turns the turbine, which then turns the generator so that electricity is produced.

Wave energy

The destructive energy of waves can be seen on the coastline of any country that has suffered from a hurricane. Even under normal conditions, the eroding effect of wave energy can be seen along our coastlines.

Waves transfer energy, as you may have found out while swimming in the sea. This, mainly kinetic, energy can be used for generating electricity. There are a number of different approaches to this, with various different designs being tested. The diagram on the right shows the rising of the waves pushing moving air through a turbine, which then turns the generator to produce electricity. The first major installation was undertaken in Portugal.

Tidal energy

This is different from making use of waves. To make use of tides, barriers (barrages) are built across the mouth of a wide river. At high tide, water is trapped behind the barrage, and, when it is released at low tide, the moving water can drive turbines to generate electricity.

However, building the barrage is expensive, can damage the environment by flooding, and stops free access for shipping. Using tidal energy is also not very useful in the Caribbean, where the differences between high and low tides are usually small.

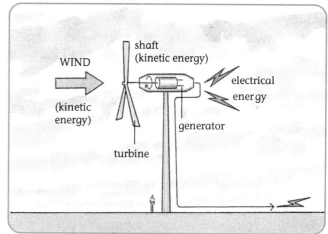

Inside a wind turbine: as the vanes turn, kinetic energy is changed to electricity

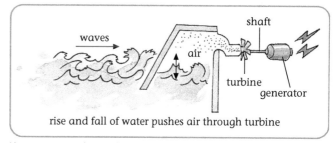

How waves can be used to generate electricity

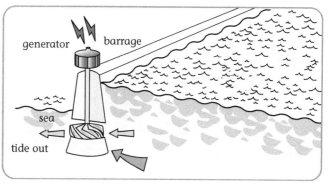

How tides can be used to generate electricity

18.3 What are some alternatives to fossil fuels? (continued)

Geothermal energy

'Geo' means 'from the Earth' and 'thermal' means 'heat'. So geothermal means 'heat energy from the Earth'. Rocks inside the Earth are very hot (see page 198), partly from the decay of radioactive materials such as uranium. There are places on Earth where the crust is relatively thin, and in these places humans can make use of the underground energy source.

- Water seeps down to deeper parts of the Earth and is then (super) heated to steam under pressure, which spurts out as a **geyser**. This is usually associated with volcanic activity. The heated steam can be captured and used to generate electricity. This has been used in Guadeloupe and is also being developed for Dominica and Nevis.
- Another method can be used in non-volcanic areas. It is possible to bore very deep holes and pump cold water down to the hot rocks underneath. The heat changes the water to steam, which comes gushing out. This is used to turn a turbine and generator to produce electricity. However, there is a very large initial cost for boring the holes and setting up the power station.

Hydroelectricity

Water is raised from the sea and lakes by evaporation to form clouds. Water vapour condenses and falls as rain, to produce streams and rivers. The water can be collected into a dam for storing water. Water travels down through large pipes, and the potential energy of the water is converted to kinetic energy. This is used to turn turbines and generators, which produce electricity. As long as there is sufficient water in the dam, this is a renewable source of energy. There are examples of the use of hydroelectricity in Dominica, Jamaica and St Vincent. The biggest producer in the Caribbean at present is the Dominican Republic. You could find out if there are any plans for your country to make use of hydroelectricity. What would be the costs, and the benefits?

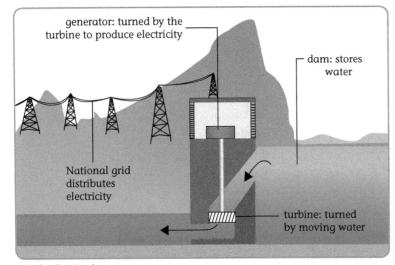

A hydroelectric plant

Superheated steam forms a geyser. The steam could be captured in pipes and used in a power station to generate electricity

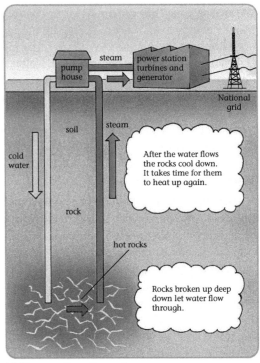

Making use of geothermal energy

Generating electricity

Many alternative sources of energy are used to generate electricity. Moving water or steam is used to turn a turbine and then a generator (see below and page 299).

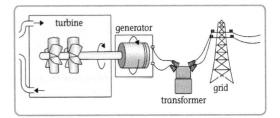

Nuclear energy

This is the energy that binds nuclear particles together. Nuclear energy is the most concentrated form of energy known. In this type of energy, matter is converted directly into energy according to Einstein's equation $e = mc^2$, where e = energy, m = mass and c = universal constant (speed of light). The universal constant, c, is a very large number. Thus, an extremely large amount of energy is produced from a relatively small amount of matter. This is a possible alternative energy resource, but is non-renewable, as radioactive substances could be used up.

- **Nuclear fission** In this type of nuclear reaction, a radioactive substance such as uranium can be bombarded with neutrons and made to disintegrate. Each uranium atom releases two neutrons, which then cause the disintegration of further uranium atoms, and so on. The uranium forms simpler elements and releases an enormous amount of energy. The rate of energy release is controlled in a nuclear power station, and used to heat water into steam. This is then used to generate electricity.
- **Nuclear fusion** In this type of nuclear reaction, the nuclei of atoms of one element, e.g. hydrogen, fuse together to make a different element. This takes place in the Sun, and in hydrogen bombs, and releases even more energy. But there are no fusion reactors to date.

How can we make more effective use of alternative energy sources?

There are many examples across the Caribbean of relatively small-scale uses of renewable energy sources. One of the major problems facing most governments now is the cost of imported fuel. If the predictions of most experts are correct, this cost is likely to go up in future years, as the price of crude oil is expected to increase. This in turn will increase the cost of fuels and therefore the costs of transport and generating electricity. It is often costly to start using a renewable energy source. Governments often need to provide financial support to assist the process.

In small groups, discuss the setting up of a project to make use of an alternative energy source in your country. Consider which source to use, and the economic and environmental costs.

Pros and cons of nuclear energy

- A gram of nuclear fuel can produce over a million times more energy than a gram of any ordinary fuel. It can therefore be used to help alleviate the world's energy problems. That is why, despite the remote possible potential dangers of nuclear energy, e.g. radioactive leakage, there are over 400 nuclear power stations in 25 countries generating 17% of the world's electricity.
- The use of nuclear energy instead of coal reduces the emissions of carbon dioxide by 1600 million tonnes, tens of thousands of toxic heavy metals (arsenic, cadmium, lead, mercury) and extremely large quantities of sulphur and nitrogen oxides, the causes of acid rain.
- Nuclear power stations are deemed to be extremely safe because of the high level of safety controls instituted.
- However, the satisfactory disposal of nuclear waste products continues to be a problem. How, where and in what containers, should waste be disposed of, to prevent seepage and contamination of water supplies?

Questions

1 Where could (a) geothermal and (b) hydroelectricity be explored and used?

2 How do you assess the pros and cons of using nuclear energy?

3 (a) Research and find out the total fuel import bill of your country. What is the cost of a unit (kWh) of electricity?
(b) What is being done about increasing the use of alternative energy sources?

Key ideas

Use these words to fill in the spaces as you write the sentences in your Exercise book.

wind   **hydroelectricity**   **geothermal**   **energy**   **renewable**   **fossil**

We need to find alternatives to non-renewable _____ fuels. Solar _____ and biofuels are examples of _____ energy. _____ makes use of the kinetic _____ of moving water to generate electricity. Energy from superheated steam is the basis of _____ energy. _____ energy might be an energy source along the Atlantic coasts of Caribbean islands.

18.4 How can we use solar energy?

How is the Sun's energy useful today?

One of the major demands for energy worldwide is for domestic use, mainly for heating: for cooking and hot water. Because of the high price of oil, and pollution problems, more and more attention is being paid to the direct use of solar energy. Solar energy is abundant in the Caribbean, and also trouble-free and dependable. You can also make some models (see page 394).

How does the solar water heating system work?

The system consists of a collector and a storage tank. The system in the picture on the right is called a thermo-siphon system because the water circulates by convection currents.

● The collector is an insulated box with a glass cover. Infrared rays pass through the glass and cause a heating effect on the black copper pipes. Water passes through these pipes and absorbs the heat.

● The storage tank is usually a steel tank lined with glass to prevent rusting, and it is strong enough to withstand the water pressure. The tank is insulated on the outside with, for example, glass wool or polyurethane foam. The tank is connected at two points to the collector.

Objectives

● Discuss the uses of solar energy.
● Discuss the variables affecting solar energy transfer.
● Assess the extent to which solar energy can be used as an alternative source of energy.

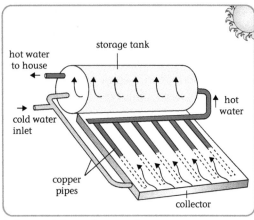

A thermo-siphon solar water heater

● Water in the collector becomes less dense as it heats up; it rises into the storage tank, which is above the level of the collector.

● At the same time, cooler water flows from the bottom of the tank to the collector again. This system does not require any external source of power to circulate the water. However, the tank needs to be placed higher than the collector for the system to work. If the tank is placed at a lower level, an electrically driven pump must be installed to provide the circulation.

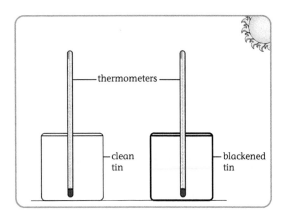

Practical 143

Using the heating effect of the Sun (MM, ORR, AI)

1 Get two identical clean tin cans with a capacity of 250–500 cm³. Tins originally used for condensed milk or fruit juice would be best, as they still have their tops.

2 Widen the holes in the top, just enough to let in water and flush out residues. Remove any paper labels and blacken one tin over a candle flame or a sooty yellow Bunsen flame.

3 Put equal volumes of tap water in each tin and place them in the Sun. The temperatures should be equal at the start.

4 Measure and record the temperature of both lots of water every 5 minutes.

5 Plot your results on a graph with time on the horizontal axis and temperature on the vertical axis. Plot your graph while the experiment is in progress, so you can decide when to stop.

6 Can you explain why the curves are different? Why did you choose to stop the experiment when you did?

7 As options to the design:
   ● use similar tins but use a different radiant heat source, e.g. a 100 watt bulb or electric fire
   ● vary the containers, e.g. use white and black film containers, and leave half with and half without their lids.

8 Try to explain all your findings.

Heat is transferred by radiation, conduction and convection (see pages 164–5). How are these involved in a solar water heater, and your model using tins?

- Solar energy is transferred by radiation. For best results the collector of the solar water heater must be fully exposed to solar radiation. Overcast, cloudy skies and shade diminish its ability to function at full capacity.
- A small amount of heat is lost by reflection at the glass surface and due to re-radiation from the collector.
- Most of the radiant energy passes through glass before being absorbed by the blackened metal pipes inside. (You have seen from your practical that a blackened surface is best at absorbing radiation.)
- Heat then travels by conduction through the metal to the water inside. Copper is used for the pipes, as it is a very good conductor of heat.
- Convection is the main method of heat transfer in the water itself, because water is a poor conductor of heat. Convection is efficient in the small tins you used, but a strong current flow is needed for an efficient hot water system. In the thermo-siphon system, two important conditions are needed: (1) a significant temperature difference between the water in the storage tank and water in the collector; and (2) the head (height) difference in water between the storage tank and the collector.
- Except on weekends, probably the greatest demand for hot water is in the morning. This is water that would have been heated the day before (unless supplementary heating by electricity was employed). It is therefore very important that the storage tank is properly insulated in order to minimize heat loss.

Solar still

The Sun's energy in the form of heat can be used to produce pure water from tap or seawater in a solar still. A simple type consists of a box containing water under a clear glass top to let the sunlight in. The bottom of the box is blackened to absorb heat. As the water is heated, vapour condenses on the slightly cooler glass top and drops run down the sloping surface into a container.

List all the parts that make up a solar still. Suggest materials to use for making each part, which would make the still most efficient. Then list and describe all the processes involved in the production of the distilled water.

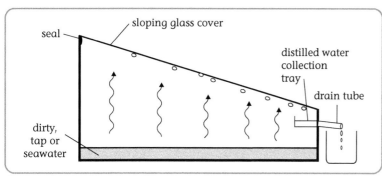

Cross-section of a box solar still

A water solar heater in use

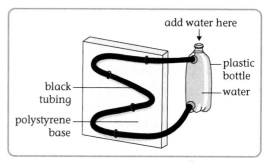

An improvised solar water heater: describe how it works, and how it could be improved

Did you know?

- The solar energy that reaches the Earth each year is more than 10,000 times greater than all our energy needs.
- It would take 167,000 nuclear power stations to produce as much energy as the Sun radiates to Earth each day.

Questions

1 In the solar water heater system, how important is the location of the collector in relation to the storage tank? Why?

2 In the afternoon, you take some water from the cold tap to drink. However, you find it is warm. How can you explain this?

3 How are (a) radiation, (b) conduction and (c) convection important in a solar water heater?

4 How is the solar still (a) similar to and (b) different from the production of distilled water using a condenser (see page 214)?

18.4 How can we use solar energy? (continued)

Solar drier

The Sun's energy has always been used for drying and preserving foodstuffs: meat, fish, tobacco and fruits (see page 232). The solar drier is an improvement on traditional methods.

A simple system would be a glass-covered box containing stones or bricks, with a shelf where materials for drying are placed. The stones absorb the Sun's heat during the day and release their heat to circulating air, which dries the foodstuff.

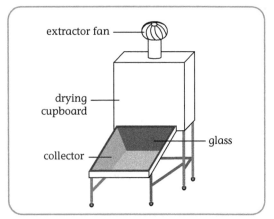

Indirect solar drier used to dry products that should not be exposed to direct sunlight: the collector is covered in glass, and hot air circulates up into the drying cupboard

Practical 144

Making a solar drier (PD, MM, ORR, AI)

- Your group is to design and make a solar water drier. You should compare the drying effect of your system with similar amounts of food left uncovered, and in plastic bags.

- Decide how to keep the food items from pests, and how you will measure how well each condition dries the food.

- Carry out your investigation, make your measurements, and report and explain your findings.

- How could you improve your system?

An improved version of a solar drier is shown in the diagram on the right, where materials sensitive to sunlight can be kept in a drying cupboard. Hot air from the collector is drawn through the cupboard by convection, to dry the contents. The air circulation can be assisted by an extractor fan.

Solar cooker

We can also focus the solar energy to produce a heating effect.

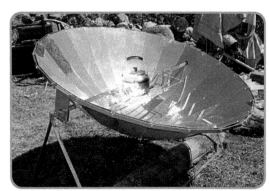

A solar cooker with a parabolic mirror: the water or food to be heated is placed where heat energy is focused. In this way the Sun's heat rays can be directly used to heat the water or food

Practical 145

Collecting solar energy (MM, PD)

- Use a concave (shaving) mirror to focus the Sun's rays. Compare this with the heat produced by using a magnifying glass of similar size.

- Can you design an efficient solar energy collector using aluminium foil? How will you decide if you have been successful? Compare and evaluate different class designs.

You will notice that the Sun's rays are brought to a focus by a concave mirror as they are with a convex lens. A large mirror is much lighter and easier to make than the corresponding lens, so a collector such as a curved mirror is the best way of obtaining high temperatures from sunlight. This is the principle of the solar cooker. The solar cooker has a parabolic mirror. This is a concave mirror with a special shape to focus the rays at a point. A similar shape is used in headlamps and dish aerials (see pages 344–5).

Questions

1 (a) What is the reason for drying foodstuffs? (b) Why is it useful to use a solar drier?

2 How are (a) radiation, (b) conduction and (c) convection important in a solar drier?

3 (a) Why does a solar cooker have a shiny surface and not a blackened one? (b) Why is the shape of the cooker important?

Can the Sun produce electricity directly?

The energy in sunlight can be turned directly into electrical energy by **photovoltaic** (PV) cells. These are also called **solar cells**, and they can be arranged together in a solar panel. Although their efficiency is low, they are robust and reliable and especially useful as a source of electrical energy in remote places away from power lines, and in space exploration.

One type of PV cell is made from two very thin layers of silicon, which are semi-conductors (see page 291). The two layers of silicon are treated to give them special properties, which enable them to transfer electrons and thus behave in a similar way to a dry cell (see page 298) to produce electricity. Light particles (photons) from the Sun striking the layers dislodge electrons from the material's atoms, causing a current to flow and so produce electricity.

Photovoltaic cells, because of their expense, were at first used mainly in space, to supply energy in the solar panels of satellites. Research and development in recent times have seen a vast improvement in efficiency as well as a decrease in production costs. They have many uses, for example in solar-powered calculators and cars.

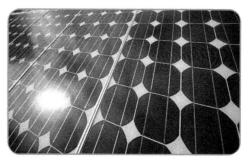
A photovoltaic unit of silicon cells encased in a frame

A solar panel generating electricity for a water pump

What does it cost to heat water electrically?

The use of photovoltaic arrays to supplement electrical supplies awaits a significant reduction in costs and increase in efficiency. Meanwhile, the use of solar water heaters comes within the reach of those aspiring and able to raise their standard of living.

Rough calculations show that an electrically powered heater, with a capacity of 250 litres per day producing water at 60°C, consumes about 10 kW h (units) of electricity. As an example, for Barbados, in 2009, this is approximately equivalent to US$900.00 per year. With the tax incentives often given, this is about half the price of a new solar water heater. Then there are no more bills for the heating of water. This means that the initial outlay, the capital cost for the solar heater, would easily be paid back in less than 3 years.

Questions

4 How does the rising price of crude oil affect the relative merits of installing a solar water heater?

5 How are solar cells used?

6 What developments are needed to make photovoltaic panels a commonplace source of electrical energy?

7 Prepare a table to compare fossil fuels, and four alternative sources of energy discussed in this topic. How are the sources different in their origin, initial costs, polluting effect on the environment and potential dangers for humans?

Key ideas

Use these words to fill in the spaces as you write the sentences in your Exercise book.

| efficient | convection | photovoltaic | solar | radiation | collector |

The solar water heater demonstrates three methods of heat transfer: _____ , conduction and

_____ ; to make best use of _____ the storage tank should be higher than the _____ .

_____ cells make use of the Sun's _____ to generate electricity directly; they are also called

_____ cells and will be used more when they become cheaper and more _____ .

19 Machines and movement

19.1 How are levers useful?

A machine does *not* reduce the overall work, but it does help us to do a job more conveniently, e.g. using a pulley to raise a load. It may also help us to do jobs we could not otherwise do ourselves, e.g. shift a heavy boulder with a crowbar, or do them more neatly, e.g. cut with a pair of scissors (also see page 395).

There are several kinds of mechanical machine, which work by using forces (pushes and pulls). The forces may be applied by humans, or with the help of electrical energy.

The lever as a machine

Levers are rigid bars with a pivot or turning point (**fulcrum**). A force is applied to the lever (as **effort**), to move a mass (the **load**). The principle behind using a lever is similar to that of balancing a seesaw, or a metre stick (see pages 354 and 398).

From the investigation with the ruler (Practical 146), you will find how a small mass (exerting a small force) can balance a larger mass (with its larger force). Small forces can balance or overcome larger forces. The key is to alter the distance through which the force is acting. You can show this by doing the following practical.

Force multipliers

The lever is arranged so that we can move a load by using less effort than the weight of the load, but we have to exert it over a longer distance. The effort is applied further from the fulcrum than the load is in class 1 and 2 levers.

Class 1 lever: the **fulcrum** is between the **effort** and the **load**. It is a force multiplier.

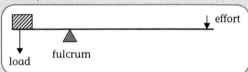

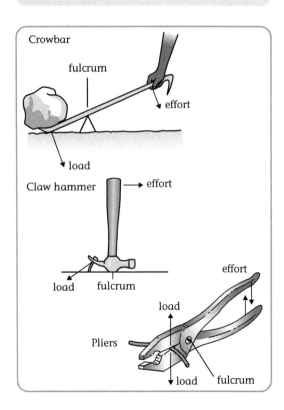

Practical 146

How does a lever work? (ORR)

1. Lie a wooden 30 cm ruler unevenly on top of a hexagonal pencil.

2. Attach a block of modelling clay as a load on the shorter side of the ruler.

3. Add standard masses at the position marked A in the diagram below, and record how many are needed to lift the load.

4. Repeat step 3, at positions B and C.

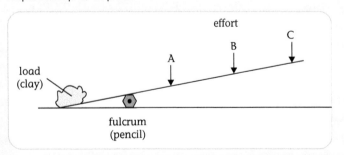

5. Compare the numbers of standard masses needed in each position to lift the load. How does the distance from the pivot (fulcrum) at which you add the masses (apply the force) affect how easily you can lift the load? How is this similar to a small child balancing a larger one on a seesaw?

Class 2 lever: the **fulcrum** is at one end, the **effort** is at the other end and the **load** is in between. It is a force multiplier.

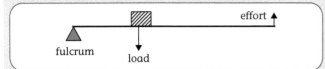

Distance multipliers

In a distance multiplier, the effort is nearer to the fulcrum than the load is. This means that we need to exert an effort that is greater than the force of the load, but over a shorter distance: class 3 lever.

Class 3 lever: the **fulcrum** and the **load** are at opposite ends, with the **effort** in between. It is a distance multiplier.

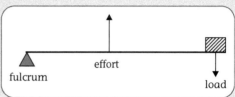

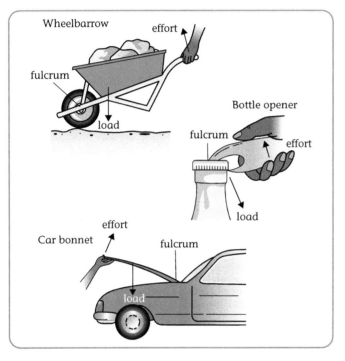

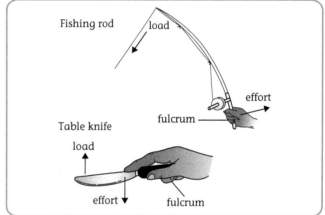

The law of the lever

This states that: the force (in newtons) times distance (in metres) on the effort side must be equal to the force (in newtons) times distance (in metres) on the load side.

$$f_1 \times d_1 = f_2 \times d_2$$

We can use this equation to find out if a lever system is a force or distance multiplier.

Questions

1 Suggest some other class 1, 2 and 3 levers not mentioned in the text.
2 What is meant by (a) force multipliers and (b) distance multipliers?
3 Explain the 'law of the lever'.

Key ideas

Use these words and numbers to fill in the spaces as you write the sentences in your Exercise book.

distance   **load**   **force**   **1**   **3**   **2**   **lever**   **fulcrum**   **convenient**

A machine makes work more _____ . A _____ is a length of rigid bar that is used to apply a _____ to another object. In a _____ multiplier, the effort is further from the _____ than the _____ is: class _____ and _____ levers. In a _____ multiplier, the effort is closer to the _____ than the load is: class _____ levers.

19.2 Are there levers in the human body?

Animals need to move from place to place to search for food, to escape predators and to find a mate. To do this they use a system of levers and muscles.

The framework of the human body that allows movement is the skeleton.

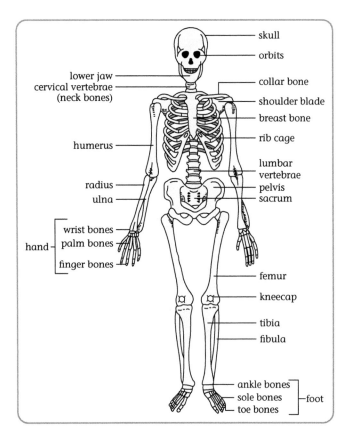

Using the skeleton for movement

- **Bone** This tissue makes up most of the skeleton, and is strong, hard and rigid. It makes up the long bones in the legs and arms, which have to be rigid to be used as levers.
- **Cartilage** This is a flexible tissue, which forms a protective layer at the ends of the bones. It acts as a shock absorber as the bones move.
- **Joints** This is where bones meet, and many of them allow for movement. There are different kinds.
- **Tendons** attach **muscles** to the bones. Muscles contract to produce the effort needed to make bones move.

Questions

1 For a named joint in the human body, identify the (a) fulcrum, (b) effort and (c) load.
2 Describe in detail how a named joint works.
3 How do we walk?

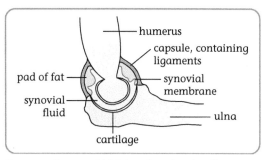

Structure of a synovial joint, as found at the elbow, knee, shoulder and hip joints

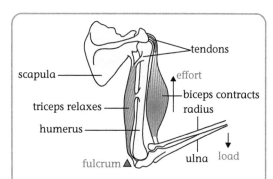

(a) The arm is raised when the biceps muscle contracts and the triceps relaxes

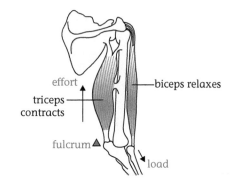

(b) The arm is lowered when the triceps muscle contracts and the biceps relaxes

Levers in the human body

Class 1: fulcrum is between effort and load, e.g. balancing the head on the top of the backbone.

Class 2: load is between fulcrum and effort, e.g. standing on tiptoe.

Class 3: effort is between fulcrum and load, e.g. raising and lowering the arm, and moving the jaws.

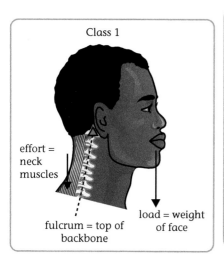

Class 1

effort = neck muscles

fulcrum = top of backbone

load = weight of face

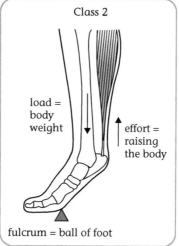

Class 2

load = body weight

effort = raising the body

fulcrum = ball of foot

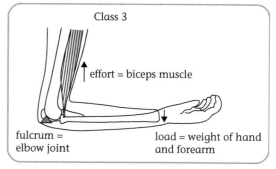

Class 3

effort = biceps muscle

fulcrum = elbow joint

load = weight of hand and forearm

Examples of levers in the human body

Action at a joint

Effort

A muscle is attached, by tendons, to at least two bones. The effort for movement is the contraction of the muscle, which pulls the bones together. Muscles are often in pairs, and when one contracts, the other one relaxes, e.g. the biceps and triceps in the arm.

Fulcrum

The fulcrum is the pivot or joint about which movement occurs, e.g. the elbow joint. The synovial fluid lubricates the joint.

Load

The load is the weight of the body itself being moved or lifted, or of something that is held by the body and lifted up. In the arm, a class 3 lever, a greater effort must always be expended by the muscle than the weight of the load that is being moved. This allows the muscle to exert its effect through a greater distance. You can make a model of a joint; see page 395.

Questions

4 Calculate the force the biceps exerts to lift a kg bag of sugar.

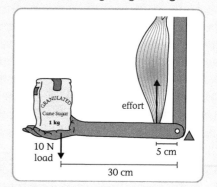

GRANULATED Cane Sugar 1 kg

effort

10 N load

5 cm

30 cm

Use the law of the lever: $f_1d_1 = f_2d_2$

Is the force of the effort more or less than the load? Which class of lever is the arm?

Key ideas

Use these words to fill in the spaces as you write the sentences in your Exercise book.

elbow　　**load**　　**muscles**　　**bones**　　**effort**　　**joints**　　**lever**

The human skeleton is made up of _____ that meet at _____ . An example of a joint is

the _____ joint. The arm is a class 3 _____ , with the _____ (fulcrum) between the muscle

(_____) and the weight (_____). Movement of part of the body occurs as one of the _____

of a pair contracts to pull the _____ closer together.

19.3 How do machines make work easier?

Besides levers, there are other machines that can make work easier. They include the inclined plane (and the wedge and screw), wheel and axle, gears and the hydraulic press, and pulleys (see page 336).

These machines make work easier by allowing a load to be moved by a smaller effort. This relationship is described mathematically as:

load/effort = mechanical advantage (MA)

Example
What is the MA of a machine that exerts an effort of 200 N and overcomes a load of 1000 N?

$$MA = \frac{load}{effort} = \frac{1000}{200} = 5$$

> The larger the mechanical advantage, the easier the machine makes doing work, but the longer the distance over which the effort must be applied.

The inclined plane

The diagram on the top right shows two men loading a truck using an inclined plane (a ramp that is higher at one end than the other). Using the inclined plane is a lot easier than lifting a very heavy box by hand directly into the truck through the distance (height, h). Note that, overall, the same amount of work is done (ignoring the friction of the rollers), when the box is pushed through the longer distance, s, of the inclined plane. For the inclined plane, the mechanical advantage is the length of the inclined plane, s, divided by its vertical height, h.

The wedge

The wedge is also an inclined plane. It is like two inclined planes joined together. In the diagram in the middle right, it is being used in the form of a chisel to split a log. E = effort (banging on the wedge), L = load (log being split). The thickness of the wedge is an important consideration. The principle of the wedge can also be applied to the cutting edges of knives, swords and razor blades. Can you explain this connection?

The screw

The screw is also an inclined plane. In the diagram on the bottom right, it is used as a car jack, which is essentially a long screw carrying a nut. The nut is joined to a steel bar, which supports the load of the car when the jack is in use. When the long nut is turned, e.g. one revolution, using the short steel bar (called a tommy bar), the car is raised a very small distance, which is equal to the pitch of the screw, and this is not usually more than 2 or 3 mm in height. But, by using the car jack, one person is able to raise the side of the car, which they could not do otherwise.

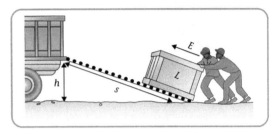
Using an inclined plane

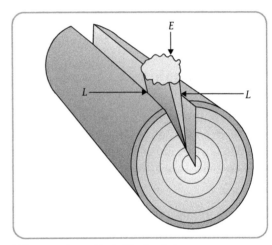
Using a wedge, a kind of inclined plane

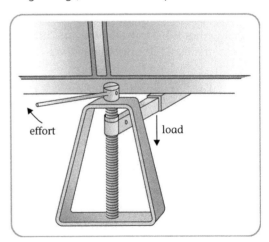
Using a screw, a car jack. The same principles apply here as for the inclined plane (above). A relatively small force is applied over a long circular distance to raise a very large weight through a very small distance. This process is repeated several times until the car has reached sufficient height off the ground

The wheel and axle

Various applications of the wheel and axle are shown. In each case, effort is applied through a relatively large circular motion (wheel) to overcome a heavier load, which moves through a proportionally smaller distance.

Wheels, connected in pairs by the metal rods, axles, are also used on vehicles. Again, the outsides of the wheels move a long distance, whereas the heavy vehicle makes a small forward movement.

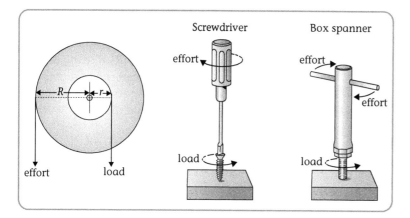

The mechanical advantage of a wheel and axle can be calculated from the equation:

$$MA = \frac{load}{effort} \quad \text{or} \quad MA = \frac{\text{radius of wheel}}{\text{radius of axle}}$$

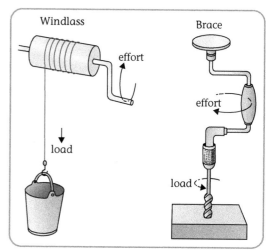

Gear wheels

Wheels with cuts in their outer rim are called **gears** (see the diagram on the right). When the teeth of two gears are meshed together, one gear can turn the other. If each of the gear wheels is connected to a shaft, then one gear can supply the effort while the other can be the load, thus getting the same advantage as the wheel and axle.

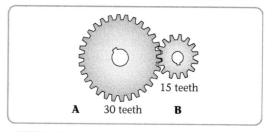

A 30 teeth B 15 teeth

Hydraulic press

This is used, for example, in the brake system of vehicles. It uses the pressure of a fluid to gain a mechanical advantage. When the foot brake in the vehicle is pushed down, it pushes a large piston against the brake fluid, which is in a closed system of pipes. The pressure on the fluid is transferred to smaller wheel pistons, which are then pushed outwards to exert a greater pressure on the brake shoes. The brake shoes make contact with a revolving brake drum, which is attached to the wheels, reducing their movement, and thus slowing down or bringing the vehicle to a stop.

Questions

1 (a) In the gear wheels shown above, if gear **A** is turned clockwise, in which direction does gear **B** turn? (b) When the larger wheel makes five revolutions, how many will the smaller wheel make?

2 Why is a screw a simple machine?

3 What is mechanical advantage? How can you work it out (a) for an inclined plane and (b) for a wheel and axle?

Key ideas

Use these words to fill in the spaces as you write the sentences in your Exercise book.

load   gears   mechanical   circular   smaller   effort

_____ advantage is _____ divided by effort. The larger the _____ advantage, the easier the machine makes doing work. Wheels with cuts in their outer rims are called _____ . In a wheel and axle, _____ is applied through a relatively large _____ motion (wheel) to overcome a _____ , which moves through a proportionally _____ distance.

19.4 How efficient are machines?

How do we use pulleys? (MM, ORR, AI)

1 Suspend a 1 kg mass from a spring balance calibrated in newtons (N). What is the weight (in N) of the 1 kg mass?

2 Make your own pulley, as in (a) below, from empty cotton reels or spools. Use your pulley to raise the mass of 1 kg by pulling on the spring balance, as shown in (a). When the mass is not moving it is balanced by the pull on the spring balance (i.e. it is in equilibrium). What is the force in newtons? What is the force when the mass is just moving upwards?

3 Suspend the mass in another way, as shown in (b) below. Now, what is the force on the string **A** (as shown by the spring balance)? Is it approximately half that in (a)? What is the force exerted on the other string, **B**? What is the force on string **C**?

- The force due to gravity that pulls a mass of 1 kg is approximately 10 N. Therefore, the pull on string C is 10 N.
- In (a), a force of 10 N is needed to raise the weight of 10 N. There is no mechanical advantage.
- In (b), because the effort force is shared between strings **A** and **B**, the pull on each of these two strings is 5 N (excluding the pull due to the mass of the pulley). What do you think would be the mechanical advantage in this case? How would you work it out?

Objective

- Discuss the principles of mechanical advantage and energy conversion.

Mechanical advantage

What force (effort) exerted by pulling on string **B** can cause the mass (load) to rise? As the pull on string **B** is 5 N when equilibrium is reached, it means that a pull of just more than 5 N would cause the mass to rise. What is the mechanical advantage of the system?

MA = load/effort = 10 N/5 N = 2

Consider (c) below. The load is supported by four ropes on two sets of pulleys, each rope taking only a quarter of the total load. So, if the pull on the rope **D** is only slightly more than a quarter of this load, the load is pulled upwards.

- This arrangement is called the **block and tackle**. The mechanical advantage is 4 and for each unit of length that the load moves, the effort rope moves four times further.

What affects the efficiency of a machine?

Consider (c) again. Do the ropes and pulleys themselves have mass that has to be moved? Will energy be used for doing this? If the load is small, a large proportion of the energy put in goes into moving the pulleys and the rope, and in overcoming friction.

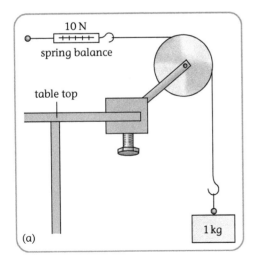

(a)

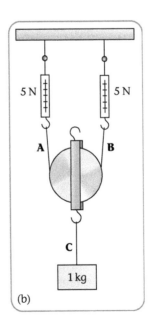

(b)

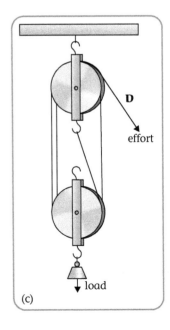

(c)

How is efficiency measured?

We need to consider the work we put in, and the useful work we get out. Other work will be 'wasted' on moving the pulleys and ropes, and overcoming friction:

efficiency (%) = work output/work input × 100

The work done (energy converted) equals force × distance in the direction of the force:

work (in J) = force (in N) × distance (in m)

So we can express efficiency in another way:

efficiency = load × distance/effort × distance

For levers and other machines, efficiency is calculated in a similar way.

You probably think that the best machine to use must be the most efficient one. But you must also consider the question of convenience. For example, an inclined plane might be the best machine for loading a truck (top right), but a pulley may be best for getting loads to the top of a building. Like the lever, the pulley can be used to change the direction along which a force is acting. A motor used with a pulley can raise a load to the top of a building (see the bottom diagram on the right).

Can machines be dangerous?

Machines, both simple and complex, must be properly maintained if they are to be used safely and efficiently. Harm may be caused by improper use, by bad selection and by failing to take necessary safety precautions. For example, in simple machines, too weak a cable in a pulley system may cause an accident, and too thin or narrow an inclined plane may fail to stop a car rolling backwards. With more complex machines, e.g. those found in your school Home Economics and Industrial Arts departments, expert advice is needed on maintenance and proper use. However, while you may learn to use the machines safely and carry out simple maintenance, rectifying of faults and carrying out repairs should be left to those who are trained and qualified to do this work.

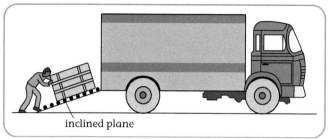

Using an inclined plane

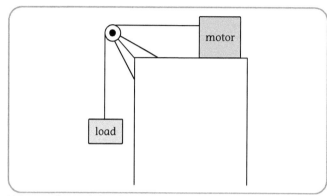

Using a pulley and electric motor

Questions

1 How can you tell the mechanical advantage of a pulley system, just by looking at it?

2 (a) What is efficiency? (b) How might you test, experimentally, the efficiency of a pulley system?

3 Give examples of machines being used more for convenience (such as changing the direction of the force), than for mechanical advantage.

4 Discuss any special precautions you must take in the operation of a complex machine you have leaned to use, e.g. a sewing machine.

5 Can a machine be 100% efficient? Why?

Key ideas

Use these words to fill in the spaces as you write the sentences in your Exercise book.

load	mechanical	input	block	effort	output

The _____ advantage of a machine is greater than 1 if the _____ needed is less than the

_____ moved. The _____ advantage of a pulley system depends on the arrangement of the

ropes. In a _____ and tackle arrangement supported by six ropes, the _____ advantage is

expected to be 6. Efficiency is work _____ divided by work _____.

337

19.5 How do we use and care for machines?

Practical 148

How is friction important? (MM, ORR, AI)

1 Place a small rectangular block on a horizontal board near the end of the bench. Tie a length of string to a hook or a screw eye on the block. Let the string pass over a free-running pulley (see the diagram on the right).

2 Add a few grams at a time to the scale pan until the block first moves. Record the frictional force (in newtons).

3 Repeat the experiment, but change the nature of the board, e.g. cover it with sandpaper, or rub it with vegetable oil. Compare the frictional forces in each case.

4 How can your results be applied to the care of machines with moving parts, such as a bicycle, sewing machine or lawn mower? Would this improve their efficiency?

Objective

● Discuss factors contributing to inefficiency of machines and ways of overcoming them.

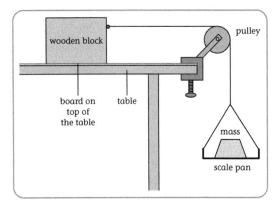

Friction: harmful and useful

● Frictional forces are undesirable when they cause breakdown through excessive rubbing of mechanical parts in machinery. Oil or grease is used for lubrication.
● However, friction is also useful. For example, many accidents are caused because of worn tread on the tyres of cars, or brake shoes that have been worn down by friction. These should both be replaced, for safety on the roads.
● Friction also allows drive belts in motors to work to transmit power and to enable brakes to work.

Corrosion and rusting

As you saw on pages 270–1, corrosion is a chemical reaction in which a metal reacts with oxygen and other chemicals to form new compounds, which damages the metal. Some metals, such as aluminium, are protected against corrosion as they form a thin, resistant layer of oxide that stops oxygen and water getting through.

Rusting of iron and steel objects is also an example of corrosion. Many machines are made of iron and steel, and we need to use methods to reduce rusting (see pages 272–3) to protect the machines and keep them efficient.

The lawn mower

A lawn mower has rotating blades to cut the grass through pushing. This can be done by human effort or with the help of a gasoline or electric engine. A lawn mower becomes inefficient if the blades become dull or if bearings and other moving parts are not well lubricated. Wet grass left in the machine can contribute to rusting. Screws, nuts and bolts can slacken because of vibration. It should be serviced regularly.

General care of machines

● Use oil on moving parts to reduce friction, loss of heat energy and wear.
● Dry the metal parts of machines and store machines under cover so they do not stay wet and rust.
● Take special care to keep machines dry near to the coast, where salt spray increases the rate of rusting.
● Use grease on metal parts that might otherwise rust.
● Paint iron or metal objects to cover and protect them from rusting.
● If the paint cover on a bicycle or car becomes damaged, get it repaired; otherwise rusting will occur.

Lawn mower with a gasoline engine

Activity

Use and care of a bicycle

1 Examine a bicycle. Make a table with four columns in your Exercise book. In a separate column for each, (a) list the different working parts, (b) write what you think could go wrong with that part, (c) state how that defective part would affect the bicycle and (d) record how you might have avoided the problem, or what you should now do about it. For example: for (a) the handle bar, it may (b) be too stiff, so that (c) the bicycle cannot steer, and you need (d) to oil it.

2 Discuss your results in class. Identify the defects that (a) only reduce the attractiveness of the bicycle, but do not affect its overall functioning, and (b) those that could be a safety hazard, e.g. stiff handle bar, tyres flat or too hard, brake pads worn.

3 Look at the list for general care of machines. How could you use these ideas in the care of your bicycle? What other things do you also need to check?

Check how your gears work and how to care for them

The motor car

As with other machines, all moving parts in a car need to be lubricated, which prevents rusting and reduces friction. For example, cogs (below) and bearings must slide and move over each other with the minimum of resistance and therefore with minimum wear and loss of energy transmission.

However, friction is important. Tyres need maximum friction to grip the road and pull the vehicle forward without slipping: for this there must be a deep tread on the tyres, which should be at the correct pressure.

Scratches to paintwork should also be attended to, because once the protective surface is damaged, the metal underneath can rust very quickly.

Care should also be taken on the road, so as not to drive into potholes or over very rough surfaces that can damage the wheel rim and the wheel bearings, and affect wheel alignment or cause a flat tyre. These can affect the efficiency.

Questions

1 How would a flat tyre affect the efficiency of a bicycle?

2 (a) What are the characteristics of an efficient machine? (b) How can you keep a bicycle in good working order?

Key ideas

Use these words to fill in the spaces as you write the sentences in your Exercise book.

dry	moving	oil	paint	tyres	friction	lubrication

_____ applied in the right places can prevent rusting and provide _____ , which reduces

_____ between _____ parts. Other ways to reduce rusting are to keep machine parts

_____ and to _____ parts that are exposed to the weather. _____ is necessary for the

contact of _____ against the road, and of brakes against wheels.

20 Conservation of energy

20.1 Energy and how it is transformed

It is difficult to give a precise yet complete definition for 'energy'. We describe it in terms of what it can do, like the purchasing power of money, so energy can be defined as the capacity for doing work. When any work is done, energy is involved in bringing about the change. The unit for energy, and the unit for work done, is the joule (J).

Energy is not 'used up': it is transformed or converted into another form. During your course you have studied many forms of energy and their effects (see the pink box and pages 16–17). You can also consider how one form changes into another.

Activity

Inter-conversions of energy

Discuss these situations in small groups. In each case list all the energy conversions that occur, if you:

1 use a toy tank (see page 16) or operate a wind-up toy
2 plug in and switch on a named appliance
3 light a Bunsen burner
4 heat the head of a pin in a Bunsen flame
5 use a hot pin to touch the head of a match
6 operate a piece of equipment that uses a dry cell
7 test a leaf that has been in the Sun, or a storage organ, for its starch (see page 48)
8 lift a heavy stone above your head, and let it drop onto a block of modelling clay
9 use scissors to cut a piece of paper
10 hold an ice cube until it melts
11 mix and cook a cake
12 switch on and use a solar-powered calculator
13 switch on and use a computer and printer
14 switch on and watch a TV.

The importance of solar energy

Photosynthesis, which involves the trapping of the Sun's energy into high-energy chemical substances, is a crucial step in making use of that energy. During photosynthesis, plants trap only 1% of the Sun's energy that reaches Earth. Photosynthesis provides for the growth of plants; and all animals, directly or indirectly, depend on it for their food.

Fossil fuels (see pages 318–19), such as coal, crude oil (and the fuels we make from it) and natural gas, depend on photosynthesis that occurred in the past, and renewable fuels, such as wood (and charcoal), depend on it now.

Solar energy (see pages 326–9) also provides us with alternatives to using fossil fuels, which, through industrial uses and the internal combustion engine in vehicles, pollute the environment (see pages 320–1). You can make solar models on page 394.

Objectives

● Explain the concept of energy, and discuss its inter-conversions.
● Discuss the conservation of mass-energy.

What does it mean?

Potential energy Stored energy with the potential to do work, e.g. **chemical** energy (in fuels, food and electrical cells), **gravitational** potential energy (because of its position above the ground, e.g. a dam) and **elastic** potential energy (in a wound-up spring, or stretched or twisted rubber band).

Kinetic energy This is the energy of a moving object, e.g. water from a dam, or a rubber band or spring uncurling.

Electrical energy This is a flow of electrons or ions in an electric current.

Nuclear energy The energy that holds together the nuclei of atoms. It is released from the Sun, atomic bombs and radioactive materials.

Sound energy Energy produced by vibrating objects that sets up sound waves in solids, liquids and gases.

Heat or thermal energy This is vibration and moving of molecules. Hotter objects, such as the Sun, have more thermal energy than colder objects.

Light energy This is visible (white) light, with wavelengths we can see, e.g. produced by the Sun or a light bulb.

Solar energy Radiation of electromagnetic waves from the Sun (the electromagnetic spectrum is shown on page 345): we can see, feel and use solar energy as light, infrared radiation, and micro- and radio waves, respectively.

Energy conversions

As you saw on pages 322–3, the Sun's energy is also involved, via photosynthesis, in the energy alternatives of biofuels, biogas and biodiesel. The Sun's energy also:

- heats the air to make winds (see page 323) that can be used to drive windmills and wind turbines, which in turn are used to generate electricity
- raises water from the sea and lakes, by evaporation to form clouds, which then falls as rain; this source of gravitational potential energy can be collected in a dam, to be used to generate hydroelectricity (see page 324)
- causes winds that make waves on the sea (see page 323)
- is used to heat water (in a solar water heater) or is directly changed to electricity (in solar or photovoltaic cells) (see pages 326–9) that can be used in solar panels to provide energy for vehicles or for spacecraft.

Mass-energy

All of the inter-conversions mentioned so far involve energy changing from one form to another. But there are some reactions in which mass (the matter of substances) can be changed into energy. These occur when the nuclei of atoms release nuclear energy (see page 325).

- **Nuclear fission** Radioactive uranium, in a nuclear power station, is bombarded with fast-moving neutrons, which cause it to undergo radioactive decay with the change of some mass into an enormous amount of energy. Simpler elements are formed (see the diagram on the right), and neutrons, which then bombard other uranium atoms to set up a chain reaction. The energy can be used to change water to steam, which turns a turbine and generator to produce electricity. In an atomic bomb nuclear fission also occurs to release an enormous amount of energy.
- **Nuclear fusion** This is the basis of the production of solar energy, on which most of our energy resources on Earth depend. It has a higher output of energy, but requires a continuous temperature of 60 million °C to occur. In the Sun and other stars, the nuclei of small atoms, such as hydrogen, fuse together to make larger atoms of another element. In the process mass is changed to energy. This is also the basis of the hydrogen bomb.

The importance of electricity

Electrical energy appears to be the most convenient form of energy to distribute and transform into other useful types.

For example, it can be changed to:

- heat, in an electric kettle
- heat and then to light, in a bulb
- sound, in a radio or telephone
- movement, in an electric car
- light and sound, in a TV or computer
- chemical energy, in a rechargeable battery.

For this reason, fossil fuels, e.g. coal, oil and natural gas, are burnt in power stations to heat water to make steam, which then drives turbines and a generator to produce electricity (see page 299). But the combustion of fossil fuels is a major contributor to acid rain and global warming (see page 321).

Using alternatives to fossil fuels, such as wind, waves, solar energy and nuclear energy, to generate electricity would help the environment (see pages 320–1).

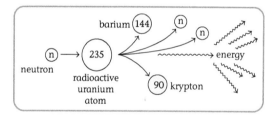

Questions

1 Trace the energy that lights a light bulb from its source, the Sun.

2 List six ways in which life on Earth depends on the Sun. Explain one way in detail, giving examples.

Key ideas

Use these words to fill in the spaces as you write the sentences in your Exercise book.

fossil   **starch**   **coal**   **energy**   **potential**   **kinetic**   **mass**

_____ can change from one form to another, e.g. the gravitational _____ energy of water in a dam can change into _____ energy and generate electricity. The organic compound, _____ , is an energy-rich compound made by plants. _____ fuels, such as _____ , also derive their energy from the Sun. The Sun's energy comes from converting _____ into energy.

20.2 Can waves transfer energy?

Practical 149

How are waves produced? (ORR)

1 Fix one end of a 5m length of rope about 1m above the ground.

2 Hold the free end and shake it up and down in a steady rhythm. Is a wave produced?

3 Increase the rate of movement of your hand. Is the motion of the wave increased? Do you think energy is transmitted along the rope?

Because your hand is holding the rope, its up-and-down movement is transmitted to the rope, which then moves up and down, transferring energy from the moving hand along the rope.

If a stone is thrown into a pond, the surface of the pond is disturbed and water waves spread out in all directions from the point of disturbance to all parts of the pond. The same effect is seen when water is disturbed by a swimming animal. Try to observe both these things, and describe what you see.

Sea waves

Sea waves are caused by the wind disturbing the surface of the water. These waves travel from the open sea towards land as barely visible 'swells'. As they reach the shore, they encounter shallower water and rise, breaking and crashing on the shore. Thus the energy picked up from the wind far out to sea is finally spent on the seashore. When there is a hurricane the waves are much more energetic because of the much higher wind energy provided by the hurricane. These are called storm surges (see page 197).

Think about the effect of sea waves on driftwood and other floating debris. It is obvious that there is very little forward movement of the water (in the direction of the wave) and more movement up and down.

In the Caribbean, there are steady easterly trade winds. The east coast of most of the islands constantly receives steady waves. The eastern coastlines are rugged and show obvious signs of continuous erosion due to this constant battering by the waves. The total amount of energy stored in sea waves in this way is enormous. In some countries, scientists are experimenting with ways of harnessing wave energy. The up-and-down wave action can be used to create compressed air to turn a dynamo, which then generates electricity (see page 323).

Objective

● Discuss the transfer and transport of energy.

A ripple tank

One of the best ways of investigating waves is by using a ripple tank. This consists of a tank of water (which may be as little as half a centimetre deep), a light bulb or spotlight supported over the centre of the tank in order to cast shadows of the waves on the bottom, a vibrator motor to produce waves and some accessories such as curved and straight bars and bars with gaps.

Practical 150

Using a ripple tank (ORR, D)

1 Use a straight bar on the water surface to generate one **plane wave** front at a time (a wave travelling parallel to the short end of the tank).

2 Observe and sketch what happens when the plane wave front hits a barrier. The plane wave front is the **incident** wave. In this case, the incident waves are straight. The resulting waves are the **reflected** waves.

3 Observe and sketch what happens when a plane wave front hits a concave reflector (curving inwards) and a convex reflector (curving outwards).

4 How do differently shaped surfaces affect the wave front? Do the waves change direction by the use of a suitable reflector?

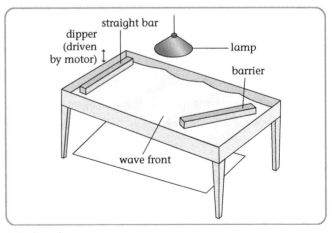

A ripple tank

Describing waves

As you have seen, waves go up and down and transfer energy from one place to another. If we could look sideways at a wave, it would look like corrugated paper (see (a) on the right).

- The tops of the waves are called crests, and the bottoms of the waves are called troughs.
- The distance from one crest to the next, or from one trough to the next, is called the **wavelength**. The number of wavelengths that pass in one second is called the **frequency**. Frequency is measured in hertz (Hz).
- The height of the crest or trough above or below the mid-line is called the **amplitude** (see (b) on the right)

Sound waves

- Water waves, and light waves and the other waves of the electromagnetic spectrum (EMS), vibrate at right angles (across) the direction in which the wave travels; we say they are **transverse** waves (see (c) on the right).
- With sound waves, the vibrations of the particles of the medium, e.g. air, are along the same direction as the waves are travelling: they are **longitudinal waves** (d).
- Light waves, and the other waves of the EMS, travel by radiation; they do not need particles to transfer them and can travel in a vacuum.
- Sound waves, however, need particles, as the particles are compressed together and spread apart in order to transfer the wave. The distance from one compression to the next is the wavelength of the sound (e).
- We can use a microphone to convert the sound waves into electrical signals, and these can be shown as wave traces on the screen of an oscilloscope (see page 129).

In other ways, sound waves are similar to water waves, and to light and other EMS waves.

Some characteristics of sound waves

- They need energy to set them up, such as the striking of a drum or plucking of a string in a musical instrument. The energy with which they are set up affects how loud the sounds are. The loudness of sound is measured in decibels (dB).
- They can transfer energy from one place to another, e.g. when we speak, or listen to a radio or TV.
- They can carry a lot of energy: e.g. very loud noises are dangerous because they can damage our eardrums.
- They can be reflected, as with echoes, or using ultrasound to make an image of an unborn baby (in ultrasonography). High-frequency sound waves with short wavelengths can also be focused with a concave surface.
- They can be changed to other forms of energy: e.g. when using a landline or mobile phone, sound waves from the speaker are converted to electric current, which is transferred to the listener and changed back to sound.
- They can be bent (refracted) and brought to a focus.

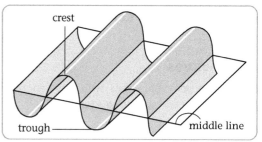

(a) Waves

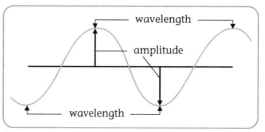

(b) Parts of a wave

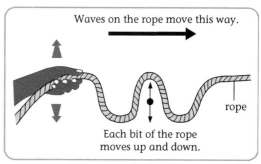

(c) Transverse waves, e.g. light

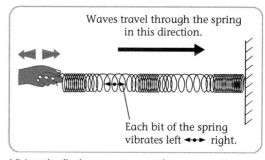

(d) Longitudinal waves, e.g. sound

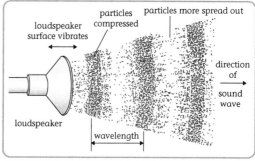

(e) Sound waves

20.2 Can waves transfer energy? (continued)

Light waves

Light waves are visible light, with wavelengths between 380 and 780 nm, which we can see (see page 314).

Some characteristics of light waves

- They need luminous objects to produce them. These can be natural sources, e.g the Sun or lightning, or artificial sources, such as a lit bulb or burning match (see page 310).
- They can transfer energy from one place to another; e.g. the light we see on Earth has travelled nearly 150 million km from the Sun.
- They can be changed into other forms of energy; e.g. the energy of sunlight is changed during photosynthesis to stored chemical energy in starch and other foods.
- They can be reflected. If the surface is not perfectly level, the image may be blurred, as in the reflection in the photograph on the right; but we can also use a flat plane mirror to form a clear image (see diagram (a)).
- They can be bent (refracted) as they pass from one medium to another, e.g. from air into glass. This is the basis of the converging of light rays by a convex lens, and diverging of light rays by a concave lens (see pages 127–8 and diagram (b), below)
- They can be reflected by a concave mirror and focused to a point (diagram (c)). Concave mirrors are used for concentrating energy. They are used, e.g. in shaving mirrors and reflecting telescopes, to give magnified images.
- They can be used with a concave mirror to give parallel beams of light, as in a headlamp or spotlight (diagram (d)).

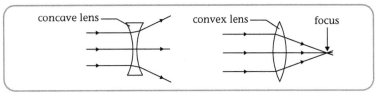

(b) A concave lens diverges; a convex lens converges

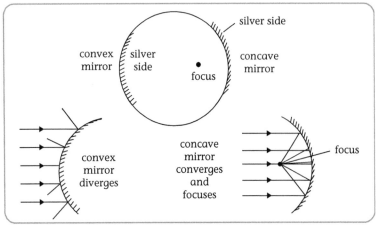

(c) A convex mirror diverges; a concave mirror converges

Reflection of light rays from a water surface. The image is not very clear

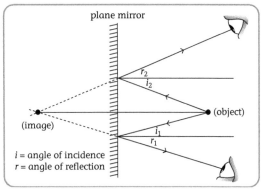

i = angle of incidence
r = angle of reflection

(a) Forming an image with a plane mirror. The light rays are reflected from the mirror's surface. The eye interprets the reflected rays as coming from an image behind the plane mirror. The object is as far in front of the mirror as the image is behind

Did you know?

- Light travels faster than sound, so we see lightning before we hear the thunder.

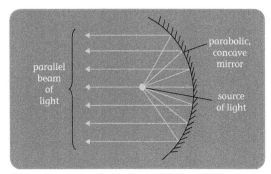

(d) In a headlamp, the source of light is at the focus of a parabolic mirror (a kind of concave mirror). The light rays it produces are reflected from the mirror to form a parallel beam of light

Electromagnetic spectrum (EMS)

The EMS has transverse waves that travel, by radiation through space, at 300 million metres per second. Their wavelengths vary from extremely small (gamma rays) to quite long (radio waves), as shown below.

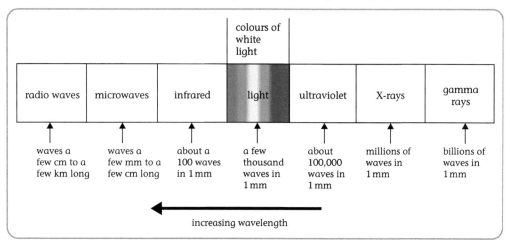

colours of white light

radio waves	microwaves	infrared	light	ultraviolet	X-rays	gamma rays
waves a few cm to a few km long	waves a few mm to a few cm long	about a 100 waves in 1 mm	a few thousand waves in 1 mm	about 100,000 waves in 1 mm	millions of waves in 1 mm	billions of waves in 1 mm

← increasing wavelength

Some characteristics of electromagnetic waves

- They are produced by energy sources, such as the Sun, or converted from electricity, e.g. microwaves.
- They can transfer energy from one place to another; e.g. waves of the EMS travel to Earth from the Sun.
- They can be changed into other forms of energy; e.g. gamma rays can cause damage to human flesh.
- They can be reflected; e.g. the microwaves used in ovens are reflected from the surfaces inside the oven to cook the food, and radio waves are used in radar (page 229) to make echoes to identify the position of objects.
- They can be bent (refracted) as they pass from one medium to another, e.g. infrared (heat) rays can be converged and focused by a convex lens to make an intense spot of heat, where an image of the Sun is focused.
- They can be reflected by a concave surface and focused to a point; e.g. a dish aerial (see photograph) that can be used to concentrate high-frequency TV and radio waves. The waves hit the curved surface and are reflected and concentrated at the focus point. They are then converted into a form we can see and hear.
- Infrared (heat) waves can also be reflected to a focus by a concave surface. This is the basis of the solar cooker (see page 328).

Questions

1 How are sound and light waves (a) different and (b) similar?
2 How do (a) a headlamp and (b) a dish aerial work?

A dish aerial. It has a concave surface that focuses TV and radio waves

Key ideas

Use these words to fill in the spaces as you write the sentences in your Exercise book.

light   **ripple**   **concave**   **convex**   **image**   **reflected**   **focus**

The behaviour of waves can be shown with a _____ tank. We know that _____ is a source of energy, as it is used in photosynthesis. _____ is _____ in a plane mirror to form an _____ .

A _____ lens and a _____ mirror diverge light rays; but a _____ lens and a _____ mirror can _____ light rays to a point.

20.3 Can collisions transfer energy?

How is energy transferred?

On pages 18–19, you saw evidence for matter being made of particles. Solid matter transmits heat energy by particle-to-particle contact (conduction). Conduction also occurs in liquids and in gases, but to a lesser extent, because the particles of matter are further apart from each other. Heat energy also causes matter to expand and changes of state to take place, e.g. solid to liquid, and liquid to gas. If heat makes matter expand too rapidly, an explosion occurs. Fast-moving particles can provide the thrust for a rocket or jet engine (see page 349), or compressed air from wave movements can turn a turbine (see page 323).

How particles transfer energy

The transfer of energy from moving to stationary objects can be demonstrated (see the diagram on the right). A loudspeaker can be connected to a sound generator. The sound makes the loudspeaker cone move in and out. At low sound levels, when the loudspeaker moves with little energy, there is very little movement of the balls and the polystyrene disc remains at its lowest level in the cylinder. As the strength of the sound signal is increased, more energy is transferred from ball to ball and they acquire more and more kinetic energy to push the disc further up the cylinder.

A moving body carries kinetic energy. It will pass on some or all of its energy to an object with which it collides. This is called the **conservation of momentum**.

Practical 151

What is momentum? (ORR, AI)

Ask three or four of your friends to help you push a garden roller, or the kind of roller used for preparing a cricket pitch. When you have got it moving freely on level ground, see if you all can quickly get it to stop. Take care!

Was that easy?

That was difficult, even with a lot of help. This is because the roller has a lot of **momentum**. Momentum depends on mass and velocity:

momentum = mass × velocity

A large momentum requires a large force to overcome it.

Have you noticed how easily cars can be wrecked even when travelling at low speeds? The large mass of the car produces a large momentum even at low speeds, and therefore requires a large force to overcome it. If a car crashes into a wall or tree, its energy is expended either in demolishing the obstruction or in bending and twisting the metal of the car (or both).

The greater the mass of a vehicle, the greater the damage it can cause in an accident. Smaller vehicles, because of their smaller mass, can accelerate and decelerate more quickly. Because they have less momentum, they are more manoeuvrable and easier to control.

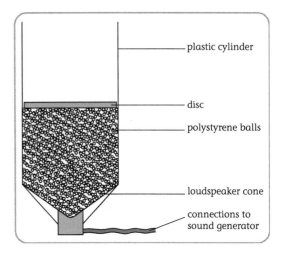

Why is the car damaged?

Questions

1 Are all forms of energy transferred by particles?
2 What are three applications of the conservation of momentum?
3 How does an object travelling through air, e.g. a bullet from a gun, lose energy and come to rest?
4 Do perfectly elastic collisions really occur?
5 Why is the law of conservation of linear momentum so important?

Practical 152

How can we calculate momentum? (MM, ORR, AI)

1 Place one of two trolleys in the middle of a slope, slightly tilted to compensate for friction. When a trolley is gently pushed on such a slope, it will continue moving at the same speed.

2 Attach one end of the other trolley to ticker tape and pass the other end through a ticker-tape timer. Fit a pin to one trolley and a cork to the other. The apparatus is shown below.

3 Give the first trolley a sharp push so that it runs down the track at constant speed and collides with the second trolley and they both move off together.

4 Use the ticker tape to find the velocity before and after the collision. A certain time interval is given by successive dots on the tape: in this case, 0.02 s. Enter your results in a table as shown (also see page 396).

$$\text{velocity} = \frac{\text{distance}}{\text{time}} = \frac{\text{length of tape}}{\text{time measured on tape}}$$

Repeat the practical on the left using one, two and three additional trolleys stacked on top of the stationary one to give two, three and four units of mass, respectively. The mass of each trolley is known (in kg), the distance travelled can be measured (in m) and the time in seconds is known. The momentum can be calculated in kg m/s.

Taking into account the limitations of the experiment, e.g. not being able to compensate properly for friction:

> The total linear momentum of the system before collision is equal to the total linear momentum after collision.

So the total linear momentum of the colliding bodies is unaltered by the collision. This fact is called **the principle of conservation of linear momentum**.

This type of collision, in which two objects collide and stick together, is called a completely **inelastic** collision. The other extreme is a completely **elastic** collision, e.g. the collision of two billiard balls or a rubber ball that bounces back up, when it has been dropped from a height onto the floor.

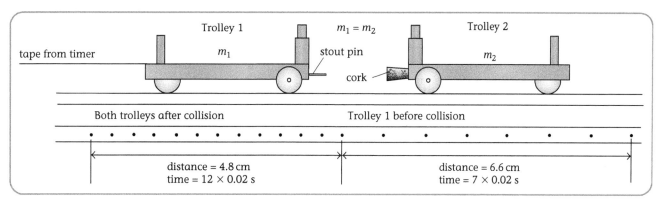

	Distance d (metres)	Time t (s)	Velocity = distance/time (m/s)	Momentum (kg m/s)
Trolley before collision				
Trolley after collision				
Two trolleys together				

Key ideas

Use these words to fill in the spaces as you write the sentences in your Exercise book.

moving   **collision**   **velocity**   **linear**   **momentum**   **mass**

A _____ ball may hit a stationary object and start it _____ as well. The distance an object

travels in a certain direction in a given time is its _____ . _____ is mass × velocity: objects with

a larger _____ or a larger _____ have a greater momentum. In an inelastic _____ between

two objects, the total _____ _____ is conserved.

21 Forces

21.1 How are forces important for movement?

Movement on land

There are two forces opposing movement on land.

Friction with the ground

Friction is the force opposing the sliding of one object over another. We can reduce friction by using a lubricant to fill in minute irregularities on touching surfaces, or we use wheels, which reduce the areas that are in contact. However, some friction between an object and the surface is necessary, in order for movement to occur.

Friction with the air (air resistance or drag)

A vehicle has an engine to produce a **thrust** force. This has to overcome friction with the ground in order to start moving, and to continue to oppose the resistance or drag of the air that tends to slow it down. To assist with this, vehicles are often **streamlined**, as are fish (see page 216).

Flying in the air

There are three main principles involved in flying.

Overcoming friction with the air (air resistance or drag)

Objects such as birds and aeroplanes are streamlined. Air flows around them rather than opposing their motion.

Overcoming the force of gravity

To overcome the downward pull of gravity, a flying object has to produce an opposing upward force, called 'lift'. To do this, birds and aeroplanes have wings in the shape of an **aerofoil** (see next page).

Birds also have a strong, light skeleton containing air spaces. They also have very powerful flight muscles, which are the most powerful muscles in the body and in some birds can be up to 35% of the body weight.

Using the action–reaction principle

Birds, insects and bats use flapping wings to assist lift and movement through the air. The downward stroke of the wing pushes against the air, which pushes back on the action–reaction principle (as for fish; see page 216), and creates a forward movement. Then the upward stroke occurs and air passes between the wing feathers.

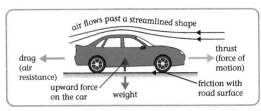

Forces important for objects moving on land

What does it mean?

Force   This is a push, pull or twist. Forces can start things moving, speed them up, slow them down or stop them, or change the direction of movement.

Unbalanced forces   Forces act in pairs. When the forces have different values, there will be movement in the direction of the larger force.

Friction   This is the force between objects sliding past each other.

Resistance or drag   This is the friction force when objects slide through water (e.g. a fish) or air (e.g. a bird or plane).

Streamlined   A shape that can reduce the effect of resistance of water or air.

Thrust   The force required for motion, to overcome drag.

Aerofoil   The shape of wings of birds or planes that helps to overcome gravity by developing an opposing force, 'lift'.

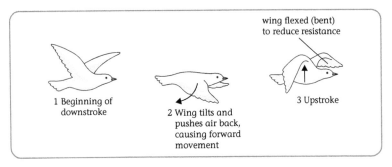

1 Beginning of downstroke

2 Wing tilts and pushes air back, causing forward movement

3 Upstroke

wing flexed (bent) to reduce resistance

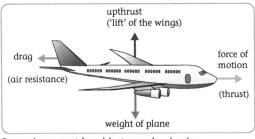

Forces important for objects moving in air

Practical 153

How does airflow create lift? (ORR)

1. Tape a piece of string to each of two table tennis (ping-pong) balls and suspend them about 4 cm apart.

2. Blow between the two balls (see diagram (a)).

3. Do they move apart? Do they come together? Is this what you expected? How can you explain your results?

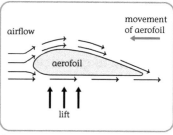

(a) Ping pong balls (b) An aerofoil – how airflow can create lift

Aerofoil

As air is blown quickly through the gap in the balls, there is less air there and less pressure. Air from the sides pushes the balls together. The same idea, of fast-moving air making an area of low pressure, is used in the aerofoil.

The aerofoil shape is a cross-section of a typical aircraft wing (see diagram (b)). The small arrows indicate the airflow over the wing as it moves through the air. The air stream divides at the front of the wing. The air around the top has furthest to travel, following the contours. But it reaches the back of the wing at the same time as air flowing along the bottom. So air going over the top must move much more rapidly. This difference in speed creates a difference in air pressure that creates the lift. Air pressure is greater below the wing than above, so the wing is lifted.

For sufficient lift a high forward speed must first be reached. This explains why aircraft must thunder along the runway before they can take off.

Action–reaction

You can set up a balloon on a string, as shown in the diagram. The cone on the front is to make it more streamlined. Blow up the balloon and then release it.

The way jet aircraft or rockets propel themselves forward is similar to this. The backward movement of air from the balloon, or of rapidly expanding gases that leave from a jet engine or rocket, produces a forward thrust to push the balloon, jet or rocket forward. This follows Newton's third law of motion:

For every action force there is an equal and opposite reaction force.

This is the **action–reaction principle**.

Questions

1. (a) What is a force? (b) Name three forces and explain how they are important for movement.

2. In what ways is movement through the air (a) similar to and (b) different from movement along a land surface?

3. How are birds adapted for flight?

4. How does streamlining assist flying?

5. What is an aerofoil and how is it important?

6. What is the action–reaction principle and how is it important?

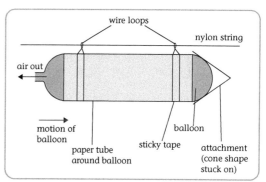

As air comes out from the balloon (action) there is an opposite and equal reaction that pushes the balloon forwards

Key ideas

Use these words to fill in the spaces as you write the sentences in your Exercise book.

| aerofoil | friction | lift | unbalanced | drag | pressure |

Movement occurs when there are _____ forces. _____ opposes motion when surfaces slide past each other. In water and the air, the resistance to movement is called _____ . Wings of birds and aeroplanes have an _____ shape, which creates _____ by differences in _____ on the two surfaces, which opposes the force of gravity.

21.2 Does gravity affect balance?

What is gravity?

A ball dropped from a height will fall to the ground. An object attached to a suspended spring causes the spring to stretch. The falling of the ball and the stretching of the spring are both due to a force called **gravity**. The Earth exerts a gravitational force on all objects near it, such as the falling ball. We say that the objects are in the Earth's gravitational field. It is the strength of this gravitational field that gives weight to matter. Weight is a force. When a 1 kg mass is attracted by the Earth's gravitational field it does so with a force of approximately 10 N.

The Earth and the planets in our solar system are subject to gravitational forces. They are in the Sun's gravitational field. They move around the Sun rather like objects being whirled at the end of a string (see page 358). The gravitational force keeping the Earth in the near circular orbit around the Sun is a **centripetal force**. The reaction force that balances the centripetal force is the **centrifugal force**. If the centripetal force were to cease, the Earth, or any other object, would go off in a straight line.

You have seen, on pages 348–9, that objects that fly have to oppose the force of gravity. But how is gravity important for the balancing of objects on land?

Centre of gravity

All objects have a **centre of gravity**. This is the point through which gravity is directed. In the case of regular geometric objects, the centre of gravity corresponds with the geometric centre of the object ((a) in the diagram on the right). How could you plan a practical to test if this was true?

Practical 154

How can you find the centre of gravity of an object? (MM)

1 Take a rectangular piece of cardboard. Carefully balance it horizontally on the edge of a ruler and mark a line along the edge of the rule where the object is balanced.

2 Rotate the object slightly and find a new position where it is again balanced on the ruler's edge. Mark the second line (see diagram (b)).

3 The point where the two lines intersect is the centre of gravity. Any other lines along which the object is balanced will pass through this point. If you make a hole through this point, the object will spin freely.

4 This method can also be used to find the centre of gravity for irregular flat objects. However, there may be some difficulty experienced in getting it to balance on the edge of a ruler. A better method is described on page 351 (see also page 397).

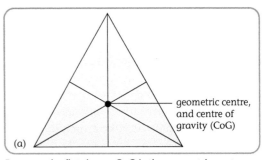

For a regular flat shape, CoG is the geometric centre

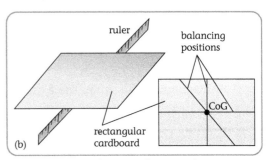

Finding the centre of gravity of a rectangle

Practical 155

The centre of gravity of irregular flat objects and solid objects (MM)

1. Make a hole in the flat object at three places along the edge, as shown in diagram (c) on the right. Suspend it from one hole from a pin held by a clamp. The flat surface will come to rest with its CoG along the vertical line (see page 397).

2. Repeat the procedure with the object hanging from a different hole. Where the two lines intersect is the CoG. Any other vertical line will also pass through the CoG.

3. Is the CoG always within the object? You can find out by using an L-shaped piece of card. Where is its CoG located?

4. Use a similar method to find the CoG of a regular solid object, such as a pencil or ruler.

How does the centre of gravity affect balance?

Another word for balance is **equilibrium**. Look at the diagrams of wooden blocks (d), (e) and (f) on the right. The position of the CoG is shown on each block.

- Figure (d) shows the block in **stable equilibrium**. If the block is tilted slightly (displaced) as in (e), the CoG is raised. But the perpendicular line from the CoG still falls within the base area of the block. If the block is let go, it will fall back to its former position at (d).

- However, if the block is tipped so that the vertical line from its CoG comes outside the base of the block, it will fall over, as in (f). It is in a state of **unstable equilibrium**.

Stability and instability

An object is stable when it returns to its original position after being displaced. An object is unstable and likely to fall over when its CoG falls outside the base area on which it was standing.

The stick (diagram (g)) is in a state of unstable equilibrium. As soon as it is tipped, the CoG is lowered and the stick falls over.

A ball (h) has a CoG that is neither raised nor lowered when it is pushed along or turned. The ball is said to be in **neutral** equilibrium.

Questions

1. How can you tell if an object will balance?
2. Match these items to stable, unstable and neutral equilibrium, and explain why in each case.

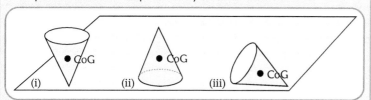

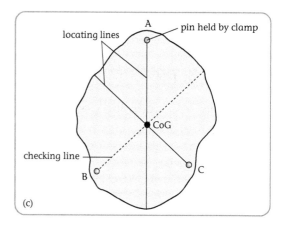

(c)

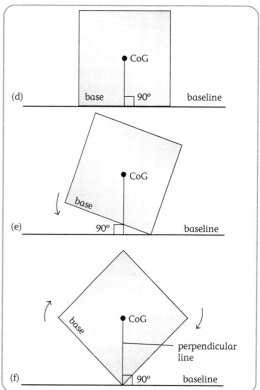

(d)

(e)

(f)

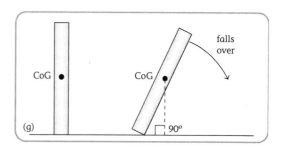

(g)

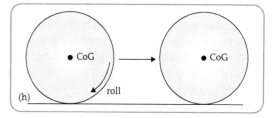

(h)

351

21.2 Does gravity affect balance? (continued)

Practical 156

Is stability related to the centre of gravity? (MM, ORR, AI)

1 Make an adjustable inclined plane (see diagram (a)). A temporary one can be made by using tape and two pieces of cardboard, whereas a more permanent one can be made from plywood using a hinge between the two boards.

2 Use the inclined plane to find the angle of tilt of a block, i.e. the angle to which you can tilt a block before it falls over. Place a wooden block, block **A**, on the plane. Put a small piece of modelling clay at the front edge to prevent sliding.

3 Raise the upper portion of the inclined plane gradually and hold it in position with a suitable prop.

4 Continue raising the slope until you reach the angle where block **A** just topples over. Measure the angle using a protractor. Try another block that is taller. Which block has the greater angle of tilt? Which block is more stable?

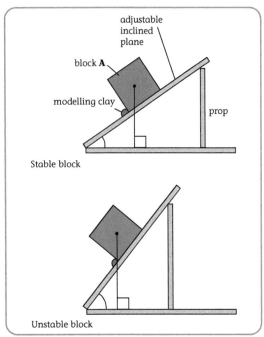

(a) Using an adjustable inclined plane

Practical 157

Does mass affect stability? (ORR, MM, AI)

1 Obtain some blocks with the same dimensions but made from different materials. Try blocks of wood, aluminium and iron. Do the masses differ? Measure the angle of tilt of each block.

2 If blocks are not available, make your own blocks using matchboxes filled with sand, marl, clay, iron filings, sawdust, lead shot, etc. Find the angle of tilt of each block using the adjustable inclined plane. Enter your results in a table.

(Note: if the blocks are not cubes, they must all be positioned in the same way on the inclined plane in order to compare the angle of tilt. Why?)

3 What are your findings? How does mass affect the position of the centre of gravity, and stability?

Questions

1 How does the centre of gravity affect the stability of an object?

2 How are (a) furniture and (b) motor vehicles constructed to enhance stability?

3 How do (a) sitting passengers, (b) standing passengers and (c) loads on top of a vehicle affect the stability of a vehicle?

4 How are loading position and stability important in loading ships?

5 Does speed affect stability?

Activity

Does the distribution of mass in a column (stack) affect the stability?

1 Look at the boxes strapped together (see diagram (b)). **X** and **Y** have different densities. The diagram shows the arrangement of **X** and **Y** blocks in stacks of four.

2 Which stack of blocks is the most stable? Which stack of blocks is least stable? Explain your answer.

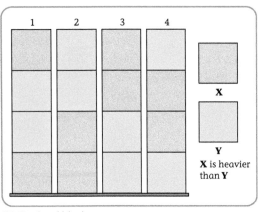

(b) Stacks of blocks

Is stability important in loading vehicles?

When loads are being transported, it is important to think about the distribution of the load so that the vehicle does not topple over. The centre of gravity is kept as low as possible and the base broad. In order to do this the loader thinks about (a) the maximum height of loading, (b) the density of the goods being loaded and (c) the way the goods of different densities are distributed. The denser materials are best placed at the bottom near the base and the less dense materials placed at the top. The type of terrain over which the vehicle is travelling is important, because unevenness and slopes in the road can upset the equilibrium. What steep slopes and rough terrain are for land vehicles, rough seas are for boats, and attention must also be given to the loading of boats. Heavy loads on deck tend to shift the centre of gravity upwards, making it also more likely that the ship might capsize.

What is the maximum loading weight?

In most Caribbean countries, vehicles that transport loads are allowed to do so after being issued with a special permit. They have to carry a sign specifying the mass of the vehicle and the carrying capacity in kilograms. For passenger vehicles, the number of people is limited.

Tare refers to the mass of the vehicle, net (or nett) to the cargo-carrying capacity, and gross to the total mass. There are limits to the quantity of material, ensuring that the centre of gravity is not raised beyond safe limits. Too many passengers in a bus will also have the same effect: that of raising the centre of gravity and causing instability over rough roads and around corners.

However, there are other reasons why the load may be restricted: too much weight over a small area of the road could damage the surface and the power of the engine must be matched to the load transported. Moving heavier loads requires more gasoline or diesel.

Loading ships: how should the load be distributed so the ship does not capsize?

Key ideas

Use these words to fill in the spaces as you write the sentences in your Exercise book.

centrifugal   **unstable**   **tilt**   **centripetal**   **loaded**   **neutral**

An object whirled on a string is held in place by a _____ force; the balancing reaction force is a _____ force. If the CoG is neither raised nor lowered when an object is pushed along, it is in _____ equilibrium. If a block falls over when it is tilted, it is in _____ equilibrium. A vehicle with a low CoG can withstand a greater _____ angle without toppling over. When a vehicle or ship is _____ the CoG rises; care is taken that it does not become _____ .

21.3 How can we balance forces?

Practical 158

Forces in equilibrium (MM, ORR, AI)

1 Suspend a metre rule at the 50 cm mark, as shown in the diagram below. Balance it with a small piece of modelling clay if necessary.

2 Make hooks of bent wire and use them to hang masses on the rule.

3 Hang a mass of 40 g at the 30 cm mark (20 cm from the pivot point). Now add 10 g masses at 20 cm from the pivot point on the other side. How many masses of 10 g do you need for balance?

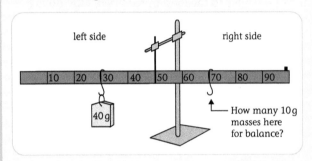

left side right side

How many 10 g masses here for balance?

4 Now place a 40 g mass on a hook 10 cm from the pivot. Where must you place one 10 g mass on the other side, so that it balances the 40 g mass?

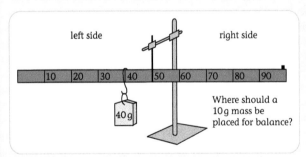

left side right side

Where should a 10 g mass be placed for balance?

5 Use different masses at different distances on one side and balance the rule by placing other different masses on the other side. Record the masses and distance from the pivot in a table.

6 What do you observe? How is it that a small mass can balance a much larger mass?

Left side			Right side		
Mass m_1	Distance d_1	$m_1 \times d_1$	Mass m_2	Distance d_2	$m_2 \times d_2$
40	10	400	10	40	400
etc.					

Objective

● Demonstrate the conditions for equilibrium under parallel forces.

When the rule is balanced:

mass (m_1) × distance (d_1) on the left side = mass (m_2) × distance (d_2) on the right side

The mass on each side of the ruler is acted upon by gravity and exerts a turning parallel force that counteracts the other one. This is called the **law of levers**. The forces on the two sides are also said to be in **static equilibrium**.

$$m_1 d_1 = m_2 d_2$$

therefore $m_1 = \dfrac{m_2 d_2}{d_1}$

or $d_1 = \dfrac{m_2 d_2}{m_1}$

You can find m_2 or d_2 by changing the subject of the formula and substituting. So, if one mass or one distance is unknown, it can be calculated from the other three known values.

Example
$m_1 = 40\,g$ $d_1 = ?$ $m_2 = 10\,g$ $d_2 = 20\,cm$

$m_1 d_1 = m_2 d_2$

$d_1 = \dfrac{m_2 d_2}{m_1}$ $d_1 = \dfrac{10\,g \times 20\,cm}{40\,g} = 5\,cm$

Moments

The masses (and therefore the forces) on each side of the pivot exert a turning force. The value of the turning force of a particular mass will vary, depending on its distance from the pivot.

Look at your table of results. You will find that a 10 g mass can balance a 40 g mass, but the smaller mass must be further from the pivot. It must actually be four times as far from the pivot as the 40 g mass to balance it (also see page 398).

The turning effect of a force is also called the **moment** of a force. If the ruler is balanced, the clockwise moments about a pivot (on the right-hand side) must equal the anti-clockwise moments (on the left-hand side). This is described as $f_1 d_1 = f_2 d_2$ where f_1 is the force (in newtons) and d_1 the distance (in metres) on the left, and f_2 and d_2 are the corresponding quantities on the right.

This principle is also important in the way we use machines such as levers (see pages 330–1). When we exert an effort force further from the pivot (fulcrum), we can move a larger load.

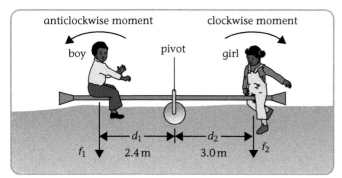

The boy exerts a force 500 N. What is the weight of the girl?

Make use of the law of levers: add in the values you know, and work out the unknown.

$$f_1 d_1 = f_2 d_2$$

The steelyard

The steelyard is an ancient type of scale using the principle of balanced parallel forces (see the diagram below). The mass to be measured is hung on the hook at **A**, a short distance from the pivot at **C**. The steelyard is suspended by a hook at **W**. The mass **P** is moved along the lever arm to balance the mass at **A**. The weight of the mass **R** is determined from the position of **P** on the scale.

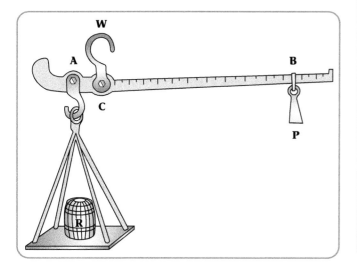

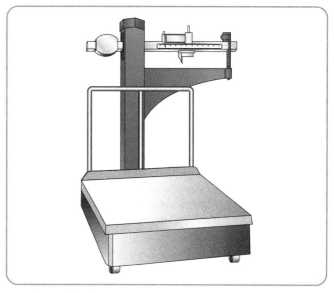

A modern steelyard. Note: a spring balance measures weight, but the steelyard scale compares and therefore measures mass

Questions

1 Use the picture above to explain how the modern steelyard can be used.

2 On the left of a metre rule is a 30 g mass at 10 cm from the pivot. How can you use (a) 10 g masses or (b) 5 g masses to make the ruler balance?

3 (a) What is the law of levers? (b) Why does a balanced rule also show forces in equilibrium?

4 What is the moment of a force? How can the principle be applied to the use of machines such as levers?

5 If a metre rule is not balanced, can balance be achieved by arranging equal forces on either side of the pivot? Explain your answer.

Key ideas

Use these words to fill in the spaces as you write the sentences in your Exercise book.

weight   **mass**   **equilibrium**   **balanced**   **clockwise**   **moment**

Gravity acting on a _____ produces a force that is called _____ . When the forces acting on

an object that is at rest are _____ , then we say that the object is in a state of static _____ .

The _____ of a force is the _____ × distance from the fulcrum. A metre rule is _____ if

the _____ _____ = the anticlockwise _____ .

21.4 Where are we in space?

To show where we are in space, we can make a diagram (see the opposite page).

- We live in one of the Caribbean countries.
- The Caribbean region lies in the northern hemisphere of the Earth between 22°N and 1°N, and from 89°W (Belize) to 56°W (Guyana).
- The Earth is our **planet** and it has a natural **satellite**, the Moon, which travels round it.
- The Earth is one of the planets that travel round (**orbit**) the Sun, which is a **star**. Between the orbits of Mars and Jupiter are many small rocky bodies called **asteroids**.
- There are eight planets and their satellites in our solar system. (Pluto is now classed as a 'dwarf' planet and not a main planet.) The planets, dwarf planets, asteroids and the Sun make up our solar system.
- This is only one of the solar systems that form a part of our **galaxy**. Our solar system is on one side of our galaxy in one of the 'arms'. We can see part of our galaxy as the Milky Way.
- Our galaxy is only one of very many that are in the **Universe**, which extends far further than we can observe with the most powerful light or radio telescopes. In the Universe are many millions of galaxies, solar systems and planets.

The planets of our solar system

The planets can be divided into two main groups (see below). The inner four 'terrestrial' planets are small, rocky and have a high density. The other four 'gaseous' planets are much bigger, consist largely of hydrogen and helium and have a low density.

Some characteristics of the planets are given below. You can also update the information, which changes with more research.

Objective

- Use models to show how planets orbit the Sun.

Did you know?

- Our Sun is an average-sized star. It looks large to us because it is much closer than other stars.
- Most planets have **natural** satellites. Earth also has **artificial** satellites, e.g. communications and weather satellites that humans have launched.

Practical 159

Making a model of the solar system (MM)

1 Make circular discs, or modelling clay balls, to represent the planets. Use the table below and let 1 mm represent 1000 km. (The diameters will be, approximately, Mercury 5 mm, Venus 1.2 cm, Earth 1.3 cm, Mars 7 mm, Jupiter 14.3 cm, Saturn 12 cm, Uranus 5.1 cm and Neptune 5.0 cm.

2 Mark a position in the classroom to represent the surface of the Sun. If we use a scale with Earth 5 cm from the Sun, then the other planets are approximately these *average* distances away: Mercury 2 cm, Venus 3.5 cm, Earth 5 cm, Mars 7.5 cm, Jupiter 26 cm, Saturn 47.5 cm, Uranus 1 m and Neptune 1.5 m.

3 Attach cotton threads to the planets and suspend them the correct distances from the Sun.

Planets	Diameter at equator (km)	Average distance from the Sun at equator (millions of km)	Approximate time to orbit the Sun (in Earth years)	Number of satellites (moons)	Mean temperature (°C)	Atmosphere
Mercury	4880	58	0.25	none	465 (day) −184 (night)	None
Venus	12,104	108	0.67	none	450	Mainly carbon dioxide
Earth	12,756	150	1	1	14	Mainly nitrogen and oxygen
Mars	6794	228	nearly 2	2	−55	Carbon dioxide
Jupiter	142,984	778	12	≥ 63 and rings	−150	Mainly hydrogen and helium
Saturn	120,536	1429	29.5	≥ 60 and rings	−180	Mainly hydrogen and helium
Uranus	51,118	2870	84	≥ 27 and rings	−180	Mainly hydrogen and helium
Neptune	49,532	4504	165	≥ 13 and rings	−220	Mainly hydrogen and helium

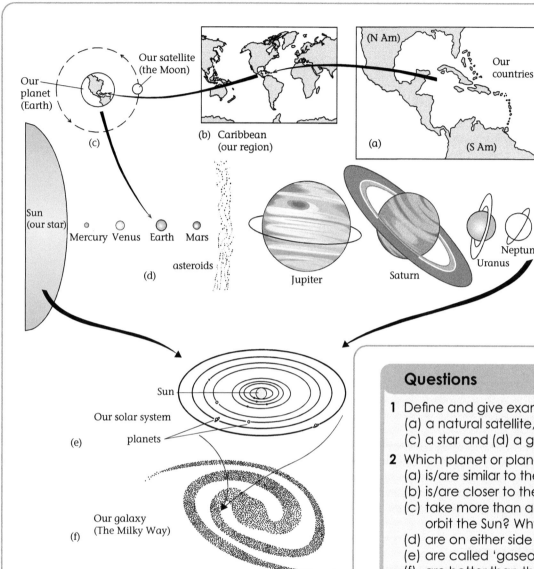

Our place in the Universe

Questions

1. Define and give examples of (a) a natural satellite, (b) a planet, (c) a star and (d) a galaxy.

2. Which planet or planets:
   (a) is/are similar to the Earth in size?
   (b) is/are closer to the Sun than Earth?
   (c) take more than an Earth year to orbit the Sun? Why?
   (d) are on either side of the asteroids?
   (e) are called 'gaseous' planets? Why?
   (f) are hotter than the Earth? Why?

3. (a) Why is life like ours possible on Earth?
   (b) Do you think life like ours exists on other planets in our solar system? Why? How might we find out?

Key ideas

Use these words to fill in the spaces as you write the sentences in your Exercise book.

galaxy   star   less   satellites   solar   planets   more

The _____ orbit a _____ ; and _____ orbit the _____ . A star can produce _____ energy.

Earth is part of our _____ system, which is part of the Milky Way _____ . _____ that are

further from the Sun than the Earth take _____ than a year to orbit the Sun; those that are closer

to the Sun take _____ than a year.

21.5 How can we travel in space?

Practical 160

The importance of gravity (MM, ORR)

1 Tie a 2 m length of string securely onto a rubber bung. Find an open area well away from windows.

2 Whirl the string above your head. Increase the speed. Does the pull on the string increase?
- You are showing how planets are attracted by the force of gravity of the Sun (the string), so they do not fly off into space (because they are travelling forward). The planets keep in their orbits round the Sun (see page 357).

3 Whirl the bung in a complete circle. Then, if it is safe, let go of the string and observe the path of the bung as it moves away. How does the bung move?
- This is like a rocket in orbit that increases its speed, so it overcomes the gravity of Earth and escapes into space. As the bung is not traveling fast enough, it will soon be attracted by Earth's gravity and fall down.

What is it like in space?

In space, objects are not close to any large bodies, and so they are weightless and do not fall. Instead of air there is a near-perfect vacuum. There is also a lot of radiation, such as ultraviolet, X-rays, gamma rays and cosmic rays from the Sun or other stars. In space, temperatures can rise very high in direct sunlight or fall very low in shadow.

How can people survive in space?

In the same way that people cannot survive at the bottom of the sea (see pages 230–1), conditions in space are hostile and so unlike what we are used to on the Earth's surface that we cannot survive without assistance. So space travellers need to have a specially created, suitable environment in a spaceship or spacesuit, with Earth-like conditions.

Protection from space

Astronauts need to leave their spacecraft to carry out tasks such as performing experiments and making repairs to the spacecraft. Spacesuits protect them from radiation and provide life support, with an air supply at the correct pressure, sealed helmet and visor, an outer suit that is pressurized and provided with warm or cold water for temperature control, heavy overshoes and communication links.

Weightlessness

Astronauts can perform acrobatics not possible on Earth. But prolonged weightlessness has bad effects on the body. We need to have the stresses caused by gravity for our muscles and organs to stay healthy and adapted to Earth's conditions.

Objective

- Describe the characteristics of space and how problems affecting human life might be overcome.

An astronaut on the Moon

Effects of weightlessness

- Space motion sickness (first 72 hours), causing headaches and vomiting.
- Bone deterioration, as calcium is lost and bones become weaker.
- Muscles die as a result of disuse, so astronauts become very weak.
- Heart muscle degenerates, heartbeat slows and fewer red cells are made (causing 'space' anaemia). Blood also tends to collect in the upper body, making the face appear swollen.
- The immune system is weakened, making astronauts open to infection.
- Balance and hand–eye coordination are affected, as the inner ear can no longer sense direction and gravity.

Questions

1 Describe natural and artificial satellites.
2 Describe three problems of space travel.

How can some problems be overcome?

Gravitational effects

Exercise regimes using springs and treadmills are used to exercise the muscles.

Temperature

A spacecraft is very well insulated, as it is usually very cold in space. However, on return to Earth the frictional forces mean that outer shields have to withstand extremely high temperatures.

Spacecraft propulsion

Spacecraft use rocket engines for propulsion, as for the jet engine (see page 349). Hot gases are produced by burning fuel in a combustion chamber. The sudden out-rush of these gases pushes the spacecraft forward. Spacecraft have to fly beyond the atmosphere and have to carry their own oxygen.

In practice, rockets are multi-stage: several rockets are mounted one on top of the other. Each stage rocket has its own fuel tanks and engine. When the fuel from the first stage is used up, it is discarded and the second stage is fired. The whole rocket becomes lighter as it travels upward and can reach a far greater speed and height than single-stage rockets.

In July 1969, after only 8 years, the US Apollo programme successfully achieved its objective of putting an astronaut on the Moon. The Saturn Apollo rocket they used weighed over 3000 tonnes at launch but only a tiny part, the command module, completed the journey to the Moon and returned to Earth.

In 1981 a new development in space travel came into being with the launching of the space shuttle (see the photograph on the right). This has a major advantage over rockets in being extremely versatile and also re-usable. It was able to launch satellites and retrieve them for repair. It has also been very useful in the building of the International Space Station (ISS) in Earth's orbit.

You can carry out research to discover and describe future space exploration achievements.

Navigation

- **Maps:** working out suitable routes for the spacecraft. These are calculated with reference to the Sun and stars using large radio telescopes, ultra-sensitive radar receivers and signal detectors able to detect radiation as weak as the radiant power from a lighted match on Mars.
- **Location:** continually checking the actual flight path during the journey from the speed and time, and direction of travel. Radar is vital to navigation in space, and also clocks capable of measuring nanoseconds (10^{-9} seconds).
- **Communication:** making corrections to the flight path. As a spacecraft travels further away, it becomes more difficult to send and receive signals with Earth, and these become delayed. A spacecraft has its own control systems, which make immediate adjustments to its flight path.

The space shuttle lifting off

Key ideas

Use these words to fill in the spaces as you write the sentences in your Exercise book.

weightlessness   **gravity**   **rockets**   **muscles**   **spacesuits**   **bones**

_____ are used to launch spacecraft; they must travel fast enough to escape Earth's _____ .

Without _____ , the astronauts experience _____ , which has damaging effects on their _____ and _____ . Astronauts wear _____ to protect them from space conditions.

The electromagnetic spectrum

Radiation		Typical wavelength	How produced	How detected
10^{-14} m		10^{-12} m (a million-millionth of a metre)	Radioactive substances, nuclear reactions	Geiger–Müller tube
10^{-12} m	**Gamma rays**			
10^{-10} m	**X-rays**	10^{-10} m (a ten-thousand-millionth of a metre)	X-ray tube	Photographic film
10^{-8} m	**Ultraviolet**	10^{-7} m (a ten-millionth of a metre)	Sun, sparks, mercury lamp	Photographic film, sun tan, fluorescent substances glow
10^{-6} m	**Visible light**	5×10^{-7} m	Sun, electric lamps, hot objects	Eyes, photographic film
10^{-4} m	**Infrared**	10^{-5} m (a hundred-thousandth of a metre)	Hot objects, Sun	Skin, photo-transistor
10^{-2} m	**Microwaves**	10^{-2} m (a hundredth of a metre)	Microwave ovens	
1 m	**TV**	1 m	TV transmitter	TV aerial
10^{2} m	**Radio**	300 m	Radio transmitter	Radio aerial
10^{4} m				

increasing wavelength →

School-based assessment (SBA)

This section may be photocopied and used by students in your school:

- as they plan their practical work (pages 361 and 362)
- to jot down notes before writing up their reports (page 363)
- as a source of practicals suitable for SBA (pages 365–98).

Science investigating			
Use this sheet to decide what to do under each skill heading			
Steps	**Skills**	**What is covered**	**My notes**
Plan	Plan and Design	Think of hypothesis Set up a fair test What materials? What method? Change plans?	
Do	Observe	Use senses safely Record accurately	
	Manipulate	Handle equipment safely and correctly	
	Measure	Handle correctly and read scales Make accurate readings, with units	
Show	Draw	Draw specimens and equipment, with labels	
	Record	Do you need to make tables, bar charts, pie charts, line graphs?	
	Report	Use headings (page 363) and write a report	
Explain	Analyse	Assess if you have achieved your aim	
	Interpret	Interpret data in tables, charts, graphs Draw conclusions	

Planning and designing
Use this sheet to help you plan a fair test

Steps	Description	My notes
Observation/ Problem	What is the question you want to investigate? *e.g. Is size important for how quickly seeds germinate?*	
Hypothesis	• What statement (hypothesis) can you make about what you expect? • How can you make it testable? *e.g. Small seeds such as Balsam germinate quicker than large seeds such as beans.*	
Set up a fair test	Change only **one** variable. You compare your experiment to a **control**. • List **one** variable to be changed. *e.g. size of seeds* • List variables to be kept constant. *e.g. water, light, temperature, number of seeds* • Repeat the experiment or, in this case, use several seeds.	
Results	Decide on the expected results. • List observations or measurements you will make. *e.g. first appearance of new root. Count numbers of seeds germinated.* • When will you record results? *e.g. every day at morning break*	
Materials and method	• What materials will you need to use? *e.g. test tubes, moist cotton wool, equal numbers of seeds* • Outline your method. *e.g. equal amounts of water to wet cotton wool, left in same conditions* • Modify your plan if necessary. *e.g. if seeds rot, set up again*	
Assessment	Will your test allow you to say if your hypothesis is supported or not?	

Outline for a laboratory report

Use a copy of this sheet as you do your practical;
then use the notes as you write your report in your SBA practical workbook

Heading	Description	My notes
Date	When done	
Title	Name of practical	
Aim	What you were trying to find out The hypothesis	
Materials and apparatus	Equipment, chemicals (can be shown as a table)	
Diagram	Apparatus used	
Method	What was done (in the passive tense)	
Results	What was found: Observations Measurements Display results in tables, bar charts, line graphs etc.	
Discussion	What do these results mean? How can they be analysed and interpreted?	
Conclusion	Has the aim been achieved? Was a fair test set up? Was the hypothesis supported or not? Sources of error?	

Practicals that can be used for SBA

Note: the following practicals have been chosen from all sections of the syllabus. Sufficient detail has been given to help guide students in doing their practical work. They should then write their reports in their Practical workbooks under the headings given on page 363.

Chapter	Title		SBA skills
3	1	Observing plant and animal cells, p. 365, (3.1)	ORR, D
3	2	Investigating osmosis, p. 366, (3.2)	MM, ORR, AI
4	3	Are chlorophyll and light needed for photosynthesis?, p. 367, (4.1)	D, ORR, AI, PD
4	4	How does pH affect salivary amylase?, p. 368, (4.9)	MM, ORR, AI
5	5	Anaerobic respiration in yeast, p. 369, (5.4)	MM, ORR, AI
5	6	Heat released from a peanut during burning, p. 370, (5.4)	MM, ORR, AI
6	7	Comparing transpiration rates, p. 371, (6.2)	MM, ORR, AI
8	8	Investigating sounds, p. 372, (8.7)	MM, ORR, AI
9	9	Observing and drawing flowers and fruits, p. 373, (9.2)	D, ORR, AI
9	10	What conditions are necessary for germination?, p. 374, (9.3)	ORR, AI
10	11	How can heat be transferred?, p. 375, (10.1)	D, MM, ORR, AI
10	12	How does speed of drying vary?, p. 376, (10.3)	PD, ORR, AI
11	13	Measuring water drainage and water retention, p. 377, (11.2)	MM, ORR, AI
11	14	Collecting land organisms, p. 378, (11.4)	ORR, D, AI
11	15	How plants and animals affect carbon dioxide levels, p. 379, (11.5)	ORR, AI
11	16	Caribbean map for tracking hurricanes, p. 380, (11.8)	ORR
12	17	Growing plants using hydroponics, p. 381, (12.1)	MM, ORR, AI
12	18	Fresh water and seawater plants, p. 382, (12.3)	MM, D, ORR, AI
13	19	How can we stop microorganisms from growing?, p. 383, (13.1)	ORR, AI
15	20	Comparing the elastic limits of materials, p. 384, (15.2)	MM, ORR, AI
15	21	How do metals react?, p. 385, (15.4/15.8)	ORR, AI
15	22	What determines the rate of rusting?, p. 386, (15.7)	PD, AI
16	23	How do acids react?, p. 387, (15.4/16.2)	PD, D, ORR, AI
16	24	Solutions, suspensions and colloids, p. 388, (16.3)	MM, ORR, AI
16	25	How can we remove stains?, p. 389, (16.2/16.3)	ORR, AI
16	26	Investigating hard and soft water, p. 390, (16.5)	PD, ORR, AI
17	27	Comparing series and parallel circuits, p. 391, (17.2)	MM, ORR, AI
17	28	Current, voltage and resistance, p. 392, (17.3)	MM, ORR, AI
17	29	Do colours contain different pigments?, p. 393, (17.11)	ORR, AI, D
18	30	Making a model that uses solar energy, p. 394, (18.4/20.1)	PD, D, MM, AI
19	31	Making a model machine, p. 395, (19.1–19.4)	PD, D, MM, AI
20	32	What happens in collisions?, p. 396, (20.3)	MM, ORR, AI
21	33	The centre of gravity of flat objects, p. 397, (21.2)	MM
21	34	Finding out about moments, p. 398, (19.1/21.3)	MM, ORR, AI

1 Observing plant and animal cells

Refer to pages 44–5

You will need:

☐ microscope   ☐ slide and cover slip

☐ leaf of Moses-in-the-bulrushes (*Rhoeo discolor*) or of a purple onion

☐ tweezers   ☐ pointed needle   ☐ prepared slide of animal cells

● SBA skills that can be assessed:

ORR, D

Observing plant cells

1 Use the tweezers to pull off a small (5 mm square) piece of the lower (purple) epidermis of a leaf of *Rhoeo discolor* or a piece of coloured epidermis from an onion.

2 Place this on a microscope slide in a drop of water.

3 Slowly lower the coverslip using the pointed needle (see page 33). (This is to stop air bubbles being trapped.)

4 Look at your slide under the low power of a microscope (page 33).

5 Notice how the cells fit closely together to make the tissue of the epidermis.

6 Look for characteristics of plant cells: thick cell wall, nucleus, cytoplasm, large vacuole. (You will not find chloroplasts, as these are not present in ordinary epidermal cells. Also, at this magnification you will not be able to distinguish the cell membrane from the cell wall, nor will you see mitochondria or chromosomes.)

7 Draw one complete cell and show how it joins to the other cells. Draw and label just what you can see. (For hints on making a good drawing, see pages 36–7.)

Observing animal cells

1 Collect a slide of prepared animal cells from your teacher. (We use prepared slides, as these have been stained to show important parts. It is also safer than making slides for yourself.)

2 Look at the slide under the low power of the microscope.

3 Notice how the cells are loosely packed together; not as tightly as in the plant tissue.

4 Look for characteristics of animal cells: outer cell membrane, nucleus, cytoplasm without large vacuoles or chloroplasts. (At this magnification you will not be able to see mitochondria.)

5 Draw one complete cell. Draw and label just what you can see.

Record your observations. Write up your reports in your Practical workbook.

Plant cell	Animal cell

2 Investigating osmosis

Refer to page 47

You will need:

- piece of potato
- ruler
- 2 Petri dishes
- 30% salt solution
- distilled water
- sharp knife
- white tile

- SBA skills that can be assessed:

  MM, ORR, AI

1 Cut two potato strips to the same size (1 × 1 × 5 cm). Dry them on a paper towel.

2 Label one Petri dish 'Water' and the other one 'Salt solution'. Pour in the correct liquids.

3 Add a potato strip to each dish.

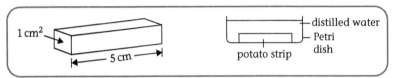

4 Every 5 minutes, take out the strips. Dry them and measure to the nearest mm. Record the lengths in the table.

Time	5 min	10 min	15 min	20 min	25 min
Distilled water					
Salt solution					

5 Use the graph paper below to make a line graph of your results. Time should be along the horizontal axis, and the length of the strips (in mm) on the vertical axis. Use different colours to show which strip was left in. Explain your graph.

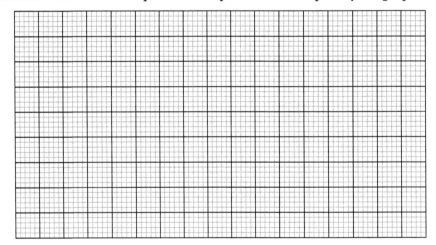

6 What is the texture of the strip left in water? How do you explain this based on osmosis?

7 What is the texture of the strip left in salt solution? How do you explain this based on osmosis?

8 Predict what would happen if you left a 5 cm strip in a salt solution of half the strength that you used. Why do you think this?

9 Predict what would happen if you first heated the strips in boiling water. Why?

Write up your report in your Practical workbook.

3 Are chlorophyll and light needed for photosynthesis?

Refer to page 48

You will need:

○ potted plant with green leaves   ○ aluminium foil   ○ scissors

○ paper clips   ○ potted plant with variegated leaves

○ apparatus and chemicals for testing leaves for starch (see page 48)

● SBA skills that can
be assessed:

D, ORR, AI, PD

Is chlorophyll needed for photosynthesis?

1 Leave a potted plant in the dark for 24 hours.

2 Test one of its leaves to make sure it does not contain starch (see the test in Practical 10 on page 48).

3 Make a cut-out shield from aluminium foil. Wrap and secure it around the leaf.

4 Leave the plant in the light for 2–3 hours.

5 Remove the leaf, and test it for starch. Draw the pattern where starch was made.

6 Compare the parts that (a) received light and (b) did not receive light.

7 What do you conclude? Explain why this is a fair test.

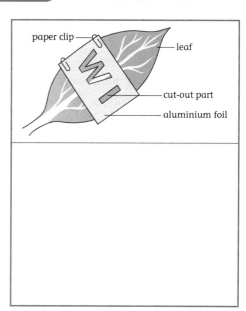

Is light needed for photosynthesis?

1 Use a de-starched plant with variegated leaves (partly green and partly white). *Tradescantia* or variegated *Hibiscus* would be suitable.

2 Draw the pattern of the green and white parts of your leaf.

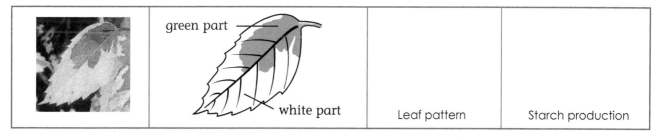

		Leaf pattern	Starch production

3 Leave the plant in the light for 2–3 hours. Remove the leaf that you drew. Decolourise it and test for starch. Draw the pattern of starch production in the space above.

4 How does the pattern of starch production compare to the distribution of chlorophyll?

5 What do you conclude? Explain why this is a fair test.

Planning and designing

You have some red algae from a rock pool on the shore. Design fair tests to show:

(a) that the algae are carrying out photosynthesis by producing oxygen in the light

(b) that they are producing starch even though they do not look green.

Write up your report in your Practical workbook.

4 How does pH affect salivary amylase?

You will need:

- cracker
- dilute sodium hydroxide
- dropping pipettes
- beaker of water
- test tubes
- amylase enzyme
- iodine solution
- heating apparatus
- dilute hydrochloric acid
- litmus paper
- white tile
- Benedict's solution

Refer to page 71

● SBA skills that can be assessed:

MM, ORR, AI

1 Cut a piece of cracker of about 1 cm². Crush it and mix it with distilled water. This is your sample of cooked starch.

2 Divide your sample equally between three test tubes, labelled **A**, **B** and **C**. The test tubes should be about half full.

3 Add 5 drops of dilute hydrochloric acid to test tube **A**. Test with litmus paper.
Add 5 drops of dilute sodium hydroxide to test tube **B**. Test with litmus paper.
Add 5 drops of distilled water to test tube **C**. Test with litmus paper.

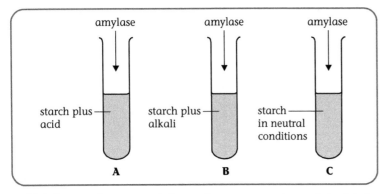

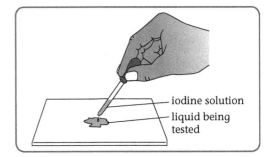

4 Add 3 drops of commercial amylase enzyme to each test tube.

5 Leave the test tubes for 5 minutes. Then use a dropping pipette to take a little solution out of test tube **A**, and test it with iodine solution on a white tile.

6 Repeat step **5** for tubes **B** and **C**.

7 Test again with iodine solution at 10 minutes and 15 minutes. Record your results.

Test tube	Acid/alkali/neutral	Tested with iodine		Conclusion
A				
B				
C				

8 Under which conditions does salivary amylase work best? Explain.

9 Salivary amylase digests cooked starch to produce a reducing sugar called maltose. Take the test tube in which you believe digestion has occurred and test it with Benedict's solution. Explain what you find.

Note: in the body, salivary amylase works best in the slightly alkaline conditions in the mouth. In very acidic or very alkaline conditions it does not work well.

Write up your report in your Practical workbook.

5 Anaerobic respiration in yeast

Refer to page 78

You will need:

☐ 4 test tubes ☐ 2 bungs with bent tubing attached
☐ water ☐ Bunsen burner ☐ thermometer
☐ vegetable oil ☐ glucose ☐ yeast
☐ teaspoon ☐ limewater

● SBA skills that can be assessed:

MM, ORR, AI

You want the yeast to respire anaerobically. This is why you will boil the water (to drive out air containing oxygen) and cool it (so it will not harm the enzymes in the yeast), and cover it with oil (to prevent oxygen getting in; but the oil does allow carbon dioxide to get through).

1 Boil half a test tube of water. Then let it cool to 35 °C.

2 Mix a teaspoonful of glucose into the cooled water.

3 Divide the glucose solution into two test tubes.

4 Into one of the test tubes add a teaspoonful of dried yeast and cover the mixture with a layer of oil.

5 Add the bung with the tubing. Arrange for the other end of the tube to dip into limewater in another test tube (see the diagram on the right). This is your experiment.

6 Set up a control in a similar way, with oil, bung, tubing and limewater, but do not add any yeast to the glucose solution.

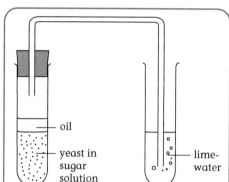

oil

yeast in sugar solution

limewater

7 Record your observations at the beginning of the activity and after 30 minutes in a warm place.

	Experiment with yeast		Control without yeast	
	Beginning	End	Beginning	End
Temperature of glucose mixture				
Appearance of glucose mixture				
Appearance of limewater				
Smell of glucose mixture				

8 Explain each of the observations you recorded in the table.

9 Write the word equation and the chemical equation for the reaction that occurred with the yeast.

10 Describe one use of this reaction.

Write up your report in your Practical workbook.

6 Heat released from a peanut during burning

Refer to page 80

You will need:

- ☐ boiling tube
- ☐ thermometer
- ☐ stirrer
- ☐ reagents for food tests (page 57)
- ☐ Bunsen burner
- ☐ measuring cylinder
- ☐ balance
- ☐ peanut (skinned)
- ☐ pin
- ☐ tin can to enclose boiling tube
- ☐ knife

● SBA skills that can be assessed:

MM, ORR, AI

You are going to burn half a peanut and use the energy released to heat 20 cm³ of water in a boiling tube. You will record the increase in temperature of the water.

1 Measure out 20 cm³ of water into the boiling tube.

2 Record the starting temperature of the water. Set up the boiling tube inside a tin (see diagram on the right).

3 Measure the mass of half a peanut and attach it firmly to the end of a pin.

4 Use a Bunsen flame to set the peanut alight, and hold it under the end of the boiling tube. If the peanut goes out, then light it again.

5 Record the highest (final) temperature of the water.

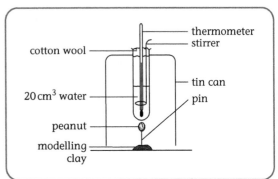

WARNING: No student with a nut allergy should do this experiment.

Starting temperature (T1)	°C
Highest (final) temperature (T2)	°C
Increase in temperature (T2 – T1)	°C
Mass of half peanut	g

6 Enter your figure for temperature increase into the equation:

Energy released (J) = increase in temperature (_____ °C) × mass of water (20 g) × 4.2 = _____ J.

7 Work out the energy released in joules. This is from half a peanut of mass (_____ g).

8 If a mass of _____ g of peanut releases _____ J of energy, then work out what 1 g would release:
_____ J of energy for each g = _____ J/g.

9 Energy release is usually given in kilojoules rather than joules. So divide your answer by 1000 to give the energy release in kJ/g: _____ kJ/g.

10 Cut and squash the other half of the peanut. Use food test reagents to test for starch, reducing sugar, fat and protein (see page 57). Record your results.

Starch ☐   Reducing sugar ☐   Fat ☐   Protein ☐

11 From your results with food tests, which food substance do you think provided the greatest amount of energy to heat the water? Explain your answer.

12 Half a peanut should provide about 5 kJ of energy. How do your results compare with this? What could be the reasons for any differences?

13 What suggestions do you have for improving the design of the experiment?

Write up your report in your Practical workbook.

7 Comparing transpiration rates

You will need:

- leafy shoot
- 10 cm scale
- paper towel
- fan or hair dryer
- rubber tubing
- beaker of water
- bread tie
- capillary tube
- clamp
- large plastic bag

Refer to page 87

- SBA skills that can be assessed:
  MM, ORR, AI

You will use a potometer to measure the rate at which water is taken up by a leafy shoot. This is taken to be the same as the water loss (**transpiration**) of the plant.

1 Cut a leafy shoot under water and attach it firmly to the end of a piece of rubber tubing.

2 Attach the other end of the tubing firmly over a length of capillary tube.

3 Hold the capillary tube so its end is in a beaker of water. Attach the scale to the side of the tube. The water should be a complete column.

4 Briefly raise the capillary tube out of the water and touch the end with some dry paper towel. This will make an air bubble.

5 Put the tube back in the water, and watch the bubble of air rise up as water is transpired.

6 Put the plant in full sunlight near a window. Record the length of time taken for the bubble to travel 10 cm (**A**).

7 Squeeze the rubber tubing to push the air bubble out, and transfer the apparatus to a cool place in the laboratory.

8 Allow a new bubble of air to enter the tube, and record the time for it to travel 10 cm (**B**).

9 Repeat steps **7** and **8**, in a cool place in the laboratory, but with:
   (a) a fan or cold hair dryer near the leaves (**C**)
   (b) a plastic bag attached and held over the top of the leaves using a bread tie (**D**)
   (c) the leaves uncovered, but with half of them removed (**E**).

10 Record and explain all your results.

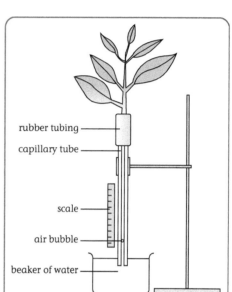

	Time to travel 10 cm	Explanation
A Full sunlight, still air		
B Cool place, still air		
C Cool place, windy air		
D Cool place, humid air		
E Cool place, few leaves		

11 What effects are you testing for, by comparing **A** and **B**, **B** and **C**, **B** and **D**, **B** and **E**?

12 From your results, list the features that *slow down* the rate of transpiration.

Write up your report in your Practical workbook.

8 Investigating sounds

Refer to page 129

You will need:

- ☐ 2 rubber bands
- ☐ sonometer (or improvisation)
- ☐ 2 rulers
- ☐ masses
- ☐ 4 pencils

● SBA skills that can be assessed:

MM, ORR, AI

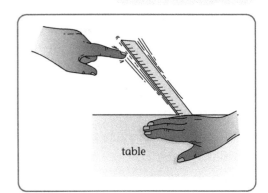

1 Set up a ruler so that 25 cm overhangs the edge of the table (as shown in the diagram).

2 With your free hand, pluck the overhanging portion and record what you see.

3 Now shift the ruler so that 20 cm overhangs. Pluck again, and compare the vibrations and the sound produced with steps **1** and **2**.

4 Repeat step **3**, reducing the overhang by 5 cm each time, down to 5 cm.

table

5 What is the effect of shortening the length of the vibrating ruler on:
   (a) the vibrations
   (b) the pitch of the sound?

6 Set up two rulers with rubber bands and pencils as shown below.

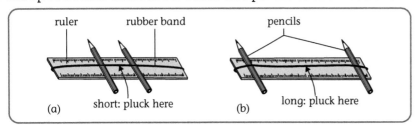

ruler   rubber band   pencils

(a)   short: pluck here   (b)   long: pluck here

7 Pluck the rubber bands between the pencils. How does the pitch of the sound in (a) the short vibrating band compare to that in (b) the longer vibrating band?

8 Set up a sonometer as shown below, or make your own improvisation.

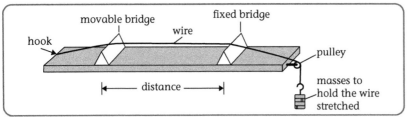

movable bridge   fixed bridge   wire   hook   pulley   distance   masses to hold the wire stretched

9 Adjust the movable bridge so that the vibrating distance is 10 cm. Pluck the wire and record the appearance of the vibrations and the sound produced.

10 Repeat step **9** with lengths of vibrating wire of 15 cm, then 20 cm.

11 Do your results agree with the previous experiments?

12 For what reasons does the sonometer give better results?

Write up your report in your Practical workbook.

9 Observing and drawing flowers and fruits

Refer to pages 136 and 139

You will need:

☐ flowers   ☐ hand lens   ☐ knife   ☐ fruits

● SBA skills that can be assessed:

D, ORR, AI

Observing and drawing flowers

1 Collect from your teacher flowers of **A** *Delonix* (flamboyant), **B** *Hibiscus* and **C** a grass.

2 Examine each flower with a hand lens. Record the number of parts in the table. (If there are too many to count, just write 'many'.)

	Number of			
	Sepals	**Petals**	**Stamens**	**Carpels**
A Flamboyant				
B Hibiscus				
C Grass				

3 For each of **A**, **B** and **C** say if you think the flower is insect or wind pollinated. In each case give two reasons for your choice.

	Insect or wind pollinated?	**Reasons**
A Flamboyant		
B Hibiscus		
C Grass		

4 Cut flower **A** in half. Draw the half flower. Show and label the following:
sepals, petals, anther, filament, stamen, stigma, style, ovary, ovules, carpel, receptacle.
Include a title and the magnification (see page 36).

Observing and drawing fruits

1 Collect from your teacher fruits of **A** tomato, **B** Pride of Barbados, **C** sweethearts (or other sticky fruit), **D** railway weed (or other hairy fruit) and **E** coconut.

2 Examine each fruit. Suggest the method by which its seeds are dispersed, and give your reasons.

	Dispersal?	**Reasons**
A Tomato		
B Pride of Barbados		
C Sweethearts		
D Railway weed		
E Coconut		

3 Make drawings of each fruit to show the features that are important for the method of dispersal you have chosen: mechanical/explosive, by water, by wind, by contact with animals, and by animals eating the fruit and passing out the seeds.

4 Select three other fruits that you know, e.g. mango, Busy Lizzie and cotton. How are they each dispersed and what special features do they have?

Write up your report in your Practical workbook.

10 What conditions are necessary for germination?

Refer to page 140

You will need:

- small seeds
- box
- 5 boiling tubes
- cooking oil
- cotton wool
- refrigerator

● SBA skills that can be assessed:

ORR, AI

1 You will need 50 small seeds, e.g. balsam or *Crotalaria*.

2 Label five boiling tubes A–E. Count out five sets of 10 seeds. Make five equal amounts of cotton wool, with four of them wet with equal amounts of water.

3 Set up a controlled experiment to find the conditions necessary for germination as shown below.

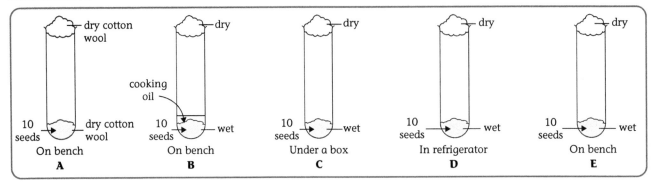

4 Leave the tubes set up until you see most of the seeds have germinated in boiling tube E. Then count and record the numbers of seeds germinated in all the tubes (see the table below).

Questions

1 Why should you not use just one or two seeds in each boiling tube? What is the advantage of using so many seeds? Why should they be small?

2 Why is this a controlled experiment to find the conditions necessary for germination?

3 Which of the boiling tubes is the **control**? Why do you think this?

4 Complete the following table to give the purpose for each boiling tube (one has been entered for you). Also record your results: how many seeds in each boiling tube germinated. Include a conclusion for each of the conditions, to say if it is necessary for germination.

	Purpose	Results	Conclusions
A	Without water		
B			
C			
D			
E			

5 Make a general statement about the conditions necessary for germination.

6 Evaluate your experiment. What further experiments would it be useful to do?

Write up your report in your Practical workbook.

11 How is heat transferred?

Refer to page 164

You will need:

- copper, iron and glass rods
- candle
- shoebox
- scissors
- coloured crystals
- heating apparatus
- 3 thumbtacks
- polythene
- sticky tape
- beaker of cold water
- stopclock
- 2 cardboard tubes
- small candle in a dish
- splint

● SBA skills that can
be assessed:

D, MM, ORR, AI

Heat transfer through solids

1 Use the candle to make a similar blob of wax on each rod, and attach a thumbtack.

2 Set up the three rods on a tripod.

3 Heat the other ends of the rods with a Bunsen flame.

4 What happens? Record how long this takes for each rod.

_____

5 Which material would you use for making a pan? Why?

_____

6 Which material would you say is an insulator? Why?

_____

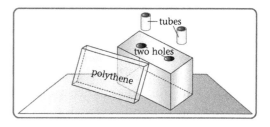

Heat transfer through gases

1 Cut two round holes in the long side of the shoebox, and push the two rolls of cardboard into them (tube **A** and tube **B**).

2 Cut away the front of the shoebox and replace it with polythene, which you should stick in place.

3 Light a small candle below tube **B**. Put on the lid.

4 Light the splint and hold it above tube **A**. Draw on the diagram what you see happening.

5 By which method has heat been transferred? _____ .
What are the characteristics of this method of transfer?

Heat transfer through liquids

1 Place a few coloured crystals into the beaker of cold water, and heat it gently directly under the crystals. Draw on the diagram what you see happening.

2 By which method has heat been transferred? _____ .
What are the characteristics of this method of transfer?

Write up your report in your Practical workbook.

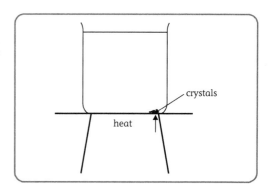

12 How does speed of drying vary?

Refer to page 170

You will need:

- hot water
- cotton wool or tissue paper
- table fan
- bungs with thermometers to fit flasks
- 3 conical flasks
- sticky tape
- bell jar
- measuring cylinder
- dishes of water
- stopclock or stopwatch

● SBA skills that can be assessed:

PD, ORR, AI

Work in a group, to set up a conical flask for each of the conditions.

1 Plan and record how you will set up three conditions.

Hot	Humid	Well ventilated

thermometer

soaked cotton wool or tissue paper

200 cm³ hot water

2 List the factors you should keep constant in each condition.

_____

_____

3 Prepare a hypothesis (what you think will happen).

_____

_____

4 Cover the outside of each conical flask with a known amount of cotton wool or tissue paper. Hold it on with sticky tape.

5 Wet the cotton wool or paper with a known amount of water.

6 Measure out quantities of 200 cm³ of hot water, and put it into each conical flask.

7 Add a bung and thermometer and record each temperature.

8 Take the temperature of each thermometer every 2 minutes for 20 minutes. Record in the table.

Conditions	Minutes										
	Start	2	4	6	8	10	12	14	16	18	20
Hot											
Humid											
Well ventilated											

9 What control(s) should you have set up for your experiment?

10 Why does the temperature fall? Account for the results in each set-up.

Hot conditions	
Humid	
Well ventilated	

11 How do the results of your experiment relate to sweating, transpiration and drying clothes?

_____

_____

Write up your report in your Practical workbook.

SBA practicals

© 2010 Cambridge University Press

13 Measuring water drainage and retention

Refer to page 179

You will need:

- hot water
- cotton wool or tissue paper
- a balance
- 4 measuring cylinders
- samples of sand, loam and clay soils
- small dishes to weigh soil
- 3 filter funnels
- water

- SBA skills that can be assessed:

  MM, ORR, AI

Work in groups of three, and each of you take measurements for one type of soil.

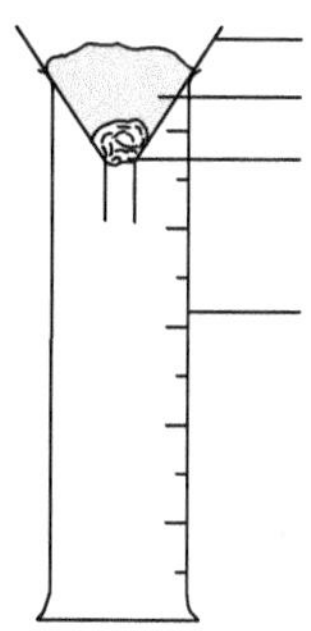

1 Set up three measuring cylinders, with filter funnels each containing a plug of cotton wool placed in them.

2 Use a small dish to weigh out exactly 20 g of each soil sample. Check with your teacher. Each student should record their measurements below.

	Sand	Loam	Clay
Dish alone			
Dish + soil			

filter funnel
soil sample
cotton wool

measuring cylinder

3 Put the soil into a filter funnel (as shown in the diagram).

4 Each student should exactly measure 100 cm³ of water in a measuring cylinder and gently pour it into their sample.

5 Leave for 30 minutes.

6 Read off the amount of water that has drained through. Check with your teacher. This is the water drainage for each sample.

7 Work out how much water has been retained by each sample. Enter your results in the table below.

	Sand	Loam	Clay
Water drainage (cm³)			
Water retained (cm³)			

8 Why did you use the same mass of each soil? _____

9 Why did you add the same volume of water to each soil? _____

_____

10 From your experiment, what do you think conditions will be like for plants growing in each kind of soil?

Sand _____

Loam _____

Clay _____

Write up your report in your Practical workbook.

14 Collecting land organisms

Refer to pages 186 and 188

You will need:

- scissors or shears
- animal traps
- notebook and pencil
- plastic bowl
- hand lens
- beaker of water
- knife or penknife
- nets
- plastic bottles
- plastic bags and ties
- plastic cup
- clamp
- long stick
- gardening gloves
- paper tape
- forceps
- light

● SBA skills that can be assessed:

ORR, D, AI

Work in a group, with each of you concentrating on three areas to collect organisms.

1 Collect or make the materials you need. Refer to page 188 for reference diagrams and to see how each collecting material is used.

2 You should examine these areas, using the appropriate collecting materials. In each case record a description or names of plants or animals you found, and their probable feeding level.

Area examined	Plants or animals found	Probable feeding level(s)
The soil (see page 186)		
Dead leaves and soil litter		
On and under leaves		
Near where water drips		
Crevices of a path		
Edges of a water channel		
Crevices of a wall		
On wall surfaces		
Rotting wood		
Underneath a stone		
Angle of tree branches		
Hanging from a tree		
Holes in a tree trunk		
Long grass		

3 Take small samples of plants, and single animal species to examine in the laboratory.

4 Draw and label one of your specimens. Include the name, date, view and magnification.

Write up your report in your Practical workbook.

15 How plants and animals affect carbon dioxide levels

Refer to page 190

You will need:

- ○ 6 boiling tubes
- ○ cloth bag
- ○ thread
- ○ paper tape
- ○ carbon dioxide indicator solution
- ○ small animals, e.g. woodlice
- ○ black paper
- ○ test-tube rack
- ○ leaves
- ○ measuring cylinder

● SBA skills that can be assessed:

ORR, AI

You will use carbon dioxide indicator (a solution of sodium hydrogencarbonate and two indicators). It changes colour with the carbon dioxide concentration, as shown below.

Colour	Amount of carbon dioxide (CO_2) dissolved
Reddish	Same as in the air
Purple	Less than in the air
Yellow	More than in the air

1 Set up six boiling tubes (**A–F**) early in the morning. Use $5\,cm^3$ of indicator solution in each tube. Enclose each small animal in a cloth bag. No specimens should touch the indicator. For tubes **C** and **F**, cover the tubes with black paper, held on with paper tape. Do not breathe on the indicator. Put the bungs into the boiling tubes as quickly as possible.

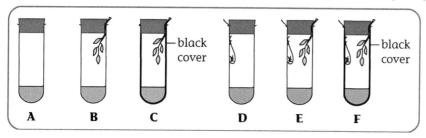

| **A** | **B** | **C** black cover | **D** | **E** | **F** black cover |

2 Record the predicted colours for each boiling tube. Then leave them all in strong sunlight for 4 hours. Add the actual colours to the table, and add your explanation for each tube.

	Prediction	Actual	Explanation
A Nothing in tube			
B Leaf			
C Leaf, covered			
D Animal			
E Plant and animal			
F Plant and animal, covered			

3 (a) Why were tubes **C** and **F** covered? (b) Why is it unnecessary to cover tube **D**?

(a) _____

(b) _____

Write up your report in your Practical workbook.

16 Caribbean map for tracking hurricanes

Use the page to record in pencil, and then in pen the names and tracks of hurricanes this season.

Refer to page 197

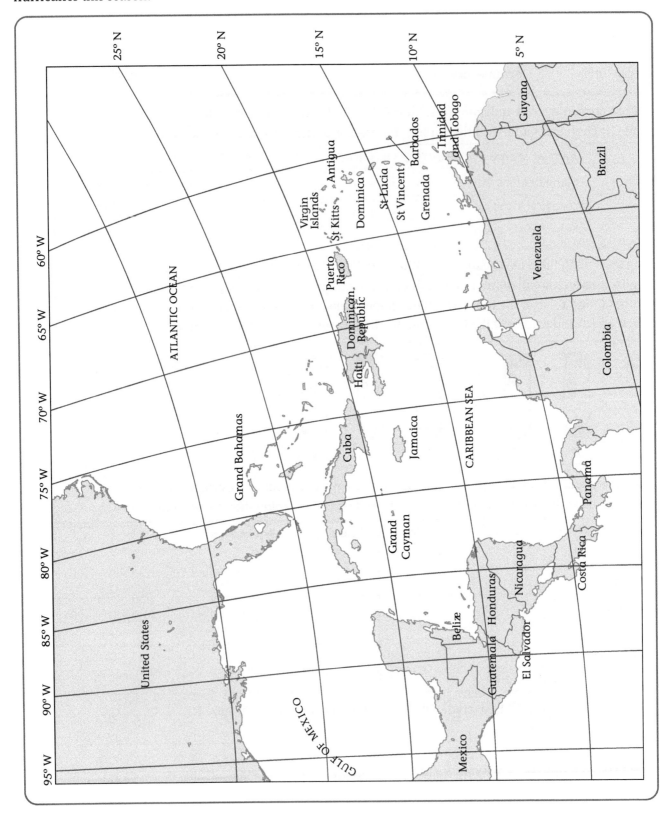

17 Growing plants using hydroponics

Refer to page 208

You will need:

- [ ] sunflower seeds
- [ ] loam soil
- [ ] 5 plastic cups
- [ ] marker
- [ ] tray
- [ ] houseplant fertilizer
- [ ] newspaper
- [ ] scissors
- [ ] distilled water
- [ ] card
- [ ] measuring cylinder

● SBA skills that can be assessed:

  MM, ORR, AI

1 Work in small groups. Leave 20 soaked seeds between several layers of damp newspaper.

2 Keep the newspaper damp, but not too wet, for 3 days – or until the seeds germinate.

3 Choose the best 15 seedlings. Choose ones that are as similar to each other as possible.

4 Cut four card discs that fit snugly inside the plastic cups. In each one, cut three small holes, into which you push the seedlings, so that they are supported.

5 Set up the plastic cups as shown below. Note that the card covers for plastic cups **A** and **C** need an extra hole to allow air in. Make up the houseplant fertilizer solution by following the instructions on the bottle (do *not* make it too strong).

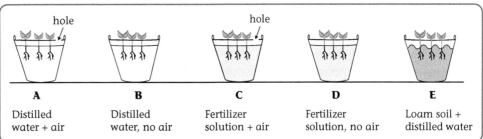

| A | B | C | D | E |
| Distilled water + air | Distilled water, no air | Fertilizer solution + air | Fertilizer solution, no air | Loam soil + distilled water |

6 Leave your plants to grow on a bench near the window. Every 3 to 4 days check the water levels in **B** and **D** and add distilled water as necessary. Keep the soil in **E** moist, but not wet. Every 3 to 4 days replace the distilled water in cup **A** and the fertilizer solution in cup **C**.

7 After 3 weeks, record the appearance of the seedlings in each cup, and write explanations.

	Appearance	Explanation
A Distilled water + air		
B Distilled water alone		
C Fertilizer + air		
D Fertilizer alone		
E Loam soil + water		

8 Explain why the experiment had to run for 3 weeks.

_____

9 Why were 3 seedlings used in each set-up?

_____

10 Why were air and replacement liquids added to cups **A** and **C**? Did it make a difference? Why?

_____

Write up your report in your Practical workbook.

18 Fresh water and seawater plants

Refer to page 218

You will need:

☐ pondweed   ☐ seaweed   ☐ samples of fresh water and seawater
☐ knife   ☐ dishes   ☐ microscope   ☐ slides and coverslips

- SBA skills that can be assessed:

  MM, D, ORR, AI

1 Strip off a thin outside layer of pondweed (from fresh water) and seaweed (from seawater).

2 Mount some of the pondweed strip in fresh water on a slide. Cover it carefully with a coverslip and examine it under the low power of the microscope.

3 Mount some of the seaweed strip in seawater on a slide. Examine it under low power.

4 Make labelled drawings of a few cells from both plants in their normal conditions.

Pondweed mounted in fresh water	Seaweed mounted in seawater

5 Mount some of the pondweed strip in seawater on a slide. Examine it under low power.

6 Mount some of the seaweed strip in fresh water on a slide. Examine it under low power.

7 Make labelled drawings of a few cells from both plants in their unusual conditions.

Pondweed mounted in seawater	Seaweed mounted in fresh water

8 Explain what happens to the:
(a) pondweed left in seawater

_____

_____

(b) seaweed left in fresh water

_____

_____

9 How do these findings compare to those described for fresh water fish and seawater fish that were moved into habitats for which they were not adapted? (See page 215.)

_____

_____

Write up your report in your Practical workbook.

19 How can we stop microorganisms from growing?

Refer to page 232

You will need:

- [ ] slice of bread
- [ ] 6 plastic bags and ties
- [ ] water
- [ ] salt
- [ ] sugar
- [ ] vinegar
- [ ] 2 test tubes

- SBA skills that can be assessed:

ORR, AI

Work in a group, to set up a plastic bag for each of the conditions.

1 Toast, or oven cook, a piece of bread to make it dry.

2 Cut it into six equal-sized pieces.

3 Dissolve salt in a test tube full of water until no more will dissolve. Make another solution in the same way, but this time use sugar.

4 Set up a control, as shown on the right.

5 Set up five other bags, as shown below.

6 Under each bag, write your prediction about what will happen.

7 Examine the bread each day for 2 weeks. Do not remove it from the bags.

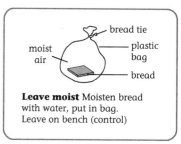

Leave moist Moisten bread with water, put in bag. Leave on bench (control)

Prediction:

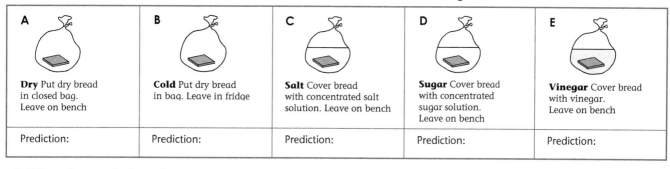

A	B	C	D	E
Dry Put dry bread in closed bag. Leave on bench	**Cold** Put dry bread in bag. Leave in fridge	**Salt** Cover bread with concentrated salt solution. Leave on bench	**Sugar** Cover bread with concentrated sugar solution. Leave on bench	**Vinegar** Cover bread with vinegar. Leave on bench
Prediction:	Prediction:	Prediction:	Prediction:	Prediction:

8 What do you find out by comparing each set-up with the control?

A	B	C	D	E

9 Which conditions (a) encourage and (b) discourage growth of mould?

(a) _____

(b) _____

10 The table below shows four sets of conditions, **W**, **X**, **Y** and **Z**, in which bacteria might be found. Record what results you would expect, and give the reasons.

	Temperature (°C)	Oxygen	Water	Expected results	Reasons
W	0	Present	Present		
X	25	Present	Present		
Y	30	Present	Absent		
Z	100	Present	Present		

Write up your report in your Practical workbook.

20 Comparing the elastic limits of materials

Refer to page 258

You will need:

- narrow and thick rubber bands
- metre rule
- clamp and stand
- slotted 10 g masses and mass hanger
- cotton and nylon threads
- paper tape

- SBA skills that can be assessed:

  MM, ORR, AI

Your group should choose to compare two rubber bands of different thicknesses, or two different threads (cotton and nylon) of the same thickness.

1 Set up one of your chosen materials. Wind the material round the bar and secure it with paper tape.

2 Measure down 5 cm, and attach the mass hanger at that position.

3 Add a 10 g mass to the mass hanger. Record any extension of your material in the table.

4 Repeat step 3 until you notice a permanent change in your material. Record all your results.

5 Repeat the activity with your other material.

	Load	0 g	10 g	20 g	30 g	40 g	50 g	60 g	70 g	80 g	90 g	100 g
Extension	Material A	0										
	Material B	0										

6 Draw graphs of your results, load against extension. Compare and explain your results.

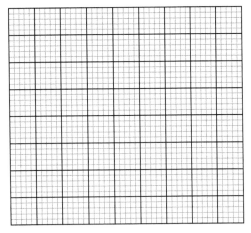 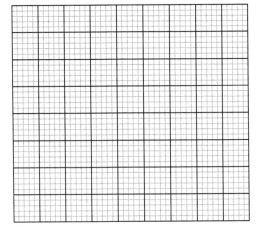

7 Account for these observations:
   (a) The strings of rackets are made from nylon and not cotton.
   (b) Rubber is used for the soles of shoes and the outside of balls.
   (c) Cricket bats are made from springy wood.
   (d) Boat sails are made from polyester and not nylon.

Write up your report in your Practical workbook.

21 How do metals react?

You will need:

- ☐ wire cutters
- ☐ emery paper
- ☐ magnesium ribbon
- ☐ rack
- ☐ 3 small beakers
- ☐ copper wire
- ☐ 3 iron nails
- ☐ tap water
- ☐ copper sulphate solution
- ☐ wire

Refer to pages 265 and 273

- SBA skills that can be assessed:
  ORR, AI

Showing how metals compete

1 Fill two-thirds of a beaker with copper sulphate solution.

2 Clean an iron nail with emery paper so it is completely clean. Put it into the solution (a).

3 Note the colour of the nail and the solution (b).

4 Leave them for 3 days (c). Note the colour of the solution. What colour is the nail? (This is a covering of copper metal.)

(a)

(b)

(c)

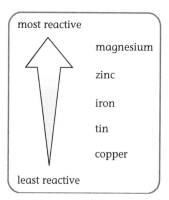

most reactive

magnesium

zinc

iron

tin

copper

least reactive

5 Explain what happened to the iron nail and copper sulphate solution. Write a word equation.

_____

Showing sacrificial protection

1 Clean an iron nail and piece of magnesium ribbon with emery paper.

2 Connect the metals with a piece of wire and place them in a small beaker of water (d).

3 Set up another iron nail and piece of copper wire in a similar way (e). Leave (d) and (e) for 3 days.

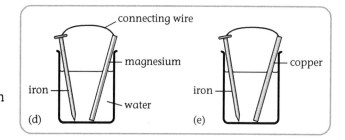

connecting wire

magnesium

iron

water

(d)

copper

iron

(e)

4 Observe the nails. Explain what you see.

(d) _____

_____

(e) _____

_____

Write up your report in your Practical workbook.

© 2010 Cambridge University Press

SBA practicals 385

22 What determines the rate of rusting?

Refer to page 271

You will need:

- 6 test tubes
- marker pen
- salt solution
- vinegar
- universal indicator paper
- calcium oxide
- tap water
- 6 nails
- measuring cylinder
- rubber bung
- distilled water
- emery paper
- bleach

● SBA skills that can be assessed:

PD, AI

Work in groups

1 Mark the test tubes **A** to **F**. Clean the six nails with emery paper.
2 Put equal amounts of liquid into tubes **B** to **F** (see the table below for liquids).
3 Record the pH of each liquid (using universal indicator paper) and whether they are acidic, alkaline or neutral.
4 Add a nail to each test tube. Use dry calcium oxide and add a bung to test tube **A**.
5 Record the appearance of the nails after 1, 3, 5 and 8 days.
6 Use the table below to record all your observations and list the rates at which rust formed from 6 (fastest) to 1 (slowest).

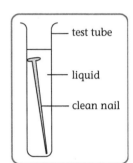

test tube
liquid
clean nail

	pH	Acidic/alkaline/neutral	Days				Rate
			1	**3**	**5**	**8**	
A Left dry							
B Distilled water							
C Tap water							
D Salt solution							
E Vinegar							
F Bleach							

7 Explain and account for the results in each test tube.

	Explanation
A Left dry	
B Distilled water	
C Tap water	
D Salt solution	
E Vinegar	
F Bleach	

8 Summarize your findings. In each case list which test tube(s) support your answers.
   (a) What conditions are necessary for rusting to occur?
   (b) Does rusting occur only in acids and alkalis?
   (c) How does rusting compare in tap water and distilled water? Why?
   (d) Why should iron and steel objects near the coast be kept dry?
   (e) Why are iron tins not used for pickling food?

Write up your report in your Practical workbook.

23 How do acids react?

Refer to pages 262 and 280

You will need:

- test tubes
- splints
- bung and delivery tube
- dropping pipette
- dilute hydrochloric acid
- limewater
- dilute sodium hydroxide
- universal indicator paper
- zinc
- sodium carbonate
- box of matches

● SBA skills that can be assessed:

PD, D, ORR, AI

Your group has been provided with the equipment and chemicals listed above. Work in pairs to carry out **one** of the activities **A**, **B** or **C**.

A How do acids react with metals, and what gas is produced?

B How do acids react with carbonates, and what gas is produced?

C How do acids react with alkalis, and how does the pH change?

In each case you will:

1 choose the equipment and chemicals you need; ask your teacher for anything you need

2 draw the apparatus you will use; use a ruler, make a section drawing and label the parts

3 carry out your activity, recording any colour changes; test and record any gases produced

4 complete your part of the table summarizing the chemical reactions of acids.

Drawing of apparatus used	Description of results

The reactions of acids	Word equation
A Acid + metal	
B Acid + carbonate	
C Acid + alkali	

5 Look at the work of other members of your group and add their results into your table. Discuss all your findings. Which of the reaction(s) do not always give the result(s) you expect? Explain.

Write up a report of your part of the practical in your Practical workbook.

24 Solutions, suspensions and colloids

Refer to pages 283–5

You will need:

- [ ] sodium chloride
- [ ] starch
- [ ] test tubes
- [ ] ethanol
- [ ] glass rod
- [ ] copper sulphate
- [ ] distilled water
- [ ] sand
- [ ] small beakers
- [ ] filtering apparatus
- [ ] calcium carbonate
- [ ] vinegar
- [ ] vegetable oil
- [ ] spatulas
- [ ] heating apparatus

● SBA skills that can be assessed:

MM, ORR, AI

● A mixture is formed from substances that do not chemically react with each other.

● Work in groups of four. Each student sets up two mixtures, describes their appearance, does the filtering and shares their results.

1 Choose and make the mixtures shown below.

2 Add the appearance of the mixture to the table (e.g. transparent/coloured/cloudy/parts visible).

3 Set up filtering apparatus for the mixtures, and record any residue left on the filter paper. Record in the table whether or not the mixture can be separated into its parts by filtering.

4 Record the type of mixture in the last column.

Mixture	Appearance	Filtering	Type
A Sodium chloride and water			
B Starch stirred into boiling water			
C Copper sulphate and water			
D Copper sulphate and ethanol			
E Crushed calcium carbonate and water			
F Vegetable oil shaken with vinegar			
G Sand shaken with water			
H Copper sulphate and vegetable oil			

5 Collect the full information for the table from other members of your group.

6 Describe the main characteristics of each type of mixture, and give an example.

(a) Solution _____

(b) Suspension _____

(c) Colloid _____

Write up a report of your part of the practical in your Practical workbook, and include the full table of results.

25 How can we remove stains?

Refer to pages 282 and 283

You will need:

☐ small pieces of cotton cloth ☐ scissors ☐ ruler ☐ glass rods

☐ stains: tea bag just covered with boiling water; a rusty nail; bottle of nail varnish; ballpoint pen

☐ removal liquids: cut lemons; borax solution; warm water; propanone (acetone); methanol (meths)

● SBA skills that can be assessed:
ORR, AI

- Stains can be removed either by neutralization or by using a solvent. The solvent may be water (with or without detergent) or an organic (carbon-containing) solvent.
- Work in groups of four. Each student should try to remove a stain using two different methods, record which method works, and give the reasons. Then they should check and share their results.

1 First make your stained cloth. Use a 5 cm square of cotton cloth and place it in the solution or wipe some of the stain material over it. Cut the square diagonally into two equal pieces.

2 Treat pieces of the stained cloth in the two ways recommended in the table. Leave the cloths to soak for 30 minutes. Then record the result in each case.

3 In the last column, record the nature of the stain (acidic, alkaline or neutral) and the reason why one of the stain removal methods worked.

Stain	Removal liquid	Result	Reason
A Tea stain	lemon juice		
	borax solution		
B Iron rust	lemon juice		
	borax solution		
C Nail varnish	warm water		
	propanone (acetone)		
D Ballpoint pen	lemon juice		
	methanol (meths)		

4 Collect the full information for the table from other members of your group.

5 What happens to the stain:
  (a) during neutralization? _____

  (b) with a solvent? _____

6 How would you remove (a) fruit juice, (b) grease, (c) paint? What principle is used in each case?

Write up a report of your part of the practical in your Practical workbook, and include the full table of results.

26 Investigating hard and soft water

Refer to pages 288–9

You will need:

- soap solution
- heating apparatus
- dropping pipette
- sodium carbonate
- test tubes and bungs
- test-tube rack
- 4 water samples, **A**, **B**, **C** and **D**, which contain: distilled water, water with calcium sulphate, water with calcium hydrogencarbonate and tap water (but not necessarily in that order)

● SBA skills that can be assessed:

PD, ORR, AI

Work individually. You first have to plan your investigation, then record and interpret your results.

1 You have been given a test-tube rack containing samples of water in test tubes labelled **A**, **B**, **C** and **D**. The samples are listed above, but the letters for each one may vary between students.

2 You are provided with the other materials as listed above, including spare test tubes. You have to identify what is in each of your samples **A**, **B**, **C** and **D**. Make up your plan, ask for any other materials you think might be useful, identify any problems you think you might have in identifying the samples, and then show your plan to your teacher.

3 Carry out your plan. Use or modify the tables given below in order to record your results. Show your tables of results to your teacher.

4 Carry out any further tests to identify the samples.

Sample	First test	Results	Conclusion
A			
B			
C			
D			

Sample	Second test	Results	Conclusion
A			
B			
C			
D			

5 What is each sample? Explain for each one how you reached your decision.

A _____

B _____

C _____

D _____

Write up your report in your Practical workbook.

27 Comparing series and parallel circuits

Refer pages 294–5

You will need:

- [ ] 4 new 1.5 V dry cells
- [ ] 4 screw-in bulbs (1.25 V, 0.25 A)
- [ ] dc ammeter (0–1 A)
- [ ] 2 circuit boards
- [ ] bulb holders
- [ ] scissors
- [ ] insulated wire
- [ ] dc voltmeter (0–3 V)

● SBA skills that can be assessed:

MM, ORR, AI

Work in small groups. Set up pairs of circuits. For each pair, complete the tables to compare the brightness of the bulbs and the readings in volts and amps. Try to explain your findings.

1

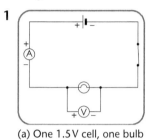

(a) One 1.5 V cell, one bulb

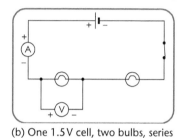

(b) One 1.5 V cell, two bulbs, series

	Brightness	Volts (V)	Amps (A)
(a)			
(b)			

2

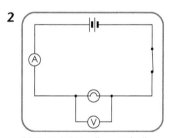

(c) Two 1.5 V cells, one bulb

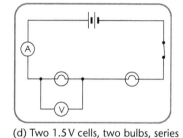

(d) Two 1.5 V cells, two bulbs, series

	Brightness	Volts (V)	Amps (A)
(c)			
(d)			

3

(e) Two 1.5 V cells, two bulbs, series

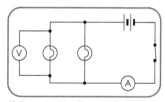

(f) Two 1.5 V cells, two bulbs, parallel

	Brightness	Volts (V)	Amps (A)
(e)			
(f)			

Conclusions (Cross out the incorrect phrases.)

(a) The greater the number of dry cells in a series circuit, for the same number of bulbs, the (brighter/dimmer) the bulbs will be.

(b) The greater the number of bulbs in a series circuit, with the same number of cells, the (brighter/dimmer) the bulbs will be.

(c) In a series circuit there (is a single path/are alternative paths) for the current. The current (is the same/varies) around the circuit. If there are two bulbs in series, the voltage across each one is (half/the same as) the voltage of the dry cell(s).

(d) In a parallel circuit there (is a single path/are alternative paths) for the current. The current (is the same/varies) around the circuit. If there are two bulbs in parallel, the voltage across each one is (half/the same as) the voltage of the dry cell(s).

Write up your report in your Practical workbook.

28 Current, voltage and resistance

Refer to page 296

You will need:

- ☐ nichrome wire (8 cm, 32 swg)
- ☐ dc voltmeter (0–5 V)
- ☐ insulated wire
- ☐ 2 × 1.5 V cells
- ☐ dc ammeter (0–1 A)
- ☐ variable resistor (rheostat)

● SBA skills that can be assessed:
MM, ORR, AI

Work in small groups.

1 Make a coil by winding the nichrome wire round a pencil. This is your fixed resistor, and you are going to find the value of its resistance in ohms (Ω).

2 Set up the circuit with the dry cells, ammeter and variable resistor in series. Place the voltmeter in parallel with the coil to measure the voltage across it.

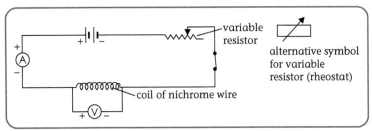

3 Adjust the variable resistor to allow more or less current to flow. For each position, record the current flowing through the coil and the voltage across the coil. Enter your results in the table.

Current (*I*) in amps						
Voltage (*V*)						
Ratio *V/I*						

4 The ratio *V/I* is the resistance of the wire. It is measured in ohms (Ω). What is the value of the resistance of your metal coil?

5 Plot a graph of current (on the horizontal, *x*-axis) against voltage (on the vertical, *y*-axis).

6 What is the shape of your graph? It should be a straight line. This shows that the current and voltage increase and decrease in proportion, and the ratio *V/I* remains constant.

We can state this as **Ohm's law**: the current flowing through a metal is proportional to the voltage across it. This is only true if the temperature stays the same.

Note: we do not use a bulb filament in this practical because it would get hotter as the current was increased, and this would increase the resistance.

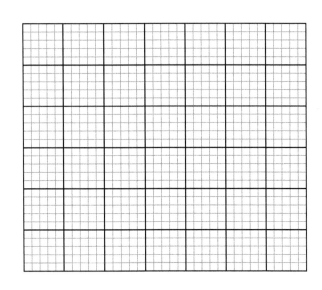

Write up your report in your Practical workbook.

29 Do colours contain different pigments?

Refer to page 317

You will need:

- filter papers
- methanol (meths)
- paper tape
- scissors
- glass rod
- ruler
- water
- small beaker
- range of colours such as food colourings, felt-tip markers, dyes

● SBA skills that can be assessed:

ORR, AI, D

Many of the colours that we use are mixtures, not single colours. You can find out what is in a colouring material by using chromatography. Work individually.

1 Each student should investigate one colouring material.

2 Cut a strip of filter paper, 2 cm wide and 1 cm longer than the depth of the small beaker.

3 At 1.5 cm from the end of the strip make a dot of colour. Let it dry, then add another dot. Repeat this process five more times to make an intense dot of colour.

4 Use the glass rod and paper tape to suspend the filter paper strip in the beaker, so it does not quite touch the bottom.

5 Remove the paper strip while you pour *either* water or methanol into the beaker to a depth of 1 cm. Return the strip to the beaker. The liquid should not touch the colour spot.

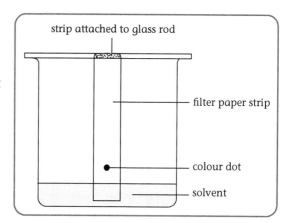

6 Examine the coloured dot every 5 minutes for half an hour. Record what you notice.

Original colour	Time (minutes)					Final result
	5	10	15	20	25	

7 How many constituent colours were in the original colour?

8 Why did they separate?

9 Choose a different colouring material, or the same colouring but with the other solvent, and see if you get similar or different results.

10 How is the process of chromatography useful in everyday life?

11 Draw coloured diagrams of your strips before and after the separation process.

Write up your report in your Practical workbook.

30 Making a model that uses solar energy

1 Work in pairs. You will be planning the whole project yourselves, in order to build a model that makes use of solar energy to convert it to another form of energy.

Refer to pages 326–8 and 340

● SBA skills that can be assessed:

PD, D, MM, AI

2 You should choose one of the following models to make:
   (a) solar water heater
   (b) solar still
   (c) solar drier
   (d) solar cooker.

3 You can follow the ideas in your textbook, or create your own design. You have to decide what materials to use, and collect these yourself (including discarded items). You will need to draw plans of your model and check these with your teacher. When you have completed your model you have to demonstrate and evaluate it to show that it works.

4 The finished models can be displayed in the class for comments from other students (peer review), which can be part of the evaluation.

5 Use this space for your planning and drawing.

Names of designers: _____   _____

Model to be built: _____

Drawing and list of materials to be used:

Results of testing the model:

Results after any necessary modifications:

Write up your report in your Practical workbook.

31 Making a model machine

1 Work in pairs. You will be planning the whole project yourselves, in order to build a model machine that works. Your machine, for example, should lift a load or cut or break food.

2 You can choose one of the following models, or make your own choice:
   (a) a scissor design to crush food
   (b) a bottle opener
   (c) an arm to lift 500 g
   (d) a skull and lower jaw to crush food
   (e) a pulley system to pull a 1 kg load up a slope to a vertical height of 30 cm.

3 You can follow the ideas in your textbook, or create your own design. You have to decide what materials to use, and collect these yourself (including discarded items). You will need to draw plans of your model and check these with your teacher. When you have completed your model you have to demonstrate and evaluate it to show that it works.

4 The finished models can be displayed in the class for comments from other students (peer review), which can be part of the evaluation.

5 Use this space for your planning and drawing.

Refer to pages 330–6

● SBA skills that can be assessed:
PD, D, MM, AI

Names of designers: _____   _____

Model to be built: _____

Drawing and list of materials to be used:

Results of testing the model:

Results after any necessary modifications:

Write up your report in your Practical workbook.

32 What happens in collisions?

Refer to page 347

You will need:

☐ 2 trolleys   ☐ 2 masses the same weight as a trolley   ☐ pin and cork
☐ board (slope)   ☐ ticker tape and ticker-tape timer   ☐ modelling clay

● SBA skills that can be assessed:

MM, ORR, AI

Work in a group.

1 Set up a board, slightly tilted, using a little modelling clay, to compensate for friction. When a trolley is gently pushed on such a slope, it will continue moving at the same speed. Check that this is so, and make any adjustments.

2 Fit a cork to the front of one of the trolleys and place it in the middle of the slope. You are going to push the other trolley to collide with it. Fit a pin to the other trolley and a ticker tape that passes through a ticker-tape timer, which will record what happens. The apparatus is shown below.

3 Give the first trolley a sharp push so that it runs down the track at a constant speed and collides with the second trolley and they both move off together.

4 Use the ticker tape to find the velocity before and after the collision. A certain time interval is given by successive dots on the tape: in this case, 0.02 s. Enter your results in a table as shown.

$$\text{velocity} = \frac{\text{distance}}{\text{time}} = \frac{\text{length of tape}}{\text{time measured on tape}}$$

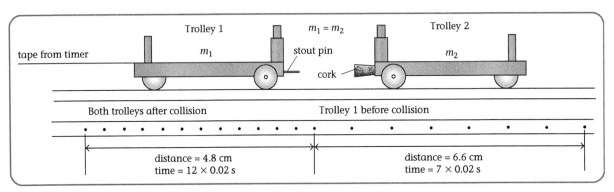

	Distance d (m)	Time t (s)	Velocity = distance/time (m/s)	Momentum (kg m/s)
Trolley before collision				
Trolley after collision				
Two trolleys together				

5 Repeat the experiment twice more, but add first one mass and then two masses on top of the second trolley to give twice and then three times the units of mass.

6 The mass of each trolley is known (in kg), the distance travelled can be measured (in m) and the time in seconds is known. The momentum can be calculated in kg m/s.

7 Do your experiments support the statement that: *The total linear momentum of the system before collision is equal to the total linear momentum after collision?* Explain any reasons why your results may not be exactly like this.

Write up your report in your Practical workbook.

33 The centre of gravity of flat objects

Refer to pages 350–1

You will need:

- card
- pencil
- set square
- 20 cm length of thread with a pin tied at one end, and a washer at the other
- scissors
- soft vertical surface
- paper tape
- ruler
- pair of compasses
- coin

● SBA skills that can be assessed:

MM

Work individually.

1 Prepare a carefully drawn and cut out circle (radius 5 cm), rectangle with sides 6 cm and 10 cm, and an irregular shape of your choosing.

2 Make three small holes near the edge of each shape. Put the pin through one of the holes (**A**) and attach it to a vertical surface. Make sure the shape can move freely.

3 Draw two crosses on the shape, in line with the thread of the plumb line. Take down the shape and connect the crosses.

4 Repeat steps **2** and **3** for another of the small holes (**B**). Where the two lines meet is the centre of gravity (CoG). Mark it.

5 Check what you have found by hanging the shape from hole (**C**). The plumb line should go through the CoG: the checking line.

6 Repeat steps **2** to **5** with the other two shapes.

7 For the circle and rectangle there is another way to find the CoG. Turn both shapes over to their other side, and work out and mark the CoG. Push the pin through your card from one CoG to the other. How accurately are the two positions in the same place?

8 Draw and cut out another card that is in the shape of an L. Predict where you think its CoG will be. Repeat the activity above to see if you were correct.

9 How could you modify your activity to find the CoG of a solid object, such as a pencil?

10 Make a model cutout of a truck, as shown below (a). Find its CoG. Then find out what happens to the CoG when the load (a stuck-on coin) is (b) high on the vehicle and (c) low on the vehicle. What precautions should be taken when loading vehicles, and why?

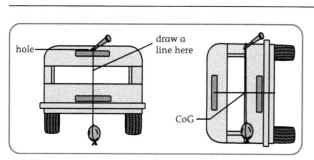

(a) CoG of unloaded truck

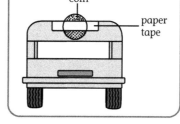

(b) High load

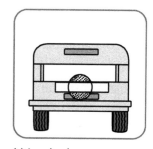

(c) Low load

Write up your report in your Practical workbook. Include your cutouts marked with their CoGs.

34 Finding out about moments

Refer to pages 330 and 354–5

You will need:

- a metre rule with a hole drilled at 50 cm
- thread
- modelling clay
- string and clamp
- metal hooks
- scissors
- masses from 10 to 100 g

- SBA skills that can be assessed:

  MM, ORR, AI

- As with a lever, the metre rule moves about its balance point, the pivot, or fulcrum. The further a force is applied from the fulcrum, the greater will be its turning effect. This turning effect is called the moment of the force and is measured as force (in newtons) × distance from the fulcrum (in m). Work in pairs.

1 Tie string through the central hole in a metre rule and suspend it from a clamp so it balances. If necessary, add a small piece of modelling clay to one side to make it level.

2 Use metal hooks, or attach threads to the masses, so you can suspend them from the ruler.

3 Hang a 40 g mass (which exerts a force of 0.4 N) on the left side of the ruler 10 cm (0.1 m) from the fulcrum. This will make the ruler unbalanced. Where should a 10 g mass (force 0.1 N) be placed to make the ruler balance again?

4 Take the masses off, and try other ones at different distances from the fulcrum. In each case you must make the ruler balance. Record your results in the table.

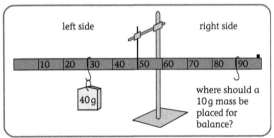

Left side			Right side		
Force f_1 (newtons)	Distance d_1 (metres)	$f_1 \times d_1$	Force f_2 (newtons)	Distance d_2 (metres)	$f_2 \times d_2$
0.4 N	0.1 m	0.4 N × 0.1 m = 0.04 N m	0.1 N	0.4 m	0.1 N × 0.4 m = 0.04 N m

5 When the ruler is balanced, what is true about the moments of the force on the two sides of the fulcrum?

6 When does a force: (a) have the greatest turning effect?

(b) have the least turning effect?

Write up your report in your Practical workbook.

Glossary and Index

buoyancy: the upthrust force of a fluid exerted on an object, 215, 216, 220, 221

burning: *see* combustion

caffeine: a stimulant, e.g. in coffee; can be damaging in large amounts, 100, 102

calcium: an element needed in the diet for strong bones and teeth, 59, 65; salts in hard water, 288–9

calorimeter: a container for burning food to find its energy value, 80

camera: a device for taking pictures; in photography, 52–3; compared with the eye, 124

cancer: uncontrolled growth of cells, causing disease, 145; of lungs, 81, 82; of reproductive organs, 149

Candida: see thrush

capillaries: blood vessels with walls only one cell thick, 90, 120; in temperature control, 123

capillarity: the rising of liquids in narrow tubes, such as xylem vessels, 86, 87

carbohydrases: enzymes that digests carbohydrates, e.g. amylase digests starch, 68, 69

carbohydrates: carbon compounds used as food, e.g. starch and sugars, 25, 56, 58; digestion of, 68, 69; tests for, 48, 57; types of, 55

carbon compounds: compounds in living and non-living things that contain carbon, 24–5; *see also* food, fuels *and* plastics

carbon cycle: the recycling of carbon in nature, 191

carbon dioxide: a gas in the air; and burning of fuels, 81, 321; and carbon cycle, 191; in fire extinguishers, 255; and photosynthesis, 49, 50; and respiration, 76, 78; transport of, 74, 89, 120; test for, 76

carbon dioxide indicator solution: changes colour to show changes in carbon dioxide concentration, 190, 379

carbon monoxide: a poisonous gas from incomplete burning of carbon compounds, 81, 248

carnivores: animals that eat animals, 186, 188–9, 219; and teeth 64

cars: vehicles burning fossil fuels, and the effects, 320

catalyst: a substance that speeds up a chemical reaction without itself being used up; in living things, *see* enzymes

cataract: clouding of the lens in the eye, 127

cell, electrochemical: uses chemicals to cause a current to flow when connected into a complete circuit, 292, 293, 298

cell, living: the building block of organisms, 13, 44–5, 365; division, 134, 150

cell membrane: partially permeable layer around the cytoplasm of cells, 44, 45, 46

cellulose: the carbohydrate in plant cell walls and roughage (fibre) in the diet, 55, 56, 58, 67

cell wall: dead, outer, permeable layer of plant cells, made of cellulose, 45

central nervous system (CNS): made of the brain and spinal cord, it coordinates activities in the body, 112–13, 116, 117

centre of gravity: the point through which gravity appears to act, 350–1, 352, 397

change of state: how a substance changes from solid to liquid to gas, and back again, 19; *see also* evaporation

charcoal: wood that has been heated in a limited supply of air, 318

charge: a characteristic, e.g., of electrons (negative charge) and protons (positive charge); a flow of charged particles, e.g. electrons or ions, make up an electric current, 21, 290, 291

chemical control measures: spraying pesticides to kill pests, 235

chemical energy: stored (potential) energy in foods, fuels and electrochemical cells, 16, 340

chemical equations: equations that show the numbers of atoms present in the reactants and products in a chemical change, 23, 51, 77

chemical weathering: breaking down of rocks by chemical reactions, 176

chemicals: made of atoms and molecules, they are the building blocks of all living and non-living matter, 20–1, 23; safe handling of, 247, 249, 274–7; *see also* acids *and* alkalis

chlorophyll: the green pigment in chloroplasts that traps light energy in photosynthesis, 48, 50, 51, 52

chloroplasts: the parts of plant cells containing chlorophyll, 50, 51

cholesterol: a chemical that has been linked to plaque formation in the arteries, and high blood pressure, 97

chromatography: the process by which the colours in a pigment are separated, 317, 393

chromosomes: found in the nucleus of a cell, they carry genetic information in the form of genes, 44, 150–1

ciliary muscles: muscles in the eye that relax and contract to change the shape of the lens, 125, 127

circulatory system: the heart and blood vessels in which the blood circulates round the body, 88

classification: the grouping of objects or living things based on their characteristics, 12–15

clay soil: soil containing a majority of very small clay particles, 178–81, 182; improvement of, 181

cleanliness: keeping surfaces free, e.g. from dirt and bacteria; of eyes, 127; personal, 238–9; of household appliances, 268–9; and stains, 282, 283

clinical thermometer: a mercury-containing thermometer used for recording human body temperatures, 169

clones: groups of genetically identical offspring; *see* asexual reproduction

clothing: body coverings; colour, insulation and fibres affect the degree of heat transfer, 171

clotting of blood: chemical changes that thicken the blood and block arteries, 88, 94

clouds: mostly made of very small droplets of water; and the weather, 194; and the water cycle, 210

coal: a fossil fuel formed from plants from long ago, 299, 318; and pollution, 81, 321

cochlea: the part of the inner ear concerned with balance, 131

cold-blooded: *see* ectothermic

collisions: when particles or objects bump into each other; elastic or inelastic, 346–7, 396

colloids: heterogeneous mixtures with particles between the sizes of those in solutions and suspensions, 284–5, 388

coloured pigments: chemicals, e.g. paints, of different colours, 316; separation by chromatography, 317

colours of light: radiation of certain wavelengths within the visible spectrum, 314–15, 345; and the eye, 315; primary and secondary, 314

combustion: the combination of oxygen with a fuel, to release energy; of fossil fuels, 318, 319, 320, 321; in respiration, 6, 80

community: a number of populations living together, 189

community hygiene: removal of garbage and sewage by sanitation services, 236, 240–3

compass: a magnet that swings so its N-pole points to magnetic north, 228

compost: produced by the aerobic decay of organic material by bacteria, 237; used to improve soils, 181, 183

compounds: pure substances in which the molecules have different atoms combined in definite proportions, 20–1; of carbon, 24–5

computers: electronic devices with a central processing unit, which deal with binary data, 28–9

concave lens: a lens that is thin in the middle and diverges light rays, 126, 344; used to correct short sight, 128

concave mirror: a mirror that curves inwards and converges light rays, 328, 344; and headlamps, 344

concentration gradient: difference in concentration that allows materials to diffuse, 46, 74, 84, 85, 120

condensation: the process of cooling that changes a gas to a liquid, 19; in the water cycle, 210; *see also* distillation

condom: sheath made of rubber, used as a contraceptive device, 160; and protection against sexually transmitted infections, 156

conduction, electrical: the flow of an electric current through a substance, e.g. metal, 256, 266, 290

conduction, thermal: the transfer of thermal energy (heat) from hotter to colder parts of a substance without the molecules moving, 164, 165, 166, 167, 256, 266, 267

conductor: a substance that readily allows electricity or thermal energy to pass through it; *see* conduction

conservation: to maintain the environment in a good state; of soils, 183, 184–5; of water, 209

conservation of momentum: the transfer of energy when objects collide, 346–7

constipation: difficulty in passing faeces, which are dry and hard, 67

consumer: an animal that cannot make its own food, and eats plants or other animals, 186, 188, 189, 219

contour ploughing: planting around the contours of a hill, 185

contraceptive: a device or drug that prevents pregnancy, 160–3

contraceptive pills: pills containing female hormones that prevent ovulation and therefore pregnancy, 161

contraction: of muscles, to become shorter and fatter, 332, 333; in the eye, 124, 127

control: the part of an experiment that has all the variables that are considered important, 30

convection: the transfer of thermal energy (heat) by the movement of particles in a liquid or gas, 164–5, 166, 173, 175; and the skin, 123

convection currents: movement of gases and liquids by convection; land and sea breezes, 165; ocean currents, 164; winds, 193, 194, 196

convex lens: a lens that bulges in the middle and converges light rays, 126–8, 344; used to correct long sight, 128

convex mirror: a mirror that curves outwards and diverges light rays, 344

corm: a plant storage organ with a swollen vertical stem, e.g. cocoyam, 133

cornea: transparent front layer of the eye, brings about some bending of light rays, 125

corrosion: the chemical action on the surface of a metal, which wears it away, e.g. rusting, 270–1; prevention of, 272–3

corrosive: chemicals that destroy equipment and living flesh, 247, 249

crop rotation: growing different crops each year on the same plot of land, 184

cross-pollination: transfer of pollen from one flower to a flower on another plant of the same kind, 138

crude oil (petroleum): a fossil fuel formed as a result of heat and pressure on the remains of small plants and animals, 318, 322; and pollution, 320–1

current: the movement of electrical charge, of electrons or ions, 290, 292

cutting sections: preparation of very thin slices, e.g. of plant material, for observation, 33

cuttings: parts of plants cut off one plant and grown into new plants, 133, 135

cyclones: *see* hurricanes

cytoplasm: main part of a cell where most chemical reactions occur, 44, 45

dam: a barrier built to enclose water at a high level, often used to generate hydroelectricity, 324

day and night: caused by the Sun shining on different parts of the Earth, 204

deafness: damage to part of the ear, nerve or brain that means a person cannot hear properly, 130

decay: process by which materials rot, brought about by fungi and bacteria, 187, 188, 232, 237, 322

decomposers: microorganisms that cause decay; to produce energy, 237, 322; to release mineral salts, 187

decompression: the slow ascent of divers in order to get rid of dissolved air in the blood, 231

defecation: removal of undigested food remains from the anus, 66, 67; compared with excretion, 104

deficiency diseases: caused by inadequate amounts of vitamins or minerals, 58, 59

dehydration: removal of water; in disease, 208, 243; in preserving food, 232, 328

denitrifying bacteria: bacteria changing nitrates to nitrogen, 187

element: a pure substance that cannot be broken down into simpler substances, 20, 21, 23; *see also* metals *and* non-metals

embryo: early stage of development, 143; in flowering plants, 138, 140; in humans, 152, 153

emotional changes: unpredictable mood swings; in adolescents, 147; and stress, 97

emphysema: difficulty in breathing caused by the stretching of alveoli, 82

emulsify: to break down fat into tiny droplets, 69

emulsion: an example of a colloid, in which two liquids are partly mixed, 285

endocrine system: a system of glands that secrete hormones into the blood, which control growth and development, 117, 118–19

endothermic: describes an animal that can control its body temperature within narrow limits, 122–123

energy: the ability to do work, 16–17, 322–5, 340–1

energy requirements: energy needed by different groups of people for different activities, 58, 99

environment: the conditions found in a habitat, 189

enzymes: proteins made in living cells that act as catalysts, 66, 68–9, 70–1, 368

epidermis: covering layer; on plant leaves, 50, 51; on the skin, 105, 115, 123

epigeal germination: germination in which the cotyledons are brought above ground, e.g. in red peas, 141

equilibrium: the balancing of an object; stable, unstable or neutral, 350–1, 352, 353

equipment: appliances used in the laboratory, 32–5

erosion: washing or blowing away of soil or pieces of rock, 176, 184–5

eruption: release of magma from a volcano or mid-ocean ridge, 201, 202, 203

ethanol: the chemical name for alcohol, 24

eutrophication: provision of extra nutrients from fertilizers and sewage; and algal bloom, 224

evaporation: process of heating that slowly changes a liquid to a gas below its boiling point, 19; and cooling effect, 123, 170, 171, 376; and water cycle, 210

excretion: the removal of wastes made by the activities of living cells, 6; in flowering plants, 110–11; in humans, 104–5, 106–9

exercise: physical activity that causes us to breathe deeply and to sweat, 98–9, 102, 103

exhaled air: the air we breathe out, 73

extractor fan: a mechanical or electrical fan set high in a wall to extract air and aid ventilation, 175

eyes: the organ for sight, 124–5, 126–8; and camera, 124; care of, 127; and colour vision, 315; defects of, 127–8; lenses and, 126, 127, 128

faeces: undigested waste that passes out through the anus, 66, 67; *see also* constipation *and* diarrhoea

fair test: an experiment set up so only one variable is changed, 30–1, 362

farming practice: methods used for farming, 183–5

fats: carbon-containing food used for energy, insulation and cell membranes, 25, 55, 56, 58, 69; and health, 97, 145; test for, 57

fatty acids: one of the building blocks of fats; *see* fats

feedback mechanism: action taken in the body to return conditions to set values, 120, 121

feeding levels: the arrangement of organisms showing their feeding positions, e.g. producers, consumers and decomposers, 188, 189, 219

fermentation: *see* anaerobic respiration

fertilize/fertilization: when a male gamete joins with a female gamete in sexual reproduction, 134; in flowering plants, 138; in humans, 149, 150

fertilizers: added to soils to provide minerals for plant growth; natural, e.g. compost, or artificial (chemical), e.g. NPK, 180, 181, 183; as household chemicals, 276; causing pollution, 224

fibre: plant cell walls in the diet, 55, 56, 58; preventing constipation, 67

fibres: natural and synthetic clothing materials, 171

filament lamp (incandescent): a lamp with a metal filament that becomes very hot, and glows, when an electric current passes through it, 310, 312, 313

film: photosensitive material used in cameras, 53

filtering: using filter paper to separate components of a mixture, 213

fire: combustion of a fuel, accompanied by flames, 245, 254–5; extinguishers, 254, 255

first aid: initial action when an accident occurs, 252–3

fish: vertebrates with fins and scales, 15; and aquatic habitat, 215–17; gaseous exchange in, 74, 75, 217; in food chains, 219, 226–7; and temperature control, 122

fishing methods: methods used to catch fish, on a small scale or as a business, 226–7; farming of fish, 226

flammable chemicals: chemicals that easily catch fire under normal conditions, 247, 255

flashlight: a device, with a bulb and dry cell(s) in a circuit, which can be switched on or off, 292

flies: insects (with only two developed wings) that can spread disease, 234

flight: moving in the air, e.g. birds and aeroplanes, 348, 349; and spacecraft, 358, 359

flotation, law of: a floating body displaces its own weight of the fluid in which it floats, 221

flowering plants: complex plants that bear flowers, 13, 136

flower structure: the parts that make up a flower, 136–7, 138, 373

fluid: either a gas or a liquid, 221

fluorescent tube/bulb: a tube containing chemicals that absorb ultraviolet radiation and give out visible light, 311, 312

fluoridation: the adding of fluorides to toothpaste or drinking water, to strengthen teeth, 65

focusing: bringing rays together to a point; heat rays, 328; light rays, 126, 127, 128, 344; sound waves, 345

foetus: unborn human after 8 weeks of growth, 152, 153

maximum and minimum thermometer: uses mercury and alcohol to record highest and lowest temperatures, 169

measurement: finding the quantity of something by comparison with a scale, 34–3; standard units of, 8–9

mechanical advantage: in a machine, the force of the load divided by the effort, 334, 335, 336

meiosis: cell division during the formation of gametes; the chromosome number is halved, 134, 150

menopause: when a woman stops having periods, 143

menstrual cycle: monthly cycle of egg production and bleeding, in human females, 146, 147; and rhythm method, 160; and contraceptive pill, 161, 163

metals: elements that are good conductors of heat and electricity; some react with acids to release hydrogen, 256, 257; cleaning of, 268–9; competition of, 385; reactions of, 262–5; uses of, 266–7; and alloys, 266–7

methane: the simplest hydrocarbon, 24; the main part of biogas, 237, 322; a greenhouse gas, 81, 321

microorganisms: very small organisms, 13; control of, 383; *see also* bacteria, protists *and* viruses

microphone: a device that can convert sound waves into electrical signals, 129

microscope: instrument for magnifying specimens mounted on slides, 33; and magnification, 44

microwaves: electromagnetic radiation used for cooking, mobile phones and TV signals, 165, 345, 360

milk teeth: the 20 teeth that children have, before the adult teeth replace them and the molars grow, 65

mineral salts: inorganic salts, such as sodium chloride; and animals, 58, 59; and plants, 54, 86; in soil, 181, 187

mirror: a surface that reflects light rays to form a clear image, 344

mitochondria: structures in the cytoplasm where the later stages of aerobic respiration occur, 44, 45, 80

mitosis: ordinary cell division involved in growth and asexual reproduction; chromosome numbers are the same in the new cells, 132, 134

mixtures: impure substances of elements and/or compounds mixed in no fixed proportions, and not joined together, 20–1; kinds of, 283–5, 388

mobile phones: send and receive signals using microwaves, 345

models: structures with a similarity to the real thing, 394, 395

molecules: atoms joined together; the atoms are of the same kind (in elements) or different kinds (in compounds), 20, 23, 24, 260

moment of a force: the turning effect of a force, 330, 331, 398

momentum: mass × velocity, 346–7

monocotyledons: flowering plants with narrow leaves and parallel veins, e.g. maize, 13; seeds of, 140–1

Moon: the natural satellite of Earth; phases of, 204; and organisms, 205, 206–7; and tides, 205

mosquitoes: insects, with a narrow pair of flying wings, which transfer disease, 234, 242

motor neurones: nerve cells that carry impulses from the brain and spinal cord to muscles, 116, 117

mouth-to-mouth resuscitation: *see* artificial respiration

movement: change in position; of particles, 18–19, 46–7; of living things, 7, 332–3

multiple fission: asexual reproduction by splitting into many offspring, shown e.g. by *Plasmodium*, 132

muscle fatigue: aching of the muscles after respiring anaerobically, due to accumulation of lactic acid, 78, 80

muscles: organs that contract to exert an effort and pull bones together for movement, 115, 332, 333

N: symbol for newton(s)

narcotics: drugs, e.g. morphine and heroin, which relieve pain and give a high, 101

nasal cavity: the space behind the nostrils that contains the sensory cells for smell, 72, 114

natural immunity: protection against specific diseases, developed in response to a microorganism, 95

natural ventilation: making use of breezes and convection to bring fresh air into a building, 173, 174

negative charge: the charge on electrons and on objects that have gained electrons, 21

nervous system: the system that coordinates the activities of the body, 112–17

netting: process of catching fish with different kinds of net, 227

neurones: nerve cells that form the nerves, 116, 117

neutralization: the reaction between acids and bases or acids and alkalis to form a salt and water, 280, 281, 282; when testing for non-reducing sugars, 57

neutral wire: the wire in the mains supply that returns the current; covered with blue plastic, 302

neutron: particle in the nucleus of atoms; with the same mass as a proton but no electrical charge, 21

newton (N): unit in which forces, such as weight, are measured; on Earth a 100 g mass has a weight of about 1 N, 330, 331, 354, 355

nicotine: an addictive drug that is part of cigarette smoke, 82, 100, 102

nitrates: important minerals in the soil, produced from the decay process, which are re-used by plants, 187

nitrifying bacteria: bacteria changing ammonium compounds to nitrites, and nitrites to nitrates, 187

nitrogen: main gas in the air, 73; cycle, 187, 191; narcosis in divers, 231

nitrogen-fixing bacteria: bacteria that change nitrogen into nitrates, 187

nitrogen oxides: gases that contribute to acid rain, 321

nodules: bumps on the roots of leguminous plants, e.g. beans, that contain nitrogen-fixing bacteria, 187; and crop rotation, 184

non-biodegradable: made of materials, e.g. most plastics that microorganisms cannot break down, 237, 261

non-conductors: *see* insulators

non-living: materials that do not possess the characteristics of life, 6–7, 10

PSA: test to check for a healthy prostate gland, 149

puberty: when egg and sperm production begins; marks the beginning of adolescence, 142, 146–7

pulley: a machine using wheels and ropes, 336, 337

pulse: the stretching of an artery each time the heart beats, 91; and exercise, 98

pupil: the opening in the centre of the iris, 124, 125; reflex, 124, 127, 313

P-waves: primary waves, the fastest seismic waves, which can travel through the core of the Earth, 200

radar: a device for using the reflection of radio waves to identify the position of objects, 229

radiation: the transfer of energy by electromagnetic waves, for example infrared waves transfer thermal energy (heat), 164, 165, 166, 326, 327, 328, 345

radioactive decay: breakdown of radioactive substances, e.g. uranium, to release nuclear energy, 341

radio waves: long wavelength electromagnetic radiation used to carry radio and TV programmes, 345

rats: pests that eat and foul our food, 234; and spread leptospirosis, 242

reactivity series: places metals in order of their chemical activity, 265, 273, 385

receptors: sensory cells, in sense organs, which detect stimuli, 114–115, 116, 117

recessive: a gene that does not show an effect if the dominant gene is present, 151

recording and reporting: presenting results in a logical order, 39–41, 363

recycling: using materials again and again; basic materials, 187, 190–1; non-biodegradable materials, 236, 237, 261; biodegradable materials; *see* biogas *and* compost

red blood cells: cells in the blood that carry oxygen as oxyhaemoglobin, 88, 89

reducing sugars: sugars, e.g. glucose, that give a red precipitate when heated with Benedict's solution, 57

reflection: the bouncing back, e.g. of water, sound or light waves, from a surface, 342, 343, 344, 345

reflex action: a quick automatic response to a stimulus, without thought; called an involuntary action, 116, 117

refraction: the bending of waves as they travel from one material to another; *see* lens *and* prism

refuse: waste materials from households, offices and industries, 236–7

relax: when a muscle becomes longer and thinner, 332

relay switch: uses an electromagnet in one circuit in order to complete another circuit, 309

renewable: energy sources, e.g. solar energy, which are being replaced and so will not run out, 322–5

repel/repulsion: the force that pushes like poles of magnets apart, 228, 308

reproduce/reproduction: to make offspring, 7; *see* asexual *and* sexual reproduction

reptiles: vertebrates with four limbs and eggs laid in leathery shells, 15; and temperature control, 122

resistance: a measure of the opposition of a material to the electric current flowing through it, measured in ohms (Ω), 296–7, 392

respiration: the breakdown of food to release energy in living cells, 6; *see* aerobic *and* anaerobic respiration

respiratory: related to respiration; diseases, 81, 82–3; substrates, 77, 80; surfaces, 51, 74, 75; system in humans, 72–3

response: the end result of the body's reaction to a stimulus, 6, 114, 115, 116, 117

retina: layer of light-sensitive cells inside the eye, 125

rheostat: a variable resistor, 297, 392

Rhesus factor: an antigen on most people's red cells (Rh+), important in pregnancy, 93, 154

rhizome: a plant storage organ with a swollen horizontal stem, e.g. ginger, 133

rhythm method: a natural contraceptive method based on determining the 'safe' days for intercourse, 160

Richter scale: a scale for describing the magnitude of earthquakes, 200

ripple tank: a shallow tank of water used to demonstrate water waves, 342

rocky shore: shoreline that is affected by tides, 206–7

root hairs: tiny hairs behind root tip that increase the surface area for absorbing water and minerals, 85

root pressure: pressure to push water up the stem as more enters by osmosis, 86

roughage: *see* fibre

runner: a method of asexual reproduction where a new stem grows out, forms roots, and makes a new plant, 133

rust: a fungal disease causing red-brown spots, e.g. on maize, 243

rusting: formation of red-brown iron oxide on iron objects left in contact with air and water, 270–3, 386 prevention of, 272–3, 385

sacrificial protection: attaching metals, e.g. zinc, to iron that are more reactive than the iron, so they corrode before the iron does, 273, 385

safety: behaving in ways that may avoid accidents; and earthquakes, 199; and field trips, 248; at home, 244–5; and hurricanes, 196; at school, 246–8; at work, 249–51; *see also* household chemicals

saliva: produced in the mouth; it contains an enzyme (salivary amylase) that digests cooked starch, 67, 69, 369

salt: sodium chloride; and blood pressure, 97; in food preservation, 232, 233; and rusting, 271, 272

sandy soil: soil containing a majority of larger sand particles, 178–81, 182; improvement of, 181

sanitary control measures: cleanliness as a method for controlling pests, 235; *see also* hygiene

satellites: objects that move in orbits around Earth or another planet; artificial, 228; natural, 204, 356

saturated fats: fats in which the fatty acid parts have as many hydrogen atoms as they can, 55, 97

SBA: school-based assessment to test practical skills; description of, 27–43; tables 361–3; worksheets 364–98 scavengers: animals that eat dead and decaying flesh, e.g. vultures and flies, 186, 188, 219

scouring: scraping a small amount of a surface away with a powder or pad, in order to clean it, 269, 287

screw: a machine based on an inclined plane, 334

scuba: self-contained underwater breathing apparatus used by divers to provide air of the correct composition and pressure, 230, 231

scurvy: a deficiency disease caused by inadequate vitamin C, 58

seashore: area where the land meets the sea, which is affected by the tides, 206–7

seawater: water with a high salt content, 215–19; and fishing, 226–7; pollution of, 224–5

secondary sexual characteristics: male and female features developed during adolescence, 119, 146, 147

sedimentation: method for allowing components of a soil to settle into layers, 177, 178

seedling: young plant after a seed has germinated, 142

seeds: structures formed from fertilized ovules in flowering plants, 138, 139; germination of, 140, 141, 474; respiration of, 76, 78; structure of, 140

seismic waves: shock waves produced by earthquakes; see L-waves, P-waves and S-waves

seismograph: instrument for recording seismic waves, 200

self-pollination: transfer of pollen from one flower to the same flower or to a flower on the same plant, 138

semicircular canals: organs of balance in inner ear, 131

semi-conductor: element, e.g. silicon, that is an insulator when cold but a conductor when warm, 290, 329

sense organs: organs that detect stimuli, 114–15

sensors: system for sensing internal changes, as part of feedback mechanisms for homeostasis, 120

sensory neurones: nerve cells that carry impulses from the receptors to the spinal cord and brain, 116, 117

series circuit: the parts in a circuit are connected in series if a current flows through each part one after another, 294–5, 391

serum: plasma with the clotting agents removed; used for finding blood groups, 92

sewage: urine and faeces, 236, 237; recycling of, 236, 237, 322

sex determination: joining of gametes to make males and females, 44, 150

sexually transmitted infections (STIs): transfer of disease microorganisms mainly during sexual intercourse, 156–7

sexual reproduction: reproduction in which two gametes join to form a new cell, producing varied offspring; in humans, 148–9, 150, 152–3, 154; in plants, 134, 135, 136–9

shock: body reaction in which a person is faint, pale and sweating, 253; see also electric shock

short sight: when the image of a distant object falls short of the retina, corrected with a concave (diverging) lens, 128

sickle cell disease: an inherited disease of haemoglobin caused by a recessive gene, 151

SI units: units accepted for scientific use, 8–9

skeleton: bony framework inside vertebrates, 332–3; in birds, 348

skin: covering layer in mammals responsible for sweating and temperature control, 105, 122–3; as a sense organ, 115

smoking: causing damage with cigarette smoke; and lung disease, 82, 83, 102; and heart disease, 83, 97, 100; and pregnancy, 154; passive, 82

soapless detergents: do not make a scum with hard water, e.g. washing-up liquid, 286–7

soapy detergents: make a scum with hard water before they lather, e.g. toilet soap, for personal use or washing wool items, 286–7, 288

sodium hydroxide: caustic soda; it absorbs carbon dioxide, 49, 76

soft water: water that lathers easily with soap, 288–9, 390

soil: made of rock particles, minerals, humus, air and water, 176–85; parts, 177–9; conservation, 183, 184, 185; erosion, 184; formation, 176; types, 178, 179, 180–2

soil air: air in the spaces between soil particles; importance of, 177; measuring, 179

soil organisms: living things in the soil or leaf litter; animals and plants, 186, 187; microorganisms, 187

soil water: water in the spaces between soil particles, 177; drainage and retention of, 179, 181, 377

solar cells: transfer solar energy into electricity, 329

solar energy: radiation from the Sun; solar cooker, 328; solar drier, 328; solar still, 212, 327; models, 394

solar system: our Sun and its planets and asteroids, 356–7

solar water heater: absorbs solar energy and transfers it as thermal energy (heat), 326–7

solid: state of matter with a constant shape and volume, 19; and heat transfer, 164, 167

solute: a substance that dissolves in a particular liquid (solvent), 283

solution: a homogeneous mixture of a solute and solvent, 283, 284, 388

solvent: a chemical in which other substances dissolve, 283, 389; organic, 283; water as a, 23, 208, 283

solvents, organic: some are sniffed as vapours, e.g. glue and paint thinner, and abused as drugs, 101

sonar: a device for using the reflection of sound waves to identify the position of objects, 229

sound: vibrations of particles set up by vibrating objects, 372; hearing, 130–1; needs a medium, 16, 129; transmission of, 343

space: area above our atmosphere, 358–9

species: members of the same group of organisms that can breed with each other, 189

spectrum: rainbow of different colours (frequencies, wavelengths) obtained by splitting white light, 314, 345

sperm: male gametes made in the testes, 149; in sex determination, 150

spermicides: chemicals that kill sperm and can be used, with a barrier method, to prevent fertilization, 160

thrombosis: a blockage, usually by a blood clot, e.g. in the coronary arteries to the heart muscle, 96, 97

thrush: an infection caused by a fungus, 156

thyroid gland: an endocrine gland in the neck that produces thyroxine, which controls metabolic rate, 118, 119

tides: the ebb and flow of the sea (about twice a day) that is caused mainly by the Moon's gravity, 205, 207; as an energy source, 323

tissue: a group of similar cells with a particular job, 10

tissue culture: growing a small piece of a plant on nutrient agar, to make a whole new plant, 132

tongue: sense organ for taste, 114; rolling of, 151

tooth decay: wearing away of the enamel to expose the inside of a tooth to infection, 65

toothpaste: used for cleaning teeth; it is usually slightly alkaline to neutralize bacterial acids, 282

toxins: poisonous substances produced by some bacteria, 94

training of athletes: special diet and exercise programmes for athletes, 102–3; and drug mis-use, 102, 103

transformer: used to increase (step-up) or decrease (step-down) the voltage of an ac supply, 299

transpiration: the evaporation of water from plants via the stomata, 87, 170, 371

transport: movement by vehicles, and problems of combustion of fuel, 320

transport systems: moving of materials in living things; need for, 84, 85; in humans, 88–91, 96; in plants, 86–7

transverse waves: the vibrations are at right angles to the direction the wave is travelling, e.g. light and other electromagnetic waves, 343

trip switch: protects an electric circuit by switching off a current if it is too big, 300

tsunamis: fast, high waves caused by raising and lowering of the sea floor due to earthquakes, 200

tubal ligation: cutting of the oviducts, as a method of sterilization, 162

turbine: a device that is turned by the kinetic energy of moving water, steam or wind; it then transfers its kinetic energy to a generator, 299, 303, 313, 324

ultrasound: high-frequency sounds outside the range of human hearing, 130; for scanning, 152, 154

ultraviolet radiation: electromagnetic radiation with a wavelength shorter than that of violet light, 126, 345

umbilical cord: the connection between the mother-to-be and foetus, 153

unit: the unit of electricity transfer as appliances work; 1 kilowatt-hour (1 kW h) of the mains supply, 304, 305, 306

universal indicator: an indicator with several pigments that change colour at various pH values, 264, 278, 279, 281

Universe: everything there is; billions of galaxies each of billions of stars, 356, 357

unsaturated fats: fats in which the fatty acid parts could contain more hydrogen atoms, 55, 97

uranium: radioactive uranium can be made to release nuclear energy, 341

urea: poisonous waste made from the breakdown of excess amino acids; excreted by the kidneys, 107, 108; made in the liver, 107, 120

ureter: a tube that carries urine from a kidney to the bladder, 106, 107

urethra: the tube from the bladder to the outside, 106, 107, 148

urination: the passing of urine, 106

urine: the liquid containing water, salts and urea excreted by the kidneys, 107, 108, 109

uterus: part of a woman's body in which an embryo and foetus develop before birth, 148, 153

vaccinate/vaccination: injection with a weakened disease microorganism, to make a person produce antibodies to that disease, 95

vacuole: space filled with cell sap in the cytoplasm of a plant cell, 45

vacuum flask: an insulated container that cuts down on heat transfer, 76, 166

vagina: opening from the uterus in human females; separate from the ureter, 106, 148

valves: flaps of tissue that stop blood flowing the wrong way; in heart, 90; in veins, 96

variables: the various conditions, e.g. temperature and water, in an experiment, 20, 362

varicose veins: swelling of the veins when the valves cannot prevent backflow of blood, 96

vasectomy: the cutting of the vas deferens, so sperm are not available for fertilization, 162

vectors: animals, e.g. mosquitoes, rats and flies, that can transfer diseases to other animals, such as humans, 234, 240, 242

vegetative reproduction: asexual reproduction in flowering plants, 133, 135

vehicles: cars and lorries, etc.; and combustion of fuel, 320; loading of, 353, 397

veins, human: blood vessels that carry blood towards the heart, 90, 91, 96

veins, plant: transport tissues (phloem and xylem vessels) and cambium, 51, 86, 87

velocity: speed in a certain direction, 346, 347

ventilation: circulation of air; *see* artificial *and* natural ventilation

ventricles: the two thick-walled lower chambers from which blood leaves the heart, 90, 91

vertebrae: individual bones in vertebral column, 112, 332

vertebrates: animals with vertebral columns (backbones), 15, 332

villi: microscopic folds in lining of the small intestine that increase the surface area for absorption of food, 46, 66

viruses: microorganisms that can only reproduce inside other cells, 13, 94, 95

vitamins: substances, e.g. vitamin C, needed in small amounts to stay healthy; in diet, 58; in supplements, 277

volcanoes: places where magma comes up from lower levels in the Earth, to emerge as lava, 198, 199, 201, 202, 203

voltage: the 'push' of an electrical supply, 294, 295, 296; danger with, 303; changed by transformers, 299

voltmeter: a meter used to measure voltage in volts (V), 293, 294, 295

volume: the amount of space an object takes up, measured e.g. in cm^3, 84

voluntary action: an action involving thought, 113, 116, 117

vomiting: being sick; partly digested food comes up, 67

W: short for watt(s)

warm-blooded: *see* endothermic

washing soda: sodium carbonate, used to soften all kinds of hard water, 289

waste: unwanted, and sometimes dangerous, materials, 236–7; and community hygiene, 240; using, 237, 322

water: a compound of hydrogen and oxygen (H_2O), 23; conservation, 209; cycle, 190, 191, 210; importance of, 208; purification of, 211, 212–14

water balance: *see* osmoregulation

water waves: the up-and-down movement of surface water, 342, 343; as an energy source, 323; and earthquakes (tsunamis), 200; and hurricanes (storm surge), 197

watt (W): the unit used to measure power (how fast work is done); 1 watt is 1 joule of energy transferred each second (J/s), 295, 296, 304, 306, 307

wavelength: the distance between a point on a wave and the same point on the next wave, 343

waves: vibrations that carry energy, 342–5

weather: day-to-day changes in temperature, rainfall, winds, etc., 194–5

weathering: breaking into smaller pieces, e.g. rock surfaces, 176

wedge: a machine based on an inclined plane, 334

weight: the force of gravity on an object, measured in newtons (N); the weight of a 100 g mass is about 1 N, 336, 354

weightlessness: the effect, when travelling in space, of not being close to a large body, such as the Earth, 358

wet and dry bulb thermometer: *see* hygrometer

wheel and axle: a machine where the effort is applied in a circular motion, 335

white blood cells: cells that help destroy, or neutralize the effect of, microorganisms, 88, 94, 95

wind generator: wind vanes that use a turbine to transfer kinetic energy from the wind to drive a generator, 323

wind pollination: transfer of pollen by the wind, 137

winds: movement of air from areas of high to lower pressure, 193, 194; breezes, 165; global winds, 193; and ventilation, 173; *see also* Beaufort scale

word equations: listing the reactants and products in a chemical reaction, 22, 23

work: the amount of energy that is transferred, measured in joules (J); *see* joules

X chromosome: human sex chromosome; males have one, females have two, 44, 150

X-rays: short wavelength electromagnetic radiation, 345; and radiotherapy, 145; and pregnancy, 154

xylem: the tissue in plants that transports water and minerals up the stem, 85, 86, 87

Y chromosome: human sex chromosome found in males, 44, 150

yeast: a single-celled fungus, 132; and anaerobic respiration, 78, 79, 80, 369

zinc sheet: *see* galvanized iron

zones: areas with different kinds of organisms found on a seashore, 206, 207

Acknowledgements

The authors and publishers are grateful for the permissions granted to use photographs.

Cover, 209, 358 Getty Images; p. 6 Philip Wolmuth/ Alamy; pp. 7, 11, 12*l*, 25, 37, 38, 50, 64, 114, 135, 137, 150, 151, 174, 184, 194, 206, 208, 217, 225, 243, 254, 257, 260, 269, 270, 275, 276, 285, 288, 304, 305, 306, 323, 324, 327, 329*b*, 338, 339*l*, 344, 345, 365, 367, June Hassall; pp. 12*r*, 316 Charles Stirling (Diving)/Alamy; pp. 29, 53 Dorling Kindersley/Getty Images; pp. 44*l*, 89 Carolina Biological Supply Company/Phototake/Alamy; p. 44*r* Grant Heilman Photography/Alamy; p. 79 Diane Ross; p. 81 Imagebroker/Alamy; p. 91 Dorothy Reisse MD/Getty Images; p. 92 David H. Lewis/iStockphoto; p. 98 Jurgen Reisch/Getty Images; p. 102 Jupiterimages/Getty Images; p. 116 Wendy Lee; p. 149 D. Philips/SPL; p. 155 Mauro Fermariello/SPL; p. 158 Steve Bly/Alamy; p. 160 Stock Connection Distribution/Alamy; p. 161 Allik Camazine/ Alamy; p. 163 BSIP/Phototake/Alamy; p. 185*t* David Frazier/Corbis; p. 185*b* Malkolm Warrington/SPL; p. 193 Justin Kaze Zelevenz/Alamy; pp. 197, 359 NASA/SPL; p. 202 Stephen & Donna O'Meara/SPL; p. 212 SPL; p. 218 Lawrence Naylor/SPL; p. 219*l* Manfred Kage/SPL; p. 219*r* Roland Birke/Phototake/Alamy; p. 221 Robert Harding Picture Library Ltd/Alamy; p. 222 Thaddeus Robertson/ iStock; p. 230 Zac Macaulay/Getty Images; p. 233 Art Directors & TRIP/Alamy; p. 234*t* Dr Morley Read/SPL; p. 234*ct* James Cotier/Getty Images; p. 234*cb* Dave King/ Getty Images; p. 234*b* Jack Thomas/Alamy; p. 236 Wilmar Photography/Alamy; p. 238*l* Richard Levine/ Alamy; p. 238*r* David Mack/SPL; p. 250 Bill Stormont/ Getty Images; p. 251*t* Joanna McCarthy/Getty Images; p. 251*c* David Leahy/Getty Images; p. 251*b* Pasquale Sorrentino/SPL; p. 258 Glyn Kirk/Action Plus; pp. 263, 264, 278 Andrew Lambert Photography/SPL; p. 266 Wayne Howard/iStock; p. 268 Bubbles Photolibrary/Alamy; p. 271*t* Justin Kase Zfourz/Alamy; p. 271*b* Malcolm Park/Alamy; p. 273 Leslie Garland Picture Library/ Alamy; p. 274 Smneedham/Getty Images; p. 282*t* Dr Jeremy Burgess/SPL; p. 282*b* Charles Bach/SPL; p. 284 Mediablitzimages (UK) Limited/Alamy; p. 286 Martyn F. Chillmaid/SPL; pp. 298, 385 Sciencephotos/Alamy; p. 318 blickwinkel/Alamy; p. 328 Cordelia Molloy/SPL; p. 329*t* Wiskerke/Alamy; p. 339*r* James King-Holmes/SPL; p. 346 Franklyn Williams/© 2009 Keen i Media Ltd; p. 353 Sonja Grunbauer/Getty Images

SPL = Science Photo Library
l = left, r = right, t = top, b = bottom, c = centre

Acknowledgement is made to the Caribbean Examinations Council (CXC) for use that has been made of the Caribbean Secondary Education Certificate, Integrated Science syllabus, effective for examinations from May/June 2011, especially regarding the specific objectives and information on School-based assessment.